POLITICAL SCIENCE SERIES

INTERNATIONAL POLITICS

POLITICAL SCIENCE SERIES

# *International Politics*

Vernon Van Dyke

UNIVERSITY OF IOWA

*SECOND EDITION*

NEW YORK

APPLETON-CENTURY-CROFTS

DIVISION OF MEREDITH PUBLISHING COMPANY

# PREFACE TO THE FIRST EDITION

The aim of this book is to describe and explain the behavior of states in their relations with each other in as clear and coherent a manner as possible.

Two principal questions are asked. The first is, why do states behave as they do? This question concerns motivations and objectives, "why" being interpreted both in a "because of" and in an "in order to" sense. The second principal question is, by what methods and under what limiting conditions do states pursue their objectives? In other words, how and within what limits do they strive to get what they want? The limits referred to may be voluntarily accepted, imposed by other states, or imposed by circumstances beyond human control.

The book is based on the assumption that the problem of war is the major problem faced in international politics. Therefore, the treatment of the above questions is heavily influenced by a desire to gain and provide an understanding of the causes of war and the conditions of peace. To facilitate the achievement of this objective, international politics is discussed within the framework of an analogy with domestic politics. This reflects the view that the political process at the international level has much in common with the process at the national level, and that an understanding of the factors making for domestic peace or civil war will contribute to an understanding of comparable factors operating among countries.

The questions posed are dealt with on a general basis rather than in relation to specific countries. Either method might be employed. An examination and explanation of the actions and interactions of enough states over a long enough period of time—in other words, an examination of diplomatic history—should lead to the answers which are sought. In truth, this route to the answers is, in a sense, an imperative one, for it is only through knowledge of specific actions in specific circumstances that generalizations about behavior can be reached. But it is not necessary for everyone to retrace the same path. Once the study of history has progressed far enough to provide generalizations (or the basis for them), as it obviously has, it seems best to seize upon them and use them, always testing them to determine the extent to which they provide reliable guides to an understanding of actual events, and always trying to perfect them so as to provide a basis for prediction. Thus, though the choice might reason-

v

ably have been otherwise, this book makes no effort to present diplomatic history, whether from the remote or from the immediate past; there is no discussion, for example, of the foreign policies of the major powers—so common in textbooks on international relations. The focus is on generalizations which the study of history has provided rather than on the myriad of factual details leading to them. Historical data are introduced here and there simply to illustrate the main points on which attention should center. And these main points are examined not only in the light of illustrative material from political history but also in the light of enriching data from other fields, especially from economics and psychology. It is hoped that clarity and understanding will thereby be enhanced.

In writing the book I have had valuable assistance from others. Special thanks go to Frederick S. Dunn, Director of the Center of International Studies at Princeton University, to Taylor Cole of Duke University, and to Arno Mayer of Brandeis University, all three having read the entire manuscript and offered welcome suggestions. Similarly, Lane Davis, James Murray, Arnold Rogow, and Paul Olson, all of the University of Iowa, and Fred Sondermann of Colorado College read various chapters with the usual result, suggestions for improvement. Both Frank A. Beach of Yale University and Harold Guetzkow of the Carnegie Institute of Technology were good enough to offer comments on an early version of Chapter 8, "Psychological Factors in War and Peace." During the summers of 1955 and 1956 I had the privilege of directing seminars on the teaching of international politics under grants from the Ford Foundation, the members of the seminars being teachers of the subject themselves; it is perhaps needless to say that discussions with them proved to be of great benefit. Finally, thanks should go to the University of Iowa, which generously granted me a research professorship for a semester and thus facilitated the completion of the work.

Any weaknesses and errors in the book, of course, remain my own.

V. V. D.

*University of Iowa*

# PREFACE TO THE SECOND EDITION

The general purpose and plan of the book remain unchanged in the second edition. The most obvious differences are the elimination of a chapter on the treatment of dependent peoples, the addition of two chapters—one on Prestige and Pride and the other on Intelligence Activities and Covert Operations—and the change in the sequence of chapters in Part III. Another difference does not show up in the table of contents, but is nonetheless real: a recognition of the phenomenal changes that have been taking place in the world in the last decade—changes in the role and importance of the peoples of Asia, Africa, and Latin America; in the relationships of the United States and the Soviet Union, and of each of them with other states, including actual or former allies; in the technology of war; and so on. It would be foolhardy to claim to have caught up intellectually with the changes, vast and portentous as they are; in truth, it would be surprising if even after these changes are superseded by others, men are not still debating their significance and trying to adjust to them. But at least the present edition reflects an effort to take the changes into account within a framework aiming at analysis and generalization, not at historical chronology.

To the list of those to whom thanks are due for whatever good features the book possesses, I want to add the name of Willard Range of the University of Georgia. He has read the entire manuscript of the revised edition, and it is much improved as a result.

V. V. D.

*University of Iowa*

vii

# CONTENTS

## PART III

## METHODS AND LIMITING CONDITIONS IN INTERNATIONAL POLITICS

PART IV

PROSPECTS FOR PEACE

PART IV

PROSPECTS FOR PEACE

# POLITICS: DOMESTIC AND INTERNATIONAL

Part I

# 1

# WHAT IS POLITICS?

All of us are involved in international politics. There was a time when relations among states seemed to matter little to most Americans, but that time is long since past. Most of what we pay in federal taxes has to do with international affairs; we pay for past wars, for the means of deterring war, for the capacity to wage war if need be, and for attempts to influence developments abroad so as to make them as compatible as can be with the kind of future we want for ourselves. Over all our lives hangs the possibility of personal involvement in war, whether in fighting it or producing the things that are needed in fighting, or whether the problem is sheer survival in a world undergoing nuclear destruction. Moreover, quite apart from the problem of war, our lives are tied up with the lives of people abroad in many ways; we are affected by their ideas, their ambitions, their cultural pursuits, their ability and willingness to engage in trade; and in turn we affect them. The foreign policies of various governments and the international political relationships that go with them are of fundamental importance in our lives.

In some ways international politics seems very simple, and in some ways it is bewildering. It seems simple in that the language of newspapers and of foreign offices is generally language that everyone can understand; practitioners in the field are not in a world of their own, using esoteric words. It seems simple, too, in that many of the most vital issues are easy to grasp—where a boundary should be placed on a map, whether trade should be permitted to flow, whether aid should be given, whether an alliance should be made or war declared. Actually much of the language of international politics and most of the issues are more complex than they seem, but still the appearance of simplicity is there.

International politics seems bewildering, too. Most of us have no particular animus toward Russian or Chinese soldiers, but the possibility is before us that we may have to try to kill them and perhaps destroy their countries. Most of us want a good education, a good income, personal freedom, and a life that is useful and interesting; but we as a nation devote an astounding proportion of our resources, both human and material, to purposes that are more closely related to war than to the kind of life that we prefer to lead. Over the past several decades, decisions made in Berlin, Tokyo, Moscow, and Peking have unleashed events that have increased the cost of living in Iowa and have sent Hoosiers and Texans to Guadalcanal, Normandy, Korea, and Vietnam. Forces that seem beyond control sweep people into battle in strange lands, although apparently no one really wants this to happen. How to prevent it from happening and how to shape the future in a desirable way are big and challenging problems.

## THE STRUGGLE OVER CONFLICTING DESIRES

### Conflicting Desires

The starting point in politics, whether domestic or international, is the fact that people have desires. From this, all else flows. Without the presence of desires, politics would no more exist among men than among stones. They are the mainspring of politics.

There are, of course, many kinds of desires, and not all of them are political. But almost all bring people into contact with each other and lead them to form groups. Groups are essential to politics, for politics is a group phenomenon. Robinson Crusoe could not play politics.

In any group—whether it is a family, a fraternity, a church, or a nation —the members share some desires and have disagreements concerning others. For example, the members of a fraternity may agree in wanting a new house; there may be complete harmony on the point that the old house is unsatisfactory and that a new one is needed. Yet, when it comes to action for raising funds, deciding where to locate the new house, selecting the plans, and settling dozens of other issues, disagreements are bound to arise. Views concerning the best course of action and perhaps the best way of organizing for action are bound to differ. One hundred per cent harmony in any group is very rare. This fact, too, is fundamental to the nature of politics. Politics does not exist without disagreement any more than it exists in the absence of desires and groups.

The disagreement must not be total. It must not be so complete and comprehensive as to exclude all possibility of cooperation or adjustment. It must not be so extreme as to break up the group, or terminate contact between groups, or produce literally a death struggle. For politics to exist, relationships must fall somewhere between complete agreement and complete disagreement. There must be both common and contradictory desires.

## Group Leadership and Group Policies

Politics does not flow automatically from all desires involving agreement-disagreement, found within or among groups. There are personal, economic, esthetic, and other questions that are not political. Questions become political when they involve the determination or selection of group policy or group organization or group leadership or the conduct of intergroup relationships. The worker who begs his boss for a raise is not in politics; he is engaged in a nonpolitical, personal activity. But if he tries to secure the election of new trade union leaders—perhaps in the hope that they will force the boss to increase wages—he is in politics. The stockbroker who argues with the Internal Revenue Service over the size of his income tax is not in politics, but he gets into it if he agitates in favor of an amendment to the income tax law.

Politics is an activity engaged in by members of a group oriented toward some action by the group. Or it is an activity engaged in by different groups oriented toward actions that concern their relationships. Politics arises from the very existence of groups and from the efforts of men to shape group policies and to create relationships under which their desires can be achieved to the maximum extent.

A number of definitions provide summary characterizations of politics. One of them has it that politics is "the activity (negotiation, arguments, discussion, application of force, persuasion, etc.) by which an issue is agitated or settled."[1] Another describes politics as "the art of influencing, manipulating, or controlling [groups] so as to advance the purposes of some against the opposition of others."[2] Another identifies politics with "all those actions more or less directly related to the making of binding decisions for a society."[3] Still another speaks of politics as a struggle among actors pursuing conflicting desires on public issues. In this definition the word *actors* may refer to an individual in politics or to a public official who is acting on behalf of a group or to a government. The definition can be stated more fully as follows: politics is (1) the activity occurring within and among groups (2) which operate on the basis of desires that are to some extent shared, (3) an essential feature of the activity being a struggle of actors (4) to achieve their desires (5) on questions of

1 Martin Meyerson and Edward C. Banfield, *Politics, Planning and the Public Interest* (New York, Free Press, 1955), p. 304.

2 Quincy Wright, *The Study of International Relations* (New York, Appleton-Century-Crofts, 1955), p. 130.

3 David Easton, "An Approach to the Analysis of Political Systems," *World Politics,* Vol. 9 (April, 1957), p. 385.

group policy, group organization, group leadership, or the conduct of intergroup relations—that is, on public issues (6) against the opposition of others with conflicting desires.[4]

Politics occurs in all groups. It occurs in university faculties, in service clubs, in churches, in business firms, in political parties, in the governmental bureaucracy, in legislatures, and among citizens or subjects grouped for the purposes of government. It also occurs among groups that are in contact with each other—among different faculties within one university, among different branches or agencies of government, and among governments themselves.

## THE STRUGGLE OVER CONFLICTING "VALUES" OR "INTERESTS"

Before proceeding further, it will probably be best to clear away some possible sources of doubt and confusion. Most discussions of politics, describing the basic source and purpose of political action, refer to the promotion of *values* or the pursuit of *interests* rather than to the struggle to achieve desires. The essence of politics is said to be the authoritative allocation of values in a society as it is influenced by the distribution and use of power. And politics is said to be a struggle in which individuals or classes or parties or nations strive to promote their interests through influencing or controlling group action. These kinds of statements are quite acceptable, and since we will be using the concepts *values* and *interests* later, we may as well explore their meaning now.[5]

### Values

In one sense *value* is a synonym for the desired. Whatever is desired is valued. A value is thus a desired event, situation, relationship, or procedure.[6] It may denote an end (desired for its own sake) or a means (desired because it will contribute to the end). Thus there are said to be *goal values* and *instrumental values*. Power, wealth, well-being, respect, pride, etc., may all be values and might go into either of the two categories depending on why they are desired. What is a goal value for one person may be an instrumental value for another.

Alternatively, the word *value* sometimes serves to designate not what is desired but what is desirable. It is used to denote a conception of the desirable, which influences the selection from available ends and means

4 Vernon Van Dyke, *Political Science, A Philosophical Analysis* (Stanford, Stanford University Press, 1960), pp. 133-135.

5 Vernon Van Dyke, "Values and Interests," *American Political Science Review*, Vol. 56 (September, 1962), pp. 567-576.

6 Harold D. Lasswell and Abraham Kaplan, *Power and Society* (New Haven, Conn., Yale University Press, 1950), pp. 16, 55-58.

of action.[7] The word is thus given a moral connotation. It suggests a standard for distinguishing between right and wrong, good and bad, and desires that are judged to be wrong or bad will not be values.

In this book, unless otherwise indicated, we shall use the first of the above two meanings; the desired will be a value. In this sense, politics can be said to be a struggle over public issues in which each actor seeks the maximum realization of his values.

## Interests

Like *value*, the term *interest* may refer either to a goal or to a method of reaching a goal; it may refer to an end or a means. An interest that is thought to be self-justifying (desired for its own sake) is said to be an *independent interest*, and one that is regarded as a means is said to be *dependent*. This distinction is sometimes ignored, and then there is danger of confusion. Suppose that a person's objective is the acquisition of wealth; he regards this as an independent interest. Given this independent interest, he can engage in rational and more or less scientific inquiry into appropriate methods—or hire others to do it for him. The inquiry would presumably reveal, on the one hand, that the construction of horse-drawn buggies would not bring wealth. On the other hand, it might reveal that the profits from the construction of houses would likely be high. Therefore he would have a dependent interest in constructing houses, but not in making buggies.

To shift the illustration, suppose that the objective of the American people is to preserve their freedom and democracy. This is an independent interest. Again rational inquiry can occur to find appropriate methods. The inquiry might show that unilateral disarmament would bring freedom and democracy into jeopardy, but that armaments and alliances would probably help to preserve them. If this is true, the American people would have a dependent interest in armaments and alliances, but not in unilateral disarmament.

Note that in the above illustrations we started with assumptions. In the first wealth was assumed to be an independent interest, and in the second freedom and democracy. But are such assumptions necessarily valid? Can a person *know* that wealth is an independent interest, or can a people *know* that democracy should be preserved? The answer is that the process of determining interests must begin with one or more assumptions or postulates; perhaps he decides that he wants wealth in order to be able to promote human welfare or happiness, and then human welfare or happiness becomes his independent interest and wealth is trans-

[7] Clyde Kluckhohn and others, "Value and Value Orientations in the Theory of Action," in Talcott Parsons and Edward A. Shils, eds., *Toward a General Theory of Action* (Cambridge, Harvard University Press, 1951), p. 395.

formed into a dependent interest. Having accepted a new and more fundamental independent interest, he may then examine the question whether the acquisition of wealth is the best way to promote it—whether it is really a "true" interest—and he may or may not decide that it is. Similarly, those who assume that freedom and democracy should be independent interests of the American people may ask themselves why, and then they too will be driven back in their thinking to some other assumption or postulate. Perhaps they will find that they want freedom and democracy in order to preserve and promote human dignity; if so, freedom and democracy become dependent interests, and inquiry may or may not show that they are the best means of promoting the newly recognized independent interest.

We have engaged in this examination of the meaning of the concept *interests* in order to permit us to avoid some of the intellectual traps that it contains. Those who apply the concept without examining it carefully are inclined toward several errors. They are inclined to regard interests as tangible, material, or selfish, and to assign no place to altruism or social conscience; or if they do acknowledge these qualities it is usually to treat them as deviant and dubious sources of political motivation. They also tend to think of interests as objectively determinable, as if they exist independently of any postulates or preferences. They speak of the "true interests" of a person or a people, which exist even if the individuals involved are not aware of them. In our terms, however, *interests* may be either selfish or altruistic. Independent interests are always subjectively selected, or accepted on faith, and cannot be proved true or false. Only dependent interests are, in principle, objectively determinable, and they can be "true" only in the sense that they effectively promote the achievement of the independent interest that is assumed to be self-justifying.

Thus interpreted, independent interests are the same as goal values, and dependent interests are the same as instrumental values. And the desired may fall into any one of these categories.

It is sometimes said that foreign policies should aim to promote the national interest. This statement can scarcely be condemned as wrong, but it is so vague that it is not very helpful. It is a little more meaningful —even though more awkward—to say that foreign policies should be based on a clear and coherent conception of relevant goal values or independent interests, and on wisdom in selecting the appropriate instrumental values or dependent interests.

## POLITICS AS A STRUGGLE FOR POWER

Sometimes it is said that politics is a struggle for power. The statement is true, but it is likely to produce a misconception. It might suggest the concept of a "political man" analogous to the concept of an "economic man" which economists have used, and just as the behavior of the "economic man" was assumed to be guided exclusively by a search for maximum profits, so the behavior of the "political man" would presumably be guided exclusively by a constant search for maximum power. But if such an "economic man" ever existed, he has been rare; practically all men, even in the conduct of their business activities, are influenced some by noneconomic desires. Similarly, a "political man" who devoted himself exclusively and singlemindedly to the greatest possible increase in his power would be very rare.[8] The proposition that politics is a struggle for power does not mean that every individual and every group are constantly seeking maximum power.

In the first place, desires are not exclusively political. People have wants that are nonpolitical in nature. They want material comforts, entertainment, esthetic and intellectual satisfactions, recognition, respect, and many other things that may or may not relate to politics. And in pursuing their other wants, they necessarily have to limit their pursuit of political power. The pursuit of maximum power is commonly incompatible with the fulfillment of nonpolitical desires. Few are willing to forgo all other desires so that a maximum of political power can be achieved.

In the second place, political desires themselves may be limited in character. Individuals are frequently indifferent to politics—and therefore to power—in some or all of the groups to which they belong. If not indifferent, they may well be satisfied with a modicum of influence or control; a person who becomes vice-president of a group does not necessarily want to be president, and a president does not necessarily want to be a dictator. Moreover, intergroup politics is not necessarily an all-out struggle for boundless power. Some groups, at least, have limited objectives and are satisfied with whatever power will permit them to achieve those objectives. For instance, if the lawyers can muster enough power to control state legislation on certain restricted matters, such as admission to the bar, they are likely to be satisfied; they are not likely to seek complete control over the state government for the bar association. A pressure group concerned with the tariff on imported textiles is not likely to seek enough power to permit it to dictate federal legislation concerning the allocation of wavelengths to radio broadcasting stations.

Therefore, though politics is a struggle for power, it is not to be pictured as a process involving constant and all-out struggle by all units involved for maximum power. The extent to which available energy and resources are devoted to the accumulation and use of power is likely to vary widely according to circumstances.

The point is significant. If every person or group involved in the polit-

8 Edward Hallett Carr, *The Twenty Years' Crisis, 1919-1939* (New York, Harper & Row, 1964), p. 97.

ical process strove constantly and exclusively for maximum power—if this were a law of politics—then there would be a basis for predicting future behavior. Each group could shape its policies in full knowledge of the dominant objective of every other group. There would be no place for sentiment or morality or friendship, or for nonpolitical pursuits. Rather, there would be a constant and cold calculation of the power advantages to be gained from this move or that. Politics would be a ruthless process in which the power of one person or group would be restrained only by the adverse power of another person or group, or by adverse circumstance. Law and morality would be articles of convenience, to be observed or cast aside as expediency dictated.

There is no doubt that politics sometimes approaches this description, particularly where relationships involve nearly total disagreement on issues that both sides regard as vital. But it would be misleading to assume that acute struggle and tension are inevitable, or even normal, in politics.[9] Equally, it would be misleading to assume that, where acute political tension does exist, all efforts to alleviate it are necessarily futile.

## IS POWER AN END IN ITSELF?

Another misconception might also arise from the statement that politics is a struggle for power. It is that power is the one and only objective—an end in itself. Of course, it may be. Individuals and groups sometimes take the view, as we shall later see, that the possession of power, that is, control over others, is the ultimate goal of action. There are political movements which seem to be inspired by nothing else than an urge to power. This, however, is not always true. Recall the proposition that politics springs out of human desires. These desires are varied. Although they include the desire to dominate, they also include many others. They include the desire for material things, for the essentials and the comforts and the luxuries of life. They include the desire for order and for security. They include the desire for respect and esteem. They include the desire for civil rights and personal liberties. Power is always an objective, but it may be just a prerequisite to the achievement of other desires rather than the ultimate goal.

If power were always the end in itself, politics could be likened to a game, the object of which is to select the current winner. It would presumably be a more bloody game than is chess or baseball, but still the outcome would be without moral significance. The victory of one participant in the game would be followed sooner or later by the victory of another, and life would be made up of endless rounds of meaningless struggle. Each victor would have demonstrated his power, and that would be that.

[9] Arnold Wolfers, *Discord and Collaboration* (Baltimore, Johns Hopkins, 1962), pp. 81-102; Carr, *op. cit.*, pp. 102 ff.

Although this kind of a situation is imaginable and although it is perhaps a theoretical possibility, it never exists in reality. Power may in practice be an end in itself for some participants in the struggle, but not for all of them. Most, if not all, want power so as to achieve more ultimate objectives, whether moral or material. The outcome of the power struggle at any one time represents not simply the victory of one side as an end in itself, but a decision as to whose desires can be achieved. It may have, in fact it is likely to have, moral significance to those involved. It determines how people will live. It determines what kind of society will exist. It determines what kind of a political, economic, and moral structure will prevail; and what kind of civilization people will have. One need only look at the impact of various revolutions—American, French, Bolshevik, Chinese—to see how fateful the political struggle may be. The struggle between the free world and the Communist world is fraught with similar significance.

Thus, though politics is a struggle for power, it should not be regarded as this alone. The earlier statement is perhaps better: that it is a struggle to determine whose desires relating to group concerns will be fulfilled. It is not simply a game in which points are scored for the purpose of seeing who wins, but a process in which the most fundamental decisions are made concerning the kind of life that people will lead.

## THE POWER STRUGGLE INVOLVES BOTH COOPERATION AND CONFLICT

Attention should also be called to the fact that the power struggle is not necessarily a struggle of each against all. It is not to be assumed that every participant is hostile to every other participant. This is rarely true, if ever. The power struggle involves cooperation as well as conflict. Persons and groups whose desires are identical or harmonious are likely to join forces in an effort to achieve what they want. Even where the desires of the participants are in conflict, there may be compromise and adjustment to permit joint efforts. Politics thus witnesses more or less intensive and effective cooperation among some individuals and groups in order that opposition to others can be more effective. Struggle between antagonists is matched by more or less harmony within each of the antagonistic groups. Politics involves friendly as well as hostile relationships.

### The Focus in the Study of Political Science and International Politics

While politics occurs within all groups and among many of them, political activity is most prominent in connection with government. Though political science is concerned with politics wherever it occurs, it focuses primarily on the struggle among individuals and groups to influence or control government and on the struggle among different governments. The student of political science wants to know how power is gained, maintained, and exercised everywhere, but especially how it is done within and among governments.

In international politics, we are primarily interested in the power struggle among the governments of sovereign states. In particular, we are interested in the problem of war. How does it happen that the international power struggle leads so frequently to war? Why do states wage war and how do they try to ward it off? This book is written on the assumption that peace is a value (desirable) but not necessarily the supreme value. A major purpose of this book is to identify values relevant to peace and war, to explore the implications both of these values themselves and of methods of pursuing them, and to see whether and how adjustments might be made to reduce the role of violence in international affairs.

We shall start our inquiry in the more familiar domestic sphere. An understanding of international politics is likely to be improved by an understanding of domestic politics—where a power struggle also occurs and where civil war is sometimes fought.

## SUGGESTED READINGS

BANFIELD, Edward C., "Note on Conceptual Scheme," in Martin Meyerson and Edward C. Banfield, *Politics, Planning, and the Public Interest* (New York, Free Press, 1955), pp. 303-329.

BUNDY, McGeorge, "The Battlefields of Power and the Searchlights of the Academy," in E. A. Johnson, ed., *The Dimensions of Diplomacy* (Baltimore, Johns Hopkins, 1964), pp. 1-15.

CARR, Edward Hallett, *The Twenty Years' Crisis, 1919-1939, An Introduction to the Study of International Relations* (New York, Harper & Row, 1964).

CURTIS, Michael, ed., *The Nature of Politics* (New York, Avon Book Division, The Hearst Corporation, 1962).

DAHL, Robert A., *Modern Political Analysis* (Englewood Cliffs, N.J., Prentice Hall, 1963).

EASTON, David, *A Framework for Political Analysis* (Englewood Cliffs, N.J., Prentice-Hall, 1965).

———, *The Political System* (New York, Knopf, 1953).

LASSWELL, Harold D., and KAPLAN, Abraham, *Power and Society* (New Haven, Conn., Yale University Press, 1950).

MILLER, J. D. B., *The Nature of Politics* (London, Duckworth, 1962).

WRIGHT, Quincy, *The Study of International Relations* (New York, Appleton-Century-Crofts, 1955).

# 2

# DOMESTIC POLITICS,
# PEACE, AND CIVIL WAR

Americans tend to think that international politics is very different from domestic politics. Domestic politics usually connotes persuasion, peaceful legislation and administration, and periodic elections; of course, legislative and electoral battles occur, but they occur within a framework of agreed rules and on the basis of a common loyalty to the constitutional system. In contrast, international politics connotes war and the threat of war; the contenders may well be bitter enemies, as the Communists and the Western democracies are today, and the issue may well be the survival of a country or a way of life or a particular kind of world order. Thus international and domestic politics seem to be quite different in kind.

This view is not surprising in a country with a well-organized and stable government exercising authority that is everywhere accepted, for in the international political arena such a government does not exist. But the differences would not appear quite so great if they were looked at from within a country that has recently experienced civil war, or from a country in which a breakdown of law and order or the overthrow of the government is an ever present possibility. The fact is that politics is struggle wherever it occurs, and the struggle within countries sometimes erupts in violence and war just as it does among countries.[1] Since World War II, civil war or quasi-civil war has been a much greater problem for some countries than international war—e.g., Greece, China, Malaya, Ko-

[1] According to Quincy Wright, 70 of the 244 wars in which European states engaged from 1480 to 1941 were civil wars; the corresponding figures for non-European states are 12 out of 113. *A Study of War* (Chicago, The University of Chicago Press, 1942), Vol. I, p. 651.

rea, Indonesia, Indochina and Vietnam, Algeria, and the Congo; in many other countries, governments have been overthrown by illegal and forceful means, even though civil war did not occur.

Still, for some countries, civil war is a much less frequent event than international war. This means that conditions and methods of action exist within those countries that somehow permit the political struggle to proceed by means that usually are peaceful. The question is, what are these conditions and methods? The answer can certainly shed some light on the problem of reducing the prevalence of war in international politics.

## GOVERNMENT AND DOMESTIC PEACE

Government is a vital factor in determining whether peace will prevail within countries or civil war occur.[2] Government includes many things. There is no need here to attempt a comprehensive description, but it is important to recall those aspects of government which contribute particularly to the preservation of domestic peace.

### The Executive: Law Enforcement and Armed Peace

Government regularly includes an executive—whether a president, a prime minister, a dictator, or a king. One of the major tasks of the executive is to administer and enforce the law. Normally this task proceeds quite peacefully; once citizens and subjects know what the law is they usually abide by it. But the important thing for our purposes is that every government aims to equip its executive with the power to enforce law against the recalcitrant. What we call peace within countries does not involve the elimination of all violence; rather, peace involves an organization of violence. Peace is always armed. Governments disarm those subject to their jurisdiction; they regulate or forbid the possession of weapons by citizens and subjects, and they prohibit the creation of private or party armed forces. At the same time, they themselves maintain both police and military forces. They want the physical power in their own command to be so overwhelming as to give potential rebels no hope of success. And, in truth, as long as executive power is clearly overwhelming, it would be madness for hostile elements to rebel.

Suppose for a moment that some government should renounce all use of violence. How long would it remain a government? Persons or groups which wished to challenge its authority could no doubt succeed in doing so. And a determined group willing and able to resort to violence could

[2] See the discussion, "War and Vital Interests Inside the State," in J. L. Brierly, *The Outlook for International Law* (Oxford, Clarendon, 1944), pp. 46-60.

no doubt completely overthrow and displace a government which committed itself to nothing but pacific methods. Or suppose that, while not renouncing violence, a government should fail to maintain overwhelming military power in relation to those subject to it; suppose that it should allow a hostile party or faction to develop an army or to subvert and win over to its own side the armed forces that are supposed to be loyal to the government. If those hostile to the government came to command sufficient military power to give them a good prospect of winning in civil war, they would at least be strongly tempted to initiate such a war.

Every civil war, every rebellion, illustrates these truths. In China after World War II the Nationalist regime failed to maintain a preponderance of power and paid for its failure by being driven to Taiwan. In many colonial areas after World War II the imperial rulers proved themselves either unable or unwilling to maintain a preponderance of power—e.g., in Indochina, Indonesia, India, Palestine, Algeria, and the Congo; and the practical implication was that they had to leave, either gracefully or in bitter defeat. And some of the governments established in the new states have themselves succumbed to violence and the threats of violence directed against them.

Peace, then, depends to some extent on power relations within the country. The executive must have sufficient power at its command to enforce obedience, whether this be on the part of single individuals or revolutionary groups. A peaceful country is a policeful country. It is usually not necessary for a government to develop its power to the uttermost, but it is necessary that it constantly maintain a preponderance that is overwhelming in relation to the power that can be mustered by any potential rebels. What we call peace, then, depends in part on the ratio of military power between the government and those who might be inclined to challenge the government in civil war.

## Legislative Authority, Making Law a Reflection of the Desires of the Strong

In addition to a law-enforcing authority armed with superior power, government also includes a law-making authority—perhaps the executive itself if the country is dictatorial, or perhaps an elected legislature. Lawmaking has much to do with the questions of war and peace within any society. Probably the most serious and threatening disputes which arise are disputes over what the law should be. Should slavery be permitted or prohibited? Should trade unions be outlawed, or should collective bargaining with trade unions be required? Should the law provide for a socialist or for a capitalist system? Should minority groups, like the Negroes in America, have fully equal membership in society? In a time of depression and mass unemployment, should the law provide some form of aid, or should life proceed on "the devil take the hindmost" principle? During the past century, in one country or another, all these questions and many more like them have produced either threats of civil war or the actual outbreak of civil war.

The important thing in any society, if war is to be avoided, is that the law should be a reasonably accurate reflection of the desires of the strong.[3] The correlation between strength and law, as indicated above, can be obtained in part by measures of the government to keep itself strong; as long as it has overwhelming police and military power at its command, it is under no compulsion to change the law. Yet, in a changing society a government which fails to change the law is likely to find it difficult to maintain a clear preponderance of power. Groups that are rising in the society will become more and more discontented with laws which confer advantages on groups that are declining. For instance, at one time trade unions were illegal in many states of the United States; at one time there was no attempt to regulate utilities or control monopolies; at one time there was no governmental effort to alleviate distress produced by economic depressions; at one time there was no federal income tax law. Now suppose that in none of these respects had the law been changed. Certainly discontent would have become widespread, and the position of the government would have become precarious. Workers would have become restive, and would have regarded government simply as an instrument through which employers maintained a system of repression and exploitation. Many consumers would have become enraged over the extortions of utilities and monopolies. The unemployed would have become bitter against a system which brought ruin to their lives. And the relatively poor would have resented a tax system which seemed disproportionately burdensome to them. Perhaps, despite all this, the government would have been able to maintain itself through repressive measures—through a rigid preservation of a monopoly of violence. However, mass discontent would have made this difficult. The discontented might well have found ways of organizing themselves for action against the government despite its measures of repression—just as various rebel groups in Russia managed to organize and act against the Tsar.

Rather than try to maintain the correlation between strength and law by exclusive concern for strength, most governments seek to maintain the adjustment at least in part through changing the law. Particularly in democratic countries, emphasis is placed on procedures through which influence and control over government can be transferred from groups that have lost strength to groups that have gained strength. There are periodic elections by which the desires of the voters are presumably

3 For a more extended discussion of this proposition, see pp. 285-290 below, Chapter 14, and the sources there cited.

determined. There are legislatures in which representation is given to parties or groups in rough proportion to their voting strength. Parties and groups which lose out in elections lose control of law-making and law-enforcing authority. Those with the greatest voting strength gain such control and, within constitutional limitations, can enact new law or amend old law to satisfy their desires. Dictatorial governments likewise have means of changing the law—even though it is simply the fiat of the dictator. In connection with all types of government, one of the main considerations in enacting and changing the law is that the law should be such, at a minimum, as to keep discontent below the point at which rebellion might break out.

The importance of adequate procedures for changing the law—or of permitting the strong to determine what the law should be—can scarcely be exaggerated; these procedures contribute mightily to the preservation of peace within the state. There is no way of knowing how often civil war would break out in the absence of such procedures; it would depend on many factors, including the speed with which change occurred in the distribution of strength among groups and classes within the society. Nevertheless, there can be no doubt that civil war would occur much more frequently than it does if government insisted rigorously on enforcing unchanging law. "No peace system can be expected to work for any length of time unless it contains adequate provision for bringing about changes in the status quo as required by changing conditions."[4] Elections and legislatures—or substitutes for them—are the fields of battle in which most of the disputes are resolved which might otherwise lead to the outbreak of violence or civil war.

In the international field, what we have just been discussing is commonly treated under the label "peaceful change." Richard Van Wagenen defines peaceful change as

the resolving or adjustment of social problems, normally by institutionalized procedures, without resort to unauthorized physical force. It should be noted that the use of authorized physical force does not violate the concept of peaceful change.[5]

He goes on to suggest that the term *policeful change* would be more appropriate than *peaceful change,* because the essential consideration is not whether the change is peaceful or warlike, but rather whether it is authorized or unauthorized. Within countries governments authorize and may enforce change.

[4] Frederick Sherwood Dunn, *Peaceful Change* (New York, Council on Foreign Relations, 1937), p. 2.
[5] Richard W. Van Wagenen, *Research in the International Organization Field* (Princeton, Center for Research on World Political Institutions, 1952), pp. 11, 14-15.

## The Judiciary, Interpreting the Law
and Maintaining an Expectation of Justice

Courts likewise are important instruments for the preservation of peace within countries. It is through them that the executive seeks to enforce criminal law, and through them (at least in most countries) that the citizen secures protection against arbitrary and illegal executive actions. Moreover, it is through them, in civil suits, that individuals can frequently secure the settlement of disputes between themselves. So far as domestic peace is concerned, the chief direct contribution of civil actions and the prosecution of those accused of crime is a reduction in scattered acts of individual violence. But it seems plausible to assume that civil war would be more likely if there were no judicial agencies to which appeal could be made for an interpretation and application of the law.

Courts, along with other governmental agencies, help to reduce the prospects of civil war especially by maintaining an expectation of justice. The existence of such an expectation of justice through political and governmental action is another of the important bases of peace within states. Whether within or among states, war is usually, though not always, a measure of last resort. As long as any substantial hope exists that strongly held desires can be fulfilled by peaceful political and governmental processes, civil war is not likely to occur. If people think that they can get what they regard as justice by resort to courts or to legislatures or to executive action, they are not likely to rebel. By maintaining institutions and procedures through which justice can be done, governments do a great deal to deter the resort to violence.

### Law Itself as a Reinforcement of Peace

There is another way, too, in which government contributes to domestic peace: it provides law. Hitherto, we have emphasized the importance to peace of means of enacting, amending, and interpreting law. But the very existence of law, whether it is statute or common law, also reinforces peace. In the first place, law helps to maintain domestic peace simply by providing reasonably clear statements of rights and duties; it is obvious that violence is more likely to occur where rights and duties are undefined or vague. Adjacent property owners, for instance, are more likely to get into a dispute over their respective obligations concerning a line fence if there is no law concerning the question than if there is a law regulating the question. Further, law reinforces peace through what may be called a socializing effect. Law helps to create and intensify the bonds of any society. Those living under one law are likely, more and more, to regard themselves as belonging to one society. Moreover, law will produce common bonds among them—particularly among those who believe that they derive benefits from the law. For instance, property owners will likely want to maintain the governmental and legal system under which their property rights are protected; parties to contracts will want to maintain the system under which they expect the contract to be interpreted and enforced; trade unions, if they regard their position in society as reasonably satisfactory, will oppose rebellion against the system, especially if the program of the rebels would render the position of trade unions less satisfactory. In short, law facilitates the development of a whole network of common interests, and the more intensive and extensive this network becomes the less likely it is that rebellion will occur.

## ATTITUDES AND DOMESTIC PEACE

The preceding discussion brought out three principal points. The first was that peace within countries depends in part on the relative power positions of different groups and organizations; more specifically, that peace depends in part on governmental possession of military and police power that is overwhelming in relation to the physical power that can be mustered by any rebellious group. The second point was that peace also depends in part on the existence of peaceful procedures, whether judicial, legislative, or executive, through which people can get what they regard as justice; these procedures relate to making, amending, and interpreting the law. The third item called attention to the fact that the very existence of a system of law tends to reinforce peace.

All these points are important, but clearly they do not provide the whole story. A government might be able to maintain itself and preserve domestic peace simply on the basis of its command of violence and on the basis of executive, legislative, and judicial processes, but in fact governments do not like to rely on these factors alone, and they commonly do not do so. Peace within countries also depends upon the attitudes of people, not simply on government and the processes of government.

## A Constitutional Consensus

In general, peace within countries is more secure the more widely a common set of fundamental desires exists.[6] When the people of any country are at odds on the fundamental principles on the basis of which life will proceed, domestic peace is obviously endangered. In Russia under the tsars, for example, agreement on fundamental principles broke down. Some wanted to retain a tsar as an absolute ruler; others wanted democracy; others wanted to establish a dictatorship of the proletariat

6 R. M. MacIver, *The Web of Government* (New York, Macmillan, 1947), pp. 3-6, 15-21, and *passim*.

and ultimately a communist society. Reconciliation of these conflicting desires was impossible, and the question whose desires would prevail was finally answered on the battlefield. Similarly, before the French Revolution, before the American Civil War, before the Spanish Civil War —and, in fact, before every major civil conflict—sharp differences have developed on issues regarded as vital. Peace is precarious in any country when powerful elements in the population reject economic or political principles which the government seeks to uphold. But where there is general acceptance of the existing system, as there is in the United States and in many other countries, domestic peace is reasonably secure.

What are the attitudes that are of fundamental importance? Perhaps the basic one concerns belief in law and order—belief in peace. In most countries people simply do not think in terms of possible civil war. Almost all of them conduct their affairs on the assumption that peace will be preserved—that the changes which occur will occur on the basis of peaceful processes. They tacitly subordinate all demands for change to a paramount desire that law and order should be maintained. They have a desire for peace that is supreme over any desire for change. And the very forgetfulness of the possibility of rebellion is the surest guarantee that rebellion will not occur. As we shall see later, in international politics the very expectation of war does much to bring war on. The absence of such an expectation within countries is probably the best assurance of domestic peace.

What is called a constitutional consensus underlies this belief in peace. In a democratic country the constitutional consensus will include such beliefs as the following: that paramount importance is to be attached, not to the government as such nor to the nation as such, but to the individual; therefore that respect for, and the promotion of, the dignity and worth and liberty and welfare of the individual should guide governmental activities; that the right to law-making and law-enforcing authority should be assigned in accordance with the outcome of free and fair elections; that the law should be obeyed; that there should be tolerance of minorities; and that minority parties should not be crushed or liquidated, but should be permitted to operate unhampered by discriminatory legal impediments to future electoral victory.[7]

Given general popular agreement on fundamental principles such as these, the possibility of civil war is rendered extremely remote. There may be—and really there are bound to be—intense disputes over the meaning of some of these principles and the best method of implementing them, but the principles themselves set limits on the ways of resolving such disputes. To resort to civil war as a method of settlement would be to abandon the principles themselves.

[7] Cf. "American Ideals and the American Conscience," in Gunnar Myrdal, *An American Dilemma* (New York, Harper & Row, 1944), Vol. I, pp. 3-25.

## Society, the Public Interest, and Loyalty

Along with common attitudes on the supreme importance of peace and on such fundamental principles as those described above usually goes recognition of membership in a society in which individuals have obligations to each other. There is a belief that in some circumstances the individual—or perhaps a great many individuals—should accept risks and sacrifices in the interest of the rest.[8] The most extreme examples relate to international war. When a country is involved in foreign war, people generally accept the view that it is right to ask some to risk their lives in behalf of the good of the society as a whole; military preparations against the possibility of future war commonly also require sacrifices from some—for instance, in the form of military service—in order that the interests of the rest may be served. In questions unrelated to war, too, there is a recognition in many ways of the supremacy of common, public interests over private interests. This is involved in the concomitant of the principle of majority rule, that is, that the minority should obey. It is involved in the idea that the law should be observed even by those who consider it bad. The principle that the good of the many transcends the good of the few is also reflected whenever the right of eminent domain is exercised.

Accompanying this recognition of the transcendent importance of the good of the whole society goes loyalty to certain symbols and principles of that society. American society, like most others, is a national society. Therefore we give great emphasis to certain national symbols. The most important of them is the flag, but there are others, too. We maintain national shrines, such as Mount Vernon, and various memorials, such as the monuments to Washington, Jefferson, and Lincoln in Washington, D.C. Visits to these shrines and memorials are supposed to kindle and maintain loyalty to the society of which we are a part. Certain government buildings, particularly the White House and the Capitol, take on symbolic significance in reminding us of common membership in one society. National holidays, particularly the Fourth of July, and the singing of the national anthem serve the same purpose. The principles on which our national life is based are set forth and symbolized in the Constitution, which is therefore hallowed. Negatively, we encourage loyalty to our society and the principles on which it is based by denouncing and excoriating those who desire the overthrow of our system, like the Russian and Chinese Communists.

Response to national symbols and belief in the principles on which our society is based commonly involve emotional overtones. Faith in the flag

---

[8] Cf. E. H. Carr, *The Twenty Years' Crisis 1919-1939* (New York, Harper & Row, 1964), pp. 166-169.

and acceptance of constitutional doctrine take on a religious flavor. Given attitudes of this sort, civil war becomes no more than a very remote possibility.

Attitudes, then, reinforce government in maintaining peace within countries. The relationship between the two is a reciprocal one. The existence of common attitudes helps make government possible, and governments themselves do a great deal to foster and preserve common attitudes. Through the educational system, through public ceremonies, through the exhortations of political leaders, and in many other ways, governments try to develop, maintain, and intensify a sense of oneness on the part of the people, a sense of loyalty to the society as a whole. And, in varying degrees, governments try to suppress those whose activities undermine the sense of common loyalty. All governments make treason a crime. Many outlaw certain political movements regarded as seditious, such as the communist movement. All try to enforce some degree of respect to the national flag—for instance, by making desecration of the flag a punishable offense.

The existence of organized government and adherence by the people to a common set of fundamental attitudes, then, are the principal pillars on which peace within countries rests.

## DOMESTIC PEACE AND THE DESIRES
## OF THE STRONG

The proposition was made above that, if civil war is to be avoided, the law should be a reasonably accurate reflection of the desires of the strong. This idea calls for some elaboration and emphasis. People do not commonly think of the fact that within countries the strong rule, and so they put international politics—where the strong more obviously rule—in a class by itself. Actually, it is in the nature of all politics that the strong rule.

We have already described politics as a struggle for power; within countries, it is a struggle to gain and maintain control over governmental offices, with a view to exercising that control to promote the fulfillment of political desires. The group, perhaps a political party, or the amalgamation of groups that can muster predominant strength establishes its right to law-making and law-enforcing authority. Theoretically, the strong may be either a majority or a minority. The desires of a people may be so harmonious that the strong include virtually the entire population. Or, particularly in the light of modern technology and of the relatively new techniques of totalitarian control, the strong may constitute only a small proportion of the population.

## Strength and the Right to Rule in Democracies

The strength which gives the "right" to rule is measured in various ways. In democratic countries it is measured in the first instance through elections. Control over government is assigned on the basis of electoral appeal.

Suppose, however, that the distribution of ballots fails to reflect the distribution of military power. Suppose that a political party, such as the Communist Party, has managed to get itself into a position where it might overthrow the government in civil war even if it cannot win a majority of the votes. Or suppose that some sort of conspiracy against the democratically elected government exists, and that the conspirators have the support of most or all of the police and military forces. What kind of a position is the government then in?

In such a situation the government will exist only on the sufferance of those who, by whatever means, have secured a preponderance of military power. It may seek to save itself by making concessions to the opposition, and then the desires of the militarily strong will largely dominate. If it fails to make adequate concessions, it will face rebellion, and the strong will establish their right to rule in civil war.

It may be that the attitudes on which domestic peace rests will be influential enough to deter rebellion even on the part of those who have the power to rebel successfully. However, these attitudes themselves are not likely to survive indefinitely if the laws and the administration of those laws go flagrantly against the desires of the strong. Men are usually reluctant to undertake the risks of war, whether civil or international, but all history shows that they do sometimes accept those risks. Sooner or later, unless the government makes great concessions to the desires of the strong, the attitudes which deter rebellion will be abandoned and rebellion will occur.

Thus if the distribution of ballots does not correspond reasonably well with the distribution of military strength—if those who win elections do not possess a preponderance of military power—sooner or later civil war is likely to occur. Battlefields replace polling booths, and bullets replace ballots in determining who the strong are, and therefore who has the "right" to rule.

## Strength and the Right to Rule in Dictatorships

The relationship between military power and control over government is all the more apparent in dictatorial countries. Dictators ordinarily establish their control over government simply because they can muster more physical power than others They secure the "right" to rule through the threat or the use of force. Before the establishment of their "right" to rule, if they take another's property, the action is punishable as robbery; if they kill an opponent, the action is punishable as murder. After they secure control of the government they become the "legitimate" authorities, and the very same actions against the very same people are regarded as "legal" and are classified as taxation or confiscation or execution. Since they secured the "right" to rule through the threat or the use of force, this method of displacing them is suggested to others. Consequently, the dictator tries, within the limits of his own principles and objectives, to win the support of as many people as possible, and to repress, perhaps bloodily, those whose support he cannot gain. The latter, in turn, will seek to escape repression and, given propitious circumstances, may conspire and seek to overthrow the dictator. Given modern devices of totalitarian control, this is often an extremely difficult task, but if success is achieved, the "right" to rule is transferred. Control over government and therefore over law goes to those who are now the strong.

The principal points of this chapter can be summarized as follows. A power struggle goes on in politics within countries just as it does among countries. Within countries the power struggle is normally carried out by peaceful means; civil war is less frequent than international war. The power struggle within countries can be carried on by peaceful means for two main reasons:

1. Government exists. The government normally possesses a monopoly, or at least an overwhelming preponderance, of power, thus making rebellion futile and thus permitting the enforcement of law. Moreover, government involves institutions and procedures through which laws may be enacted, changed, interpreted, and administered.

2. Attitudes exist which reinforce peace. The presence of common desires and of common loyalties and the very assumption that the political process will be carried on peacefully all work together to relegate the possibility of civil war into the background.

Nevertheless, within countries the strong rule; the law normally reflects the desires of the strong. As the distribution of power within a country changes, as some groups rise in power while others fall, the law will be changed to reflect the new situation. It will be changed peacefully if adequate peaceful procedures are available. If adequate peaceful procedures are not available, then violence is sooner or later likely to occur. The strong will not indefinitely support a legal order which runs drastically counter to their desires.

## SUGGESTED READINGS

BLOOMFIELD, Lincoln P., "Law, Politics, and International Disputes," *International Conciliation*, No. 516, January, 1958.

BOASSON, Charles, *Approaches to the Study of International Relations* (Assen, Van Gorcum, 1963).

CLAUDE, Inis L., Jr., *Power and International Relations* (New York, Random House, 1962).

DEUTSCH, Karl, *The Nerves of Government* (New York, Free Press, 1963).

FOX, William T. R., ed., *Theoretical Aspects of International Relations* (Notre Dame, University of Notre Dame Press, 1959).

HARRISON, Horace V., ed., *The Role of Theory in International Relations* (Princeton, Van Nostrand, 1964).

KNORR, Klaus, and VERBA, Sidney, eds., *The International System. Theoretical Essays* (Princeton, Princeton University Press, 1961).

LERCHE, Charles O., Jr., and SAID, Abdul A., *Concepts of International Politics* (Englewood Cliffs, N.J., Prentice-Hall, 1963).

MANNING, Charles A. W., *The Nature of International Society* (New York, Wiley, 1962).

ROSENAU, James N., ed., *International Politics and Foreign Policy. A Reader in Research and Theory* (New York, Free Press, 1961).

SINGER, J. David, ed., *Human Behavior and International Politics, Contributions from the Social-Psychological Sciences* (Chicago, Rand McNally, 1965).

WALTZ, Kenneth N., *Man, the State, and War: A Theoretical Analysis* (New York, Columbia University Press, 1959).

WRIGHT, Quincy, *The Study of International Relations* (New York, Appleton-Century-Crofts, 1955).

———, *A Study of War* (Chicago, The University of Chicago Press, 1942). Abridged edition, University of Chicago Press, 1964.

# THE WHY'S
# OF STATE BEHAVIOR:
# MOTIVES AND
# CAUSAL CONDITIONS

# *Part* II

# INTRODUCTORY NOTE

In the chapters of Part II we shall be analyzing the why's of state behavior. We shall interpret "why" to mean both "in order to" and "because of," and so shall take up both motives and causes. The assumption is that political behavior reflects both choice and governing conditions. People choose and pursue goals; they strive to accomplish purposes; they have conscious reasons for doing what they do. At the same time, choices are at least influenced if not determined by factors beyond the control (and perhaps beyond the understanding) of those who make them.

In analyzing the "why's" we shall first discuss sovereignty and security, and the desire to preserve them. Then we shall deal with some ideas which those who act in the name of the state espouse and which presumably influence their decisions: the idea of the nation and the associated ideology of nationalism, and the ideas of liberals, fascists, and communists. Thereafter attention will be focused on the economic forces and objectives which in various circumstances contribute either to international cooperation or to international conflict. War itself, and the expectation of war, will be seen to play a significant role in causing war. The character of human nature will be analyzed with a view to assessing psychological factors making for peace and war. Manifestations of the demand for prestige and pride will be examined. Finally, in summary, Chapter 10 will list and briefly discuss the various objectives that states commonly pursue.

Later, in the chapters of Part III, the focus will be on the "how's" of state behavior—the methods employed to achieve the goals.

# 3

# SECURITY AND
# SOVEREIGNTY

States generally seek self-preservation or security above all. They regard survival as their paramount interest. Normally they are willing to sacrifice every other interest, if need be, to promote this one effectively.

The words *self-preservation, security,* and *survival* appear to have plain, common-sense meanings, and to a large extent they do, but complexities and ambiguities are hidden in them which deserve to be explored. The meaning of concepts which play such an important role in international politics cannot simply be taken for granted. Further, if states put such stress on preserving themselves, it is proper to ask what leads them to do it and whether the objective is justifiable.

## THE "SELF" IN "SELF-PRESERVATION"

When states seek self-preservation, precisely what is the "self" that is to be preserved? The answer is not always obvious.

### Territory and People

Naturally, the self includes territory and the accompanying people. Self-preservation is regularly taken to require the preservation of "territorial integrity." The general rule is that states want to preserve their jurisdiction over whatever territory they possess.

However, different portions of a state's territory may not be regarded as equally valuable parts of the self, and states may in fact survive the loss even of territory that they regard as essential. Britain defended its colony,

Burma, during World War II in the struggle for self-preservation, and then voluntarily granted it independence; Burma was apparently not an essential part of the self that was to be preserved. The United States did the same with regard to the Philippines. Poland survives as a state, but with boundary lines far different from those of 1939. Germany lost territory that it considered an essential part of its self after World War I, but did not lose its character as a state. Frequently, in history, states have ceded or exchanged territory without any sign of a feeling that this was contrary to self-preservation.

Sometimes uncertainty arises when boundary lines change, or when there are changes in the limits of effective jurisdiction. What were the limits of the French national self after Alsace-Lorraine was ceded to Germany in 1871? What is the extent of Germany's territorial self today? What does "China" include? Does it include Taiwan and the offshore islands? The territories lost to the Tsars in the 19th century? To what territory does the notion of self-preservation apply in Korea? In Vietnam?

Similarly, uncertainty sometimes arises when new states come into existence, as so many have in Africa and Asia in connection with the dissolution of empires. A number of these states are unnatural in the sense that their existence and their boundary lines reflect arbitrary judgment and capricious event rather than accepted principle. The result is obvious doubt about the appropriate or desirable extent of the territorial self, and some reshuffling has been going on as states divide up or seek to merge or federate into a larger whole.

Thus, though states have self-preservation as a major objective, the territorial self that is to be preserved is subject to definition. It normally includes the territory under the actual jurisdiction of the government in question; it is likely to include any territory thought of as part of the homeland, even if some of it is under the control of other governments; and it may include other territory as well.

## Sovereignty and Equality

In addition to territory and people, the self that is to be preserved has another attribute usually described as sovereignty or independence. The meaning of these words is very elusive. This is indicated by the fact that the League of Nations accepted both Britain and its colony, India, as sovereign, and by the fact that the United Nations accepts as sovereign both the U.S.S.R. and two constituent republics within the U.S.S.R.

However, the term does have a legal meaning. From a legal point of view it denotes a status. A political entity that is free to make and enforce law as it sees fit, subject only to the requirements of international law, is said to possess sovereignty or independence. In other words, where law-making and law-enforcing authority is unlimited, except by international law, there sovereignty resides.[1] The fact that sovereigns are subject to international law implies that they are able to enter directly into relations with other states.

The legal conception of sovereignty can be clarified by considering political entities that are not sovereign. Among these are the political subdivisions into which states are divided. In this country, for example, the fifty states are not sovereign; the constitution not only limits their law-making and law-enforcing authority, but it also confers on the federal government the right to make laws which will be enforced within the various states. Neither are counties and cities sovereign, for their authority is dependent on legislation enacted by state governments. Puerto Rico is not sovereign; rather, it is a dependent territory to which the United States has granted self-government. Similarly, the colonies or dependent territories within the British or other empires are not sovereign; they have been annexed by a "mother country" and have only such law-making and law-enforcing authority as the mother country permits them to have.

Not only do these various kinds of subordinate political entities have law-making and law-enforcing authority that is limited by some other political entity; another key fact is that they are not directly subject to international law. Their actions may violate international law, but responsibility for the violation rests with the sovereign. If a foreign government wishes to lodge a formal protest claiming, for example, that Iowa has violated a treaty obligation or a rule of general international law, it will address the protest not to Des Moines but to Washington, D.C. Similarly, protests concerning the actions of a British colony would go not to the colonial government but to London. In other words, nonsovereign, dependent political entities lack a capacity to enter freely into foreign relations; they lack the capacity to assume the rights and undertake the duties provided for in international law.

Thus it can be said that sovereignty involves two closely related elements: freedom to make and enforce domestic law, and a capacity to invoke rights and assume obligations under international law. It may be helpful to think of the sovereign as standing on a line across the middle of this page. The upper part of the page is the field of international law; the lower part is the field of domestic law. The sovereign is limited by regulations in the upper field of international law, but can do as he pleases in the lower field of domestic law. However, the line between the two fields is a shifting one. As international law develops, by treaty or otherwise, the line cuts across the page at a lower point. The sovereign is still there, subject to the one field of law and supreme over the other, but the line between the two fields has shifted. The field of domestic law has contracted, and the field of international law has expanded.

[1] Quincy Wright, *A Study of War* (Chicago, The University of Chicago Press, 1942), Vol. II, p. 896.

For example, certain Malay states once concluded treaties with Great Britain under which they became protectorates. They conceded various rights to Britain in connection with their governmental affairs. In so doing they expanded the realm of international law to which they were subject, and contracted the realm of domestic law over which they were supreme. But still they retained supremacy in a domestic realm, and so remained sovereign, even if their sovereignty lost some of its significance. Somewhat similarly, it is common for states to make treaties accepting reciprocal limits on their freedom to levy tariffs and to regulate trade in other ways. Some of the states of Western Europe are developing a Common Market, meaning that they are eliminating all trade barriers between themselves; this in turn requires some of them to change various domestic policies, e.g., policies that keep agricultural prices artificially high. There is no question that they all retain their sovereignty, but still the realm to which sovereignty applies is shrinking, and the realm regulated by international law is expanding.

Let it be noted that however important sovereign independence is to the "self" that is to be preserved, it is far from being the only attribute that counts. Suppose, for example, that after a vastly destructive thermonuclear war the tattered survivors in each of a number of countries should congratulate themselves that, though they had lost everything else, they had preserved sovereignty. Would the "self" have been preserved?

Sovereign states are said to be equal.

Superficially, this statement looks absurd. States are obviously unequal in many ways. They are unequal in terms of the size of their population and territory. They are unequal in terms of resources, wealth, and power. These inequalities are obvious. Not so obvious is the fact that states are also unequal in terms of legal rights. Some states possess rights which others do not have. This is illustrated by the above reference to British relationships to certain Malay states; by treaty these states gave up certain rights to Britain. It is also illustrated, say, in the United Nations, where some states have permanent seats on the Security Council and others are elected for limited terms. It is often illustrated by the situation of states defeated in war; the peace treaties imposed on them commonly deny or limit rights which other states freely exercise, such as the right to maintain armed forces of the size and kind that they want.

Actually, of course, the principle of the equality of states does not mean that they are equal in every respect. Rather it means this: that states are equally entitled to have their rights respected. In other words whatever the rights of a state may be they are to be respected in the same way in which the rights of other states are respected.[2]

2 J. L. Brierly, *The Law of Nations* (New York, Oxford, 1963), pp. 130-133.

The principal implication of this is that power, as such, gives no special rights. One state has no right, simply because it is stronger, to impose its will on another. Nor does a group of states have the right to override the sovereign equality of any outside state; if the outside state is observing existing law, it is legally free to rest on its rights and to refuse to acquiesce in the demands or suggestions of others.

This point is tremendously important. To assure clarity it is desirable to make the same point in another way. Within democratic states, people are generally regarded as equal; our constitution assures to every person the equal protection of the laws. This is not, however, interpreted to prevent majority rule. Laws may be enacted and enforced on everyone, even though a substantial minority opposes the law. The principle of equality does not give the individual a right of veto on changes in the law.

In the international realm, the situation is different. The principle of sovereign equality is interpreted to mean that no changes in the law affecting the rights of a state may be made without its consent. International law itself is said to be based on the consent of the states which it binds. Treaties come into effect only when states agree to them, and they bind only those states that do agree. Unless some specific contrary arrangement has been agreed to, each state has a veto on the creation of new law affecting it. There is no international legislature which can enact law by majority vote.

Further, within states the principle of equality is not interpreted to forbid hailing an individual into court against his will. He can be sued, or he can be prosecuted for violation of criminal law. But here again the situation is different in the international realm. The principle of sovereign equality is interpreted to mean not only that a state may veto changes in the law affecting its rights, but also that a state cannot be hailed into court without its consent. There are, of course, judicial methods which states may use for the purpose of settling their disputes, but they are not obliged to accept such methods. They can neither be sued nor criminally prosecuted. If they take their case to court, it must be with the consent of all parties.

Finally, within states the principle of equality is held to be compatible with the existence of an executive organ of government which will enforce law. Among states this does not prevail. Although some halting steps have been taken toward the creation of international executive organs, particularly in the United Nations, such organs as now exist have very limited powers. Sovereign states have not wanted to place themselves under an international executive with effective power over them. Among the considerations deterring them has been the fear of losing the rights and privileges that sovereign equality provides.

## A Political and Economic System

Square miles of land, numbers of people, and a legal status of sovereignty and equality fall far short of including all the aspects of the self which states seek to preserve. Within the various sovereign states, there are different traditions, different customs, and different ways of living. There are democratic governments, which vary more or less among themselves. There are oligarchies and dictatorships. Economic systems differ, the principles of communism, socialism, and capitalism being implemented in varying degrees in different countries. Scales of living and the distribution of wealth vary. The list of differences among the political and economic systems in different states is almost endless.

Within each country some or all people want to preserve the political and economic system under which they live. A dictator is likely to think that governing the state is a good thing for himself, and perhaps for others as well; he will not want the political system in which he has come to power to be destroyed. Where political power is held by an oligarchy or ruling class, the rulers involved are also likely to think that it is good and right to preserve the system under which they enjoy a privileged position. Similarly in democracies, where political power is widely dispersed, the politically influential are commonly jealous of the independence of their state and want to preserve its democratic system. Whatever the economic system, there will be some who are favored by it and who therefore want it preserved.

The self that is to be preserved thus normally includes a political and economic system—a social system; it includes a way of life, a culture. The aim of governments is not simply to preserve the state, but to preserve a particular kind of state. This sometimes raises a problem of priority, for measures that will perhaps contribute to the preservation of territorial integrity may be more or less incompatible with principles on which the social system is based. Should women be mobilized on the same basis as men when dire threat confronts the state? Should lies be told if it seems likely that they will render the state more secure? Should a country which prizes freedom adopt measures of regimentation to increase its survival capacity? Should surprise attack or "preventive" warfare be regarded, in principle, as proper? Or perhaps the question should be, in what circumstances, if any, should a state adopt methods of preserving territorial integrity and sovereignty which are incompatible with the principles by which it wants to live?

The fact that the self includes a particular type of social system also raises questions concerning relationships with foreign states. Should alliances be made with states which champion antithetical social systems? Should similar social systems be protected or promoted in other states? If a desirable kind of self is to be preserved, does this necessitate action, and, if so, what kind of action, to establish or maintain an appropriate world environment? We shall discuss these questions further in Chapter 5.

## SECURITY AND ITS PROBLEMS

Although the terms *self-preservation, survival,* and *security* are sometimes used interchangeably, the term *security* often has a broader connotation. It relates not only to the ultimate desire that the state survive, but also to the desire that it should live without serious external threat to interests or values that are regarded as important or vital.

The policies that states follow to promote their security rest on a series of judgments and choices.[3] In the first place, the interests or values to be rendered secure must be decided upon. We have listed what are usually regarded as the basic ones in the above attempt to define the self that is to be preserved; these items might be subdivided and other items might be added. The list offered may appear to be an obvious one, yet it is of some importance that each government decide explicitly for itself precisely what it is that it wants to preserve and thereafter give conscious attention to the problems involved. Otherwise they may find themselves preserving something which is really not vital to them, or unprepared to preserve the vital.

In the second place, judgment must be exercised in identifying the sources and appraising the extent of foreign threats to whatever it is that is to be kept or rendered secure. This means that attention must be paid to changing conditions which may affect relationships with other states, and that estimates must be made of their intentions and capabilities. As we shall see later, the tasks involved are very difficult.

In the third place, the degree of security aimed at must be decided upon. Absolute security, involving the complete absence of any external threat, is normally unobtainable. No security at all, involving complete helplessness in the face of external threats, is normally unacceptable. The security goal chosen must fall somewhere between these extremes. Even under similar threats, different states seek different degrees of security, which means that some devote a relatively high and others a relatively low proportion of their resources to the security effort; it also means that states differ in the emphasis which they put on alliances and other international security arrangements.

In the fourth place, the methods of promoting security must be chosen —a topic to be discussed in various chapters of Part III. Dangers may be warded off or countered through negotiations with other states, which implies that decisions must be made on the specific objectives to be pursued and on the specific arguments and pressures to be employed. Economic measures may be adopted to affect the power or welfare of other states. Propaganda may be spread, and fifth columns may be developed. Armed power may be increased or reduced at home, and military aid may be extended or denied to other states. Alliances and other agreements affecting security may be concluded. War itself may be waged in the name of security. The number and variety of available methods is very extensive, and they can be employed in various combinations. The choice of method is often both difficult and crucial.

## WHY SELF-PRESERVATION IS DESIRED

Why do states seek to preserve themselves, and why do people make sacrifices for this purpose? Many considerations are involved, some rational and some nonrational. Within the same state, different persons and different classes may be moved by different considerations. Those who feel that the state serves their good may be expected to want to preserve it. Governmental leaders themselves will almost certainly be in this category. The ruling class, if any, is very likely to be. All the elites within the society, that is, all those who get the most of the best, usually want to preserve the political structure under which they enjoy a favored position. Perhaps almost the entire population of the state will believe on quite reasonable grounds that their interests will be served better if the state survives than if it should become a part of some larger political entity.

Further, rational expectations are usually supplemented by emotional forces—especially by nationalist and patriotic feelings, which we shall discuss in subsequent chapters. The emotional forces are commonly so strong that the desirability of preserving the state becomes a matter of faith. Even to raise the question whether the state should be preserved may produce the impression of apostasy or sacrilege. People in one country may be able to be dispassionate about whether a foreign people are really better off because they constitute an independent state, but the same people are unlikely to take a detached view of thir own position. Americans, for example, may take it almost as a matter of course that the people of Western Europe would be better off if they would abandon the idea of national independence and join in a federation, but those who suggest that the American people themselves should take a comparable step risk being accused of virtual treason.

## SECURITY AND COMPETING INTERESTS

There are qualifications to the general proposition that self-preservation, survival, or security constitute the paramount objective of states, and some of them should be enumerated. Political leaders and those who influence them sometimes place such stress on other objectives that they are willing to resort to aggressive war, thus risking the very existence of the state. The prospect of gain of some sort may appear to be great enough to justify the risk. Hitler and the Nazis illustrate this point. Individuals, groups, and whole social classes may place such stress on private or class interests that the question of the survival of the state becomes secondary if not insignificant. There are always some who are out to feather their own nests regardless of social need. Commonly there are dissident groups within the state who may welcome its extinction, even through foreign conquest. A privileged class which is in danger of losing out in a domestic political struggle may, in effect, abandon the idea of preserving the independence of the state if there is a good prospect that by so doing the social order under which they have prospered can be maintained. Conversely, a class which feels underprivileged may seek foreign aid and may compromise or abandon the principle of national independence if there is a good prospect that by so doing the desired domestic changes can be brought about. Thus, some conservatives in France in the late 1930's are said to have endorsed the slogan "Better Hitler than Blum," that is, they are said to have taken the view that it would be better for France to be subjected to Germany under Hitler than for France to be ruled by socialists. Also, communists needing Soviet help have often been willing to subordinate the question of the independence of the state to their paramount objective of achieving and maintaining the triumph of communism.

Governments and people regularly face a problem in allocating resources between their efforts in behalf of security and their efforts in behalf of welfare. Although people generally want security for their state, they also want to enjoy not only the necessities but also some of the comforts and luxuries of life. Prosperity, pleasure, and esthetic satisfactions are desired in some measure. To some extent the promotion of welfare is quite compatible with the promotion of security, for many measures contribute to both power and welfare simultaneously. Frequently, however, a choice must be made, and it is by no means a foregone conclusion that the choices will be for power or security rather than for welfare. Sometimes the politically influential are so insistent on what they regard as welfare that they neglect the security program.

Conscientious objectors do not make the survival of the state the paramount objective; in refusing to fight, they reflect attachment to what they regard as a more important value. Moreover, the possibility of unlimited nuclear war is leading many to ask whether anything—even the continued existence of the state—will justify the cost, and the question is very probably expanding the roll of conscientious objectors. It is leading others to be "nuclear pacifists," meaning that they reject the use of nuclear weapons even if, in principle, they accept nonnuclear war as a possible means of preserving national independence and other values; the logical implication is a willingness to concede domination to the ruthless. Pragmatically, if not cynically, some undoubtedly endorse the principle, "Better Red than dead," meaning that it is better to accept Communist rule, even if it means the loss of national independence, than to be killed in the effort to avert it.

Those endorsing the political unification or federation of two or more states—e.g., those who call for a United States of Africa, or a world federal government—are implicitly or explicitly attacking the principle of state sovereignty; though they may wish to preserve the state against external aggression, they seek a voluntary abandonment of independence on certain agreed conditions. American advocates of world federation take heart from certain precedents illustrating the voluntary abandonment of sovereignty, such as the union of the original thirteen American states and the merger between the United States and the Republic of Texas.

Despite qualifications and exceptions, however, the general rule remains that the paramount objective of states in the field of international politics is self-preservation.

## PRESERVING SOVEREIGN INDEPENDENCE

Human experience demonstrates that government and the state are necessary and inevitable; men cannot have a satisfactory life in anarchy. It does not demonstrate, however, that the world must be divided into precisely the states which exist, or, perhaps, that it must be divided at all. The world has not always been divided as it now is, and present divisions must be regarded as temporary. Political history is full of the stories of the rise and fall of states. Some states have been swallowed up by others, and sometimes the process has gone on, as it did in the days of Rome, until all the known world was included in one empire. At other times, empires have had to disgorge peoples who then established themselves in separate states with their own governments. States which have been divided have sometimes voluntarily united, and states which have been united have sometimes voluntarily divided. The shifting of boundary lines between states has occurred again and again. Mountains and seas are pretty well fixed on the map, but political boundaries recurrently change.

So far as the division of the world into states has a rational justification, it is to be found in the diversity of human aspirations, interests, and ways of thought and action. We Americans, with our own sovereign and independent state, can govern ourselves pretty much as we please. Were the United States to be united with Canada, both Americans and Canadians would have to make adjustments, many of which would be unwelcome on one or both sides. Were the union also to include other peoples, still greater reciprocal adjustments would be required. The division of the world into states permits the politically influential to govern each country as they see fit; it recognizes diversity and facilitates the creation and preservation of attitudes and practices which the different portions of mankind regard as desirable. If the world were united under one government, and if this world government were given significant functions and powers, its survival would be doubtful. Differences between communists and others, to say nothing of the multitude of other differences which divide the human race, would probably tear it asunder.

The state system has the advantage, then, of recognizing and reflecting human diversities, but it has powerful disadvantages as well. It results in substantial international anarchy. The principle of sovereign equality, as interpreted, has prevented the development among countries of anything really comparable to the governments which exist within countries. We have seen that, within countries, government constitutes one of the principal foundations of peace. Deprived of a central government, then, the world is much more likely to suffer war, with all the destruction and tragedy that it involves, than is an individual country. Likewise, an anarchic world can make only lame arrangements for the economic, social, and cultural services and functions which normally go with government.

In the international realm, therefore, one of the main problems is to develop world government, or to find substitutes which will be adequate in performing the functions that government normally performs, while at the same time permitting the survival of diversity. A world government which did not recognize and respect human diversity could not be established; if it were somehow established, it could not succeed. A world without one government, divided into states, reflects human diversities, but is plagued by war.

## SUGGESTED READINGS

BRIERLY, J. L., *The Law of Nations*. 6th ed., Sir Humphrey Waldock, ed. (New York, Oxford, 1963).

GROSS, Feliks, *Foreign Policy Analysis* (New York, Philosophical Library, 1954).

HALLE, Louis J., *Civilization and Foreign Policy* (New York, Harper & Row, 1955).

KEETON, George W., *National Sovereignty and International Order* (London, Peace Book Co., 1939).

WOLFERS, Arnold, *Discord and Collaboration* (Baltimore, Johns Hopkins, 1962).

WRIGHT, Quincy, *A Study of War* (Chicago, The University of Chicago Press, 1942).

# 4

# NATIONALISM AND WAR

The argument of the preceding chapter was based tacitly on the assumption that the units with which we deal in studying international politics are states. States were said to pursue the objective of self-preservation, survival, or security.

Though it is correct, in a way, to say that states are the units with which we deal, this is by no means the whole story. The sovereign state and its government are not living beings who can think or write or speak. We talk about the policies of states; we say that governments negotiate with each other; more generally, we speak of the behavior of states and governments. But such statements involve a considerable amount of fiction. No one could draw a picture of a state adopting a policy or of two governments negotiating.

The fact is that governments are made up of human beings and that the human beings who hold government offices act in the name of the state. It is not the government which thinks or acts; it is the men who compose the government. And they, in turn, are always influenced more or less by other men, the citizens or subjects, whose obedience and support they must have. In other words, if the policies of states are to be understood, one must understand the desires and thoughts and emotions that govern the actions of individual men. States behave as men decide they should behave.

The proposition that the units with which we deal are states must be qualified in another way, too. Ever since the beginning of the western state system, the list of states into which the world is divided has undergone periodic change. New states have come into existence, and old states have disappeared. These changes have not all occurred as a result

40

of the will or actions of states. Many of them have been brought about against the will of existing states by the revolutionary action of private groups. And, as with states, such groups behave as men decide they should behave.

What influences the judgment and behavior of those who act in the name of the state or in the name of revolutionary movements is a long and complex subject. We shall be exploring it in a number of chapters. One of the factors is the idea of the nation and the ideology of nationalism. This factor is, in truth, probably the most important of all in influencing those who help determine what the policies of most states should be, and it has probably also been the most important of all in the revolutionary movements of modern times. The idea of the nation and the ideology of nationalism are therefore of great importance to an understanding of international politics.

The ideology of nationalism involves two rather simple basic propositions. The first is that all members of the nation—or at least all who are territorially concentrated—should be politically united, presenting a common front to other nations; almost always the political unity sought is within one nation-state, and this is to be sovereign. This proposition reflects the alleged right of national self-determination. The second is that all members of the nation should be loyal primarily to their nation or nation-state. We shall discuss these propositions in turn.

## THE NATION AND THE STATE

Toward the close of World War I Woodrow Wilson declared:

Peoples and provinces are not to be bartered about from sovereignty to sovereignty as if they were mere chattels and pawns in a game. . . . Peoples may now be dominated and governed only by their consent. Self-determination is not a mere phrase. It is an imperative principle of action, which statesmen will henceforth ignore at their peril.

The statement was an outgrowth of the democratic principle that people should form their own constitution and choose their own government. It is not unnatural that those who accept this principle should go on to say that groups of people, especially those located in border regions, should be permitted to decide to which state to attach themselves or whether to constitute a state of their own.

Wilson's Secretary of State, Robert Lansing, was hostile to such an extension of democratic principle. He held that the idea of self-determination was "loaded with dynamite," and said,

It will raise hopes which can never be realized. It will, I fear, cost thousands of lives. In the end it is bound to be discredited, to be called the dream of an idealist who failed to realize the danger until too late to check those who attempt

to put the principle in force. What a calamity that the phrase was ever uttered!
What misery it will cause![1]

Wilson himself later appeared to regret having endorsed the principle
of self-determination, saying that he had not known that nationalities
existed which sought to have it applied to them. Nevertheless, the principle continues to be endorsed. The Charter of the United Nations and
various other international documents of the post-World War II period
speak of it, however ambiguously. Even more important, nationalist leaders throughout the former colonial world have appealed to it, and, in
accordance with it, almost all colonies have since World War II achieved
their independence. Several dozen new states have come into existence
in Africa alone. Of the 117 members of the United Nations in October,
1965, 49 had been dependent territories when the Charter was drafted two
decades earlier. Many problems remain, as we shall see; still, the spread of
nationalism and the extent of the implementation of the principle of
national self-determination have been phenomenal.

We might ask why nationalism develops. Obviously, it does not spring
suddenly upon the scene. Vast numbers of people are not completely
lacking in national consciousness at one moment and ardently nation-
alistic the next. The idea comes to be endorsed by a few, and then others
follow along. To find out why, we would have to plumb deeply into the
well-springs of human behavior. Presumably we would conclude that
people become nationalists because they think that nationalism will
serve some need or want; perhaps, it is useful in promoting an economic
interest, or in satisfying a craving for distinction, prestige, and pride, or
in providing a basis for social unity and order.[2] But we will not pursue
this line of thought, though some of the possibilities will be treated in a
later chapter. Here, rather than focusing on the reasons for the development of nationalism, we shall simply accept it as a phenomenon with
important implications for international politics and explore these implications.

The basic proposition to be made is this: that if the principle of nationalism and self-determination were given general application, the
theoretical end point would be a world in which each nation constitutes
a state, provided it wishes to do so. But the satisfactory, general application of the principle is impossible, for it leads, necessarily or potentially,
into a series of difficulties. The object now is to identify and explore
these difficulties.

[1] Wilson's and Lansing's views are quoted and discussed in Alfred Cobban, *National
Self Determination* (Chicago, The University of Chicago Press, 1944), esp. pp. 19-22.
[2] See Hans Kohn, *The Idea of Nationalism: A Study of Its Origins and Background*
(New York, Macmillan, 1961); Paul E. Sigmund, Jr., *The Ideologies of the Developing
Nations* (New York, Praeger, 1963). Karl W. Deutsch, *Nationalism and Social Communi-
cation, An Inquiry into the Foundations of Nationality* (New York, Wiley, 1953).

In the first place, the principle implies that the nation as a concept can be defined, and that a nation as an entity can be identified and set apart from other nations. Second, efforts to create a nation-state are likely to run counter to the interests of states organized on other-than-nationalist lines; more specifically, empires and multinational states—and nonnational states—are threatened by the principle and are likely to resist its implementation. Third, the principle ignores considerations other than nationality which are frequently important in the location of boundary lines—historic claims, and economic and military desires. Fourth, nationalists are not always satisfied with the creation of a nation-state; rather, they tend to go beyond this, seeking glory for the nation in the form of dominion over foreign territory and people. In other words, nationalists tend to become imperialists, denying to others the right of independence that they claim for themselves. Struggle, perhaps war, is likely to ensue.

We will now examine these difficulties in turn.

## The Problem of Identifying Nations

The concept of the nation is vague.[3] The nation is not a physical substance the properties of which can be measured or analyzed in a scientific way. It exists in the external, physical world, to be sure, and therefore has objective attributes, but it also exists in part in the minds of men, and therefore it includes subjective elements. There is no one definition of the term which all would accept. The problem of identifying a nation is therefore often plagued with doubt and difficulty, as is the problem of determining on the map precisely where one nation ends and another one begins.

   *1. The vagueness of the identifying characteristics.* All agree that the nation must include both people and territory. Precisely how many people and how much territory it would be impossible to say. The people must be in reasonably close contact with each other and must regard themselves as constituting a distinct society, set apart from other societies, which are considered alien or foreign. Again it is impossible to say how intense this feeling of membership in a distinct society must be. Further, the attributes that distinguish one group of people from another vary a good deal. Most often it is language, although language is obviously far from reliable as a test of nationality; Englishmen and Americans speak the same language, but regard themselves as members of different nations, and the Swiss speak four different languages. Moreover,

3 Hans Kohn, *Nationalism, Its Meaning and History* (Princeton, Van Nostrand, 1955). Elie Kedourie, *Nationalism* (New York, Praeger, 1961). Carlton J. H. Hayes, *Nationalism, A Religion* (New York, Macmillan, 1960). Louis L. Snyder, *The Meaning of Nationalism* (New Brunswick, N.J., Rutgers University Press, 1954). E. H. Carr, *Nationalism and After* (New York, Macmillan, 1945).

in some regions of the world languages shade off into each other so imperceptibly, through the dialects of border regions, that it is impossible to tell where the dividing line between them is. Race and color are sometimes cited as distinguishing nations from each other, but often people of different race or color are combined in one nation and people of the same race or color are divided into different nations. The same may be said with regard to religion as a distinguishing characteristic. Similarly, different traditions or customs or culture patterns sometimes set nations apart from each other, but they do not always do so. In short, the attributes that distinguish one nation from another are not always clearly discernible.

Another element normally marking the existence of a nation is a desire on the part of its members for political unity. Though in rare cases (as in the old Austro-Hungarian Empire) some nationalists may be satisfied with a status providing a degree of self-government within a multinational framework, the usual demand is for complete independence or sovereignty. Either the people involved must have their own government, whatever its form, and constitute an independent state, or they must, as a general rule, aspire to self-government and independence. Again, however, it is impossible to say how widespread or how intense those desires must be before a nation can be said to exist. And to complicate the problem still more, there is Arab nationalism, which takes different forms; while some Arab nationalists think in terms of uniting the Arab world in one sovereign state, others think more in terms of a common front of separate Arab states in dealing with the non-Arab world.

For a nation to exist, there must be not only people, territory, a sense of membership in a distinct society, and (usually) a desire for common government within an independent state, but there must also be some degree of common feeling or will; there must be a sense of oneness, of unity, of common purpose; there must be a recognition of the existence of common bonds and common interests which set the national society apart from foreign societies. The people must believe that they have more in common with each other than with outsiders. They must "feel that they belong together in the double sense that they share deeply significant elements of a common heritage and that they have a common destiny for the future."[4] There must be a conception of a national self whose purposes are to be advanced and protected. If men thought of themselves primarily as farmers or factory workers or businessmen or clergymen and identified themselves primarily with their counterparts all over the world, nations could not exist. To constitute a nation, they must think of themselves primarily as Americans, Frenchmen, Germans, and

4 Rupert Emerson, *From Empire to Nation* (Cambridge, Harvard University Press, 1960), p. 95. Quotations from this book are reprinted by permission of the publishers; copyright 1960 by the President and Fellows of Harvard College.

regard the bonds that tie them to the country as more important than any bonds that they may have with people in other countries.

In short, though some of the elements requisite to the existence of a nation are fixed and objectively determinable, others are impermanent and subjective. The existence of a nation depends in part on the attitudes of men. The nation is not divinely ordained, nor is it the product of some inescapable law of nature. Rather, people think nations into existence and could think them out of existence. The nation is a historically constituted society, created by the decisions of many men.

2. *Resulting problems.* The nationalist proposition that all members of a nation should be included within an independent state thus meets with a serious difficulty at the outset. If there is no reliable definition of the term *nation,* how can nations be distinguished from each other? Further, in practice the difficulty is intensified. Even where the criteria of nationality are agreed to, it is often difficult or impossible to apply them. In border regions between clearly recognizable nations—for example, in the area where the Serbs, Greeks, and Bulgars border on each other—the distinguishing characteristics of nationality are sometimes so fused and intermixed that they no longer provide guidance for the drawing of political boundary lines. In still other areas, people of clearly distinct nationalities are so interspersed that it is impossible to locate a boundary in such a way as to put all members of each nationality on the same side of the line.

In much of Africa—and in some other parts of the world—many people have no more national feeling than did the people of Europe at the time of the Crusades. Existing boundary lines in Africa reflect not so much divisions between nations as the outcome of the nineteenth century struggle among imperial powers for colonies, and much of Africa is beset by the question whether existing states should (or can) remain united and whether existing boundary lines should (or must) be changed. (Included is the question whether international integration or federation of some sort should not occur.) How Africa will fare in implementing the principles of nationalism remains to be seen.

The significance of all this to international politics is rather simple and clear. If members of adjacent nations insist, as they commonly do, that state and national boundary lines shall coincide, and if there is no objective and reliable way of determining where one nation ends and the other begins, disputes are likely and the disputes may lead to war. Even assuming that each nation is willing to follow the principle of nationality in formulating its territorial claims, each is likely to make the most extensive claims for which it can find a shadow of justification, for it is not customary for nations to give each other the benefit of the doubt on such questions. Conflicting claims thus arise, and peaceful settlement of them has often proved to be impossible.

Problems of this kind have abounded in European history, particularly in the Balkans. For example, in 1911 nationalist aspirations led Greece, Serbia, Bulgaria, and later Montenegro to join in a Balkan League, the object of which was to seize territory from the Ottoman Empire. The parties agreed in advance to a division of the seized territory along lines of nationality, except for one area in Macedonia where their claims were in conflict; they could not agree what the limits of their respective nations were in relation to this contested zone. The prewar agreement was that the ultimate assignment of this zone should be left to the judgment of the Russian Tsar.

When the war against the Turks was over, however, Greece occupied Salonica, and Serbia occupied the contested Macedonian zone. Bulgaria was unwilling to allow either state to keep what it held, and it treacherously attacked them both. A Second Balkan War was therefore fought among the victors over the division of the spoils, a war in which Rumania also joined. The principle of nationality thus broke down as a basis for delimiting states; nationalist aspirations produced war not only against the imperial overlord, but also among the victor nations themselves. Power rather than principle ultimately determined where the various boundary lines should be.[5]

## Nationalist Claims and Multinational or Nonnational States

The second difficulty with the principle that each nation should be free to constitute itself as a united and independent state is that it threatens empires and multinational states, as well as nonnational states, and they are likely to resist its implementation.

The boundaries of states and of nations have never fully coincided—not when the idea of nationalism developed, and not today, after a century and a half of changes in the political geography of the world.

That this is almost inevitable is implied in what has already been said. Where the dividing line between nations cannot be determined, or where people of clearly distinct nationalities are territorially interspersed with each other, or where there is little or no consciousness of nationality, there can be no identity of state and nation.

The same truth can be arrived at historically. As the nationalist idea that the nation and state should be coterminous spread over the world, it rarely found a situation where in fact they were coterminous. The idea first came to the fore in Europe at the time of the French Revolution. Few if any of the states of Europe were then nation-states. All of southeastern Europe was included in two great empires, the Ottoman and the Hapsburg. The Poles were divided between Prussia, the Hapsburg Em-

[5] A. J. Grant and Harold Temperley, *Europe in the Nineteenth and Twentieth Centuries* (New York, Longmans Green, 1952), pp. 375-380.

pire, and the Russian Empire. At this time Germany and Italy did not exist
in a political sense; instead, the Germans and Italians were divided into
many states. Neither was there a Belgium. Further, outside Europe the
coming of nationalism has found few, if any, nation-states already in
existence. At one time or another, European states have held most of the
rest of the world as subject or colonial territory.

   1. *Irredentas and national minorities.* Where the nation and state are
not coterminous, *Irredentas* and national minorities are said to exist. The
term *Irredenta* came into prominence while Italy was being united as a
nation-state. The process of national unification was substantially completed by 1870, but many Italian-speaking people remained within the
Austro-Hungarian Empire. From Rome's point of view the Italians who
remained under alien rule constituted an Irredenta, that is, they were
"unredeemed." One of the principal objects of Italian nationalists thereafter was to bring about the redemption of their compatriots by annexing
them and the territory on which they lived to Italy. From Vienna's point
of view, these Italians constituted a national minority. The term *national
minority* designates a sizable but minority element in the population of
the state; the minority is more or less concentrated in a given territory;
its members may possess citizenship or nationality in a legal sense, but
are not really regarded in a spiritual sense as comembers of the nation;
rather, they are regarded either as constituting a nation which may want
its independence or as belonging in a spiritual sense to some foreign nation-state, usually an adjacent one, which they may wish to join.

   The fact that nation and state do not always coincide should be coupled
with another fact that is simple but significant: states commonly want to
retain territory that they possess. Admittedly, this proposition can be ques-
tioned in the light of the action of Britain and France in recent years in
peacefully granting independence to many former colonies. But let the
French wars in Indochina and Algeria, the Dutch struggles in Indonesia,
and the British troubles with the Mau Mau be recalled. Also, note Portugal's efforts to retain its overseas "provinces," and South Africa's refusal to
alter the status of territories mandated to it after World War I. Many of
the newer states of Africa and Asia contain national or ethnic minorities
that seek independence or some kind of special status; many include irredentas. Relationships among a number of them are troubled by the fact
that boundary lines make no sense in terms of national or ethnic or lin-
guistic divisions. There are few signs as yet that these states will be more
magnanimous and disinterested than the former imperial powers of Europe
in resolving their territorial problems. Conflict is already in progress, and
some of the conflict may express itself in war.

   2. *A corollary concerning divided nations.* A corollary proposition
ought also to be made. There have been times when a nation, though not
subject to alien rule, has been divided into different states. The govern-

ments of these different states commonly wish to preserve themselves. A contradiction develops, then, between nationalists seeking unification and governments seeking survival. In this situation the governments threatened by nationalism have sometimes joined hands to suppress it, as the German states did under the leadership of Metternich in the first half of the nineteenth century. More often one of the governments—the one regarding itself as in an especially favorable position—has become the champion of nationalism and has sought unification of the nation by subordinating or liquidating the other governments that stood in its way. Prussia under Bismarck played such a role, and so did Cavour, the Premier of Sardinia-Piedmont, in connection with the unification of Italy. Wars were involved in each case.

Today Germany, Korea, and Vietnam are all divided. The six governments all proclaim that they seek reunification, and they all declare themselves champions of the national cause. But note that they all want unification on their own terms. In each country the two governments are threats to each other. The two in Korea have already fought a war, and the two in Vietnam are engaged in an indirect form of war.

3. *Making the state a nation.* Sometimes the proposition that the nation should be a state gets reversed and is made to read that the state should be a nation. Perhaps the state has been created before nationalism has really taken hold, or perhaps there is a dominant nationalism that wants to eliminate, or prevent the development of, extraneous elements.

One commentator has gone so far as to say, "The nation is not the cause, but the result, of the State. It is the State which creates the nation, not the nation the State." [6] This view is conveyed in the expression, "We have made Italy, now we must make Italians." [7] Such attitudes are extreme, yet they suggest a widely applicable truth. Nationalist sentiments existed in the American colonies before the Declaration of Independence, but the process of creating the nation went on largely after independence had been achieved. In most of the countries of Latin America the question is moot whether a nation exists; many of the people are to all intents and purposes outside the political system—not politically mobilized; many others recognize that they are affected by government, but are simply mute subjects; usually the portion identifying themselves with the body politic and participating somehow in its life is small. Should those who participate—usually a minority of the total population—be called the nation? If so, the term *national minority* acquires a second meaning. What about the Republic of South Africa, where the dominant white minority insists on a policy of *apartheid*, not wishing to integrate all inhabitants of the country into one nation? Are the whites a nation? Obviously India and Pakistan became states before they were nations; the

---

6 Rudolf Rocker, quoted by Emerson, *op. cit.*, p. 114.
7 Quoted by Emerson, *op. cit.*, p. 95.

principles of nationalism would have made it just as sensible to divide the India of 1947 into twenty countries as to divide it into two; and either of the two could still be subdivided without necessarily violating the principles of nationalism. Whether the state of Burma is to be described as a nation or as a multinational state or as a composite mixture of nations and tribes or simply as a heterogeneous, nonnational, plural society is a matter of more or less arbitrary choice. The boundary lines between Thailand and Laos, and between Cambodia and South Vietnam, do not coincide with what can reasonably be called national boundary lines. Malaysia has become a state, but is scarcely yet a nation. Indonesia has acquired western New Guinea, regardless of whether there is an Indonesian nation and whether the New Guineans are a part of that nation. Rupert Emerson says that "everywhere in Africa, including the independent states of Ethiopia, Liberia, the Sudan and Ghana, the sense of national existence is hesitant and precarious, and the outlines of the presumptive African nations are often still dim. . . . The African nationalist still has before him almost the entire task of creating the nations in whose name he professes to speak." [8] How to create a nation is thus an urgent practical question. And the task of identifying the kinds of conditions and activities that give rise to attitudes of nationalism has become a major one for scholars.[9]

The problem is different for those countries in which a powerful nationalism already exists that is simply to be extended or preserved. They attack the problem in various ways. Some of them restrict or prohibit the immigration of aliens, one of the reasons being the fear that large numbers of immigrants might adulterate the character of the nation. Thus, the United States has had a national origins quota system for regulating immigration, so devised as to restrict especially the immigration of those considered most likely to retain their alien ways after coming into the country. (New legislation provides for the termination of this system in 1968.) For several decades Orientals were prevented from immigrating to the United States at all. Similarly, Australia, though no longer speaking openly of a "white Australia" policy, sharply restricts the immigration of Orientals. Once an immigrant comes into a country, those seeking national homogeneity want to bring about his assimilation: they do various things to induce him to drop distinctly alien culture patterns and to take on the language and customs of the nation that he has joined.

The regulation of immigration may prevent the creation of a new national minority, but does not solve the problem of a national minority which is already within the country. It must somehow be eliminated if the state is to be made into a homogeneous nation. Elimination may be

[9] See Karl W. Deutsch and William J. Foltz, eds., *Nation-Building* (New York, Atherton, 1963). The book includes an excellent bibliography.

[8] Emerson, *op. cit.*, pp. 93-94.

attempted through assimilation, transfer, dispersal, or extermination. Assimilation has been the most common, although perhaps not the most successful, method. The effort here is to induce or force the minority to abandon its own language and customs and adopt those of the majority; the hope is that eventually the minority will cease to be distinguishable as such, and that the loyalties of the people involved will go to the nation-state which they have fully joined. Thus the Tsar tried to "Russify" some of the minorities under his jurisdiction, and Mussolini tried to "Italianize" the German-speaking inhabitants of South Tyrol—an Austrian province transferred to Italy after World War I.

The transfer of populations, designed to eliminate national minorities, may be voluntary or involuntary. Members of the national minority may simply be given the right to move out of the country—as with the Hungarian "optants" who found themselves in Rumania after a shift in the boundary line following World War I; these Hungarians were given the right to choose between Hungarian and Rumanian citizenship, but if they chose to retain Hungarian citizenship they had to abandon their homes and move across to the Hungarian side of the new boundary line. Involuntary transfers of population may result from persecutory measures which leave the people involved with little choice but to flee, or they may result from direct governmental action. Greece and Turkey made a direct attack on the problem after World War I, when they formally agreed to an exchange of populations; under the agreement, Greeks in Turkey were deported to Greece, and Turks in Greece were deported to Turkey; people who had lived all their lives in a given home suddenly found themselves uprooted and sent to another country in response to the demands of nationalism. The agreement did not apply to Cyprus, then under British control, as is attested by the troubles of the middle 1960's between the Turks and Greeks who live there.

Dispersal as a means of eliminating a national minority has been practiced mainly, if not exclusively, in the Soviet Union. During World War II the Soviet government uprooted and dispersed over its own territory four different minority groups, apparently on suspicion of disloyalty, and a similar fate evidently befell a substantial portion of the people of the Baltic Republics. Extermination as a method of eliminating a people regarded as a national minority was attempted by the Nazis against the Jews with an appalling degree of success in both Germany and Poland.

Both the seriousness and the intractability of the problem of national minorities are reflected in European experience. The very fact that Greece and Turkey would exchange minorities after World War I suggests their fear that the persistence of the problem would impair good relations between them. Similar fears led the victors in World War I to require that several of the states in eastern and southeastern Europe agree to special treaties designed to protect remaining minorities against certain kinds of discriminatory treatment. But no effective way of enforcing these treaties was ever found. Poland denounced its obligation in the 1930's. With the rise of Nazi power, the German minorities in eastern Europe became an acute problem, and Hitler used the alleged mistreatment of them as an excuse for an aggressive program. After World War II minorities treaties in Europe were not revived.

*4. Plebiscites as instruments of self-determination.* The effort to make the nation and the state coterminous has sometimes—especially after World War I—involved the use of plebiscites; that is, the people in question have been asked to choose their future status by voting. Thus, when Germany protested the plan to transfer the province of Upper Silesia to Poland after World War I, the Allies agreed to let the people of the province vote on whether they wanted to be included in Germany or Poland.

Although superficially attractive in terms of democratic principles, the idea of holding plebiscites to determine the national status of a given group of people runs into a number of practical difficulties.[10] The overwhelming one is that one or more existing governments are likely to be opposed. The general expectation in the West is that if the people of East Germany were allowed to do so, they would vote to join West Germany; if so, they would be voting the East German regime out of existence and would again be creating a major German state that might sometime be a threat to the Soviet Union. It is not surprising that they are denied the opportunity. For that matter, in a period of tension between the Communist and the non-Communist worlds, it is doubtful whether either side would permit plebiscites if there was much prospect that they would significantly enhance the power or prestige of the other.

Quite apart from such general international complications, plebiscites are likely to be opposed by whatever government now rules the territory in question. The proposition made above is applicable here again: that governments ordinarily want to keep what they have. To allow a minor nationality to secede and become a sovereign enclave is almost unthinkable. And above all, if part of the main homeland is involved rather than an overseas territory, it is almost as unthinkable that a plebiscite should lead to a transfer of territory to a neighboring state. In a utopian world, the Soviet Union and Communist China, Ethiopia and Somaliland, Cambodia and Thailand, India and Pakistan would all be disinterested and benign while people in border regions voted to choose the state to which they would belong, but in the actual world this is scarcely to be expected.

The counterpart of the proposition that governments usually want to keep what they have is the proposition that if they can safely get what

[10] See Cobban, *op. cit.*, pp. 25-27, and the references there cited.

they want by seizing it, they will be strongly tempted to do so (without risking an adverse vote in a plebiscite). Thus, the Soviet Union and Poland acquired former German territories after World War II, no one suggesting plebiscites; as a result both East and West maintain powerful forces in Europe to deter the other from attempting to solve the German problem by a quick seizure of desired territory.

There is another general difficulty in the use of plebiscites. They naturally can take into account only the wishes of the people who vote. This may mean that the economic and strategic interests and historic claims of one or more states are ignored. Such considerations are sometimes held to be so vital as to preclude the use of plebiscites. More will be said on this topic in a moment.

Even if these difficulties with plebiscites are somehow overcome, problems still remain. Within which territorial unit will the plebiscite be held? By adjusting its size appropriately, or by something analogous to gerrymandering, the outcome may be controllable. Who will be permitted to vote? The answer to this question might also determine the outcome, especially where transfers of population have occurred. If plebiscites were now held to determine who should possess former German territory beyond the Oder-Neisse line, the choice would surely go to Poland and the Soviet Union, for the German inhabitants have fled. Who will supervise or administer the plebiscite, and how will its freedom and fairness be assured? Strong national passions are likely to be involved, and partisans of one side or another are likely to attempt to control the outcome through intimidation or fraud. Supervision by outside powers, presumably neutral, is perhaps the answer, but the supervisory personnel will then be strangers whose regulations and controls may be circumvented by adept, local political leaders. What can be done if the people involved are unfamiliar with democratic electoral processes? If all these problems are solved and a plebiscite held, should the entire area involved be awarded as a unit in accordance with the wishes of the majority, or should the area be divided so as to place each local voting district, so far as possible, within the state of its choice? Finally, on what occasions should plebiscites be permitted and who would decide when to permit them? Frequent shifts of territory from one state to another would obviously cause undesirable instability.

It is, of course, possible that the various problems connected with plebiscites can be solved in specific situations with reasonable satisfaction. The fact remains, however, that it is difficult to do so. This perhaps explains why there was no attempt to use plebiscites in connection with the territorial problems that emerged in Europe after World War II, and why there has been so little discussion of the possibility of using them to solve problems faced by many of the new states of Africa and south and southeast Asia.

## Nonnationalist Considerations and
## National Boundaries

A third major difficulty in the proposition that the nation and the state should coincide comes from its neglect of considerations other than nationality. Nationalists themselves grant that historic claims and economic and military needs should all be taken into account in fixing boundary lines, yet the principles of nationalism provide no solution for the problems involved. Consider again, for example, the former German territory beyond the Oder-Neisse line. Germans have fled from this territory and have been replaced by Poles and others. Suppose that this situation persists for many decades. Let it not be assumed that Germany will abandon its claim to this territory simply because it has come to be inhabited by people of another nationality. Given the opportunity to make its voice heard, Germany is likely to say that its historic claim is paramount over every other consideration. The recovery of territory lost in previous wars is a common objective of states, regardless of changes in the nationality of the inhabitants of the territory.

Palestine offers an extreme illustration of the point. The Arabs have a historic claim to Palestine based on many centuries of uninterrupted occupation. During the whole period the Jews constituted an infinitesimal portion of the population, and they remained a minority in 1948, when Israel was born, even after several decades of immigration. Self-determination based on the outcome of a plebiscite would surely have precluded the establishment of Israel. But the Zionists gained widespread support—including the diplomatic support of the United States—for their claim, based (at least ostensibly) on the fact of Jewish possession of the area in ancient times.

Not only historic claims but also economic and military desires compete with considerations of nationality in the fixing of boundary lines. Most governments are concerned about both the wealth of their citizens and the economic basis of power; they may therefore wish to bring areas under their control because of the economic advantage to be derived, regardless of the nationality of the inhabitants. Moreover, when boundaries are being located, concern for the economic livelihood of the people in border regions may compete with purely nationalist considerations in influencing the decision made.

Military considerations are probably even more important. Assuming future war as a possibility, governments seek security. Among other things, this involves a desire for strategically defensible frontiers. Thus, after World War I, Italy not only wanted to include all Italians within its new borders, but also sought a frontier on the Brenner Pass in the Alps. That this involved the annexation of territory inhabited by German-speaking people made little difference in Rome, so long as Italy was made militarily more secure and powerful. Similarly, after World War I, Czechoslovakia received the Sudetenland even though its inhabitants were Germanic, largely because the territory included the mountainous rim on which the defense of the state had to rest. Losing this region to Hitler in 1938, Czechoslovakia was awarded it again after World War II. Military considerations have likewise influenced the fate of much additional territory during and since World War II. The Soviet Union has gained and regained territories both in the Far East and in Europe, largely to enhance its security. Poland has theoretically been compensated for its territorial losses to the Soviet Union by the acquisition of former German territory. The United States has taken numerous Pacific islands which were previously under the control of Japan, most of them being held in the form of a trust territory. In all these territorial transfers, nationality considerations had scant significance.

Contradictions between nationalist claims, on the one hand, and historic, economic, and military considerations, on the other, are virtually inevitable. The problems may be temporarily resolved, usually by letting the powerful have their way, but new solutions are likely to be sought later when power relationships have changed. The demand for new solutions is almost certain to involve friction and perhaps war.

## Nationalism and Imperialism

Experience has revealed a fourth major difficulty in the nationalist proposition that each nation should constitute a united and independent state. It is that nationalists are often not satisfied to be nationalists in the strict sense. Rather, they tend to become imperialists, that is, they seek control over territory beyond the confines of the nation. They become advocates of extranational expansionism. As a French writer puts it, "Patriotism, conventionally defined as love of country, turns out rather obviously to stand for love of more country."[11]

Although perhaps not inevitable, the desire for extranational expansion is a common characteristic of nationalism and a natural one. It stems from a number of sources, most of which will be discussed elsewhere; imperialism is a broad subject.

Nationalists sometimes seek extranational expansionism out of concern for the security of the nation, thinking that the acquisition of a given piece of foreign territory will be strategically advantageous. Sometimes they seek extranational expansionism for economic reasons: they want to control foreign territories in which important raw materials are located, or in which investments can be profitably made, or to which surplus

[11] René Johannet, quoted by Quincy Wright, *A Study of War* (Chicago, The University of Chicago Press, 1942), Vol. II, p. 1038, footnote 81.

products can be sold, or to which surplus population can migrate. Sometimes, if the nation is in some way disunited or beset by domestic dissension, they seek foreign adventure as a means of promoting national unity.

However sound or unsound these reasons for extranational expansionism may be in specific instances, they are relatively rational. Irrational and emotional forces are also often powerful. The nationalist glorifies the nation. He identifies himself with its fortunes and wants for it a place in the sun so that he can bask in its reflected rays. Defeat for the nation is ignominy for such an individual, and victory for the nation gives him prestige. National honor and pride become intertwined with personal honor and pride. It may or may not be true that individuals who thus identify themselves with the nation could secure full satisfaction out of its cultural, scientific, or other such achievements. The fact is that they often do not. Rather, they commonly interpret glory in terms of conquest and dominion, in terms of size and power.

In glorifying the nation the nationalist is also likely to glorify the principles on which the life of the nation is based. These principles he is likely to regard as moral and good; since they are good for him and his nation, he may assume that they would be good for all the world. Contrary principles espoused abroad may come to be regarded not merely as less desirable but as positively bad and evil. A missionary and crusading spirit may well enter in, the nationalist becoming convinced that it is his duty to give light and guidance to the backward and benighted. The French revolutionists of 1789, determined at the outset to gain liberty, equality, and fraternity for themselves, soon found themselves caught up in a crusade to spread the blessings of these principles over all of Europe, if not over the world. Englishmen responded to Rudyard Kipling's plea on the white man's burden:

> Take up the White Man's Burden—
> Send forth the best ye breed—
> Go bind your sons to exile
> To serve your captives' need.

A similar spirit has existed in the United States at various times; an extreme form of it is illustrated in the following declaration by former Senator Albert J. Beveridge:

God has made us [the English-speaking and Teutonic peoples] the master organizers of the world to establish system where chaos reigns. He has given us the spirit of progress to overwhelm the forces of reaction throughout the earth. He has made us adepts in government that we may administer government among savage and senile peoples. Were it not for such a force as this the world would relapse into barbarism and night. And of all our race He has marked the

American people as His chosen nation finally to lead in the regeneration of the world.[12]

President McKinley justified the taking of the Philippines partly on the basis of such considerations as these. Generally speaking, imperialism commonly involves national pride: a belief that the principles and practices associated with one's own nation are superior to contrary principles and practices, and that they should therefore be made to prevail universally.

The nationalist proposition that each nation should constitute a united and independent state is thus fraught with difficulties. The problem of defining the concept of the nation and the problem of actually identifying nations are plaguing. If these problems are solved, there remains almost inevitable conflict between the "rights" asserted by nationalists and the rights possessed by those established states which include national minorities or which rule over colonial territory. Likewise, disagreement, friction, and possible war are inherent in the fact that historic claims and economic and military-strategic desires sometimes run counter to claims based on nationality. Finally, nationalism fails to provide a basis for a stable international order because of its tendency to develop into imperialism.

The fact is that the questions whether a particular state should exist and, if so, what its boundary lines should be have more commonly been decided on the basis of war and threats of war than on the basis of common consent that the principle of nationality and consequent nationalist claims ought to be respected. This is to say that the political geography of the world has been fixed, however temporarily, more by power than by principle. If power is a more important factor than principle, it is not surprising that the principle has never been fully implemented; it would not be surprising if it never were. The principle that each nation should constitute a united and independent state invites unending conflict.

Nevertheless, we should emphasize that the principle is endorsed very widely. The ideological factors contributing to the demands of colonial peoples for independence since World War II have been mixed. As we will see in a later chapter, the yearning for a basis for personal pride and dignity has been an important factor. But nationalism has been coupled with this yearning in the minds of many of the political leaders. "The most powerful motivating force determining the policy of the uncommitted nations is . . . nationalism and the desire for national independence and prestige."[13] Whether the people who have achieved independence are better governed than they were is, to the nationalist, an

[12] *Congressional Record*, Vol. 33, Part 1 (January 9, 1900), p. 711.
[13] Sigmund, *op. cit.*, p. 36.

irrelevant question. It is not good government that the nationalist primarily seeks; it is self-government—whatever the meaning of "self" may be. As Rupert Emerson says, "Nationalists the world over have revolted against alien domination and, in occasional outbursts of frankness, have stated their case in such classic phrases as that they would rather be governed like hell by themselves than well by their imperial rulers."[14]

## LOYALTY TO THE NATION

The second main proposition to which all nationalists agree is that the individual should be loyal primarily to his nation, above all where relationships with foreign nations are involved.[15] The question is, what does loyalty require? A universal requirement has already been discussed: that the patriot shall endorse and uphold the idea that the nation should be united, usually in a sovereign nation-state, presenting a common front to other nations. Beyond this point, the meaning of loyalty varies, depending on who defines the term. Governments may define loyalty in one way, privately organized groups and organizations in another, and the individual may adopt a personal definition of his own.

### Governmental Definitions of Loyalty

Governments in defining national loyalty always require general obedience to law and support for the constitution. In dictatorial countries this is likely to mean that any word or act will be regarded as disloyal if it in any way impedes achievement of the purposes of the government, and, above all, if it might contribute to the downfall of the government. In other words, loyalty to the nation is defined to mean loyalty to the particular government which rules the nation. In democratic countries, the usual governmental definition of loyalty is not so sweeping. In the United States, for example, no question of national loyalty is involved if one seeks to bring about the defeat of the party in power at the next election. But it is disloyal to advocate the overthrow of the government by force and violence. The offense against the requirements of national loyalty is particularly heinous if those advocating such overthrow are associated in any way with a foreign power. The ultimate form of disloyalty, from the point of view of governments, is treason.

Not only do governments define loyalty to prohibit certain things like subversion and treason, but they also define it to require certain things in a positive way. This is true above all in connection with military

14 Emerson, *op. cit.*, p. 43.
15 For a discussion of the meaning, sources, and expression of loyalty, and of interrelations among loyalties, see Harold Guetzkow, *Multiple Loyalties: Theoretical Approach to a Problem in International Organization* (Princeton, Center for Research on World Political Institutions, 1955).

affairs. Where foreign danger to the nation exists, service on behalf of the nation becomes a paramount obligation of the patriot. He is expected not only to support the idea of national defense, but to give service for national defense if he is called upon to do so. Governments expect loyalty to the nation to supersede literally all other loyalties. They require those who owe them allegiance to leave home and family, school and career, in order that the national cause may be served. They extol sentiment such as that attributed to Nathan Hale, who is said to have regretted that he had but one life to give for his country.

Most democratic governments respect the views of those citizens whose religious or ethical beliefs prohibit or restrict the rendering of military service. That is, they permit the individual to put loyalty to his interpretation of the injunctions of God or conscience ahead of loyalty to the nation or state. They therefore grant the right of conscientious objection to military service, and may arrange alternative types of service for conscientious objectors to perform. Generally, however, governments simply imprison or otherwise punish those who place loyalty to anything else ahead of loyalty to the nation.

We ought to note that sometimes two governments exist for the same state, or two or more persons claim to speak for the government. This raises very special problems for those who normally want to guide themselves by the governmental definition of loyalty. During much of World War II, for example, what were Frenchmen to do who wanted to follow the lead of "the government?" Were they to adhere to Petain or to De Gaulle? If an officer in the army issued orders reflecting loyalty to Petain, what was the subordinate to do who believed that loyalty to France required support for De Gaulle?[16] Correspondingly, in the Congo in the early 1960's, what did loyalty require in the province of Katanga? Were the people to follow Tshombe, who claimed to rule the province, or Adoula, who claimed to rule the whole country? Obviously, those who are willing to follow "the government" wherever it leads are not always spared difficult and perhaps fatal choices.

## Private Definitions of Loyalty

Private organizations and individuals, in defining the requirements of national loyalty, may or may not agree with governmental definitions.[17] Some go beyond the government in fixing the demands of loyalty, and at the other extreme some disagree totally with the government on the subject. Militantly patriotic organizations and individuals often go be-

---

[16] Cf., Raoul Girardet, "Civil and Military Power in the Fourth Republic," in Samuel P. Huntington, ed., *Changing Patterns of Military Politics* (New York, Free Press, 1962), esp. pp. 121-123, 142-143.

[17] Henry Steele Commager, *Freedom, Loyalty, Dissent* (New York, Oxford, 1954), esp. pp. 135-155.

yond governmental requirements. In the United States, for example, the government does not interpret loyalty to require support for a capitalist or free enterprise system, but some "100 percent Americans" do. They regard the particular economic system that the country has had as so precious and essential an aspect of the nation that they denounce advocacy of socialism as disloyal. A few have gone so far as to claim not only that the advocacy of socialism is disloyal, but also that it is subversive to include books about socialism or communism in libraries or to teach them in schools. In the days of the League of Nations there was much opposition to American membership, some of it based on a fear that membership might somehow lead to a loss of national sovereignty and independence; there is some opposition to the United Nations today on the same ground. Loyalty to an international organization is not to supersede loyalty to the nation.

At the other extreme, some private individuals and organizations completely reject their government's definition of the requirements of loyalty. Consider, for example, the position of a German nationalist in the part of Germany under Communist dictatorship. He has considerable reason for regarding the Communist dictatorship as an instrument of the Kremlin —an instrument through which Russians control East Germany. From his point of view, therefore, East Germany is under hated alien rule. Further, he is likely to blame both the Russians and their German accomplices for the fact that Germany remains divided. In this situation, what does nationalism require of him? Thinking that the German Communists who constitute the government have betrayed the country, he may conclude that, as a good patriot, he must seek their overthrow. Perhaps he will decide that he can do this best by fleeing to West Germany. There he may join with others in efforts designed to liberate his part of Germany from foreign rulers and native traitors. He may make radio broadcasts, encouraging dissidence and perhaps rebellion in East Germany. He may engage in various plots or conspiracies against "his" government. He may even try to bring about war in the hope that East Germany can thus be liberated and all Germany united once more. Or the German nationalist may elect to stay within East Germany to carry on activities that are officially regarded as subversive and thus engages in sabotage against his own government if war should come. Whichever course of action he takes, the Communist dictatorship will consider him a traitor, but from his own point of view he will be serving the national cause which the Communists have betrayed.

Those in the civil and military service of government sometimes find themselves in an especially difficult position. Consider, for example, those who served Hitler in Germany and Stalin in the Soviet Union. Hitler's rule was catastrophic for Germany, and Stalin's was heinously immoral even by Communist standards. Were the civil and military servants of these regimes to let Hitler and Stalin be the keepers of their consciences? Were they to give faithful service and blind obedience to notoriously evil leaders? And what about those who since then have served Trujillo in the Dominican Republic, Duvalier in Haiti, and Verwoerd in South Africa?

In sum, loyalty to the nation may be interpreted differently. The general requirement is that the interests of the nation be served, but what is in the interest of the nation is a question on which patriots may differ.

## Nationalism and Internationalism

Internationalism of various sorts creates problems concerning loyalty. Communists extol "proletarian internationalism" and get themselves into a dilemma concerning nationalism; we will analyze their reaction to the dilemma in the next chapter. Some alliance systems and international organizations, such as the United Nations, call for a measure of internationalism, and thus call nationalism into question in some degree. A few groups of states (notably those of Western Europe and those of Central America) have been experimenting with arrangements for economic integration and political consultation—with some kind of political union as a theoretical ultimate possibility; an attenuation of nationalism necessarily goes with such developments, which explains why so many nationalists are hesitant if not obstructionist. Sometimes it is necessary to choose between loyalty to the nation and support for the development of broader political systems in which the nation as such plays a lesser role.

## The Inculcation of Loyalty

It goes without saying that those who concern themselves with the meaning of loyalty are likely to engage in activities designed to secure general acceptance of their ideas. Governments do so, and often do it very vigorously. They commonly use public schools for the purpose, insisting that teachers and textbooks shall inculcate loyalty at least to the constitutional system of the country if not to the government itself. The teachers themselves are to be loyal nationalists, not disloyal or subversive. Textbooks are to present and discuss the utterances of the founding fathers and the traditions of the country in a favorable light. Perhaps there will be a requirement that, on occasion, the national anthem be sung, the flag saluted, or pledges of allegiance given. Outside the schools, governments or the dominant political party may organize youth movements to capture the minds of the young. They may regulate or control means of mass communication—the press, radio, television, movies—to see to it that subversion is avoided and loyalty inculcated. They always establish national shrines and declare national holidays to commemorate persons or principles or past events which have been significant in the life of the nation, hoping that such memorials and the ceremonies connected with them will create or reinforce national loyalties.

The efforts of private organizations and individuals to inculcate loyalty will reflect their conception of the meaning of the term. If they agree with the government's definition, they will simply reinforce and extend the government's program. In most countries, whether because the people control the government or because the government shapes popular attitudes, substantial agreement with the government's definition exists. Thus private organizations often voluntarily assist in inculcating and maintaining a spirit of loyalty to the nation, according to the official definition. So, commonly, do the press, the radio, and other means of mass communication even if they are under private control. Those who adopt a more extreme definition of loyalty than the government are likely to try to secure general conformity with their views. Thus the American Legion or the D.A.R. may try to prevent "radicals" from speaking at public meetings or to prevent the use of "socialistic" books in the schools. In the case of persons suspected of supporting or sympathizing with communism, pressures may be brought to bear to exclude them from radio broadcasting, even if the program involved is purely for entertainment purposes. Similarly, people who reject the government's definition of loyalty and who think that loyalty to the nation requires the overthrow of the government may do what they can to secure the acceptance and support of others for their views.

## Conclusions Concerning Loyalty

Two principal conclusions are to be drawn from this discussion of national loyalty. The first is that under the nation-state system governments seek and usually obtain the fervent loyalty of the people under their jurisdiction. A "nation of patriots" is the ideal of the nationalist. For Americans, "politics" should stop at the water's edge. In Britain, during World War II, a "national" government was formed: a coalition government involving the submergence of partisan rivalries. In other countries too, in times of crisis, national unity in the face of foreign danger has been the watchword. National loyalty and patriotism thus provide a basis for unity and power.

The second conclusion is intimately related. It is that, if primary loyalty goes to the nation, loyalty to anything other than the nation must be secondary or nonexistent. This has very serious implications for the problem of international peace. We said in Chapter 2 that attitudes reinforce government in maintaining peace within countries. Where the nation constitutes a state, loyalty to the nation-state is one of the most significant and potent of these attitudes. Nationalism thus commonly makes an immense contribution to the preservation of domestic peace. However, national loyalty is usually interpreted in a way that precludes international loyalties, and so it tends to prevent the development of attitudes which might reinforce international peace. The idea of sovereignty and the idea of nationalism work together to keep the world as a whole deprived of the bases of peace which people within countries enjoy. They are major obstacles to the development of an international political structure which might be effective in reducing the role of war.

Nationalism is the strongest ideology extant. It is the most potent of the dynamic forces which guide the behavior of statesmen. Desires connected with nationalism—to establish the nation as an independent state, to complete the unification of the nation, to create national homogeneity, to preserve the territorial integrity or independence of the nation, or to glorify the nation through foreign aggrandizement—have influenced international relations in the last century and a half to an extent which would be difficult to exaggerate. By every sign they will continue to do so.

Although all nationalists subscribe to the two main propositions which we have been discussing in this chapter, they differ among themselves on related issues. Some of the differences stem from the ideology to which they subscribe and will become apparent in the following chapter.

## SUGGESTED READINGS

AKZIN, Benjamin, *State and Nation* (New York, Hillary House, 1964).

CARR, E. H., *Nationalism and After* (New York, Macmillan, 1945).

COBBAN, Alfred, *National Self-Determination* (Chicago, The University of Chicago Press, 1944).

COMMAGER, Henry S., *Freedom, Loyalty, Dissent* (New York, Oxford, 1954).

DEUTSCH, Karl W., and FOLTZ, William J., eds., *Nation-Building* (New York, Atherton, 1963).

DEUTSCH, Karl W., *Nationalism and Social Communication* (New York, Wiley, 1953).

EMERSON, Rupert, *From Empire to Nation* (Cambridge, Harvard University Press, 1960).

GUETZKOW, Harold, *Multiple Loyalties: Theoretical Approach to a Problem in International Organization* (Princeton, Center for Research on World Political Institutions, 1955).

HAYES, Carlton J. H., *Nationalism: A Religion* (New York, Macmillan, 1960).

KAUTSKY, J. H., *Political Change in Underdeveloped Countries: Nationalism and Communism* (New York, Wiley, 1962).

KEDOURIE, Elie, *Nationalism* (New York, Praeger, 1961).

KOHN, Hans, *Nationalism: Its Meaning and History* (Princeton, Van Nostrand, 1955).

————, *The Idea of Nationalism* (New York, Macmillan, 1961).

PLAMENATZ, John, *On Alien Rule and Self-Government* (London, Longmans, 1960).

PYE, Lucian W., *Communication and Political Development* (New Haven, Conn., Yale University Press, 1962).

SHAFER, Boyd C., *Nationalism, Myth and Reality* (New York, Harcourt, Brace & World, 1955).

SIGMUND, P. E., Jr., ed., *The Ideologies of the Developing Nations* (New York, Praeger, 1963).

SILVERT, K. H., ed., *Expectant Peoples. Nationalism and Development.* By the American Universities Field Staff (New York, Random House, 1963).

SNYDER, Louis L., ed., *The Dynamics of Nationalism. Readings in its Meaning and Development* (Princeton, Van Nostrand, 1964).

ZNANIECKI, Florian, *Modern Nationalities: A Sociological Study* (Urbana, Ill., University of Illinois Press, 1952).

# 5

# IDEOLOGICAL
# MOTIVATIONS
# AND OBJECTIVES

In discussing nationalism we have already been discussing ideology, for nationalism is an ideology. We have seen how nationalist ideas affect political life within states and, even more, how they lead to friction and conflict among states. Other ideologies operate similarly. We shall discuss liberalism, fascism, and communism.

Certain assumptions underlying the discussion should be made explicit: that ideas influence action; that the desire to promote or defend certain principles is a factor in the power struggle; that the ideology of a state—liberal, fascist, communist, or whatever—helps to determine both the methods it will adopt and the objectives it will pursue in foreign affairs.

The point will perhaps be clearer if the situation within countries is recalled. We have seen that politics within countries involves struggle over the principles on the basis of which political, economic, and social life should proceed. Some may want democracy, others dictatorship. Some may want free enterprise, others socialism. As long as significant portions of the population disagree on such fundamental questions, there is danger of civil war. Those favored by the existing system will want to preserve it, but those who think that another system would make life better for themselves will want change. If most or all the people ever agree on one common set of fundamental principles, domestic peace is made relatively secure.

The situation is similar among countries. Whatever the prevailing ideology within the state, the government is likely to regard it as good and to want to preserve it. A government based on liberal-democratic principles will want to preserve those principles; a fascist dictator will want to preserve fascism, and so on. Where the social system in a number of states is based on the same set of ideological principles, the governments involved have a common interest in preserving the conditions that permit the survival of the ideology; thus a basis of cooperation is provided. Conversely, where ideologies are antithetical—and particularly where one or more of them calls for the aggressive extension of certain principles over the world—a basis is laid for hostility and conflict.

Although ideas influence action, they are not necessarily the ultimate or the sole mainspring of action. They themselves may be reflections of something more basic, as when the rich man objects in principle to the graduated income tax, or they may be rationalizations of desires which it would be improper to express publicly, as when a politician who is greedy for personal power professes concern only for the public interest. Whether or not a particular idea is developed or endorsed does not depend only on the native ability of men to think or on the intrinsic merit of the idea; to be endorsed, ideas must somehow correspond to personal and social wants and needs. There is an interplay between economic, social, and psychological conditions, on the one hand, and the ideas that men develop and endorse, on the other. An emperor is not likely to endorse the ideas of nationalism, and a millionaire is not likely to endorse communism. Ideas alone thus do not provide a full explanation of political behavior.

Even so, they are significant. Though they may be reflections of something more basic or rationalizations of secret desire, knowledge of them frequently makes the behavior of states more understandable and more nearly predictable. Moreover, ideologies which originally are reflections or rationalizations may take on an independent force of their own and continue to influence action long after the reasons for endorsing them have disappeared. Nationalism itself, for example, was originally championed largely by the rising merchant class as a tool in its struggle against certain vestiges of feudalism, but it continues as a powerful force, evoking support from all classes and influencing their conduct.

Aside from nationalism, two of the most potent ideologies in the world are those of liberalism and communism, and a third, socialism, offers a kind of cross between the two. Fascism, weakened by the defeat of its champions in World War II, plays a lesser role, but it is scarcely safe to assume that it will not revive; in any event it is desirable to give some attention to it if only to see to what extremes certain ideas may lead. One of the questions confronted in liberalism and fascism, and in nationalism as well, concerns the relationship of the individual to the state. If the individual is to give primary loyalty to the nation-state, which comes first, the individual or the nation-state? Is supreme importance to be attached to the nation or to the individual human being? Is one the master and the other the servant? If so, which is which? If not, what is the relationship between the two?

## LIBERALISM

### Basic Principles

*Liberalism* is a much abused term, assigned various meanings.[1] The most common features of the liberal outlook are a concern for the welfare of human beings, considered more as individuals than as a mass, and a belief in individual liberty and equality. If anyone says that his concern is primarily with the nation as an organic entity, or with social classes as such, or with races, or if he says that he wants dictatorship, he is also likely to deny that he is a liberal. Liberals emphasize the importance of human dignity. They stress the notion of the worth of the individual—a worth that should be accorded to him simply because he is a human being whether or not he contributes loyally and effectively to the society of which he is a part. They stress the notion that all men are created equal, denying that nature has made some better than others and that some are by nature entitled to special rights or privileges. Liberals deny the existence of any objective or scientific way of determining what men should be like, or what goal-values ought to be pursued; they have no mold into which to cast either the human personality or society as a whole. Their emphasis is on the view that each man should determine for himself what is good for him, and that he should be free to seek his own good. With the goal of individual liberty goes the requirement of political democracy.

Given concern for individual welfare and liberty as the test of liberalism, there are nevertheless differences among liberals. In fact, in a strict sense we should not speak of "the" liberal outlook, for liberals differ significantly among themselves. Nineteenth century liberals were inclined to stress individualism and to minimize the role of government—to advocate *laissez faire*. They distrusted government. To them, freedom existed in the absence of restraint. Government should be not much more than a policeman, keeping order while individuals pursued their own good. The pursuit of that good, it was thought, would show that a harmony of interests existed—that the way to maximize social welfare was to permit individuals to maximize their personal welfare. As it worked out, however, though *laissez faire* liberalism permitted some to get rich, it in practice left a considerable portion of the population in squalor, disease, and degradation. Moreover, despite exceptions, there was in practice considerable social immobility: people tended to stay in the same class and to remain at about the same relative economic level, as their parents. It was something of a travesty to say, in effect, that the rich and the poor were

[1] Kenneth N. Waltz, *Man, the State and War* (New York, Columbia University Press, 1959), pp. 85-123. Harry K. Girvetz, *The Evolution of Liberalism* (New York, Crowell-Collier Books, 1963).

equally free to publish newspapers, to get monopoly control over the market for steel, to employ the best attorneys, and to send their children to the best universities (and something of a travesty to say that they were equally free to be ill-housed, ill-clothed, and ill-fed). Many liberals came to take the view that concern for welfare demanded a different interpretation of liberty and equality: that these values existed not simply in the absence of restraint, but in a positive capacity and opportunity. They therefore sought to modify the *laissez-faire* system by bringing about governmental intervention in the operation of the economic system, and thus use government in an affirmative way to build up capabilities and to create and equalize opportunities. *Laissez-faire* liberals—noninterventionist liberals—have, in fact, come to be called conservative, if not reactionary; and liberalism has come to be associated more with reformist efforts to promote individual welfare through governmental action (i.e., with interventionism). Interventionist liberals are commonly thought of as progressive.

As described above, liberals span the Center of the political spectrum in the Western democracies. Beyond them on one side of the spectrum are the fascists and the members of the "radical Right," who reject one or more of the major historic liberal values. Some of them stress the nation as an entity, or strive above all to preserve the position of a dominant class or race; most of them want to modify freedom and democracy somehow—perhaps by substituting outright dictatorship. Beyond the liberals on the other side of the spectrum are the socialists and communists, whose declared goal values are similar to those of the interventionist liberals but whose methods differ; even the mildest socialists want more stress on cooperative-collectivist efforts to promote welfare through government, and others on the Left are in varying degrees willing to use violent and dictatorial methods to achieve their ends. Toward the Left on the political spectrum, too, there is more willingness to call for (in fact, to require) present sacrifices in behalf of hoped-for future good. Let this generation be regimented and deprived so that the next generation can be free and affluent! On the Left, as on the Right, there is more of a tendency than there is on the part of liberals in the Center to focus on men-in-the-mass—on the group (e.g., the proletariat, or the working class) rather than on the individual. The counterpart is more willingness to sacrifice individuals on behalf of the group, more tendency to deny that people should be granted worth and respect simply as human beings.

## Implications for International Politics

The general ideological positions sketched out above developed in relation to domestic politics. The classical political theorists of the English-speaking world gave scant explicit attention to questions arising in the international realm. They were concerned primarily with relationships between the individual and his own state, not with attitudes about foreign policies and practices in foreign states. Sir Thomas More provided an early example. He dealt almost exclusively with Utopia itself and did not attempt to offer prescriptions concerning Utopia's relationships with foreign countries. He simply described his Utopians as reluctant to go to war and eager to reduce its costs.[2] And subsequent writers did little more.

The original neglect has not been remedied, perhaps because of the intractable nature of the problems. Most liberals could probably agree on a list of objectives to be sought in the realm of international politics, but the record shows considerable disagreement about the relative emphasis to be placed upon them and about the choice of means for pursuing them. Liberals want liberty and democracy throughout the world, as well as at home. It is notable that early liberal pronouncements were couched in universal terms. The references were, for example, to *human* dignity, not simply to the dignity of Englishmen. The American Declaration of Independence asserted that "all men" are created equal, and the French revolutionaries championed not only the rights of Frenchmen but the rights of man. With the concern for the rights of man goes some degree of concern for the welfare of man. The very term *humanitarian* is universal, not national. Liberals also want peace and stability throughout the world, just as they do at home. And, in general, they join with others in a concern for national security and survival.

Where do these concerns lead the liberal? Confusion showed up long ago. The French revolutionaries quickly encountered the fact that kings and other autocrats ruled in some countries, denying liberty and equality to their subjects and threatening war to put an end to the subversion emanating from Paris. One of the revolutionary responses was the use of the sword to carry liberty, equality, and fraternity to other countries: France would force men to be free. There was no rejection of the desirability of peace, but rather a greater emphasis was placed on other values. In more recent times, liberals have likewise tended, in some circumstances, to put more emphasis on liberty than on peace. Woodrow Wilson wanted to make the world safe for democracy. Franklin D. Roosevelt felt it vital to support democracy against Hitlerism; he listed four freedoms and championed them for the world. Since World War II most liberals have regarded communism as the main enemy. The Truman Doctrine declares that the United States will assist free peoples in defending their freedom; and in accordance with the Doctrine, the United States has intervened in struggles in various parts of the world—notably in Greece, Korea, Vietnam, Cuba, and the Dominican Republic—even at the risk of major war. Many liberals regard racial discrimination anywhere as in-

[2] Arnold Wolfers and Laurence Martin, eds., *The Anglo-American Tradition in Foreign Affairs* (New Haven, Conn., Yale University Press, 1956), pp. 1-10.

tolerable and are willing to try to force change (whether in the American South or in the Republic of South Africa).

As the above makes clear, the problem of peace impinges on the problem of human liberty, and liberals have reacted differently to the problem. A few have seen the solution in the triumph of liberalism throughout the world. Just as communists believe that world revolution is a prerequisite to peace, so some liberals have believed that the destruction of tyranny would make peace prevail. As governments became more representative of their people, there was no reason why they " 'should not arrive at a passionless impartiality in dealing with each other.' "[3] Rule by the people would be a rule of reason.

Woodrow Wilson believed that peace requires interventionism of a different sort. His championship of the League of Nations marked the adoption of the view that governments must combine in positive action to deter or defeat aggression, reinforcing peace and security in this way. Many who support the United Nations and various schemes of "world peace through world law" take a similar view. In sum, many liberals seek peace by an interventionist kind of policy, aimed perhaps at the promotion of liberalism over the world, perhaps at the deterrence and defeat of aggression, or perhaps at international institutional arrangements to which all subscribe.

Obviously, liberals (like others) face a dilemma in assigning relative importance to liberty and peace, a dilemma greatly accentuated in recent years by the development of weapons of mass destruction. No one has a satisfactory solution to the problem that they pose. Many continue to endorse one or another of the interventionist lines of action identified above, hoping either to avoid nuclear war or to hold its destructiveness far short of the ultimate possibilities. Others are so appalled by the truly catastrophic nature of these ultimate possibilities that they want to go to great lengths to avoid them. A few would make peace the paramount value, or at least forswear war as a means of action. Many more want simply to minimize the risks, e.g., by adopting a drastically limited conception of the kinds of circumstances or challenges abroad that justify an interventionist stand.

Further, liberals face a dilemma in that the more they stress some of the values named above, the more they weaken the principle of sovereignty. The problem shows up rather sharply in the Charter of the United Nations. On the one hand, it obliges the members to promote human rights and fundamental freedoms; and on the other hand, it asserts the principle of sovereignty and abjures intervention in matters that fall within the domestic jurisdiction of states. When liberals stress the sovereignty of states and the rights of domestic jurisdiction, the implica-

---

[3] T. H. Green, as quoted by Waltz, *op. cit.*, p. 114.

tion is an acceptance of diversity in the world—perhaps including the survival in some countries of conditions and practices that are abhorrent.[4]

Where does concern for human welfare lead the liberal? Again, as in connection with other liberal values, confusion showed up long ago. *Laissez faire* liberals in the eighteenth and nineteenth centuries could act abroad much as they did at home, seeking their own welfare and ostensibly letting others do the same. But, just as was the case at home, they dealt with many in different parts of the world who were relatively helpless. Liberals did not invent imperialism, but most of them accepted it and took advantage of it. One of the results was the exploitation and oppression of the weaker peoples abroad, accompanied variously by appeals to the idea of a harmony of interests, a *mission civilisatrice,* or the acceptance of the "white man's burden." Attacks on the *laissez faire* system in the advanced countries were followed by attacks on its overseas manifestations, but ambivalence developed about the matter. Some of the progressive liberals who were demanding governmental action on behalf of welfare at home confined themselves to anti-imperialism when they looked abroad; interventionist in one realm, they became noninterventionist if not isolationist in the other. Let other people rule themselves, or be ruled by whatever person or group manages to get and keep power! We may be our brothers' keeper, but only in our home country! In contrast, other progressive liberals have wanted to match governmental action on behalf of welfare at home with corresponding action abroad. This motivation, in part, explains the programs of economic aid that so many governments have adopted in the last decade or two.

The upshot of all this is considerable doubt and ambiguity about the meaning and implications of liberalism for foreign policy and international affairs. The fundamental principles mentioned at the outset hold —the concern for the dignity, welfare, and freedom of man, and the concern for security and peace. But attitudes differ about the actions to which these principles should lead.

## Liberalism and Nationalism

Where do the nation-state and nationalism fit into the liberal's tenets?[5] The liberal, speaking as a liberal, must treat them from a utilitarian point of view. If the nation-state and the ideas of nationalism are good for the individual, they are good. If they are bad for the individual, they are bad. They do not justify their own existence except in serving the individual. Thus the liberal has a clear answer to the question, "Which

[4] Cf., Quincy Wright, "Policies for Strengthening the United Nations," in James Roosevelt, ed., *The Liberal Papers* (Garden City, N.Y., Doubleday, 1962), esp. pp. 315-320.

[5] See the discussion of liberal nationalism in Carlton J. H. Hayes, *The Historical Evolution of Modern Nationalism* (New York, Richard R. Smith, 1931), pp. 120-163.

comes first?" He says that the individual does, and that the nation-state is therefore secondary and subordinate.

Nevertheless, the answer is really not as clear nor as definitive as it seems. The liberal nationalist, regarding the nation-state as a useful instrument for the protection and promotion of the welfare of the individual, naturally wants to preserve it. He probably will also want to preserve, in the main, the social and political system associated with the nation-state. What then happens to the individual whose words or actions either make it more difficult for the nation-state to survive or tend positively to undermine it? Further, though regarding the nation-state and its accompanying institutions and practices as means of serving the individual, the liberal rather naturally tends to turn the means into an end in itself. When he glorifies the nation-state, even as a means, does he not thereby attach value to it, and may he not thereby attach so much value to it that its preservation becomes the supreme end? If he does this, the question may be asked again: what happens to the individual? May he not be relegated to a place of secondary importance? May he not become the servant rather than the master?

Liberalism requires that the individual be afforded certain rights: the right to freedom of speech, press, and religion, the right to own property, the right to due process of law, the right to organize into trade unions and to strike, and so on. What happens to such rights when the nation-state is in danger? Are they to be modified or abolished?

The right of trade unions to call strikes is a good case in point. Suppose that in time of extreme national emergency—perhaps in time of war —the railway unions call a strike. Now, the whole economy of any advanced country is dependent on railroads. If the trains do not run, the country will be paralyzed. An extended strike in wartime might lead to complete national disaster. Will the right to strike be upheld even then? The question puts the liberal nationalist in a dilemma. If he denies the right to strike, he goes against a fundamental tenet of his creed, but if he upholds the right to strike it is conceivable that his country will be conquered. Conquest by a communist state, to assume the worst, would mean not only the virtual or complete elimination of the independence of the nation-state, but also the abolition of most of the rights which the liberal holds dear.

The liberal may confront the same kind of dilemma in connection with many other issues. In the broadest possible terms, he may be driven to choose, at least temporarily, between the preservation of democracy and the preservation of the nation-state. In every national emergency the tendency in democracy is to concentrate power in the hands of the executive. The greater the emergency, the greater is this tendency. In time of war, if the nation-state is in mortal peril, democratic procedures may be too slow and unreliable to afford a maximum chance of countering the threat. Will the liberal then stick to democratic procedures and individual rights, or will he sacrifice all so as to give the nation-state the best chance of survival?

In actual practice, the tendency of liberals when faced with such dilemmas has been to attach increased value to the nation-state. When the social and political life of the country is going smoothly and when no serious external threats exist, democracy can be enjoyed to the full, and substantially free rein can be given to individuals in the pursuit of their welfare. But in times of stress, the idea of loyalty to the nation-state and the idea of subordinating individual welfare to the common national good take on added significance. The possibility is that the emphasis on the nation-state might go so far as to make it, rather than the individual, the object of supreme value. Then emotional attachment to the nation may replace belief in the worth and dignity of man; glorification of the nation may replace glorification of the individual. And, whatever the glorification of the nation might mean, it has often in practice meant the enhancement of the power of the nation and the subjection of the individual. "Nationalism has more often than not been the enemy of democratic institutions."[6]

## FASCISM

Fascist thought starts with an assumption diametrically opposed to that underlying liberal thought. Where the liberals postulate the supreme value of the individual, fascists postulate the supreme value of the nation-state or, as in Nazi Germany, the *Volk*. Where the liberals appraise the nation in terms of its utility in promoting the welfare of individual human beings, the fascists appraise the individual in terms of his utility to the nation. To the fascist, it is the nation which comes first, the individual being secondary and subordinate, deriving such rights as he has from service to the nation or to the racial society. The Italian fascists went on from this point to endow the nation-state with a life of its own, distinct from the lives of the human beings who composed it. They regarded the nation not simply as an aggregation of individuals but as a corporate body, a living organism, a Being. The Charter of Labor formulated in Mussolini's time most clearly expressed this conception. It asserted that

the Italian nation is an organism having ends, life, and means of action superior to those of the separate individuals or groups of individuals which compose it. It is a moral, political, and economic unity that is integrally realized in the fascist state.[7]

This kind of an outlook involves obvious fiction. It flies in the face of reason. It is based on a mysticism, deriving belief from emotion or feeling.

[6] Alfred Cobban, *National Self-Determination* (Chicago, The University of Chicago Press, 1944, copyright 1944 by The University of Chicago), p. 65.
[7] Herbert W. Schneider, *Making the Fascist State* (New York, Oxford, 1928), p. 333.

So also was the attitude of the German Nazis, who placed supreme value on race.

Far from denying the mystical basis of their beliefs, the fascists and Nazis affirmed it and gloried in it. They were contemptuous of reason, extoling instinct, intuition, or drive of will. They deliberately and avowedly created a myth, believing that people would more likely do great things when inspired by a myth than when guided by reason. Thus the Nazis decried the fact that the nation which they took over had become a nation without a myth, and they regarded it as their mission to create "by means of a new myth a new standard of value by which all things are to be judged." Their view was that:

During great historical movements the forces of nature operating in the human soul overleap the confining wall of logic. . . . The life of a race or a nation is not a logically developing system, nor yet a process which takes place in strict accord with natural laws. It is rather the unfolding of a mystical synthesis, an activity of the soul, which cannot be explained by logical formulae.[8]

On this nonrational basis the fascists and Nazis proceeded to glorify the nation-state or the ethnic *Volk* organized in the nation-state. It became the supreme value, its greatness the supreme end. Thus Mussolini declared:

We have created our myth. . . . Our myth is the nation, our myth is the greatness of the nation. . . . The foundation of Fascism is the conception of the State, its character, its duty, and its aim. Fascism conceives of the State as an absolute, in comparison with which all individuals or groups are relative, only to be conceived of in their relation to the state. . . . Everything for the state; nothing against the state; nothing outside the state.[9]

In their ecstatic frenzy for the power of the nation or race, the fascists and Nazis of course lost sight of the individual. He was simply a tool, perhaps useful or perhaps harmful to the pursuit of extrahuman ends. He had no value simply as a human being. No more possessing a soul than does a pig or a horse, he could be slaughtered or worked according to the convenience of his masters. He really lost his individuality, being either absorbed into the body of the nation-state or treated as an animal fit only for slavery or death. "There are no longer any private people. All and every one are Adolf Hitler's soldiers." "All honor, after all, is political honor; with the honor of one's country, one's own is lost as well."[10]

---

[8] Quoted by William M. McGovern, *From Luther to Hitler* (Boston, Houghton Mifflin, 1941), p. 627.

[9] Herman Finer, *Mussolini's Italy* (New York, Holt, 1935), p. 218; Benito Mussolini, "The Political and Social Doctrine of Fascism," *International Conciliation*, No. 306 (January, 1935), p. 13.

[10] Statements by S. Behn and Robert Ley, quoted by Aurel Kolnai, *The War Against the West* (New York, Viking, 1938), p. 169.

The implications of fascist or Nazi nationalism for international relations are both more clear-cut and more extreme than those of liberalism. Positing the nation and the greatness of the nation as the supreme value, Mussolini went on to assert:

The Fascist State is an embodied will to power. . . . For Fascism, the growth of empire, that is to say the expansion of the nation, is an essential manifestation of vitality, and its opposite is a sign of decadence.[11]

Hitler arrived at the same general conclusion on the basis of his racial myth. He believed in the "worth of Blood," and held that differences in blood created differences in the value of races and men. The "basic idea of nature" was to him "aristocratic," those endowed with the best blood being the aristocracy entitled to rule over the others and those possessing the worst blood being subhuman and entitled only to die. "A State which, in the epoch of race poisoning, dedicates itself to the cherishing of its best racial elements, must some day be master of the world." Hitler felt an "obligation in accordance with the Eternal Will that dominates this universe and to promote the victory of the better and stronger, and to demand the submission of the worse and the weaker."[12] The acceptance of such attitudes by a government controlling considerable power makes war virtually inevitable.

## COMMUNISM

Communism is not a single, coherent ideology any more than liberalism is. Peking now leads one school of thought, Moscow another; and Communist parties over the world, or factions within them, choose between the leaders or develop deviations of their own. But there is a core of thought on which Communists are substantially agreed. We will describe it and note the surrounding issues on which disagreements have developed.

### The "Science" of Marxism

The declared purpose of Communists is world revolution. Underlying the demand for it is a rejection of the tolerance and freedom that liberals proclaim (a rejection based on the "science" of Marxism). Lenin, a leading apostle of Marx and still revered by Communists as the founder of Russian Bolshevism, long ago declared,

. . . The theory of Marx is the objective truth. . . . Following in the direction of the Marxian theory, we shall draw nearer and nearer to the objective truth

---

11 Mussolini, op. cit., p. 16.
12 Adolf Hitler, Mein Kampf (New York, Reynal & Hitchcock, 1939), pp. 103, 580, 994.

(without exhausting it); following another path, we shall arrive at confusion and falsehood.[13]

Subscribing to the same view, Stalin depicted communism as a science which reveals the laws of historical development, a science which permits the discovery of "authentic data" about society, data "having the validity of objective truths." According to the journal issued by the Cominform—an international organization of Communist parties existing from 1947 to 1956—"Marxism-Leninism is all-powerful because it is correct."

In other words, Communists regard themselves as having a relationship to society similar to that of a medical doctor.[14] They believe that they have a science which permits them to diagnose social ills and prescribe remedies just as a doctor does with human patients. Moreover, they believe that they alone are in a position to do this; non-Marxist approaches lead only to "confusion and falsehood." Just as quacks are prevented from practicing medicine because of the damage to patients which they might do, so, according to the Communists, those not guided by Marxism-Leninism should be barred from political activity and deprived of political influence. Armed with "truth" provided by "science," Communists believe that they know what is good for mankind, who and what obstruct the achievement of the good, and how to overcome all obstacles to world-wide triumph.

## Alleged Contradictions in Capitalism

According to the science of Marxism-Leninism, capitalism, though once a progressive system, has lost its usefulness and become a barrier to human progress. It is said to be beset by a series of contradictions which doom it to destruction, if only the Communists give the forces of history a little help. The basic alleged contradiction is between the private ownership of the means of production and the social nature of the productive process. The claim is that, if production requires cooperative group efforts, then it is contradictory to have the means of production under individual ownership. From this basic contradiction, others are said to flow: between classes, between imperialist states and colonies, among imperialist states themselves, and between the capitalist world and the Communist world, once the latter emerges.[15]

[13] V. I. Lenin, *Collected Works* (New York, International, 1927-1932), Vol. XIII, p. 114.

[14] Several passages in this discussion of Communism are repeated from the author's chapter, "The Foreign Relations of the Soviet Union," in Charles P. Schleicher, *Introduction to International Relations* (Englewood Cliffs, N.J., Prentice-Hall, 1954).

[15] For a brief summary of Communist theory see Historicus, "Stalin on Revolution," *Foreign Affairs*, Vol. 27 (January, 1949), pp. 175-214; cf. R. N. Carew Hunt, *The Theory and Practice of Communism* (London, Geoffrey Bles, 1950).

All history, to Communists, is the history of class struggle. In a capitalist system, the owning class (the bourgeoisie) is said to be dominant, both economically and politically. Owning the means of production, it employs others and makes them "wage slaves." Employers are held to be exploiters, failing to pay the workers their just due. Further, the owners of the means of production get control of the state; the machinery of government thus allegedly becomes an instrument in the hands of the bourgeoisie, used to maintain and enhance its privileges. Through the state the owners impose their oppressive rule. The bourgeoisie thus consists of exploiters and oppressors, and the workers constitute the exploited and oppressed.

Particularly among the industrial workers, the proletariat, class consciousness arises. The proletariat becomes aware of the fact that it is being exploited and oppressed and of the fact that a different kind of economic and political system is possible—a system in which exploitation and oppression would not occur. A struggle then ensues between the bourgeoisie and the proletariat; control over the government is the immediate issue. Claiming to know the "true interests" of the proletariat on the basis of the "science" of Marxism, the Communists become the self-styled "vanguard" of the proletariat in this struggle. Their immediate object is revolution, that is, the seizure of state power.

Other contradictions impinge upon this struggle and facilitate the victory of the proletariat. Capitalism is said to lead necessarily into imperialism, and thus to the reduction of foreign peoples to colonial or semicolonial status. Colonial peoples are then exploited and oppressed, just as the proletariat is in the imperialist country itself. They, too, engage in a struggle against their exploiters and oppressors, striving to throw off the yoke of imperialism and secure national independence. They are thus allies in the class struggle, every victory they win contributing to the eventual triumph of the revolution within the imperialist country itself.

Further, according to communist theory, imperialist states inevitably become involved in struggle with each other. Driven to imperialism, they compete with each other in the search for colonies; they struggle over the division of the world, and, once the world is divided up, they struggle over a redivision. Wars occur in the process, weakening one or more of the imperialist states involved and facilitating a revolutionary seizure of power.

Finally, once revolution has occurred in one or more of the capitalist countries, a new contradiction arises, a contradiction between the two worlds of socialism and capitalism. According to the Marxist-Leninist point of view, capitalism will be weakened by the very fact that part of the world has been removed from its sphere of exploitation. Further, the Communists are convinced that their system will work better than any other, and that the very example of their success will contribute to revolution elsewhere. Moreover, as will be seen in a moment, Lenin made it a prime duty of the socialist state to promote revolution abroad.

Communists believe both that the various contradictions make their ultimate victory inevitable and that they must organize and work to achieve victory. They must act as the agents of history in giving effect to its ineluctable laws. Their party must consist of selected and strictly disciplined revolutionaries, thoroughly dedicated to their cause. They must be willing to use literally any means that will promote their triumph, for the end will justify the means. Existing laws may be disregarded, for they are laws enacted for the benefit of the bourgeoisie. Prevailing morality may be ignored, for morality, too, is simply a class instrument. For communists, anything will be moral "which serves to destroy the old exploiting society and to unite all the toilers around the proletariat." The party must work openly where the laws permit, but in any event it must also have an underground apparatus which can persist in revolutionary activity despite repression on the part of the bourgeois state. Crime and sin are dismissed as concepts of the class enemy; nothing will be really criminal or sinful which serves the cause. Deception, robbery, murder, and treason are all justifiable.

## Democracy Means Dictatorship

Communists endorse democracy, but give the word their own special meaning. In fact, they deny that there is any such thing as democracy pure and simple. The state is a class instrument, and the principles on the basis of which the state is governed are class principles. Where democracy exists under capitalism, it is therefore bourgeois democracy, just as a capitalist state is bourgeois. And bourgeois democracy, Lenin long ago declared,

. . . is always bound by the narrow framework of capitalist exploitation, and consequently always remains in reality a democracy for the minority, only for the possessing classes, only for the rich. Freedom in a capitalist society always remains just about the same as it was in the ancient Greek republics: freedom for the slave owners.[16]

There might be freedom within the bourgeoisie; the ruling bourgeois party in a democracy might permit other bourgeois parties to operate, but a real challenge to bourgeois rule would be met by martial law and the threat or the use of violence. In short, Lenin held, "The most democratic bourgeois republic was never, nor could it be, anything else than [a] dictatorship of the bourgeoisie."[17]

Communists demand the transfer of power to the proletariat, propos-

16 V. I. Lenin, op. cit., Vol. XXI, Bk. 2, p. 217.
17 Selected Works (New York, International, 1935), Vol. X, p. 35.

ing to replace the dictatorship of the bourgeoisie with a dictatorship of the proletariat. The function assigned to the dictatorship of the proletariat is to "expropriate the expropriators," that is, to socialize the means of production; this involves the liquidation of the bourgeoisie as a class. The ultimate goal is the creation of a classless (one-class) society in which exploitation and oppression will be eliminated. Such a society would operate on the basis of the principle, "From each according to his ability, to each according to his need." Class divisions having disappeared, there would be no more need for the state; it would wither away.

Communists engage in some subtle sleight of hand in connection with the demand for a transfer of power to the proletariat and for the liquidation of the bourgeoisie. When power goes to the proletariat, precisely who gets it? Who are included in the bourgeoisie? The answer to the first question is that power goes actually to the Communists. It goes to the Communists not because they have been elected to represent the proletariat but because the "science" of Marxism-Leninism designates them as the "vanguard" of the proletariat. They constitute themselves as a self-appointed elite. It is a dictatorship of Communists which they establish, acting in the name of the proletariat. The answer to the second question (Who are included in the bourgeoisie?) is equally arrogant. The revolutionary struggle is ostensibly between the proletariat and the bourgeoisie. The Communists assert that they speak for the proletariat. Those who are against the Communists must therefore be for the bourgeoisie. They are bourgeois, and are therefore to be liquidated.

Nevertheless, the dictatorship of the proletariat is ostensibly democratic, is "a million times more democratic than the most democratic bourgeois republic." It is democratic not because it has the electoral support of any particular portion of the people nor because it wins out in electoral competition with other parties. Rather it is democratic because it serves the "true interests" of the masses of the people, these true interests being determined not by the people themselves but by those schooled in the "science" of Marxism-Leninism.

The democratic or anti-democratic nature of public life of a state, of a government's policy, is determined not by the number of parties but by the substance of the policy of this state, of these parties—by whether this or that policy is carried out in the interests of the people, in the interests of its overwhelming majority, or in the interests of its minority.[18]

## Extending the Revolution

The Communists expect to triumph now in one country and now in another, the revolutionary tide ebbing and flowing in correlation with

---

[18] Georgi Aleksandrov, *The Pattern of Soviet Democracy* (Washington, Public Affairs Press, 1948), p. 23.

periods of stability and crisis in the capitalist system. There is no time-table in accordance with which this historical process is expected to un-fold, but there is no doubt in the minds of the faithful that world tri-umph finally will be theirs. There is ultimately to be "the closest union and complete merging of the workmen and peasants of all nations into a single world-wide Soviet Republic."

How will triumph in the various countries be achieved? And what of relationships between those countries in which the revolution has already triumphed and those in which non-Communist regimes still prevail? The emphasis in Marxist-Leninist theory is on the expectation that the Com-munist party of each country will play the major role in seizing power for itself; for long the assumption was that the seizure would occur through revolution. But still an international duty—a world mission—is assigned to the country in which the revolution first triumphs. Lenin long ago declared:

> The victorious proletariat of that country, having expropriated the capitalists and organized socialist production at home, would rise against the rest of the capitalist world, attracting the oppressed classes of other countries, raising among them revolts against the capitalists, launching, in case of necessity, armed forces against the exploiting classes and their states.[19]

Once the Bolsheviks had seized power in Russia in 1917, Lenin declared it "inconceivable that the Soviet Republic should continue to exist in-terminably side by side with imperialist states. Ultimately one or the other must conquer. Pending this development a number of terrible clashes between the Soviet Republic and the bourgeois states must in-evitably occur." He championed "proletarian internationalism," which he defined as "hard work at developing the revolutionary movement and the revolutionary struggle in one's own land, and the support (by propa-ganda, sympathy, material aid) of such, and only such struggles and policies in every country without exception."

In line with this conception of proletarian internationalism, Lenin encouraged the formation of Communist parties abroad and led in the establishment of an international organization of those parties, called the Third International, in 1919. Acceptance of the "science" of Marxism-Leninism was, of course, prerequisite to membership in the organization. Soviet leaders naturally set themselves up as the supreme interpreters of the science, as revealers of the "truth." Able, as they were, to lend prestige and to give financial, diplomatic, and military support to non-Soviet parties, they established their control over the international move-ment. Loyalty to the Soviet Union and its leadership became the touch-stone for foreign Communists. Foreign parties became fifth columns

---

[19] *Collected Works,* Vol. XVIII, p. 272; Vol. XX, Bk. 1, p. 145; cf. also J. V. Stalin, *Leninism* (London, Communist Party of Great Britain, 1928), Vol. I, p. 56.

abroad, controlled from Moscow (a situation that survived for some years after the formal dissolution of the Third International in 1943).

The extreme to which Lenin was willing to go in promoting the triumph of the Communist ideology is indicated by the fact that he endorsed not only civil but also international war as appropriate methods in the struggle. He was not concerned with the question whether international wars were aggressive or defensive; the question was whether they were "just" or "unjust." "Just" wars included, among others, those "waged . . . to liberate the people from capitalist slavery, or, lastly, to liberate colonies and dependent countries from the yoke of imperialism." He took the view that, "if war is waged by the proletariat after it has conquered the bourgeoisie in its own country and is waged with the object of strengthening and extending socialism, such a war is legitimate and 'holy.' " Along the same lines, a Congress of the Third International later enacted a resolution denying the existence of any contradiction "between the Soviet Government's preparations for defense and for revolutionary war and a consistent peace policy." "Revolutionary war of the proletarian dictatorship," it declared, "is but a continuation of revolutionary peace policy 'by other means.' "[20]

All of this would suggest a display of great revolutionary zeal and militancy on the part of the Russian Communists, and in truth, they did display these qualities in the first years after their revolution. Now and again the qualities have been revived, and they may come to the fore again. But as early as 1919, the Bolsheviks—in bitter struggle among themselves— decided that saving the revolution in Russia was more important than extending it abroad; this means that, in effect, they decided against trying to help Communists in other countries if this meant great risks and costs for themselves. Since that time they have repeatedly demonstrated their adherence to this principle. Their caution has obviously been accentuated by the development of nuclear weapons and missile delivery systems. Moreover, it is plausible to suppose that it may also have been accentuated simply by the passage of time, the rise of new generations and new leaders, the very costly experience of World War II, and the fact that domestic economic developments have given the Russians more to lose. Long ago Lenin accepted the need for a policy of "peaceful coexistence" with non-Communist countries in certain periods, and in recent years it is this policy that the Soviet Union has proclaimed.

The differences between Moscow and Peking, in so far as they are ideological, turn largely on the relationship of peaceful coexistence and revolutionary duty. The words and the principles that are involved, the state-

[20] *History of the Communist Party of the Soviet Union (Bolsheviks), Short Course* (New York, International, 1939), pp. 167-168; V. I. Lenin, *Selected Works,* Vol. VII, p. 357; Communist International, *The Struggle Against Imperialist War and the Tasks of the Communists, Resolutions of the Sixth World Congress, July-August, 1928* (New York, Workers Library, 1934), p. 33.

ments by Lenin and others concerning them, and the relevant precedents are all vague. The two sides can thus use approximately the same language, but still mean something very different. The fact is that they do use approximately the same language, making it terribly difficult to determine with any precision just what each side stands for and what the differences are. Both sides claim, of course, to be engaged in struggle against capitalism and imperialism, and neither construes *peaceful* coexistence to be placid or harmonious. The question is what kinds of struggle are to be engaged in and what kinds avoided. The Soviet Union has been placing great stress on struggle by economic means: it will bury the West through peaceful economic competition and through the force of the example of its domestic success. Furthermore, the Soviet Union has been emphasizing the urgency of avoiding nuclear war and avoiding lines of action that might accentuate the danger that nuclear war might occur. It has tended to emphasize the possibility of a peaceful transition to socialism in some countries, if not throughout the world, and has been willing to take certain actions (e.g., accept a nuclear test ban treaty) designed to ameliorate relations with the West. On all these counts (and others too) the Chinese are scornful. They claim that "the prophets who pin all their hopes on 'peaceful transition' proceed from historical idealism, ignore the most fundamental contradictions of capitalism, repudiate the Marxist-Leninist teachings on class struggle, and arrive at a subjective and groundless conclusion."[21] To them, peaceful coexistence applies not to international relationships in general but only to relationships between "countries with different social systems."

It should never be extended to apply to relations between . . . oppressed and oppressor countries . . . and never be described as the main content of the transition from capitalism to socialism. . . . Peaceful coexistence cannot replace the revolutionary struggles of the people. The transition from capitalism to socialism in any country can only be brought about through the proletarian revolution and the dictatorship of the proletariat in that country.[22]

Moreover, according to the Chinese, it must be a major principle that socialist countries are "to support and assist the revolutionary struggles of all the oppressed peoples and nations." They deny they want world war. They point out that "the wars of national liberation and the revolutionary people's wars that have occurred since World War II have not led to world war."[23] And they claim that those who accuse China of wanting to spread socialism by "wars between states" are themselves "opposed to revolutions by the oppressed peoples and nations of the world and op-

---

[21] John Wilson Lewis, ed., *Major Doctrines of Communist China* (New York, Norton, 1964), p. 252.
[22] *Ibid.*, p. 261.
[23] *Ibid.*, p. 259.

posed to others supporting such revolutions."[24] From their point of view Khrushchev and his successors in the Soviet Union are revisionists, and "revisionism is the main danger." The rejoinder of the Russians is that the Chinese espouse "dangerous" views, that their alleged recommendations "for an armed struggle everywhere" are nothing but an attempt to push a policy of "reckless adventure," that their claimed love of peace is in glaring contrast to their deeds, and that their real concern is not for the interests of the peoples of Asia, Africa, and Latin America, as they assert. According to the Russians, the Chinese leadership "is clearly trying to establish control over the national liberation struggle in order to make it an instrument for the implementation of its own hegemonic plans. That probably sheds more light than anything else on the true object of the Chinese leaders' policy. . . ."[25]

## Attitudes Toward Nationalism

With the objective of world revolution, Communism is internationalist in outlook. What attitude does it take toward nationalism? The question arises in regard to three major groupings: the developing countries, the "imperialist" countries, and the countries in which the Communists themselves rule.

With a qualification to be noted shortly, Communists have long been champions of nationalism in the developing countries. In their eyes all of these countries have been under the yoke of imperialism. Whether or not formally in colonial status, they are the international counterpart of the proletariat: just as the bourgeoisie of the advanced countries exploits and oppresses the proletariat at home, so does it exploit and oppress the less advanced peoples abroad. Moreover, imperialism allegedly strengthens itself through such exploitation and oppression. Thus one way of weakening imperialism and of contributing to its ultimate overthrow is to champion the cause of national liberation; this means that nationalism gets endorsed in the name of internationalism.

The qualification on the above stems from the fact that some nationalists in the developing nations are anti-Communist and, especially in the nations that are formally independent, pro-Western. Somewhat different reactions to this fact seem to be among the sources of conflict between the Russians and the Chinese. The Russians have been more inclined than the Chinese to woo the leaders and peoples of the developing nations without regard to their political outlook. The Chinese express their view as follows:

24 *Ibid.*, p. 256.
25 *Tass* summary of report of February 14, 1964, by Mikhail A. Suslov. *New York Times,* April 4, 1964, pp. 8-9. Cf., Alexander Dallin, ed., *Diversity in International Communism, A Documentary Record, 1961-1963* (New York, Columbia University Press, 1963), esp. pp. 629, 641, 747, 752, 756.

The policy should be to unite with the bourgeoisie, insofar as they tend to be progressive, anti-imperialist, and antifeudal, but to struggle against their reactionary tendencies to compromise and collaborate with imperialism and the forces of feudalism. On the national question the world outlook of the proletarian party is internationalism, not nationalism. In the revolutionary struggle it supports progressive nationalism and opposes reactionary nationalism.[26]

The early attitude of Communists toward nationalism in the more advanced countries was one of contempt. They regarded nationalism as an ideology of the merchant class developed in the struggle against feudalism and retained as a device for persuading the workers under capitalism to support those who held them in subjection. Nationalism, like religion, was opium for the people. During and after World War II, however, this line changed, and Communists in the advanced countries came to describe themselves as the true national patriots. The obvious inference is that the Communists concluded that nationalism was too powerful an ideology to be combatted frontally and that it was more prudent to try to capture and take advantage of it.

The general line that the Communists have adopted for this purpose is that just as the "science" of Marxism-Leninism reveals the true interests of the proletariat, so does it reveal the true interests of the nation. The working class is the authentic national class, incarnating the national interest. Whatever is good for the working class, as determined by the Communists, is good for the nation. Only the Communists and those aligning themselves with the Communists are true patriots. All others are unpatriotic betrayers of the nation.[27] On this basis the Communists set themselves up as the correct interpreters of the national tradition and as the vanguard of the nation as well as the working class. They may go to great lengths in imbuing themselves and others with the national spirit. For example, a Chinese Communist ping-pong player and coach, facing international competition in 1965, gave as one of the prescriptions for victory: "A player should not consider personal success or failure in his activity but must consider the honor of the fatherland in the first place." As it turned out, his team won the world championship.

Communists have been somewhat ambivalent about nationalism in subdivisions of the countries that they rule. Cultural manifestations of nationalism are encouraged and some political manifestations of it are at least formally recognized. For example, within the Soviet Union national differences are reflected in the division of the country into constituent republics and in the further division and subdivision of the constituent republics themselves. Formally, the republics have a right of secession from

26 Lewis, op. cit., p. 249.

27 See Vernon Van Dyke, "The Communists and the Foreign Relations of France," in Edward Mead Earle, ed., Modern France (Princeton, Princeton University Press, 1951), pp. 240-247. Lewis, op. cit., pp. 266-67.

the USSR. Two of them, the Ukraine and White Russia, are members of the United Nations. But there are limits beyond which the political expression of nationalism is not to go. Ukrainians who agitated for complete independence from Moscow, for example, would surely be found to be tools of the class enemy.

Nationalism in the satellite countries has been a serious problem. As devotees of "proletarian internationalism," Communists must deplore politically divisive nationalism among themselves. They could use nationalist appeals in their struggle for power, but they were not to interpret nationalism in such a way as to set them off from the USSR. Loyalty to socialism, as interpreted in Moscow, was to be paramount. But the Poles and Hungarians and Serbs and other peoples of Eastern and Southeastern Europe had their own proud national traditions, and for some of these people the Russians had been the historic national enemy. In the end, events proved that nationalism of a divisive sort could not be entirely eliminated. Such nationalism was a major factor in Titoism and in the establishment of Yugoslavia as a Communist-ruled state that was nevertheless independent of Moscow. In 1956 developments going in a similar direction were handled by bloody Red Army repression in Hungary and by a compromise arangement in Poland under which Poland has a considerable degree of freedom from Moscow both in theory and in practice. Since then and above all with the development of the split between Moscow and Peking there has been a considerable loosening of the ties that once bound the non-Russian parties in a rather strict subordination to Moscow's control.

## Implications for International Politics

In so far as ideology affects the behavior of Communist states, what are the implications for international politics? In the first place, Communism provides Moscow and Peking with a basis for the development of fifth columns—some of them very powerful—in other countries. Aggression by subversion and by unconventional war has taken a much more prominent place in world affairs than ever before. In the second place, ideology has provided a basis for a familial sort of relationship among those states endorsing it. To a considerable extent, the familial relationship has been and is cooperative, but between Moscow and Peking it has become bitterly hostile. The notion that Marxism-Leninism is a science revealing truth makes for conflict when different practitioners of the science come up with different truths; in fact, the stage is set for something akin to religious wars. Internecine struggles within various Communist parties, especially the Soviet party, provide little basis for expecting peace even if all the world should go Communist. In the third place, and most important of all, statesmen whose thoughts are shaped by Marxist-Leninist theory must, somehow and some time, seek the overthrow of non-Communist governments. They must assume the existence of basic and irreconcilable mutual antagonism in relations with such governments; neither side can expect fundamental reconciliation and trusting cooperation with the other.

Differences between the policies of the liberal-democratic and the Communist states are usually not as complete as the above sketch suggests. The basic objective of every state is normally to preserve and protect itself against external attack, or more generally, to avoid having an outside will imposed upon it. In other words, all states, including Communist states, seek to preserve their independence and their security. Moreover, though Communism endorses aggressive civil and international war as a useful instrument of policy, it would be unsound to infer from this that Communist governments are forever plotting war. As indicated above, the Soviet leaders long ago accepted the principle that they would not undertake serious risks and costs simply to promote revolution abroad. In any event, governments do not ordinarily go to war unless they see a good prospect of winning. Aware of the potential destructiveness of nuclear warfare, and denied substantial hope of victory, even a Communist government may be devoted to peace. Further, even though world revolution is the Communist objective, neither the Soviet nor any other Communist government can pursue this objective forever in utter disregard of the people under its control; some minimum standard of well-being must be maintained, and there will be pressures for something above a minimum standard. Concentration on world revolution and an all-out effort to promote it may be possible for a time, but zeal and sacrifice for the achievement of a single objective cannot be maintained indefinitely. Human desires are too varied, and human beings are too concerned with their own personal interests, to permit this.

Though differences between the policies of the liberal-democratic and the Communist states are perhaps not as great as the ideologies suggest, they are nevertheless sharp. The basic difference probably derives from the fact that liberal-democrats do not claim to know the "truth" whereas the Communists do. Not claiming to possess "truth," not asserting absolute knowledge of the interests of individual men or of society, the liberal emphasizes procedures by which decisions should be made and certain limitations within which decisions should be made. He stresses majority rule, minority rights, and constitutional safeguards of liberty. He seeks to keep the future open, to maintain conditions under which individuals can choose the paths which seem likely to lead to satisfaction. Emphasizing liberty he must also emphasize tolerance of differing ideas and practices to which liberty leads. His world is one of diversity, involving respect for the choices of others—within limits that are still being explored. He must insist upon restraint, for liberty is like a kite which is kept flying by the string which holds it down.

The Communist is intolerant. Claiming to know what should be done, why should he tolerate error? Why should he permit liberty, when liberty may lead to wrong choices? Why keep the future open, when he knows without doubt what it should be? His duty is, rather, to remake individual men and whole societies—to remake the world—in accordance with the prescriptions of science. In the titanic struggle to remake mankind, he does not even grant the right of silence; those who are not liquidated must be compelled to shout, if not to work, for the cause. He permits diversity only where the obstacles to its elimination are too great to be overcome. Commanding "truth," he has no respect for what he regards as error. Such restraint as he displays reflects only his prudence rather than respect for the right of others to be wrong.

Both liberal-democracy and Communism may thus make for either co-operation or conflict among states. Each ideology facilitates cooperation among those adhering to it. At the same time, each ideology is a challenge —each is subversive—to the other. This very fact makes for friction and conflict, and the prospect of conflict is greatly enhanced by the belief of Communists that it is their historic mission to overthrow non-Communist systems and bring world-wide triumph to their cause.

## SOCIALISM

A considerable portion of the politically active throughout the world are socialist, social-democratic, or Christian-socialist. The beliefs that go with the labels are indistinguishable from liberalism at the one extreme and from communism at the other. The stress is on the promotion of human welfare through governmental action: government is to assume a greater degree of responsibility than capitalist principles suggest for deciding how to allocate resources, for providing capital and deciding how it is to be invested, for increasing the level of production, for managing productive enterprise, and for providing various kinds of social services. In greater or less degree this means a planned, collectivist economy with a higher proportion of productive power in the hands of government and less reliance on the individual investor or entrepreneur. Among the objectives is a reduction of the amount of exploitation that occurs (or is thought to occur) under capitalism and to promote a greater degree of social and economic equality. Non-Communist socialists generally think less in terms of class struggle than in terms of closing the gaps separating the classes and obtaining the support of all classes in the social development that they seek. They regularly claim to believe in democracy, but often fail to assign the term a clear meaning. In Egypt Nasser speaks of a "Socialist-Democratic Cooperative society"—which he will lead indefinitely. In Indonesia, Sukarno champions what he calls "guided democracy, or democracy with leadership," rejecting the kind of democracy associated with what he calls "free-fight liberalism."

Socialism has implications for foreign policies and international politics, just as the other ideologies do. The farther a socialist is along the scale ranging from liberalism toward communism, the more distrustful and suspicious he is likely to be of countries and governments thought of as capitalist. The United States is sometimes handicapped in its relations with other countries by this fact, and the Soviet Union gains a relative advantage. In Western Europe, socialists in times past were inclined to oppose imperialist policies of their own governments and in more recent times have been especially responsive to demands that colonial areas be granted independence. In the former colonies themselves, the anti-imperialist attitudes of socialists are more pronounced. They generally combine belief in socialism with an emphasis on nationalism and a jealous regard for national independence; they are sensitive to signs of "neo-colonialism," which they of course oppose. Their attitudes are sometimes such as to discourage foreign investment in their countries, and international difficulties sometimes arise when socialist governments nationalize property owned by foreigners. Socialists profess a love of peace, just as liberals do.

## REALISM AND UTOPIANISM

Though realism and Utopianism are not ideologies, they are similar to ideologies in their relationship to political behavior; they are perspectives, or sets of attitudes, that are associated with certain kinds of motivations, analyses, and prescriptions, just as are liberalism, fascism, communism, and socialism. We will thus give them brief attention here. Meanings assigned to the terms are usually vague, and the vague meanings differ among themselves. Also, *Utopianism* and *idealism* have a great deal in common, and sometimes are used as synonyms. When the contrast is between realism and idealism, confusion is sometimes increased by the claim that idealism is more realistic than realism, or by the claim that the same policy can be both idealistic and realistic—idealistic in the goals pursued and realistic in the methods employed. The object here is to present characterizations of the two points of view, drawn largely from the work of Edward Hallett Carr.[28] They may or may not be applicable in their entirety to any specific persons.

The words themselves suggest that the realist starts with reality—with what was and what is—whereas the Utopian or idealist starts with what ought to be. Realists are inclined to be pessimistic about the possibility

[28] Edward Hallett Carr, *The Twenty Years' Crisis 1919-1939* (New York, Harper & Row, 1964), pp. 11-21.

of shaping the course of events by deliberate effort and will; they are inclined to be determinists and to think that causal forces are at work beyond conscious control—or that objective laws operate—making certain patterns of behavior and certain kinds of development more or less inevitable; or they may believe that so many factors are at work and so much about them is unpredictable—their identity, their relative force, their interrelationships, etc.—that planned control of the course of events is impossible, above all in international politics. This means that realists have little faith in the efficacy of human reason. They may espouse moral principles and claim to act in accordance with them (after all, very few people profess to be amoral or immoral), but their morality is likely to reflect conditions and practices in whatever environment is significant to them (not the conditions and practices that prevail elsewhere or the conditions and practices that allegedly ought to prevail); realism may thus prescribe somewhat different moral judgments in, say, Moscow, Peking, and Washington. Thus realism has about it an aura of opportunism and an emphasis on expediency. Some realists like to explain and predict behavior in terms of *interests:* individuals and groups (including nations and states) act as their interests dictate, and the possibilities of cooperation and conflict are determined by relationships among the interests that are involved. Those stressing interests ordinarily assume that they are selfish interests—that all actors pursuing interests are pursuing their own advantage. Hans Morgenthau prescribes that the interests of states be "defined in terms of power," though without saying what kinds or elements of power he has in mind or how much power is enough. In his view, *interests* become a kind of mystical eternal force or spirit, temporarily incarnated in existing states and destined to be reincarnated when other actors come to dominate the scene.[29] Others suggest, as indicated in Chapter 1, that there are different kinds of interests (independent and dependent), identified or determined in different ways; power, however defined, is one interest among others and must be considered in relation to the others.

Utopians or idealists, in contrast to realists, are more inclined to believe that men can be masters of their fate, and that through reason and will they can shape the future (their own future and the world's) in a desirable way. They regard men and society as perfectible through deliberate effort. They are likely to be less opportunistic than the realists, less attracted by expediency, more inclined to be moralistic and doctrinaire, and more inclined to think and act in universal terms. They are thus more optimistic about human nature and human affairs, and may well be impatient with those at home and abroad, who in their eyes, are not contributing to the development of the good society.

[29] Hans Morgenthau, *Politics Among Nations,* 3rd ed. (New York, Knopf, 1960), pp. 9-10.

Realists and idealists are likely to differ, too, in their attitude toward the role of armed power and war. For the realist, armed power and war are simply features of what has been and is, to be accepted and used as expediency dictates—not with a view to reforming the world or achieving any other general, long-run goal but rather with a view to serving immediate and relatively limited needs. For the idealist, armed power and war are evils whose role is to be reduced if not eliminated: differences are to be resolved by nonviolent competition, through reason and persuasion, not by the threat and use of violence. Realists may thus use war and the threat of war to serve their limited ends, and if war is thrust upon them they may accept it as a regrettable but unavoidable feature of the political system, to be fought and terminated—if at all possible—in such a way as to minimize risks and costs. Idealists are much more inclined to regard war, if it occurs, as the work of evil men or an evil foreign system; for them war is thus much more likely to be thought of as an Armageddon, a final struggle between good and evil, leading to a warless world. The outlook of idealists and of interventionist liberals is suggested by the statements of Woodrow Wilson when he asked Congress to declare war on Germany in 1917.

We have no selfish ends to serve. . . . We are but one of the champions of the rights of mankind. . . . We shall fight for the things which we have always carried nearest our hearts—for democracy, for the right of those who submit to authority to have a voice in their own governments, for the rights and liberties of small nations, for a universal dominion of right by such a concert of free peoples as shall bring peace and safety to all nations and make the world itself at last free.

The difference between idealists and realists is typified by the statement that Bismarck "fought 'necessary' wars and killed thousands; the idealists of the twentieth century fight 'just' wars and kill millions."[30] And the idealist view is expressed in the statement: "Either war is a crusade, or it is a crime. There is no half-way house."[31]

## SUGGESTED READINGS

*The Conservative Papers* (Garden City, N.Y., Anchor Books, Doubleday, 1964).
CRANKSHAW, Edward, *The New Cold War, Moscow v. Pekin* (Baltimore, Penguin, 1963).
DALLIN, Alexander, ed., *Diversity in International Communism, A Documentary Record 1961-1963* (New York, Columbia University Press, 1963).
GIBSON, John S., *Ideology and World Affairs* (Boston, Houghton Mifflin, 1964).
GIRVETZ, Harry K., *The Evolution of Liberalism* (New York, Collier Books, 1963).

30 A. J. P. Taylor, as quoted by Waltz, *op. cit.*, p. 114.
31 Michael Straight, as quoted by Waltz, *op. cit.*, p. 111.

KAPLAN, Morton A., ed., *The Revolution in World Politics* (New York, Wiley, 1962).

KAUTSKY, John H., *Political Change in Underdeveloped Countries: Nationalism and Communism* (New York, Wiley, 1962).

LEWIS, John Wilson, ed., *Major Doctrines of Communist China* (New York, Norton, 1964).

MORGENTHAU, Hans J., *In Defense of the National Interest* (New York, Knopf, 1951).

———, *The Purpose of American Politics* (New York, Knopf, 1960).

ORTON, William Aylott, *The Liberal Tradition, A Study of the Social and Spiritual Conditions of Freedom* (New Haven, Conn., Yale University Press, 1945).

OSGOOD, Robert E., *Ideals and Self-Interest in America's Foreign Relations* (Chicago, The University of Chicago Press, 1953).

PERKINS, Dexter, *The American Way* (Ithaca, N.Y., Cornell University Press, 1957).

PROCTOR, J. Harris, ed., *Islam and International Relations* (New York, Praeger, 1965).

ROOSEVELT, James, ed., *The Liberal Papers* (Garden City, N.Y., Anchor Books, Doubleday, 1962).

SIGMUND, Paul E., Jr., *The Ideologies of the Developing Nations* (New York, Praeger, 1963).

VON DER MEHDEN, Fred R., *Politics of the Developing Nations* (Englewood Cliffs, N.J., Prentice-Hall, 1964).

WALTZ, Kenneth N., *Man, the State and War* (New York, Columbia University Press, 1959).

WOLFERS, Arnold, and MARTIN, Laurence W., eds., *The Anglo-American Tradition in Foreign Affairs* (New Haven, Conn., Yale University Press, 1956).

6

# ECONOMIC OBJECTIVES
# AND ECONOMIC FORCES

Any inquiry into the question why states behave as they do
—and that is the inquiry in which we are engaged—must take economic
factors into account. They obviously play a significant role in international politics, just as they do in domestic politics.

There is danger of confusion in considering the subject, so we must be
clear on what we are and what we are not discussing. The object in this
chapter is to explain and assess the influence of economic considerations
and economic forces on foreign policies. We want to know to what extent
and in what ways economic factors make for cooperation or conflict
among states. We want to know how and in what ways international relations are affected by the desire to retain or secure control over scarce
resources. We want to know what follows in the international field from
the fact that men desire wealth and from the fact that they operate under
a particular kind of economic system—under capitalism, in particular.

Of course, economics plays not only an influential but also an instrumental role. It is not only a determinant of foreign policy but also a tool
of foreign policy. A state may pursue objectives selected for economic reasons, or it may adopt economic methods in pursuing objectives selected
for whatever reasons. We are here interested in the influential role of
economics, not in its instrumental role. For example, we are not interested
in the economic methods by which governments may seek to win friends
or influence people; we are not interested in the economic methods by
which the power of a state may be increased or reduced. Discussion of economic methods for the promotion of political purposes will be reserved
for a later chapter.

The influence of economic considerations and forces on the behavior of states is in some respects a highly controversial subject. Economic determinists, and particularly the Marxists, interpret and explain virtually all political actions, domestic and international, in economic terms. Others reject such sweeping views, yet grant that economic factors play a powerful role. We shall first deal with the less controversial aspects of the subject, and then discuss economic theories of imperialism and war.

## ECONOMIC CONSIDERATIONS AND
## FOREIGN POLICIES

That men desire the necessities and comforts and luxuries of life goes without saying. If they could secure all that they wanted within their own countries, the pursuit of economic objectives would presumably have less impact on international politics. The fact is, however, that many of the things that people want can be secured only, or more advantageously, in foreign countries. Resources are not distributed among countries in proportion to the demand for them. Raw materials in short supply in one country may exist in abundance in another; Britain, for example, produces no oil, but various states in the Middle East produce far more than they require. Climate and soil may permit one country to produce agricultural commodities which can only be produced with difficulty, if at all, in another; coffee, for example, can be grown in Brazil, but not in the United States. There are differences among nations in the productive skills and productive facilities available; the Swiss, for example, possess in an unusual degree the skills and facilities necessary for watchmaking, yet do not manufacture automobiles. More generally, differences exist among countries in the possession of capital available for investment and in the rate of profit that can be secured on investments.

International commercial and financial relationships develop naturally and almost inevitably out of factors such as these. Needing oil, the British go abroad to buy it. Wanting coffee, Americans import it from Brazil and elsewhere. Desiring watches, the people of many countries secure them from Switzerland. Requiring capital for the development of their resources, governments and private entrepreneurs often seek to attract foreign investors or to borrow abroad.

These statements are all rather simple and obvious, yet they are fraught with great significance to international politics. Governments themselves desire revenue, and they commonly look upon international commercial activities, particularly on the importation of goods from abroad, as a source of revenue. At the same time, governments commonly seek to protect the domestic economy against the possible adverse effects of foreign trade. More important to an explanation of the impact of economic pursuits on international relations is the fact that individuals who go abroad do not always leave their own governments entirely behind them. It is said that a Chinese emperor in the eighteenth century was unmoved by the fact that a number of Chinese traders had been killed in Java; he said that he was not interested in the fate of those who were so greedy for gain that they left the Heavenly Kingdom and went abroad among barbarians to seek it. This kind of attitude is alien to the western world. Tourists and traders who go abroad—and often even emigrants—take the flag with them, in effect, and the flag also follows the dollar. Governments are concerned with the wealth and well-being of their citizens abroad, and with the security of their lives and property. They therefore commonly seek to promote the economic activities of their citizens abroad, to see to it that justice is done to them in foreign countries, and generally to facilitate profitable and desirable international trade. Citizens abroad, in turn, look to their home governments for protection, and sometimes seek even more than protection, as will be shown below.

These attitudes are basic to an explanation of the influence of the pursuit of economic objectives on the behavior of states. Sometimes they produce cooperation among states in service to the mutual advantage of their citizens. Often, however, the activities of citizens abroad lead to international friction and conflict.

## The Economic Factor in Colonial Imperialism

The establishment of European colonies abroad—involving the conquest of most of the rest of the world since the fifteenth century—resulted from the pursuit of a number of different objectives. The first explorers crossed the seas partly out of pure curiosity. They and their successors, having contacted alien lands and peoples, pressed on partly out of a desire to extend the Christian religion, or to secure religious liberty for themselves, or, more recently, to take up the alleged White Man's Burden. Many colonies were seized either because the possession of colonies was thought to lend glory to king or nation or because of their strategic value in rendering existing possessions more secure. There is no simple explanation of overseas imperialism. Yet among the factors which have operated, economic considerations have certainly been powerful.

*1. The search for profits and the seizure of colonies.* Economic objectives were particularly important in the early expansion of Europe across the seas. Voyages down the African coast sponsored by Prince Henry the Navigator were encouraged when the first ships returned with gold dust and Negro slaves. Later expeditions were lured on by thought of the riches to be obtained from importing the spices and other rare products of India and the East. Once the Portuguese reached India, they found that they could not capitalize on their discovery merely through peaceful trade. They had to destroy the fleets of the Arab merchants and to establish naval bases on the shores of India and other eastern lands. These things they did, enriching themselves and establishing colonies, some of which Portugal retains, though in some jeopardy, to this day.

Later the Dutch entered the trade, the States-General creating the Dutch East India Co. in 1602 and authorizing it to make war or peace, seize foreign ships, establish colonies, construct forts, and coin money. The British likewise entered with their East India Co. Soon the two were fighting each other as well as the Portuguese while reducing the peoples of the East to colonial subjection. Gradually the Dutch, in an effort to make their trade secure, established political control over the East Indies, which they retained until after World War II. The British, and later the French, developed their trade and power primarily in India, the British eventually winning out and reducing all India to colonial control. It should be noted that neither the Dutch nor the British began their activities in the East for the purpose of establishing empire. Rather, the main purpose was profit, but once European lives and property were at stake in the East, activities could not remain purely commercial. To protect themselves and their interests, the Europeans felt compelled to take part in the political and military affairs of the governments and peoples of the region; moreover, other motives welled up—such as the "daemonic will to conquer and to rule"—and the combination led gradually to the establishment of colonial controls.[1]

Similar developments occurred in relationship to the Western Hemisphere. Desire to find a way to the Indies and to the profits to be secured through trade with them played a major role in the voyages of Columbus and others who sailed west across the Atlantic. It took much exploring before what someone has called the "depressing fact" became clear that the route to the West led only to a sparsely populated new world. Meantime the explorers laid claim to newly discovered lands on behalf of the crown which sponsored their voyages. Adventurers and settlers took up residence temporarily or permanently across the seas, extending the realm of European control. Spanish *conquistadores* established the "silver empire," looting the wealth of the Aztecs and Incas and winning a vast empire for Spain. Colonizers set out from Britain for North America, usually sponsored by a joint stock company. There were a number of arguments for sponsoring such colonization, the most important being economic. "The colonies were to enrich the investors, and the realm in general, by producing commodities which were in demand in Europe; to enrich the Crown by means of customs duties; and to enrich the merchants and manufacturers of England by serving as markets for English products."[2] Britain and Spain, especially, enacted navigation and other acts designed to preserve for their own people the profits of trade with

---

[1] John Strachey, *The End of Empire* (New York, Random House, 1960), p. 23.
[2] J. H. Parry, *Europe and a Wider World* (London, Hutchinson's University Library, 1949), p. 108.

the colonies and to enhance the revenues which the governments themselves would derive from that trade. The French and Dutch were likewise lured on largely by the prospects of profit to participate in the exploration and colonization of the new world.

In the Western Hemisphere, as in the East Indies, the pursuit of wealth led to conflict both with native peoples and among the European countries involved. Privateering, bordering on piracy, was common for long periods in the relationships between the ships of different European countries in the Atlantic. Numerous colonial wars were fought among the imperial powers.

During the nineteenth century the European powers reduced one part of Africa after another to colonial control. The motivating considerations in most of the acts of expansion were mixed. The desire for profits was certainly among them. When King Leopold II of Belgium took steps leading to the establishment of the Congo Free State, of which he became King, he professed the most altruistic motives:[3] "To open to civilization the only part of our globe where it has not yet penetrated, to pierce the darkness which envelopes whole populations, is a crusade, if I may say so, a crusade worthy of this century of progress." In fact, however, his rule over the natives of the Congo turned out to be ruthless and inhumane, though very profitable. He and others associated with him made millions of dollars. Whatever Leopold's original motives, his actions eventually led to the acquisition of the Congo Free State by Belgium as a colony. Elsewhere in Africa, too, the desire to protect the lives and property of citizens who themselves were pursuing profit, the desire for prestige and power, ostensible response to the idea of the White Man's Burden, and other considerations combined to produce imperialism. By the end of the century very little of the continent remained free.

2. *The role of population pressure.* The pressure of population on resources has figured, especially in more recent times, as both a reason and an excuse for imperialism. Note that it is not population density which is necessarily involved; the pressure of population on resources may be great even in sparsely settled territories. Note too that there is no direct correlation even between pressure of population on resources and imperialism; many countries where such pressure is great have been non-imperialistic. Something must be added to population pressure before imperialism is produced, and even then it may or may not materialize. Perhaps the most general formulation is this: when the politically influential believe that scales of living are unduly low, that resources in the homeland provide an inadequate basis for improvement, and that improvement could be accomplished through a program of territorial aggrandizement, the stage is set for an expansionist program. Japan's im-

[3] Parker Thomas Moon, *Imperialism and World Politics* (New York, Macmillan, 1927), pp. 75-97.

perialism in the half-century leading to World War II is frequently explained in these terms, the allegation being that she needed colonial territories both as an outlet for surplus population and as a source of raw materials. In the period between the wars Mussolini cited population pressure in Italy as a factor necessitating territorial expansion (and at the same time tried to encourage population growth so as to obtain the manpower that a program of aggrandizement seemed to require). In fact, migration from an imperialist country to its colonies has rarely if ever served significantly to reduce population pressure, but the belief that it would may at times have stimulated colonial ventures.[4]

Present population trends, if they persist, will certainly create great domestic problems for a number of states, and international relationships are bound to be affected; the effect might be profound. Estimates made in the early 1950's (which "now seem minimal") indicated that a continuation of trends would bring a 65% increase in the population of the underdeveloped countries between 1950 and 1975, and then a doubling of the 1975 population by 2000. Total population of these countries would increase from 1.6 billion in 1950 to 5.4 billion in 2000. By 2000 as compared to 1950, the population of Asia and Africa would in each case be more than tripled, and the population of Latin America quadrupled. Whereas the developed part of the world (Europe, USSR, Northern America, Australia, New Zealand, and Japan) included 33% of the earth's total population in 1950, it would include only 21% in 2000. A series of *ifs* suggests that the population of China alone may exceed one billion by 1978.[5] Now it may be that existing trends will not persist and that these population levels will not be reached. But the possibility must be recognized. And there is an obvious call for thought and planning with regard to the potential problems. Much depends on the choices that peoples and governments make. It is one thing if they seek solutions through domestic measures and another if they resort to programs of imperialistic adventure.

3. *Economic factors in American imperialism.* The history of American foreign relations offers numerous examples of the influence of economic considerations in producing imperialism, whether it took the form of the acquisition of territory or of military intervention in the affairs of other states. While Texas was still a part of Mexico, people from the United States emigrated to the territory primarily for economic reasons. They naturally took their own language and customs and expectations with them. In a sense they constituted an alien fifth column infiltrating the territory of a friendly state. Mexican rule proved uncongenial and even-

---

[4] Grover Clark, *A Place in the Sun* (New York, Macmillan, 1936), pp. 85-129.
[5] Irene B. Taeuber, "Population Growth in Underdeveloped Areas," in American Assembly, *The Population Dilemma* (Englewood Cliffs, N.J., Prentice-Hall, 1963), pp. 35, 37.

tually unacceptable to them. They rebelled, established their independence, and later secured admission into the United States. War between the United States and Mexico developed over the issue.

Hawaii became a possession of the United States by a somewhat similar process. Missionaries began the penetration of the islands and were soon followed by traders and pineapple growers. Again a clash of culture developed, and the Americans on the island—with unauthorized help from local United States representatives—eventually rebelled against the native government and seized control. Cleveland, inaugurated as President soon after the Hawaiian revolution, had pangs of conscience over the role of the United States in the events and tried to find a way to restore a legitimate Hawaiian regime, but he could not do so without placing the lives of the American rebels in jeopardy. The revolutionary government therefore survived, and in the surge of American imperialism at the time of the Spanish-American War it secured the annexation of Hawaii to the United States.

American advocates of the annexation of the Philippines after the Spanish-American War used economic arguments, among others, to support their program. They were enamored of the possibilities of trade in the Far East, and thought that control of the Philippine Islands would facilitate the penetration of markets in the region. Senator Albert J. Beveridge, a leading exponent of annexation, made perhaps the most flamboyant plea, appealing at once to economic considerations, to the idea of the White Man's Burden, and to national chauvinism:

American factories are making more than the American people can use; American soil is producing more than they can consume. Fate has written our policy for us; the trade of the world must and shall be ours. And we will get it as our mother [England] showed us how. We will establish trading posts throughout the world as distributing points for American products. We will cover the ocean with our merchant marine. We will build a navy to the measure of our greatness. Great colonies, governing themselves, flying our flag and trading with us, will grow about our posts of trade. Our institutions will follow our flag on the wings of our commerce. And American law, American order, American civilization, and the American flag will plant themselves on shores hitherto bloody and benighted, but by those agencies of God henceforth to be made beautiful and bright.[6]

In these cases—Texas, Hawaii, and the Philippines—it is obvious that the economic argument alone does not explain the imperialistic expansion which occurred. In each one, considerations of national pride and a longing for something vaguely regarded as greatness clearly played a significant role.

The United States on numerous occasions has been involved in friction

6 Claude G. Bowers, *Beveridge and the Progressive Era* (New York, Literary Guild, 1932), p. 69.

and conflict with several of the Caribbean republics. Again noneconomic considerations have often been influential. The desire to forestall European intervention, to safeguard the route through Panama, and perhaps the psychological satisfaction derived from dominance have all played a role. But economic considerations have usually been important in the difficulties that have arisen. One of the most flagrant examples is that relating to Nicaragua in the period from 1909 to 1912. American business concerns operating there, dissatisfied with the government of President Zelaya, apparently encouraged and financed revolution against it. The United States government officially intervened to support the revolutionaries in the struggle that ensued. The justification for the intervention, which prevented Zelaya's forces from re-establishing control over the port city of Bluefields, was that American life and property there would be endangered if the rebel forces were defeated. In other words, by military action the United States assured the rebels a safe haven in Bluefields. Later, when the legitimate government sought to blockade the port so as to prevent "the revolution from continuing to receive, as before, arms, supplies, and funds from New Orleans," the United States frustrated the action by threatening war. Unable to cope with American support for the rebels, both President Zelaya and his legitimate successor abandoned the struggle and fled the country. The rebels thus won out. Negotiations with the rebel government led to agreement between the United States and Nicaragua satisfactory to American commercial interests operating in the country. Soon the former secretary of one of the American concerns became Nicaragua's president.[7]

This is a clear instance in which the actions of a state were influenced by the economic interests of its nationals abroad. Similarly, American relations with Mexico were strained for over a decade after the 1917 Mexican constitution asserted national ownership over subsoil deposits, including ownership of oil under land owned or leased by American companies. Mixed considerations—among them economic ones—led to American intervention in Cuba, the Dominican Republic, Haiti, and Panama.

4. *The relative influence of economic and political factors.* The developments and episodes described above scarcely permit any generalization other than that sometimes and to some extent economic factors have contributed to international friction, colonial imperialism, and war. Systematic studies have been made, however, from which more pointed conclusions have been drawn. Jacob Viner, for example, has investigated

[7] Charles A. Beard, *The Idea of National Interest* (New York, Macmillan, 1934), pp. 170-182. Cf. Samuel Flagg Bemis, *The Latin American Policy of the United States* (New York, Harcourt, Brace & World, 1943), pp. 161-163. In a sense the American practice of extending diplomatic protection to its citizens in Caribbean countries, sometimes involving military intervention, served as a substitute for reducing them to the status of colonies. See pp. 303-304, below.

relationships between international finance and balance-of-power diplomacy, mainly in Europe, from 1880 to 1914. In all the transactions studied he found that the bankers, far from taking the initiative in actions which dragged governments into difficulties, were "passive and in some cases unwilling instruments of the diplomats."

. . . The bankers in general seem to have been pacifically inclined, and to have been much more favorably disposed than were their governments to international cooperation and reconciliation. . . . Bankers rarely favor an aggressive policy toward powerful adversaries, or even toward weak countries if the latter have powerful friends. Whatever their attitude toward weak and friendless countries, in the diplomacy of the Great Powers they are a pacific influence. . . . For the claim sometimes made that the bankers exercised a controlling influence over pre-war diplomacy, the available source material offers not the slightest degree of support.[8]

Similarly, Eugene Staley, in his *War and the Private Investor*, made an analysis of all cases roughly in the half-century after 1880 in which pressures from private traders and investors are alleged to have been the source of serious international disputes. Only rarely did he find that the economic factor operated alone, and often he discovered it to be less influential than political factors. Where serious disputes arose such factors as concern for national power and prestige almost always supplemented economic factors in producing difficulties. This was particularly true in relationships among the great powers. Where the potential antagonist was a great power, and where no significant military or political interest was involved, governments extended only hesitant support, if any at all, to citizens trading and investing abroad. They did not want to fight a major war, or seriously to risk it, solely for the benefit of a few. Several statements by Staley are in point:

Private investments seeking purely business advantage (i.e., unmotivated by political expansionism, balance of power strategy, military considerations, or other reasons of state) have rarely of themselves brought great powers into serious political clashes.

Where there has been really serious friction between major powers over investment matters, examination will disclose in most instances that the political opposition existed before the investment issue arose, and either expressed itself through them or crystallized around them.

Investments used in the service of naval and political strategy, colonial expansion, quests for national glory, and the like, have been more productive of international friction in the past than investments actuated solely by private profit motives.[9]

[8] Jacob Viner, "International Finance and Balance of Power Diplomacy, 1880-1914," *Southwestern Political and Social Science Quarterly*, Vol. 9 (March, 1929), pp. 450-451.
[9] Eugene Staley, *War and the Private Investor* (Garden City, N.Y., Doubleday, Doran, 1935), pp. xvi, 359, 360.

The Moroccan crisis of 1911 is one of the few incidents in which a private enterpriser has dragged an unwilling government into serious diplomatic difficulties. There is every evidence that the German government wanted the German concern involved in this case to reach an amicable understanding with its French counterpart. The French government took a similar view. Nevertheless, the German firm persisted with incomprehensible stubbornness in rejecting even the most generous offers; at the same time it engaged in a propaganda campaign, arousing German nationalist and patriotic emotion over the issue. A serious crisis ensued in the relations between Germany and France; it was resolved peacefully, yet it certainly contributed to an embitterment of relationships. The very rarity of such a case, however, is at least as significant as the fact of its occurrence.

The influential role of the economic factor in modern times has been somewhat greater in relationships between great powers and small, "backward" countries. As Staley puts it, "Private investments have been important as instigators (as distinguished from tools) of diplomatic action mainly in connection with the relations of relatively weak capital-importing countries with relatively strong capital-exporting countries."[10] Most of the episodes described on the preceding pages illustrate the point.

*5. Exploitation, mutual advantage, and independence.* The above examples allude only to cases of more or less active or aggressive measures on the part of erstwhile imperialist countries. Two comments might be added. It should not be assumed that all economic relationships between great powers and underdeveloped areas (even when the latter became colonies) have necessarily been to the disadvantage of the weaker party. Even in the heyday of imperialism, many such relationships provided mutual benefit. Some colonial areas gained more than the imperial country, and some very probably progressed more under alien rule than they would have had they been left alone.

Despite this, the establishment of colonial and quasi-colonial relationships led to long-range difficulties. Colonial peoples commonly became resentful both of white settlers who entered their territory and of the alien governments to which they were subjected. Especially after World War II anti-imperialist nationalism became a powerful force in much of the colonial world; an almost pathological hatred of the imperial overlord sometimes developed. Economic motives are rarely emphasized in this connection, though undoubtedly they have played a role. It is much more common to explain independence movements in colonies in terms of a fanatical desire to bring to an end the humiliations accompanying subjection to foreign control. The "daemonic will to conquer and to rule" that contributes so much to an explanation of imperialism brought about

10 *Ibid.,* p. 366.

its counterpart: the daemonic will to be free. Colonial peoples, it turned out, also had their pride.

## International Effects of Domestic Economic Measures

International relations are affected by the pursuit of economic objectives at home as well as by the pursuit of economic objectives abroad. Governments are concerned not only with the prosperity and well-being of nationals doing business in foreign countries but also with the prosperity and well-being of citizens within the country. They want to prevent foreign trade from having an adverse effect on the domestic economy; they sometimes regulate the character and extent of participation by foreigners in domestic economic life; and they normally seek to maintain or improve the level of domestic well-being. Measures taken for any of these reasons may produce repercussions abroad.

*1. Protection of domestic producers.* During the seventeenth and eighteenth centuries the countries of western Europe regulated foreign trade relationships on the basis of the principles of mercantilism. Both power and plenty were the objectives, and a long-run harmony between the two was assumed.[11] Money was thought to command them both, so foreign trade relationships were regulated with a view to amassing money. A so-called favorable balance of trade was sought, mainly by encouraging exports and restricting imports. Though the theory alleged to justify mercantilist methods has been proved unsound, some of them are still employed.

Tariffs are the traditional device for protecting the domestic economy —or simply for conferring advantage on special interest groups at the expense of others. More recently, states have resorted to fixing quotas on imports, that is, to specifying that no more than a certain quantity of an item can be imported in a given period of time. They have also resorted to exchange controls, to regulating the purchase of foreign currencies needed to pay for imports. Furthermore, sanitary regulations are sometimes imposed; whether the desire to protect domestic plant and animal life from disease is the real or only the ostensible reason, the effect is to curtail imports.

Although perhaps protecting the domestic economy, tariffs, quotas, exchange controls, and sanitary regulations are likely to do damage to other countries. A reduction in one's country's imports means a reduction in another country's exports. An increase in the United States' tariff on watches amounts to an attack on the prosperity of Switzerland. A French quota on the importation of automobiles reduces profits in Detroit. British exchange controls which restrict the importation of cotton from the

11 Jacob Viner, "Power Versus Plenty as Objectives of Foreign Policy in the Seventeenth and Eighteenth Centuries," *World Politics*, Vol. 1 (October, 1948), esp. p. 10.

United States help cause unemployment in the South. An American ban on the importation of Argentine beef because of the presence of hoof-and-mouth disease in Patagonia contributes to depression in Argentina. Not only do these measures sometimes reduce trade, but, of course, they curtail increases in trade which might otherwise occur.

The adoption of protective devices often leads to international protest. Governments do not like to have their economies damaged or undermined from abroad. They do not like it when others seek to "export unemployment." Some thirty different countries protested to the United States when the Smoot-Hawley tariff was enacted in 1930. A country shut out from foreign markets—and therefore substantially prevented from buying the things it needs abroad—may take drastic measures to remedy the situation. It may retaliate in kind, or it may take even more extreme measures. As Jacob Viner puts it, "Trade barriers . . . are undoubtedly the major economic contribution, directly or indirectly, to international conflict, tension, and war."[12] There is no doubt that the protective measures taken by other countries played a role in producing the economic difficulties that contributed, however significantly, to both German and Japanese aggressiveness in the 1930's.

These problems sometimes lead also to international cooperation. After all, international trade may serve mutual advantage. Beginning in 1934, the United States took the lead in efforts to secure a general relaxation of trade barriers, through a Reciprocal Trade Agreement program. The most spectacular development along this line since World War II is the establishment of a Common Market by six of the states of Western Europe. The goal of the Common Market—achieved in large part already—is the complete elimination of all trade barriers among the members.

2. *Regulation of foreign participation in economic life.* Governmental regulations of the character and extent of participation by foreigners in domestic economic life are far less significant than trade barriers to international politics. Moreover, such regulations are usually designed to promote objectives that are more political than economic, as when governments are moved by national pride or by concern for security to prevent aliens from securing control over vital sectors of economic life. Nationalist and racialist factors are often involved. Former American policies concerning the immigration of Orientals, and concerning the treatment of those who had already entered the country, provide a case in point. Welcomed when cheap labor was needed, the Chinese were excluded from the country when fear developed, especially in the trade unions, that their willingness to accept low wages would depress the scale of living of American workers. The Japanese were likewise subjected to dis-

---

[12] Jacob Viner, "The Economic Problem," in George B. de Huszar, ed., *New Perspectives on Peace* (Chicago, The University of Chicago Press, 1944, copyright 1944 by the University of Chicago), p. 102.

crimination for various reasons, including economic ones. Diplomatic difficulties ensued, leading to a gentlemen's agreement between the United States and Japan under which the latter agreed to deny passports to its nationals wishing to emigrate to the United States. Later, California and other states enacted legislation prohibiting aliens ineligible for citizenship (principally the Chinese and Japanese) from owning or leasing land for agricultural purposes. Still later the federal government heaped indignity on both China and Japan through the immigration law of 1924; while permitting immigration from other countries on a quota basis, the law entirely prohibited immigration from these and other Oriental countries. There was resentment over this especially in Japan, and the resentment was undoubtedly a factor in the exacerbation of relations with Japan which later occurred.

Regulations concerning the participation of foreigners in domestic economic life have also contributed to other episodes involving international friction. Economic considerations were among those which induced the Boer Republic to enact legislation discriminating against aliens, and this legislation in turn helped to bring on the Boer War. Economic considerations have commonly also figured among those leading to the socialization or nationalization of resources or industries—for example, by the Bolsheviks after the October Revolution, by the Mexicans in connection with subsoil deposits and the oil industry, and by Iran of the Anglo-Iranian Oil Co. The implications for international politics are obvious.

3. *Deficit financing and war preparations.* Governmental efforts to maintain or improve the general level of domestic prosperity are probably most serious for international relations when they involve an armaments program. It should not be forgotten that such a program may be designed for pump-priming as well as for power. When governments try to spend themselves out of depressions, or spend to avoid depressions, they sometimes find it easier to spend on armaments than on anything else. People may be divided about the wisdom of adopting a work-relief program or providing a dole; they are less likely to be divided over proposals to increase the power of the armed establishments, particularly if a foreign enemy exists or can be created. As a writer in *Punch* put it many years ago,

> The heart of a nation, as never before,
> Is united when making munitions of war.

The United States Congress in 1934 explicitly declared that one of its purposes in appropriating money for the construction of naval vessels was to provide work. Usually, however, such explicit admissions are not made. It becomes difficult to tell, therefore, where concern for power stops and where the desire to provide employment begins in influencing governments to enact arms programs. Hitler's rearmament of Germany in the 1930's certainly was a major factor in eliminating unemployment in the country, whether or not this was a conscious purpose. Certainly, too, the armaments program in the United States has come to be so important an element in the national economy that changes must be considered not only in terms of military needs but also in terms of the prospective effects on the level of prosperity. International agreement on disarmament is deterred far more by other considerations than by fear of its effects on domestic economic life; still, these effects might be significant.

It should be pointed out that pump-priming is called for only in deflationary periods. Further, advances made in the field of economics in recent years have revealed means of curbing deflation which are superior to large-scale armaments expenditures. It is therefore not to be assumed, whether in periods of deflation or inflation, that armaments programs are undertaken (solely, largely, or at all) for economic reasons. Dangers to national security may be very real.

To sum up, we have seen that the pursuit of economic objectives both abroad and at home may influence foreign policies and contribute to international friction and war. Citizens who travel or trade or invest abroad sometimes drag their governments after them into colonial ventures or into difficulties with foreign states; this occurs more often in relations between strong and weak powers than in relations between strong powers themselves. Governments seeking to promote domestic prosperity sometimes take measures which create international friction and increase the probability of war; they enact trade controls which undermine prosperity abroad, they discriminate against aliens in domestic economic life, and they may use armaments programs to relieve or avert unemployment. Conversely, too, states sometimes cooperate with each other in the pursuit of common economic interests.

*4. State-controlled economies and the problem of war.* This discussion of the relationship between economic forces and the behavior of states has so far related mainly to free-enterprise economies. Is there reason to believe that the collectivization of economic life significantly reduces the role of economic factors in contributing to international friction and war? Apparently not, either on the basis of empirical evidence or on the basis of theoretical expectations. In a number of cases where the Soviet Union has gained the upper hand politically—in Eastern and Southeastern Europe after World War II, in Manchuria, and perhaps in Sinkiang—it has imposed exploitative economic relationships. In so doing it has aroused bitter resentment even on the part of Communists in the countries involved. This is one of the factors that led to the split between the Soviet Union and Yugoslavia in 1948, and the issue subsequently appeared in relationships between the Soviet Union and other Communist countries. The Hungarians rebelled against the Russians in 1956, and the Poles defied them for a variety of reasons, this one among others. A similar statement applies to relationships between the Soviet Union and

Communist China. The record is adequate to demonstrate that economic rapaciousness is not confined to capitalists.

Nor is it theoretically to be expected that Communists would refrain from economic exploitation unless faced with some kind of external deterrent. After all, Communist governments have economic interests to protect and promote, just as other governments do. If anything, they are even more committed to the pursuit of economic ends, and if the achievement of these ends seems to call for some kind of diplomatic or military action against other states, Communist rulers will at least be sorely tempted to take the action. Jacob Viner even suggests that classless societies, if organized on a national basis, will be "readier to engage in war than bourgeois capitalist societies." He further states,

As compared to class-divided states, a classless state will be more unified with respect to national policy because of the absence of internal conflicts of class interest and the absence of opposition parties organized on class lines and tending even to take antinational positions. It is hard to think of any economic ground for going to war which may not be as much present in a world of classless nation-states as in a world of capitalist states, and there is no basis for supposing that classless societies would not share with capitalist societies most of the political or sentimental or moral reasons for going to war, while producing some novel ones of their own.[13]

In short, in view of the probability that some degree of state intervention in economic life is likely to continue indefinitely, economic factors influencing the behavior of states are likely to continue to operate. The adoption of socialist proposals might well accentuate rather than reduce the economic sources of international friction and war.

## ECONOMIC THEORIES OF IMPERIALISM

It is one thing to say that economic factors sometimes contribute to the development of friction or the outbreak of war among states, and quite another thing to explain friction and war mainly or exclusively in economic terms. This is what some do. Though perhaps recognizing that other factors play some kind of a role, they assert that economic factors are decisive or crucial. An Englishman, J. A. Hobson, advanced this kind of an interpretation in a book on imperialism, which was first published in 1902. Lenin's theory of imperialism goes along the same line. We will focus on these two authors in turn.

### Hobson's Theory of Imperialism

Hobson's theory rests on the idea of overproduction-underconsumption, the idea that a capitalist country tends to produce more than it can con-

[13] *Ibid.*, p. 96. Cf., Jacob Viner, "International Relations Between State-Controlled National Economies," *American Economic Review*, Vol. 34, Part 2 (March, 1944), p. 328.

sume. There results, Hobson argued, a surplus of goods and a surplus of capital, and the presence of the surpluses in turn leads to a search for foreign markets in which the surplus goods can be sold and the surplus capital invested. Out of the search, Hobson claimed, imperialism and war arise.

According to Hobson, capitalism commonly involves "a distribution of general income which puts too small a share in the hands of the working classes, too large a share in the hands of the employing and owning classes."[14] The employing and owning classes, possessing "too large" a share of the total income, either save or invest much of it. If they save it, they leave products on the market for which there is inadequate demand. If they invest it within the country in new factories and other means of production, they simply accentuate the difficulty, creating still more surpluses for which effective demand is inadequate. If the working classes— the mass of the consumers—had a greater share of the national income, they might buy up the products which otherwise are surplus, but the distribution of income is said to prevent them from doing so. Thus, in Hobson's words,

Everywhere appear excessive powers of production, excessive capital in search of investment. It is admitted by all business men that the growth of the powers of production in their country exceeds the growth in consumption, that more goods can be produced than can be sold at a profit, and that more capital exists than can find remunerative investment.[15]

What is the way out? According to Hobson, the way out which is commonly chosen is imperialism. "It is this economic condition of affairs," he said, "that forms the taproot of imperialism." Those with surplus products and surplus capital seek to sell or invest abroad. "Imperialism is the endeavor of the great controllers of industry to broaden the channel for the flow of their surplus wealth by seeking foreign markets and foreign investments to take off the goods and capital they cannot sell or use at home."[16]

Hobson did not argue that the economic factor operated alone in producing imperialism. He pictured finance as the "governor" rather than the "fuel" of the imperial engine. It did less to generate imperialist strivings than to direct and concentrate them. "Finance manipulates the patriotic forces which politicians, soldiers, philanthropists, and traders generate; the enthusiasm for expansion which issues from these sources, though strong and genuine, is irregular and blind; the financial interest has those qualities of concentration and clear-sighted calculation which are needed to set Imperialism to work."[17]

14 J. A. Hobson, *Imperialism* (London, George Allen & Unwin, 1938), p. vii.
15 *Ibid.*, p. 81.
16 *Ibid.*, p. 85.
17 *Ibid.*, p. 59.

Neither did Hobson argue that imperialism is necessarily of economic benefit to the imperialist country as a whole. Rather, he took the view that imperialism is "bad business for the nation"; its risks and costs are greater than the rewards which come to the country as a whole. Yet, though imperialism is "irrational from the standpoint of the whole nation, it is rational enough from the standpoint of certain classes in the nation." Some stand to gain, and they manipulate public policy so as to secure gain for themselves even though others suffer. According to Hobson, "The famous words of Sir Thomas More are as true now as when he wrote them: 'Everywhere do I perceive a certain conspiracy of rich men seeking their own advantage under the name and pretext of the commonwealth.' "[18]

Hobson did not argue that imperialism is inevitable under capitalism. Rather, it results from "a false economy of distribution," a wrong distribution of income. "Imperialism is the fruit of this false economy; 'social reform' is its remedy. The primary purpose of 'social reform' . . . is to raise the wholesome standard of private and public consumption for a nation, so as to enable the nation to live up to its highest standard of production."[19] Hobson declared that a completely socialist state which kept good books would soon discard imperialism, and that an intelligent laissez-faire democracy which gave duly proportionate weight in its policy to all economic interests alike would do the same.

John Maynard Keynes's *The General Theory of Employment, Interest and Money* contains an explanation of imperialism and war similar in some respects to that of Hobson. Keynes pointed out[20] that in a laissez-faire capitalist system "full, or even approximately full, employment is of rare and short-lived occurrence." Though governments desire to alleviate or eliminate unemployment, traditional laissez-faire theories provide them with no orthodox means of doing so. If they are to reduce unemployment they are therefore impelled to struggle for an export surplus and for an import of the monetary metal at the expense of their neighbors. International trade thus became to him "a desperate expedient to maintain employment at home by forcing sales on foreign markets and restricting purchases, which, if successful, will merely shift the problem of unemployment to the neighbor which is worsted in the struggle."

Never in history [he said] was there a method devised of such efficacy for setting each country's advantage at variance with its neighbors' as the international gold (or, formerly, silver) standard. For it made domestic prosperity directly dependent

---

[18] *Ibid.*, p. 46.

[19] *Ibid.*, p. 88.

[20] John Maynard Keynes, *The General Theory of Employment, Interest and Money* (New York, Harcourt, Brace & World, 1936), esp. pp. 250, 349, 381-383. For a discussion of various economic explanations of imperialism, see E. M. Winslow, *The Pattern of Imperialism* (New York, Columbia University Press, 1948).

on a competitive pursuit of markets and a competitive appetite for the precious metals. [The struggle] has tended to become increasingly internecine.

Keynes recognized that war had "several causes," but over and above the others he placed the economic causes, "namely, the pressure of population and the competitive struggle for markets." He argued, however, as did Hobson, that the economic causes of war could be counteracted within the framework of the capitalist system.

## Lenin's Theory of Imperialism

Hobson obviously influenced Lenin. Lenin based his theory on the "general and fundamental law" that under capitalism both the means of production and the money available for investment are concentrated in fewer and fewer hands. In other words, capitalist economies come to be dominated by monopolies or trusts, supplemented internationally by cartels. At some point in this process capitalism is transformed into imperialism. According to Lenin's "briefest possible definition," imperialism is "the monopoly stage of capitalism."

Capitalism in its monopolist or imperialist stage, according to Lenin, is necessarily expansionist. It is expansionist in part because the monopolists come to control "surplus" capital. They will not use the surplus for the purpose of raising the standard of living of the masses, for this would mean a decline in profits. They cannot keep on investing within a strictly national economy, because as capitalism matures the rate of profit on investments within the country tends to decline. So they invest abroad, in less advanced countries, where the rate of profit promises to be higher. Having invested, they want their investment to be secure. "The necessity of exporting capital gives an impetus to the conquest of colonies, for in the colonial  market it is easier to eliminate competition, to make sure of orders, to strengthen the necessary 'connection,' etc., by monopolist methods  (and sometimes it is the only way) ."

Monopoly capitalism is also expansionist, Lenin held, because of the need for foreign raw materials and because of the competition among capitalists of various countries for control over them. "Colonial possession alone gives complete guarantee of success to the monopolies against all the risks of the struggle with competitors. . . . The more capitalism is developed, the more the need for raw materials is felt, the more bitter competition becomes, and the more feverishly the hunt for raw materials proceeds throughout the whole world, the more desperate becomes the struggle for the acquisition of colonies."

As the reference to the acquisition of colonies suggests, Lenin was not speaking solely of economic expansion. Under his analysis, monopoly capitalists dominated not only the economic but also the political life of imperialist countries. In general, he regarded all governments simply as instruments of a ruling class. Whether governments were monarchical or republican, dictatorial or democratic—in fact, regardless of their form —they would be class instruments in societies divided into classes. Under monopoly capitalism, they would be tools of the monopolists. Thus, if the monopolists wanted to render their foreign investments secure, and if they wanted to gain control over the sources of needed raw materials, they would simply use government to serve this end. Whether the nation as a whole gained or lost through imperialist expansion was an irrelevant question; it was only the interests of the monopolists which counted. Thus through their economic power and through their use of the state the monopoly capitalists engaged in struggles for territorial expansion. The fundamental forces at work were economic, but Lenin admitted the existence of a "non-economic superstructure" which stimulated the striving for colonial conquest. What he meant was that the monopoly capitalists developed ideologies and principles which justified and reinforced their pursuit of economic interests.

In Lenin's description, the process of imperialism went on until the whole world had been divided up among the imperialist powers, but even then it did not stop. Enduring stability was out of the question. Lenin held that capitalism develops unevenly in different countries. Power relationships among countries therefore change, and as they change there are demands for a redivision of the world. Imperialist countries which in the days of their strength seized foreign territories are thus compelled to disgorge their gains when other imperialist countries become more powerful.

Lenin simply assumed that wars arise naturally out of the imperialist struggle. He thought it "naive" to talk about peace under imperialism. There would be wars among the imperialist states themselves over the division and redivision of the world, and wars between imperialist states and the colonial areas. Nowhere did he explicitly claim that all wars arise out of economic causes even under capitalism; in fact, when explaining the origin of particular wars he cited reasons which seem to have little to do with capitalism or with economics. Nevertheless, the inference of his argument was that wars would be inevitable as long as capitalism endured.[21]

## AN APPRAISAL

There is no denying the fact that economic forces and economic considerations sometimes contribute to international friction and war, just as do many other forces and considerations. The principal question is

[21] E. Varga and L. Mendelsohn, eds., *New Data for V. I. Lenin's "Imperialism, The Highest Stage of Capitalism"* (New York, International, 1940), esp. pp. 138-140, 182, 186, 192; cf. Lionel Robbins, *The Economic Causes of War* (London, Jonathan Cape, 1939).

whether any of the theories presuming to explain war largely or exclusively in economic terms is sound.

It is rather striking that none of those who stress economic theories of imperialism and war have developed or defended those theories on the basis of a serious analysis of the formulation of foreign policies or the actual developments leading to the outbreak of war. None of them traces the precise route from the existence of an economic desire to the firing of the first shot. Rather, they engage in economic analysis and are satisfied when they have found an economic desire or circumstance which makes resort to war more or less plausible. They are then inclined to assume that, when war occurs, it occurs because of the reasons they have found plausible.

In contrast, those who approach the question of the causes of imperialism and war through a study of the formulation and execution of foreign policies in concrete situations rarely emerge with an answer that is exclusively economic. Almost always noneconomic factors are found to be heavily involved, and very often they appear to play a decisive role.

Certainly studies such as those made by Viner and Staley, referred to earlier in this chapter, have refuted any theory which ascribes imperialism and war, as a general rule, to the influence of particular and identifiable capitalists on government. As Staley demonstrates, it is the exception rather than the rule when serious friction and war can be explained on this basis. Governments rarely undertake serious risks promoting or protecting the interests of individual persons, groups, or corporations, except when those interests coincide with larger interests of the state. To the extent that Hobson's theory, or any other theory, rests on the idea that war generally results from a conspiracy of rich men seeking personal profit, it is plainly unsound.

Moreover, differences in the behavior of the various capitalist states render any theory questionable that ascribes war to capitalism as such. Switzerland and Sweden, which Lenin would have regarded as capitalist, have avoided participation in war for almost a century and a half, and have not pursued imperialistic policies. In the twentieth century, Denmark, the Netherlands, and a number of other states commonly regarded as capitalist have not been imperialistic in the sense of acquiring colonies, and have become involved in war only because they were attacked. If underconsumption or unemployment or monopoly capitalism were a compelling cause of imperialism and war, how can so many states have avoided its force? It is no answer to say that the states named are too small to fight, for they could have allied themselves with more powerful neighbors.

Further, it is plain that wars occur under capitalism which are hardly explicable in terms of any of the economic theories that have been advanced. Certainly none of them explains in any direct way the Spanish-

American War, the Russo-Japanese War of 1904-1905, the Turco-Italian War of 1911, or the Balkan Wars. Lenin's theory to the contrary notwithstanding, they hardly explain the Austrian attack on Serbia in 1914 and the subsequent transformation of this war into World War I. Nor, to take a more recent illustration, do they explain the North Korean aggression of 1950. The very fact that wars have occurred throughout history, waged by both capitalist and noncapitalist powers, demonstrates that causes of war operate which are independent of capitalism.

Lenin's theory is particularly vulnerable. It is simply not true in any meaningful sense that monopolists control government as a regular matter in advanced capitalist countries. For the United States, one need only recall Roosevelt's New Deal and Truman's election in 1948—major events which are hardly attributable to Wall Street. For Britain it is sufficient to recall the election of a Labor government with a socialist program after World War II. If it is contended that the New Deal in the United States and the Labor program in Britain are simply alternative expressions of the political power of monopolists, the obvious answer is that the monopolists are sharply divided against themselves, favoring quite different types of economic policies with different implications for international politics. The record shows that capitalist democracies tend to become welfare states, a possibility which Lenin's analysis denies. Moreover, since World War II the actions of the Soviet Union on the one hand and of the Western powers on the other scarcely lend credence to the view that imperialism is peculiarly associated with capitalism.

The views of Hobson and Keynes were not so extreme. Although Hobson no doubt exaggerated and distorted the role of economic factors in producing imperialism and war, both he and Keynes granted that noneconomic factors were also in part responsible. Moreover, both granted the possibility of reforms within the framework of capitalism that would reduce or eliminate economic forces which, among others, make for war, and the development of the idea of the welfare state has in fact been accompanied by such reforms.

It might be noted that Quincy Wright, though, of course, granting that economic factors sometimes help produce imperialism and war, does not associate these phenomena especially with capitalism. In fact, the reverse is true. He says:

Capitalistic societies have been the most peaceful forms of societies yet developed. . . . Wars have occurred during the periods of capitalistic dominance, but they have been least frequent in the areas most completely organized under that system. . . . In the modern period, in which alone capitalism has been fully developed, war has more frequently been initiated by states dominated by agrarianism or by socialism than by those dominated by capitalism.[22]

[22] Quincy Wright, *A Study of War* (Chicago, The University of Chicago Press, 1942, copyright 1942 by the University of Chicago), Vol. II, pp. 1162-1164.

It is perhaps understandable that those who have stressed economic causes of war should have neglected to point out that economic pressures actually work both ways. While bringing economic advantage to some, war brings loss and destruction to others. Major wars necessarily disrupt trade patterns, both within and among states. War means the severance of trade with the enemy and the actual or potential loss of investments in enemy territory. The fact is that the economic interests of traders and investors have often led them to exert their influence on behalf of peace. Moreover, even those who stand to gain economically from war may recoil from it for noneconomic reasons.

A curious commentary on economic motives in political behavior, and on economic interpretations of imperialism, is contained implicitly in *The End of Empire* by the late John Strachey, a Labor Party leader in Britain. A final chapter goes "Towards a Theory of Imperialism" with a predominantly economic interpretation. Imperialism first developed in human history when techniques of production became such as to provide a surplus—something over and above what was required for subsistence. It then became possible for some to live off the labor of others, and so they became imperialist, either enslaving others or holding them in subjection and servility while exploiting them. In more modern times, mercantile empires arose (e.g., through the operations of the East India Company) and, more recently, the fully developed capitalist empires. In explaining the latter, Strachey goes along with Hobson and Lenin. Capitalist societies develop "a distribution of income and other characteristics which leave their directing classes little choice but to attempt the conquest, colonisation and exploitation of as much of the world as they can get hold of." Strachey grants, however, that such societies can be modified—and that some have in fact been modified—so as to reduce or eliminate the economic pressures that bring about imperialism.

The curious thing is that Strachey puts much less stress on economic motivations when actually describing the steps leading to empire and in prescribing for Britain now that it has come to "the end of empire." In India, he says, Clive pursued economic gain, but "when all this is realized there still remains something unaccountable" about crucial decisions that he and those with him made leading to the subordination of India to British political control. Strachey then accounts for the unaccountable by asserting that the decisions marked "the moment in history when a daemonic will to conquer and to rule seized the British, an imperial will to rule which possessed them for the next two centuries." He asks later what purposes Britain should pursue now that it is no longer possessed by such a will. "We shall stagnate unless we can find other purposes to satisfy our hearts." In searching for suitable substitutes he asserts (correctly or not) that the United States has made personal enrichment the ideal, and he rejects the motive as not sufficiently satisfying. Even national enrichment is not enough. Economic motives will not do! "If Britain is to be great in the future as she has been in the past (note the assumption that *greatness* is the goal), we shall have to take the things of the mind and the spirit much more seriously than we have hitherto done." And after identifying various domestic ways of tending to things of the mind and spirit, he goes on:

It is by lifting our eyes and looking outwards upon the whole world that we shall find an ideal high enough, difficult enough of attainment, and therefore inspiring enough, to fire the national imagination. The highest mission of Britain in our day is to help the underdeveloped world. . . . This is above all the field in which Britain is called upon to lead the world. . . . It will be by serving the peoples of the world that we can be great.[23]

What does this say about the primacy of economic forces and economic motives?

## SUGGESTED READINGS

AMERICAN ASSEMBLY, *The Population Dilemma* (Englewood Cliffs, N.J., Prentice-Hall, 1963).

BEARD, Charles A., *The Idea of National Interest* (New York, Macmillan, 1935).

CLARK, Grover, *A Place in the Sun* (New York, Macmillan, 1936).

DEANE, Phyllis, *Colonial Social Accounting* (Cambridge, Cambridge University Press, 1953).

HOBSON, J. A., *Imperialism* (London, George Allen & Unwin, 1938).

KNORR, Klaus, "Theories of Imperialism," *World Politics*, Vol. 4 (April, 1952), pp. 402-431.

KOEBNER, Richard, and SCHMIDT, Helmut Dan, *Imperialism* (Cambridge, Cambridge University Press, 1964).

KOLARZ, Walter, *Communism and Colonialism* (New York, St Martin's, 1964).

LANGER, William L., "A Critique of Imperialism," *Foreign Affairs*, Vol. 14 (October, 1935), pp. 102-119.

———, *The Diplomacy of Imperialism, 1890-1902* (New York, Knopf, 1935).

MEYER, Alfred G., *Leninism* (Cambridge, Harvard University Press, 1957).

MOON, Parker Thomas, *Imperialism and World Politics* (New York, Macmillan, 1926).

ORGANSKI, Katherine, and ORGANSKI, A. F. K., *Population and World Power* (New York, Random House, 1961).

PARRY, J. H., *Europe and a Wider World* (London, Hutchinson's University Library, 1949).

ROBBINS, Lionel, *The Economic Causes of War* (London, Jonathan Cape, 1939).

SNYDER, Louis L., ed., *The Imperialism Reader, Documents and Readings on Modern Expansionism* (Princeton, N.J., Van Nostrand, 1962).

STALEY, Eugene, *War and the Private Investor* (Garden City, N.Y., Doubleday, Doran, 1935).

23 Strachey, *op. cit.*, pp. 244, 246, 247.

STRACHEY, John, *The End of Empire* (New York, Random House, 1960).

THORNTON, A. P., *The Imperial Idea and its Enemies* (New York, St Martin's, 1959).

VARGA, E., and MENDELSOHN, L., eds., *New Data for V. I. Lenin's "Imperialism, The Highest Stage of Capitalism"* (New York, International, 1940).

VINER, Jacob, "The Economic Problem," in De Huszar, George B., ed., *New Perspectives on Peace* (Chicago, The University of Chicago Press, 1944).

WINSLOW, E. M., *The Pattern of Imperialism* (New York, Columbia University Press, 1948).

# WAR AND THE
# EXPECTATION OF WAR

Many years ago an English writer, R. G. Hawtrey, made the rather enigmatic statement that "the principal cause of war is war itself." He explained himself to some extent as follows:

When I say that the principal cause of war is war itself, I mean that the aim for which war is judged worth while is most often something which itself affects military power. Just as in military operations each side aims at getting anything which will give it a military advantage, so in diplomacy each side aims at getting anything which will enhance its power. Diplomacy is potential war. It is permeated by the struggle for power, and when potential breaks into actual war, that is usually because irreconcilable claims have been made to some element of power, and neither can claim such preponderance as to compel the other to give way by a mere threat.[1]

This explanation is helpful, but it by no means exhausts the subject. Hawtrey's own explanation bears some clarification, and additional implications of his central proposition can be found.

Our purposes will be served best if we broaden Hawtrey's proposition a little and then explore its meaning. We can say that war and the expectation of war exert a major influence on the behavior of states. Both past war and the expectation of future war are involved, and they not only help cause war but they also help to shape foreign policies and international relationships both in peacetime and in wartime. If it were not for the fact that wars occur and are expected to occur, states would behave very differently than they do.

[1] R. G. Hawtrey, *Economic Aspects of Sovereignty* (New York, Longmans, 1930), p. 107.

## WAR AND THE
## SEEDS OF FUTURE WAR

War affects the behavior of states and sows the seeds of future war in various ways.

### Struggles over Peace Terms

War is likely to produce tensions among the victors—and it may produce new war—because of disagreements over the terms of a peace settlement. This is, of course, not to be expected if the war has involved only two states and if one of them has emerged as a clear victor; however, if there are two or more states on the winning side, the problem of arriving at a peace settlement may involve serious difficulties among them. Each will want to satisfy the aspirations which led it to go to war or which it developed during the course of the war. Expecting (or planning) future war, each will want to assure for itself a strong power position. The resulting desires and demands of one victor may be incompatible with those of another. A struggle will then ensue, involving international tension and possibly leading to war.

One of the best illustrations dates from the Balkan wars of 1912-1913. Once the first war was over (against the Ottoman Empire), the victors fell out among themselves over the division of the spoils, and a new war ensued, this one among the victors. Similar strains in the fabric of allied relationships have been evident after each of the general wars in the last century and a half. During the Congress of Vienna after the Napoleonic wars, three of the principal powers actually made an alliance against the remaining two, and there was real danger that the struggle over the terms of peace would lead to new war. During the Paris Peace Conference after World War I, tension developed especially over the demands of Italy. After World War II, there was no attempt to arrive at a general settlement in one conference, but great tension soon developed over various aspects of the piecemeal settlement. "Cold war" set in between East and West, and hot war occurred in Korea.

### Dissatisfactions of Parties to the Peace Settlement

Once a peace settlement is made, its terms are likely to be unsatisfactory to some states, and the dissatisfied may then pursue policies designed to upset the settlement. Some of the victorious states themselves may be dissatisfied, even though they formally agreed to the peace terms. After World War I, for example, many Italians took the view that Italy had "won the war, but lost the peace." Under Mussolini, Italy became a revisionist power, and ultimately joined Germany in attacks on the peace treaties. Defeated states are, of course, most likely to resent a peace settlement and to seek change in it. France never reconciled itself to the loss of Alsace-Lorraine after the Franco-Prussian War in 1871. The Versailles settlement, in turn, embittered Germany and contributed to the rise of Nazism with its aggressive foreign policy. If the division of Germany which occurred after World War II can be called a settlement, certainly it is one which Germans and others will seek to upset.

## Dissatisfactions of Former Neutrals

Neutrals in war may be dissatisfied with its outcome and may seek change. They may see danger for themselves in the new power relationships established as a result of war. A country which felt reasonably secure as long as a potential enemy was held in check by a third power may suddenly become insecure if the third power itself is defeated. Thus, for example, France felt reasonably secure against Prussia as long as Austria seemed able to hold Bismarck in check, but after the Seven Weeks' War many Frenchmen demanded "Revenge for Sadowa," that is, they sought somehow to regain security for France after the battle in which Austria was decisively defeated; their attitude contributed to the coming of the Franco-Prussian War. The same kind of considerations sometimes lead neutrals to enter a war which is already in progress, as will be noted below.

## The Diversion or Reduction of Power, and Demands for Change in Situations Maintained by Power

Another point is closely related. It is that whenever a given situation is maintained more by power than by consent, there are likely to be demands for change whenever the power is diverted or significantly reduced. War and the threat of war may divert or reduce power, and may therefore be an occasion or a cause of troubles outside the original area of friction. Examples of the operation of this principle are numerous. After the Crimean War the victors (Britain, France, and Sardinia) prohibited Russia from fortifying the shores of the Black Sea or maintaining naval vessels on its waters, but when the Franco-Prussian War occurred Russia defied the prohibition, and the Crimean victors were too preoccupied in Western Europe to enforce it. Likewise during the Franco-Prussian War French power could no longer preserve the Pope's control over the area of Rome; Italian nationalists were thus free to take—and did take—one more step toward the unification of Italy. A Japanese leader offered a very cynical version of the principle under discussion many decades ago; anticipating troubles in Europe (which eventually took the form of World

War I), he looked forward to them. He saw that the diversion of European power from the Far East would leave Japan relatively free to work its will, and he declared, "When there is a fire in a jeweler's shop, the neighbors are not to be blamed for helping themselves." Japan subsequently utilized World War I as the occasion for taking over German rights in the Pacific and Far East, and for making its Twenty-one Demands on China. Similarly, while the powers of Western Europe were locked in struggle during the early stages of World War II, the Soviet Union took advantage of the situation to fight a war against Finland and to annex Estonia, Latvia, Lithuania, and parts of Poland and Rumania. Should the Soviet Union come to face great danger of war with Communist China, or should actual war break out, changes in Central and Eastern Europe are highly probable. Preoccupation with China might mean that the Soviet Union could no longer sustain the East German regime, and so Germany might be reunited under non-Communist control. The Communist governments in the other satellite countries might or might not survive, depending (among other things) on the boldness of domestic anti-Communist elements and of the Western powers. Communist parties everywhere would be greatly weakened.

The diversion of power has sometimes transformed relations between an imperial country and its colonies. For example, when Spanish power declined drastically during the Napoleonic wars, most of Spain's colonies in the Western Hemisphere revolted and established their independence. When the power of France, the Netherlands, and Britain declined during World War II, all three faced severe colonial difficulties. It is probably more than a coincidence that the British granted independence (or dominion status with the right of secession from the Commonwealth) to Burma, Ceylon, India, and Pakistan after the relative decline of British power in World War II. More certainly, it was the relative decline in Dutch and French power which made feasible the rebellions that confronted the two countries after World War II in Indonesia and Indochina, respectively.

## War, Domestic Change, and Future Troubles

War on any considerable scale necessarily has a significant impact on the social, economic, and political situation within the belligerent countries, especially in those which are defeated. This, in turn, is likely to affect their subsequent behavior. It was World War I which permitted the Bolsheviks to seize power in Russia, and World War II which provided the occasion for an extension of Communist control in Eastern and Southeastern Europe, China, and North Korea. These developments have obviously had a tremendous impact on international politics, leading both to cold and to hot war. Similarly, World War I and its aftermath produced changes in Germany which facilitated the rise of Hitlerism and thus contributed to the coming of World War II. Unrestricted thermonuclear war would no doubt transform political conditions and relationships within and among the states most affected.

## Success in War Recommends War

War affects the behavior of states by the very example and lessons which it involves. Gains made by one state through war recommend the use of war to other states as an instrument of policy. In a sense, war is sometimes contagious. Consider, for example, the record of the 1930's. Japan's success in Manchuria and China certainly encouraged Mussolini to think that he could engage in aggression against Ethiopia without encountering substantial opposition from other powers. Success in Ethiopia, in turn, encouraged both Italian and German intervention in the so-called Civil War in Spain. Cumulative successes encouraged Hitler's aggressiveness, leading to World War II. Although no one can know what might have been, it seems to be a fair guess that the early frustration of Japan's program by a combination of powers determined to suppress any aggression might have deterred Mussolini and Hitler from taking the course they subsequently did take. The assumption that successful war encourages more war is certainly one of the factors that induced President Truman to order American intervention in Korea in 1950; he hoped that the defeat of one Communist act of aggression would discourage similar subsequent acts.

## War and the Assumption of Violence

Finally, the occurrence of war strengthens the expectation that it will recur. It confirms a basic assumption on which statesmen must operate —the assumption of violence. And, as we shall see, this expectation and this assumption have a profound effect on foreign policies and do much to bring war on.

It might be noted that there is little that is automatic or inevitable about the effect of war on the behavior of states. Almost all the above propositions suggest what may happen rather than what definitely will happen. No law of politics is involved. Though quarrels among victorious allies over the peace settlement usually occur, they are not always serious; for example, the victors in the Crimean War had no great difficulty in agreeing on the terms to be imposed. Defeated states do not always seek to upset a peace settlement imposed upon them; Bismarck's terms to Austria-Hungary after the Seven Weeks' War, for example, were so generous that it was soon possible for him to make an ally of his former enemy. Similarly, after World War II, though former allies have become actual or potential enemies, former enemies have in a number of cases become allies. Colonies do not always rebel when the mother country is in difficulty, else many of the colonial difficulties that occurred after World War II would have occurred after World War I, if not before. This discussion of war and the seeds of war has dealt with tendencies and possibilities, not with certainties. Even if war did always sow the seeds of future war, the future war might never come. After all, seeds do not always sprout.

Another warning note might be entered. The statement that war is likely to influence future behavior obviously does not mean it will be the only influencing factor. The statement that war is a cause of certain developments does not necessarily mean that it is the only cause. The statement that war is an occasion for certain developments—such as rebellion on the part of a colony—clearly implies that other factors are also operating. The dynamics of international politics are complex.

# THE INFLUENCE OF THE
# EXPECTATION OF WAR

## A Domestic Analogy

In Chapter 2 we saw that one of the attitudes which contributes mightily to the preservation of peace within countries is the very assumption that peace will prevail. Within stable countries, people normally assume that disputes which arise will be settled without resort to violence. Individuals do not ordinarily carry lethal weapons, and political leaders do not ordinarily calculate their moves in terms of possible civil war.

Suppose that the situation were different. Suppose that every time a hand was raised, one would have to fear that it might contain a dagger. Suppose that anyone reaching into a pocket was suspected of reaching for a gun. Suppose that the usual consequence of a personal antagonism or a grudge was an effort to injure or to kill. Would not the very atmosphere of aggression and suspicion and fear accentuate violence? A person would have to arm himself and train himself to use arms. With death as the possible consequence of inaction, he would have to act quickly and decisively on the slightest sign of a need for self-defense. He would have to act and then inquire whether the need for action was real.

Similarly, if political leaders regularly assumed the possibility of civil war, they would have to jockey for advantage, or at least for safety, in terms of military power. Command over votes would not be enough. A political leader who saw an opportunity to strike in such a way as to establish his power definitely or to eliminate a threat to his position would at least be strongly tempted to do so. One who saw the distribution of power shifting against him would be tempted to strike while victory seemed possible of achievement. Concern for power and security, concern for survival, would tend to overshadow what are normally regarded as the substantive issues of politics. It can hardly be doubted that in such a situation civil war would be more common than it in fact is.

The same kind of considerations apply in the international field. Between some countries—the United States and Canada, for example—there is no expectation of war and therefore no power struggle in a military sense. But between other countries—the United States and the Soviet Union, for example—the expectation of war is ever present; even if neither side really wants war, which may or may not be true in this instance, each must regard it as a distinct possibility.

## Types of Preparedness Measures

Assuming that defensive war may be necessary, states must prepare for it. They must seek to maintain or build up their power, exerting themselves more or less in proportion to their estimate of the extent and imminence of the danger.

Discussion of the elements of power, and therefore of the various areas of activity in connection with an effort to maintain or increase power, will be postponed until later. But the most prominent of these areas of activity must be mentioned here. Expecting war, states must make military, economic, psychological, and diplomatic preparations.

The character of the military preparations normally made is fairly obvious. States which feel threatened seek to build up their armed establishments. They train men, plan strategy, develop new weapons, manufacture the thousands of items needed in war, and seek to build up the morale of the armed forces, perhaps by inculcating hate of the prospective enemy. The richer states may also help poorer allies to build up their armed power.

Economic preparations are usually labeled as manifestations of *economic nationalism*—a term which denotes "the point of view that it ought to be the object of statesmanship in economic matters to increase the power rather than the economic well-being of a given society." Various kinds of economic regulations and activities may increase power. Tariffs, quotas, exchange controls, and the licensing of foreign trade are devices to this end. State subsidies, special concessions on taxes, or other measures may be employed to develop and support economic activities which are of special significance to the power of the state, like the operation of a merchant marine or airlines, or the production of synthetic oil or rubber. The state itself may engage extensively in vital economic activities, as the United States has done in the field of atomic energy and in connection with the stockpiling of strategic materials. It may control foreign trade and foreign investments in such a way as to strengthen potential allies and weaken potential enemies. It may engage in pro-natalist policies, seeking to increase the human war potential, as Hitler and Mussolini did. And economic nationalism may merge into imperialism if the government seeks to secure political control over foreign sources of supply of essential materials. Along a somewhat different line, aid may be given to prospective allies, who are attempting to build up their economic foundations for military power.

Psychological preparations are expressed in propaganda, generally designed to convince the people of the state that the cause for which it stands is just and that this righteous cause is threatened by an outside power, which is evil. Love for the country and devotion to its cause are obviously desirable if the mobilization of power is to be adequate; suspicion, distrust, and hatred of the potential enemy are also to be desired.

Diplomatic preparations usually involve efforts to isolate the potential enemy, if possible, or to cut it off from outside support to the greatest extent possible. At the same time, they involve efforts to win friends and allies. Moreover, diplomacy must be so conducted as to put the country in the best possible light when and if war comes.

## Effects of Preparedness Measures

States following defensive policies and engaging in these preparations normally justify them in the name of peace. The hope is that the power of the state can be made so great, as compared to the power of the potential enemy, that it will not dare attack. Preparations for war sometimes have this effect; perhaps they usually do—it is difficult to say when a war has been averted which otherwise would have occurred. But certainly such preparations also have an opposite effect. A state engaged in them is unlikely to be able to convince its potential antagonist that its purposes are purely defensive; even if it does succeed in doing so, the other state is bound to wonder how long those purposes will remain defensive. The antagonist is therefore likely to build up its own power, if only as a precautionary measure. In so doing, it accentuates already existing fears, and so encourages still more vigorous preparations in the other state. A vicious circle is thus created, a so-called armaments race. Thought of the possibility of war begins to dominate domestic and foreign policy in the states involved. Every move is appraised in terms of its effect on power relationships. There is an inclination to read a hostile intent into the various moves of the potential antagonist. Both international tensions and personal anxieties are likely to become acute, and they may become intolerable.

War tends to break out in such circumstances. Perhaps one side will make a move which the other regards as aggressive. Perhaps one side, assuming that war has become virtually inevitable and fearing that it will lose out in a prolonged armaments race, will decide to precipitate hostilities, that is, to wage a preventive war. Psychological factors strengthen the temptation to do this, for the anxieties of peace sometimes seem greater than the horrors of war. Many observers of the British scene in the fall of 1939 noted that the declaration of war seemed to bring relief.

States which recognize the possibility of war, but desire to avoid it are thus in something of a dilemma. On the one hand, if they neglect their power and allow themselves to get into an inferior power position, they invite inadmissible demands if not attack. On the other hand, if they pay great attention to power relationships and seek to develop a safe power position, they may create or accentuate tensions and thus help to bring on the war which they seek to avoid. A middle course is obviously desirable, but precisely what constitutes a middle course in a necessarily vague situation is a question on which even those trained to judge such matters may differ.

## Fears of Third States and the Extension of War

Not only does the expectation of war lead to preparation for war, which may help to bring it on. Fears for the future also often lead to the extension of existing wars. Once war has broken out between any two states, its outcome will be of concern to other states. This might not be so if it were known that the war would be the last one ever to be fought, but if future wars are to be expected the possible results of an existing war must be appraised in this light.

*1. A hypothetical illustration.* Suppose that there were only three states, A. B, and C. They do not command precisely the same amount of power, but the differences are not great. Now suppose that state A attacks state B. If state C could be sure of living in peace regardless of the outcome of the struggle between A and B, it might well remain neutral, but it cannot be sure of this. All history teaches it that it must assume the possibility of future war. The outcome of the present war is therefore of vital importance. If A should conquer and annex B, C might not be able to survive a future war. A would have gained such power as to render C helpless. By all means, state C must try to prevent such a development. C may have no particular interest in the issues over which A and B are fighting, but this makes no great difference. The overwhelmingly important requirement is that C maintain a relative power position that will permit it to survive.

There are various ways in which C can attempt to do this. If the belligerents are fairly evenly matched and seem headed for a stalemate, C can bide its time. If state A seems to be headed for victory, C can give aid to State B. Perhaps the aid can be in the form of supplies or perhaps C can formally join in the war on the side of B on mutually agreeable terms regarding the ultimate peace settlement. Or C could join with A in despoiling B if mutually agreeable terms were arrived at.

In other words, recognizing the possibility of future war, C must attempt to prevent an outcome of the existing war that would have a serious adverse effect on its own relative power position. The attempt may well involve C itself in the war. In this example the expectation of future war has led to an extension of the existing war.

This helps to explain what Mr. Hawtrey meant when he said that "the aim for which war is judged worth while is most often something which itself affects military power." If, in the hypothetical case described above, state C should enter the war, it would not be fighting, immediately at least, for freedom or justice or wealth or any similar value, for nothing which it holds dear has been attacked; rather it would be fighting to maintain a relative power position that would permit it to maintain its values if they were threatened in the future.

2. *Illustrations from the two world wars.* History is full of illustrations of the operation of these considerations. Of course, third states may enter a war to promote immediate interest or advantage, but a large proportion of them do so to protect themselves against putative future dangers—dangers which might or might not in fact develop. If an enigmatic statement is permitted, it might be said that states are often fighting a future war rather than a present one, that is, they fight now rather than later because of a fear that if they wait their chances of victory will have been reduced.

Consider World War I, for example. It began with an attack by Austria-Hungary on Serbia. How did this war between two states in the heart of Europe turn into a world war? Among the numerous operative factors, the concern of other states for their future relative power position was certainly important. Russia and France had agreed that it was vital to them to preserve a "balance" of power. We shall discuss this concept more fully later; here it suffices to say that they had agreed that they must maintain a distribution of power that would leave them reasonably safe. They had further agreed that changes in the Balkans might make the distribution of power unsafe. When Austria-Hungary attacked Serbia, therefore, Russia and France immediately became concerned. Russia, especially, feared that Austria-Hungary would win, that Austria-Hungary would be strengthened by victory, and that an increase in Austro-Hungarian power would be dangerous for the future. Other influences also operated, of course. Together they led to Russian mobilization, the obvious Russian intention being to intervene in the war.

This alarmed Germany, for Russia and Serbia combined might defeat its ally, Austria-Hungary. Then Germany might be left in a relatively less favorable power position. Germany was not attacked; there was no immediate menace to her, but she feared for the future. This fear, among other considerations, led her to deliver ultimatums both to Russia and to Russia's ally, France. So, almost immediately, the war between Austria-Hungary and Serbia was extended over most of the continent of Europe.

When Germany attacked Belgium in an effort to get at and crush France, Britain became involved. There was no attack on Britain. Had she chosen to do so, she in all probability could have remained neutral in the war, but the war might then have ended with Germany and Austria-Hungary dominant on the continent, with bases just across the Channel from which mortal attacks might in the future be launched on Britain. It had always been British policy to prevent any such development, and the policy was continued in 1914. Britain entered the war largely to ward off the danger which might develop in the future out of a victory on the part of the Central Powers.

Similar considerations were among those which finally induced the United States to abandon neutrality and declare war. Secretary of State, Robert Lansing, gave clear expression to them in 1916:

It is my opinion that the military oligarchy which rules Germany is a bitter enemy of democracy in every form; that, if that oligarchy triumphs over the liberal governments of Great Britain and France, it will then turn upon us as its next obstacle to imperial rule over the world; and that it is safer and surer and wiser for us to be one of many enemies than to be in the future alone against a victorious Germany.[2]

Nothing could be more explicit in showing that the expectation of future war contributed to an extension of the existing one.

Virtually the same sequence occurred in connection with World War II. In the fall of 1939 Germany attacked Poland. She did not attack France and Britain, yet they declared war. Why? Among other things, they believed that an increase in Germany's power would ultimately endanger them. Each felt, as Lansing had before, that it was "safer and surer and wiser . . . to be one of many enemies than to be in the future alone against a victorious Germany." In guiding American policy Franklin D. Roosevelt was influenced by the same thoughts. In his State of the Union message in 1940 he declared that "it becomes clearer and clearer that the future world will be a shabby and dangerous place to live in—even for Americans to live in—if it is ruled by force in the hands of a few." A defense policy based on withdrawal within our own boundaries would, he declared, merely "invite future attack." He thought it a delusion that the United States could safely be permitted "to become a lone island, a lone island in a world dominated by the philosophy of force."

[2] Robert Lansing, *War Memoirs* (Indianapolis, Bobbs-Merrill, 1935), p. 103. The influence of the expectation of war is also discussed in E. H. Carr, *The Twenty Years' Crisis, 1919-1939* (New York, Harper & Row, 1964), pp. 109-113.

Such an island represents . . . a helpless nightmare, the helpless nightmare of people without freedom; yes, the nightmare of a people lodged in prison, handcuffed, hungry, and fed through the bars from day to day by the contemptuous and unpitying masters of other continents.

In another address Roosevelt declared:

If Great Britain goes down, the Axis powers will control the continents of Europe, Asia, Africa, Australasia, and the high seas—and they will be in a position to bring enormous military and naval resources against this hemisphere. It is no exaggeration to say that all of us in the Americas would be living at the point of a gun—a gun loaded with explosive bullets, economic as well as military.[3]

Thus the United States took the road to war in part because it feared the results of a future war fought in less favorable circumstances. It fought, in part, against hypothetical future danger.

The same kinds of considerations have operated since World War II. American Secretaries of State have referred again and again to the danger that the future would bring if Communists loyal to Moscow were to come to power throughout Europe or throughout Asia. One of the objectives of the containment policy has been to prevent such a shift in the distribution of power from occurring. The possibility of future war is one of the main determinants of present policy.

Wars seem to spread especially when they involve at least one great power on each side for a significant period of time. Quincy Wright reports that during the past three centuries "there have been fourteen periods in which war existed with a great power on each side for over two years."[4] In eleven of the fourteen, every other great power became involved. Among the factors operating, concern over the distribution of power which would follow the war was undoubtedly significant.

## Future Security and Present War Aims

Once states become involved in war, there is a tendency for them to develop objectives which have little or nothing to do with their initial decision to fight. In particular, victors commonly seize territory from the defeated even though they did not go to war for that purpose. The British Empire was built up to quite an extent in this way, governments in London seizing on the opportunities that victory provided to take territory which was either commercially or strategically valuable. The United States has done the same thing. Certainly few Americans entered the Spanish-American War with a view to annexing the Philippines, yet this

[3] Franklin D. Roosevelt, *Roosevelt's Foreign Policy, 1933-1941* (New York, Wilfred Funk, 1942), pp. 214, 242, 251, 312.

[4] Quincy Wright, *A Study of War* (Chicago, The University of Chicago Press, 1942, copyright by the University of Chicago), Vol. I, p. 240.

is what occurred at the end of the war. Certainly too, the desire to take Japanese territory had nothing to do with American participation in World War II, yet at the war's end the United States secured the former Japanese mandated islands under a trusteeship arrangement and simply remained in occupation of the Ryukyu Islands, including Okinawa.

The expectation of future war is among the factors contributing to such aggrandizement. Assuming that more war will occur, those who make decisions on high policy are necessarily under pressure to shape each peace settlement in such a way as to promote future security or future victory. Seizures of foreign territory—defensive imperialism—may serve this purpose.

## JINGOISM AND MILITARISM

A number of attitudes and motivating forces sometimes become closely associated with the thought and expectation of war. Whatever the causes of their development, they may well play an influential role.

### Jingoism

Jingoism is perhaps the most transient and superficial of these attitudes and forces. The term entered the English language in the course of an Anglo-Russian crisis in 1878. Russia had defeated the Ottoman Empire and threatened a penetration of its power to the Mediterranean. This Britain was determined to prevent. In the course of the agitation over the issue a jingle appeared in England, declaring:

> We don't want to fight, but by jingo if we do
> We've got the ships, we've got the men, we've got the money, too.

Ever since, the term *jingoism* has served to denote a cocky and bellicose national spirit, one which almost invites and welcomes war. Whipped up by what is taken to be a challenge from abroad, it involves brash willingness and even eagerness to take up the challenge. A government controlled by jingoists has a chip on its shoulder and is spoiling for a fight. Such an outlook obviously makes war more likely.

### Militarism: The Use of Armed Forces
### for Other than Military Purposes

Militarism is a rather vague concept. It refers to an attitude or spirit which is more stable and durable than jingoism. In its least significant form it denotes various attitudes and practices associated with armies and wars, yet transcending true military purposes.[5] It regards armed

5 Alfred Vagts, *A History of Militarism* (New York, Norton, 1937), p. 11.

establishments as having purposes to which security and war are incidental and peripheral. There was a time in Europe, for example, when some of the royalty regarded armies (or units thereof) more or less as playthings. They derived gratification out of command itself and out of the ceremony and display associated with peacetime military activity. The attitude is typified by the Russian grand duke who said that he hated war "because it spoils armies."

In Europe and elsewhere, armies have also served as means of providing status, honor, and income to the nobility or to others. Until fairly recent times in some of the European countries, commissions as officers in the armed forces were reserved for the nobility, the needs of the service and the competence of the individual having little to do with the appointments made. Commissions were often sinecures, granted more as favors or rewards or as bribes designed to assure the support of the recipient for king or government than because of military need. Sometimes far more officers were appointed than were needed. Conversely, sometimes the principle that officers must be noblemen restricted a military expansion regarded as desirable. In the decade before World War I, for example, Germany curtailed the expansion of its army "because not enough officers 'of class' could be found, and the military were unwilling to descend to 'little-suited elements' and thus expose the officer body to 'democratization.' "[6]

Militarism, both in its mild and in its more serious forms, may include the idea that military activity is a good means of promoting values and instilling virtues regarded as desirable. Military training has often been described as a device for inculcating loyalty, discipline, and a sense of civic responsibility, and as a means of promoting health, physical hardihood, and education. Soldiers are often looked upon as being somehow more heroic than civilians, additional prestige going to the man because of the uniform he wears. Military service, in peace as well as in war, is regarded as ennobling.

These manifestations of militarism may or may not have much to do with international politics. So long as armies remain playthings, or means of providing status, honor, and income, or devices for promoting domestic values or instilling virtues, they are of relatively small moment on the world scene. Accompanying these purposes of armies, however, there may be tendencies which promote resort to war. After all, few would argue that these functions fully justify the existence of armies. Those who wish armies to serve these purposes must therefore find some ulterior justification. They may thus be inclined to create or magnify foreign dangers and perhaps to bring about actual war. Moreover, a military caste—whether or not consisting of noblemen—may be inclined to regard war as a kind of glorified sport.

6 *Ibid.*, p. 221.

## Militarism: The Political Supremacy
## of the Military

The "supremacy of military authorities over civilian authorities" has been described as "the very essence of militarism."[7] The implication is that militarism prevails in the degree to which the policies of the state are under the effective control of military men—whether or not the military men hold the positions of formal political supremacy. Sometimes counts are made of the number of governments controlled by military men—whether or not they are a result of the seizure of power—and then inferences are drawn relating perhaps to the prospects for democracy in the world or perhaps to prospects in the international field. The assumption is that military men in general share an outlook that is distinctive from one that civilians generally share.

This assumption is hazardous. Even within any one country military leaders are likely to have differing points of view, and when the comparison is between military leaders of differing countries and cultures, the differences are likely to be even greater. It is not even to be assumed that military leaders will put special stress on military traditions and virtues. Some civilian leaders seem more inclined than military leaders to stress military approaches and solutions to problems.

Given these caveats, however, we might note attitudes that are said to reflect the "military mind" or "the professional military ethic." The following characterization—an abstract model or ideal type, which may or may not fully apply to any one person—is drawn from the work of Samuel P. Huntington.[8] (1) The military mind stresses the fact of human conflict (the selfishness and evil in men) and the threat and use of violence in resolving conflict. (2) It stresses the group against the individual. The individual is weak, inclined to be fearful and irrational, and unable to realize his own potentialities. Some degree of compensation for these failings can be found in organization, leadership, and discipline—in the subordination of the individual to the group and its traditions and interests. "The 'weak, mediocre, transient individual' can only achieve emotional satisfaction and moral fulfillment by participating in 'the power, the greatness, the permanence and the splendour' of a continuing organic body. The military ethic is basically corporative in spirit. It is fundamentally anti-individualistic." (3) It stresses the security and preservation of the state; after all, the state is the *raison d'être* of armed forces. (4) It assumes that "the problem of military security is never finally solved." Human nature is such that war must always be expected; if one

[7] Statement quoted by Samuel P. Huntington, *The Soldier and the State, The Theory and Politics of Civil-Military Relations* (Cambridge, The Belknap Press of Harvard University Press, 1957), p. 109.

[8] *Ibid.*, pp. 61-79.

enemy is checked or laid low, another will arise. Diplomacy, international law, and international organization (e.g., the United Nations) cannot be entirely relied upon. As a minimum they must be reinforced by armed power, and on occasion they are superseded by armed power. (5) It tends to view with great alarm potential threats to the security of the state, to assume the worst concerning the intentions and power of other states, and thus to call for greater emphasis on the development of armed power. The preference is for power in being, including every kind of weapon and skill that could conceivably be required. (6) It desires to avoid war. This attitude reflects awareness of the uncertainties and dangers of war and a realization that war may disrupt the structure within which the military operates. At the same time, if war seems unavoidable and if time seems to be on the side of the prospective enemy, the military mind may endorse preventive war.

Another of the general characteristics attributed to the military mind is that it tends to be apolitical and nonideological. This implies aloofness from domestic political issues, an inclination to react to foreign policy questions in peacetime solely in terms of security considerations, and an inclination to shape military strategies in wartime solely in terms of military considerations. At the same time, where military and political concerns become interrelated, there is willingness to be guided and limited by the political decisions of appropriate authorities. If "the military mind" establishes its supremacy in the state, of course, the fact indicates that some kind of modification of these attitudes has occurred.

In so far as militarism of the above sort comes to influence the domestic politics of any country, authoritarianism is promoted. In international relationships, the effect necessarily varies depending on the specific attitudes that are dominant.

## Militarism: Emphasis on War
## as a Method or a Goal

As indicated in part above, militarism may involve one or more of several attitudes that make war more likely. The militarist, as the term is sometimes used, may regard war and the preparation for war "as the chief instruments of foreign policy and the highest form of public service."[9] He may extol and glorify military exploits. He may welcome foreign danger and foreign war as means of promoting domestic unity, and he may regard war as good in and of itself. (Note that militarism in this sense is distinct from the supremacy of the "military mind" as just discussed.)

*1. War as normal.* It is perhaps natural that repeated war and threats

[9] C. Delisle Burns, "Militarism," *Encyclopedia of the Social Sciences,* Vol. X, pp. 446-451.

of war should militarize thought and life, and that they should make war appear both as an almost normal instrument of foreign policy and as a normal pursuit. The whole life of a people—the social, political, and economic structure—may be so conditioned by war that war becomes a habit or a necessity. Schumpeter's theory of imperialism, to be discussed below, is based on this proposition. It is also perhaps natural that in an atmosphere of war added weight is commonly given in the councils of state to the generals and admirals (with results that are bound to vary, depending on their personal attitudes and characteristics). Almost certainly they will favor the development of greater military strength. They may or may not be more inclined than others to see and to seek military solutions.

*2. War as a source of glory.* Pride in past military exploits is a common phenomenon. Among the heroes in the history of every country, victorious military leaders are accorded a high place. Whether they fought aggressively or defensively makes little difference. Whether they contributed in any significant way to the cultural or material betterment of their country or of mankind is a question which is commonly neglected or ignored. The destruction and death that they wrought are forgotten. Whether their cause was good or bad, their memory is honored at least in the country in whose name they fought. Those who conquer are considered great. Defeat disgraces the leader involved and casts down the pride of the country from which he comes. The usual remedy is victory, perhaps in another war.

Surely such attitudes affect current behavior. If war has been a historic path to glory, it is recommended to those of the present and future who seek glory, and they are numerous. Perhaps no one would deliberately begin a war for the sake of the glory it might bring, but certainly the view that war, and more especially victory, are glorious must condition the thoughts of military and civil leaders—and even of the rank-and-file citizens—who make the fateful decisions concerning peace and war. People are drawn to do those things which bring praise.

It might be recalled that Frederick the Great, dispatching his officers to war in 1740, sped them on to what he called the "rendezvous of fame, whither I shall follow you without delay." Some months later he explained that

> My youth, the fire of passions, the desire for glory, yes, to be frank, even curiosity, finally a secret instinct has torn me away from the delights of tranquillity. The satisfaction of seeing my name in the papers and later in history has seduced me.[10]

*3. War as a unifying activity.* War long ago demonstrated its usefulness as a means of producing or reinforcing social cohesion and political

[10] G. P. Gooch, *Frederick the Great* (New York, Knopf, 1947), pp. 12, 15.

unity within belligerent countries. It is a recognized means through which a government threatened by domestic discontent and disaffection can seek to strengthen its position. If the government can direct antagonisms abroad and occupy people with foreign war, they are less likely to engage in domestic, internecine strife. This function of war has frequently been noted. An observer in 1604 is said to have described "forreigne warre" as "a sovereigne medicine for domesticall inconveniences."[11] Shakespeare ascribed similar thoughts to King Henry IV, who

> I . . . had a purpose now
> To lead out many to the Holy Land
> Lest rest and lying still might make them look
> Too near unto my state. Therefore, my Harry,
> Be it thy course to busy giddy minds
> With foreign quarrels; that action hence born out
> May waste the memory of former days.

There are, of course, more recent illustrations. Secretary of State Seward early in Lincoln's first administration submitted "Some Thoughts for the President's Consideration," urging a militant foreign policy and probable war. His belief apparently was that foreign war would be a cure for internal dissension. Some interpreters believe that Bismarck shifted to a policy of overseas imperialism in the hope that it would serve as a "lightning rod for the Social-Democratic danger" and generally as a means of promoting domestic unity.[12]

A Japanese diplomat is said to have explained Japan's resort to war against China in 1894 as a means of improving the situation at home "by arousing the patriotic sentiment of our people and more strongly attaching them to the Government."[13] Before the Russo-Japanese War of 1904-1905, the Russian Minister of the Interior expressed the view that "we need a small victorious war to stem the tide of revolution."[14] Hitler before his accession to power publicly declared,

> If I wish to bind our people together in unity, I must first create a new front which has a common enemy before it, so that every one knows that we must be one, since this enemy is the enemy of us all.[15]

*4. War as good in itself.* Militarism in its most extreme form glorifies war as good in itself. In recent times, the attitude is illustrated best in

[11] Quoted by Jacob Viner, "International Relations between State-Controlled National Economies," *American Economic Review*, Vol. 34, Part 2 (March, 1944), p. 326.
in the play advised his successor as follows:

[12] Vagts, *op. cit.*, p. 418.

[13] *Ibid.*, p. 421.

[14] D. J. Dallin, *The Rise of Russia in Asia* (New Haven, Conn., Yale University Press, 1949), p. 79.

[15] Frederick L. Schuman, "The Third Reich's Road to War," *Annals of the American Academy of Political and Social Science*, Vol. 175 (September, 1934), p. 34.

fascist and Nazi writings. Mussolini, for example, expressed himself as follows:

Fascism, the more it considers and observes the future and the development of humanity quite apart from political considerations of the moment, believes neither in the possibility nor the utility of perpetual peace. It thus repudiates the doctrine of Pacifism—born of a renunciation of the struggle—as an act of coward-ice in the face of sacrifice. War alone brings up to its highest tension all human energy and puts the stamp of nobility upon the peoples who have the courage to meet it.[16]

E. Banse, a Nazi writer, took a similar position:

War means the highest intensification not of the material means only, but of all spiritual energies of the age as well. . . . War provides the ground on which the human soul may manifest itself at its fullest height, in richer forms and surging from more profound wells than it might in any scientific or artistic ex-ploit as such. Nowhere else can the will, the achievements of a race or a state rise into being thus integrally as in war. War is a purifying bath of steel, breed-ing new impulses, and an infallible test of fitness.[17]

Similarly, Robert Ley, head of the German Labor Front under Hitler, described war as "an expression of the highest and best in manhood."[18]

It is difficult to say how widespread each of these attitudes toward war may be. Their prevalence varies in different times and in different countries. (Surely the development of nuclear weapons and missile de-livery systems makes them less acceptable than ever before.) The point need not be labored, however, that where such attitudes exist—and par-ticularly when they are entertained by individuals with considerable in-fluence over foreign policy—the implications for international politics are profound.

## SCHUMPETER'S THEORY OF IMPERIALISM

### His Definition: "Objectless" Expansionism

The above discussion of militarism leads naturally into a discussion of Schumpeter's theory of imperialism. Note should be made first of all of the definition of imperialism which Schumpeter adopted, for it is a re-strictive one. He excluded from consideration many acts and policies which others describe as imperialist. He refused to call an expansionist policy imperialist when it appeared reasonable, that is, when it was de-signed to promote a "concrete interest." Thus his theory does not cover policies which a landlocked state might pursue to obtain access to the sea,

16 Benito Mussolini, "The Political and Social Doctrine of Fascism," *International Conciliation*, No. 306 (January, 1935), pp. 7-8.

17 Quoted by Aurel Kolnai, *The War Against the West* (New York, Viking, 1938), p. 411.

18 *New York Times*, March 28, 1940, p. 3, col. 3.

or policies which a state in need of land or raw materials might pursue to get them. He acknowledged that there are reasons for every aggressive policy, but insisted on calling such policies imperialist only when the true cause of them lies beyond the reasons given and is not included among the war aims.

Whenever the word imperialism is used [said Schumpeter], there is always the implication . . . of an aggressiveness, the true reasons for which do not lie in the aims which are temporarily being pursued; of an aggressiveness that is only kindled anew by each success; of an aggressiveness for its own sake, as reflected in such terms as "hegemony," "world dominion," and so forth. And history, in truth, shows us nations and classes—most nations furnish an example at some time or other—that seek expansion for the sake of expanding, war for the sake of fighting, victory for the sake of winning, dominion for the sake of ruling.[19]

Regarding expansion for its own sake as really objectless, Schumpeter defined imperialism as "the objectless disposition on the part of a state to unlimited forcible expansion."[20] He declared that "numberless wars—perhaps the majority of all wars—have been waged without adequate 'reason'—not so much from the moral viewpoint as from that of reasoned and reasonable interest."[21]

## Underlying Reasons for "Objectless" Expansion

There must be reasons, of course, even for objectless expansion, whether or not those involved are conscious of them; Schumpeter's object was to reveal the reasons. To do this, he examined a series of examples of imperialism in ancient and modern times. He found that states which became imperialist faced needs and desires at some time which led them to create a war machine and to wage war. Initially the war machine and the wars fought were designed to promote "concrete interests," and therefore state policies were, by Schumpeter's definition, non-imperialistic. But the very existence of the war machine and the very prosecution of war resulted in conditioning both attitudes and the social structure of the state. Economic, political, and social life became more or less adjusted and adapted to the needs of war. Then, when "concrete interests" had been served and reasons for war had disappeared, there was a threat of maladjustment. A social order geared to war would be out of place if international relations became harmonious. Of course, the social structure might be changed and adapted to conditions of peace, but such readjust-

[19] Joseph A. Schumpeter, *Imperialism and Social Classes* (New York, Augustus M. Kelley, 1951, copyright 1951 by Elizabeth Boody Schumpeter; quotations by permission of the trustees of the estate of Elizabeth B. Schumpeter), p. 6. Cf. Klaus Knorr, "Theories of Imperialism," *World Politics*, Vol. 4 (April, 1952), pp. 402-431.

[20] Schumpeter, *op. cit.*, p. 7.

[21] *Ibid.*, p. 83.

ment threatened rulers and vested interests generally; rather than run the risks of peace, they sometimes preferred to wage war even though no "concrete interest" would be served thereby. "Created by wars that required it, the machine now created the wars it required."[22]

Schumpeter summarized his findings in three points. First, he held "that 'objectless' tendencies toward forcible expansion, without definite, utilitarian limits—that is, nonrational and irrational, purely instinctual inclinations toward war and conquest—play a very large role in the history of mankind." Second, he found the explanation of this drive toward war "in the vital needs of situations that molded peoples and classes into warriors—if they wanted to avoid extinction—and in the fact that psychological dispositions and social structures acquired in the dim past in such situations, once firmly established, tend to maintain themselves and to continue in effect long after they have lost their meaning and their life-preserving functions." Third, he found that the survival of warlike dispositions and structures is due both to the "domestic interests of ruling classes [and to] the influence of all those who stand to gain individually from a war policy, whether economically or socially."[23]

Schumpeter drew his prime illustrations of this sequence from antiquity, but argued that it operates also in modern times. He explained the wars of Louis XIV in these terms. He assumed that, by the end of France's war with Spain in 1659, the "concrete interests" of France had been served; there was no serious external threat, and disarmament might have occurred. "But the foundations of royal power rested on [the] military character of the state and on the social factors and psychological tendencies it expressed." In particular, Louis XIV felt compelled to cater to the aristocracy for its support.

Unless the nobles were to be allowed to revolt, they had to be kept busy. Now all the noble families whose members were amusing themselves at Versailles could look back on a warlike past, martial ideas and phrases, bellicose instincts. To ninety-nine out of a hundred of them, "action" meant military action. If civil war was to be avoided, then external wars were required. . . .

Thus the belligerence and war policy of the autocratic state are explained from the necessities of its social structure, from the inherited dispositions of its ruling class, rather than from the immediate advantages to be derived by conquest.[24]

## The Anti-Imperialistic Nature of Capitalism

Though tracing the forces making for imperialism down to modern times, Schumpeter contended that they are declining in strength. To him, imperialism was "atavistic in character."

22 *Ibid.*, p. 33.
23 *Ibid.*, pp. 83-84.
24 *Ibid.*, pp. 76-77.

It . . . stems from the living conditions, not of the present, but of the past—or, put in terms of the economic interpretation of history, from past rather than present relations of production. It is an atavism in the social structure, in individual, psychological habits of emotional reaction. Since the vital needs that created it have passed away for good, it too must gradually disappear, even though every warlike involvement, no matter how non-imperialist in character, tends to revive it.[25]

In contrast to Lenin and others, Schumpeter argued that capitalism is anti-imperialistic. Under it people are "democratized, individualized, and rationalized," and "everything that is purely instinctual, everything insofar as it is purely instinctual, is driven into the background by this development."[26] Thus, throughout the world of capitalism, there has arisen opposition to war. Peace movements have appeared. When war is fought it must be fought in the name of defense against attack; imperialism must be repudiated, or ascribed exclusively to the enemy. Schumpeter acknowledged that developments may occur under capitalism producing economic causes of war; specifically, he cited tariffs and other trade barriers as elements permitting the development of monopolies, which in turn required export markets for their most profitable operation, and he granted that the competitive struggle for export markets might lead to friction and war. But he described trade barriers themselves as essentially atavistic, resulting from attitudes surviving from the precapitalist period more than from attitudes developed under capitalism, and he thought that gradually such attitudes would disappear. He held it to be "a basic fallacy to describe imperialism as a necessary phase of capitalism, or even to speak of the development of capitalism into imperialism." He held that under capitalism, "imperialisms will wither and die."[27]

Schumpeter's study of imperialism was first published in 1919. Events since then, especially the rise of fascism, Nazism, and perhaps Communism, give rise to the question whether he may not have been too optimistic about the democratizing, individualizing, and rationalizing effect of capitalism, and about its tendency to make imperialisms wither and die. Perhaps, too, he exaggerated when he said that "numberless wars—perhaps a majority of all wars" are to be explained by his theory. Yet, even if the theory explains only a few wars—or even if the factors on which he dwelt serve merely to reinforce others which made for war—his contribution to an understanding of the behavior of states is significant.

25 *Ibid.*, pp. 84-85.
26 *Ibid.*, p. 89.
27 *Ibid.*, pp. 118, 130.

## SUGGESTED READINGS

ALLPORT, Gordon W., "The Role of Expectancy," in CANTRIL, Hadley, ed., *Tensions That Cause War* (Urbana, Ill., University of Illinois Press, 1951).

BURNS, C. Delisle, "Militarism," *Encyclopedia of the Social Sciences*, Vol. X, pp. 446-451.

CARR, E. H., *The Twenty Years' Crisis, 1919-1939, An Introduction to the Study of International Relations* (New York, Harper & Row, 1964).

HUNTINGTON, Samuel P., *The Soldier and the State, The Theory and Politics of Civil-Military Relations* (Cambridge, The Belknap Press of Harvard University Press, 1957).

LASSWELL, Harold, *World Politics and Personal Insecurity* (New York, McGraw-Hill, 1935), esp. Chapters III and IV.

SCHUMPETER, Joseph A., *Imperialism and Social Classes* (New York, Augustus M. Kelley, 1951).

VAGTS, Alfred, *A History of Militarism* (New York, Norton, 1937).

# PSYCHOLOGICAL FACTORS
# IN WAR AND PEACE

We have been discussing the behavior of states. This has involved a fiction for, strictly speaking, states do not behave. The state is an abstraction and—to the contrary, fascist theory notwithstanding—is not a living thing. The state, therefore, does not think or feel or act. The thinking and feeling and acting which constitute what we call the behavior of states are done by individual human beings. They are done by those officially charged with authority to make decisions on behalf of the state, by advisers of the decision makers, and by all those throughout the population who, by vote or otherwise, influence public policy. This being so, if we wish to understand what we call the behavior of states we must understand the factors, at least the major ones, which help to explain the political attitudes and actions of individual men.

This thought is, of course, not a new one. We have been proceeding on the basis of it all along. We said that some or all men in each state like the idea of sovereignty, and that one of the major objectives of those controlling public policy is to preserve sovereignty and security. We discussed nationalism and patriotism and the ideological conflict in terms of the thoughts of men. We took up the question of the extent to which men's behavior is governed by economic conditions, and therefore of the extent to which state policy is determined by economic factors. In the preceding chapters we discussed the effect of war and the expectation of war on state policy (i.e., on the thoughts of those who make decisions in the name of the state) .

Thus, in seeking to explain the behavior of states, we have already been discussing the attitudes of individual men and some of the forces and conditions that help shape those attitudes. We have been identifying the major goal values (independent interests) that men consciously pursue in the realm of international politics and the causes or conditions that help to release and direct their energies.

So far we have been assuming that men are rather deliberate and self-conscious about what they do—that they know their own motives and can give reasons for their behavior. Obviously, this is often true: people *do* decide upon much of what they do and are able to explain their decisions by citing reasons that are entirely plausible and satisfying. In very many cases the best way to find out why someone acts as he does is to ask him. But obviously this is not always true. Sometimes people do not want to confess their motives, or at least not all of them, and so they may knowingly lie or distort or conceal. Moreover, often it is not a question of being willing to identify motives but of being able to: people do not always know what their motives are. They act without really knowing why. To be sure, they are likely to think that they have a reason, but observers can see that reasons really operate other than or in addition to those that are avowed.[1]

It is with this latter kind of decision-making that we are concerned in this chapter; that is, we are concerned with factors affecting choice other than the entirely conscious and rational factors. We are concerned with the irrational and the nonrational. More specifically, we are concerned with some psychoanalytic explanations of behavior, with the question of the relationship between frustration and aggression, and with the various other findings and hypotheses of psychologists that shed light on decisionmaking —including decisionmaking relating to war and peace.

## HUMAN NATURE VERSUS LEARNED BEHAVIOR

It is sometimes said that "you can't change human nature" and that "human nature makes war inevitable." Few psychologists, if any, would agree with either proposition. In fact, many psychologists would question whether there is any such thing as human nature in the sense of biologically determined behavior patterns which are common to all mankind. They point out that man, as compared to other animals, is least controlled by instinct; man is guided and controlled far more by what he learns than by what he biologically is. His personal attributes are determined less by the fact that he is human than by the fact that he has certain experiences in a given environment. The behavior of human beings, then, is shaped less by heredity than by what they learn. The culture into which they are born and in which they live does more to influence their behavior than do their genes and chromosomes. As Mark May puts it, "Man's biological nature is neither good nor bad, aggressive nor submis-

[1] Cf., R. S. Peters, *The Concept of Motivation* (New York, Humanities Press, 1958), pp. 1-26.

sive, warlike nor peaceful, but neutral in these respects." Man may develop in any of a number of different directions "depending on what he is compelled to learn by his environment and by his culture. It is a mistake to assume that he can learn war more easily than peace. His learning machinery is not prejudiced. . . . The bias is in his social environment."[2]

## Freud: Eros and Thanatos

Sigmund Freud led in the development of psychoanalysis. We must limit our reference here to just one aspect of his findings. He was tremendously impressed with the prevalence among his patients of intense drives of love and hate, of which the individuals themselves were often unconscious—so impressed that he came to regard these drives as instinctive or innate. He postulated the existence of what he called Eros, the impulse of love and of life, and the simultaneous existence of Thanatos, the impulse toward death or destruction. He became convinced that man has an innate drive toward evil, aggressiveness, destructiveness, and cruelty.

. . . Men are not gentle, friendly creatures wishing for love, who simply defend themselves if they are attacked. . . . A powerful measure of desire for aggression has to be reckoned as part of their instinctual endowment. The result is that their neighbor is to them not only a possible helper or sexual object, but also a temptation to them to gratify their aggressiveness on him, to exploit his capacity for work without recompense, to use him sexually without his consent, to seize his possessions, to humiliate him, to cause him pain, to torture and kill him. *Homo homini lupus;* who has the courage to dispute it in the face of all the evidence in his own life and in history? This aggressive cruelty . . . manifests itself spontaneously and reveals men as savage beasts to whom the thought of sparing their own kind is alien. Anyone who calls to mind the atrocities of the early migrations, of the invasion of the Huns or by the so-called Mongols under Jenghiz Khan and Tamurlane, of the sack of Jerusalem by the pious Crusaders, even indeed the horrors of the last world-war, will have to bow his head humbly before the truth of this view of man. . . . Civilised society is perpetually menaced with disintegration through this primary hostility of men towards one another[3]

Some have been unkind enough to point out that the situation is relatively worse than Freud said: that if man were really like a wolf among wolves he would rarely attack his own kind but would release his destructive impulses against other species. The fact recalls the view of man expressed by Mephistopheles in Goethe's *Faust:*

[2] Mark A. May, *A Social Psychology of War and Peace* (New Haven, Conn., Yale University Press, 1943), p. 20.
[3] Sigmund Freud, *Civilisation and Its Discontents* (London, Hogarth, 1949), pp. 85-86.

> Life somewhat better might content him,
> But for the gleam of heavenly light which
>    Thou has lent him:
> He calls it Reason—thence his power's increased,
> To be far beastlier than any beast.

Freud was probably wrong in holding that the cruel and destructive behavior of men is attributable to instinct. It results, rather, from a socially
conditioned learning process. Those who find such behavior distressing
may derive hope from this and look for long run change, but in the short
run the origin of cruelty and aggressiveness makes little difference.

## Alfred Adler: Inferiority and Superiority

Alfred Adler was another early psychoanalyst. He sometimes styled
himself the "father of the inferiority complex," and declared it to be his
"most general supposition that the psyche has as its objective the goal of
superiority." He posited the proposition that the individual is predominantly "guided and spurred on by his longing for superiority." From this
basic postulate, Adler and his disciples proceeded to explain the loves
and hates and fears of men. His prescription for the good of men was
"the conscious evolution of a feeling for the common weal and the conscious destruction of the will-to-power."[4]

## Karen Horney: The Search for Glory

Karen Horney, another prominent psychoanalyst, identified herself
more with Sigmund Freud than with Adler, but the premise with which
she started is similar to that of Adler. Her premise was that in our culture
the individual develops "an urgent need to lift himself above others."
Disappointed with his "real self," he creates "an idealized image of himself," which he endows "with unlimited powers and with exalted faculties; he becomes a hero, a genius, a supreme lover, a saint, a god." He becomes a Walter Mitty. The qualities of the idealized image may remain
in the background, permitting "healthy striving" without significant
neuroticism. But neuroticism develops when the qualities of the idealized
image are permitted to come to the fore, leading perhaps to a Dr. Jekyll
and Mr. Hyde type of personality. Neuroticism triumphs when the real
self is forgotten and when the individual regards his ideal self as real.

Since the idealized image regularly provides for self-glorification, the
search for glory becomes the comprehensive and dominant drive. According to Horney, this involves a drive toward perfection, toward external
success, and toward vindictive triumph. The drive for perfection involves

[4] Alfred Adler, *The Practice and Theory of Individual Psychology* (New York, Harcourt, Brace & World, 1929), esp. pp. 7-15.

an assumption of omnipotence, an assumption that anything is possible for the idealized self. The drive toward external success, involving neurotic ambition, requires that one excel—whether in intellectual or artistic activities, in social relationships, in saintliness, in leadership, or whatever. The chief aim of the drive toward vindictive triumph "is to put others to shame or defeat them through one's very success; or to attain the power, by rising to prominence, to inflict suffering upon them—mostly of a humiliating kind." Or the drive toward vindictive triumph may manifest itself in efforts to frustrate, outwit, or defeat others in personal relations. It is a vindictive drive, according to Horney, "because the motivating force stems from impulses to take revenge for humiliations suffered in childhood—impulses which are reinforced during the later neurotic development."

Among recent historical figures Hitler is a good illustration of a person who went through humiliating experiences and gave his whole life to a fanatic desire to triumph over an ever-increasing mass of people. In his case vicious circles, constantly increasing the need, are clearly discernible. One of these develops from the fact that he could think only in categories of triumph and defeat. Hence the fear of defeat made further triumphs always necessary. Moreover, the feeling of grandeur, increasing with every triumph, rendered it increasingly intolerable that anybody, or even any nation, should not recognize his grandeur.[5]

What proportion of people may suffer from such neuroticism Horney does not say, though the implication is that tendencies of this sort are endemic in modern society.

## Erich Fromm: Escape from Insignificance

In one of the most interesting efforts to apply the intuitions and insights of psychoanalysis to the political process, Erich Fromm selects for emphasis the necessity which men feel to "belong," to "avoid isolation and moral aloneness," to avoid powerlessness and insignificance.[6] He argues that the development of Protestantism and capitalism, though enhancing freedom from regimentation, has produced the very things that men want to avoid. Alone, insignificant, and powerless in modern society, men cannot go on bearing the burden of freedom as long as it is interpreted in a negative way, as freedom from restraint or interference. "They cannot go on bearing the burden of 'freedom from'; they must try to escape from freedom altogether unless they can progress from negative to positive freedom." There are three mechanisms of escape: authoritarianism, destructiveness, and automaton conformity.

Authoritarianism is said to develop from

[5] Karen Horney, *Neurosis and Human Growth* (New York, Norton, 1950), esp. pp. 21-27.

[6] Erich Fromm, *Escape from Freedom* (New York, Rinehart, 1941), pp. 22-23.

. . . the tendency to give up the independence of one's own individual self and to fuse one's self with somebody or something outside of oneself in order to acquire the strength which the individual self is lacking. . . . The more distinct forms of this mechanism are to be found in the striving for submission and domination, or, as we would rather put it, in the masochistic and sadistic strivings as they exist in varying degrees in normal and neurotic persons respectively.[7]

Masochism, as Fromm defines it, aims "at dissolving oneself in an overwhelmingly strong power and participating in its strength and glory"; sadism aims "at unrestricted power over another person more or less mixed with destructiveness." Fromm speaks of a sado-masochistic person as having an "authoritarian character." He is both ready to submit to power, that is, to domination by the strong, and at the same time ready to impose power, to attack, to dominate, and to humiliate the weak.[8]

Destructiveness Fromm attributes not only to isolation and powerlessness but also to "anxiety and the thwarting of life."

Life has an inner dynamism of its own; it tends to grow, to be expressed, to be lived. It seems that if this tendency is thwarted the energy directed toward life undergoes a process of decomposition and changes into energies directed toward destruction. . . . The more the drive toward life is thwarted, the stronger is the drive toward destruction.[9]

The third mechanism of escape, automaton conformity, is almost self-explanatory. By this means, the individual loses his sense of isolation by ceasing to be himself and by becoming "exactly as all others are and as they expect him to be." The distinction between the self and society thus disappears.[10]

The personality characteristics described by Freud, Adler, Horney, and Fromm may, of course, be expressed in nonpolitical pursuits. Not everyone who feels an urge to lift himself above others or to belong need satisfy his desires through political action. Moreover, those who enter the political arena may secure their satisfactions exclusively within the realm of domestic politics. However, the realm of international politics obviously includes opportunities to express Eros and Thanatos, and to seek superiority and glory. It is noteworthy that both Freud and Horney illustrated their analyses by citing political leaders (Genghis Khan and Hitler) who profoundly affected the course of world affairs. Fromm's whole book was an effort to explain the development of fascism, which obviously had international implications. Since the decisions affecting international politics are made by human beings and not by an abstract entity called the state, the personality characteristics of the human being involved are bound to have effect.

7 *Ibid.*, p. 134.
8 *Ibid.*, pp. 141-142, 164-168, 221.
9 *Ibid.*, pp. 183-184.
10 *Ibid.*, pp. 185-186.

# THE FRUSTRATION-AGGRESSION THEORY

## The Importance of Other People and the Group

The pursuit of goals usually involves contact with other people, and usually a goal can be achieved only if other people provide assistance. Neither an infant nor, in a complex industrial civilization, an adult can meet even his most elementary needs by his own unaided efforts. If interpersonal relations could somehow be cut off, if all human beings could be isolated from each other, a substantial portion of them would starve, to say nothing of the lesser deprivations which they would suffer. Survival and other satisfactions are not only personal but also interpersonal or group matters. Cooperation and mutual aid are recognized essentials of a satisfactory life.

Securing satisfactions through group relationships, the individual learns to identify himself with the group. He comes to regard himself as a member of the group and to believe that his wants and needs can be satisfied only, or best, through association with the group. A sense of solidarity with the group thus develops. The individual learns to be loyal to the group. He develops a sense of duty or obligation. Through penalties and rewards he learns that he must help sustain the group both against internal disruption and against external attack, lest the satisfactions associated with membership in the group be lost. He learns that peace should be maintained within the group, that reliance should be placed on peaceful processes for the resolution of any conflicts which arise. The general trend in history has been toward the enlargement of the peace group—from family through clan or tribe to the modern nation-states and empires. The problem of extending the peace group to include mankind is, in part, the problem of teaching men to believe that this would give fuller and surer satisfaction to their wants and needs.[11]

## The Inevitability of Frustration

The social conditioning of the individual and the development of group loyalties do not occur without great strains and tensions. Whereas many values can be obtained through cooperation and mutual aid, the search for others involves competition. Not everyone can have enough. One man's gain may be another man's loss. Similarly, if the desire for superiority or the search for glory is the dominant drive, all men cannot

[11] Cf. Harold Guetzkow, *Multiple Loyalties: Theoretical Approach to a Problem in International Organization* (Princeton, N.J., Center for Research on World Political Institutions, 1955).

be satisfied in equal measure. The result is frustration, that is, in varying degrees men find themselves unable to secure what they want.

## Aggression and Its Targets

Theories explaining the effect of frustration on human behavior are still in a tentative stage.[12] It is generally agreed, however, that frustration often leads to aggression. The aggression may be overt or covert—covert aggression taking the form, perhaps, of a plan for revenge which is never executed. The aggression may be undirected, as when one swears, or it may be directed. When it is directed, various targets may be chosen. The individual himself may be the target, that is, the aggression is directed inward. Or the external source of the frustration—perhaps another person—may be the target. Or an entirely innocent person or object may become the target; then a displacement of the aggression is said to occur.

*1. Self-blame and projection.* When the self is made the target, there is likely to be a feeling of guilt or sin or inadequacy of some variety. In extreme cases this leads to suicide. There is, however, a mechanism by which self-blame and hatred of the self can be alleviated or avoided. The individual can simply imagine that it is someone else who is blaming and hating him; he "projects" onto others his own tendencies to punish himself. They are plotting against him, persecuting him. It is they, therefore, not he, who deserve punishment. Those who see evil in themselves, whether they are frustrated or not, may likewise project the evil onto others: not my intentions, but theirs, are bad; it is their aspirations which are wicked and destructive.

The advantage of this mechanism is . . . obvious. It reduces anxiety to force the enemy outside the gate of one's soul. It is better to hate other people for meanness and to bear the fear of their ill-will than to hate oneself. . . . To see wickedness in others, though terrifying, is better than to be divided against oneself. It avoids the terrible burden of guilt.[13]

*2. The displacement of aggressions.* When aggression is directed against the source of frustration it is directed against whatever it is (animate or inanimate) that stands in the way of the achievement of desires. Thus a child denied candy by the mother may strike at her. Displacement is a more involved process. Suppose, for example, that a stu-

---

[12] John Dollard and others, *Frustration and Aggression* (New Haven, Conn., Yale University Press, 1939); N. R. Maier, *Frustration, the Study of Behavior Without a Goal* (New York, McGraw-Hill, 1949); Hilde Himmelweit, "Frustration and Aggression, a Review of Recent Experimental Work," in T. H. Pear, ed., *Psychological Factors of Peace and War* (London, Hutchinson, 1950), pp. 159-191; Elton B. McNeil, "Psychology and Aggression," *Journal of Conflict Resolution*, Vol. 3 (September, 1959), pp. 195-293.

[13] E. F. M. Durbin and John Bowlby, *Personal Aggressiveness and War* (New York, Columbia University Press, 1939), p. 23.

dent is frustrated by his professor. Suppose, further, that in the circumstances it is not politic for the student to direct an aggressive response at the professor. The student may then turn unconsciously to a safer target. Instead of releasing his aggression against the professor, he may take it out in some way on a classmate. In turn, a professor frustrated by his students may displace his aggressions on his wife. It is not unusual for aggressive impulses generated by a series of frustrations to be bottled up or repressed until they are finally released all together on a single hapless target. Then the aggressive responses are far out of proportion to the nature of the offense.[14]

3. *Displacement, Thanatos, and sadism.* It is perhaps in these terms that Freud's conception of Thanatos should be explained. Perhaps, too, the frustration-aggression theory explains such episodes as the lynching of a colored woman in the United States in 1918. She was lynched because she had declared that if she knew the names of the persons who had lynched her husband the Saturday before she would have them prosecuted. She was in the eighth month of pregnancy.

Her ankles were tied together and she was hung to the tree, head downward. Gasoline and oil from the automobiles were thrown on her clothing and while she writhed in agony and the mob howled in glee, a match was applied and her clothes burned from her person. When this had been done and while she was yet alive, a knife, evidently one such as is used in splitting hogs, was taken and the woman's abdomen was cut open, the unborn babe falling from her womb to the ground. The [infant's] head was crushed by a member of the mob with his heel. Hundreds of bullets were then fired into the body of the woman. . . .[15]

Tendencies toward similar acts of sadism (and, on the other side, tendencies toward masochism) show up clearly in the racial struggles that continue today. And they have appeared—and continue to appear—in other connections as well. The Nazi movement was surely reinforced by the destructive impulses of the German people.

Many are convinced (and base this conviction on long personal experience) that the most effective instrument in the Nazi propagandist's hands has been the spectacle of cruelty. When masses of men have been repressed for a long time by adverse social, political and economic conditions, they seem to accept the open expression—above all the open demonstration—of hatred with deep satisfaction. . . . When the Nazis drove dissenters—or imaginary dissenters—from their meetings with cudgels, their audiences grew larger. Few people in Germany were at bottom anti-Semitic, but the joy large numbers felt in promises of blood-curdling treatment to be meted out to the helpless minority made them responsive to the suggestion. Smashing windows and street fighting were relied upon to win the

[14] Dollard and others, *op. cit.*, pp. 39-54.
[15] A report by Walter F. White, "The Work of a Mob," *The Crisis*, Vol. 16 (September, 1918), p. 222. Cf., Leonard W. Doob, *Social Psychology* (New York, Holt, 1952), pp. 286-295.

crowd. . . . "We shall reach our goal," declared Goebbels, "when we have the courage to laugh as we destroy, as we smash, whatever was sacred to us as tradition, as education, as friendship, and as human affection."[16]

However little or much the Nazis may have laughed, they became responsible for one of the greatest, if not the greatest, destructive orgy in human history.

The outbreak of war in 1939, and the overrunning of almost all Europe in 1940, put some nine million Jews in the hands of the Nazis, and of these two-thirds perished. Death came in every possible form, from starvation and exhaustion to suffocation in the appalling trains in which the victims were transported across Europe, from poison and torture in "medical" experiments, to the bullets and gas of the extermination camps. . . .

Exact civilian losses in the Soviet Union have never been published, but a careful estimate is that they amounted to between twelve and fifteen million. Normal warfare could not explain one half, perhaps even one quarter, of these casualties, and by far the greater number must have perished by cold-blooded murder. Exclusive of the Jewish victims, some three million Poles, one million four hundred thousand Yugoslavs, six hundred thousand Frenchmen, half a million Greeks, and Czech, Dutch, and Belgian victims to the number of another half million, all perished by Hitler's command. Thus the five to six million Jews formed considerably less than half the total holocaust.[17]

Note that the above speaks only of civilian deaths. Note also that these illustrations come from what we are pleased to regard as the most highly advanced, cultured, and civilized parts of the world, not from parts of the world that we think of as backward or savage.

*4. Some qualifications and caveats.* It should not be assumed that aggressive behavior results exclusively from frustration and that it will necessarily end when frustration is no longer encountered. Neither should it be assumed that the problem of aggressiveness might be solved by somehow providing targets on which aggressions can be displaced harmlessly. Rather, aggression often becomes the normal and habitual means by which an individual attempts to secure what he wants. In many situations, aggressive attitudes tend to be general, extending over large areas of conduct regardless of opportunities for harmless displacement.[18] Moreover, the very nature of some of the goals which men pursue makes aggressive behavior of some sort rational and logical. If men placed greater value on brotherly love and were possessed of a passion for personal anonymity, political life within and among countries would be far different from what it is.

16 Adolf Hitler, *Mein Kampf* (New York, Reynal & Hitchcock, 1939), footnote, pp. 231-233. For a more comprehensive explanation of the motivations leading Germans to support the Nazis, see Fromm, *op. cit.;* also May, *op. cit.,* pp. 179-187.
17 James Parkes, *Antisemitism* (Chicago, Quadrangle Books, 1964), pp. 100-101.
18 H. J. Eysenck, "War and Aggressiveness: A Survey of Social Attitude Studies," in Pear, *op. cit.,* pp. 52-53.

### The Significance of Projection and Displacement in Political Life

Projection and displacement obviously play a significant role not only in private interpersonal relations but also in public affairs. The story is told of a psychiatrist whose prescription for a neurotic patient was that he should engage in soapbox oratory against almost anything he pleased. He might denounce Wall Street or the Communists, capitalism or creeping socialism, Republicans or Democrats. The point was to release repressed feelings of hatred and repressed impulses to aggression. Of course, the story ends with the report that the patient showed marked improvement after following his psychiatrist's advice. No one has yet devised a way of measuring the prevalence of this kind of motivation for political behavior, but surely it is common. What proportion of the political fanatics have an intelligent grasp of the issues on which they take their stand? What proportion of them, conversely, simply need some outlet for their aggressions, no matter what the target may be? One can scarcely read Nazi diatribes against the so-called Jewish pluto-democracies, or Soviet Communist diatribes against the so-called imperialist warmongers without thinking that they reflect deliberate efforts to bring about a displacement of aggressions onto foreign targets. Scapegoats are sometimes useful, even if creating them causes international complications. Projection is also apparent in the international field, above all in the list of evil practices and intentions that Communists attribute to the capitalist world.

### Animism

Projection and displacement overlap with, if they do not account for, another nonrational phenomenon, revealed especially by anthropological research.

It consists in the universal tendency to attribute all events in the world to the deliberate activity of human or para-human will. All happenings, whether natural and inevitable, or human and voluntary, are attributed to the will of some being either human or anthropomorphically divine. If a thunderstorm occurs, or a hurricane visits a village, or a man is killed by a tiger, the evil is attributed either to the magic of a neighboring tribe or the ill-will of demons and gods. In the same way, good fortune, however natural, is attributed to the deliberate intention of some other human being. This universal tendency in the human mind is termed animism.[19]

Illustrations of animism abound in primitive societies. Relevant activities often take the form of ceremonies to drive away spirits or appease gods

---

[19] Durbin and Bowlby, *op. cit.*, p. 13.

who are held to bring evil to men. But they are also often directed against other human beings who are regarded as masters of magic or witchcraft.

The Motu of southeast New Guinea have a superstitious fear of the neighboring Koitapu, to the magical power of whom they attribute any calamity befalling them. In 1876 they lost much of their sago in a storm at sea, their frail canoes being unable to withstand the rough water and carry the cargo. They charged the Koitapu with bewitching their canoes and killed many of them in revenge. Again, in 1878, after a prolonged drought, for which they held a Koitapu village responsible, they attacked the village and killed all they could.[20]

A little reflection suggests that animism is hardly confined to primitive societies. The Nazis who killed Jews were no more rational than the Motu who killed the Koitapu. The same is probably true of the Russian Communists who starved the kulaks in connection with the collectivization of agriculture and who brought about the great purge of the late 1930's. It is a commonplace in American politics that voters in a drought-stricken area are likely to turn against the party in power at the next election. There may be some elements of animism in the denunciations which Communists and non-Communists currently exchange. Durbin and Bowlby declare, "We think it difficult to exaggerate the frequency and importance of this cause of fighting in human societies of all degrees of civilization."[21]

## Man's Inhumanity

After briefly surveying events in the period between the two World Wars, Durbin and Bowlby conclude, "No group of animals could be more aggressive or more ruthless in their aggression than the adult members of the human race." They do, however, find two differences between the aggression of more primitive beings and that of adult men.

In the first place the aggression of adults is normally a group activity. Murder and assault are restricted to a small criminal minority. Adults kill and torture each other only when organized into political parties, or economic classes, or religious denominations, or nation states. A moral distinction is always made between the individual killing for himself and the same individual killing for some real or supposed group interest.

In the second place, the adult powers of imagination and reason are brought to the service of the aggressive intention. Apes and children when they fight, simply fight. Men and women first construct towering systems of theology and religion, complex analyses of racial character and class structure, or moralities of group life and virility before they kill one another. Thus they fight for

[20] Maurice R. Davie, *The Evolution of War* (New Haven, Conn., Yale University Press, 1929), p. 115.
[21] Durbin and Bowlby, *op. cit.*, p. 14.

Protestantism or Mohammedanism, for the emancipation of the world proletariat or for the salvation of the Nordic culture, for nation or for kind. Men will die like flies for theories and exterminate each other with every instrument of destruction for abstractions.[22]

Adult fighting, in other words, is a product of society, culture, and adherence to principle.

When the Nazi leader, Goering, was being interviewed at the time of the Nuremberg trials, one of his statements was:

Why of course the *people* don't want war. Why would some poor slob on a farm want to risk his life in a war when the best he can get out of it is to come back to his farm in one piece? Naturally, the common people don't want war; neither in Russia, nor in England, nor in America, nor for that matter in Germany. That is understood. But after all, it is the *leaders* of the country who determine the policy, and it is always a simple matter to drag the people along. . . .[23]

Along the same line, difficulties in securing volunteers for the armed forces suggest that blood lust is relatively rare as the dominant drive. If some are guided primarily by Thanatos, others are guided by Eros. Although many Americans seem to enjoy witnessing suffering and destruction—goading prize fighters to murder their opponents and attending 500-mile automobile races in Indianapolis to see cars smashed and drivers killed—the proportion actually participating in acts of violence is small. Further, it is clear that the psychological factors under discussion cannot alone account for war; they do not indicate, for example, why war broke out in 1939 but not in 1938 or 1937. At the same time, even Goering's statement attributes qualities to the people to which the leaders can appeal; men have aggressive impulses and hates which leaders can channel, and in many circumstances men can switch to other leaders in their search for outlets for their hostility. If they don't literally want war, they sometimes want lines of action (whether rational, nonrational, or irrational) that involve great danger of war.

## PROBLEMS OF PERCEPTION

Social psychologists and others speak of *stereotypes* and of unreliable perception. When a stereotype is expressed in words rather than simply remaining an unarticulated image, it is a generalization about some aspect of reality "based not on carefully collected data but on hearsay, on anecdotes, on partial and incomplete experience, on what 'people' have said."[24] The generalization may be either true or false. Potentially most significant for international politics are those stereotypes relating to the

[22] *Ibid.*, pp. 12-13.
[23] G. M. Gilbert, *The Psychology of Dictatorship* (New York, Ronald, 1950), p. 177.
[24] Otto Klineberg, *The Human Dimension in International Relations* (New York, Holt, Rinehart and Winston, 1964), p. 34.

characteristics of various peoples and the policies of various governments. If those who influence decision making think of Orientals as cunning, Indians as incompetent, and black Africans as primitive, the decisions are very likely to be affected. Some of Hitler's decisions were apparently affected by his scornful generalization that the British were a nation of shopkeepers, and the decisions of others have no doubt been influenced by the characterization of Britain as Perfidious Albion. The image of the Latin American as the easy-going lover of siestas is likely to have a somewhat different influence on policies than the image of the Latin American as an eager and industrious person working with determination in adverse circumstances. It is probably inevitable that people will think and act in terms of stereotypes, but by definition they are not reliable as bases of policy decisions.

A number of conditions lead to unreliable perception.[25] (1) Training and experience make people alert to somewhat different things; what is perceived by one may go undetected by another. (2) Expectations affect perception. The Japanese attack on Pearl Harbor, for example, was so unexpected that various people failed to perceive (or to properly evaluate) warning evidence that, from hindsight, was clear. Since World War II expectations based on ideology have on various occasions obviously led the governments in Moscow, Peking, and Washington to misread each other's intentions and capabilities. (3) Desires affect perception. The person who wants to pursue a given course of action is likely to be especially perceptive to indications that it will be successful. (4) The attitudes or reports of others influence perception. Rigged experiments indicate that sometimes perceptions—at least those reported—are influenced less by plain evidence than by what others say; if half a dozen people assert that they see something in an experiment, the seventh is likely to say that he sees the same thing, whether or not he in fact does. One implication is that in any group people may concur with the dominant view of the characteristics of another group even when the evidence before them is to the contrary. (5) Likes and dislikes affect perception. Precisely the same kind of activity may be perceived differently, depending on whether we like or dislike the person or group or state engaging in it. At the extreme, everything done by an enemy is bad, and everything done by a friend is good. This phenomenon is sometimes spoken of as a straining for consistency: "we strive to keep our views of other human beings compatible with each other."

Stereotypes and unreliable perceptions obviously play some role in, say, relations between the United States and the Soviet Union. After talking to a number of people in the Soviet Union, an American social psychologist reports that "the Russian's distorted picture of us was curi-

25 *Ibid.*, pp. 90-99. Cf., Charles E. Osgood, *An Alternative to War or Surrender* (Urbana, Ill., University of Illinois Press, 1962), pp. 26-31.

ously similar to our view of them—a mirror image."[26] In each country people claim virtue for their own side and attribute evil to the other; for example, *we* are peace-loving, *they* are aggressive. And in each country people tend to perceive events in such a way as to confirm their views. It is, of course, not to be assumed that this tendency makes both sides wrong, or that their perceptions are equally distorted; it is not to be assumed that each is simply creating a bogeyman, and that tensions and struggles would cease if only each could bring its perceptions entirely into line with reality. Sometimes reality itself is fearsome. But the tendency to think in terms of stereotypes and unreliable perception is common enough to recommend constant double checking.

## LASSWELL'S POLITICAL TYPE

Harold D. Lasswell has been one of the leaders in the effort to relate the study of human psychology explicitly to political problems. Two related aspects of his work are especially pertinent for our present purposes.

### Values Pursued

In the first place, he lists and defines values (desires, interests) that he regards as especially significant to the study of political behavior. They fall into two groups: the welfare values and the deference values.

Among the welfare values we are especially concerned with well-being, wealth, skill, and enlightenment. By *well-being* is meant the health and safety of the organism. *Wealth* is income: services of goods and persons accruing to the individual in any way whatever. *Skill* is proficiency in any practice whatever, whether in arts or crafts, trade or profession. By *enlightenment* we mean knowledge, insight, and information concerning personal and cultural relations.

Most important among the deference values, for political science, is *power*. Other important deference values are respect, rectitude, and affection. *Respect* is the value of status, of honor, recognition, prestige, the "glory" or "reputation" which Hobbes classes with gain and safety as one of the three fundamental human motivations. *Rectitude* comprises the moral values—virtue, goodness, righteousness, and so on. *Affection*, finally, includes the values of love and friendship.[27]

Lasswell defines power as participation in the making of decisions—a decision being a policy involving severe sanctions or deprivations.[28] Similarly, he uses the term to designate "relations in which severe deprivations are expected to follow the breach of a pattern of conduct."[29]

[26] Urie Bronfenbrenner, "The Mirror Image in Soviet-American Relations: A Social Psychologist's Report," *Journal of Social Issues*, Vol. 17, No. 3 (1961), pp. 45-56.
[27] Harold D. Lasswell and Abraham Kaplan, *Power and Society* (New Haven, Conn., Yale University Press, 1950), pp. 55-56.
[28] *Ibid.*, pp. 74-75.
[29] Harold D. Lasswell, *Power and Personality* (New York, Norton, 1948), p. 12.

Each value which he lists may be desired either for its own sake or because it is useful in the pursuit of other values. Lasswell makes no general assumption concerning the order of priority that individuals and groups assign to these values, or about the relative intensity with which they are pursued. In fact, he warns against sweeping generalizations.

It is impossible to assign a universally dominant role to some one value or other. No single principle of motivation can be elaborated into a tenable "philosophy of history"—as though always and everywhere human conduct can be interpreted as a striving only for economic gain, or for political power, or for prestige and glory, or for love and affection. In a specific situation, any or all of these—and others as well—might be involved in different degrees. What values are operative to what extent can be determined only by specific empirical inquiry.[30]

This observation obviously calls into question some of the theories described earlier in this chapter, especially those of Karen Horney. Similarly, it adds to the doubts already expressed in the chapter "Economic Objectives and Economic Forces" concerning theories which purport to explain imperialism and war largely or exclusively in economic terms. With men pursuing a number of different values (and Lasswell's list does not presume to be exhaustive) an understanding of politics becomes more difficult to achieve. At the same time, it is helpful to be alert to the range of values that help shape behavior.

## Deference Values, Especially Power, and the Political Type

Though heeding his own warning that no one value plays a universally dominant role, Lasswell is inclined to put special emphasis on the deference values. More particularly, he treats the desire for power as a ubiquitous political phenomenon, and he assumes that it is dominant in guiding the behavior of some individuals. To facilitate an understanding of such individuals, he constructs a model—a fictitious person—of what he calls the political type. The political type is the power seeker. "The notion of a political type is that of a developmental type who passes through a distinctive career line in which the power opportunities of each situation are selected in preference to other opportunities." The basic characteristic of the political type is "the accentuation of power in relation to other values within the personality when compared with other persons." More broadly, the political type feels an intense and ungratified craving for deference. He seeks to gratify these cravings through political activity, and rationalizes his activity in terms of the public interest.[31]

[30] Lasswell and Kaplan, *op. cit.*, p. 57.
[31] Lasswell, *op. cit.*, pp. 21, 22, 38.

There is no implication that all those who are active in politics, or even all those who hold leading political positions, are political types in Lasswell's sense. Throughout history, examples abound of individuals who have sought to give up power rather than expand it. At the same time, there are also many instances of individuals who have been driven on by a craving for power which seemed insatiable. In some the lust for power has been so intense as to create a merciless disregard and even contempt for the interests and welfare of other men. "According to our speculative model, the perfect power type is wholly absorbed with advancing the value position of the 'sacred me' (not 'us'). Hence he sacrifices anyone and everyone at convenience for his power, and does not conceive of power as a means of advancing the value position of family, neighborhood, nation or any other group."[32] Endless accumulation of power becomes an all-consuming passion. The question is why? Why do some persons tend toward the extreme of Lasswell's political type?

## The Sources of the Craving for Power

Lasswell's hypothesis is that "low estimates of the self" are at the bottom of the craving for power. The individual somehow feels deprived; he does not command the values which, for some reason, he thinks he should command. Perhaps he suffers from a physical handicap, a lack of well-being. Perhaps his income is low. Or perhaps, while thinking that he deserves deference, he feels that he does not actually obtain it—that others hold him in unduly low esteem. Alternatively, if the individual does not feel currently deprived, he may fear the loss of values in the future.

In some circumstances the individual accepts the actual or threatened deprivation without struggle; he becomes reconciled to low estimates of the self. In other circumstances he seeks to compensate for deprivation or to safeguard himself against future deprivation which he fears. The struggle for compensation or for a guarantee for the future takes the form of a struggle for power. Power is expected to overcome low estimates of the self. Lasswell's summary statement is as follows:

The accentuation of power is to be understood as a compensatory reaction against low estimates of the self (especially when coexisting with high self-estimates); and the reaction occurs when opportunities exist both for the displacement of ungratified cravings from the primary circle to public targets and for the rationalization of these displacements in the public interest.[33]

Appropriate skills, of course, must also be possessed.

The same factors that lead individuals to crave power are also said to operate on groups. Individuals identify themselves with the group, and

32 *Ibid.*, p. 56.
33 *Ibid.*, p. 53.

want it to command welfare and deference values in which they can share. The respect which individuals feel that they command, for example, varies with the respect commanded by a group with which they are identified. The nation or state is commonly the most important among such groups. When estimates of its value position are low, or when there is fear for its future value position, the stage is set for a compensatory struggle for power. The point is illustrated by the statement of a Nazi leader at a congress of the League for Germans Abroad in the 1930's: "We have a common fate. Your star became dim with Germany's decline. When Germany came to be held in contempt, your prestige disappeared."[34] It is also illustrated currently by demands on the part of colonial peoples for independence.

The desire for respect is now understood to be one of the most important influences on men's conduct. Social tensions arise from resentment at not being respected as much as from any other source. Movements to give freedom to dependent peoples derive their strength primarily from the desire on the part of these peoples to participate in the sharing of respect.[35]

## Healthy and Sick Personalities

Lasswell's political type represents an extreme which few, if any, individuals or groups actually reach. In his conception people range in their desire for power from some undetermined minimum to an absolute maximum. What proportion of individuals within any society and throughout the world are grouped at different points along the power scale is unknown. Further, the question how they should ideally be distributed along the scale can be answered only on the basis of some assumptions concerning the nature of the good society. In most conceptions of the good society, there would be a cutting point somewhere along the scale; individuals on one side of the cutting point would be regarded as having socially desirable or healthy personalities, and those on the other side (i.e., those who come closest to being political types) would be regarded as having sick personalities. Measures might then be taken to promote the development of healthy personalities and to exclude sick personalities from positions of political influence and control. The effect on the course of history might well be great. Plainly, by standards most likely to be acceptable to believers in liberalism and democracy, many of those who have done much to shape history in the past have been sick.

Lasswell's explanation of the sources of the lust for power obviously has something in common with psychoanalytical explanations of behavior and with the frustaration-aggression theory. He does not generalize as

---

[34] Rudolf Hess, *Reden* (München, Zentralverlag der N.S.D.A.P., 1940), p. 264.
[35] Frederick Sherwood Dunn, *War and the Minds of Men* (New York, Harper & Row, 1950), p. 41.

much as Karen Horney, for example, but his political type could well be a person who, in her terms, is dominated by a drive for self-glorification. Similarly, low estimates of the self presumably mean frustration for the individual, and the compensatory striving for power presumably involves aggression.

## IMPLICATIONS FOR INTERNATIONAL POLITICS

Some implications of the study of human psychology for international politics are reasonably clear, and others are shrouded in uncertainty and doubt.

### Long-Run Possibilities

In the long run, perhaps the most important point is that human behavior is largely a reflection of the learning process. This process largely governs the selection of values, the order of priority among them, and the intensity with which they are pursued. It, rather than instinct, is the source of what Freud called Eros and Thanatos, of what Adler called the goal of superiority, of what Horney called the individual's feeling of an urgent need to lift himself above others, and of what Fromm called the desire of men to avoid powerlessness and insignificance. The learning process, moreover, largely governs the selection of methods for satisfying needs and wants, and the nature of reactions to frustration. It is on the basis of the learning process that estimates of the self are made and that reactions to low estimates of the self are selected. If the learning process governs so much of human behavior, it obviously follows that behavior can be shaped and changed. Very little of what men do is really inevitable.

Identification with the nation and loyalty to it are among the things learned. There is nothing in the nature of man which precludes identification with larger entities, up to and including the world as a whole. Loyalties could theoretically be developed to an entity encompassing all mankind.

These thoughts suggest the possibility of developing a peaceful and stable world order comprised of harmonious and good societies. The very expression of the thought, however, is enough to suggest how far men are from achieving such a goal.

### Short-Run Dangers from "Mad Caesars"

For the short run, little can be said with real assurance. Presumably a fairly high proportion of those who rise to the top politically throughout the world are driven on by some such desires as those emphasized by

Freud, Adler, Horney, and Fromm. It seems plausible to assume that many are driven on by frustration, reacting to it in aggressive ways. Displacement of aggressive impulses, projection, and what Durbin and Bowlby call animism appear to be common in political life. Obviously there are many in public life in various countries with tendencies toward the extreme illustrated by Lasswell's political type.

There have been many "mad Caesars" in history—sick personalities in positions of great political power. Some have ruled in states so small and weak that the damage they have done was almost automatically restricted; others have had great military power behind them, and have been able to do damage on a far-reaching scale. Genghis Khan might be cited, along with his statement that

. . . a man's highest job in life is to break his enemies, to drive them before him, to take from them all the things that have been theirs, to hear the weeping of those who cherished them, to take their horses between his knees, and to press in his arms the most desirable of their women.[36]

Hitler was no doubt a sick person in the sense that the word is being used here. Probably Stalin was, as well. Reporting to the Twentieth Congress of the Communist Party of the Soviet Union, Khrushchev is said to have described Stalin as "a very distrustful man, sickly suspicious. . . . Everywhere and in everything he saw 'enemies,' 'two-facers,' and 'spies.' . . . His persecution mania reached unbelievable dimensions." Khrushchev also referred to Stalin's "mania for greatness," and asserted that he "completely lost consciousness of reality."[37] These statements suggest not only that Stalin was driven on by a lust for power but also that he was mentally sick in other ways. Given the extent of mental illness—or at least of some degree of disturbance—in populations generally, it is not surprising if some who reach high office succumb in similar ways.[38]

Where sick personalities have autocratic control over great military power, the danger to the world is obviously very real. With the development of nuclear weapons and the prospect that most states will come to possess them, the proportion of statesmen who are in a position to do great damage will certainly increase.

Of course, statesmen do not act alone. They always have advisers, even the "mad Caesars." Frequently they share power with many others—with an oligarchy or an elite. In democracies the whole electorate, and especially the elected representatives of the people, share in decision-making. The more power is shared the less likely is it that the special personality

[36] Quoted by Lasswell, *op. cit.*, p. 43.
[37] *New York Times*, June 5, 1956, p. 15, cols. 1, 7, 8.
[38] Arnold A. Rogow, *James V. Forrestal* (New York, Macmillan, 1963), pp. xi-xii, 340-351.

characteristics of some one leader will be decisive. His actions will be influenced and perhaps controlled by those who participate in shaping public policy. In most governments, most of the time, very strenuous efforts are made to see to it that issues, above all issues involving questions of war and peace, are thoroughly and rationally considered by a large number of able people. The chance that unconscious or subconscious or irrational motives will control decisions on fateful issues is small, yet it happens.

Even democracy does not necessarily assure wisdom and rationality. Just as all members of the Motu tribe may have believed that the Koitapu bewitched their canoes, so may all or most members even of advanced societies share in the drives, motives, and attitudes of their leaders. The advisers of a "mad Caesar" may to some extent share his personality characteristics. Identifying with the nation or state, they may seek glory and power through it. The group as a whole may approach the characteristics of the political type. Low estimates of the individual or group self may lead to a compensatory struggle for power. Humble citizens may be frustrated, and be ready to displace their aggressions onto a foreign enemy. The problem of shaping the development of the human personality in such a way as to obtain socially desirable responses to stimuli in interpersonal and intergroup relations is not an easy one to solve.

## Dangers in Psychological Approaches

Psychological approaches to politics, domestic or international, can easily give wrong impressions. One of them is that there are no real political issues. Especially when considerable attention is paid to the irrational aspects of behavior, the tendency is to conclude that if statesmen and others would only consult psychiatrists and accept psychotherapy the troubles of the world would be over. Or the conclusion may be that a focus on the learning process, with a view to creating healthy personalities, would permit the solution of all problems. In truth, these conclusions have a measure of truth in them, but the problem of creating a desirable world order is far too complex to be solved in these ways alone. Not all behavior is irrational. Neuroticism does not dominate the world scene. People with quite healthy personalities sometimes clash. The simple fact is that thoroughly rational people may want different things, or, when they want the same thing, there may not be enough of it to go around. Moreover, even if there is potentially enough to go around, it may be impossible to secure agreement on the best way of making it available. Problems arising out of such situations are quite real. Their solution may be complicated by the presence of irrational or neurotic behavior, but even the most perfectly adjusted and rational people would scarcely find answers that are easy and pat. If answers are to be found, the resources of many fields in addition to the field of psychology will have to be taxed.

## SUGGESTED READINGS

BRAMSON, Leon, and GOETHALS, George W., eds., *War. Studies from Psychology, Sociology, Anthropology* (New York, Basic Books, 1964).

CANTRIL, Hadley, ed., *Tensions That Cause War* (Urbana, Ill., University of Illinois Press, 1951).

DURBIN, E. F. M., and BOWLBY, John, *Personal Aggressiveness and War* (New York, Columbia University Press, 1939).

FROMM, Erich, *Escape from Freedom* (New York, Rinehart, 1941).

GILBERT, G. M. *The Psychology of Dictatorship* (New York, Ronald, 1950).

GLOVER, Edward, *War, Sadism, and Pacifism* (London, George Allen & Unwin, 1945).

HORNEY, Karen, *Neurosis and Human Growth* (New York, Norton, 1950).

KELMAN, Herbert C., ed., *International Behavior, A Social-Psychological Analysis* (New York, Holt, Rinehart and Winston, 1965).

KLINEBERG, Otto, *The Human Dimension in International Relations* (New York, Holt, Rinehart and Winston, 1964).

——, *Tensions Affecting International Understanding, A Study of Research* (New York, Social Science Research Council, 1950).

LASSWELL, Harold D., *Power and Personality* (New York, Norton, 1948).

LASSWELL, Harold D., and KAPLAN, Abraham, *Power and Society* (New Haven, Conn., Yale University Press, 1950).

McNEIL, Elton B., ed., *The Nature of Human Conflict* (Englewood Cliffs, N.J., Prentice-Hall, 1965).

MAY, Mark A., *A Social Psychology of War and Peace* (New Haven, Conn., Yale University Press, 1943).

MUNROE, R. L., *Schools of Psychoanalytic Thought* (New York, Holt, Rinehart and Winston, 1955).

PEAR, T. H., ed., *Psychological Factors of Peace and War* (New York, Philosophical Library, 1950).

SINGER, J. David, ed., *Human Behavior and International Politics, Contributions from the Social-Psychological Sciences* (Chicago, Rand McNally, 1965).

9

# PRESTIGE AND PRIDE

This chapter is essentially a continuation of the preceding one. Recall particularly the references to the search for glory as a pervasive human motive, and recall Lasswell's emphasis on the deference values, especially power. Here the purpose is to elaborate on these ideas and to stress them, and to do this by introducing somewhat different terminology and applications. We will speak of the search for prestige and pride.

## PRESTIGE

The prestige of a nation in world affairs is sometimes thought of simply as its reputation for power. Charles Burton Marshall was evidently thinking in these terms when he said,

Prestige is the faculty enabling a great power to avoid final, miserable choices between surrender and war. Prestige is the ingredient of authority in international affairs. One may point up its meaning by an account of a geneticist who crossed a tiger and a parrot. When asked about the results of the experiment he replied: "When it talks, I listen." The quality which demands being listened to is prestige—and a nation suffers loss of it at great peril.[1]

In other words, prestige is reputation that reflects and suggests authority or importance or ascendancy. To broaden the statement, it is the reputation for distinctive success in meeting whatever tests are thought to be significant. It is the reputation for an ability to achieve goals of a challenging sort, for a will to achieve them, and for a future in which these

[1] Charles Burton Marshall, "Cuba—Why the Russians Are There," New Republic, Vol. 147 (October 1, 1962), p. 9.

qualities will be preserved if not enhanced. Failure to meet significant challenge means loss of prestige, and so does evidence of declining ability or weakening will. Conversely, successful response to challenge reinforces prestige, and so does a reputation for being on the wave of the future. A state with adequate prestige can be reasonably sure that others will not lightly encroach on its rights and interests, and it may obtain the deference of others—their respectful submission or yielding—on issues to which the prestige is relevant.

Prestige is clearly among the goals that states pursue. This is one of the reasons for armed establishments, as we will note in the chapter on arms and arms control, and one of the reasons for testing weapons and staging war games or other displays of armed power. More broadly, it is one of the reasons why states are so sensitive about the handling of any matter that may be taken to be indicative of their power and determination. Thus the kings of Europe paid great attention to questions of ceremony and protocol, partly on the assumption that the resolution of such questions would be indicative of relative status and prestige; and governments all over the world have followed suit. Governments do not want to accept the slightest indignity, even if the concrete issue seems insubstantial, lest this be construed to indicate that they lack the ability or determination to protect or advance their interests. Moreover, a considerable portion of the international issues that arise are handled not so much on the basis of their intrinsic significance as on the basis of their potential symbolic significance; they are handled not on their merits but as tests of strength and will—tests that indicate how other more or less comparable future issues may be handled. Thus the intervention of the United States in Korea in 1950 was dictated not so much by the substantive importance of South Korea to the United States (e.g., its strategic or economic significance, or the significance of the fate of the South Koreans themselves) as by a belief that our response to the challenge would indicate our probable responses to future challenges: by intervening we would demonstrate our determination to block the forceful extension of Communism and so convince Communist regimes that other acts of aggression would not pay. Also, Secretary of State Dulles permitted the case of the offshore islands of China to become a test of our support for the government on Taiwan and our opposition to the government on the mainland. Questions pertaining to the fate of Vietnam and Berlin are also being handled at least as much in terms of their symbolic significance as in terms of their substantive significance.

Developments in space after the first Sputnik went into orbit in 1957 illustrate concern for national prestige. The booster that put Sputnik into orbit also dramatically enhanced Soviet prestige. Moreover, subsequent Soviet successes and the less spectacular American achievements accentuated the effect. Public opinion polls in various countries indicated

that a large proportion of the people had come to think of the Soviet
Union as the world leader in science, and this had reasonably clear implications for beliefs about potential military power. The result was a
welling up of demands in the United States for action to recoup national
prestige. As John F. Kennedy put it when he was running for the presi-
dency in 1960:

> The people of the world respect achievement. For most of the 20th century they
> admired American science and American education, which was second to none.
> But now they are not at all certain about which way the future lies. . . . If the
> Soviet Union was first in outer space, that is the most serious defeat the United
> States has suffered in many, many years. . . . Because we failed to recognize the
> impact that being first in outer space would have, the impression began to move
> around the world that the Soviet Union was on the march, that it had definite
> goals, that it knew how to accomplish them, that it was moving and we were
> standing still.[2]

Not long after Kennedy was inaugurated, the first manned orbital
flight occurred—the Gagarin flight. Kennedy feared "the impact of this
adventure on the minds of men everywhere, who are attempting to make
a determination of which road they should take," and he concluded that
the time had come "for this nation to take a clearly leading role in space
achievement." Among other things, he called for—and got—a commitment to the effort to get a man to the moon and back by 1970. "No single
space project in this period," he said, "will be more impressive to mankind."

Kennedy's point that American science and education affect national
prestige might be broadened: the prestige of every country depends to a
considerable extent on the quality of its domestic life. No one standard
of judgment is foreordained, and we do not have precise knowledge of
the standards that are in fact employed. Few assign the greatest prestige
to the country whose population best succeeds in renouncing earthly
desire. The much more common demand is for achievement that relates
somehow to earthly satisfactions, and probably achievement in a number
of different areas; moreover, in the eyes of many it is not so much achievement that counts as continuing progress toward greater achievement. A
country that wallows in backwardness, or that seems unable to see or
solve problems, or that fails to come up with distinctive accomplishments
is likely, in most eyes, to enjoy little prestige. Conversely, a country's
prestige is enhanced the more it achieves in areas that the observer considers significant, e.g., in the stability, adaptability, and stimulating
quality of its political and legal order, in the effectiveness of its economic
system in meeting human needs in ever-increasing measure, in the level of

[2] The source of this quotation, and of all other quotations relating to space in this
chapter, are given in Vernon Van Dyke, *Pride and Power, The Rationale of the Space
Program* (Urbana, Ill., University of Illinois Press, 1964), Chapters 2, 8, and 9.

public and private morality maintained, in the quality of health, education, and welfare provided, in the results of its scientific, technological, artistic, and literary pursuits, in its record in sports, etc. Very often prestige goes simply to those who display virtuosity, regardless of the area of activity involved.

## PRIDE

Pride is often thought of as one of the seven deadly sins and is rarely listed among the motives that inspire political behavior in either domestic or international politics. But the term is not necessarily pejorative. It does not necessarily mean inordinate conceit. There is an alternative lexical meaning: "a reasonable delight in one's position, achievements, possessions, etc."; "pleasure or satisfaction taken in something done by or belonging to oneself." Thus national pride may be taken to reflect appropriate gratification stemming from past, current, or confidently anticipated achievements. It is a counterpart of prestige, and the same constituent elements are involved: belief that the nation has the capacity to respond to significant challenges with distinctive success, belief that it has the will to do so, and belief in an assured future in which these qualities will be preserved if not enhanced. If self-evaluations are in accord with the evaluations made by people abroad, pride and prestige go together.

In international politics, and in many other realms as well, the search for pride and prestige is associated with the search for greatness and glory. Negatively, it is associated with a desire to avoid, terminate, or seek revenge for humiliation.

### Pride in Conquest

That the search for a basis for pride has been a powerful motivating force in history is abundantly clear, especially in view of the fact that one source of pride has been conquest, territorial aggrandizement, and the subjection of people. The nature and force of the motive are illustrated in a conversation which, according to Plutarch, took place between Cineas and Pyrrhus, when Pyrrhus was preparing to invade Italy.

"The Romans, sir [said Cineas], are reported to be great warriors and conquerors of many warlike nations; if God permit us to overcome them, how should we use our victory?"

"You ask," said Pyrrhus, "a thing evident of itself. The Romans once conquered, there is neither Greek nor barbarian city that will resist us, but we shall presently be masters of all Italy, the extent and resources and strength of which any one should rather profess to be ignorant of than yourself."

Cineas after a little pause, "And having subdued Italy, what shall we do next?"

Pyrrhus not yet discovering his intention, "Sicily," he replied, "next holds out her arms to receive us, a wealthy and populous island, and easy to be gained. . . ."

"You speak," said Cineas, "what is perfectly probable, but will the possession of Sicily put an end to the war?"

"God grant us," answered Pyrrhus, "victory and success in that, and we will use these as forerunners of greater things; who could forbear from Libya and Carthage then within reach . . . ? These conquests once perfected, will any assert that of the enemies who now pretend to despise us, any one will dare to make further resistance?"

"None," replied Cineas, "for then it is manifest we may with such mighty forces regain Macedon, and make an absolute conquest of Greece; and when all these are in our power what shall we do then?"

Said Pyrrhus, smiling, "We will live at our ease, my dear friend, and drink all day, and divert ourselves with pleasant conversation."

When Cineas had led Pyrrhus with his argument to this point: "And what hinders us now, sir, if we have a mind to be merry, and entertain one another, since we have at hand without trouble all those necessary things, to which through much blood and great labor, and infinite hazards and mischief done to ourselves and to others, we design at last to arrive?"

Such reasonings rather troubled Pyrrhus with the thought of the happiness he was quitting, than any way altered his purpose, being unable to abandon the hopes of what he so much desired.[3]

The desire to provide a basis for pride through achievement has been manifested by many others. Before becoming King of Prussia, Frederick the Great envisaged himself as always advancing "from country to country, from conquest to conquest, selecting, like Alexander, new worlds to conquer." Later he declared, "The policy of great monarchies has never varied. Their fundamental principle has been ceaseless aggrandizement." "The passions of princes," he said, "know no other restraint than the limit of their power."[4] Napoleon seemed to be similarly motivated. Speaking to French sailors in 1797 he declared, "Comrades, when we have secured peace for the continent, we shall join you in conquering the freedom of the seas. . . . Without you, we can carry the glory of the French name only to a small portion of the continent; with you we shall sail the seas and the most remote regions shall behold our national glory."[5] On another occasion he said, "We must go to the Orient. All great glories are won there. . . . Europe is a mole-hill. There have never been great revolutions and great empires except in the Orient, where six hundred million men live." Hitler explained himself largely in terms of racial principle, but it is implicit in what he said that he

[3] Plutarch's *Complete Works, Parallel Lives,* Vol. II (New York, Crowell, 1909), pp. 54-55.

[4] G. P. Gooch, *Frederick the Great* (New York, Knopf, 1947), pp. 283-284; Hans Kohn, *The Idea of Nationalism* (New York, Macmillan, 1944), p. 362.

[5] George Gordon Andrews, *Napoleon in Review* (New York, Knopf, 1939), pp. 176-177.

sought glory and power through aggrandizement: "The pacifist-humane idea is perhaps quite good whenever the man of the highest standard has previously conquered and subjected the world to a degree that makes him the only master of this globe." "The Nordic race has a right to rule the world. We must make this right a guiding star of our foreign policy."[6] A principal leader of the Nazi movement, Goering, admitted while he was on trial after World War II at Nuremberg that Hitler had gone to war not so much to regain territory or to gain anything else that was tangible as to get revenge for the defeat of 1918.[7] And Goering himself looked forward to revenge for 1945: "My people have been humiliated before. Loyalty and hatred will unite them again. Who knows but that at this very hour the man is born who will . . . avenge the humiliation we suffer now."[8] Concerned with "greatness," Goering rejected humanitarianism: "The empire of Genghis Khan, the Roman Empire, and even the British Empire were not built up with due regard for principles of humanity, . . . but they had achieved greatness. . ."[9]

## British Pride and the British Empire

Whatever the British concern for humanitarianism, pride in achievement has clearly played a major role in British imperialism. Recall John Strachey's analysis, alluded to at the end of the chapter on economic ob-jectives and economic forces. He asserts that economic motives contrib-uted to the conquest of India, but that they were not sufficient to explain it. His emphasis is on the "daemonic will to conquer and to rule [that] seized the British, an imperial will which possessed them until very recent times."[10] Further, asking why many men in India were willing to fight under the British banner rather than for native rulers, he answers that their "pride as men" was the explanation: the native rulers were inefficient and ineffective, bringing humiliation to those identified with them, whereas the British were resolute, well-organized, and successful; they ran a "better show."

The immense power of the satisfaction which men get merely from belonging, without much personal advantage, to a successful "show" should never be forgotten by the student of history and politics who is searching for the reasons which have made things happen in the otherwise inexplicable way in which they *have* happened.[11]

6 Adolf Hitler, *Mein Kampf* (New York, Reynal & Hitchcock, 1939), pp. 394-395. The second statement, attributed to Hitler, is quoted from Frederick L. Schuman, *The Nazi Dictatorship* (New York, Knopf, 1935), p. 128.

7 G. M. Gilbert, *The Psychology of Dictatorship* (New York, Ronald, 1950), p. 302.

8 *Ibid.*, pp. 306-307.

9 *Ibid.*, p. 111.

10 John Strachey, *The End of Empire* (New York, Random House, 1960), p. 23.

11 *Ibid.*, p. 39.

Others have also treated British imperialism as a phenomenon welling up from forces that are largely of an emotional nature. One of the Englishmen who opposed freedom for Canada more than a century ago said that it would not be Canada valued in pounds, shillings, and pence which would be cast off, "but the proudest trophies of British valour, but the character of British faith, but the honour of the British name."[12] Richard Cobden commented that "so grateful to our national pride has been the spectacle [of imperial rule] that we have never, for once, paused to inquire if our interests were advanced by such nominal greatness." And Goldwin Smith, writing on empire in 1863, found that what he called "the pride of Empire" ran through all the arguments for retaining colonies; the imperial system rested on "unreflecting pride."[13] A more recent English writer on imperialism speaks of the importance of powerful and enduring political ideas that can "catch and fire the imagination."

In the last generation of the Victorian era, many men thought they had found just such an idea. It became their faith, that it was the role of the British Empire to *lead the world* in the arts of civilization, to bring light to the dark places, to teach the true political method, to nourish and to protect the liberal tradition. It was to act as a trustee for the weak, and bring arrogance low. It was to represent in itself the highest aims of human society. It was to command, and deserve, *a status and prestige shared by no other*. It was to captivate the imagination and hold fast the allegiance of the million by the propagation of peculiar myths —one among which was the figure of Queen Victoria herself, who became depersonalized, as an idea: the idea of the Great White Queen. While encouraging and making profit from the spirit of adventure, it was nevertheless to promote the interests of peace and commerce. While it was to gain its greatest trophies in war, it was to find its main task in serving the ends of justice, law and order. It was an idea that moved, an idea that expanded, an idea that had to continue to move and to expand in order to retain its vitality and its virtue.[14] [Italics supplied.]

The same writer cites a reference to "that greater pride in Empire which is called imperialism and is a larger patriotism." It was a part of the imperial idea, he says that "a British subject in a foreign land must be able to feel and proud to say that he was a citizen of a Power whose fame and influence spanned the world, and whose reputation was his sufficient shield."[15]

Given this kind of a role for the imperial idea, it is understandable that Strachey should be concerned about the consequences of the disso-

---

[12] Quoted by Klaus E. Knorr, *British Colonial Theories 1570-1850* (Toronto, University of Toronto Press, 1944), pp. 362-363.

[13] *Ibid.*, p. 365.

[14] A. P. Thornton, *The Imperial Idea and Its Enemies* (New York, St Martin's, 1959), pp. ix-x. Quotations reprinted by permission of St Martin's Press, Inc., the Macmillan Company of Canada, Ltd., and Macmillan & Co., Ltd.

[15] *Ibid.*, pp. x, 4.

lution of the British Empire. "The morale, the spirit, the mental health even, of all of us in Britain are involved. . . ." He believes that the identification of individual Britishers with the Empire is such that many of them "feel a sense of personal loss—almost an amputation—when some colony or semi-colony . . . becomes independent. The hauling down of the Union Jack in yet another part of the world has a depressing effect."[16] Strachey goes on to discuss the problems of psychological adjustment that other peoples had faced in connection with the loss of what he calls greatness and what is here treated as a source of pride.

From Assyria, with her specialty for total ruthlessness, to Hitler with his, what most men have meant by national greatness has had little or nothing to do with a particular political institution. What has been idoliscd has been simply the capacity to conquer and to enslave, or otherwise exploit, other peoples. For by far the greater number of states over by far the greater part of their histories, this has been the single test of national greatness. No state which had not subdued, and was not exploiting, other peoples, has been considered great.[17]

Athens perished, according to Strachey, not because of material losses in war but because after these losses "she could never again feel satisfaction with herself." So far as Spain is concerned, "What undid her was that the Spaniards were unable to see any tolerable way of life [after] their country's grandeur was gone," i.e., after the loss of empire.[18]

Strachey then goes on with the statements that we have already quoted at the end of Chapter 6 but which bear repeating. Now that "the enlargement or maintenance of empire" can no longer be the British "national purpose," he fears that "we shall stagnate unless we can find other purposes to satisfy our hearts." He speaks of personal self-enrichment, saying that it has been adopted as the national ideal in the United States, Belgium, and Germany, but he thinks that this ideal will not suffice. "Nations which have known empire may simply break their hearts if they do not find a higher ideal than personal enrichment by which to live."[19] Even national enrichment—concern for the material welfare of the whole community—is not enough. He then goes on to suggest a number of additional possibilities, such as the promotion of educational equality and the perfecting of democratic political institutions. "If Britain is to be great in the future as she has been in the past, we shall have to take the things of the mind and the spirit much more seriously than we have hitherto done." But there is more beyond this.

It is by lifting our eyes and looking outwards upon the whole world that we shall find an ideal high enough, difficult enough of attainment, and therefore

16 Strachey, *op. cit.*, p. 204.
17 *Ibid.*, pp. 210-211.
18 *Ibid.*, pp. 212-213.
19 *Ibid.*, p. 229.

inspiring enough, to fire the national imagination. The highest mission of Britain in our day is to help the underdeveloped world. . . . This is above all the field in which Britain is called upon to lead the world. . . . It will be by serving the peoples of the world that we can be great.[20]

One might ask how this differs from Kipling's call to take up the white man's burden. But the much more significant point for present purposes is the tacit assumption, the underlying premise, that it is important to find an activity in which Britain can lead the world—important to be great. This attitude recalls the view of one of the most famous of Englishmen, Thomas Hobbes, that life can reasonably be compared to a race. "This race we must suppose to have no other goal, nor other garland, but being foremost, and in it . . . to consider them behind is glory; . . . continually to be out-gone is misery; continually to out-go the next before is felicity; and to forsake the course is to die."[21]

In this context it is interesting to note the reactions of a Chinese observer, Yen Fu, to British life and thought at the end of the nineteenth century—at a time of great wealth and power for Britain and of further ignominy for China because of additional defeats in war. To Yen Fu the difference in the fortunes of the two countries, and more broadly the difference between East and West, lay not so much in weapons or productive power or political organization as in the realm of ideas and values, in the realm of motivations. In the China that he knew, the sages "were not unaware that the universe is an inexhaustible storehouse [of infinite possibilities] and that if the subtle powers of the human mind are given free vent, human ingenuity and intellectual capacity can attain unfathomable results." But the sages preferred harmony to striving. Instead of calling for achievement of some sort, they "preferred to preach contentment with one's lot." Struggle was "man's greatest calamity." "The energetic pursuit of survival and mastery as ends, the prospect of strife and conflict, respresented the demonic—the ultimate evil. They thus shrank back from the actualization of men's potentialities, settling for peace, harmony, and order on a low level of human achievement." A Western scholar concludes:

Here we find the very crux of the difference between East and West. On the one hand, we have a vision of reality which stresses the primacy of force in the universe at large and the thrust of energy in the biological and human world. The key terms are energy, dynamism, struggle, self-assertion, and the fearless realization of all human potentialities on ever higher levels of achievement. . . . On the other hand, we have a vision which exalts passivity and quietude,

20 *Ibid.*, pp. 244, 246, 247.
21 Thomas Hobbes, *The English Works of Thomas Hobbes*, ed. by Molesworth (London, John Bohn, 1839-1845), Vol. IV, pp. 52-53.

which shrinks from struggle and strife, and positively fears the assertion of human vital energies.[22]

## Pride and Anti-Imperialist Nationalism

Imperialism gives pride at the expense of the subjugated people, through their humiliation. Given the general conception of human motives asserted here, it is not surprising that the humiliated should rebel. That they have done so and are doing so is one of the themes that runs through the literature on anti-imperialism and anticolonialism. Thus in assessing the reasons for demands for independence, Rupert Emerson acknowledges resentment against economic practices in colonies, but relegates it to a secondary position. "The more fundamental elements were the sense of inferiority inherent in colonialism, the indignation aroused by determination of status on racial grounds, and the gnawing consciousness of being a second-class citizen in one's own country. . . . Colonialism created . . . the conditions which made nationalism . . . an appropriate response for those who would regain their self-esteem"[23] Emerson speaks of practices and attitudes of whites in Africa where "the humiliation which is inflicted runs so deep as to be almost beyond repair. What is involved is . . . a charge of inherent inferiority against a race as a whole. . . . Imperial arrogance and racial discrimination have been the prime sources of the vehemence of Asian and African nationalism."[24] As another commentator has said, "People do not like being exploited, but they can put up with it. What they cannot put up with is being considered inferior."[25]

The struggle of colonial peoples to restore their pride has expressed itself above all, of course, in independence movements. They do not necessarily expect that self-government will be good government. In terms of the efficiency of administration, the preservation of law and order, the extent of freedom, and even in terms of economic well-being, it is not at all clear that independence means improvement, at least in the visible future; it is already obvious that in a number of cases it means the reverse. But these considerations are not controlling. A Pakistani writer has ex-

[22] Benjamin Schwartz, *In Search of Wealth and Power, Yen Fu and the West* (Cambridge, The Belknap Press of Harvard University Press, 1964), pp. 54-56. Quotation reprinted by permission of The Belknap Press of Harvard University Press; copyright 1964 by the President and Fellows of Harvard College.

[23] Rupert Emerson, *From Empire to Nation* (Cambridge, Harvard University Press, 1960), pp. 55, 381. Quotations from this book are reprinted by the permission of Harvard University Press; copyright 1960 by the President and Fellows of Harvard College. Cf., Eugene Staley, *The Future of Underdeveloped Countries* (New York, Harper & Row, 1961), pp. 21-24.

[24] *Ibid.*, p. 382.

[25] W. R. Crocker, quoted by Emerson, *op. cit.*, p. 426.

pressed the dominant thought in asserting, "National freedom or sovereignty is a good in itself. It has an absolute value, for which good government by an alien people is no substitute."[26] Nkrumah of Ghana says the same: "It is only when a people are politically free that other races can give them the respect that is due them. . . . It is far better to be free to govern or misgovern yourself than to be governed by anybody else."[27]

In addition to demanding (and getting) independence, colonial peoples have sought to restore their pride in other ways. As Emerson points out, "for the restoration of their self-respect it is essential that their own cultures and histories be restored to a place of honor."

Thus Cheikh Anta Diop has written a large book whose central purpose is to establish that it is not white men to whom we owe civilization but Negroes. . . . To this version of Africa's past . . . another African writer adds further laurels in demonstrating that virtually all mankind's achievements are to be traced to Negro sources. As Georges Balandier summarizes Akwa's elaborations on the theme, Moses and Buddha become Egyptian Negroes, Christianity derives from a Sudanese people, and such European philosophers as Nietzsche, Bergson, Marx, and the existentialists reflect the philosophy of the Bantus.[28]

James S. Coleman also speaks of an effort to bring about a cultural renaissance in Africa.

It has usually been accompanied by a quest for an African history which would in general reflect glory and dignity upon the African race and in particular instill self-confidence in the Western-educated African sensitive to the prejudiced charge that he has no history or culture. In short, there has emerged a new pride in being African.[29]

More or less similar attitudes have manifested themselves outside of Africa. Nehru, for example, once spoke of the desire of middle class Indians to have "some cultural roots to cling on to, something that would give them assurance of their own worth, something that would reduce the sense of frustration and humiliation that foreign conquest and rule had produced"[30]

Two comments on the Suez crisis of 1956 further illustrate the role of pride in imperialism and anti-imperialism. Recall that after Nasser's government in Egypt nationalized the Suez Canal, Britain (together with France and Israel) launched a military attack. There followed "an undoubted profound psychological pleasure throughout England in seeing,

---

26 F. K. Khan Durrani, quoted by Emerson, *op. cit.,* pp. 346-47.

27 Quoted by Emerson, *op. cit.,* p. 185.

28 Emerson, *op. cit.,* pp. 152, 155-56.

29 James S. Coleman, "Nationalism in Tropical Africa," reprinted from *American Political Science Review* in Karl Kautsky, *Political Change in Underdeveloped Countries* (New York, Wiley, 1962), p. 174.

30 Quoted by Emerson, *op. cit.,* p. 152.

as you hear people say, 'the old lion wag its tail again.' "[31] And, on the other side, "what could never be forgiven or forgotten [by the Arabs after Suez] was the unconscious revelation by the British . . . that they regarded the whole affair, not as a quarrel between equals, but as the attempted chastisement of a black servant by his white master."[32]

## Pride Through Competitive Achievement in Space

Mention is made above of the fact that in the United States Sputnik was regarded as a blow to national prestige over the world. Even more obvious was its blow to national pride, and the determination to restore a basis for pride became one of the major motives of the space program. Secretary of State Dulles, picturing the Soviet leaders "gloating" over their success, described Sputnik as "mocking" the American people, and said that a "wave of mortification" swept the country. The first administrator of the space agency sensed that being second in space meant to many people that we were second-best, and he pointed to the "out-pouring of public opinion . . . demanding that we regain first place." On almost all sides the demand arose that the United States make itself "the leader" in space. A House committee took the view that the United States "had no alternative" to committing itself to a major space program. "There was the painful fact of hurt national pride to overcome." The London *Times* spoke of the "demon of inferiority which . . . disturbed American well-being." On becoming President, Kennedy took steps to move the country into what he called "its proper place in the space race," and he did not feel it necessary to specify what he meant by the "proper place." "No nation which expects to be the leader of other nations can expect to stay behind in this race for space." The new space administrator, appointed by Kennedy, held that "the United States could not do less than its best in space if we were to remain a first-class Nation"; and, along with virtually everyone else, he simply assumed that it was imperative to be "first-class." To accept "second-class" status was unthinkable! This kind of attitude supplemented concern for prestige in inducing Kennedy in 1961 to endorse the goal of a manned lunar landing by 1970. Beating the Russians in a spectacular space achievement was to shore up both national prestige and national pride. In 1962 came the Glenn flight—the first American manned orbital flight—releasing an orgy of expressions of pride in Congress and elsewhere. The importance attached to the achievement is indicated by the fact that Glenn was invited to speak to a joint session of Congress. "I am certainly glad to see," he said, "that pride in our country and its accomplishments is not a thing of the past." To the

---

[31] *Ibid.*, p. 384.

[32] John Marlowe, *Arab Nationalism and British Imperialism* (New York, Praeger, 1961), p. 139.

administrator of the space program, Mr. Webb, the "pre-eminence" of the United States was the goal, desired as both an independent and as a dependent interest, i.e., as good-in-itself and as good because of the contribution to the achievement of other goals, such as security. A onetime director of Manned Space Flight in NASA made statements similar to those that in earlier times went with imperialism. Response to the challenge of the unknown "has been the measure of society's vitality." The lunar project "exemplifies our urge to act, to discover, and to excel." Reaching the moon has become "a matter of America's pride."

Great nations cannot mark time. . . . The study of history discloses that the lives of nations and civilizations are filled with change. They do not stand still. They grow or they shrink. . . . If we do not make these efforts, we will not be first on the moon, we will not be first in space, and, one day soon, we will not be first on earth.

## CONCLUDING COMMENTS

That statesmen are concerned with the prestige of their states is obvious. Sometimes, as when the concern expresses itself in seemingly exaggerated emphasis on a minor question of protocol, the reaction of observers is one of amusement or scorn. At other times, as when a government chooses to regard a substantively unimportant issue as a test case and so risks war, the reaction of observers may be to denounce what appears to be foolhardiness. Mistakes are made, and such reactions may be well-founded. But the important general point is that serious consequences may well flow from the level of prestige that a state enjoys. The higher the level, the more likely it is to be able to protect and promote its rights and interests without serious challenge, and the more influence it is likely to have on the course of events. The lower the level, the more likely is it that the state will become a pawn in a political process dominated by others. All of this is commonly recognized.

It is less often said that statesmen are concerned with national pride, but it is clear that they are.[33] The desire to enhance pride has figured prominently among the motives of the great conquerors of history. It has played an important role in both imperialism and anti-imperialism. Time and again in history, ruling groups and those who identify themselves with ruling groups, have shown that they take pride in subjugating others. Plainly, the psychological satisfactions associated with superiority are often more important than any economic rewards that may be forthcom-

---

[33] For a discussion of "Pride and the Will-to-Power" see Harry R. Davis and Robert C. Good, eds., *Reinhold Niebuhr on Politics* (New York, Scribner, 1960), pp. 76-81. Also see Tamotsu Shibutani, *Society and Personality, An Interactionist Approach to Social Psychology* (Englewood Cliffs, N.J., Prentice-Hall, 1961), Chapter 13, "Self-esteem and Social Control," pp. 432-467.

ing; in material ways, those held in subjection may even be treated beneficently. And conversely, the determination to avoid or terminate humiliation is often equally powerful as a motive, sometimes superseding all others. People reduced to slavery or some other form of physical control may have no choice but to accept their lot, and may be so beaten down as to lose all pride. But sooner or later some of the humiliated find ways to assert themselves, perhaps in uprisings and war. Where prestige and pride—and humiliation—flow from victories and defeats in continued free competition, as in space, successive reversals of fortune seem less likely to have severe international consequences.

## SUGGESTED READINGS

EMERSON, Rupert, *From Empire to Nation* (Cambridge, Harvard University Press, 1960).

GILBERT, G. M., *The Psychology of Dictatorship* (New York, Ronald, 1950).

McCLELLAND, David, *The Achieving Society* (Princeton, N.J., Van Nostrand, 1961).

SCHWARTZ, Benjamin, *In Search of Wealth and Power. Yen Fu and the West* (Cambridge, The Belknap Press of the Harvard University Press, 1964).

SHIBUTANI, Tamotsu, *Society and Personality, An Interactionist Approach to Social Psychology* (Englewood Cliffs, N.J., Prentice-Hall, 1961).

STRACHEY, John, *The End of Empire* (New York, Random House, 1960).

VAN DYKE, Vernon, *Pride and Power, The Rationale of the Space Program* (Urbana, Ill., University of Illinois Press, 1964).

# COMMON OBJECTIVES
# OF STATES

In the preceding chapters we have been analyzing the dynamics of international politics; we have been trying to find out what reasons and causes lead states to behave as they do. We discussed the desire of states to preserve their security and sovereignty. We discussed nationalism and some of the ideas connected with it, such as self-determination and patriotism. We discussed the ideological conflict, in particular the influence of liberal and communist ideas on the formulation and execution of foreign policies. Then came discussions of the role of economic factors, the role of war itself and of the expectation of war, the role of psychological factors, and finally the role of the determination to enjoy prestige and pride.

Three observations should be made about this list of topics. In the first place, it is not a complete list. Who knows how many factors affect the behavior of states? Some would insist that climate is the ultimate determinant. Some would want stress placed on geography, or on the implications of scientific and technological developments. Some would say that religion and morality should be included. The list of relevant topics might conceivably include even astrology. Yet, though the topics discussed do not include all which are or might be relevant, they no doubt include the most important of them.

In the second place, there has been no effort to rank the various topics in an order that reflects their influence on the behavior of states. It would be extremely difficult to determine their order of importance in relation to the policies of only one state in one particular situation. To attempt a generalization which would be applicable to all states and all policies would be out of the question.

In the third place, there has been no effort to discriminate rigorously between influencing factors which may be fundamental and factors which may be derivative or superficial. Are ideologies fundamental, or do they simply reflect class or other interests based on economics? Is nationalism fundamental, or is it simply a reflection of economic or psychological needs? Are war and the expectation of war fundamental, or do they simply reflect the fact that the world is divided into sovereign states? There is no agreement on such questions. To specify an ultimate factor or to list a group of ultimate factors which control the behavior of states would be quite arbitrary. In any case influencing factors which originally were derivative have often achieved independence and have come to exert influence in their own right. In the present state of knowledge all that can be said with assurance is that all the elements discussed do influence the behavior of states, and collectively they appear to be the most important influencing factors.

The purpose in this chapter is to present a summary statement and discussion of the objectives that states commonly pursue. In part, this will involve a synthesis of what has been said in the preceding chapters on the dynamics of international politics. In part, pursuing different categories of thought, it will involve a somewhat different angle of approach to the general question of what makes states behave as they do.

## SECURITY AND SOVEREIGNTY

The paramount objective of every state, as a general rule, is self-preservation or survival. More broadly, the objective is security. When necessary, governments normally sacrifice every other objective, and require that citizens and subjects do likewise, to preserve the state. Peace is often sacrificed for this purpose; states wage war, if survival requires it. Efforts to enhance prosperity are also curtailed or abandoned, if survival is at stake. The greater the threat of destruction, the stronger will be the tendency to abandon political and economic principles and practices, such as free speech, free enterprise, and free elections, which seem to stand in the way of survival. Those moral and religious principles which interfere seriously with measures for self-preservation are likely to be reinterpreted. At the same time, citizens of the state who can contribute to its preservation are expected and required to do so, even though it cost them their lives.

Although these generalizations are sound, they are subject to interpretation and qualification. What are the attributes of the self that is to be preserved? Precisely what is to be rendered secure, and how much security is desired? In the eyes of individuals and governments, what desires sometimes qualify or supersede the desire for security?

We have seen that the self which is to be preserved regularly includes territory and people, though it is often difficult to say precisely what territory and people. Generally, the territorial self is defined in terms of the status quo, but it may also be defined in terms of a past situation or a future expectation. The basic proposition is that governments wish to retain what they have, or, more accurately, to avoid being compelled by other states to give up what they have. It is an involuntary loss which is to be guarded against especially.

The self also regularly includes sovereignty and equality. Sovereignty, it will be recalled, denotes the status of an entity supreme over domestic law but subject to international law. Each state wants to be able to fix and enforce law within its own domain as it pleases; it wants to retain an area of law over which it is supreme. There is therefore a strong tendency to restrict the development of international law and of international executive, legislative, and judicial agencies. Equality means that the rights of one state are entitled to as much respect as the rights of any other state; there is a determination to maintain the principle, in which even the most powerful acquiesce, that power as such gives no special rights. Title to sovereignty and equality is commonly regarded as so precious that it is to be preserved at any cost. However, just as territory is sometimes ceded voluntarily without any sense of damage to the territorial self, so are treaties sometimes voluntarily accepted which restrict the sphere of sovereignty and establish unequal rights.

The self is also usually considered as including a particular political and economic system. States want to avoid being compelled by external pressures to modify the social system under which they live. Communist states want the world to be safe for Communism, and democratic states want the world to be safe for democracy. The elites in every society (i.e., those who get the most of the best) are almost certain to think that the system under which they have secured privileges should be preserved, and others may share the belief; the social system or way of life becomes an essential part of the self whose survival is sought. Perhaps, in addition, attempts may be made to extend the social system to other states.

Security is a somewhat broader concept than self-preservation or survival. It relates not only to the ultimate desire that the state survive but also to the desire that it should live without serious external threat to values or interests which are regarded as important or vital. The concept is a vague one. The values or interests to be kept secure must be selected and defined; the nature and extent of foreign threats must be appraised; the degree of security sought must be determined; and the methods of promoting security must be selected. Each step involves judgment and choice. States may make judgments and choices which render the concept incapable of general application; a number of states, all genuinely seeking security, may do it in such a way that security for one means insecurity for another. International friction and war may develop out of incompatible conceptions of the requirements of security.

Whether all existing states should be preserved or kept secure is a question about which detached observers might well have doubts. It is difficult to believe that a rational, omniscient, and omnipotent being would divide the world precisely as it is divided; such a being would presumably amalgamate or federate many states, possibly all of them. But the situation is somewhat analogous to that faced by the director of a children's camp who, when confronted with problems of children whom he did not like, said that he always had to keep reminding himself that somebody loved every precious one of them, even though he could not see why; he could not disregard them without unpleasant consequences. Similar forces operate in relation to love for, or loyalty to, the state. It may be based on rational or irrational considerations, or both, but still it exists.

However, as we have seen in Chapter 3, there are qualifications to the proposition that governments and people attach paramount value to the preservation of the state. Sometimes there is a willingness to risk the very existence of the state in an effort to achieve other values. On rare occasions some states have voluntarily accepted annexation by, or amalgamation with, other states. Sometimes there are disaffected elements in the population (e.g., national minorities, colonial peoples, Communists in a non-Communist state, and non-Communists in a Communist state) who attach little or no value to the preservation of the state. Conscientious objectors refuse to defend the state by military means. Advocates of one or another form of international federation or world government, though presumably willing to defend the state against external threats, nevertheless want it to go out of existence as a sovereign entity on agreed conditions.

But despite qualifications and exceptions, the general rule is that states seek self-preservation and security above all.

## PEACE

Statesmen frequently say that they seek peace. Affirmations of a desire for peace have become almost a universal feature of diplomacy. In many treaties, including the Charter of the United Nations, states have pledged themselves to peace. War itself is sometimes said to be fought on behalf of peace, as when President Truman declared that "our men [in Korea] are fighting for the proposition that peace shall be the law of this earth."[1] In most countries, and particularly in democratic countries, popular sentiment virtually compels the endorsement of peace. Even Hitler, while making statements which the discerning could only interpret as endorsements of war, also felt it necessary to make rather frequent protestations of a desire for peace.

As usually defined, peace means the absence of war. Yet, when states-

[1] *State Department Bulletin,* Vol. 23 (September 11, 1950), p. 407.

men and others say that they seek peace, so defined, there is always an
explicit or implicit proviso. No statesman wants peace at any price. There
are always some things which they want more than they want peace. It
may be survival or security; it may be unification of the nation or other
aggrandizement; it may be the protection and promotion of commercial
interests or ideological principles; it may be freedom or justice. The very
fact that wars occur demonstrates that peace is not the paramount value.
This is not to say that professions of a desire for peace are necessarily
hypocritical, although sometimes they undoubtedly are. It is rather to say
that, although statesmen and others commonly want peace, they regularly
want other things more. They want peace, provided that it is compatible
with the preservation and promotion of other values which are more
precious.

This point is obvious and simple, yet it is one which is often ignored,
and the results of ignoring it are sometimes unfortunate. The objective
of peace calls for international negotiation, and successful negotiation
commonly requires compromise. The danger is that, if peace is made an
absolute value and war is ruled out as a possibility, compromise may lead
to futile concessions and appeasement. It is perhaps no accident that the
British Prime Minister who declared in 1938 that peace was the greatest
interest of the British Empire should have been the principal author of
the policy of appeasing Hitler. Moreover, it is easy, however unsound, to
jump from the premise that peace is the objective to the conclusion that
armaments and a military establishment are unnecessary. The American
peace movement between the wars, for example, was largely a movement
for disarmament. The danger in this is that the state will find itself in a
position of weakness when it realizes that it regards some values as more
precious than peace and when it feels bound to fight for them.

Peace is not always defined negatively, as the absence of war. Sometimes it is given a positive meaning; it is equated to law and order or to
order and justice. In this sense, peace presupposes law and recognized
means of changing, interpreting, and enforcing law. In other words, it
presupposes governmental or quasi-governmental organization. This in
turn may involve police action to enforce law, and the police action may
be on a scale so extensive that the acts involved become indistinguishable
from acts of war. Thus, by one interpretation peace is the antithesis of
war. By the second, it may require enforcement action, perhaps including
virtual war. It is the latter meaning of the word *peace* which President
Truman evidently had in mind when he said that American forces in
Korea were fighting for peace.

The creation of such institutions as the League of Nations, the United
Nations, and the International Court of Justice testifies to the fact that
states sometimes seek peace defined as a situation of law and order, just
as they sometimes seek it defined as the absence of war, but provisos and

qualifications arise again. States are commonly willing to insist that their own legal rights must be respected and to take action to enforce their own rights. When they are convinced that attacks on the legal rights of other states involve serious potential menace to their own rights and interests, they may join in action, including military action, against the aggressor; the defense of national interest may then parade under the cover of support for law and order or support for an international organization. When they are not convinced that attacks on other states involve menace to themselves, they may give verbal support to the principle that law and order are to be preserved, but participation in enforcement action is another matter. It will occur, if at all, only on the condition that risks and costs in terms of objectives other than peace are not too severe. This general question will be discussed more fully in a later chapter.

In this general context peace does not mean placidity or serenity or harmony. It does not have the same connotation as such phrases as "peace of mind" or "the peace of the countryside." In our terms, if placidity or serenity or harmony prevailed it would mean not simply the absence of war but the absence of politics. Struggle always occurs in politics, both within countries and among countries; when the struggle takes some forms peace is said to exist, and when it takes other forms there is war, but struggle is there in any case. "Peaceful coexistence," therefore, does not mean placid or serene or harmonious coexistence; rather, it means that the struggle is carried on with something less than the full range of possible methods.

In sum, peace is among the objectives that states pursue, but their pursuit of it is not unqualified. When peace is defined as the absence of war, states sometimes abandon it and go to war for the preservation or promotion of goals deemed more important. When it is defined as a situation of law and order, to be supported by war (police action) if necessary, states usually abandon it when the prospective short-run risks and costs in terms of other values appear to be greater than the prospective gains.

## PROSPERITY

Protection and promotion of the economic well-being of some or all of the population constitute a regular objective of states, pursued by means of both domestic and foreign policies. This proposition holds, regardless of the economic system involved.

Pursuit of prosperity through foreign policy contributes to both cooperation and conflict in international affairs. In many ways the economic interests of states are mutual. The exchange of goods and services, and the borrowing and lending of money, commonly serve the mutual advantage of individuals, whether they occur within countries or among countries. In economic relationships one man's gain is not necessarily another man's loss. All involved have a common interest in developing and maintaining conditions in which mutual advantage is served, and international cooperation in peace is normally one of those conditions.

At the same time, economic activities are competitive. Those with things to sell compete for markets. Those who want to buy scarce products compete for available supplies. Sellers and buyers compete with each other in the sense of bargaining over prices and other terms of transactions. In international affairs several types of problems are likely to accentuate the frictions that commonly accompany competition. There are the problems attendant on the fact that different currencies are involved. There are the problems created for one country when another establishes trade regulations and barriers for its own advantage. There are the problems which arise when economic relationships develop between peoples with differing power positions, differing cultures, and differing conceptions of the rules and principles by which relationships should be governed.

The very fact of competition means tension among individuals involved. Because of the pressure of special interests or because the over-all outcome of the competitive struggle is likely to affect whole populations, the tension which arises from international commercial activities spreads in some degree to foreign offices. They commonly seek a peaceful adjustment of difficulties. After all, war is rarely profitable to a country as a whole, and is unlikely to be profitable even to a ruling class as a whole. Noneconomic factors usually become involved in policies and negotiations on economic questions, perhaps reinforcing factors making for peaceful adjustment and perhaps reinforcing factors making for conflict. War sometimes ensues.

It is one thing to acknowledge that economic considerations exert a substantial influence on foreign policies and quite another to contend that economic conditions and forces control foreign policies. Marxists generally make this claim, though they differ among themselves in explaining and supporting the conclusion they reach. The extreme view that all wars under capitalism are economic in origin is not supported by historical evidence; nor, in the light of the numerous factors influencing the behavior of states, is such a claim even superficially plausible.

## THE PROTECTION AND PROMOTION
## OF IDEOLOGY

Along with sovereignty goes the right of each state to establish and maintain the social, economic, and political system of its choice, which implies adherence to the ideology of its choice. One of the regular objectives of states is to preserve this right and to preserve the favored ideology.

When states adhere to substantially the same ideology, this causes no difficulty; in fact, it constitutes a force making for cooperation. However, sharp ideological differences are a source of discord and possible war.

The reasons for this are fairly obvious. No social system and no ideology are totally good or totally bad. In varying proportions, all of them have good and bad features. Moreover, no social system operates through the years with uniform success and effectiveness; economic, political, and other difficulties periodically arise. The natural consequence of the bad features of a system and of its periodic special difficulties is that it will not evoke loyalty uniformly among different groups and classes. Varying proportions of the population of every state are always more or less disaffected. Given some knowledge of an alien ideology, some or all of the disaffected will be attracted by it. The very existence and example of an alien social system and an alien ideology are therefore to some extent subversive. The subversive influence may be so slight as to be politically insignificant (Oriental ideologies, for example, have never produced much impact in the West), or it may be so great as to produce intense demands for change. The ideology of the French Revolution proved to be quite subversive to the monarchical system in Europe, and today liberalism and Communism are subversive of each other.

The threat of an alien ideology is all the greater when its adherents are imbued with missionary fervor and, even more, when they receive support and encouragement from their government in efforts to extend the ideology abroad. Aggression by subversion is no more welcome than aggression by military means. The more threatening it becomes, the greater becomes the prospect of war.

It might be noted that domestic and international factors combine in creating a threat of war rising from subversive influences. A country with faith in its own ideology and hope for the future need have little fear of the subversive influence of an alien ideology, and international relations need not be troubled by a theoretical ideological conflict. However, a country without faith and hope, or a country with allies who are without faith and hope, has much to fear. International tensions arising out of an ideological conflict are as much a measure of domestic doubts and insecurities as of efforts from abroad to create revolution.

## JUSTICE

All states profess to seek justice for themselves and to desire it for others. To the extent that international law is deemed to incorporate justice, support for justice becomes support for law and order. Where international law is deemed to be unjust, support for justice involves demands for change, and demands for change may lead to conflict and war.

Even within countries where there is at least vague agreement on standards of justice, it is often difficult to determine precisely what would be just in concrete circumstances. There are judicial struggles over what the law is and legislative struggles over what the law should be. These are struggles to determine the official definition of justice. Where there is little or no agreement on standards of justice, the struggles are naturally all the more intense and are all the more likely to be resolved on the basis of power. The official definition of justice then becomes a reflection of the desires of the strong.

The struggle over justice among countries is similar to the struggle over justice within countries. Where international law is deemed to incorporate justice, the struggle over the application of law can be a judicial matter. Where there is general agreement on standards of justice but belief that existing law scarcely reflects those standards, there is basis for negotiation and agreement. But where conceptions of justice are markedly different, resolution of such disputes as arise will occur on the basis of a power struggle which may take the form of war.

Among some countries, particularly among those with similar ideologies, standards of justice are likely to be similar, and there is a fair prospect that the struggle for justice will be conducted by peaceful means. Among other countries, particularly among those with radically differing ideologies, standards of justice are so divergent that the settlement of disputes becomes almost automatically a question of power, whether brought to bear in conjunction with diplomatic negotiations or on the battlefield.

Dedication to justice and the fact of differing conceptions of justice are well illustrated in statements made on successive days in June, 1945, by Premier Suzuki of Japan and by General Eisenhower. The war with Germany had already ended, but the war with Japan was still in progress. Premier Suzuki's statement was as follows:

From the very beginning the Greater East Asia war has been a holy war. . . . "Our fundamental policy is based on justice and righteousness. . . ." This means that Japan is fighting a war to uphold the principle of human justice and we must fight to the last.[2]

Eisenhower spoke the next day, presumably without knowing of Suzuki's statement. "This was a holy war. More than any other war in history, this war has been an array of the forces of evil against those of righteousness."[3]

There is no reason to impugn the sincerity of either spokesman. It is probable that both conscientiously believed what they said. When conceptions of justice held in different states are so contradictory, it is understandable that the pursuit of justice leads to international difficulties.

[2] *New York Times,* June 10, 1945, p. 3, col. 2.
[3] *Ibid.,* June 11, 1945, p. 5, col. 4.

# PRESTIGE AND PRIDE

Throughout history those making decisions in the name of states have obviously been concerned with prestige, pride, greatness, glory, and honor. Prestige is sometimes sought as an instrumental value, sometimes as a goal value. Pride, greatness, glory, and honor are more commonly goal values—good in themselves. That they are desirable is simply taken for granted. Their desirability is beyond discussion. Men do not like to live, when they can help it, in degradation, humiliation, ignominy, shame, or dishonor. And many have paid with their lives in efforts to avoid this fate.

Individuals may, of course, gain the desired values on a purely personal basis, through personal achievement, and some are so apathetic politically, or so alienated, as to be indifferent to the fortunes of the nation or state. But governments and all those who are patriotic must struggle against such views. They must encourage citizens to identify themselves with the state, linking their pride with its fortunes. Pericles demonstrated the fact many centuries ago when exhorting his fellow citizens to continue their struggle against Sparta:

I am of opinion that national greatness is more for the advantage of private citizens than any individual well-being coupled with public humiliation. A man may be personally ever so well off, and yet if his country be ruined he must be ruined with it. . . . Your country has a right to your services in sustaining the glories of her position. These are a common source of pride to you all, and you cannot decline the burdens of empire and still expect to share its honours. . . . That which makes for the splendour of the present and the glory of the future remains forever unforgotten. Make your decision, therefore, for glory and honour now.[4]

Though it is perhaps conceivable that states could acquire prestige and pride by meeting standards of excellence on a noncompetitive basis, the fact is that competition occurs; and gain for one side is loss for the other. Moreover, as indicated in the chapter on Prestige and Pride, the competition has very frequently taken the form of struggle for supremacy, ending perhaps in the establishment or enlargement of empire, and implying the subjection and perhaps the enslavement of the losers. This in turn sets the stage for a resumption of the struggle when the losers seek to throw off their humiliation and restore their pride.

# AGGRANDIZEMENT

In modern times it is rare for statesmen to say that they seek territorial aggrandizement, yet it is obvious that they engage in it. A number of rea-

4 Thucydides, *The Peloponnesian War* (New York, Modern Library, Random House, 1934), Bk. II, Ch. 7, pp. 116, 118, 119.

sons have been given in the preceding chapters. Nationalism itself calls for expansion on the part of those states which do not already encompass what is deemed to be national territory. Messianic movements, whether religious or secular, likewise sometimes call for expansion. Islam was extended by military means, in part for the greater glory of Allah. Various Christian statesmen, more in earlier than in recent times, have been moved to engage in expansion ostensibly to save foreign souls. A *mission civilisatrice* or the idea of taking up the white man's burden has sometimes been cited as an excuse or reason for aggrandizement, as in King Leopold's venture into the region of the Congo and as in Mussolini's attack on Ethiopia. Economic penetration has frequently led to the establishment of political control, particularly for weak and backward countries. The habit of war and domestic economic and political conditions that help bring war on have produced wars which in turn have led to aggrandizement. Schumpeter's theory of imperialism rests on this fact.

War and the expectation of war have combined with the desire for survival or security in bringing about many acts of aggrandizement. Machiavelli long ago observed that "fear to lose stirs the same passions in men as the desire to gain, as men do not believe themselves sure of what they already possess except by acquiring more."[5] Thomas Hobbes endorsed this observation in paraphrasing it.[6] Even the most superficial survey of diplomatic history establishes its truth. It is rare for war to break out simply because a state desires control over a strategic point which may be of value in future war, but once war has broken out, for whatever reasons, belligerents commonly seek to take advantage of the opportunities which it provides for seizing strategically desirable territory from the enemy. Neutrals may enter a war partly for this reason, as Japan did in relation to World War I.

On top of all this, aggrandizement sometimes occurs because of cultural and psychological forces that drive men toward signal achievement, toward competitive success, toward status that lends prestige and bolsters pride, toward power, glory, greatness, and honor. Men so driven are no doubt disproportionately represented among the statesmen of the world, for some measure of this kind of characteristic is practically prerequisite to achieving and retaining positions of political responsibility.

The various forces making for expansion are so strong and have been so often manifested in history that some describe expansion as a virtual law of politics. Martin Wight, for example, declares:

It is the general nature of all Powers to expand. The energies of their inhabitants expand economically, culturally, and politically, and unless there is a

5 Niccolo Machiavelli, *The Prince* and *The Discourses* (New York, Modern Library, Random House, 1940), p. 124. This general thesis is developed particularly by John H. Herz, *Political Realism and Political Idealism* (Chicago, The University of Chicago Press, 1951).

6 Thomas Hobbes, *Leviathan* (Oxford, Blackwell, 1946), p. 64.

strong counter-reason, all these tendencies will be summed up in territorial expansion. . . .[7]

Wight goes on to say that "every Power tends to expand until it reaches an equilibrium that is the product of two factors: external pressure and internal organization." In other words, they continue to expand as long as internal organization and resources permit the mustering of the necessary strength, or until they are stopped by some countervailing force. The countervailing force might be a natural barrier, such as an ocean or a mountain chain, or the armed might of other states. Similar conclusions will be cited below when power as an objective of states is discussed.

It is a historic fact that some states have set out on programs of aggrandizement without evident limits. World conquest seems to have been the goal, but to transform such intermittent and scattered efforts into a law of politics is too extreme, and even to describe it as a general tendency is questionable. Probably most statesmen most of the time give no thought to the possibility of taking other people's territory. Other values and goals are often more important. Yet the desire for aggrandizement, though not universal and constant, has appeared frequently enough that it must be listed among the significant goals that states sometimes seek.

## POWER

### What Is Power?

No definition of power has gained general currency, partly because of the number of different contexts in which the word is used and partly because of the existence of intellectual problems that have not been solved.[8] It is common to think of power as a particular kind of influence, and to define influence as an ability to affect the actions, thoughts, or feelings of others. If something about A (e.g., A's presence or activity) makes a difference in the actions, thoughts, or feelings of B, A has influence over B. The influence may not be intentional, and B may or may not be aware that he is responding to it.

The more fully A's influence rests on an ability to coerce B (and here the concern is with B's actions, not with B's thoughts or feelings), the

[7] Martin Wight, *Power Politics*, "Looking Forward" Pamphlets, No. 8 (London, Royal Institute of International Affairs, 1946), pp. 39-40.

[8] See William H. Riker, "Some Ambiguities in the Notion of Power," *American Political Science Review*, Vol. 58 (June, 1964), pp. 341-349. E. V. Walter, "Power and Violence," *American Political Science Review*, Vol. 58 (June, 1964), pp. 350-352. Felix E. Oppenheim, *Dimensions of Freedom* (New York, St Martin's, 1961), esp. pp. 91-108. Robert A. Dahl, *Modern Political Analysis* (Englewood Cliffs, N.J., Prentice-Hall, 1963), pp. 40, 50-51. Edward C. Banfield, *Political Influence* (New York, Free Press, 1961), pp. 3, 348. Harold D. Lasswell and Abraham Kaplan, *Power and Society* (New Haven, Conn., Yale University Press, 1950), pp. 48, 76. Arnold Wolfers, *Discord and Collaboration* (Baltimore, Johns Hokpins, 1962), pp. 103-105.

more the relationship is one of power. In other words, it is the use or the threat (latent or active) of sanctions that distinguishes power from influence. As long as the effect of A on the actions of B depends on such things as logic, knowledge, skill in presenting a case, the promise or hint of rewards, etc., A is exercising influence. But the more the effect comes to depend on the possibility of threat or the imposition of some kind of punishment or deprivation, the more fully does influence become power. Broadly, we can speak of persuasive influence and coercive influence, and identify the latter with power.

## The Desire for Power
### as an End and as a Means

States clearly desire some power. Whatever their goals—whether security or national independence or prosperity or prestige or pride—they need to have power (power-in-being and potential power), and they may need to employ it. A state without any power lives at the mercy of its neighbors. They may, of course, permit it to survive; rivalries among the neighbors may prevent any one of them from attacking even a powerless state, or their adherence to certain principles of law or morality may operate for the benefit of the weak. However, states do not like to have to rely on such uncertain prospects if they can avoid it. They prefer to command power, and if their own power is inadequate for their purposes they are likely to seek allies. Concern for relative power position is regularly among the considerations that influence decisions on both domestic and foreign policy; especially in times of international tension, this concern may be the dominant factor in decision-making. Concern for power, in fact, is the irreducible common denominator of the foreign and domestic politics of states. Both a state seeking security and a state seeking aggrandizement must command power.

Not only is power necessary as a means for the achievement of objectives; it may well be an end in itself. It may become an end simply because it is pursued so regularly as a means and because it proves itself so regularly to be useful that it tends to take on value in itself. It may become an end, too, as a result of psychological forces at work in those who participate in the decision-making process.

The importance that states attach to power is suggested by the term *power politics*, employed especially in discussions of international relationships, usually in a pejorative sense. The term connotes a stress on coercive influence rather than on persuasive influence. To one writer it designates "the politics of force—the conduct of international relations by force or threat of force without consideration of right and justice."[9] The importance of power is suggested even more by the very fact that

[9] Wight, *op. cit.,* p. 11

states are called powers. The terms *state* and *power* are used synony-mously. We speak of world powers and great powers and small powers. "A Great [or a world] Power is a Power with general interests, and with such strength that it can attempt to advance or protect those interests in every sphere. . . . Small Powers are Powers with the means of defending only limited interests, and of most of them it is true that they possess only limited interests."[10] Great powers normally achieve (and lose) their status in war. The importance of power in politics is also attested by the uni-versal view that, whatever else international politics may be, it is also a struggle for power.

## How Much Power?

The question is, how much power? Is there a desire for irresistible power over all other actors on all possible issues, or are there limits be-yond which states do not care to go? The questions are similar to those raised above in connection with the discussion of aggrandizement as an objective.

Just as many have seen no limits to the craving for aggrandizement, so have many seen no limits to the lust for power. Whether attributing the lust for power to psychological or economic or political or other forces, some observers in all periods of history have taken the view that it is in-satiable. During the Peloponnesian Wars, according to Thucydides, an Athenian spokesman declared, "Of the gods we believe, and of men we know, that by a necessary law of their nature they rule wherever they can."[11] Thomas Hobbes described "a perpetual and restless desire for power after power, that ceaseth only in death," as "a general inclination of all mankind."[12] Bertrand Russell asserts, "Men desire to expand, and their desires in this respect are limited only by what imagination suggests as possible. Every man would like to be God. . . . Of the infinite desires of man, the chief are the desires for power and glory."[13] Bertrand de Jouvenel asks rhetorically, "Can it be doubted . . . that Power admin-isters to conquer and conquers to administer? The instinct of growth is proper to Power; it is a part of its essence."[14]

Such generalizations, however, are somewhat too glib and simple to be true. Hobbes himself spoke only of an inclination of men, and not of an absolute law of human behavior; even then he modified his statement:

Kings whose power is greatest turn their endeavours to the assuring it at home by laws, or abroad by wars; and when that is done there succeedeth a new desire;

10 *Ibid.*, pp. 18, 27.
11 Thucydides, *op. cit.*, Bk. V, Ch. 17, p. 334.
12 Hobbes, *op. cit.*, p. 64.
13 Bertrand Russell, *Power, a New Social Analysis* (New York, Norton, 1938), p. 11.
14 Bertrand de Jouvenel, *On Power* (New York, Viking, 1949), p. 137.

in some, of fame from new conquest; in others, of ease and sensual pleasure; in others, of admiration, or being flattered for excellence in some art, or other ability of the mind.

In short, as Hobbes saw it, kings pursued various objectives, including ease, sensual pleasure, admiration, and flattery; these appear to have little to do with a power quest. Bertrand Russell, too, spoke of the "infinite desires" of men, granting that there are others beside power and glory.

In fact, other desires than the desire for power do exist, and pursuit of them precludes an effort to maximize power. To revert to the formulations of Lasswell, listing various welfare and deference values, it is clear that the pursuit of some of these values is often incompatible with the pursuit of unlimited power. The study of psychology reveals that human behavior is influenced by a whole galaxy of innate and acquired drives many of which militate against the concentration of all resources on an effort to develop maximum power.

Even in societies placing great emphasis on power, such as Germany under the Nazis, various forces interfere with a really total mobilization and an all-out drive for power. Attitudes toward the role of women generally preclude full exploitation of their power-potential. Popular demand for many of the comforts and luxuries of life cannot be wholly ignored even by the most power-hungry dictator. Personal rivalries, the pursuit of private interests, and class conflict are likely to impede achievement of the theoretical maximum of power.

True, there have been in history both "mad Caesars," with psychopathic cravings for power, and "hysterical Caesars" with psychopathic fears which led to defensive imperialism. Enough rulers have sought apparently unlimited power and territorial aggrandizement to give reason to suspect that they may exist today and will appear in the future. Still, there have also been many rulers so avid for the pleasures of life, and many governments so concerned with such values as prosperity and peace, that they have neglected the power of the state. Moreover, most governments have little or no desire to exercise influence on some other governments or in relationship to certain kinds of issues.

Perhaps the best statement is that governmental attitudes range between two theoretical extremes, the one calling for an all-out struggle for maximum power and the other reflecting complete indifference to power.[15] In practice, neither extreme is ever reached. Accurate methods for measuring attitudes contributing to the power drive have not been developed, but it is a fair guess that during most of the twentieth century the attitude of at least one or another of the great powers has been closer to the first extreme than to the second. And a drive for maximum power by one major state is of tremendous importance in influencing the

[15] Wolfers, *op. cit.*, Chapter Six, "The Pole of Power and the Pole of Indifference," pp. 81-102.

policies of all states. Prudent governments do and must take care lest their relative power position becomes such as to preclude the effective defense of cherished values.

## THE CLASSIFICATION OF OBJECTIVES

This chapter and the preceding chapters have dealt with the reasons and causes leading states to behave as they do. No effort has been made to group the reasons and causes into general categories, but the possibility ought at least to be noticed. Robert E. Osgood has suggested a scheme that is relevant—a scheme that applies to the conscious reasons or motives of statesmen and thus to the goals that they pursue.[16] According to his scheme the goals of foreign policies fit roughly into two broad categories, depending on whether they reflect national self-interest or national idealism. National self-interest stems from the motive of national egoism, "marked by the disposition to concern oneself solely with the welfare of one's own nation; it is self-love transferred to the national group." In contrast, national idealism is "the disposition to concern oneself with moral values that transcend the nation's selfish interests; it springs from selflessness and love." Goals of national self-interest are security or self-preservation, the protection and advancement of whatever are thought to be "vital interests," the preservation or establishment of a position that permits an independent foreign policy ("the conduct of foreign relations without reference to other nations or to matters beyond unilateral national control"), the preservation of national prestige and national honor, and finally national aggrandizement ("the increase of national power, wealth, or prestige"). Goals of national idealism are more difficult to label. Those derived from the Christian-liberal-humanitarian tradition of Western civilization are based on the fundamental value assigned to the dignity and worth of man and on the notion of the inalienable rights of man. They emphasize the brotherhood of man, the importance of promoting human welfare, and the importance of resolving conflict through the application of reason, morality, and law. From these ideals spring various "ethical restraints upon egoism—honesty, truthfulness, fidelity to obligations, kindness, fair play, lawfulness, nonintervention in other people's affairs, and all the rest—which operate by force of conscience, custom, or law." From the ideals also spring various universal goals, such as the promotion of peace, good will, justice, freedom, and welfare. Obviously, the pursuit of a universal goal may demand some degree of altruism. Carried to the extreme, it calls for a denial of the principle that the preservation of the state is the paramount end.

Osgood disavows the thought that any state is likely to follow policies

---

[16] Robert Endicott Osgood, *Ideals and Self-Interest in America's Foreign Relations* (Chicago, The University of Chicago Press, 1953), pp. 4-7.

that are purely self-interested or purely idealistic. Actually, it is often difficult to know which kind of motive is dominant.

Useful as the above classification scheme may be, it should be noted that it does not accommodate all of the influencing factors listed in the preceding chapters. It concerns itself with ends and motives, and more particularly, with those ends and motives that are consciously pursued or entertained. It does not concern itself with causal conditions, nor does it concern itself directly with such an underlying problem as the influence of the expectation of war.

Arnold Wolfers suggests several other possible classification schemes, limiting himself, as Osgood does, to ends or motives and not attempting to encompass underlying conditions or causes. He distinguishes between "possession goals" and "milieu goals."[17] "Possession goals" relate to values that are particular to the state pursuing them—its rights, its territory, its prerogatives, its power—whereas "milieu goals" relate to the environment in which the nation operates and are not particular or exclusive, e.g., the preservation of law and order over the world or the economic development of other states. This scheme avoids a difficulty inherent in the use of such labels as realism, self-interest, and idealism, which have acquired emotional connotations that are difficult to escape, thus prejudicing inquiry, and which raise such questions as whether, after all, idealism may not serve self-interest best.

Wolfers also suggests the categories "direct national goals" and "indirect national goals." National goals are "direct" when direct benefit to the nation is sought and "indirect" when benefit to the nation is sought via benefit to individuals. Independence, for example, is a "direct" national goal and prosperity an "indirect" national goal. Obviously, questions of relative importance and priority arise with regard to such goals. In the nuclear age it is conceivable that "the indirect national goal of keeping citizens alive and their possessions intact [might win out] over the goal of national self-preservation in the traditional sense." A third pair of categories of goals suggested by Wolfers includes ideological or revolutionary goals on the one hand and traditional national goals on the other.

Finally, and more comprehensively, Wolfers suggests the possibility classifying goals into three categories, "goals of national self-extension," "goals of national self-preservation," and "goals of national self-abnegation."[18] Goals of national self-extension call for change in the status quo, however defined, and therefore require great emphasis on power. Goals of self-preservation usually call for preservation of the status quo and require varying degrees of concern for power. Goals of self-abnegation, such as the pursuit of human justice, universal well-being, or the preservation

17 Wolfers, op. cit., pp. 73-77.
18 Ibid., pp. 91-99.

of a civilization which transcends national frontiers, may or may not require concern for power. There might be sacrificial efforts which disregard considerations of power, or, for example, there might be sacrificial efforts among allies which are designed to facilitate the mobilization of maximum power against a common enemy. Goals of national self-abnegation may or may not be covers for the pursuit of goals of one of the first two types.

# THE CLASSIFICATION OF STATES BY MOTIVATION OR OBJECTIVE

The motivations and objectives of each state are bound to differ more or less from the motivations and objectives of every other state. Nevertheless, common elements do often exist that permit the classification of states into groups. In recent decades the following classification schemes have been used.

## Power States and Welfare States

Especially in the 1930's, when the Axis powers—fascist Italy, Nazi Germany, and Japan—were threatening, states were sometimes divided into those pursuing power (guns) and those pursuing welfare (butter). The terms were somewhat misleading. All states pursue power in some degree, which means that all of them give up butter to some extent for guns. Moreover, the stress on guns was to some extent a reflection of the amount of sacrifice that their possession required: the states that were rich enough to have guns and butter too did not need to talk so much about the guns. Nevertheless, given these qualifications, the labels were reasonably apt. The Axis countries in fact pursued power more avidly and aggressively than their prospective and actual victims.

## "Haves" and "Have-nots"

It was also common between the wars to classify states into the "haves" and the "have-nots"; the "haves," of course, were those states relatively rich in material resources and affording relatively high standards of living; the rest were "have-nots." The assumption was that the "haves" would as a general rule, follow pacific and defensive policies, whereas the "have-nots" would be inclined toward aggression. This basis of classification, however, has fallen into disuse, and for good reasons. Material resources and standards of living do not, in and of themselves, provide a reliable basis for classification or prediction. The poorest states have not historically been the most aggressive, nor have the richest states been the most pacific. Until very recent years, for example, China was an anvil rather than a hammer in international politics despite her poverty. Ethiopia, though poorer than Italy, was a victim of aggression and not the aggressor. Neither the Central Powers of World War I nor the Axis Powers of World War II were really "have-nots" in terms of relative standards of living. A little consideration suggests that the extremely poor scarcely can be aggressive, at least without outside help, for they do not have the wherewithal with which to fight. Moreover, there is no necessary relationship between actual standards of living and feelings of deprivation. Those who know of nothing better are likely to be apathetic in their poverty, whereas those who live fairly well may be bitterly discontented and aggressive if they think that they deserve a better lot and have hope of achieving it. It is not so much the nature of one's existence as the nature of one's aspirations which influences behavior.[19]

## Satiated and Unsatiated States

Bismarck once described Germany as a "satiated" state, the inference being that states are sometimes "unsatiated." These terms have been used ever since. The assumption is that satiated states, like the "haves," pursue defensive and pacific policies, whereas the unsatiated, like the "have-nots," are aggressively inclined. The chief difference between the two bases of classification is that the question of having or not having relates simply to the objective facts of a state's situation, whereas the question of satiation also includes the attitude of a government toward those facts. Since foreign policies derive from governmental attitudes, the classification of states as satiated or unsatiated provides a somewhat better guide to their probable behavior.

## Status Quo and Revisionist Powers

States are also sometimes classified as "status quo" or "revisionist" powers. Status quo powers follow policies designed generally to maintain an existing situation. They may or may not "have" much in this situation, and they may or may not be satiated, but they assume that any change would likely be to their disadvantage. The situation they want to maintain is usually one which has been established by treaty. Status quo powers thus are supporters of existing law, and they pursue defensive policies. Revisionist powers, on the other hand, seek change. They may already "have" a great deal but are still unsatiated. The change which they seek usually relates to a treaty. They thus seek to overthrow at least some aspects of existing law, and they are inclined toward militant and aggressive policies. The terms *status quo* and *revisionist*, it might be noted, as-

19 Eric Hoffer, *The True Believer* (New York, Harper & Row, 1951), pp. 8-9.

sume the existence of some settled or fixed situation. Following the Paris peace settlement after World War I, France could properly be called a status quo power, for she wanted to maintain the settlement. Later, Germany and Italy could properly be called revisionist powers, for they wanted to upset the settlement. Since World War II, however, so many situations remain fluid and unsettled that only confusion can result from trying to classify states according to these categories.

## Status Quo and Imperialist Powers

The term *status quo power* has a somewhat different meaning in another context. Sometimes it is used as the antonym of the term *imperialist power*. In this context, a status quo power is one which seeks to preserve or restore or moderately improve a given power relationship. The given power relationship may be the existing one or one which existed at a certain time in the recent past. States following a status quo policy are thus states which aim to keep the order of power in what is regarded as a customary pattern or to restore it to that pattern after temporary disruption. They are, in general, defensive and pacific. An imperialist power, on the contrary, is defined in this context as one which seeks to upset a given power relationship for its own advantage. It regards its given or customary power position as unsatisfactory and inferior, and it aims to move from inferiority to superiority.[20] It is likely to be militant and aggressive. According to these definitions, as to those of the preceding paragraph, France was a status quo power in the interwar period, and Germany and Italy were imperialist. For the period since World War II, the non-Communist part of the world should probably be classified as following status quo policies, whereas the Soviet Union and other Communist states should probably be described as imperialist.

These classifications for the period since World War II are stated as probable rather than certain because they reflect a judgment of Western and Soviet aims and intentions. It is assumed that the West is trying to retain or restore what it regards as a customary order of power, and that the Communist bloc is attempting to create a new order of power in which it will have a superior rather than an inferior position. This assumption might be wrong. The possibility calls attention to one of the crucial questions in conducting diplomacy: how to determine whether another state seeking change or adjustment is really imperialist and therefore potentially dangerous, or whether it can be satisfied and induced to support the status quo, defined either as a legal situation or as an order of power, once concessions have been made. This is a problem which will come up again in Part III.

[20] Cf. Hans Morgenthau, *Politics Among Nations* (New York, Knopf, 1960), pp. 39-40.

## Aligned, Neutral, Neutralized, and Neutralist States

Since World War II a classification scheme has developed relating to the East-West struggle. The states on each side are *aligned* or *committed*. Most of them are members of an alliance system, either the one led by the Soviet Union or the one led by the United States. *Neutral* has traditionally designated the wartime status of a state, not its peacetime status. When war breaks out, a state may voluntarily declare itself neutral, meaning that it intends to stay out of the war and to treat the belligerents impartially. It may abandon neutrality, if it chooses, and its neutrality is not guaranteed in any special way by other countries. Sweden aims at neutrality in this sense. A *neutralized* state enjoys its status on the basis of international agreement. Switzerland, for example, was formally neutralized after the Napoleonic wars, and in 1955 Austria became party to an international agreement binding it "to practice in perpetuity a neutrality of the type maintained by Switzerland." A neutralized state may not enter into any agreement in peacetime that may involve it in war, e.g., it may not make an alliance or permit the establishment of foreign military bases on its soil. The implication of an international agreement neutralizing a state is that others will respect its neutrality should war come, and the neutralized state is to be prepared to enforce such respect if need be. *Neutralist* and *neutralism* are newer and vaguer terms. India and many of the former colonial countries are said to be neutralist. They refuse to join in either of the major alliance systems, but this does not necessarily mean that they intend to be neutral if war should come. Their focus is on peacetime situations and policies, and they are not content to be passive onlookers, as neutrals and neutralized states tend to be. They are more activist. They deplore alliances—at least those of the United States and the Soviet Union. Whatever their attitudes about the usefulness of armed forces in relation to their own problems, they deplore tendencies in the United States and the Soviet Union to emphasize the military and to think in terms of military dangers and possible military solutions. Except where their own overriding interests are at stake, they seek to avoid any kind of action that might maintain or increase East-West tensions. They want peace among the major powers and hope that it can be maintained and made more secure through understanding and *détente*.

## SUGGESTED READINGS

CARR, E. H., *The Twenty Years' Crisis 1919-1939* (New York, Harper & Row, 1964).
DE JOUVENEL, Bertrand, *On Power* (New York, Viking, 1949).

EMENY, Brooks, *Mainsprings of World Politics,* Headline Series, No. 42 (New York, Foreign Policy Association, 1943).

GROSS, Feliks, *Foreign Policy Analysis* (New York, Philosophical Library, 1954).

MACHIAVELLI, Niccolo, *The Prince* and *The Discourses* (New York, Modern Library, Random House, 1950).

HERZ, John H., *Political Realism and Political Idealism* (Chicago, The University of Chicago Press, 1951).

OPPENHEIM, Felix E., *Dimensions of Freedom* (New York, St Martin's, 1961).

OSGOOD, Robert E., *Ideals and Self-Interest in America's Foreign Relations* (Chicago, University of Chicago Press, 1953).

RUSSELL, Bertrand, *Power, a New Social Analysis* (New York, Norton, 1938).

WOLFERS, Arnold, *Discord and Collaboration* (Baltimore, Johns Hopkins, 1962).

WOLFERS, Arnold, and MARTIN, Laurence W., *The Anglo-American Tradition in Foreign Affairs* (New Haven, Conn., Yale University Press, 1956).

# METHODS AND LIMITING CONDITIONS IN INTERNATIONAL POLITICS

*Part* **III**

## INTRODUCTORY NOTE

In Part II we described and analyzed the motivations and causal conditions that influence those who make decisions in the name of the state. We focused on the question why states behave as they do.

In Part III we shall deal with the methods by which states pursue their objectives and the limits under which they act. We shall focus on the question what states do and how they do it.

The dividing line between Part II and Part III is neither absolute nor clear-cut. Questions concerning the why, what, and how of behavior are closely interrelated. Ends and means interact on each other, and means may become ends. Nevertheless, as will be seen, there are differences in subject matter between the two parts, and even where the subject matter is similar there will be differences in focus and emphasis.

# 11

# POWER

Power, as we have already seen, plays a vitally important role in international politics. It is necessary to security, peace, justice, prestige, pride, and most of the other values that states seek to preserve and promote. It is also a limiting condition in politics, for both natural obstacles and the adverse power of other states prevent any one state from achieving omnipotence and so restrict it in what it can do.

Though we have stressed the importance of power, we have not identified its component elements. That is the purpose of this chapter. What must a state have to be strong? What are the bases or sources of power, and how can it be calculated or measured? We are interested in present power, in mobilizable power, and in long-range trends, for statesmanship must be guided not only by existing facts but also by future probabilities. The truth of this statement and the reasons for it will be made clearer later on.

We have defined power as coercive influence, distinguished from persuasive influence. At the same time, we have recognized that the distinction between the two kinds of influence is not complete and clear-cut. Persuasion plays a role in mobilizing and exercising power, and the possession of power often adds markedly to an ability to persuade. In what follows, the stress is on the sources and the measurement of coercive influence, but there is no effort to rigidly exclude the sources and measurement of the ability to persuade.

Power is a complex phenomenon. Many elements contribute to it or detract from it. We shall describe these elements under the following headings: (1) the geographic base; (2) the demographic base; (3) productive capacity: resources and plant; (4) transportation and communications;

(5) scientific and inventive potentialities; (6) governmental organization and administration; (7) the economic system; (8) strategic position; (9) ideas; (10) intelligence; (11) armed establishment; and (12) the wisdom of leadership. This classification scheme is rather arbitrary and involves some overlapping. It is also open to question because it does not call special attention to nuclear weapons and missile delivery systems, which imply a magnitude of power and a speed of attack that might render every other source of power irrelevant. But so far very few states have nuclear weapons and missile delivery systems. In any event, other classification schemes also have weaknesses, and this one is useful even if imperfect.

## THE ELEMENTS OF POWER

### The Geographic Base

Among the factors that govern the strength and weakness of states, climate, natural resources, terrain, size, and location (in relation to the oceans and other states) play important roles.[1]

*1. Climate and natural resources.* The importance of climate is rather obvious. The Antarctic and the Sahara are clearly not suitable for the development of great power. All polar, desert, and tropical regions are handicapped from a power point of view. A temperate climate is most propitious. "In general, history is made . . . between 25° and 60° north latitude."[2]

Natural resources for agricultural and industrial production are likewise of great importance. Fertile, arable soil is basic to agricultural production. Metallic ores, like iron ore, and inanimate sources of energy, like coal and oil, are essential to all kinds of productive activity. A country without a good supply of such resources within its own borders is vulnerable to outside pressures, and a country without access to them is doomed to weakness. It is almost unthinkable that great power could develop in certain regions—for example, the Middle East—in view of the fact that nature has not provided them with anything like a balanced and adequate supply of natural resources. If such countries were somehow to get possession of nuclear warheads and delivery systems, they might, of course, terrorize the world; and this kind of a development is remotely conceivable. Who knows if or when the production of such weapons may become relatively cheap and easy? But so far the technological revolutions have accentuated discrepancies in power rather than close the gaps; the

[1] See Harold and Margaret Sprout, *Foundations of International Politics* (Princeton, N.J., Van Nostrand, 1962), pp. 287-391. See also the various articles on "The Geography of Conflict" in *Journal of Conflict Resolution*, Vol. 4 (March, 1960), pp. 1-161.

[2] Nicholas J. Spykman, "Geography and Foreign Policy, I," *American Political Science Review*, Vol. 32 (February, 1938), p. 41. See also the second installment of this study in the April, 1938, issue of the same journal.

powerful have been made more powerful. The nuclear powers, and the states most likely to join them, are all rather well endowed with many kinds of resources and skills.

2. *Terrain.* The power of a state is also in part a function of terrain. More specifically, terrain may influence the size and shape of a state and its potentialities for offense and defense. Where expansion occurs, it tends to occur along the lines that nature makes easiest and to stop when serious natural obstacles (oceans, mountains) are encountered. Historically, states have sought frontiers that they regarded as strategically desirable, and their capacities for defense and offense have presumably been affected by the degree of success achieved. Similarly, terrain affects decisions concerning strategy and tactics, and thus may work to the advantage of one side more than another, as in Vietnam. Some kinds of terrain add to the power of guerrilla forces, and other kinds give the power advantage to more conventional forces, conventionally employed.

3. *Size and location.* Pure size is important to power, though nothing follows automatically from it. Great size does not necessarily assure great power, as Brazil attests, but it usually creates the possibility of great power. Great size commonly implies the presence of large expanses of arable land, a considerable variety and quantity of raw materials, and thus the capacity to sustain a large population. Liechtenstein and Luxembourg can scarcely expect ever to be great powers. In terms of the weapons and strategies of the past, great size was important because it allowed room for retreat and maneuver. Large states, when at war, could buy time with space, that is, they could retreat before the enemy, escape crushing blows, and still have space left in which to mobilize power and organize for counterattack. Both China and the Soviet Union did this in World War II; if they had not had great reaches of land at their disposal, they would surely have succumbed or would have had to establish governments-in-exile, as many smaller countries did. Hitler conquered far more Russian than Polish territory, but Russia still had space left, and Hitler's logistical problems increased with his conquests. Generally, small countries that were subjected to heavy attack in World War II were quickly overrun. Given conventional warfare, great size is likely to be advantageous in the future too, despite the leaps that have occurred in the speed of aircraft; but the advantage of size will be greatly reduced, if not eliminated, should missiles with nuclear warheads be employed.

Geographic location is potentially significant to the power of a state, but generalizations on the point are hazardous. A given location may make little difference, or may make either for strength or weakness, depending on time and circumstance. We must therefore deal with concrete examples, though few can be found that are representative of a class. Belgium and Poland have historically been in dangerous positions, being relatively small states located between powerful neighbors. Switzerland's position, though somewhat similar, has proved to be less dangerous. Britain, France, and the United States have derived advantage from their location on the Atlantic Ocean, but Cuba has scarcely derived a similar advantage. Britain is an island state, and this circumstance is combination with others has until recently made her relatively safe from invasion, but the insular character of Ceylon and the East Indies did not save them from conquest. Britain has in the past gained strength from its strategic location in relation to maritime routes and the principal ports of Europe; whether the location will be an advantage in the future, given the new weapon systems, remains to be seen. Other states have suffered more than they have gained from their strategic location. Egypt, strategically located, was for decades under varying degrees of foreign control, whereas Ethiopia remained independent in part because its territory was of such little strategic significance. Colombia lost Panama, and Panama itself was obliged to turn the Canal Zone over to the United States.

In past wars, remoteness from other centers of great power contributed defensive strength to the United States, but turned out to be a handicap when the problem was to exert American power abroad. China's location was disadvantageous during World War II, when she was remote from her friends and close to a powerful enemy; but the same location was an advantage to the Chinese Communists and their regime in Peking as long as they were on good terms with the Soviet Union. The republics of the Caribbean and of Central America are so located as to be militarily helpless in the face of American power, yet their fate has been substantially different from the fate of the countries of Eastern and Southeastern Europe, which lay helpless in the face of Soviet power at the close of World War II. Many more statements like these could be made concerning the significance of geographic location to the power of states. They substantiate the rather obvious point that location is significant to power, but they hardly lead to a single sound generalization. Further, they suggest that any generalizations encountered should be scrutinized with great skepticism.

*4. The relevance of technological conditions.* As is already clear, the importance of terrain, size, and location must be appraised in terms of other factors, especially in terms of the level of technology. With the developments of the last century in the fields of communication and transportation, rivers have almost lost significance as defensive bastions, and neither mountains nor oceans have the significance they once had. As late as World War II the United States and the interior areas of the Soviet Union were regarded as immune from attack, but now both Chicago and Tomsk might be obliterated in the first minutes of a war. Until the post World War II era, attack across the Arctic was out of the question; then in the middle 1950's there were feverish efforts to build a warning system in the Canadian Arctic in case of a Soviet aerial attack, and no sooner was the system built than it was rendered obsolete by the coming of the missile age. The prospect that the Red Army might, like the *Wehrmacht* have difficulty crossing the English Channel (to say nothing of the Atlantic Ocean) may yet be significant, but there can be no assurance on the point in view of the fact that ballistic missiles with nuclear warheads could be launched from Soviet bases and wipe out a substantial portion of the population of Britain, or of the United States, or of any other country in the world.

## The Demographic Base

*1. Power and manpower.* The problem of assessing relationships between population and power is comparable in its complexity to the problem of assessing relationships between geographic factors and power: considered alone, neither geography nor demography determines very much. In both cases, other factors are of vital significance and are so varied as to make almost all generalizations dubious. Of course, given existing scientific and technological circumstances, states with very small populations cannot be great powers, but many states with large populations are not great powers either. The amount of power possessed per ten million inhabitants varies widely when comparisons are made between, say, China, France, and the United States. Differences in age distribution, in sex distribution, and even in health do little to account for the variations. Probably the most important differences relating directly to population are connected with education, training, skills, and motivations. An illiterate population, untutored in modern agricultural methods and unable to use modern machinery or to capitalize on other fruits of modern science and technology, provides a very poor base for power. One of the major problems of the Soviet Union has been to reduce these sources of weakness, and the same problem in even more intense form confronts both China and India, to say nothing of many of the smaller countries of the world. In some degree, it confronts all countries. The complicated weapons of modern war can be neither manufactured nor maintained, nor can the armed forces be effectively organized and commanded, unless a considerable portion of the population is literate and in possession of various mechanical and other skills. Moreover, people must be highly motivated —they must care very deeply about the course of events—if a significant portion of their power potential is to be realized.

*2. Population projections.* For the purpose of projecting power calculations into the future, which all statesmen must do, population projections are useful. Such projections, based on hypothetical future birth and death rates suggested by past trends, indicate roughly the probably size and age distribution of a population for several decades hence. We have noted some of these projections briefly in Chapter 6.

*3. Governmental efforts to influence population trends.* Where death rates are high, governments have an opportunity to bring about fairly rapid population increases by adopting public health measures. Where birth rates are high, they may be able to bring about a significant reduction, as Japan has done, by permitting abortion. The effect on birth rates of legislation concerning the sale of contraceptives is less certain. Similar uncertainty has attended efforts to assess the effects of measures designed to encourage marriage and child-bearing, e.g., discriminatory tax policies, loans to newlyweds which can be paid off through child-bearing, monetary grants to parents upon the birth of a child, wage differentials based on the number of children whom the worker supports, and so on. In the 1930's this subject was generally discussed in terms of the efforts of Nazi Germany and Fascist Italy to increase their populations for purposes of power. In the 1960's, in view of the population explosion in progress over most of the world, it is discussed in terms of the possibility of curtailing growth rates in the name of promoting higher standards of living, and concomitantly, political stability.[3]

## Productive Capacity: Resources and Plant

Power requires production. A country which lacks resources and plant for the production of great quantities of goods is doomed to weakness; a country with extensive resources and a well-developed plant for utilizing them possesses a major element of power. It is likely to be all the stronger if its productive capacity is high not only in absolute but also in per capita terms. At a given time, the human and material resources of a country may or may not be employed to any considerable extent for the maintenance of military power, but the resources for this must be available if the state is to possess a commanding position on the world stage. As Sherman Kent puts it, the amount of fat, slack, and flexibility present in an economy is important to the mobilization of military power. By fat he means the possession of various kinds of resources in such abundance that a substantial proportion of them can be diverted to military purposes without intolerable sacrifice. By slack he means latent, unused productive power: "such things, as the 40-hour week, twelve to sixteen years of education for youth, small proportion of women in the labor force, unemployment of both labor and capital, only partial utilization of equipment, etc." By flexibility he means "the capacity of the economy to beat plowshares and pruning hooks into swords, and that in jig time."[4]

[3] See Sprout, *op. cit.*, pp. 392-425. American Assembly, *The Population Dilemma* (Englewood Cliffs, N.J., Prentice-Hall, 1963).
[4] Sherman Kent, *Strategic Intelligence for American World Policy* (Princeton, N.J., Princeton University Press, 1949), p. 51.

Productive capacity is important not only as it contributes to the actual or potential military power of the country possessing it; it is also important, as we shall see in Chapter 15, because it provides a basis for exerting influence on other states. Especially during and since World War II, for example, the United States has used its productive capacity as a major weapon, selling or giving goods to favored states and withholding goods from others. The discriminatory treatment of other states in economic matters has proved to be a major weapon in the power struggle.

The correlation between productive capacity and power is not necessarily direct, any more than is the correlation between population and power. To possess power states must not only produce, but they must also utilize what they produce for power purposes. During World War II both Japan and the Soviet Union developed power which, by western standards, was greatly disproportionate to their production of material things, largely because they used so great a portion of their output for military purposes. Similarly the production of goods gives a state an opportunity to manipulate international economic relationships for power purposes, but taking effective advantage of the opportunity depends on human purpose and ingenuity. Productive capacity sets limits to the level of power that can be achieved but does not govern with any precision the level that will be achieved.

## Transportation and Communications

Railway and highway networks, navigable rivers and canals, air transport, and the various kinds of electronic communication devices are all elements of a country's power. Transportation and communication facilities are essential to production, to the movement of goods and men, to the coordination of domestic activities, and to the preservation of unity. The greatest of states would become helpless almost immediately if all mechanical means of transportation and communication could somehow be suddenly destroyed. In fact, it is scarcely conceivable that large countries such as the United States and the Soviet Union could even remain united for long if the integrating forces based on transportation and communication systems should disappear. Questions of logistics (procuring needed materials, and delivering them to the points where they are needed) are among the major problems of war; their solution depends in part on the facilities that are available for transportation and communication.

## Scientific and Inventive Potentialities

Just as the present power of a state depends to quite an extent on inventions and scientific discoveries of the past, so does its power-potential depend on the inventions and scientific discoveries of the present and future. Suppose, for example, that in 1930 the states which later became allies in World War II had somehow been compelled to put a stop to all new inventions and discoveries within their borders, and Germany had continued to press scientific investigations to the limit. Presumably, the Allied powers would then have fought World War II (if they had dared to fight it at all) without radar and without many other electronic devices. The aircraft and other weapons and vehicles of 1930 would not have been substantially improved, and new ones would not have been developed. Atomic weapons would not have become available to them. Antibiotics would not have been discovered, and other developments relating to public health would not have occurred. In Germany the situation would have been different. German aircraft would have developed so as to give Hitler mastery of the skies over Europe and Britain. German weapons and vehicles would almost certainly have become superior to those at the disposal of Britain and the United States. Had the war lasted, Germany might first have developed atomic weapons. Although certainty in such matters is not possible, the odds are that Germany would have won the war, laying Britain, the Soviet Union, and the whole continent at her feet. If so, the inference is that a decade of Allied research meant the difference between victory and defeat.

Now suppose that after World War II the West had imposed a moratorium on further inventions and scientific discoveries, and the Soviet Union had taken an opposite course. What would the effect have been on power relationships today? At the least, the West would have no thermonuclear weapons, no weapons depending on fission other than the Hiroshima-type bomb, no boosters for launching nuclear warheads into long-range ballistic flight, no submarines propelled by nuclear energy and capable of firing Polaris missiles, etc. Again, it is quite conceivable— in truth very probable—that long before now the scales of military power would have been tipped decisively in favor of the Soviet Union.

The revolutionary scientific and technological developments of the future are difficult to imagine (though some are intimated by the experimental aircraft that fly many times the speed of sound and by the vehicles that achieve orbital and even escape velocities). But if recent decades are any guide, power in the future will rest on discoveries yet to be made. It is a sobering thought that Hitler would probably have won World War II and that Nazism might now be dominant over the earth had some twist of fate put nuclear weapons in his hands at Christmas time, let us say, in 1941. Such thoughts illustrate the possibility that both the distribution of power among states and the course of civilization may be drastically affected if one side or the other neglects science or manages somehow to bring off a great scientific or inventive coup.

## Governmental Organization and Administration

Effectiveness of governmental organization and administration within a state is another element of its power. How stable is the government? Does it exercise effective control over its entire territory and command the loyalty of those under its jurisdiction? To what extent, if at all, are its operations impeded by factional or party strife? To what extent is it free, in terms of the constitution and in terms of public opinion, to do those things which concern for the power position of the state may demand? Do the various agencies of government cooperate well with each other? Does the government command knowledge of the resources and capacities of the country sufficient to permit it to exploit and allocate resources wisely? Is it organized so as to be able to reach decisions with reasonable speed? Is the decision-making process one which gives reasonable assurance that decisions will be wise? Does the administrative structure facilitate efficient operations? Are the civil servants trustworthy and competent?

Questions such as these often lead to different answers in relation to different countries. Some, such as Britain, emerge from scrutiny in a favorable light, but weaknesses are revealed in many. For decades, China was weak because, among other reasons, the central government lacked effective control over major portions of the country. Until De Gaulle took control in France in 1958, political power had for several decades been divided among a number of parties. This not only led to frequent cabinet crises but rendered it difficult for the French government to pursue resolute policies on an enduring basis. It has been suggested that if anything were to disrupt the Communist Party in the Soviet Union, that country "might be changed overnight from one of the strongest to one of the weakest and most pitiable of national societies,"[5] and comparable statements might be made about Communist China and some other countries as well. Relatively new governments (and most of the governments in Africa, the Middle East, and South Asia are relatively new) are commonly handicapped by the smallness of the pool of educated persons from which leaders can be drawn and by the inexperience of those who become leaders and administrators.

Whether dictatorship or democracy is best for a country from a power point of view is a question on which opinions differ. The usual argument in favor of dictatorships is that they can act with speed and with whatever consistency or flexibility the situation seems to demand. The usual argument in favor of democracies in connection with power politics is

[5] George F. Kennan, "The Sources of Soviet Conduct," reprinted in his *American Diplomacy, 1900-1950* (Chicago, The University of Chicago Press, 1951), p. 125.

that public criticisms and widespread participation in the decision-making process make it more probable that decisions will be sound. Both arguments are questionable. Sometimes democracies act with greater speed than a dictator, and sometimes a dictator may act more wisely than a democracy. The evidence is not sufficient to permit the establishment of a general rule. In World Wars I and II the democratic regimes seem generally to have fared better than those which were autocratic or dictatorial, excepting the Soviet Union. However, prolonged war or prolonged international tension tends to undermine democracy and to accentuate movements for regimentation and dictatorial controls.[6]

## The Economic System

Effective economic organization is likewise important. To what extent do the economic system and surrounding practices stimulate and facilitate economic development? Would changed practices substantially increase production? How effective are the stimulants to inventiveness and ingenuity, and to the making of investments which involve risk? How does the per capita rate of production compare with that prevailing in similar industries in other countries? Is the economic system reasonably stable, or is it subject to debilitating crises? To what extent do relationships between various groups involved in production, for example, management and labor, involve actual and potential cooperation or strife? Is the system flexible enough to permit rapid and effective conversion to war purposes? To what extent will peacetime economic practices also serve power purposes, and to what extent must new practices be inaugurated and tested when and if the maximum mobilization of power becomes the object?

Again, questions such as these lead to different answers in relation to different countries, and thus are suggestive of actual or potential power differentials. Some countries are economically stultified, whereas others are surging forward in terms of capital investment and economic development. Production, both on an absolute and on a per capita basis, varies tremendously between countries. Some countries are plagued by industrial strife far more than others, though even where open strife does not appear there may be considerable underlying discontent, which is potentially significant to power. Most major countries have by now become experienced in some degree of economic planning, which has proved to be vital if military power is to be sharply increased, but differentials still exist in the acceptability of planning and the skill with which it is handled.

It is, of course, a major question whether socialist or relatively free

[6] Quincy Wright, *A Study of War* (Chicago, The University of Chicago Press, 1942) Vol. II, pp. 833-848.

economic systems will in the long run provide a better base for state power. Marxists contend that "capitalist" countries inevitably experience periodic depressions and that they are doomed to weakness and ultimate destruction. Exponents of free enterprise make analogous dire predictions concerning socialism. The issue may well prove to be a fateful one. Should the American economy seriously falter in the next several decades while the Soviet economy booms, or vice versa, the effect might be decisive to the outcome of the East-West struggle.

## Strategic Position

Strategic position is in part an aspect of the elements of power already discussed. We have seen that geography has definite implications for the military-strategic position of a country and that resources and supplies may govern a country's strategic position from an economic point of view; it may be able to exert influence or pressure on other states simply by regulating its international trade.

Numerous other factors also affect the strategic position of a country, whether for purposes of persuasion or coercion. The variety of counters that can be employed in international bargaining, and the variety of leverages that can be used for coercive purposes, is almost endless. Illustrations from interpersonal relations may shed light on the point. A dentist is in a good strategic position in relation to a person with a toothache. A skilled workman is in a good strategic position when two employers are in urgent need of his services. A person with a legal right to a piece of property is in a good strategic position in relation to another person who is desperately eager to obtain the property and who restricts himself to legal methods. A college student requesting tuition money from his father is in a good strategic position if the father has the money and is committed to the desirability of a college education. A blackmailer may hold a good strategic position, derived from knowledge or documents which he possesses. A kidnapper is in a good strategic position as long as the kidnapped person is at his mercy.

Similar situations occur in international politics. One state may derive strategic advantage from the commitment of another to legal or moral principles or by playing on the desires, interests, fears, or aversions of another; it may derive advantage from the rivalries of others. Iceland, though physically far weaker than the United States, can bargain effectively with the United States concerning bases on its territory because its legal position is impregnable and because the United States is committed to law observance. Western Germany, though unarmed, can negotiate effectively with the West because it possesses manpower and other bargaining counters which the West regards as valuable. After the Korean armistice, Syngman Rhee could bargain with the United States on the basis of the threat that unless he received concessions he would precipitate a renewal of the war. The Soviet Union at the time of the collapse of Germany in World War II could bargain concerning the fate of Eastern Europe and certain Far Eastern matters more effectively than otherwise because of the American desire to secure Soviet help and to reduce the loss of American lives in connection with the defeat of Japan. Communist China could intervene in the Korean War and give aid to the rebels in Vietnam because of fears in the West that drastic action against China might bring on World War III. Iran could nationalize the Anglo-Iranian Oil Co. and defy a militarily more powerful Britain both because British military intervention might have been countered by the Soviet Union and because it would have cost Britain good will in many parts of the world. Britain, in turn, could take advantage of its control of oil tankers and shipping lanes to exclude Iranian oil from the world markets and so induce Iran to come to terms. The United States, militarily preponderant in the British Isles during part of World War II, might conceivably have made Britain an American colony; the probability that few, if any, Americans thought of doing this or would have wanted to do it was an asset in Britain's strategic position.

The list of such situations could be expanded indefinitely. Often the ability of a state to exercise influence, even coercive influence, may have little to do with its command over violence. Countries that are physically small and weak sometimes occupy a strategic position of some sort which permits them virtually to dictate terms to great powers, or they can negotiate without regard to military power relationships, knowing that the character of the issue or of surrounding circumstances is such that military power will not be resorted to. Switzerland, for example, knows with practical certainty that the United States will not use military power in an effort to bring about a reduction of Swiss trade barriers. This means that great powers sometimes find themselves in situations where vast armed strength does them little good. However, governments must be cautious in relying on a strategic position which is not based on physical strength. Pushed too far, the physically strong may flout the law or moral principle, or may sacrifice some hopes and forget some fears, in order to get what they want.

## Ideas

Napoleon is said to have taken the view that the pen is mightier than the sword. Machiavelli's observation was somewhat different: that all armed prophets have conquered, and unarmed prophets have failed. Some endorse the epigram that you can't stop ideas with bullets, whereas others observe that, since ideas are commonly spread by means of bullets, they might also be stopped in the same way. Certainly the fate of Communist ideas would have been somewhat changed had Kerensky commanded enough bullets to prevent the Bolsheviks from seizing power in Russia in 1917, or had other countries intervened against the Bolsheviks in a more determined fashion in 1918-1919, or had Hitler won World War II. It was bullets which stopped the extension of Communism to South Korea after the North Korean attack in 1950.

Whether the pen is more or less mighty than the sword, it clearly has might. Ideas and ideologies are elements in the power of a state.[7] In the first place, the ideas that a government champions do a good deal to determine the extent of popular sympathy and support for it at home and abroad. In the second place, ideas influence the development and use of command over power and violence.

To be strong, a government must stand for ideas which command support at least at home, and it will be stronger if they also command support abroad. We have already noted the role of nationalism in providing unity, and therefore strength, for the nation-state. Where a nation is not yet united, the appeal to nationalism may strengthen it in a struggle to redeem an Irredenta, and by the same token the appeal is likely to weaken the state which includes the Irredenta. Colonial peoples derive strength from the appeal of nationalism, and by the same token imperial countries are weakened. We have noted that the ideologies of liberalism, fascism, and communism have international appeal. Hitler took advantage of this fact by organizing fifth columns abroad, seeking to use them as adjuncts of German power. Soviet and Chinese Communist leaders champion ideas in the struggle for the loyalty and support of Communists of other countries, no doubt believing that the outcome will affect their personal power at home and the power of their countries throughout the world. Liberal governments have not generally sought to organize adherents abroad in a formal fashion, but they engage in propaganda designed to win them foreign sympathy and support.

Ideas may also weaken a state. Nazism certainly aroused more antagonism and hostility abroad than sympathy and support. It is perhaps too early to say what the result will be for Soviet Communism in the long run, but certainly the advantage from a power point of view is not all on the side of Moscow and Peking. Neither does liberalism always evoke a positive response.

The means which a state has at its disposal for advertising and propagating its ideology should be counted, as well as the ideology itself, among the elements in its power position. Thus the facilities employed in Voice of America broadcasts are elements of American power; similar facilities, as well as foreign Communist parties, are elements of Soviet power.

[7] Bertrand Russell, *Power, a New Social Analysis* (New York, Norton, 1938), pp. 145-156.

## Intelligence

We are not using the word *intelligence* here to refer to the mental ability of political leaders, though this clearly would have something to do with the power position of the state. Rather, in this connection the word *intelligence* refers to knowledge and to the activities designed to produce knowledge. The knowledge referred to is not all knowledge, of coures, but rather whatever knowledge will contribute to the wisdom of governmental decisions concerning foreign affairs. As Sherman Kent puts it in relation to American intelligence operations, the aim is to produce "the kind of knowledge our state must possess regarding other states in order to assure itself that its cause will not suffer nor its undertakings fail because its statesmen and soldiers plan and act in ignorance."[8]

Such knowledge is power. At least, this is the common statement. According to the definitions advanced in Chapter 10, we should make the more pedantic statement that such knowledge is a basis for either persuasive or coercive influence. This is most obvious in time of war, when advance knowledge of the time, place, and strength of an enemy attack may contribute more to victory in the battle than will an armored division. Similarly, knowledge of specific weaknesses of the enemy may contribute more to defeating him than will many bomber wings. It is not so obvious, but it is nevertheless true, that knowledge may also be power in times of peace. Suppose that the object is to strengthen or weaken a country economically or militarily. The activities which ensue must not be aimless. Intelligence must provide knowledge of the particular things which it is feasible to do and which will most effectively promote the objective; in the absence of such knowledge, the objective is not likely to be achieved. Suppose that the object is to induce another state to accept a treaty of alliance. Again knowledge may be power. In fact, the very decision to seek the alliance is presumably based on intelligence reports to the effect (a) that the power position of the state is weaker than it should be in view of the intentions and capabilities of a potential enemy, and (b) that the particular alliance sought would significantly improve the situation. Once negotiations get under way, the negotiator who knows nothing of the fears and hopes and capabilities of the country with which he is dealing is in a difficult position indeed. He cannot tell what he can reasonably demand and what he may be obliged to concede. He cannot tell what timing to employ, what bargaining counters are available and useful, what promises or threats may be effective. Failure in such a situation is to be expected. Conversely, a negotiator who is fully cognizant of all relevant data is much more likely to succeed.

Put more broadly, a government without an effective and reliable in-

8 Kent, *op. cit.*, p. 3.

telligence service may go without warning of potential dangers, and thus may fail either to forestall them or to prepare itself against them, or it may become the victim of false fears, and might even plunge itself and others into unnecessary war. Governments which are blind and deaf, which fail to see and hear, live dangerously, if they survive at all. Knowledge may not provide omnipotence, but it enhances the prospect that objectives will be wisely selected and effectively promoted.

## Armed Establishments and Military Leadership

One of the more obvious facts about power is that it is expressed, among other ways, in armed establishments and given its ultimate test in war. States commonly maintained armed establishments even in time of peace, and expand them substantially in time of war.

The problem of calculating the actual and potential power of an armed establishment without actually testing it in war is a complex one, for so many elements are involved—including almost all those which we are discussing under other headings. However, certain aspects of the problem might be noted. The supremely important questions concern nuclear weapons. Does the state have them? In what quantity and variety? Does it have boosters capable of launching ballistic missiles with nuclear warheads for various distances, including intercontinental distances? How accurate are the guidance systems for such missiles? How vulnerable are the launching sites?

As of 1965, only the Soviet Union and the United States have both nuclear weapons and missile delivery systems. Either might inflict vast damage on the other, killing tens of millions of people and destroying cities by the dozen. In a war fought in this way, all other sources of power and all other means of struggle would surely be superfluous and irrelevant to the outcome. Moreover, if either state should somehow gain a decisive advantage over the other in terms of these weapons—or in terms of other revolutionary weapons, such as bacteriological or chemical weapons—it would have the world at its mercy; it might in fact be merciful, but this does not gainsay the portentous significance of the development.

In the near or more distant future, additional states will undoubtedly add nuclear missiles to their arsenals, making the situation more complex and probably more dangerous.

Both the Soviet Union and the United States could place thermonuclear weapons in a parking orbit ready for detonation at any time and capable of destroying all life in line-of-sight from the point of detonation. But on each side the decision so far is that the prospective advantages of such an action, if any, are not sufficient to justify it. In fact, the advantage seems to be on the side of keeping the thermonuclear weapon on the ground, where it is under control and easily accessible for checking and repair; it could be especially launched at the time its use is decided upon and could be exploded over the target area without ever going into orbit. The most likely military uses of orbiting vehicles have to do with observation, communication, meteorology, navigation, and geodetics.

The United States claims that even if the Soviet Union were to launch a surprise attack with missiles carrying thermonuclear warheads it could survive the blow with enough second-strike capacity left to be able to destroy Soviet society in retaliation. The Soviet Union may either have or develop a smiliar capability. In any event, the capacity of each side to inflict major nuclear damage on the other, whether in a first strike or in a retaliatory blow, has led to a nuclear impasse: each side suffers a kind of partial paralysis, fearing to take steps leading in the direction of an exchange of nuclear blows. At the same time, the partial paralysis of the nuclear powers seems to embolden some of the other states, both politically and militarily.

Despite the awesome destructive power of nuclear weapons, conventional weapons obviously remain significant. For most states, they are the only weapons available. Moreover, they may turn out to be the only weapons that even the nuclear powers dare to use. This being so, armed establishments equipped and employed in traditional ways retain their significance, and questions can appropriately be asked about them in connection with assessments of power. The number of men under arms, the availability of trained and untrained reserves, the quality and quantity of weapons and other equipment on hand and potentially available, the training and morale of personnel, the teamwork of the various branches of the armed forces, the provisions for mobility, and the quality of military leadership are all of potentially vital importance. So is the vulnerability of the state to specific forms of military action, such as an aerial bombardment that might destroy some specific crucial industry, or a blockade. Many other questions must still be answered if conventional military power is to be appraised. Not the least of them relate to conceptions of strategy and tactics. Those who plan for the last war usually suffer, and those who are imaginative enough to develop new weapons and new ways of using weapons usually reap significant rewards.

Lest the task of appraising armed establishments be made to appear even more complex and difficult than it is, note might be made of the fact that certain kinds of significant knowledge are ordinarily obtainable. For example, each country knows with some degree of accuracy how many divisions others have under arms and what the fire power of a division is; each one knows, at least roughly, what the size and composition of the air and naval forces of the others are. Each knows within limits what weapons the others have available or in prospect, and what military strategies and tactics appear to find favor. The knowledge shared by both the United States and the Soviet Union that each possesses both thermonuclear weapons and the means of delivering them to all the major civilian and military centers of the other constitutes considerable knowledge of reciprocal military capabilities.

## The Wisdom of Leadership

We have mentioned leadership as an element of power in connection with the military establishment. It is even more important in the political sphere, for it is in this sphere that the most fateful policy decisions are made, including decisions on high military strategy. Political leaders determine in what proportions to allocate resources between military and civilian programs, that is, how great the military-power-in-being should be. They allocate appropriations among the branches of the armed services. They determine when to seek alliances, with which states to seek them, and on what terms. They decide when and what to concede in relations with other states, and whether and when to stand firm. They declare war and make peace. What they do or fail to do may have a fundamental and lasting impact on the power of the state and, for that matter, on the whole course of history.

Illustrations of the point abound. Of course, many changes in the power positions of states have resulted from forces of history completely beyond the control of the political leaders of any one country or time, but usually there are alternatives to the decisions which statesmen make. Suppose, for example, that the United States had joined the League of Nations and participated actively in efforts to promote security and peace in Europe and the world thereafter. Suppose that Britain's leaders had supported Poincaré of France in a vigorous enforcement of the Treaty of Versailles. Suppose that neighboring countries had taken military action against Hitler's Germany at the time Hitler announced German rearmament or at the time of the remilitarization of the Rhineland. Suppose that toward the close of World War II American intelligence estimates concerning the need for Soviet support against Japan had been more accurate, and that American leaders had then taken a firmer stand against Soviet policies in Eastern and Southeastern Europe. Suppose that President Truman had not ordered American intervention in the Korean War or had sided with those who opposed the development of thermonuclear weapons. Suppose that the United States had stayed out of South Vietnam, had sought to prevent the construction of the Berlin wall, and had permitted the emplacement of Soviet missile launching sites in Cuba. All of these alternatives to choices actually made were within the realm of the possible and would surely have led to very different circumstances and to a very different distribution of power from what actually prevails. Hitler's decisions led to a series of events after 1933, which first transformed Germany from a weak into a very powerful state and then transformed her once more from a dominant European power to a defeated, divided, and virtually helpless power. Certain kinds of decisions by leaders in Peking and Moscow might bring on war and so transform the pattern of world power.

Thus calculations of power must include evaluations of the actual and potential quality of a country's leadership. A country is bound to be stronger and to have a greater power potential if it is led by men of strength and wisdom who are united in service to what is regarded as the national cause than if it is led by those who are weak or rash or stupid or divided against themselves in pursuit of personal or partisan advantage. The capacity of a political system to bring able leaders to the top and then actually permit them to lead is one of the tests of its effectiveness from a power point of view.

## SHORT CUTS IN THE CALCULATION OF POWER

The above analysis of the elements of power is stated in very broad terms; a thorough effort to estimate the power of a given state would require the categories listed to be broken down in considerable detail. The task would be huge, so huge that there is a temptation to avoid it in favor of short cuts. In truth, there are so many uncertainties even in thorough calculations that some short cuts may produce results that have an equal degree of reliability. Perhaps the best short cut is to consider the record of a state in wars which have actually been fought. Recent war is especially useful in this connection; barring special circumstances, the odds are that the factors which made for great strength or great weakness in a recent war will persist and will thus make for similar strength or weakness again. That this short cut is not always reliable, however, has been proved again and again; an example is the changed fortunes of France and Russia in the two world wars.

Steel production and productive capacity are also often considered as yardsticks of power, or at least as yardsticks of power-potential. The device has some merit, too. Steel is a vital sinew of strength. Quantitatively, it is probably the most important element in the weapons and equipment with which armies are provided. Moreover, the amount produced, measured in both absolute and per capita terms, is likely to reflect a great many of the attributes of the state: its resources of many kinds, its technological level and the skills of its population, its manufacturing capacity. Again, however, this index of power is not always reliable, for the proportion of steel that is or can be devoted to power purposes may vary considerably from country to country.

The Department of Economic and Social Affairs in the United Nations Secretariat publishes statistics on the production and consumption of energy throughout the world.[9] The results are even more indicative of the various qualities of a state than are statistics on steel production. The fuels counted (coal, coke, petroleum and its products, natural and manufactured gas, and electricity) are transformed for statistical purposes into metric tons of coal equivalent. Absolute and per capita figures are given on the production and consumption of the separate kinds of fuel and of all combined. Such statistics tell a great deal about the level of economic development and social organization within a country and about the amount of power that it can muster. In 1962 the United States consumed approximately 34% of the energy consumed on earth; the Soviet Union, 15%; mainland China, North Korea, North Vietnam, and Mongolia, 9%; the United Kingdom, 6%; the German Federal Republic, 5%; France and Japan each 3%; Canada and India each 2%. Together, the countries named consumed 79% of the total. On a per capita basis, kilograms of coal equivalent were consumed in 1962 as follows: the United States, 8263; Canada, 6015; United Kingdom, 4948; German Federal Republic, 3884; U.S.S.R., 3046; France, 2591; Japan, 1388; mainland China, North Korea, North Vietnam, and Mongolia, 561; Brazil, 367; India, 161; Indonesia, 117; Ethiopia, 10. Each American thus had about 820 times as much energy working for him as each Ethiopian.

These figures are suggestive of power relationships, but need to be considered with some caution. Countries that consume vast quantities of energy may use a large part of it to provide for the comforts and luxuries of life, whereas countries that consume relatively less may devote it largely to military purposes. Thus actual power relationships might depart considerably from the relationships that the statistics suggest.

## THE RELATIVITY OF POWER

Whether short cuts are resorted to or not, the calculation of power is even more complex than has so far been suggested. The reason for this is that the amount of a state's power in an absolute sense is not the significant thing. A person able to run 100 yards in 10 seconds may or may not win the race, depending on the conditions under which the race is held and the speed of the competing runners. Similarly a state possessing $x$ units of power may or may not have enough.

For power calculations to be significant they must be relative. It is not so much the absolute power of a state as its power position in relation to other states that counts. Thus power calculations must encompass all those states whose power may or will be brought to bear when a test of power comes.

[9] United Nations, Department of Economic and Social Affairs, *World Energy Supplies 1959-1962*, Statistical Papers, Series J, No. 7 (New York, 1964).

Further, to be really significant, the calculation must be made in terms of a specific form of power and a specific situation. It is one thing to give more or less surreptitious aid to refugee fighters at the Bay of Pigs, another to apply economic sanctions to make Castro's position impossible, yet another to intervene in Cuba with American armed forces, and still another to direct thermonuclear missiles at Cuban targets. Moreover, it is one thing to confront Cuba when it is isolated, another to confront it when the Soviet Union has a free hand to give Cuba whatever assistance it pleases, and still another to confront it when the Soviet Union is more or less restricted in what it can do by its dispute with Communist China. Again, it is one thing to prevent the Soviet Union from developing missile bases in Cuba, and another to induce Vietnamese peasants to refuse to give aid to guerrilla fighters of the Vietcong. The power that the United States can bring to bear in case the test occurs in New Jersey is considerably different from the power (at least the nonnuclear power) that it can bring to bear in Poland, Iran, or Laos. In sum, uncertainties in the calculation of power are very numerous.

## SUGGESTED READINGS

HILSMAN, Roger, *Strategic Intelligence and National Decisions* (New York, Free Press, 1956).

KISH, George, and SINGER, J. David (issue editors), "The Geography of Conflict," *Journal of Conflict Resolution*, Vol. 4 (March, 1960), pp. 1-161.

KNORR, Klaus, *The War Potential of Nations* (Princeton, N.J., Princeton University Press, 1956).

SPROUT, Harold and Margaret, *Foundations of International Politics* (Princeton, N.J., Van Nostrand, 1962).

# THE DISTRIBUTION
# AND BALANCING OF POWER

We have said that politics is a struggle for power, but rarely an all-out struggle for maximum power. In international politics governments seek power (coercive influence), but it is far from being their sole concern. For the pursuit of some of their desires, they rely on persuasive influence. Moreover, domestic concerns limit the pursuit of influence abroad, whether coercive or persuasive: people pursue values having to do with the good life and (in greater or less degree) object to politics that call for undue sacrifice. Only part of the resources at the disposal of governments are marshaled for the development and preservation of power; the remaining resources are devoted to other purposes. What should the allocation of resources be? How much power is enough? What kind of a relative power position do statesmen regard as satisfactory? And how do they go about securing or preserving a satisfactory relative power position? What standards of judgment do they employ, and how sound are the standards? These are the questions to which this chapter is addressed.

The *balance of power* will be our focal concept, vague and elusive as its meaning is. It provides a good approach to the questions raised. Moreover, both statesmen and scholars use the concept frequently, making its focal nature as much a matter of fact as a matter of choice.

## THE MEANINGS OF BALANCE OF POWER

The *balance of power* is variously used to designate a situation, a policy, or a system.[1]

---

[1] Inis L. Claude, Jr., *Power and International Relations* (New York, Random House, 1962), pp. 11-25.

In every day usage the term *balance* has two meanings relating to a situation. Sometimes it denotes an equilibrium, as when a scale is brought into balance by adjusting the weights, or when a mobile or chandelier is balanced through the interrelationships of a number of parts. Sometimes, *balance* denotes a remainder—an amount left over when one sum is deducted from another, as when one speaks of his bank balance; this means that *balance* may be a situation of disequilibrium rather than equilibrium, and that the balance may be more favorable to one party than to another. The upshot, found in actual usage, is that *balance of power* may designate simply the distribution of power, whatever the distribution may be.

Whether balance exists as equilibrium depends in part on the kind of struggle that is in view. If unrestricted war is assumed, it is probably reasonable to say that balance (equilibrium) exists between any two states when either of them can inflict unacceptable damage on the other. Once that point has been reached, additions to the power of either side—whether in the form of nuclear or nonnuclear weapons—have little significance, perhaps none at all. If some kind of restricted or limited war is assumed, then balance must be calculated in terms of the assumed restrictions. (We will discuss the idea of limited war in a later chapter; for the time being, we can think of it as a war between countries that possess nuclear weapons but that refrain from using them.) If guerrilla warfare is assumed, still different elements enter into the balance.

Considered as a policy, *balance of power* has corresponding variations in its meaning. The object of the policy is to create a desired power relationship, whether it falls short of equilibrium or goes beyond it to a "favorable balance." Or, the statement that a balance of power policy is pursued may simply mean that power relationships are among the important considerations when a decision is made—that there is a persisting, conscious concern for power.

Those who speak of *balance of power* as a system rarely stop to say explicitly what they mean (and not surprisingly, for the meaning of *system* is about as vague and elusive as the meaning of *balance of power* itself). Inis Claude's analysis suggests that the concept *balance-of-power system* designates a collection of states some of which guide themselves by "a general principle of action: when my state or bloc becomes, or threatens to become, inordinately powerful, other states should recognize this as a threat to their security and respond by taking equivalent measures, individually or jointly, to enhance their power."[2] Though Claude prefers to treat *balance of power* as a system rather than as a situation or a policy, he grants that it is "a most unsystematic system"—"a system only by courtesy."[3] "The balance of power system," he says, "is a system only in

[2] *Ibid.*, p. 43.
[3] *Ibid.*, p. 147.

the loosest sense. . . . It is more a framework for arrangements . . . than a setting for the systematic ordering of relationships among states."[4]

In sum, those who use or encounter the term *balance of power* or *balance-of-power* system had better be on guard. The words obviously connote a concern for power relationships, but beyond that statements about their meaning are apt to be slippery and treacherous.

## THE PURPOSES OF BALANCING POWER

Security and peace are the main purposes of balancing power.

Though peace is often stated as the purpose, security is usually the more fundamental concern. The fundamental concern is ordinarily the protection of vital rights and interests—those for which the state is willing to wage war if need be. In these terms, the desire for a balance of power situation becomes a desire for a distribution of power that will deter attack or that will permit a state to avoid defeat, if not win victory, in war.

Stated in more general terms, the prime object of the balancing of power is to establish or maintain such a distribution of power among states as will prevent any one of them from imposing its will upon another by the threat or use of violence.

The idea is an old one.[5] When Carthage was at war with Rome, Syracuse sent aid to Carthage "lest by its fall the remaining [Roman] power should be able, without let or hindrance, to execute every purpose and undertaking." The principle was that no state which might ultimately attack Syracuse should be allowed to amass sufficient power to do so with assurance of success. Fenelon stated a similar principle, writing in the seventeenth century to instruct a grandson of Louis XIV. His assumption was that in international politics the strongest state will in the long run tend to prevail over the others and overthrow them unless they unite to establish a balance. And he declared that "to hinder one's neighbor from becoming too strong is not to do harm; it is to guarantee one's self and one's neighbors from subjection. . . . The excessive aggrandizement of any one [nation] may mean the ruin and subjection of all the [others]." Vattel, an early writer on international law, defined the balance of power as "an arrangement of affairs so that no state shall be in a position to have absolute mastery and dominate over the others." In a famous memorandum written for the British Foreign Office in 1907, Sir Eyre Crowe explained the idea of the balance of power as follows:

History shows that the danger threatening the independence of this or that nation has generally arisen, at least in part, out of the momentary predominance

4 *Ibid.*, p. 274.
5 See Sidney B. Fay, "Balance of Power," *Encyclopedia of the Social Sciences*, Vol. II, pp. 395-399.

of a neighbouring state. . . . The only check on the abuse of political predominance . . . has always consisted in the opposition of an equally formidable rival, or of a combination of several countries forming leagues of defense. The equilibrium established by such a grouping of forces is technically known as the balance of power, and it has become almost a historical truism to identify England's secular policy with the maintenance of this balance by throwing her weight now in this scale and now in that, but ever on the side opposed to the political dictatorship of the strongest single state or group at a given time.[6]

Ordinarily, peace is also a purpose of the balancing of power. To deter attack by maintaining balance is to preserve peace. Similarly, to deter attack through the operation of a collective security system (to be discussed in Chapter 20) is to preserve peace. And it is reasonable to say that one of the criteria for judging a balance of power system or a collective security system is its effectiveness as a deterrent. Nevertheless, peace is not normally the paramount goal. The very idea of balancing power suggests that something is more important than peace; the term *collective security* has a similar implication. Whichever system is in question, concern for security is normally paramount. This is suggested by the fact that states sometimes deliberately resort to war for the purpose of establishing or preserving what they call balance, just as they sometimes resort to war in the name of collective security.

## ASSUMPTIONS UNDERLYING THE BALANCE OF POWER SYSTEM

Five major assumptions underlie the balance of power system.[7] Some of them are obviously valid, and others are questionable.

The first is that states are determined to protect their vital rights and interests by the means at their disposal, including war. It is up to each state to decide for itself which of its rights and interests are vital. They commonly include such values as independence, territorial integrity, security, preservation of the domestic political and economic system or the domestic way of life, and the protection of certain legal rights, like the right to the freedom of the seas. If states were not determined to protect some such rights and interests, they would logically have to be indifferent to power relationships and willing to accede to whatever demands were made upon them by other states. Complete self-abnegation is extremely rare, if it ever occurs at all. The nearest approach to it comes when one state voluntarily accepts absorption by another, as with the

---

[6] Great Britain, Foreign Office, *British Documents on the Origins of the War, 1898-1914* (London, H. M. Stationery Office, 1926-1938), Vol. III, p. 403.

[7] Cf. Quincy Wright, *A Study of War* (Chicago, The University of Chicago Press, 1942), Vol. II, pp. 743-759; Ernest B. Haas, "The Balance of Power as a Guide to Policy Making," *Journal of Politics*, Vol. 15 (August, 1953), pp. 370-398.

Republic of Texas. In general, the first of the assumptions must be regarded as sound.

The second underlying assumption of the balance-of-power system is that vital interests of the state are or may be threatened. Otherwise, there would be no need for a state which wants to preserve the status quo to concern itself with power relationships. The validity of the assumption is obvious. All history shows that threats to the vital interests of states sometimes arise. They may be ever present.

The third underlying assumption is that relative power positions can be measured with a significant degree of accuracy, and that these power calculations can be projected into the future. If such measurement and projection could not be made, a conscious effort to balance power would be out of the question.

The analysis of the elements of power contained in the preceding chapter has already demonstrated that the calculation of power is a complex problem. Some of the elements are quite intangible and therefore difficult to assess. How does one measure the power a government derives at home and abroad from the ideas that it champions? How does one measure the effect on power of the quality of military and political leadership, and how can this factor be projected into the future? How can one know whether treaties of alliance will be honored, or new ones made? Questions like these indicate that estimates of power can be no more than approximations. The probable margin of error is rather wide.

The availability of nuclear weapons affects calculations in contradictory ways. On the one hand, if it is clear that such weapons will be used in an unrestricted way, calculations are greatly simplified; if the nuclear weapons are plentiful and the delivery systems reliable, fewer calculations are necessary. On the other hand, if it is uncertain whether such weapons will be used, or which ones will be used, or on the basis of what strategy they will be used, calculations are made much more complex and the possibility of serious error is considerably increased.

Nevertheless, if governments are determined to preserve their vital interests and if these interests are in any danger of attack, power calculations must perforce be made. There is no real choice. Without a calculation or a guess, governments would have no basis for deciding what proportion of their resources to allocate to an armed establishment and military preparations. They therefore, in fact, engage in calculations and in guessing, even though they know that the results are not entirely accurate. The more thorough the calculations are, the narrower becomes the area in which pure guesswork prevails.

This third assumption, though questionable, is thus probably sound. The relative power position of a state is of such vital importance that any calculations that reduce the area of guesswork are significant.

The fourth underlying assumption is that a situation of "balance" (whether a not-too-unfavorable disequilibrium, an equilibrium, or a favorable balance) will either deter the threatening state from launching an attack or permit the victim to avoid defeat if an attack should occur. In other words, it is assumed that states are not likely to attack unless they command enough of a preponderance to make victory reasonably sure; or, if they attack without a preponderance, it is assumed that they cannot win. The latter part of the proposition—that preponderance is necessary to victory—is obvious. The first part—that the existence of "balance" will deter attack is no doubt true most of the time, but still questionable. The implication is that acts of state are rationally controlled, which is not always true. Another implication is the one discussed briefly above: that the existence of a balance or the possession of a preponderance is something that can be determined with some assurance in advance of war. But, given the pitfalls in the calculating process, an aggressive state may think it possesses a preponderance only to be proved wrong; or an aggressive state, facing uncertain power relationships, may simply take a gamble on war, hoping that the distribution of power will turn out to be in its favor.

The fifth underlying assumption of the idea of balancing power is that statesmen can and will make foreign policy decisions intelligently on the basis of power considerations. If this were not possible, the deliberate balancing of power could not occur.

## AN EXAMINATION OF THE FIFTH ASSUMPTION

### The Problem of Identifying Vital Interests

A number of factors militate against the deliberate and intelligent balancing of power. In the first place, if the vital interests of the state are to be protected through the balancing of power, those vital interests must be known and clearly defined; there must be some measure of agreement on the part of decision-makers in identifying them. Such agreement always exists to some extent, but it is rarely complete. All American decision-makers agree, for example, that the preservation of the independence and territorial integrity of the United States is a vital interest. Is it also a vital interest, that is, one for which the United States should fight, if necessary, that all countries should treat American citizens within their borders according to the requirements of an international standard of justice? Is it a vital interest that American traders should have access to certain foreign markets? Is it a vital interest that democracy should be preserved, as a good in itself, in Italy? Is it a vital interest that protection should somehow be extended to Jewish or other minority groups whom a foreign dictator is exterminating? Is it a vital interest that Communists should not be permitted to take over Berlin or Laos or South Vietnam or Indonesia or Quemoy and Matsu? Such questions are not unanswerable, but the answers are not always obvious. Different groups within the United States, and different persons and groups among the decision-makers in Washington, are likely to come up with different answers. A government which defines the concept of vital interests one way this year may conclude next year that the definition was wrong. During the early part of World War I, for example, the United States regarded the preservation of certain neutrality rights as a vital matter, only to abandon those rights voluntarily just before World War II. Given such problems in identifying the interests to be protected, it is difficult to make intelligent decisions on the amount of power that may be needed.

## The Problem of Identifying and Assessing Threats

In the second place, a government pursuing a balance-of-power policy must not only know what its vital interests are but must also be able to determine whether and when a threat to them exists or is likely to develop. In other words, it must be able to determine what the capabilities and intentions of other states are and are likely to be. Are other states able to attack or encroach upon interests regarded as vital? What is the prospect that they actually will do so unless somehow prevented?

We have already noted that it is difficult to assess the power of states with accuracy, and this in itself militates against the intelligent application of balance-of-power principles. It is often even more difficult to assess their intentions. Further, the two problems become vastly more difficult when anticipation of the future is required, as it often is in balance-of-power operations.

For example, in the chapter "War and the Expectation of War," we saw that before World War I Russia and France agreed that the acquisition of territory by Austria-Hungary might affect the balance of power in Europe, so that when Austria-Hungary later attacked Serbia, Russia mobilized, partly on the assumption that the conquest of Serbia would strengthen Austria-Hungary and make it more threatening to Russia. This kind of assumption is commonly made. Britain has repeatedly acted on the assumption that conquest of the Low Countries by a major European power would threaten her. She entered World War II on the assumption that Hitler's Germany would become an intolerable threat if Poland were conquered. In the United States, Secretary of State Robert Lansing desired American participation in World War I on the ground that a victorious Germany would be a threat to vital American interests, and before Pearl Harbor President Franklin D. Roosevelt assumed that an Axis victory would endanger this country. American policy since World War II has been based on the assumption that any extension of Communism would be a threat to the United States, because it would enhance Soviet and Communist power.

Such assumptions and anticipations may or may not be correct. Had Austria-Hungary been permitted to conquer Serbia in 1914, would she in fact have been strengthened? Might she not have had so much trouble governing unruly Serbs that the conquest would have weakened her? Might she not have become less rather than more dangerous to Russia? Suppose that the United States had not entered World War I. Would the outcome have been such as to endanger the United States? To the extent that America's entry was based on balance-of-power considerations, were these considerations sound? Suppose that we had not entered World War II. How likely is it that, in this event, the Soviet Union and Germany might have exhausted and destroyed each other, leaving the United States in a better power position than she obtained by fighting? Suppose that since World War II the United States had done nothing to halt the spread of Communism. How much would it have spread? How much would this have endangered the United States? Do not the divisions that have already appeared in the Communist movement show that extensions are more likely to weaken than to strengthen it? What would be the effect on American security if the venture in South Vietnam were to fail, or if Laos or Indonesia were to go Communist?

It takes a very good crystal ball to answer such questions, yet the balance-of-power principle requires that on occasion they be answered. On this basis, can a balance of power policy be intelligently pursued?

Not only does the intelligent pursuit of an acceptable relative power position require an ability to predict the future capacity of other states to threaten vital interests, but it also requires an ability to divine their intentions. This is not always easy. For example, after Hitler came to power in 1933 he took a series of steps which greatly strengthened Germany. He announced German rearmament in 1935. In 1936 he remilitarized the Rhineland. In 1938 in the name of the principles of nationalism and self-determination he took Austria, and a few months later the Sudetenland. He had made statements claiming for the Nordic race the right to rule the world, yet at the same time he had repeatedly professed a love of peace and had assured the world after each territorial acquisition that this was his last demand. Further, according to principles endorsed throughout the Western world, there was some justice in Hitler's demands down to the spring of 1939. As the British Prime Minister, Neville Chamberlain, put it, "there was something to be said, whether on account of racial affinity or of just claims too long resisted . . . for the necessity of a change in the existing situation."[8] The question was, could Hitler be appeased by conceding to his just demands, or would concessions simply lead to the making of new demands without end? Did Hitler really threaten Britain and other states? Down to the spring of 1939

[8] Neville Chamberlain, *In Search of Peace* (New York, Putnam, 1939), p. 274.

Chamberlain was not entirely convinced that he did, and he therefore followed an appeasement policy and did not rigorously pursue a balance of power. Then, concluding that Hitler's intentions were definitely menacing to Britain, he switched to an emphasis on power.

Analogous questions exist today. The government in Peking is by all odds the most threatening. How powerful is it likely to become, and how rapidly? When will it obtain missile delivery systems, together with a significant number of nuclear warheads? Are its intentions such that Moscow itself has reason for fear? What kinds of troubles does the United States face in relations with Peking, given the embroilment in South Vietnam and the commitment to the Nationalist regime on Taiwan? Should the stress of those threatened by Peking be on military capability or should it be on the search for a settlement aimed at stability and order? To what extent, if at all, are the two possible lines of action incompatible? If war should break out between any two of the major powers, what roles can the other states be expected to play? The intelligent pursuit of an acceptable relative power position requires that such questions be answered.

## The Problem of Contradictory Principles: Balance vs. Law, Morality, and Justice

Once statesmen pursuing a balance of power have identified the vital interests that they want to defend and have determined what threats exist or are in prospect, they have met two of the prerequisites of the intelligent application of the balance-of-power principle, but there are still others. The third one is that pursuit of the desired power position should not be limited unduly by concern for law, morality, or justice. Otherwise a balance may be destroyed, or prove unobtainable. The question is whether statesmen and peoples are prepared to do what an intelligent application of balance-of-power principles sometimes requires.

Suppose, for example, that in a free election France should go Communist, presumably meaning that it would withdraw from the North Atlantic Treaty Organization and enter the Soviet alliance system. The probability is that the example set by the French people and government would be followed in other European countries, such as Italy, which are now aligned with the United States. What would the United States do, if anything? Intervention to set aside the verdict of the polls would be difficult to justify in the light of America's endorsement of both law and democracy, yet intervention would probably be required by the principle of the balance of power. It might be said that the United States, on the basis of balance-of-power and other considerations, should seek to influence opinion in France long before the election occurs so as to prevent the development of the dilemma; still, such dilemmas sometimes arise regardless of preventive action.

Suppose that it were feasible to come to an understanding with the Soviet Union concerning the establishment of mutually satisfactory power relationships. Suppose, however, that a division of the world into spheres of interest is a necessary aspect of the understanding; this would imply that the United States would not interfere in any way with action taken by the Soviet Union to preserve or extend Communist domination within its sphere. This aspect of the agreement would be widely regarded in the United States and elsewhere as immoral. If it seemed desirable on the basis of balance-of-power considerations, would it nevertheless be accepted?

Suppose that Yugoslavia or Greece or Turkey should deliberately attack Bulgaria. Let us assume that the aggression is clearly illegal and that it is generally regarded in the United States as immoral or unjust. Military events quickly make it plain that the aggressor, left unaided, will be defeated. The almost certain consequence of defeat will be the reduction of the aggressor to the status of a satellite of the Soviet Union. The power of the Soviet Union will thus presumably be enhanced, and this threatens to upset a pre-existing balance of power. What would such countries as the United States do? Under balance-of-power considerations, they would have to act. They might attempt to secure a termination of the war short of a Communist victory, or, failing that, they might have to enter the war on the side of the aggressor. The question is, would they do so? Would devotion to the principle of balancing power lead to an abandonment of the principles of law and morality which the aggressor has violated?

Spain provides an actual case in point, and consideration of the issue has produced different answers in different Western countries. Various attributes of the Spanish government, which Franco brought into existence with the indispensable help of Mussolini and Hitler, make it morally distasteful to many people and governments. At the same time, Spain controls some resources and possesses a strategic location which are of value to the West in relation to the Soviet Union. Should Spain have been brought into the Western alliance structure? The French and British said no, largely on moral grounds. The United States said yes and made its own arrangement with Spain.

The Cuban missile crisis of 1962 also provides a case in point. The Soviet Union was in the process of developing launching sites in Cuba from which intermediate range missiles with nuclear warheads could have struck at targets in the United States. Had the United States guided itself entirely by legal considerations, it apparently would have had to stand by and do nothing. At least a very good case can be made for the view that the Soviet Union and Cuba were acting within the law, giving the

United States no legal basis for any kind of preventive action.[9] But if legal considerations suggested noninterference, power considerations (and no doubt other kinds of considerations too) suggested the opposite. The result was an American ultimatum and a Soviet retreat.

## The Problem of Domestic Political Conditions and Attitudes

A fourth prerequisite of an intelligent application of the balance-of-power principle is that domestic political conditions and attitudes should be suitable. Sometimes they are not. Sometimes they call for measures of a jingoistic and provocative sort, ill-suited to an effort to achieve "balance," and sometimes they militate against, and even preclude, the kind of measures that "balance" requires. These possibilities exist particularly in democracies, where political leaders are apt to regard victory at the polls as the primary objective.

Except for the period since World War II, American public opinion has generally prevented the United States government from engaging in a balancing of power—and even now it must be done in the name of collective security, which seems to be a more acceptable term. According to Colonel E. M. House, Woodrow Wilson said privately in 1915 that he "had never been sure that we ought not to take part in [World War I], and if it seemed evident that Germany and her militaristic ideas were to win, the obligation upon us was greater than ever."[10] Yet he fought the electoral campaign of 1916 with the slogan, "He kept us out of war." After the outbreak of World War II, President Roosevelt gave clear and sharp warnings of the dangers of an Axis victory for the United States, but in the interests of electoral victory in 1940 felt obliged to pledge that American boys would not be called upon to fight in foreign wars.[11] The tradition of isolation and neutrality was so strong in the United States that many were blind to the possibility that events abroad might produce serious threats to vital American interests. Had Wilson and Roosevelt urged in an election year that balance-of-power considerations required participation in war, the electoral victory which each in fact won would clearly have been put in jeopardy.

Not only must domestic political conditions and attitudes permit intervention in war, but they must also permit conducting the war and terminating it in the interest of the balance of power. This may involve peace

---

[9] Quincy Wright, "The Cuban Quarantine of 1962," in John G. Stoessinger and Alan F. Westin, eds., *Power and Order. 6 Cases in World Politics* (New York, Harcourt, Brace & World, 1964), pp. 179-213. See, however, various articles in the July, 1963, issue of the *American Journal of International Law* (Vol. 57).

[10] Charles Seymour, *The Intimate Papers of Colonel House* (Boston, Houghton Mifflin, 1926), Vol. II, p. 84.

[11] Franklin D. Roosevelt, *The Public Papers and Addresses of Franklin D. Roosevelt,* 1940 volume (New York, Macmillan, 1941), p. 517.

without victory, a slogan which Wilson championed before America's intervention in World War I only to abandon it later. It may require that a Kaiser or a Hirohito or a Stalin be allowed to remain in office on the basis of a negotiated peace.

George Kennan, in his appraisal of American diplomacy, poses the question whether a democracy can either wage war or make peace on the basis of the cold calculations which the balancing of power requires.

I sometimes wonder whether in this respect a democracy is not uncomfortably similar to one of those prehistoric monsters with a body as long as this room and a brain the size of a pin: he lies there in his comfortable primeval mud and pays little attention to his environment; he is slow to wrath—in fact, you practically have to whack his tail off to make him aware that his interests are being disturbed; but, once he grasps this, he lays about him with such blind determination that he not only destroys his adversary but largely wrecks his native habitat. You wonder whether it would not have been wiser for him to have taken a little more interest in what was going on at an earlier date and to have seen whether he could not have prevented some of these situations from arising instead of proceeding from an undiscriminating indifference to a holy wrath equally undiscriminating.[12]

Opposite kinds of questions can also be raised. The Cuban missile crisis occurred, for example, during an election campaign, when demands were rather widespread—especially among Republicans—for a tough line against Castro and the Soviet Union. The general view is that Kennedy's handling of the crisis helped a number of Democratic candidates to win. The question is to what extent Republicans and Democrats alike were influenced in selecting their stands by a concern for the outcome of the election. Comparable questions can be raised about the attitudes of members of both parties toward events in Vietnam before the elections of 1964.

Difficulties in establishing or preserving a satisfactory relative power position are automatically accentuated when important persons or groups either reject the goal or assign it only secondary importance. A tradition of isolation, a yearning for peace at almost any price, a belief that law and morality count above all else, and a willingness to do anything that will contribute to victory in the next election are among the many attitudes in point.

## The Problem of Choice of Method

Finally, it is one thing to conclude that balance-of-power considerations require action of some sort, and quite another thing to decide precisely what the action should be. Statesmen may be intelligent about the

---

[12] George F. Kennan, *American Diplomacy, 1900-1950* (Chicago, The University of Chicago Press, 1951, copyright 1951 by the University of Chicago), p. 66.

choice of objective but mistaken in their choice of method for reaching it. For example, in appraising American policy in relation to World War I, George Kennan does not criticize response to the principle of the balance of power but rather the timing and precise character of the response. He argues that we should have recognized before 1914 that troubles were brewing in Europe which threatened American interests, and that we should therefore have seen to it "that this country provided itself right then and there with something in the way of an armed establishment, so that our word would carry some weight and be listened to in the councils of the power."

When the war broke out, you could have ignored the nonsensical timidities of technical neutrality and used our influence to achieve the earliest possible termination of a war that nobody could really win. Admittedly, if there were any possibility of this, it was in the first months of the war, and we would have had to be armed. If this had not succeeded, then you would have had to carry on through the war, exercising what moderating influence you could, avoiding friction with the belligerents on minor matters, holding your power in reserve for the things that counted. And if you finally had to intervene to save the British from final defeat (which I am quite prepared to accept as a valid ground for intervention), then you could have gone in frankly for the avowed purpose both of doing this and of ending the war as rapidly as possible; you could have refrained from moralistic slogans, refrained from picturing your effort as a crusade, kept open your lines of negotiation to the enemy, declined to break up his empires and overthrow his political system, avoided commitments to the extremist war aims of your allies, retained your freedom of action, exploited your bargaining power flexibly with a view to bringing its full weight to bear at the crucial moments in order to achieve the termination of hostilities with a minimum prejudice to the future stability of the Continent.[13]

How often have states and statesmen, attempting to pursue the principle of balancing power, made mistakes in the way in which they went about it? Many of the failures in the balancing process have no doubt resulted less from the principle involved than from poor judgment on the part of those applying it.

The stress so far has been on factors which militate against the validity of the fifth assumption underlying the balance-of-power principle, that statemen can and will make foreign policy decisions intelligently on the basis of power considerations. Such factors exist in good number. For good or ill, states which desire to establish or preserve a balance of power are also guided by other desires, some of which may be incompatible with the balancing of power. Nevertheless, the record shows that states can and do follow the principle. They may not always do it with coldly calculated precision and with uniform success, but they do it. This will become abundantly clear through an analysis of the methods of balanc-

[13] *Ibid.*, pp. 71-72.

ing power—methods which every major power and many others have at
one time or another employed.

# METHODS EMPLOYED IN THE BALANCING
# OF POWER

## The Adjustment of Power by Domestic Measures

A number of methods are employed in the effort to establish or maintain an acceptable relative power position. The adjustment of national
power by domestic measures is prominent among them. A state that feels
threatened by the growing power of another may simply bring about a
growth of its own power in order to safeguard its position. It may build
up its armaments; it may initiate or expand an economic program designed to enhance its fighting capacity; it may develop a domestic propaganda campaign designed to stimulate love of country and hatred of the
potential enemy; it may, in fact, go through the whole inventory of the
elements of power, seeking to increase its strength in every way that is
reasonably possible. When and if the other state ceases to be so powerful
or so threatening, these measures may be relaxed and national power
allowed to decline.

For example, the United States, after engaging in demobilization at
the end of World War II to a much greater extent than the Soviet Union,
became convinced that the Soviet Union was a potential enemy state.
It therefore began a program of rearmament, which it greatly intensified
after it became clear that the Soviet Union had developed atomic weapons and after the North Korean aggression in 1950 gave increased evidence of Communist hostility. Fat, slack, and flexibility in the American
economy made it possible through purely domestic measures to do a
good deal to redress the balance between East and West. This method
of pursuing a balance of power, however, is not always adequate or feasible. Where there is a vast discrepancy in the power potential of two
states, it is futile for the weaker of the two to seek to establish balance
by its own unaided action. Domestic American measures might, but
domestic Iranian measures could not, bring about a balancing of Soviet
power.

## Winning and Strengthening Friends and Allies

If domestic measures are inadequate, and perhaps in any event, they
may be supplemented by measures taken abroad. The range of action
which can be taken abroad is at least as great as the range of action
which can be taken at home. Treaties of alliance may be concluded,
providing for various degrees of cooperation in military and related

affairs. Treaties of neutrality and nonaggression may be concluded, designed to give assurance that the power of neither party will be directed against the other. A state may extend military or economic aid, or both, to another in order to strengthen it, on the assumption that an increase in the power of the recipient will contribute to a balancing of power. Propaganda campaigns may be launched to win support for the national cause abroad and to deprive the potential enemy of support. In fact, once again, the state seeking a balance of power can go through the whole inventory of the elements of power, seeking to strengthen actual or potential allies in every way that is reasonably possible.

Treaties of alliance should be noted especially as devices employed in the balancing process. Selected illustrations follow. In 1892 France and Russia completed their alliance by signing a military convention. In the preamble they affirmed their common desire to preserve the peace and declared that they had "no other aim than to prepare for the necessities of defensive war." Article 1 then provided:

If France is attacked by Germany, or by Italy supported by Germany, Russia shall employ all her available forces to fight Germany.

If Russia is attacked by Germany, or by Austria supported by Germany, France shall employ all her available forces to fight Germany.

In 1899 France and Russia added to this an understanding that they would seek to maintain "the European balance of power." Still later there was a tacit agreement that a territorial acquisition on the part of Austria would affect the general balance of power in Europe.[14] When Austria then attacked Serbia, Russia mobilized, and France stood by her. Moreover, the Tsar sent a telegram to the King of England appealing for British aid in the name of the balance of power. The object of the Austrian ultimatum to Serbia, he said,

was to crush Serbia and make her a vassal of Austria. Effect of this would have been to upset balance of power in Balkans, which is of such a vital interest to my Empire as well as to those Powers who desire maintenance of balance of power in Europe. . . . I trust your country will not fail to support France and Russia in fighting to maintain balance of power in Europe.[15]

Before World War II the British Prime Minister issued an oral guarantee to Poland, pledging to support Poland "in the event of any action which clearly threatened Polish independence, and which the Polish Government accordingly considered it vital to resist with their national forces." This guarantee was later transformed into a formal alliance, the two parties pledging themselves to give one another all the support in their power in the event that either became "engaged in hostilities with

14 Bernadotte E. Schmitt, *The Coming of the War* (New York, Scribner, 1930), Vol. I, pp. 10, 18-21.
15 Great Britain, Foreign Office, *op. cit.*, Vol. XI, p. 276.

a European Power in consequence of aggression by the latter against that Contracting Party."[16] In 1939, also, Germany and Italy made an alliance with thinly veiled aggressive intentions. The treaty included the following article:

> If, contrary to the wishes and hopes of the contracting parties, it should happen that either of them is involved in military entanglements with another Power or Powers, the other contracting party will immediately rally to its side as ally and support it with all its military resources on land, at sea and in the air.[17]

The most notable treaty since World War II aiming at a balance of power is the North Atlantic Treaty (the text of which is in the appendix of this book). In it the parties assert their determination to safeguard the freedom, common heritage, and civilization of their peoples, to promote stability and well-being in the North Atlantic area, and to defend peace and security. For these purposes they pledge "separately and jointly, by means of continuous and effective self-help and mutual aid, [to] maintain and develop their individual and collective capacity to resist armed attack." They further agree "that an armed attack against one or more of them in Europe or North America shall be considered an attack against them all." Consequently, each party agrees to "assist the Party or Parties so attacked by taking forthwith, individually and in concert with the other Parties, such action as it deems necessary, including the use of armed force, to restore and maintain the security of the North Atlantic area." Similar provisions are included in the Rio Pact of 1947 among the American republics. The treaty of 1951 between the United States, Australia, and New Zealand involves a more limited obligation. In it "each Party recognizes that an armed attack in the Pacific area on any of the Parties would be dangerous to its own peace and safety and declares that it would act to meet the common danger in accordance with its constitutional processes."[18]

Most treaties of alliance are deliberately couched in somewhat vague language because the governments concluding them are motivated by conflicting desires. They want to give strong warning to the potential enemy, but at the same time want to assume only a weak obligation. They want to receive assurances that their allies will spring to their aid, yet many of them wish at the same time to retain the right to decide by their own constitutional processes whether and when the circumstance calling for action (i.e., the *casus foederis*) has arisen. They want assur-

[16] *Documents on International Affairs 1939-1946* (New York, Oxford University Press, 1951), Vol. I, pp. 126, 469.

[17] *Ibid.*, p. 169.

[18] The treaties here mentioned are Nos. 1964, 1838, and 2493 in U.S. Department of State, *Treaties and Other International Acts Series* (Washington, Government Printing Office, 1946-).

ances of maximum help from an ally while retaining freedom to decide how much help they themselves will give. Finally, they have to reconcile aggressive intent, if it exists, with the necessity of appearing to aim only at the defense of peace, security, and other socially accepted values.

## Curbing the Power of the Potential Enemy

In pursuit of an acceptable power position, positive measures to build up power at home or through alliances are likely to be supplemented by negative measures designed to curb the power of the potential enemy. Thus, the United States, while granting extensive aid to its allies, has attempted to cut off the flow of strategic materials to the countries behind the Iron Curtain and has been even more restrictive in its policies on trade with Communist China. It has spread propaganda in Communist countries designed to keep popular support for policies hostile to the West at a minimum. It wooed Yugoslavia for the West after Tito split with Stalin in 1948, and has made economic and other arrangements with the various Soviet satellite countries designed to encourage them to be more independent of Moscow. The United States did not dare, however, to help Hungary escape from the Soviet alliance system in 1956.

## Negotiating Agreements with the Potential Enemy

Additional kinds of measures may also be taken in pursuit of a balance of power. They may involve negotiations with the potential enemy.

1. *The level of armaments.* Particularly since World War I states have negotiated persistently over the level of armaments to be maintained— the central factor in a balance of power. Among the many objectives of such negotiations two are relevant here. In the first place, disarmament may be proposed as a propaganda maneuver designed to demonstrate one's own desire for peace and friendship among nations and to reveal to all the world the intransigence and bellicosity of the potential enemy. It thus may be designed to affect the balance of power by influencing public opinion in various countries. In the second place, it may be proposed in the hope, which is usually forlorn, that agreement on a mutually satisfactory distribution of military power can be reached. We shall see in a subsequent chapter how difficult this is and how unlikely it is that agreement can be achieved.

2. *Applying the principle of compensation.* Negotiations concerning the balance of power have on occasion involved what is called the principle of compensation. The best illustration dates from the partition of Poland in the last part of the eighteenth century. Prussia, Russia, and Austria-Hungary, which surrounded the weak state of Poland, each knew that the other two would not permit it to conquer Poland, for that would

upset the balance of power among them; yet Poland was a tempting morsel for all of them. In the end they agreed upon successive partitions, each one taking a portion of Poland deemed equivalent in terms of power to the portions taken by the others; each was "compensated" for the enhancement of the power of the others by gaining a similar increment of power for itself. The power of all three was presumably increased, but the ratio of power among them presumably remained the same.

3. *Buffer states, spheres of influence, and neutralization.* Whether or not as a result of negotiations, buffer zones or buffer states sometimes play a role in the balancing of power. Buffers are areas which are weak but which possess considerable strategic importance to two or more stronger powers. Each of the stronger powers may seek to bring the buffer within its sphere, but regards it as important, if not vital, that no other strong power be permitted to do so. If one of them manages to bring the buffer within its sphere, the usual result is annexation, or the establishment of a protectorate, or the conclusion of an alliance. Otherwise, the stronger powers will seek to maintain the independence and neutrality of the buffer. Formal neutralization may occur.

Korea, for example, has served as a buffer between Japan, China, and Russia. After defeating both China and Russia around the turn of the present century, Japan annexed Korea, only to be ousted after World War II. Then Korea, divided at the thirty-eighth parallel, became a buffer between the United States and the Soviet Union, later joined by Communist China. When North Korea attacked and threatened to take all of Korea into the Moscow-Peking sphere, the United States intervened on behalf of South Korea. The tentative result is the continued division of the country, with the southern part allied to the United States and the northern part remaining under Communist control.

Iran has historically been a buffer between Britain and Russia, and more recently has become a buffer between East and West. To minimize their rivalries in connection with the formation of the Triple Entente, Britain and Russia in 1907 agreed to a division of Iran into three zones. The northern and southern zones were to be Russian and British spheres of influence, respectively, each country pledging itself not to seek political or commercial concessions in the sphere of the other. In the central zone, neither country was to seek concessions except in agreement with the other.[19] After Russian power had collapsed because of World War I and the Bolshevik Revolution, Britain concluded a treaty with Iran which made it a virtual protectorate. (A protectorate has all the rights and powers of an independent state, except those taken away by international agreement. Among other things, the agreement usually restricts the free-

---

[19] Sidney B. Fay, *The Origins of the World War* (New York, Macmillan, 1932), Vol. I, p. 220.

dom of the protectorate in the conduct of its foreign relations.) Iran subsequently repudiated this agreement, regaining full independence. During World War II the Soviet Union and Britain occupied Iran by mutual agreement, with the United States joining in later. After the war, when the Soviet Union was slow to withdraw its troops, Britain and the United States brought coercive pressures to bear, and later when pro-Soviet elements seemed to be getting too powerful in Teheran, a *coup d'état* occurred in which the U. S. Central Intelligence Agency reputedly played a role.[20]

Belgium has historically been a buffer between France and Germany. When it first achieved independence, it was neutralized. As noted in Chapter 10, this means that other states bound themselves to respect Belgium's territorial integrity, and Belgium bound itself to remain neutral, save in its own urgent defense.[21] The scheme broke down when Germany struck at France through Belgium in 1914, and a comparable breakdown occurred again in 1939.

## War, and the Terms of Peace

War is the most extreme method of trying to establish or maintain an acceptable relative power position. We have already seen that Britain has historically sought to prevent any strong and potentially hostile power from gaining control over the Low Countries or from gaining mastery over Europe as a whole; she repeatedly has waged balance-of-power wars to execute one or another of these purposes. Russia went to the aid of Serbia in 1914 partly for balance-of-power reasons. Secretary of State Lansing desired American participation in World War I as a means of preventing Germany from gaining domination on the continent, on the assumption that Germany would thus be strengthened and that she would eventually become hostile to the United States. President Roosevelt and others favored aiding the Allies in the early part of World War II largely on the basis of the same considerations as moved Secretary Lansing, and as the war progressed the United States took such strong measures to affect its outcome that Japan attacked at Pearl Harbor in retaliation, and Germany then also declared war. Balance-of-power considerations were among those which influenced American intervention in Korea after the North Korean attack in 1950, the fear being that Communist success in Korea would encourage attacks elsewhere until eventually the United States might find itself in a very disadvantageous power

[20] George Lenczowski, *Russia and the West in Iran, 1918-1948* (Ithaca, N.Y., Cornell University Press, 1949), pp. 42-47. John Marlowe, *Iran* (New York, Praeger, 1963), pp. 97-100. David Wise and Thomas B. Ross, *The Invisible Government* (New York, Random House, 1964), pp. 110-114.

[21] Cf., Fred Greene, "Neutralization and the Balance of Power," *American Political Science Review*, Vol. 47 (December, 1953), pp. 1041-1057.

position. Some have favored "preventive war" against the Soviet Union on the basis of balance-of-power considerations: that if we do not strike now, Soviet power may become so great as to preclude effective defense of vital American rights and interests later on.

Just as war may be fought, so may peace be made with the balance of power in mind. The Peace of Utrecht (1713) contained arrangements made with the expressly stated purpose *ad conservandum in Europa equilibrium*. The same consideration was a major element in the settlement made at the Congress of Vienna a century later, and is reflected also, implicitly or explicitly, in other treaties as well.

## The Holder of the Balance

The happiest position for a state in the balancing process is that of the holder of the balance—or that of the "laughing third party" as it is sometimes called. For example, suppose that in a system including only three states, A and B are approximately equal in power and are so bitterly hostile to each other that an alliance between them is out of the question. State C can then become the laughing third party. If it lines up with A, the two could crush B, or if it lines up with B, the two could crush A. Both A and B are therefore likely to woo C diplomatically, and C can commit itself or remain noncommittal as its interests seem to dictate. Neither A nor B is likely to be able to make a major move without making sure in advance that C would not be alienated thereby. State C can thus largely dictate relationships among the three where she chooses to bring her power to bear.

In practice, it is rare for a state to enjoy a position as favorable as the one we have assigned to C in the above illustration, but sometimes states achieve somewhat analogous positions. Britain has traditionally played the role of a holder of the balance in relation to the continent of Europe, "throwing her weight now in this scale and now in that." It is thus that she came to be known as perfidious Albion. Since World War II, no state or group of states can really be described as a holder of the balance. The neutralists have probably exerted a little restraining influence on both the United States and the Soviet Union, for neither wants to alienate them. Communist China may or may not prove at all susceptible to their pressures. Moreover, within each alliance system states other than the Soviet Union and the United States can play roles more or less analogous to that of the laughing third party. China's defection from the Soviet camp has had a drastic effect on the power position of the Soviet Union, and a reconciliation (if it is conceivable) would transform the situation once more. Similarly, the NATO allies of the United States, even if they haven't threatened to switch sides, have been able to exert significant influence by blowing hot or cold on American plans.

# AN APPRAISAL OF THE BALANCE-OF-POWER SYSTEM

In analyzing the purposes and the underlying assumptions of the balance-of-power system, we have already engaged in some appraisal of it, but additional remarks are called for.

## Balance as a Basis for Security and Peace

Obviously, the balance of power—whether considered as a situation, a policy, or a system—leaves much to be desired as a basis for security and peace. That it is inadequate as a basis for peace is automatically indicated by the occurrence of two world wars in this century, to say nothing of the dozens of other major and minor wars of modern times. What proportion of the states involved in these wars actually served their security interests by participating in balance-of-power operations is a question that will be commented on below. Certainly in the history of modern Europe a great many states have failed even to survive, regardless of the balance-of-power system. The unification of Germany and Italy, in particular, meant that a great many states disappeared, and most of them disappeared involuntarily.

When balance is thought of as equilibrium—or as disequilibrium that is unfavorable to status quo powers—it follows almost automatically that it would not be very reliable as a basis for security and peace. After all, equilibrium suggests in principle that the aggressor has an even chance of winning, and a disequilibrium in his favor jeopardizes security and peace all the more. Woodrow Wilson may have been thinking along these lines when he described the "great game" of the balance of power as "forever discredited"; in the League of Nations he sought legal and institutional arrangements assuring that there would be a preponderance of power on the side of law and order. (The relationship between the balance-of-power principle and the League system of "collective security" will be discussed in a later chapter.) The French statesman, Edouard Herriot, was similarly influenced when he said that the League (meaning France?) was determined "to put an end to the old policy of equilibrium and balance which in the past has, in effect, engendered more wars than it has averted."[22] He wanted a preponderance of power in the hands of the satisfied. Similarly, Winston Churchill in 1946, facing the Soviet threat, was quite blunt in rejecting balance in the sense of equilibrium. "The old doctrine of a balance of power is unsound," he said. "We can-

---

[22] Arnold Wolfers, *Britain and France Between Two Wars* (New York, Harcourt, Brace & World, 1940), p. 173.

not afford, if we can help it, to work on narrow margins, offering temptations to a trial of strength."[23]

However, if any state or limited group of states seeks preponderance, even with the most peace-loving intentions, the basic principle of the balance of power gives warning to other states. That principle or assumption is that no state or group of states is to be trusted with undue power, and history goes far to validate the principle. When France and Britain joined in the attack on Egypt in 1956, and when the United States arranged for and surreptitiously participated in the attack on Cuba in 1961, they demonstrated that even ostensibly peace-loving states may at times succumb to the temptations that come with power.

In sum, both an equilibrium and a disequilibrium are unsafe and inadequate as bases for security and peace.

## Unnecessary War, and the Unnecessary Extension of War

Another major criticism of the balance-of-power principle is that it leads to unnecessary war and to the unnecessary extension of war. Recall that the application of the principle requires that the capabilities of other states be estimated and their intentions divined. Recall that it also requires prediction of the probable effect on power relationships of hypothetical future events. Such estimates and divinations and predictions may be wrong. States may fear power that isn't there. They may seek to counteract intentions that do not exist. They may enter an existing war, which otherwise might have been localized, because of fear for the future that may not be justified.

When threats are putative rather than direct and immediate, statesmen are in fact in a dilemma in relation to the balance of power. If they attempt to counteract a putative threat, they may actually increase present danger, perhaps becoming involved in a war which could have been avoided. Yet if they take no action they may find themselves helpless when and if the putative threat materializes. Which way out of the dilemma do they, and should they, take?

From hindsight, we know that the Russian Tsar in 1914 took the wrong way out; at least, his personal fate and the fate of Russia could hardly have been worse had he refused to go to Serbia's defense. He transformed a hypothetical future danger into an immediate catastrophe. Did France likewise take the wrong way out? Once Austria-Hungary and Germany were lined up against Serbia and Russia, what should France have done? By going to war, she incurred great risk and suffered tremendous losses, but what would her fate have been had she abstained from a war which

[23] Winston Churchill, *The Sinews of Peace, Post-War Speeches* (Boston, Houghton Mifflin, 1949), p. 103.

the Central Powers won? No one can know; France may or may not have chosen the lesser evil.

What of the choices made after the rise of Hitler to power in Germany in 1933? From hindsight it seems clear that Britain and France (and the United States) made mistakes in failing to anticipate the future danger; they could have acted against Hitler with very little risk at the time he announced the rearmament of Germany in 1935 or at the time he reoccupied the Rhineland and set about remilitarizing it in 1936. Here it was a lack of sufficient concern for power relationships which led to "the unnecessary war," as Churchill once suggested that World War II be called. Suppose that Britain and France had also refused to act against Hitler when the invasion of Poland occurred. They would at least have delayed their own participation in war. In the long run would they then have been worse off or better off?

And what of the choices being made since World War II? The United States, for example, has been increasing present dangers for itself by the course which it has been pursuing. At least, it seems very likely that the danger of war with the Soviet Union or China would be less if the United States had reverted to isolationism. But what of the long-run prospect? If the United States reverted to isolationism, what are the odds that it might some time be confronted with such overwhelming Communist power as to render impossible the preservation of vital American interests?

Assuming that the balance-of-power principle sometimes leads to unnecessary war, or to the unnecessary extension of existing war, it would be rash to conclude that statesmen should ignore the principle. If they ignore it, they may also bring on unnecessary war, or find that another state or coalition of states has mustered such overwhelming power that resistance to its demands is hopeless. At bottom, the question is not whether statesmen should be concerned with the distribution of power and with the achievement of a satisfactory relative power position; as long as states exist and are determined to preserve vital interests which may be attacked, prudence dictates that this should be done. The question is how wise the choices of the decision-makers will be. When they are wise, unnecessary wars are unlikely to occur, and vital rights and interests are likely to be preserved.

## Balance and Nuclear Weapons

What is the relationship between weapons of mass destruction and the balance of power system? The question is a crucial one, but the answer is still problematic.

As between the United States and the Soviet Union, the current references are to a nuclear stalemate. With thermonuclear bombs delivered by missile or orbiting satellite, each country could presumably destroy as many target areas in the territory of the other as it chose. Each is thus thought to have the capacity to inflict unacceptable damage on the other. A "balance of terror" is thus said to exist—the two sides standing in approximately equal terror of the colossal losses of life and property that the other could cause. This kind of balance obviously gives a modicum of assurance of security and peace, for the deliberate initiation of unrestricted nuclear war would clearly be irrational. Winston Churchill spoke some years ago of the time when "safety will be the sturdy child of terror, and survival the twin brother of annihilation," and that time has come—however precarious the safety may be. Thus, for countries possessing nuclear capacities, the balance of power is reinforced as a deterrent to war. Once the destructive capacities of a country go beyond a certain point—and it does not take very many thermonuclear bombs to get a country to that point—it has an adequate deterrent against nuclear attack regardless of other elements of power and regardless of the question whether literal equilibrium exists.

At least two kinds of qualifications need to be briefly discussed with the above. The validity of the statements made depends, among other things, on the belief on each side that the other could withstand a surprise attack and still retain power to inflict unacceptable damage in retaliation; that is, it depends on the belief that the other side could absorb a first strike and still have a powerful second-strike capability. It is the expectation of unacceptable retaliation that constitutes the deterrent. Moreover, each side should not only convince the other that it will maintain a devastating second-strike capability, but should also convince itself; otherwise it may feel compelled in a time of crisis to attempt to get in the first strike—to engage in preventive or pre-emptive attack. Or it may, in effect, become trigger-happy—so fearful and anxious that it may launch its nuclear missiles in what turns out to be the false belief that attack from the other side is imminent or under way. A country confident of its second-strike capability is likely to be more prudent and restrained in its responses than a country that fears it might be knocked out by the enemy's first blow.[24]

The other qualification is that the deterrent value of a nuclear capability is limited in scope. Most obviously, it does not give real assurance against attack on third parties, even if the third party is an ally. North Vietnam can attack South Vietnam without much fear of American nuclear power; China can attack Burma or India; the Soviet Union could even attack Turkey. As long as such attacks are made with nonnuclear weapons, it is extremely unlikely that the United States or any other

---

[24] Albert Wohlstetter, "The Delicate Balance of Terror," *Foreign Affairs*, Vol. 37 (January, 1959), pp. 211-234. See Chapter 18 below on "The Utility of War," especially the sections on "preventive and pre-emptive war" and "deterrence."

country would engage in nuclear retaliation. Moreover, if the Soviet Union should attempt to seize West Berlin, attacking American troops in the process but confining itself to nonnuclear weapons, it is doubtful what the response would be. A military struggle would ensue, but whether the United States would engage in nuclear retaliation for a nonnuclear attack is uncertain. In effect, then, there are two or more balances of power in Soviet-American relations, nuclear and nonnuclear. A nuclear balance or stalemate does not necessarily mean balance in terms of other weapons. A state that wants to promote security and peace through "balance" must seek a satisfactory relative power position in terms of each possible kind of attack.

## Conditions of Success for the Balance of Power System

Inis L. Claude, Jr., argues that in most respects during the last century the world has become less and less suitable for the operation of a balance of power system.[25]

According to his analysis, a cogent one, the following conditions would maximize the prospects of success: (1) Power should be shared by a number of states, not highly concentrated. (2) Policy should be controlled by "skilled professional players of the diplomatic game," free of ideological commitments and all other impediments to action on the basis of power considerations. (3) The elements of power should be simple and stable—simple enough to permit accurate calculations and stable enough to permit a projection of the calculations into the future. (4) The potential costs of war should be sufficient to have deterrent value, but not so great that the threat of war becomes incredible. "War should be imaginable, controllable, usable." (5) The challenges to the existing order should not be revolutionary. At least, the main protagonists in the state system should limit themselves to demands that are compatible with the "essential pluralism" of the system. And (6) there should be, if possible, a holder of the balance—a state that can throw its weight now in this scale and now in that.

None of these conditions exists today as fully as a century ago. In a strict sense, power may not be bipolar, but it is closer to being so than at any time since the Napoleonic wars. Those managing power relationships today are under more restrictions than ever before; they are restricted by ideologies, by domestic constitutional systems and democratic controls, and by the changed requirements of law and morality reflected in the United Nations Charter. The elements of power are more complex and varied than ever before and are changing ever more rapidly, making both calculations and projections extremely difficult. The Soviet Communists

[25] Claude, *op. cit.*, pp. 90-93.

may or may not be reconciled to a world of diversity and pluralism; the Chinese Communists surely are not; and for that matter, many in the non-Communist world are not entirely reconciled to a diversity that goes so far as to provide for the accommodation of Communists. Finally, as indicated above, no real holder of the balance exists.

On the other side of the argument is the fact that fear of war is undoubtedly greater today than ever before. Available weapons of mass destruction are potentially so catastrophic that they necessarily make all rational men pause. Not only does the deliberate initiation of nuclear war seem unlikely, as indicated above, but the possibility that any war might be transformed into a nuclear war militates against resort to war at all.

Thus, changes have been working both against and for a greater degree of security and peace. War has occurred in Korea, and very sizeable military actions have occurred elsewhere (e.g., in Vietnam and in the Sino-Indian border region), but both the goals pursued and the means employed have been limited. The future alone can tell us what the role of war may be.

## Balance and the Inevitability of Change

A final consideration relating to the balancing of power should be mentioned. A policy of balancing power is a means by which states seek to preserve existing rights and interests. In a dynamic world society, however, it is out of the question that all existing vital rights and interests can be preserved indefinitely. Change could be avoided only if the world were static. The manipulation of power can be no more successful among countries than within countries in freezing the status quo. The question is not whether but how change will be brought about. The balancing process must therefore be supplemented somehow so as to permit adjustment or change, or it will break down. Possibilities along these lines will also be examined below.

## SUGGESTED READINGS

CARR, E. H., *Britain, a Study of Foreign Policy* (New York, Longmans, 1939).

CLAUDE, Inis L., Jr., *Power and International Relations* (New York, Random House, 1962).

DEHIO, Ludwig, *The Precarious Balance, Four Centuries of the European Power Struggle* (New York, Knopf, 1962).

GAREAU, Frederick H., *The Balance of Power and Nuclear Deterrence, A Book of Readings* (Boston, Houghton Mifflin, 1962).

GRANT, A. J., and TEMPERLEY, Harold, *Europe in the Nineteenth and Twentieth Centuries* (New York, Longmans, 1952).

GREENE, Fred, "Neutralization and the Balance of Power," *American Political Science Review*, Vol. 47 (December, 1953), pp. 1041-1057.

GULICK, Edward Vose, *Europe's Classical Balance of Power* (Ithaca, N.Y., Cornell University Press, 1955).

HAAS, Ernst B., "The Balance of Power as a Guide to Policy Making," *Journal of Politics*, Vol. 15 (August, 1953), pp. 370-398.

KENNAN, George F., *American Diplomacy, 1900-1950* (Chicago, The University of Chicago Press, 1951).

LANGER, William L., *European Alliances and Alignments, 1871-1890* (New York, Knopf, 1931).

LERNER, Max, *The Age of Overkill, A Preface to World Politics* (New York, Simon and Schuster, 1962).

LISKA, George, *International Equilibrium, A Theoretical Essay on the Politics and Organization of Security* (Cambridge, Harvard University Press, 1957).

WOLFERS, Arnold, *Britain and France Between Two Wars* (New York, Harcourt, Brace & World, 1940).

WRIGHT, Quincy, *The Study of International Relations* (New York, Appleton-Century-Crofts, 1955).

WRIGHT, Quincy, *A Study of War* (Chicago, The University of Chicago Press, 1942).

# DIPLOMACY AND SETTLING INTERNATIONAL DISPUTES

Diplomacy is "the management of international relations by means of negotiation; the method by which these relations are adjusted and managed by ambassadors and envoys; the business or art of the diplomat."[1] It stands in contrast to war as the means by which states conduct relationships with each other and with international institutions. Whatever objectives a state pursues, diplomacy is sure to be employed as a method of promoting their achievement. The sending and receiving of diplomats is the common practice.

It is through diplomacy that states arrange alliances called for by balance-of-power considerations or seek to isolate a potential victim of attack. Through diplomacy they negotiate concerning the level and type of armaments to be maintained. Through diplomacy they seek to coordinate economic policies designed to enhance their welfare or power, or designed to restrict the welfare or power of other states. Through diplomacy they contribute to the development of international law and appeal to the law when it is useful to them. Through diplomacy they establish international organizations, like the United Nations, in which they conduct more diplomacy. There is hardly an aspect of international affairs on which diplomacy does not touch.

Diplomacy may, of course, be reinforced and supplemented in various ways. In fact, in classifications of the methods of international politics, diplomacy as such scarcely figures as a major, separate category. The cynical are inclined to classify methods under the headings of force, fraud, and favor. The more lighthearted refer to the method of the carrot, fig-

[1] Harold Nicolson, *Diplomacy* (New York, Oxford University Press, 1964), pp. 4-5.

uratively dangled in front of the donkey's nose, and the method of the stick, applied at the other end; they may vary the figure of speech and speak of the "big stick" and the "sugar stick." The more serious speak of persuasion and coercion—perhaps adding corruption, though corruption might be subsumed under the other two. Harold Lasswell classifies political methods into four categories: those which employ symbols, violence, goods, and practices, respectively.[2] A symbol may be a thing, like the national flag, or a word, like *freedom*. When states use propaganda to get what they want, they are manipulating symbols. The method of violence is self-explanatory, in the extreme taking the form of war. The use of goods as a method of achieving objectives will be discussed in Chapter 15; it takes such forms as foreign aid programs and trade regulations designed to strengthen or weaken other states. Lasswell's fourth method includes such practices as those which are observed by legislative and executive branches of government in formulating and implementing policies.

Diplomacy may apply, or be supplemented and reinforced by, all these methods. Between some states at some times, diplomacy may be completely supplanted by other methods, as when states formally declare war.

Whether or not diplomacy is classified as a major political method, it is obviously a prominent element in international relations. As such, it deserves separate attention. Moreover, the methods available to governments for seeking the settlement of international disputes also need to be examined if the processes of international politics are to be understood.

## RECOGNITION AND THE ESTABLISHMENT OF DIPLOMATIC RELATIONSHIPS

### Recognition of What? When?

The question of extending recognition arises both in relation to foreign states and in relation to foreign governments. The recognition of a state remains effective regardless of changes in the character and composition of its government. Governments are recognized as they come to power. Whether there is an obligation to recognize either a state or a government (and whether the other party has a corresponding right to demand recognition) is a vexing question on which students of international law differ. In practice, most governments deny any obligation. The practice is for each government to decide for itself whether and when to extend recognition, and to base the decision on whatever grounds seem expedient.[3]

[2] Harold D. Lasswell, *Politics, Who Gets What, When, How* (New York, Whittlesey House, 1936).

[3] Ti-chiang Chen, *The International Law of Recognition* (New York, Praeger, 1951).

## The Exchange of Diplomatic Missions

Given mutual recognition, governments normally enter into diplomatic relationships, whether through diplomatic missions that they exchange or through the missions that they maintain at the United Nations. If either government decides that it would like to sever diplomatic relationships, it is free to do so; this means that any diplomatic missions that have been exchanged will return home.

## General and Special Reasons for Recognition

When a new state comes into existence by a grant of independence (and more than fifty have in recent decades), other governments normally accord recognition, following the lead of the "mother country" without question. Similarly, when a new government comes into power by orderly processes, or when it in fact exercises uncontested jurisdiction in the state, other governments normally extend recognition. There is never any question, for example, whether the United States will recognize a new government in Britain or in Canada.

The reason for this is that governments generally find it to their advantage to recognize and to establish diplomatic relationships with other states and governments. The security and welfare of each state depends in part on establishing and maintaining satisfactory relationships with other states with which there is contact. Through diplomatic relationships one government may be able to influence the policies of another. It may build up good will for itself and perhaps obtain positive support for the policies which it chooses to pursue. It may allay hostility and reduce or eliminate obstacles to the achievement of its objectives. Advantageous commercial and cultural exchange may be promoted. The interests of citizens who travel and do business abroad can be more surely protected. Valuable information can perhaps be secured which might otherwise be unobtainable. Other advantages may accrue as well. The calculation of advantage turns out in favor of extending recognition and establishing diplomatic relationships so regularly that these actions ordinarily occur as a matter of course.

Sometimes governments have very special reasons for extending recognition. They may combine recognition with other measures to encourage or support a change which they desire, and when they do this they may meet opposition from governments which are against the change. France recognized the United States in 1778 as a means of weakening Britain, and accompanied recognition with an alliance which meant participation in war. Theodore Roosevelt, frustrated by Colombia's stand regarding the construction of a trans-isthmian canal, encouraged revolution in Panama; once revolution occurred he promptly extended recognition and took other measures to assure the survival of the new state. During World War I the Allies recognized a government of the new state of Czechoslovakia before it had actual control over any territory at all. Early in the Spanish Civil War, both Italy and Germany extended recognition to Franco's rebel faction as one of a number of measures to assure its victory. During World War II the Soviet Union coupled recognition with other measures to make sure that the government of its choice would survive in Poland after the war. In such circumstances as these, recognition takes on special significance, but it is hardly recognition itself which determines whether or not the desired change will occur; the measures which accompany or follow recognition are more important.

## Some Reasons for Withholding Recognition

Sometimes when governments oppose or dislike a change, they withhold recognition. The United States has been especially prone to do this in connection with revolutionary governments. At one time or another it has refused to recognize a number of Latin American regimes because they came to power by unconstitutional means. Similarly, it has been very reluctant to recognize Communist governments, usually on the ground of their unwillingness to abide by international obligations but partly also because of a dislike for Communism and an assumption that recognition would enhance the strength or prestige of the government recognized. There is a feeling, with regard to newly established Communist regimes, that the withholding of American recognition may encourage domestic opposition to them and perhaps bring about their overthrow, whereas recognition would stamp them as stable. So far as the Communist government of China is concerned, the withholding of recognition is also a part of a program designed to prevent that government from displacing the Nationalist government as the representative of China in the United Nations.

The refusal of the United States to extend recognition to certain Latin American governments in times past has caused them difficulties, particularly when they wanted to borrow money from American bankers, and has even contributed on occasion to their downfall. But with Communist governments nonrecognition has proved so far to be rather ineffective as a weapon. Apparently it has not weakened any of them seriously, nor has it induced any of them to make significant changes in policy. On the contrary, it may have intensified their hostility toward the outside world, and certainly it has deprived the United States itself of the usual advantages of diplomatic relationships. After more or less protracted delays, the United States has, in effect, admitted the failure of the policy of non-recognition and has extended recognition; China remains the outstanding exception.

## The Severance of Diplomatic Relationships

Sometimes the question is not whether to recognize a government and establish relations with it but whether to sever or curtail relationships. Disputes between states sometimes become so bitter that one or the other of them severs diplomatic relations as a mark of its hostility or as a means of exerting pressure. Thus the United States severed diplomatic relations with Bulgaria in 1950 in retaliation for restrictions placed on American diplomats in Sofia, and Iran severed relations with Great Britain in 1951 in the course of the Anglo-Iranian oil dispute. Frequently, though not always, the severance of relationships is a prelude to war. Displeasure with the Franco regime in Spain after World War II led the General Assembly of the United Nations to recommend that members of the United Nations should withdraw their ambassadors from Madrid, leaving diplomatic missions in the hands of officers of lower rank. The hope was that the action might lead to the downfall or reform of Franco's government, but his position in Spain seems to have been strengthened rather than weakened. Most of the American republics severed diplomatic relationships with Castro's regime in Cuba within a few years after it came to power, and all were asked to do so in 1964, when the ministers of foreign affairs of the other American republics adopted a resolution declaring Cuba guilty of aggressive and interventionist acts against Venezuela.

## Consular Relationships

International relations are not entirely intergovernmental. Citizens engage in travel and trade abroad and are frequently in need of some kind of assistance. To serve them, governments normally seek to station consuls in the principal foreign centers. Assent of the foreign government involved is necessary and is ordinarily granted, especially where diplomatic relationships exist. Again, however, assent may be withheld, or the number of consuls permitted to operate may be limited, as a means of exerting pressure on the sending government.

# SOME GROUND RULES OF DIPLOMATIC RELATIONSHIPS

Questions of rank, precedence, and protocol once plagued international relations. Sometimes they seriously delayed the conduct of diplomatic business. Persistently they led to friction, and on occasion even brought on the threat of war. In a more or less conscious effort to reduce such difficulties, states have gradually developed certain rules and principles governing diplomatic intercourse. In other words, they have developed international laws defining common interests and putting certain relationships on an orderly and predictable basis. Law thus serves, however effectively, as a method of pursuing certain objectives and, once developed, as a limiting condition of subsequent actions.

As a result of an agreement originally made at the Congress of Vienna in 1815, subsequently modified, diplomatic agents are divided into four categories and ranked as follows: ambassadors, ministers, ministers resident, and chargés d'affaires. Within each rank, precedence is based upon the date of the official notification of the arrival of the diplomat in the receiving country.[4] A diplomatic post headed by an ambassador is called an embassy, and a post headed by a person of lower rank is called a legation. States exchanging diplomats agree on the rank to be accorded them. The original expectation was that the great powers would exchange ambassadors among themselves, and the lesser powers would send and receive diplomats of lesser rank. Largely because of sensitivity to signs of prestige, however, states of all degrees of power now generally exchange ambassadors.

The individual diplomat must be *persona grata* in the eyes of the receiving government, that is, he must be personally acceptable. The practice of *agréation* has thus developed: the sending state asks for assurance in advance that the diplomat whom it proposes to send will be received. Once received, a diplomat who becomes *persona non grata* may be dismissed, or his recall may be requested. It might be mentioned in this connection that diplomats are not to interfere in any way in the domestic affairs of the country to which they are accredited, and it is up to the receiving government to determine what kinds of actions constitute interference.

The general principle is accepted that states receiving diplomatic missions will permit them to exercise their duties free from local interference and will assure them safety and respect. The implications of this principle are numerous. For example, diplomats are to be free to communicate with their home governments; diplomatic personnel cannot be sued or prosecuted, nor can diplomatic premises be invaded by the police; protection must be accorded to diplomatic personnel and property in proportion both to the needs of the situation and the means at the disposal of the receiving state. Questions persistently arise over the meaning of such rules in particular circumstances; still, the existence of the rules clearly serves to facilitate diplomatic intercourse.

---

[4] Sir Ernest Satow, *A Guide to Diplomatic Practice,* 4th ed., Nevile Bland, ed. (New York, Longmans, 1957), p. 171. See also Lassa F. L. Oppenheim, *International Law,* 7th ed., Hersh Lauterpacht, ed. (New York, Longmans, 1948-1952), Vol. I, pp. 687-757.

Consuls likewise have some immunity from local jurisdiction, but on a much less extensive scale.

## THE FUNCTIONS OF DIPLOMATS AND CONSULS

Governments assign a number of different functions to their diplomats. Ordinarily one of them is to help shape the policies that the diplomat is to follow—a process in which his influence may range from the negligible to the dominant. At the very least, the diplomat provides some of the information on which policy decisions are based. Consciously or unconsciously, he may select the information so as to promote his conception of proper policy. He may do much more. Modern means of communication permit his government to make him a full partner in the decision-making process. In comparison with those in his ministry of foreign affairs back home, he may have fuller and more intimate knowledge of the problems and possibilities that he confronts, which would lend special weight to his recommendations. In unusual cases, he may be a man of considerable political stature in his own right, and therefore be especially influential in the policy-making process.

Another function of the diplomat is to conduct negotiations with the government to which he is accredited. In this connection he is to act within the limits of the policy of his government, regardless of his own role in shaping that policy. He negotiates verbally and delivers formal notes. He receives communications from the government to which he is accredited and dispatches them home, perhaps along with his own comments and advice. The end point in intergovernmental negotiations naturally varies—a point that we will take up shortly.

The diplomat is likewise an intelligence agent in a foreign country charged with the duty of observing and reporting on everything which may be of interest to his home government. He or members of his mission normally report on a multitude of subjects: on all kinds of political developments in the country to which he is assigned, on relationships between it and other foreign states, on all aspects of its military posture and potentialities, on the facts and trends of agricultural and industrial production, on the attitudes and activities of leading public figures and on personal relationships among them, on public attitudes, and so on.

Another major function of the diplomat is to provide information concerning his country to the people of the country in which he is stationed. So far as possible the diplomat usually seeks to develop public understanding and sympathy for the policies of his government and appreciation of various aspects of life in the country which he represents. He may stress its power, its cultural achievements, its economic or scientific progress, or its future potentialities. He sponsors and attends social gatherings, gives speeches, holds press conferences, issues printed materials, participates in or provides radio and television programs, and spreads propaganda favorable to his country in every possible way. In conjunction with the American diplomatic service, libraries of information are maintained in many foreign centers, containing materials on all aspects of American life. All these informational and propaganda activities are conducted, of course, only with the consent of the government of the receiving state, which can restrict or curtail them at will.

Finally, the diplomat shares with the consul certain duties concerning nationals of his own state. He assists them in relations with the government to which he is accredited and provides information which may be helpful to them in commercial or other pursuits.

It is sometimes said that the diplomat, in contrast to the general, is a man of peace, and that his first and most important duty is to maintain friendly relations with the government to which he is accredited. The generalization is inaccurate and misleading. To be sure, the diplomat gives advice that makes for peace much more often than for war (and so does the general). Moreover, even rather strict instructions to a diplomat are likely to leave him with some discretion in the performance of his duties and so may give him an opportunity to deflect the course of events somewhat in the direction of peace or war, as he chooses. But the primary duty of the diplomat is not to promote friendly relations or peace but to serve his government faithfully. If the government's policies, as influenced by the diplomat, make for peace, then he can be a man of peace; otherwise that is hardly possible, and he may be guilty of contumacy if he attempts it. In some circumstances, it may be his assigned task to set the stage for war. This is certainly what Hitler and Mussolini called upon some of their diplomats to do.

Consuls perform varied functions. They give different kinds of assistance to nationals of the sending state who live and travel abroad, including assistance with problems that arise vis-à-vis local and other governmental agencies in the receiving state. They issue visas to foreigners who want to enter the sending state. They seek to promote the commerce of the sending state and perform various duties relating to ships flying its flag. They seek knowledge of all sorts, especially political and economic knowledge, that may be useful to the state they serve.

## AMICABLE METHODS OF HANDLING
## INTERNATIONAL PROBLEMS

The methods that states have developed for handling international problems may be classified as amicable and nonamicable. The amicable methods are either political, involving negotiations, or judicial, involving arbitration or adjudication. The principal distinction between them is that negotiations imply no obligation to reach or accept a settlement, whereas resort to judicial procedures implies an obligation to accept an award or decision as binding.

## Political Methods: Negotiation

*1. Purposes of Negotiations.* The ostensible purpose of negotiations is agreement about some issue or problem, or at least exploratory inquiry into the possibility of reaching agreement. The ostensible purpose may or may not be the real purpose.

Negotiations proceed on the tacit assumption that the parties have a common interest of some sort. Each party must be responding to the view that by negotiating it may be able to gain more, or to lose less, than by refusing to negotiate. At the same time the parties are very likely to have conflicting interests, or conflicting ideas about how a common interest can best be served; or one or more parties may be uncertain about how best to serve the common interest. The relative prominence of the common and conflicting interests varies greatly in different situations. Where the common interests are dominant, the negotiators face the happy problem of developing terms that maximize the gains of all parties. Where the conflicting interests are dominant, one side is presumably seeking to maximize its gains and the other side to minimize its losses.

Fred Charles Iklé identifies four types of issues or problems (sometimes interrelated) that figure in international negotiations, and four corresponding purposes.[5] (1) The extension of an existing arrangement, with or without modification. (2) The normalization of a relationship or situation, e.g., establishing or restoring diplomatic relationships. (3) Redistribution. That is, one side demands change requiring sacrifice by the other. In connection with issues of this kind, conflicting interests are much more prominent than common interests; in fact, the common interest (e.g., in getting the problem settled without mutual suicide) may not be talked about explicitly at all. (4) Innovation. That is, one or more parties seek change that is allegedly in the common interest; conflicting interests are allegedly secondary, and may or may not be talked about. For example, the negotiations in Western Europe associated with the establishment of the Common Market.

Thomas C. Schelling employs a somewhat simpler classification scheme; he distinguishes between the "efficiency aspect" of bargaining, where the object is a mutually profitable adjustment, and the "distributional aspect," where, even if both sides gain, more for one means less for the other and where "each party is guided mainly by his expectations of what the other will accept."[6]

[5] Fred Charles Iklé, *How Nations Negotiate* (New York, Harper & Row, 1964), pp. 26-42.

[6] Thomas C. Schelling, *The Strategy of Conflict* (New York, Oxford University Press, 1963), p. 21.

The real purpose of one or more states engaged in negotiations may, however, have little or nothing to do with the ostensible purpose of achieving agreement. Sometimes, as Iklé puts it, negotiations occur for their side effects, and he lists six of them.

(1) The object of one or both sides may be simply to maintain contact —to keep the channels of communication open—perhaps in the thought that personal contact may somehow do good, perhaps to facilitate exchange on issues unrelated to the main subject, or perhaps in the belief that it is good to make communication habitual.

(2) Sometimes the hope is that (even in the absence of agreement) negotiations may substitute for violence, either terminating hostilities already in progress or deterring their outbreak. The hope may or may not be realized. Negotiations do not always safeguard peace.

(3) Sometimes states negotiate as a means of gaining fuller information and knowledge (intelligence); negotiations may reveal the intentions of the other side; they may show how much importance he attaches to this or that, and what methods he may employ in defending or promoting his interests.

(4) The real purpose may be deception. For example, in the early stages of the Hungarian revolution in 1956 the Soviet ambassador apparently negotiated as a means of gaining the necessary time for counterrevolutionary action by the Red Army, and the charge has been made that in the same year Dulles negotiated deceptively with Britain and France over the Suez issue.

(5) Time and again states have made proposals to each other with no hope that they will be accepted or that they will ever provide a basis for serious negotiations but rather for their propaganda value. The negotiating forum, e.g., a meeting "at the summit" or a meeting of the United Nations or a related agency, may provide the best sounding board available; formal proposals at a conference are likely to have more impact over the world than a simple news release or public pronouncement. Statemen sometimes engage in negotiations mainly for the personal publicity or prestige that they can gain; it may help them at home politically if they seem to play a striking role on the world stage. Moreover, governments sometimes negotiate "to show rectitude like the Pharisee saying his prayers." Much of what passes for negotiation over general disarmament is really an effort to win approval and favor throughout the world and to show up the other side as hypocritical or sinister.

(6) Finally, one or both sides may negotiate primarily with a view to the effect on a third party. The real purpose may be to use the threat of agreement as a means of bringing a third party to terms. Thus some governments have surely negotiated with the Soviet Union in recent years as a means of putting pressure on Washington. (We might note, too, that the effect on third parties is sometimes unintended, as when American or

French negotiations with the Soviet Union undermine German confidence in the North Atlantic Treaty.)

Given the numerous possible purposes, hesitations are usually in order in judging the success of international negotiations and conferences. Sometimes those that are dismal failures in terms of their ostensible purposes are resounding successes in terms of the side effects that they achieve.

2. *Is It Always Desirable to Negotiate?* The obvious answer is no. If the genuine purpose of both sides is agreement, there is no point in negotiating in the absence of some possibility of success. It contributes little to agreement to have negotiators meet, present utterly irreconcilable demands, and then glare at each other across a table. Moreover, a party that expects circumstances to change in its favor is likely to want to delay negotiations, and a state that wants to maintain the friendship and support of other states endangers this purpose if it enters into negotiations relating to their rights and interests without their consent. Frequently, statesmen say that they will not negotiate under a threat, but they cannot always maintain this rule. Negotiations make sense (still assuming that the genuine purpose is agreement) only on negotiable issues. A state facing a demand for modification of its rights—rights that it is sure of being able to maintain—usually stands pat, seeing nothing to negotiate about. If Mexico were to demand the return of Texas, it is not to be expected that the United States would appoint negotiators.

The problem is more complicated if the purpose of one or both parties is not agreement but rather the pursuit of a side effect. The question of the desirability of negotiations then turns to an assessment of the probable relative gains and losses in relation to whatever goals are sought. A propaganda triumph may make negotiations worth while for the side that enjoys the triumph.

3. *The Strategy of Bargaining.* There has been surprisingly little analysis of the principles applicable to negotiating situations, perhaps because the subject is so complex and intractable. Both Schelling and Iklé have recently made notable contributions to the subject. In their discussions of strategy, both are concerned primarily with the pursuit of the ostensible purposes, not the pursuit of side effects. Schelling limits himself to what he calls the distributional aspects of bargaining (where more for one side means less for the other), and we will follow his example. The object here is to provide not a coherent and comprehensive analysis but simply an impression of the nature and complexities of the problems.

In explicit bargaining, as distinct from tacit bargaining, proposals or demands are submitted and a response occurs. Each side gives evidence of its intentions and expectations (however misleading) and explores the intentions and expectations of the other. Each aims at the most favorable possible terms and in private may also identify the minimal terms that it would accept. Concessions may be made in the direction of the minimal terms. But how much is it necessary to concede? How can the other side be induced to accept less favorable terms than it wants?

The cogency of argument may play a role. Each side can present evidence and reasoning supporting its view of the consequences of different terms and may make predictions that are in the nature of warnings.

Apart from the possible role of reasoned argument, Schelling points to "the power to bind oneself" as a crucial factor in bargaining—the power to make the other side believe that one is irrevocably committed to a particular course of action. Perhaps the commitment is simply a promise to act or refrain from acting in a certain way; how can it be made trustworthy? Or perhaps the commitment is in the nature of a threat: a prediction by a party that it will follow a course of action costly to the other side (and perhaps also costly to itself) unless specified terms are accepted. How can a threat be made credible? In sum, how can the other side be made to believe warnings, promises, or threats, and so be induced either to make the final concessions that are necessary for agreement or to accept responsibility for a breakdown?

The ability to convince the other side that a commitment is absolute and that no further concessions are possible varies with what Schelling calls the institutional and structural characteristics of the bargaining situation. Agents are in a somewhat different position from principals. Public commitments are likely to be more credible than secret commitments. If concession by one side would adversely affect its position in comparable negotiations with other parties, a warning that it will not make the concession acquires enhanced credibility. If the two sides engage in more or less continuous negotiations over a series of issues as they arise, the implications may differ: on the one hand, attitudes may stiffen, lest concession be construed as weakness, but, on the other hand, a tacit or explicit understanding may develop that the conceding side acquires an I.O.U. which it can cash in subsequently. The possibilities of a settlement may be either increased or decreased by putting additional issues on the agenda or bringing additional parties into the fray. Commitments are more likely to be convincing if they rest on principle or precedent, and concessions may be easier to obtain if a case can be made for the view that the other side is really not backing down, or better, if a case can be made for the view that it is demonstrating virtue. One of the functions of the United Nations and the International Court of Justice, for example, is to make it easier for states to extricate themselves from untenable positions without too much loss of face.

What of threats whose execution would obviously be costly? The most extreme example of the problem concerns the threat of war, particularly unrestricted nuclear war. (We will discuss the problem briefly here and give a more detailed discussion later in connection with the subject of deterrence.) Manifest consensus of all who influence policy-making on the threatening side is obviously helpful, if it can be managed, and so is a consistent record in carrying out threats to the letter. The execution of some kinds of threats can be turned over to third parties who will gain rather than lose through their execution. Sometimes physical arrangements are available that make the threatened action automatic, or nearly so, if occasion for it arises. Perhaps the prospective costs to the threatener can be minimized, or at least the pretense can be maintained that they will be small. Arrangements can be made so that execution of the threat occurs on a piecemeal basis, giving progressive demonstration of underlying determination. Also, the other side can be convinced that in certain circumstances the behavior of the threatener will no longer be rational, and that the threat will be executed as a matter of honor even if it be suicidal.

What of promises? As we will later see, negotiations over disarmament have bogged down, among other reasons, because neither side trusts the promises of the other. The West has been particularly insistent that procedures for verification should be an integral part of any agreement. Again, manifest consensus of all policy-makers that promises should be observed is helpful, if it can be managed, and so is a consistent record of promise-keeping. Similarly, arrangements calling for the piecemeal execution of promises may be possible, confidence and trust developing as each step is taken.

Other factors also affect the outcome of negotiations. Sometimes the advantage goes to the side that is rational, intelligent, and in complete control of its own affairs, and sometimes it goes to the irrational, the obstinate, and the disorganized. On occasion, limits placed on the negotiator lead quickly to a breakdown, and at other times they induce the other side to concede. Also, sometimes it is terribly imprudent to take a position from which there is no possibility of retreat, and again sometimes this is an effective stratagem.

Since the Munich Conference in 1938 the term *appeasement* has come into prominence in connection with international negotiations. Originally a neutral word designating efforts to relieve tensions and reduce the danger of war by a policy of concession and compromise, *appeasement* thereafter became a bad word. The Munich connotation is that appeasement occurs when a concession is made (perhaps at the expense of a third state) in fear of force and in violation of avowed principle, on the assumption that the demanding state has only a limited objective and will be pacified by the concession when in fact the demanding state has extensive or unlimited objectives and will react to the concession by presenting new demands. So defined, appeasement is obviously something to be avoided.

2. *The use of third parties: good offices, mediation, and conciliation.* A third party sometimes supplements or facilitates negotiations. The third party may be a government not directly involved, or several governments acting jointly, or an international agency such as the Security Council of

the United Nations, or individual persons appointed somehow, for example, by the Security Council, The third party may provide good offices or mediation, or it may engage in an investigation of the facts or in conciliation. Distinctions between these roles are not always agreed upon or observed. The term *good offices* usually denotes various kinds of actions by a third party designed to bring about negotiations or a resumption of them. If two disputing states have severed diplomatic relations, for example, a third party may offer its good offices, meaning that, as a minimum, it will transmit messages back and forth. The term *mediation* usually applies to active participation in the negotiations by the third party, who proposes terms of settlement. A "commission of inquiry" may seek to ascertain the facts relevant to the issue and report on them, on the assumption that impartial findings of fact may facilitate negotiation and agreement. If the commission not only reports on relevant facts but also proposes terms of settlement, it is usually said to engage in conciliation.

It should be emphasized that, when third parties are employed in any of the capacities described above, their function is strictly limited. They arrive at findings or make suggestions which the disputants are free to reject. Commissions of inquiry, mediators, and conciliators are not empowered to make awards or decisions which will be binding on the disputants. Their function is to facilitate agreement, not to impose terms of settlement.

## Judicial Methods

Amicable methods of handling international problems include not only the political methods described above but also judicial methods: arbitration and adjudication. The end point in judicial procedures is a determination and application of existing law.

*1. Arbitration.* The term *arbitration* is used rather loosely. Sometimes it denotes all methods of peaceful settlement, as in the debate in the interwar period over the order in which "arbitration, security, and disarmament" should be sought. When it denotes a judicial procedure, however, the meaning is much narrower. An appropriate definition appears in the first Hague Convention of 1907. "International arbitration," it says, "has for its object the settlement of disputes between states by judges of their own choice on the basis of respect for law. Recourse to arbitration implies an engagement to submit in good faith to the award."

States referring a dispute to an arbitral tribunal normally draw up a *compromis*, which is a written agreement specifying the various arrangements and conditions under which arbitration will occur. It is usually agreed that each party to the case will name two arbitrators, no more than one of whom is to be its national, and that the four arbitrators so named shall select a fifth. Each party is expected to argue its case before the tribunal, and the tribunal arrives at its ultimate award by a majority vote. Once the dispute is disposed of, the tribunal dissolves. The first Hague Convention provided for the establishment of a Permanent Court of Arbitration, but the name is misleading. The so-called Permanent Court is simply a list of persons deemed qualified to serve as arbitrators and presumably available for appointment to arbitral tribunals.

2. *Adjudication.* Arbitration is an age-old method of settling international disputes. Adjudication, the second of the judicial methods, developed on a significant scale only after World War I. Then a Permanent Court of International Justice was established, succeeded after World War II by the International Court of Justice. The latter is one of the principal organs of the United Nations, and membership in the United Nations automatically involves adherence to the Statute of the Court. Nonmembers of the United Nations may also adhere. Headquarters of the Court are at The Hague, Netherlands.

The International Court of Justice consists of fifteen judges elected for nine-year terms by the concurrent action of the Security Council and the General Assembly. They are not representative of the states from which they come. No two are to be nationals of the same state, and elections occur on the basis of the principle that "the representation of the main forms of civilization and of the principal legal systems of the world should be assured." The Court may make binding decisions settling legal disputes between states, and may give advisory opinions to various agencies of the United Nations or to independent organizations associated with the United Nations. Decisions and opinions are arrived at by majority vote.

### The Jurisdiction of the International Court of Justice

What kind of problems come before the court for settlement? How do they get there? What is the extent of the court's jurisdiction?

In principle, the Court has jurisdiction over any legal disputes that the parties choose to submit, but as noted above, they usually choose to handle their disputes politically even if they turn on legal issues. For a number of reasons, most of the time most states hesitate to turn problems over to the court.[7]

In the first place, many of the problems are more in the nature of general tensions than specific issues. The cold war, for example, resulted as much from ideological differences and from changed power relationships wrought by World War II as from specific, identifiable issues. Soviet in-

[7] Lincoln Bloomfield, "Law, Politics and International Disputes," *International Conciliation,* No. 516, January 1958. Max Sorensen, "The International Court of Justice: Its Role in Contemporary International Relations," *International Organization,* Vol. 14 (Spring, 1960), pp. 261-76. Shabtai Rosenne, *The International Court of Justice* (Leyden, Sythoff, 1961), pp. 66-72.

tentions and capabilities were as much responsible as specific Soviet actions. Similarly, after Castro came to power in Cuba, tensions developed in relationships between Havana and Washington almost independently of specific issues that could be identified. De Gaulle's general style and outlook make for problems within the NATO alliance structure, and ideological differences between Peking and Moscow impose strains on relationships within the Communist world. How could problems of these types be settled by a court?

In the second place, even where specific issues are identified, they often relate to policy choices that fall within the realm of discretionary action, no legal question arising. Thus the Soviet Union could protest when various neighboring states allied themselves with the United States and permitted the establishment of American bases on their soil. And the United States could take action when the Soviet Union sought to establish missile bases in Cuba. But these are not the kinds of problems that are suitable for judicial action; under existing law, a court could only confirm that governments are free to make alliances, and to extend and receive aid, as they choose. Similarly, at the close of World War II the Soviet Union could recognize one government in Poland and the Western powers could recognize another—both sides claiming to act within a legally permitted realm of discretion; and a comparable situation exists with regard to the question which government is the government of China.

In the third place, issues sometimes arise over a demand for the modification of law—for some change in the legal order. Thus some time after India gained independence she demanded Goa, a territory on the coast of India that had been under Portugal's jurisdiction for several centuries. Had the issue been turned over to a court, there is little question but that it would have simply confirmed Portugal's legal title.[8] But India was not after a confirmation of the law or even a clarification of the law. She wanted Goa whether or not her legal claim was good. And she got it—by force.

In the fourth place, many governments are hesitant and ambivalent about accepting international law, and at the very least are suspicious of procedures of settlement aiming at its application. To a very considerable extent, international law is the creation of the major powers of the Western world, reflecting their conception of right and justice (or more crudely, their conception of their interests). Communist governments do not share all of these conceptions and neither do the governments of some of the weaker or newly independent states. In the Goa case, for example, a number of governments of former colonial countries rejected the legal principles on which Portugal based its claims. Even the advanced states that have largely created international law show some ambivalence about it, in part

[8] Quincy Wright, "The Goa Incident," *American Journal of International Law*, Vol. 56 (July, 1962), pp. 617-632.

because the legislative process is so slow and cumbersome. Even if the law is clear, it may reflect the desires of the law-makers of several centuries ago rather than the desires of those who want their will to count today.

In the fifth place, many of the rules and principles of international law are even more vague—and thus even more open to varied interpretations —than are some of the provisions of the United States Constitution. Judges thus often have considerable leeway in reaching their decisions. Even governments that are willing to settle a particular dispute on the basis of law may nevertheless be reluctant to submit themselves to the hazards of judicial choice. This is especially true of Communist states in relation to the International Court of Justice (on which 13 of the 15 members are non-Communist), but it is also true sometimes of the major Western powers. The reluctance shows up more obviously, as we will see below, in connection with the question of promising to submit future legal disputes to adjudication. Rather than submit themselves to a court, governments sometimes prefer to use political procedures in determining what settlement the law suggests.

The upshot of the above is that the court plays a rather restricted role in international affairs. Relatively few cases go to the International Court of Justice for settlement, and of those submitted, few involve issues on which feelings of any great intensity have been aroused.

Approximately the same might be said, parenthetically, of the role of courts within countries. Those who believe that the path to international peace is through a requirement that all disputes be submitted to adjudication cannot support their view by reference to domestic governmental practices. Though some decisions of the United States Supreme Court have had a profound effect on American life, it is still true that by and large the great issues are handled by political rather than judicial means; they are fought out in electoral campaigns, in the halls of legislatures, in the tug of war that surrounds executive and administrative offices, and perhaps, ultimately in civil war—this despite the fact that in many connections individuals and companies can be forced to come to court whether they want to or not.

On the latter point, international practice is different, and the difference further explains the restricted role of the International Court of Justice. The accepted principle internationally is that a state cannot be hailed into court without its consent. To put it differently, states that are parties to a dispute must consent if the case is to be heard by the court. In general, one state has no right to arraign another in court, whether in a civil suit or a criminal prosecution.

For the most part, consent is *ad hoc,* specifically given after a dispute has arisen. It is given when both parties not only define their claims in legal terms (i.e., when the issue concerns conflicting claims of legal right) but also when they both think it desirable to resort to a judicial procedure. They may think it desirable for any number of reasons; e.g., they may want to support the principle of the rule of law; or they may attach importance to getting the dispute settled somehow, whatever the terms; or, they may welcome a situation in which the terms of settlement are, in a sense, imposed on them, for this may permit them to abandon claims without an undue loss of face and to minimize domestic criticism; or, if the dispute is between a weak and a strong power, the weak one may consent to adjudication as a lesser evil, fearing what its antagonist might otherwise do.

Consent is also given in advance to apply to specified kinds of disputes. Treaties often include a provision obliging the parties to submit disputes over their meaning to arbitration or to the International Court of Justice. Advance consent can also be given by accepting Article 36 (2) of the Court's Statute, the so-called optional clause, which reads as follows:

The states parties to the present Statute may at any time declare that they recognize as compulsory *ipso facto* and without special agreement, in relation to any other state accepting the same obligation, the jurisdiction of the Court in all legal disputes concerning:
a. the interpretation of any treaty;
b. any question of international law;
c. the existence of any fact which, if established, would constitute a breach of an international obligation;
d. the nature or extent of the reparation to be made for the breach of an international obligation.
In the event of a dispute as to whether the Court has jurisdiction, the matter shall be settled by the decision of the Court.

As of 1962, when 107 states were parties to the Statute, only 37 were committed under the optional clause, and they came quite disproportionately from Europe and the English-speaking countries. No Communist state and relatively few of the developing nations were included. Moreover, most states making declarations under Article 36 (2) have attached reservations. The Connally Amendment states the reservations of the United States; among other things, they exclude from the Court's compulsory jurisdiction "disputes with regard to matters which are essentially within the domestic jurisdiction of the United States as determined by the United States." A number of states accept the optional clause only for a specified number of years or reserve the right to terminate their acceptance at any time.[9]

In addition to its jurisdiction over contentious cases submitted to it by

---

[9] International Court of Justice, *Yearbook, 1961-1962*, pp. 193-215. Julius Stone, "The International Court and World Crisis," *International Conciliation*, No. 536 (January 1962), pp. 20-30.

states, the International Court of Justice may render advisory opinions on questions submitted to it by various international agencies. Thus the General Assembly obtained an advisory opinion on the question whether members of the United Nations were obliged to help defray expenses incurred in the Congo even if they opposed UN activities there. The answer was yes, thus reinforcing the rule that members who were refusing to pay should lose their vote in the General Assembly. Note that the reference here is to an *advisory* opinion to an international agency, not to a binding decision settling a dispute between parties. In the case just cited, the General Assembly did not in practice enforce the rule that the Court upheld.

## NONAMICABLE METHODS OF SETTLEMENT

We have already noted that negotiations among states may involve both persuasion and coercion. The two, in fact, are often difficult to distinguish, for the power to coerce ordinarily enhances the ability to persuade. States may achieve what they want ostensibly on the basis of persuasion when in fact their latent power to coerce is the principal persuasive factor. Moreover, it is not uncommon for negotiations to be accompanied and supplemented by active efforts to coerce, including ultimately the threat of war. Those who bargain are likely to use more than verbal blandishments if they are in a position to do so. States often resort to economic pressure of all degrees of severity to induce compliance with their wishes. In some circumstances appeal to opinion, perhaps involving subversive efforts, may put another government in a position in which it is virtually obliged to accept a settlement. Military leverages and threats may be employed.

Since coercion is not uncommon in negotiations, there is no sharp dividing line between amicable and nonamicable means of settling international disputes. The one category merges into the other. Coercion, however, is the characteristic, dominant, and perhaps the exclusive feature of nonamicable methods.

There are four types of nonamicable means: retorsion, reprisal, intervention, and war.

An act of retorsion is a legal but deliberately unfriendly act with a retaliatory or coercive purpose. For example, the severance of diplomatic relations or an embargo on the exportation of strategic materials to a particular state may constitute acts of retorsion.

An act of reprisal is an illegal and deliberately unfriendly act with a retaliatory or coercive purpose, deemed justified by prior violation of law by the other party; war is not intended but may follow if the victim of the reprisal chooses to fight. For example, after North Vietnamese PT boats attacked American destroyers patrolling the Gulf of Tonkin in 1964,

American planes struck in reprisal at PT-boat bases and at oil-storage facilities within North Vietnam.

Intervention denotes dictatorial interference (or, in a looser sense, any interference) by one state in the internal or external affairs of another. States resort to intervention for a considerable variety of purposes, among them the settlement of disputes. It may involve the occupation of some of the territory of another state, as when President Wilson ordered the occupation of Veracruz upon the refusal of the Mexican government to make amends for a violation of American rights and as when, at various times in the first several decades of this century, marines were sent ashore in Nicaragua, Haiti, and the Dominican Republic. It may involve the establishment of a blockade, as when Great Britain and France blockaded the coast of Holland in 1833 to force it to acknowledge the independence of Belgium, or a limited blockade, as when President Kennedy threatened to sink Soviet ships carrying missiles to Cuba in 1962. It may involve dictatorial interference of a third state in the dispute of two other states, designed to force a settlement on them, as when Hitler's government required Rumania to give up Transylvania to Hungary. The landing of American forces in the Lebanon in 1958, and of British forces in Jordan, is sometimes described as intervention even though it occurred on the invitation of the governments of these countries and therefore was not dictatorial. The forms and purposes of intervention are numerous. Sometimes it is legal and sometimes illegal. Both the League of Nations and the United Nations, as well as other international agencies, have engaged in collective intervention to terminate hostilities or defeat aggression. This aspect of the subject will be treated below.

War itself is the ultimate means of settling international disputes. More generally, it is the ultimate means by which states seek to impose their will on each other. When all other means have failed, or even before other means have been exhausted, states may resort to war to get what they want. The fact that war serves a function and that it is not a purposeless activity is an obvious and an important fact—a fact which those who wish to reduce its role in world affairs must not forget. If war served no function, it might simply be outlawed; people could get along without a useless activity. But reducing the role of an activity which has a useful purpose—in fact, many useful purposes—is a more complex and difficult matter.

## DIPLOMACY BY CONFERENCE

### The Increasing Use of the Conference Method

So far in the discussion of diplomacy we have confined ourselves to its traditional form, the exchange of diplomatic agents on a bilateral basis. Periodically in history, however, and especially after wars, diplomacy has been conducted in conferences, and diplomacy by conference has taken on ever-increasing importance since the time of World War I. During that war the Allies established many joint groups which functioned more or less continuously to determine and implement common policies on different aspects of the war effort. After the war came the establishment of the League of Nations, and under it there were annual and special conferences of all the members (meeting as the Assembly of the League) and more frequent conferences of a selected group (meeting as its Council). In addition, there were meetings of a number of international agencies associated with the League, as well as many conferences, such as several of the disarmament conferences, outside the framework of the League.

During World War II there was a great elaboration of the conference method of handling international problems among the Allies. The heads of the governments of the Big Three met on several occasions. Foreign ministers likewise conferred directly and personally. Britain and the United States maintained a Combined Chiefs of Staff to plan and guide the execution of military strategy. A number of other joint international agencies were also in operation. Though there was no general peace conference after the war, the conference technique has been applied to draft treaties and to handle other problems emanating from the war.

At the close of the war came the establishment of the United Nations. Its Security Council is so organized as to function continuously. Its General Assembly, in which all members are represented, meets for a number of months each year. The Economic and Social Council (ECOSOC) is a principal organ of the United Nations, and associated with the United Nations are many specialized agencies the activities of which involve numerous conferences. The NATO Council is in almost continuous session, and there is scarcely a time when one or more of the many agencies involved in European and North Atlantic cooperation is not meeting. The Organization of the American States calls for periodic Inter-American conferences, for meetings of consultation of the ministers of foreign affairs, for meetings of a council (at the ambassadorial level), and for meetings of various lesser agencies. The Council of the Arab League meets twice yearly, and various meetings occur in connection with CENTO (Central Treaty Organization), SEATO (Southeast Asia Treaty Organization), and ANZUS (an alliance of Australia, New Zealand, and the United States). In 1955 there was a conference of 29 Afro-Asian states in Bandung, Indonesia, and there have been numerous conferences of African states, the one at Addis Ababa in 1963 leading to the establishment of the Organization of African Unity, of which the Assembly is to meet at least once a year and the Council of Ministers at least twice a year. Conferences also occur in connection with the Warsaw Treaty Organization and Comecon (The Council for Mutual Economic Aid, established by the Soviet Union and a number of other Communist states).[10]

The delegates to most international conferences are below the ministerial rank. But since World War II—far more frequently than ever before—foreign ministers themselves and even the heads of government, meet in council. The principal victors in World War II set up a council of foreign ministers which met irregularly in prolonged sessions over number of years. In 1955 Britain, France, the Soviet Union, and the United States held a conference "at the summit" (i.e., the heads of government met), and another "summit" conference was scheduled in Paris in 1960. This was cancelled at the last minute when Eisenhower offended Khrushchev by publicly acknowledging that he personally had approved the U-2 spy-plane flights over Soviet territory and by intimating that they would continue. It was a "Summit Conference" in Addis Ababa that formed the Organization of African Unity in 1963. Moreover, in addition to attending conferences of a number of states, foreign ministers, and even heads of government, have come to travel to each other's capitals on diplomatic business with increasing frequency.

## An Evaluation of the Conference Method

Judgments of the conference method vary, depending largely on the standard employed.

The traditional view, stemming no doubt from the fact that the great conferences of modern European history were peace conferences, is that the purpose of conferences is to settle outstanding issues, and those who assume that this is the purpose are commonly critical of them, particularly when (as is usually the case) they think only of conferences that deal with great political problems. The criticisms come mainly from Western commentators who point to what is regarded as Soviet insincerity and the tendency of the Soviet delegates to use conferences simply as means of wearing down the other side and disseminating propaganda. In other words, the criticisms come mainly from those who assume that the purpose is agreement rather than the production of side effects. The same commentators are likely to say that the crucial question is not whether a conference is held but whether the issue is "ripe for settlement," and even then, they maintain that the conference is largely for ceremonial purposes. Dean Acheson takes this general view, pointing for his example to the problem raised by the Berlin Blockade in 1948-49.

[10] For a convenient listing and description of various international organizations and their component agencies see D. W. Bowett, *The Law of International Institutions* (London, Stevens, 1963). Also, *Yearbook of International Organizations* (Brussels, Union of International Associations, 1948 —). On the Organization of African Unity see Boutros Butros-Ghali, "The Addis Ababa Charter," *International Conciliation*, No. 546 (January, 1964).

The ending of the blockade of Berlin could never have been brought about by an international conference. Indeed, the intervention of the United Nations was utterly fruitless. The settlement was brought about by signals from Moscow, which were recognized but not proclaimed, and were then followed up by conversations in corridors by persons who appeared to have no authority or connection with the matter at all. It was only after secret negotiations and understanding that public changes of position became possible.[11]

Harold Nicolson likewise finds serious shortcomings in conferences as methods of handling diplomatic problems.[12] The evaluations are no doubt justified in part. At the same time, even considered as means of promoting the settlement of disputes, conferences are sometimes useful.

Much less doubt attends the usefulness of conferences for a variety of other purposes. They are means of exchanging information, coordinating policies, and arranging for cooperation; they are means of testing reactions to a proposed policy and of mobilizing support for a given line of action; and they are means of waging political warfare. All of these purposes—as well as the purpose of settling disputes—show up in a number of the conferences held since World War II, including the meetings of the Security Council and the General Assembly. Sometimes all of them show up more or less simultaneously in connection with the same problem, as when the Security Council and the General Assembly took up North Korea's aggression against South Korea in 1950.

Another purpose of conferences, a purpose of a different sort, is simply to speed the communication and decision process. In fact, it is in this respect that diplomacy by conference differs most clearly from traditional bilateral diplomacy. Diplomatic business has increased so much that it would be extremely cumbersome and inefficient if it all had to be handled in bilateral negotiations. Conferences, by their very nature, bring together the representatives of a number of governments, facilitating communication among them. Each can make its views known to all the others simultaneously and can learn the views of others very quickly. Delegates can seek out informal contacts to whatever extent they please and can engage in informal caucusing and lobbying. Disinterested third parties, if the conference includes any, can provide communication channels as well as suggestions to states that are at odds. Though speed of communication and decision is not always good, for it may lead to hasty action that is later regretted, it is usually desired.

Diplomacy by conference might be judged, too, in terms of its relationship to the unanimity rule, to the principle of state sovereignty, to the development of an international legislature, and to the wisdom of the

11 Dean Acheson, *Meetings at the Summit: A Study in Diplomatic Method* (Durham, The University of New Hampshire, 1958), p. 22.

12 Sir Harold Nicolson, *Diplomacy*, 3rd ed. (New York, Oxford University Press, 1964), esp. pp. 84-87.

actions taken. The usual rule of diplomacy is that each state decides for itself whether or not to take a particular action and whether or not to permit a modification of its legal rights. Of course, its decision, though technically free, may be made under various internal and external pressures. The conference method often adds to the pressures, for good or ill. Some of them come from within the conference itself, where there is pressure to go along with—or at least not to obstruct—the majority. Though a state is free to say no while all the others say yes, it is likely to hesitate before using such freedom; isolation is not ordinarily agreeable. Other pressures come from outside the conference. Public attention in the home countries of the diplomats is likely to focus somewhat more on a conference than on bilateral negotiations, and it is commonly assumed, whether rightly or not, that the public is more concerned with the appearance of agreement than with the terms of agreement. Moreover, governments which are concerned with the issues being discussed at the conference, but which are not represented, will also watch the results. This intensifies pressures for agreement. The various pressures may really produce agreement which might not otherwise have been obtained, or they may induce the statesmen involved to resort to what is called a diplomatic formula—a statement which registers agreement, but which is so vague that no one knows precisely what the agreement is. Each party hopes to have its own meaning read into the agreement later on. This may or may not solve the problem.

In connection with diplomacy by conference there is a strong tendency to modify the unanimity rule formally.[13] As amended, the Charter of the United Nations provides that the Security Council may make its decisions on the basis of nine votes out of the fifteen. On procedural questions any nine votes will suffice, and on nonprocedural questions the nine must include the votes of the permanent members (China, France, Great Britain, the U.S.S.R., and the United States). Either way, the vote of the nine is binding on all fifteen and, for that matter, on all United Nations members. The General Assembly decides some questions by an absolute majority and others by a two-thirds majority; in neither case is there any requirement that the great powers be included in the majority. Theoretically, all the great powers might be in the defeated minority. Similarly, aside from the Security Council and the General Assembly, other international agencies and conferences operate on something other than a unanimity rule.

As we shall see when we discuss the United Nations in later chapters, these qualifications to the general rule that states must consent to measures affecting them are not as important as they appear at first sight. Yet they are not without their significance. The development of diplomacy by

13 Inis L. Claude, Jr., *Swords into Plowshares, The Problems and Progress of International Organization*, 3rd ed. (New York, Random House, 1964), pp. 111-132.

conference is having a corrosive effect on the general rule. The tendency is toward the development of voting rules for conferences that are analogous to the voting rules in parliaments, and the development of such rules is bound to have significant effects. On the one hand, there is danger that the United Nations may be destroyed, for voting power bears so little relationship to other forms of power. In theory, at least, the impoverished and the weak could call for actions and even impose obligations that the wealthy and powerful refuse to undertake. Serious difficulties have already arisen with the Soviet Union, for it refuses to pay assessments voted by the General Assembly to meet the costs of UN operations in the Middle East and the Congo. Especially in view of the admission of so many new states in recent years, the United States also faces the possibility that it might find itself in an unhappy, minority position. On the other hand, the tendency toward qualified majority rule modifies the meaning of sovereignty and suggests the growth of a conception of an international public interest to which national interest must in some degree give way.

## THE CHOICE OF METHODS

In this chapter we have made a brief survey of practices concerning recognition, of ground rules on the basis of which diplomatic relationships are maintained, of the methods of settling international disputes, and of conferences as a method of diplomacy. We divided the methods of settling disputes into those regarded as amicable and those regarded as nonamicable. The amicable means are political, featuring negotiations in which third parties may or may not take part, or judicial. The nonamicable means include measures of retorsion and reprisal, intervention, and war. Diplomacy by conference, though discussed separately, belongs in the category of political methods.

What considerations influence states in their choice of methods? The question will arise repeatedly in subsequent chapters, and we shall attempt only a partial answer here.

The nature of the objective pursued may have considerable influence on the choice of method. At the end of Chapter 10, we described the various categories into which states are sometimes classified—the welfare states and the power states, the "haves" and the "have-nots," the satiated and the unsatiated, the status quo states and the revisionists, the status quo states and the imperialist states. The point was made there that states in the first category in each classification system are inclined toward peaceful methods, and states in the second category are inclined toward aggressive methods, including war.

As a general rule, a status quo state naturally wants to rely on peaceful methods rather than on war. In negotiations, the status quo state is theoretically free to preserve the status quo. It can refuse concessions and reject compromises; as long as the other side restricts itself to peaceful methods, the status quo power is normally in a position to preserve what it wants to preserve. If it feels that it might be at a disadvantage in bilateral negotiations, it can call for third-party participation or seek a general conference, especially if the third party or the members of the conference seem likely to side with it. Or the status quo power is likely to be happy to have disputes settled by judicial means, for the law to be interpreted and applied is itself a part of the status quo.

The revisionist or imperialist power is likely to have the opposite attitudes. If it is strong, it may favor negotiations, and then mix considerable coercion with its efforts to induce concessions. It is likely to prefer bilateral negotiations to those involving third powers, for an isolated state will be more likely to succumb to pressures. It is likely to prefer political rather than judicial methods of settlement, for settlement on the basis of law is not likely to be as favorable as settlement according to power. If the other party stubbornly refuses to make the desired concessions, the strong imperialist power can give more and more signs of a willingness to abandon persuasion and resort to coercion, perhaps to war.

Although helpful and largely true, these generalizations are also hazardous. A status quo power may resort to preventive war if time seems to be on the side of a rising, imperialist power. Moreover, a state which is generally an upholder of the status quo may want to upset a particular aspect of it, and then it will choose the methods of imperialism in a portion of its relationships. Furthermore, the usefulness of these generalizations depends upon the reliability of the classifying process; it is not always possible to tell whether a state is satiated or unsatiated, and even if this could be determined for any one month or year, sudden changes might be brought about by either external or internal developments.

## SUGGESTED READINGS

ACHESON, Dean, *Meetings at the Summit: A Study in Diplomatic Method* (Durham, University of New Hampshire, 1958).

ANAND, Ram Prakash, *Compulsory Jurisdiction of the International Court of Justice* (New York, Asia Publishing House, 1961).

BLOOMFIELD, Lincoln, "Law Politics and International Disputes," *International Conciliation*, No. 516 (January 1958).

BOWETT, D. W., *The Law of International Institutions* (London, Stevens, 1963).

BRAUNIAS, Karl, and STOURZH, Gerald, eds., *Diplomatie Unserer Zeit, Contemporary Diplomacy* (Vienna, Verlag Styria, 1959).

BRIERLY, J. L., *The Outlook for International Law* (Oxford, Clarendon, 1944).

CLAUDE, Inis L., Jr., *Swords Into Plowshares, The Problems and Progress of International Organization*, 3rd ed. (New York, Random House, 1964).

CORBETT, P. E., *Law and Society in the Relations of States* (New York, Harcourt, Brace & World, 1951).

COTTRELL, Alvin J., and DOUGHERTY, James E., *The Politics of the Atlantic Alliance* (New York, Praeger, 1964).

FISHER, Roger, ed., *International Conflict and Behavioral Science. The Craigville Papers* (New York, Basic Books, 1964).

HANKEY, Lord Maurice, *Diplomacy by Conference* (New York, Putnam, 1947).

IKLÉ, Fred Charles, *How Nations Negotiate* (New York, Harper & Row, 1964).

KERTESZ, Stephen D., and FITZSIMONS, M. A., eds., *Diplomacy in a Changing World* (Notre Dame, Ind., University of Notre Dame Press, 1959).

NICOLSON, Sir Harold, *Diplomacy*, 3rd ed. (New York, Oxford University Press, 1964).

——, *The Evolution of Diplomatic Method* (New York, Macmillan, 1955).

PEARSON, Lester B., *Diplomacy in the Nuclear Age* (Cambridge, Harvard University Press, 1959).

ROETTER, Charles, *The Diplomatic Art* (Philadelphia, Macrae Smith, 1963).

ROSENNE, Shabtai, *The International Court of Justice* (Leyden, Sythoff, 1961).

SATOW, Sir Ernest, *A Guide to Diplomatic Practice*, 4th ed., Nevile Bland, ed. (New York, Longmans, 1957).

SCHELLING, Thomas C., *The Strategy of Conflict* (New York, Oxford University Press, 1963).

STOESSINGER, John G., and WESTIN, Alan F., eds., *Power and Order, 6 Cases in World Politics* (New York, Harcourt, Brace & World, 1964).

STONE, Julius, "The International Court and World Crisis," *International Conciliation*, No. 536 (January 1962).

——, *Legal Controls of International Conflict, A Treatise on the Dynamics of Disputes- and War-Law* (New York, Rinehart, 1954).

THAYER, Charles W., *Diplomat* (New York, Harper & Row, 1959).

# INTERNATIONAL LAW, MORALITY, AND PEACEFUL CHANGE

In various chapters we have already made some references to both law and morality. The immediately preceding chapter contained a brief summary of certain legal principles, especially those relating to the exchange of diplomatic agents. In Chapter 2 there was a discussion of the nature of law within countries and an appraisal of its role in preserving domestic peace. Many aspects of international politics involve legal and moral questions.

In this chapter the general object is to appraise law and morality as limitations on the behavior of states and as instruments which they use in pursuing their interests. To what extent and in what ways do they contribute to peace, and why do they not assure peace? What relationships exist between law, morality, peaceful change, and power? To answer such questions we shall consider what international law is, what kinds of rules it contains, how they are brought into existence and enforced, and what purposes they serve. We shall also briefly examine the role of morality in international affairs. The discussion of these topics will provide a suitable background for an analysis of the important problem of peaceful change.

## WHAT IS INTERNATIONAL LAW?

Some doubt that anything exists which deserves to be called international law. The question is hardly worth arguing, for the answer depends upon the definition with which one starts. Some definitions of law —for example, those requiring the existence of a determinate superior enforcing authority—lead to the conclusion that there is nothing which can properly be called international law. Other definitions lead to the opposite conclusion. Since all foreign offices talk and act as if international law exists, it seems best to adopt a definition which permits it to exist. The following is as good as any:

The term international law may fairly be employed to designate the principles and rules of conduct declaratory thereof which states feel themselves bound to observe and, therefore, do commonly observe in their relations with each other.[1]

International law is said to be general when it applies to all states; it is said to be particular when it binds only some of them. Thus customary rules concerning the immunities of diplomatic agents constitute a part of general international law. A bilateral treaty constitutes particular international law, binding only the parties. From another point of view, international law is divided into three branches: the law of peace, the law of war, and the law of neutrality. Students of international law call the whole field of domestic law (national, state, and local) municipal law.

## THE INTERNATIONAL LEGISLATIVE PROCESS

States bring international law into existence mainly through custom and treaties, though judicial agencies and scholarly research do a good deal to clarify and even to expand the law thus established.

### The Development of Customary Law

The process of establishing customary law is somewhat analogous to the one by which English common law was created. If a number of states are repeatedly faced with a particular issue and if they accept the same rule for solving the problem over a considerable period, they establish what is known as a usage. When they begin to follow this rule out of a sense of obligation, the usage is transformed into custom and therefore into law. Or a state may assert a claim of right with regard to an issue and may be willing reciprocally to acknowledge that other states possess the same right. When enough states have acknowledged that the right exists, it becomes a part of international law. It is as difficult to say when states create customary law as it is to say when people who walk across a lawn create a path. No one knows how many states must accept a particular principle for how long a time before a customary rule of law can be said to have been created. At best, however, the process is a slow and uncertain one; a number of decades are likely to be required. Further, there are often so many variations in the circumstances surrounding the

[1] Charles Cheney Hyde, *International Law Chiefly as Interpreted and Applied by the United States* (Boston, Little, Brown, 1945), Vol. I, p. 1.

precedents or the claims of right that customary law is frequently vague or ambiguous.

It has been noted that "such [customary] law as has emerged has rested both theoretically and practically upon a well-nigh universal consent or acquiescence. This is to say, of course, that the law has made substantial progress where there was no substantial controversy. . . ." [2]

## Legislating by Making and Terminating Treaties

Law may be brought into existence more deliberately and more rapidly through treaties and other international agreements.[3] Treaty-making normally includes several steps. First, a treaty is initialed or signed by representatives of the states which expect to become parties to it; this usually follows negotiations among them all, but with treaties of peace may result from the dictation of the winning side. Ratification is the second step, accomplished by each state through its own constitutional processes. Finally, instruments attesting to ratification are exchanged or are deposited with a designated party. If the treaty is between only two states, it normally comes into effect when they exchange ratifications. When many states are involved, the terms of the treaty normally specify how many of them must exchange or deposit instruments of ratification in order to bring it into effect among the ratifying powers. Once a treaty has come into effect, states which were not among the original signatories may be permitted to adhere to it.

As suggested above, a treaty creates law only for those states which become party to it. France and Belgium may make a treaty creating law for themselves, but they cannot thereby add to or take away from the legal rights of the Netherlands. Even if a majority of states adhere to a treaty, they are still creating particular rather than general international law. However, treaties may be designed to be declaratory of existing general law. Further, treaties are said to create general international law when they are ratified by nearly all states. The Kellogg-Briand Pact outlawing war, for example, was ratified by so many states that its principles no doubt constitute a part of general international law. Sometimes treaties ratified by a large number of states are described as constituting "international legislation," but the practice is misleading; actually all treaties, unless they are simply declaratory of existing law, are legislative so far as the parties are concerned.

The principle *pacta sunt servanda* (agreements are to be observed) is a basic one in international law. A state cannot free itself at will from the

---

[2] Edwin D. Dickinson, "International Law: An Inventory," *California Law Review,* Vol. 33 (December, 1945), p. 539.

[3] The term *treaty* is commonly interchangeable with a number of other terms, such as *pact* and *convention.*

obligations of a treaty. Nevertheless, treaties can be terminated, and their termination is an aspect of the legislative process. They may be terminated in accordance with their own terms; for example, the treaty may provide for its expiration after a specified period of years or on notice from one party that it desires termination. They may be terminated by the general consent of the parties; the technical requirement that *all* parties consent is frequently ignored. Violation of the treaty by one party gives the other party a right to denounce it; assuming that respect for treaties is desirable, the difficulty here is that each state decides for itself whether another has violated its obligations, and the judgment rendered may not be unprejudiced. Nazi Germany, for example, presumed to free itself from a number of treaties on the basis of the dubious assertion that another party had previously violated them. Other conditions in which termination is legitimate theoretically exist but rarely occur in practice. A treaty may not be terminated simply because it was initially accepted under duress; otherwise, most treaties of peace would not be binding.

## "Legislative" Functions of Judicial Agencies and Scholars

Theoretically, judicial agencies (the International Court of Justice, arbitral tribunals, and national courts) do not participate in the legislative process. Their task is to determine what the law is, not to create new law. Yet, the very fact that a case has come before a judicial agency usually means that the law is not clear on the point in question, and when a judicial agency clarifies the law or reads meaning into a legal principle, it engages in something closely akin to a law-making function. Theoretically, the research work of scholars does not make law either, but the convenience of their findings and the thoroughness of their work often give them considerable influence on moot points.

## The Problem of Codification

Implicit in the above is the fact that the evidences of law are widely scattered. There is no comprehensive official code to which one can turn to find a statement of what the law is. The Hague Conferences of 1899 and 1907 led to the conclusion of a number of conventions which codified certain portions of international law, notably portions concerned with war and neutrality; many of the rules have, however, become obsolete because of technological and other changes. The League of Nations took it upon itself to promote the codification of international law, and called a conference in 1930 for the purpose of drawing up codes in the three areas deemed most ripe for codification: (1) nationality; (2) territorial waters; and (3) the responsibility of states for damage done in their territory to the person or property of foreigners. The results were meager. A few special conventions on certain questions pertaining to nationality were formulated, but were ratified by only a small number of states. There was much disagreement on the other topics and no comprehensive code was accepted on any of the three.[4] The Charter of the United Nations instructs the General Assembly to "initiate studies and make recommendations for the purpose of . . . encouraging the progressive development of international law and its codification." The task has been assigned to an International Law Commission, which has focused mainly on the law relating to (1) the sea, (2) treaties, (3) the responsibility of states, and (4) the succession of states and governments. Progress has been slow. There were sharp exchanges in the Sixth Committee of the General Assembly in 1960 on the question of an alleged decline in the role of international law and the adequacy of the efforts of the Commission.[5]

## THE SCOPE AND CONTENT OF INTERNATIONAL LAW

Although it would be impossible in a few pages to state the rules of international law which have developed as a result of the legislative process described above, some knowledge of the scope and content of the law is essential to an understanding of international politics.[6] At a number of different points, in fact, we have already been obliged to refer to the legal rules and principles which states accept.

### The Law of Peace

*1. Sources, sanctions, persons.* Textbooks which survey international law commonly include a discussion of the sources and evidences of law, which we have referred to above under the heading of the legislative process. They discuss sanctions, which we shall take up shortly. They define the persons, mainly states, subject to international law, and discuss the rules and principles relating to the birth of states and the recognition and succession of states and governments.

*2. The extent of the national domain.* International law includes rules and principles concerning property and control. States are said to have dominion over territory. The boundaries of a state's domain are fixed under customary law or by treaty. In a surprising number of cases, however, especially in less civilized areas, legal rights to territory are in dispute,

---

[4] Lassa F. L. Oppenheim, *International Law*, 7th ed., Hersh Lauterpacht, ed. (New York, Longmans, 1948-1952), Vol. I, pp. 57-59; P. E. Corbett, *Law and Society in the Relations of States* (New York, Harcourt, Brace & World, 1951), pp. 48-49.

[5] *Yearbook of the United Nations*, 1960, pp. 547-549.

[6] The article by Dickinson, cited in footnote 2 above, contains a good brief survey of international law. See also J. L. Brierly, *The Law of Nations* (New York, Oxford, 1963).

and in many other cases one state asserts a political claim to territory in the possession of another. There is agreement that the domain of maritime states includes a maritime belt, but disagreement on the width of the belt. Rules governing the use of straits, international waterways like the Suez Canal, and international rivers are commonly fixed by treaties. The air space above a state is under its exclusive control; among other things, this means that aircraft from one state may legally fly over the territory of another only with its consent and under such regulations as it chooses to impose. Questions pertaining to the law of outer space are new. The high seas, outside the domain of any state, are said to be free. Various legal methods exist, of course, by which states may acquire additional territory; the law includes rules concerning the transfer of rights and obligations when one state takes over all or part of the territory of another.

3. *Jurisdiction and its limits.* Within the national domain states enjoy very extensive freedom and, with minor qualifications, exercise exclusive jurisdiction. Under general international law they have retained the right to deal with domestic affairs as they see fit, even in many areas where their actions have profound implications for foreign states and peoples. They remain free to adopt the political and economic system of their choice; whether a government is fascist or communist or liberal, or whether the economy is socialized or free, makes no difference in general international law. With minor qualifications governments may adopt whatever domestic policies they choose to adopt, and may make actions within their borders legal or illegal as they wish; each state has exclusive police power within its own territory. Governments may permit the private manufacture of armaments on an unlimited scale and may themselves manufacture whatever armaments they can. They may allow or engage in the exportation and importation of armaments. They may maintain armed establishments of any composition and size, and may locate all or part of their armed establishment on the vulnerable border of another state. Pistols and thermonuclear weapons are on the same plane, so far as general international law is concerned. Governments are free to regulate the movement of goods, capital, and persons across national frontiers, even though the regulations inflict injury abroad.

There are, of course, limitations on the jurisdictional rights of a state even within its own domain. A large body of law exists regulating the treatment of agents of one state who enter the domain of another. Foreign diplomats and consuls, for example, are largely immune from the jurisdiction of the state in which they operate. War vessels paying a friendly visit in a foreign port remain under the jurisdiction of the flag state. Merchant ships in a foreign port come under the jurisdiction of the foreign state for some purposes and remain under the jurisdiction of the flag state for other purposes. Jurisdiction over the maritime belt is qualified by the requirement that foreign vessels be granted a right of "innocent passage." On the high seas, each state asserts jurisdiction over ships flying its flag, but such jurisdiction is not exclusive; it is shared to an uncertain extent with other maritime states, which assert jurisdiction even over foreign vessels where they consider it necessary for their safety or the enforcement of their laws.

The jurisdiction of a state extends over its nationals abroad, and even for some purposes over nonnationals abroad, though enforcement of this jurisdiction is often impossible. Through treaties, states generally accept an obligation to extradite those found under their jurisdiction who have fled from justice in another state, though a right to grant asylum to political refugees is recognized.

*4. Other topics.* International law also deals with the problem of determining the nationality of persons and with the problems which may arise when the same person is a national of two or more states. States commonly extend diplomatic protection to their nationals abroad, and this practice has given rise to an extensive body of law concerning the responsibility of states for injury to aliens or for damage to their property. We shall refer to this subject again.

Another important area of international law is concerned with intergovernmental communication, particularly with rules and regulations governing the status and treatment of diplomats. As we have already indicated, international law also fixes rules and procedures for the conclusion and termination of agreements among states and for the settlement of disputes which arise among them.

Increasingly, states have been concluding treaties assuring a wide variety of protections to individuals. Many of them, concerning labor and working conditions, have been concluded through the International Labor Organization. More broadly, "human rights" of various sorts have come to be recognized. The Universal Declaration of Human Rights, to be discussed in Chapter 21, deals with both the civil and political rights traditional in the Western world and also with economic and social rights; though designed to set forth "a common standard of achievement" toward which signatories would aspire, a number of states have accepted many of the principles as obligatory. A genocide convention is in force, prohibiting such measures as those which Hitler directed against the Jews.

## The Law of War

The above topics are covered in the law of peace. States have also allowed a "law of war" to develop, regulating the conduct of hostilities and the treatment of enemy nationals and their property. They have, however, reserved the right to act in conformity with military necessity, regardless of the law; moreover, they have had difficulty in keeping the law adjusted to changing technological conditions. As scientific developments bring new weapons into existence and permit the adoption of more effective military strategies, those rules concerning the conduct of hostilities which are rendered obsolete receive scant attention.

## The Law of Neutrality

Along with the law of war, states have developed a "law of neutrality," defining the rights and obligations of neutrals and belligerents in relationships with each other. A state is neutral when it does not participate in a war which is in progress and when it treats the belligerents impartially. The law of neutrality represents a compromise between the desire of neutrals to keep wartime interference with normal practices and pursuits at a minimum and the desire of belligerents to prevent the enemy from bolstering its strength by receiving supplies or other forms of aid from foreign sources. It gives no assurance that the neutral will refrain from entering the war or that the belligerent will refrain from attacking. Neutrals have in fact frequently abandoned their neutrality and have become belligerents; belligerents have frequently decided that they could gain more by attacking a neutral than by respecting its rights. But the law of neutrality facilitates the preservation of peace between neutrals and belligerents when both desire peace. It minimizes the possibility that the war will be extended simply because of the absence of rules on the basis of which special wartime conflicts of interest can be resolved.

## The Law Concerning Resort to War

Aside from concluding treaties vaguely pledging friendship and eternal peace, the various states did not permit the development of any serious legal restriction on their freedom to go to war until after World War I. When they chose to be at peace with each other, the law of peace prevailed; when they chose to go to war, the laws of war and neutrality came into operation. The law was indifferent to the choice which was made. Thus a monstrous situation existed in which states were "legally bound to respect each other's independence and other rights, and yet free to attack each other at will." [7] States were entitled to rights, provided that other states did not take them away by war. Moreover, since the law recognized the freedom of states to go to war, it could scarcely be clear in prohibiting coercive measures short of war. On many occasions, states resorted to intervention (dictatorial interference) in the affairs of other states, thus infringing on their independence or other rights, and the problem of classifying acts of intervention as legal or illegal was a vexing one.

The Covenant of the League of Nations severely restricted the freedom of the members of the League to resort to war, though leaving "gaps"

[7] J. L. Brierly, *The Outlook for International Law* (Oxford, Clarendon, 1944), p. 21.

through which war might legally be waged. Nearly all the states of the world ratified the Kellogg-Briand Pact of 1928. In it the parties "condemn recourse to war for the solution of international controversies, and renounce it as an instrument of national policy." Further, they pledge never to seek the settlement of any dispute except by pacific means. Similarly, the United Nations Charter binds the members to "settle their international disputes by peaceful means" and to "refrain in their international relations from the threat or use of force against the territorial integrity or political independence of any state."

It is obvious that these treaties have not prevented states from resorting to war. We shall discuss some of the reasons for the failure later on. Suffice it to point out here that a right of self-defense is always assumed. The Charter explicitly provides that nothing in it "shall impair the inherent right of individual or collective self-defense if an armed attack occurs. . . ." In practice, states regularly claim to be fighting in self-defense, however flimsy the claim may be. Moreover, war may arise out of essentially domestic struggles, as when two governments claim jurisdiction in the same state and when each of them secures the aid of outside states in attempting to vindicate its claim. Further, when a belief exists that justice or vital interests can be promoted or protected effectively only by the threat or use of force, the strain on obligations to eschew force is very great.

<h2 style="text-align:center">RESPECT FOR LAW AND THE<br>ENFORCEMENT OF LAW</h2>

### Voluntary Observance

By and large, international law is freely observed. The methods by which it is established suggest that this would be so. Customary law develops out of the practice of states, reflecting rules which they have proved themselves willing to observe. As Brierly puts it, ". . . states have only allowed [customary] law to control their relations in matters which, though they are not unimportant in themselves, are of secondary importance, and therefore present them with no very strong temptation to defy it." [8] Most treaties are also concluded on a thoroughly voluntary basis, establishing rules of action which the parties expect to be of benefit to them. States thus commonly observe law because they find it advantageous to do so.

Nevertheless, disputes arise. They do not arise so much because of deliberate defiance of the law, for this is relatively rare, as because of vagueness or ambiguity in the law, or because, on many questions, alternative legal principles are applicable. Where vagueness or ambiguity or alternative choices exist, it is rather natural, even when two states are equally

[8] *Ibid.*, p. 17.

willing to observe the law, that each will take the legal stand which is most advantageous to it.[9] Moreover, each state may be so convinced of the rightness of its own stand that it will regard the different stand of the other party as contrary to law.

## Sanctions and Self-help

Respect for international law does not depend entirely on the willingness of states to abide by it. Action designed to induce respect can occur, that is, sanctions can be applied. A wide variety of sanctioning measures are available. A state which seeks to induce another to observe the law may protest an impending or actual violation. If it chooses, it may threaten and take retaliatory action of various kinds. Among the possibilities are the severance of diplomatic relations, a boycott of the products of the offending state, an embargo on the shipment of some or all goods to that state, a prohibition of loans to it, or a freezing of its assets. Sanctioning measures may also take the form of military action. The United States has on many occasions intervened militarily in certain Latin American countries, occupying some or all of their territory, to prevent or terminate what it regarded as a violation of international law; some other great powers have done the same thing. Blockades have been used. If the offending state chooses to fight back against the military force brought to bear upon it, the ensuing hostilities may or may not be regarded as war. When the initial violation of law takes the form of a military invasion, war is the likely result, and, from the point of view of the invaded state, the war will be designed as a sanction of law. Sanctioning measures short of war can be classified as measures of retorsion or reprisal, defined in the preceding chapter.

Assuming the desirability of law and order in international affairs, it is obviously objectionable to have the offended state stand over the offending state as policeman, prosecutor, judge, jury, and executioner. It is as if, within countries, each individual were allowed to decide for himself whether his rights were threatened or violated, and, if so, to take such preventive or punitive action as he saw fit. The principle that every man defines and defends his own rights is a principle that prevails only in societies without effective government, which is precisely the characteristic of the society of nations.

Of course, disputing states have always been free, on the basis of mutual consent, to refer disputes over their respective rights to arbitration, and they have often availed themselves of this procedure. Since the establishment of the Permanent Court of International Justice after World War I and the International Court of Justice after World War II, the voluntary

[9] Frederick Sherwood Dunn, *The Protection of Nationals* (Baltimore, Johns Hopkins Press, 1932), pp. 25-26; Brierly, *The Law of Nations*, pp. 71-78.

submission of disputes to adjudication has also been easily possible. As indicated in the preceding chapter, many states have accepted the optional clause of the Court's Statute, binding themselves in advance to submit legal disputes to the Court. Thus, if states are willing to do so, they can avoid sitting in judgment on their own cause and can, instead, secure the presumably impartial judgment of a third party. Even so, however, the enforcement of a judgment is left to the benefited state. Neither an arbitral tribunal nor the International Court of Justice has the right or power to apply sanctions. The absence of such a right is not as serious as it might be, however, for when states accept third-party judgment they also normally accept the results; enforcement action is rarely needed.

## Sanctions through Alliances and Regional Organizations

Sanctions are sometimes provided for and imposed not simply by the offended state but by a number of states in an alliance or in a regional organization. For example, according to the Rio Pact of 1947, the Organ of Consultation of the Inter-American System may agree on the sanctions that members are to impose in case any one of them is the victim of an armed attack or is endangered in various other ways. In 1964 the Organ actually called for sanctions after finding Cuba guilty of "an aggression and an intervention . . . in the internal affairs of Venezuela." It asked the governments of the American republics not to maintain diplomatic and consular relations with Cuba and to suspend all trade with Cuba and all sea transportation between their territories and Cuba, except where humanitarian considerations dictated otherwise. The Rio Pact, however, does not curtail the right of self-help; it provides simply for supplementing it.

## Sanctions Under the United Nations

The proposition that each state is its own policeman, prosecutor, judge, jury, and executioner has been modified by various treaties, such as the League of Nations Covenant, the Kellogg-Briand Pact, and the United Nations Charter, restricting the freedom of states to resort to war. Under the United Nations Charter members are free to enforce respect for their rights only so long as they confine themselves to peaceful means, except in a case of self-defense against armed attack. When there is a "threat to the peace, breach of the peace, or act of aggression" the United Nations itself becomes concerned. The Security Council may identify the guilty state. The guilty state may be the one which is trying to enforce respect for its rights, if the means used are impermissible, or the one which is threatening or infringing upon the rights of another. Once the guilty state has been identified, the Security Council may call upon members of the United Nations to apply sanctions against it. Article 41 of the Charter specifies that these measures "may include complete or partial interruption of economic relations and of rail, sea, air, postal, telegraphic, radio, and other means of communication, and the severance of diplomatic relations." If these measures are not adequate, the Security Council under Article 42 "may take such action by air, sea, or land forces as may be necessary to maintain or restore international peace and security. Such action may include demonstrations, blockade, and other operations by air, sea, or land forces of Members of the United Nations." Similarly, the General Assembly may recommend sanctions, though it has no right or power to order them.

In short, under the United Nations Charter each state still defines and defends its own rights. But where the issue is serious, peaceful settlement must be sought, and in the event of threats to the peace, breaches of the peace, and acts of aggression the sanctioning measures taken by a member may be reinforced through action of the Organization. This subject—the role of the United Nations and the principle of "collective security" —will be discussed more fully in a later chapter.

## Strains on Treaty Obligations

The problem of maintaining respect for treaty obligations is often a special one. Strains on treaty obligations are often very great, especially as concerns treaties which affect the power position of a state or other interests which it regards as vital. Dictated treaties of peace offer an extreme illustration; imposed through violence, they are likely to be defied when the victor loses either the strength or the determination to enforce their terms. E. H. Carr speaks more generally on the subject:

> The element of power is inherent in every political treaty. The contents of such a treaty reflect in some degree the relative strength of the contracting parties. Stronger states will insist on the sanctity of the treaties concluded by them with weaker states. Weaker states will renounce treaties concluded by them with stronger states so soon as the power position alters and the weaker state feels itself strong enough to reject or modify the obligation.[10]

Even after treaties have been quite voluntarily accepted, states sometimes conclude that they will gain more by violating than by observing them. This is especially true of treaties of alliance; a state which finds that time has seriously reduced the benefits of an alliance or increased its risks is not likely to abide by its obligation.

[10] E. H. Carr, *The Twenty Years' Crisis 1919-1939* (New York, Harper & Row, 1964), p. 190.

Since the possible effect of an alliance is to draw a third party into a war which is not of his doing, the strain on the treaty is very great unless *both* allies feel at the time that they are equally threatened. It seems too much to expect that a nation which has no interest in the outcome of a war will risk its very life merely to fulfill a promise contained in a treaty of alliance.[11]

One of the fears associated with proposals to outlaw the possession of nuclear bombs is that the temptation to violate the agreement would be too great to be resisted.

In a world made bombless by treaty, the first to violate the treaty would gain an enormous advantage. Under such conditions the opportunities for world dominance would be breathtaking! Hence we come to the paradox that the further the nations go by international agreement in the direction of eliminating bombs and installations, the stronger becomes the temptation to evade the agreement.[12]

Machiavelli's advice was that "a prudent ruler ought not to keep faith when by so doing it would be against his interest and when the reasons which made him bind himself no longer exist." The injunction seems to deny that prudent rulers should ever be moved simply by a desire to maintain good faith. In practice states comonly regard it as one of their interests that the principle *pacta sunt servanda* should be maintained. They know that, if they violate treaties, others will do the same. And a world in which no state's word could be counted on would be an undesirable world for all. This is not to say that treaties are always honored. Violations do occur, but they are the exception rather than the rule.

## THE FUNCTIONS OF LAW

International law is useful to states. If it were not useful, they would not have created it, nor would they be adding to it and clarifying it as time goes on. In what ways is it useful? Is it equally useful to all? What role does law play in world affairs?

### Law Within Countries as the Instrument of the Strong

In Chapter 2 we gave a partial answer to these questions in relation to the political struggle within countries. Some of what was said there needs now to be recalled.

The general theme there developed was that law is largely an instrument of the strong, reflecting the desires of the strong. The theme was

11 Frederick Sherwood Dunn, "The Common Problem," in Bernard Brodie, ed., *The Absolute Weapon* (New York, Harcourt, Brace & World, 1946), p. 9.
12 *Ibid.*, p. 15.

similar to one advanced by Rousseau, that "the spirit of the laws of all
countries is always to favor the strong against the weak and him that has
against him that has not." [13] The notion that there can be a "rule of law,
and not of men" was rejected. The contention was that even under the
rule of law, law remains an instrument of men; more specifically, it is
used by those men who command power. Although their power may derive from different sources, such as control over wealth, control over skills,
or adherence to ideas which command support, it is ultimately expressed
in force and violence. As Brierly puts it, "There is no such phenomenon
in human society as 'the rule of law' in the literal sense of that term;
force rules always. . . ." [14]

## Strength and Law in Unstable Countries

This view of politics and of the role of law is most easily illustrated by
reference to countries which are politically unstable. In some countries of
Latin America and in some in the Middle East control over government
(and therefore over law-making and law-enforcing authority) is commonly
obtained by those who command a preponderance of violence; the correlation between political power and military power is direct and plain.
When a person or group which has seized control of the government loses
command over a preponderance of violence, a revolution or *coup d'état*
is likely; through it, those who have somehow gained control over a preponderance of violence achieve political power, which means that they
achieve law-making and law-enforcing authority. They can enact or
amend law as they please. It will reflect their desires. The truth of this is
not changed if they choose to buttress their political power by shaping the
law so as to placate those who might otherwise rebel against them.

Every civil war provides an illustration of the proposition that the law
is a reflection of the desires of the strong. When the Bolsheviks achieved
victory in Russia, they obviously changed the law to make it reflect their
will. The outcome of the Civil War in Spain in the late 1930's gave law-
making authority to Franco. Civil war in China determined that the
Communists would rule. Often, also, governments retain law-making and
law-enforcing authority not because their actions reflect the desires of
most of the people whom they rule but because revolutionary elements
are unable to muster sufficient military power to make rebellion feasible.

## Strength and Law in Democratic Countries

What of countries like the United States and Britain, where scarcely a
thought is given to the possibility of civil war? Does the law here likewise

[13] Carr, *op. cit.*, p. 176.
[14] *The Outlook for International Law*, pp. 73-74.

reflect the desires of the strong? The answer must be that it does, but the strong must be identified in several ways.

1. *The strong defined as those sharing the constitutional consensus.* The outstanding characteristic of stable, democratic societies is that a moral and constitutional consensus exists, accepted and supported by practically the entire population. This means that the population shares fundamental desires and values, including the desire that governmental affairs shall be conducted in accordance with agreed constitutional procedures and within agreed constitutional limitations. On the level of fundamental principles and procedures, then, the strong include all those who share the consensus. Their strength is so great and so nearly uncontested that it is forgotten. When all agree—when violence is not needed —the fact that it is available fades from men's minds.

2. *The strong defined as the winners in elections.* On the level of action under the constitution, the strong are identified and defined somewhat differently. At least in democratic countries, strength is measured in terms of votes. The more votes a party wins the stronger it is said to be and the more nearly complete does its control over law-making become. With sufficient electoral support, it can bring about drastic legislative and even constitutional changes. When no one person or no one monolithic party wins complete control over government, the law must reflect a compromise or adjustment of the desires of competing groups. This appears most clearly in a parliamentary democracy where a coalition controls the government and where legislation necessarily reflects bargaining among parties in the coalition. Collectively they are the strong, but their strength is qualified both by the existence of an opposition and by some degree of disunity among themselves. Compromise on the law becomes essential, and it comes to reflect common elements in the desires of various groups.

Whether strength is defined in terms of command over violence or in terms of command over votes, it should not be assumed that the desires of the strong necessarily go against the desires of the weak. In some areas, the desires of the two coincide, and then the law will serve what is generally regarded as the common good. Moreover, when the strong face an opposition and when they are more or less divided among themselves, compromises and adjustments prevent the law from reflecting the narrow desires of any one group.

3. *The strong defined as the victors in civil war.* Though command over violence may fade into the background in a democratic society operating under a constitutional consensus, the importance of violence should not be ignored. In a large society, no consensus is ever complete. At a minimum, there will be criminal elements which reject it, and it is taken for granted that they are to be suppressed. Probably, too, there will be political elements which reject some or all aspects of the constitutional consensus. Sometimes this leads to a gradual change in the consensus

through a process of agreement, but when the challenge to the consensus is revolutionary (as the Communist challenge is, for example), the challengers are considered subversive. As such, they may or may not be tolerated. When they are suppressed, the act reflects strength, even though expressed by legal means. If they are not suppressed and if, instead, they gain great strength themselves, force and violence are likely to come to the fore again as the ultimate means of determining whose will is to prevail. As many revolutions attest, the counting of votes or the use of other peaceful devices for determining who is entitled to exercise law-making and law-enforcing authority provides only a tentative decision. The tentative decision may prevail, but if it is challenged the ultimate decision will be made on the battlefield.

## Strength and Law in International Politics

If the above statements are true of the relationship between strength and law within countries, are they also true in the international realm? The answer must be in the affirmative.

*1. The strong and treaty law.* The most obvious and clear-cut illustration of the relationship between strength and law in international politics comes at the end of a war between two states when one is at the mercy of the other. The victor dictates terms. The situation is complicated a little if the winning side is a coalition of states of varying strength. The coalition as a whole dictates terms, but what governs the relative influence of its members? Again power is crucial if not decisive. A quick reading of the history of the peacemaking process after the Napoleonic Wars and both World Wars indicates that the militarily weak members of the winning side have relatively little influence; the stronger members bargain among themselves, weapons in hand, over the terms to impose. Threats of war among them are not unusual, and a state that is in a position to take what it wants commonly gets it, perhaps by consent. If there has been no victor, belligerents from both sides presumably share in fixing the terms of settlement, and the terms agreed upon are likely to reflect their respective calculations of what they could take should the war go on.

In peacetime the role of power in determining treaty law is rarely as clear-cut. In fact, peacetime treaties often reflect the common desires of the parties. Where differing desires exist, however, the stronger usually have an advantage, whether they exert strength through the "big stick" or the "sugar stick"; in the geographical region where the Soviet Union can most easily bring its power to bear, it has both imposed treaties on the weak and prevented them from concluding treaties that were objectionable. Other great powers have acted similarly.

*2. The strong and customary law.* The best statement about customary law is probably that the strong can prevent its development. The rules of law that are created through usage, or through the assertion of a claim of right on the basis of reciprocity, must be rules that are at least acceptable to the powerful. If they reject the usage, they prevent it from crystallizing into law, and if they deny the asserted right it is doubtful that it can be established. Customary law may reflect the desires and interests of all states; it may be in the common good, but the crucial fact is that it is acceptable to the strong.

The above is obviously true if "the strong" include all of the major powers. But can any one of them, e.g., the Soviet Union, prevent the development of a customary law? Probably so. At least it can refuse to guide its own behavior by what others cite as newly developed customary law. The problem has arisen most clearly in the United Nations. The Charter specifies that in the Security Council nine affirmative votes are required, including the concurring votes of the permanent members, if certain kinds of resolutions are to be enacted. But what if a permanent member abstains from voting? In the early years of the United Nations the Soviet Union or any other permanent member could surely have maintained that its abstention killed any resolution to which this voting rule was applicable. But neither the Soviet Union nor any other permanent member took this view. They all joined in accepting a customary rule that, though a negative vote would kill the resolution, an abstention would not. Then when the Korean crisis came along in 1950 (at a time when the Soviet delegate was boycotting the sessions of the Security Council) the question arose whether an absence was equivalent to an abstention. The others said yes and proceeded to enact resolutions directed against North Korea. The Soviet Union said no and claimed that the resolutions were not legally enacted. In this situation, can it be said that a customary law developed against the opposition of the Soviet Union? This ambiguous situation is made all the more so by the fact that the Soviet Union has not consistently taken the view that the absence of the delegate of a permanent member precludes legal action.

The powerful cannot create customary law quite as readily as they can prevent its creation, but when they are not divided against each other the possibility exists. They have substantially had their way, for example, on the question of an international standard of justice concerning the treatment of aliens. Weak and ill-governed countries have generally taken the view that aliens are on the same basis as citizens so far as the protection of the laws is concerned, entitled only to local remedies for any injury allegedly done to them; in other words, they have held that aliens can expect only such justice as the local law provides, and that other states have no right to insist on any other standard. Powerful states (the United States among them) have refused to accept this principle, asserting that there is a minimum international standard of justice which all states are to be expected to meet. They have extended diplomatic protection to their nationals abroad, interceding verbally and sometimes resorting to military intervention to make sure that justice was done. Faced with such attitudes and actions, the weak have perforce succumbed to the pressures of the strong. They have had to accept the dictation of the strong and, in a sense, have been fortunate when the strong chose law rather than overt force and violence as the instrument of their will.

There is no reason at all to believe that, in the absence of the institution [of diplomatic protection], the stronger states would have been content to stand by and do nothing while their citizens in Latin American countries were receiving treatment which appeared unjust or improper. . . . In other parts of the world, territorial conquest was then taking place on much slighter provocation than was being offered in some Latin American countries. . . . The legal institution of diplomatic protection, in other words, served as a substitute for territorial conquest in bringing the Latin American states within the orbit of international trade and intercourse. . . .[15]

Powerful states have thus contributed significantly to the development of law concerning diplomatic protection and international claims; in particular circumstances they have forced acceptance of legal principles which took the place of outright violence in the achievement of their desires.

3. *Some qualifications.* The proposition that the law reflects the desires of the strong must be qualified in relation to international law just as in relation to municipal law. On some points the strong and weak agree. Further, quite obviously, the powerful states are rarely united in determining the content of the law. Rather, divided against each other, they sometimes adjust their conflicts by accepting legal principles that weak states can later invoke in their own favor. Moreover, powerful states struggling with each other may seek the support of weaker states, and may therefore champion principles that the weaker states likewise favor. The strong are not, in fact, always guided by narrow and ruthless self-interest. They commonly prefer that their self-interest be "enlightened"; the term is vague, but it presumably involves a belief that self-interest is best served through some regard for the desires and interests of others in the society. Moreover, the strong join others in claiming to act in accordance with the requirements of morality and justice; though definitions of the moral and the just often differ, they also often include common elements. The result is that international law does not bestow its favors quite as unequally as the general proposition suggests. Treaties, and above all treaties of peace, often discriminate harshly against the weak, but many rules of law serve the weak as well as the strong. More or less unwittingly, the power struggle often produces rules which reflect common interests.

---

[15] Dunn, *The Protection of Nationals*, pp. 57-58.

## The Uses of Law

In which ways is law useful? The answer can be the same whether with reference to international or to municipal law. Law helps to establish and preserve order and regularity in public affairs. It permits prediction of the consequences of certain acts and warns subjects of the law not to commit those acts which would be followed by consequences they wish to avoid. It "is a means of enabling the day-to-day business of states to be conducted in normal times along orderly and predictable lines, and that is no small service." [16] Where the law is clear, it reduces the possibility that conflicting legal claims will be advanced, and it thus reduces the occasion for friction. To the extent that it promotes order and regularity in public affairs, it provides a framework within which commercial, cultural, and personal interchange can occur and interdependence can develop; such interchange and interdependence may, of course, lead to friction, but it also may create or reinforce common bonds, contributing to the development of a society. Finally, it should be noted that throughout history those who have made and enforced law have sought to make it hallowed. They have sought to inculcate the idea that obedience to law is a virtue. To the extent that they have succeeded, a final function can be assigned to the law: that it carries an air of sanctity and therefore lends sanctity even to the achievements of force and violence.[17]

## THE ROLE OF MORALITY

What role do principles of morality play, either as a limitation on the actions of states or as an instrument for promoting national advantage?

Although those acting in the name of states may sometimes do things which they themselves regard as immoral, it is reasonable to assume that this is uncommon. Certainly statesmen regularly claim that they act in accordance with high moral principles. As a general rule, it can be assumed that the moral principles endorsed by decision-makers influence the decisions they make. People commonly act in accordance with their conception of the good and the right.

### The Tendency Toward Egocentric Definitions of the Good and Right

But within what frame of reference are the good and the right defined? And what definitions are arrived at? If all those who influence decisions affecting international relations were inspired and guided by a desire to promote the good and the right equally for all mankind, and if their

16 Brierly, *The Outlook for International Law*, p. 17.
17 Cf. George W. Keeton and Georg Schwarzenberger, *Making International Law Work* (London, Stevens, 1946), pp. 31-48.

conceptions of the good and the right coincided, the world would be far different than it is. In fact, the tendency is very strong to focus on the nation or state, rather than on all mankind, in defining the good and the right; it is the national society which counts primarily, rather than a putative world society. There is a very marked reluctance to take the view that the nation or state is a unit in a world society whose good transcends the good of its individual parts.[18] The result is that those who act in the name of the state tend to regard the state as an end in itself. Supreme moral value becomes attached to such objectives as the establishment, the preservation, and perhaps the aggrandizement of the nation-state, to the way of life and the ideology for which the state stands, and to the welfare or prosperity of some or all the people within the state.

### The Morality of Satiated States

Given the national frame of reference within which the requirements of morality are defined, it is not surprising that there should be a correlation between the desires of a government and the moral principles it accepts. States which are satiated, or states which in the main wish to preserve the status quo, generally place a high moral value on peace. Thus the French Foreign Minister, Aristide Briand, speaking in the days when France was favored by the Treaty of Versailles, declared that "peace comes before all; peace comes even before justice." [19] Thus also Prime Minister Neville Chamberlain of Britain, faced with Hitler's challenge to the status quo, declared that

His Majesty's Government have constantly advocated the adjustment, by way of free negotiation between the parties concerned, of any difficulties that may arise between them. . . . In their opinion there should be no question incapable of solution by peaceful means, and they would see no justification for the substitution of force or threats of force for the method of negotiation.[20]

There is no need to doubt the sincerity of either Briand or Chamberlain; at the same time it can scarcely be pure coincidence that the moral values which they espoused tended to reinforce the favored positions which their countries held.

### The Morality of Unsatiated States

Hitler was not impressed by the morality of the status quo powers.

. . . Either the wealth of the world is divided by force, in which case this division will be recorrected from time to time by force.

[18] Carr, *op. cit.*, pp. 166-169; see also Hans J. Morgenthau, *In Defense of the National Interest* (New York, Knopf, 1951), and George F. Kennan, *Realities of American Foreign Policy* (Princeton, N.J., Princeton University Press, 1954), pp. 47, 50.
[19] Carr, *op. cit.*, p. 73.
[20] Neville Chamberlain, *In Search of Peace* (New York, Putnam, 1939), p. 279.

Or else the division is based on grounds of equity and therefore also of common sense. . . .

But to assume that God has permitted some nations first to acquire a world by force and then to defend this robbery with moralizing theories is perhaps comforting and above all comfortable for the "haves," but for the "have-nots" it is just as unimportant as it is uninteresting and lays no obligation upon them. . . . At bottom it is only a question of power, in which common sense and justice receive no consideration.[21]

Rejecting the moral conceptions of the satisfied states, Hitler advanced moral conceptions of his own. He said that the "folkish" view

. . . by no means believes in an equality of the races, but with their differences it also recognizes their superior and inferior values, and by this recognition it feels the obligation in accordance with the Eternal Will that dominates this universe to promote the victory of the better and stronger, and to demand the submission of the worse and the weaker. . . . It cannot grant the right of existence to an ethical idea, if this idea represents a danger for the racial life of the bearers of higher ethics. . . .

Hitler also declared that "peoples which bastardize themselves, or permit themselves to be bastardized, sin against the will of eternal Providence, and their ruin by the hand of a stronger nation is consequently not an injustice that is done to them, but only the restoration of right." [22]

Similarly the Communists, dissatisfied with a status quo in which capitalism survives, adopt a moral outlook which permits resort to revolution and war to accomplish their purposes. Thus Lenin long ago declared that "if war is waged by the proletariat after it has conquered the bourgeoisie in its own country and is waged with the object of strengthening and extending socialism, such a war is legitimate and 'holy.' " [23] Along the same line, Lenin and Stalin both included among "just wars" those wars which are waged "to liberate people from capitalist slavery or . . . to liberate colonies and dependent countries from the yoke of imperialism."

## Egocentric Morality as a Limit on Behavior

The existence of divergent conceptions of morality does not necessarily mean that morality is without effect in limiting the behavior of states. As suggested above, the adoption of moral principles implies the voluntary acceptance of certain limitations on conduct. Hitler's moral principles permitted him to seek the extermination of the Jews, but not the extermination of Danes and Norwegians. Moral principles now prevailing in the United States render an attack upon Canada unthinkable and pre-

---

[21] Adolf Hitler, *Speech Delivered in the Reichstag January 30th, 1939* (Berlin, Müller, n.d.), pp. 27-29.
[22] Adolf Hitler, *Mein Kampf* (New York, Reynal & Hitchcock, 1939), pp. 452, 579-580.
[23] See above, pp. 79-80.

clude any attempt to establish imperial control over Latin America. Many Englishmen favored granting dominion status to India and Pakistan because they regarded the action as morally right and even imperative. Moral principles endorsed by the Soviet Union did not prevent it from seizing eastern Poland in 1939, but they caused considerable discomfort in those who had to concoct a justification of the action.

## Egocentric and International Morality

Neither does the existence of divergent conceptions of morality necessarily mean that morality is exclusively national. International morality exists just as international law exists, consisting of moral principles which a number of states endorse. In fact, customary international law is to quite an extent a reflection of principles of morality which states jointly accept; it is sanctioned international morality. Similarly, the United Nations Charter reflects international morality in many of its provisions—for example, in calling for respect for human rights and fundamental freedoms without distinction as to race, sex, language, or religion. The moral desirability of peace is formally affirmed almost universally, though with provisos and conditions attached.

Those rules of morality which have not crystallized into law are even more vague and ambiguous than those which have. Moreover, as in connection with law, there are often several moral principles which are applicable in a concrete situation, permitting choice of the one to be stressed. The result is that national governments are left with considerable discretion in interpreting the requirements of international morality. In the exercise of this discretion, the decision-makers within a country may find it expedient to give heed to moral conceptions held abroad, for it is not always safe to commit acts which foreign governments and peoples regard as morally outrageous; still, the interpretation of the requirements of international morality is likely to be influenced primarily by the moral outlook prevailing at home.

The vague nature of what Carr calls the "code" of international morality is indicated by the following statements:

One of the most important and clearly recognized items in this code is the obligation not to inflict *unnecessary* death or suffering on other human beings, i.e., death or suffering not necessary for the attainment of some higher purpose which is held, rightly or wrongly, to justify a derogation from the general obligation.[24]

When is the infliction of death or suffering "necessary"? What "higher purpose" may justify it? These questions are answered, in the first instance at least, by national governments. They are guided by some widely

[24] Carr, *op. cit.*, p. 154.

accepted standards, a number of which have crystallized into law, but considerable freedom of choice remains. It is needless to say that the "higher purpose" which is taken to justify the infliction of death or suffering is likely to be a national purpose.

Moral issues arise most urgently in relation to war. As a practical matter, governments can scarcely take the view that war *per se* is immoral, but they have accepted moral (and legal) limits on methods of waging it. One of the limits long accepted was that a military action should not be undertaken with the primary, direct intent of killing noncombatants. The innocent were not to be killed as a means of getting at the guilty. But in World War II both sides deliberately bombed urban centers. Britain and the United States engaged in saturation area bombing in Germany. The United States destroyed Japanese cities with explosive and incendiary bombs, and obliterated Hiroshima and Nagasaki with atomic bombs. The development of thermonuclear weapons and missile delivery systems now makes it possible that all the major cities of the United States and the Soviet Union might be wiped out in the first hours of a war, with tens of millions of people killed. Depending on the kinds of bombs used and the way the wind blows, radioactive fallout might kill many millions in neutral countries. What of the morality of the World War II practices and of the possibilities for the future? We will discuss the question in the chapter on "The Utility of War."

## The Universal Validity of Egocentric Principles

The observations made above on the role of morality in international politics involve no judgment on whether there are absolute and universally applicable moral standards which spring from either divine or natural sources. For present purposes there is no need to make such a judgment. Regardless of the existence or nonexistence of absolute moral standards, the fact is that the same moral standards are not everywhere accepted. Even among individuals and groups within national societies there are marked differences of moral outlook, and the differences are all the greater where different societies and cultures are involved.

Nevertheless, the tendency of governments, like the tendency of individuals, is to claim universal validity for the moral principles which they accept. They picture themselves as promoting the good not only for their own peoples but for other peoples as well, perhaps for all mankind, and they seek to heap moral opprobrium on governments which pursue adverse policies. Thus conceptions of morality become not only guides to action but also instruments of struggle, each government seeking to strengthen its position by claiming moral credit for itself and seeking to weaken the position of unfriendly states by casting moral discredit upon them.

## Morality as a Basis for Harmony and for Strife

Where moral standards are similar, as they are among the countries of the English-speaking world, for example, they do much to facilitate harmony and cooperation; they reinforce law by providing an international constitutional consensus. Such a consensus virtually prevents certain kinds of disputes from arising and provides a basis on which the issues that do arise can be resolved. Where moral standards clash, as they did between the fascist states and others, and as they do between the Communist and non-Communist worlds, the area of consensus is bound to be very narrow, if it exists at all, and the possibilities of friction and conflict are correspondingly enhanced. The danger is particularly great when a moral outlook calls for national aggrandizement or for the liberation of foreign peoples from the evil system under which they are thought to live.

## Morality and Power

Differing conceptions of morality have been in competition with each other throughout history. Many factors affect the outcome of the competition, including the ability of the moral idea to commend itself and secure acceptance. Certainly, however, the power factor operates here, just as it does in law. Moral ideas provide one of the elements of power, and power in turn does much to determine which moral conceptions will prevail.

# THE PROBLEM OF PEACEFUL CHANGE

## Changing Power Relationships Require Changing Law

In dynamic societies power relationships change. Neither the weak nor the strong forever maintain the same relative power position. Within countries the strength of political parties waxes and wanes; some parties go out of existence, and others are created. Over the years, too, the strength of those who support the constitutional consensus and the strength of the subversives change. Among countries change is also the rule. The history of world affairs is, among other things, a history of the rise and fall of states. Some weak states have grown strong, and, sooner or later, all strong states have grown weak. The process of change continues.

If law is largely a reflection of the desires of the strong, and if strength shifts from party to party or from state to state, it is to be expected that the law would change. This does not mean that every rule of law must be replaced by another, for many of them endure indefinitely. The desires of those who are rising in power often coincide in many ways with the desires of those whose power is declining, and the same rule of law may thus serve successive wielders of power equally well. But the newly strong do not always agree with those whom they are displacing, and where their desires differ, they will insist that the law be changed. As President Eisenhower once said, "We must not think of peace as a static condition in world affairs. . . . Change is the law of life, and unless there is peaceful change, there is bound to be violent change." [25]

## Peaceful Change and Its Limits Within Countries

One of the outstanding characteristics of societies operating under a constitutional consensus is that provision is made for peaceful change. Within a country the consensus may be that a king has a divine right to rule and that others are to obey; then the king may change the law; perhaps he will act in accordance with his own arbitrary will or perhaps in response to pressures brought to bear upon him. The consensus may be that a communist or fascist dictatorship should prevail; then the party or the individual dictator may shape the law. The consensus may call for democracy; then the law may be changed by those who win elections. Nowhere within countries does the rule prevail that the law may be changed only by the slow process of developing custom or by the unanimous consent of the affected parties.

At the same time it should be noted that the possibility of peaceful change within countries is ordinarily not unlimited. Fear of various forms of resistance, including rebellion, limits even the dictator in what he can do. Within democratic countries, the constitution or the constitutional consensus imposes limits. In most federal systems, for example, the central government is not free to alter the boundary lines of the constituent units without their consent.[26] If New Jersey should adamantly demand that part of Pennsylvania be handed over to it, there is apparently no way in which this transfer can be peacefully accomplished unless Pennsylvania agrees, or unless the Constitution is amended. In effect, the problem of peaceful change is handled within countries in part by tacit or explicit agreement that certain kinds of change will not be demanded. If they are demanded nevertheless, the demand constitutes a challenge to the constitutional system, and if such a challenge is pressed it may lead to civil war.

In short, peace within countries depends not only on the existence of machinery for peaceful change but also on the absence of adamant demand for certain kinds of change.

## Change Among Countries: Peaceful and Violent

Among countries, the machinery for peaceful change is more primitive. The law can be changed through the slow accumulation of prece-

[25] *State Department Bulletin*, Vol. 33 (September 5, 1955), p. 376.
[26] Brierly, *The Outlook for International Law*, pp. 134 ff.

dents, shaping customary law. It can be changed through the voluntary conclusion of treaties. Disputes may be handled in the ways described in the preceding chapter. Direct negotiations may occur. Countries may try mediation, conciliation, or commissions of inquiry. International conferences or the agencies of an international organization may be used. Yet these devices can lead to a settlement only with the consent of the parties. Sometimes consent to change can be obtained, but on vital matters the consent of the party adversely affected is likely to be withheld. States are particularly reluctant to accept a change which deprives them of territory or which reduces their power or prestige. If they refuse to give their consent, what happens then?

Confronted by the opposition of others, a state demanding change may give up the attempt, resigning itself to a continuation of the legal status quo. But if it regards the change as urgent and vital, and if it commands sufficient power, it may resort to coercion, including military intervention and war itself. "The use or threatened use of force is . . . a normal and recognized method of bringing about important political change. . . . Normally, the threat of war, tacit or overt, seems a necessary condition of important political changes in the international sphere."[27] Heinrich von Treitschke came to a similar conclusion:

When a state realizes that existing treaties no longer express the actual relations between the Powers, then, if it cannot bring the other contracting state to acquiescence by friendly negotiations, there is nothing for it but the international lawsuit—War.[28]

## Peaceful Change Under the League

The framers of the League of Nations Covenant recognized that some provision should be made for peaceful change in addition to such devices as negotiation, mediation, and conciliation. They therefore specified in Article 19 that the Assembly of the League might "advise the reconsideration . . . of treaties which have become inapplicable and the consideration of international conditions whose continuance might endanger the peace of the world." Note that the Assembly was empowered only to advise; it could not enact or amend law, nor could it enforce acceptance of its advice. Interpreters of the Covenant disagree on the voting rules under which advice might have been rendered, but the details of the dispute are scarcely worth examining now.[29]

Article 19 and the League devices for peaceful change broke down not

[27] Carr, op. cit., pp. 215-216.
[28] Quoted by Brierly, The Outlook for International Law, p. 19.
[29] Frederick Sherwood Dunn, Peaceful Change (New York, Council on Foreign Relations, 1937), pp. 106-111. Lincoln P. Bloomfield, Evolution or Revolution? The United Nations and the Problem of Peaceful Territorial Change (Cambridge, Harvard University Press, 1957), pp. 23-60.

so much because of voting rules and inadequacies in the machinery as because of the attitudes of states. There was no constitutional consensus fixing the limits within which change might occur, as there commonly is within countries. There was no agreement to bow to the recommendations of the Assembly in certain matters; in fact the states were jealous of their sovereignty and fearful of anything resembling an international legislature. Neither was there renunciation of demands for change which were sure to be resisted. In fact, the demands for change that led to war (particularly Italy's demands on Ethiopia and Albania, and Germany's demands on Poland) were demands that no conceivable system of change could have been expected to satisfy.

I cannot see any real connection between the rigidity and consequent impracticability of Article 19 and the wars which have been waged against Members of the League in the course of the last years. No matter how generously the framers of the Covenant might have provided for the pacific revision of international treaties, they could not have made legally possible such events as the rape of Manchuria, Abyssinia [Ethiopia], Czechoslovakia, Albania, and Poland.[30]

In the absence of recognized limits within which the system of peaceful change might operate and beyond which it could not be expected to operate, Article 19 was a dead letter from the first.

## Peaceful Change Under the United Nations

The United Nations Charter in various articles similarly empowers the General Assembly to make recommendations for peaceful change. The recommendations may be made on the basis of a two-thirds vote, making action possible despite the opposition of a few adversely affected parties. Recommendations made by such a majority, particularly when supported by the major powers, necessarily carry considerable moral authority, but still they are only recommendations. As with the League Assembly, the United Nations General Assembly cannot enact or amend law, nor can it enforce acceptance of its recommendations. However, if the Security Council finds that the rejection of a recommendation of the General Assembly constitutes a threat to the peace, breach of the peace, or act of aggression, it can order enforcement action. The theoretical possibility thus exists that the General Assembly and the Security Council, acting in cooperation, might assume the role of a legislature and an executive, providing for change in the law and for such enforcement action as might be necessary to assure acceptance of the change; that is, the possibility exists that peaceful change among countries might be made more nearly what it is within countries: policeful change.[31]

30 William E. Rappard, *The Quest for Peace* (Cambridge, Harvard University Press, 1940), p. 176.
31 See Chapter 2, pp. 15-17.

We shall discuss this possibility more fully in a subsequent chapter. Suffice it to refer here to the principal case in which the possibility has been tested. In 1947 the General Assembly was confronted with the problem of Palestine. The area had been a British mandate, but Britain had announced its determination to give up its role as the mandatory power. Change of some kind was thus made unavoidable, and the Arabs and Jews who inhabited the area could not agree on a new governmental arrangement. After considerable deliberation the Assembly recommended that separate Arab and Jewish states be created in the area, but the Arabs rejected the recommendation and resisted Jewish efforts to implement it. War between the two groups resulted. When the matter came before the Security Council, various members took the view that the Charter did not authorize them to enforce recommendations of the General Assembly. Moreover, the Security Council failed to rule that the fighting in Palestine involved a threat to the peace, breach of the peace, or an act of aggression. Enforcement of the General Assembly's recommendation was thus left to the party which wanted the recommendation carried out, the Jews themselves.

Peaceful change occurs among nations, of course. Common interests frequently lead to its acceptance. The moral authority of an agency such as the General Assembly might induce a state to accept change even at some sacrifice, if the sacrifice is not too great. A state which finds itself in a position of hopeless military weakness may accept great sacrifice—as Czechoslovakia did when Britain and France joined Germany and Italy at the Munich Conference in 1938 in advising Czechoslovakia to cede part of its territory to Germany. But there is nothing in the record of the League of Nations, of the United Nations, or of diplomacy generally to give the basis for hope of peaceful change in situations where a state having the power to resist is asked to give up something which it regards as vital. On matters regarded as important, change is likely to remain a function of the power relations between states which demand it and states which oppose it.

If the problem of peaceful change among nations is ever solved, the solution will probably have to include both the elements which are ordinarily present within countries. Machinery for change is not enough. There must also be agreement on the limits within which peaceful change will be allowed to occur. If demands for change going beyond these limits are not renounced, the issue will presumably become one of naked power, as with revolutionary challenges to the constitutional consensus within countries.

## THE OUTLAWRY OF WAR

We have noted that the League of Nations Covenant, the Kellogg-Briand Pact, and the United Nations Charter all contain restrictions on the freedom of states to go to war. War nevertheless occurs. One of the major reasons for this is now clear. If the law goes drastically against the desires of the strong on matters which the strong regard as vital, and if effective means for changing the law peacefully do not exist, the issue is likely to be submitted to the arbitrament of the sword.

Merely to outlaw war, as the Kellogg-Briand Pact presumed to do, cannot possibly solve the problem. War and the threat of war have in fact proved useful to states. They have been useful, among other ways, as methods of forcing change in the law. Until alternative methods for bringing about change have been developed, and until conditions permit those methods to be effective, it cannot be expected that war and the threat of war will in practice be abandoned.

This is all the more true because war, whether legal or illegal, is not always considered morally wrong. Most systems of morality justify defensive war, and men are ingenious in finding reasons for classifying the wars they fight as defensive. Some systems of morality glorify war and call for aggression, and even those which condemn aggressive war as evil often permit it to be considered a lesser evil. The good which men hope to accomplish through war is taken to justify the evil which war itself involves.

. . . The attempt to make a moral distinction between wars of "aggression" and wars of "defense" is misguided. If a change is necessary and desirable, the use or threatened use of force to maintain the status quo may be morally more culpable than the use or threatened use of force to alter it. . . . The moral criterion must be not the "aggressive" or "defensive" character of the war, but the nature of the change which is being sought and resisted. "Without rebellion, mankind would stagnate and injustice would be irremediable." Few serious thinkers maintain that it is always and unconditionally wrong to start a revolution; and it is equally difficult to believe that it is always and unconditionally wrong to start a war.[32]

A mature legal system must be expected to include a prohibition of revolution against itself. In the international realm this means that a mature system of international law must be expected to include a prohibition of war. Yet the prohibition is not likely to be respected if effective alternatives to war are not provided for the accomplishment of change.

International law is a means which states employ in the power struggle, and a limitation on their behavior. It is a means by which they arrange to conduct a host of relationships in an orderly and peaceful fashion. It is a means by which they define common interests and through which they adjust conflicting claims and expectations. It is a means which the strong employ to register and define their will—a means by which they give status to the achievements of power. At the same time, in defining rights

---

[32] Carr, *op. cit.*, p. 208. The quotation within the quotation is from Bertrand Russell.

and imposing obligations, law limits the claims which states can rightfully assert and the actions in which they can rightfully indulge.

Law can be effective in limiting the behavior of states either as long as its rules reflect the common desires of affected states or as long as they reflect the desires of states which have both the strength and the determination to enforce them. Otherwise legal limitations on state behavior are not likely to be effective, and change of some kind will almost certainly occur. With existing attitudes and organizational arrangements, especially with divergent and essentially national conceptions of morality, there is no assurance that change can be peacefully accomplished. If it cannot be, those states which desire change and which have sufficient power are likely to seek it by threatening or using coercive measures, perhaps including war.

## SUGGESTED READINGS

BLOOMFIELD, Lincoln P., *Evolution or Revolution? The United Nations and the Problem of Peaceful Territorial Change* (Cambridge, Harvard University Press, 1957).

————, "Law, Politics, and International Disputes," *International Conciliation*, No. 516 (January 1958).

BRIERLY, J. L., *The Outlook for International Law* (Oxford, Clarendon, 1944).

————, *The Law of Nations*, 6th ed., Sir Humphrey Waldock, ed. (New York, Oxford, 1963).

CARR, E. H., *The Twenty Years' Crisis 1919-1939* (New York, Harper & Row, 1964).

CLAUDE, Inis L., Jr., *Swords Into Plowshares, The Problems and Progress of International Organization*, 3rd ed. (New York, Random House, 1964).

CORBETT, P. E., *Law and Society in the Relations of States* (New York, Harcourt, Brace & World, 1951).

FRIEDMANN, Wolfgang, *The Changing Structure of International Law* (New York, Columbia University Press, 1964).

JENKS, Clarence Wilfred, *The Common Law of Mankind* (London, Stevens, 1958).

————, *Law, Freedom, and Welfare* (Dobbs Ferry, N. Y., Oceana Publications, 1963).

————, *The Prospects of International Adjudication* (Dobbs Ferry N. Y., Oceana Publications, 1964).

KAPLAN, Morton A., and KATZENBACH, Nicholas de B., *The Political Foundations of International Law* (New York, Wiley, 1961).

OPPENHEIM, Lassa F. L., *International Law*, 7th ed., Hersh Lauterpacht, ed., 2 vols. (New York, Longmans, 1948-1952).

RAMSEY, Paul, *War and the Christian Conscience: How Shall Modern War Be Justly Conducted?* (Durham N.C., Duke University Press, 1961).

RAPPARD, William E., *The Quest for Peace* (Cambridge, Harvard University Press, 1940).

SCHWARZENBERGER, Georg, *A Manual of International Law,* 4th ed., 2 vols. (New York, Praeger, 1960).

———, *The Frontiers of International Law* (London, Stevens, 1962).

STONE, Julius, *Legal Controls of International Conflict, A Treatise on the Dynamics of Disputes- and War-Law* (New York, Rinehart, 1954).

WOLFERS, Arnold, *Discord and Collaboration* (Baltimore, Johns Hopkins Press, 1962).

WRIGHT, Quincy, *Contemporary International Law: A Balance Sheet* (Garden City N.Y., Doubleday, 1955).

———, *The Role of International Law in the Elimination of War* (Dobbs Ferry, N.Y., Oceana Publications, 1961).

# 15

# THE PURSUIT OF OBJECTIVES BY ECONOMIC MEANS

The chapters of Part II indicate that states pursue a number of different kinds of objectives. They are concerned with their security, with nationalism (whether they want to foster or combat it), with ideological and moral objectives, with prosperity and the economic basis for power, with prestige, and with a status and record that give a basis for pride. Further, as the above chapters of Part III indicate, states use a variety of methods in promoting the achievement of their objectives, e.g., they seek a satisfactory relative power position and attempt to handle various problems through diplomacy.

Whatever the objective and whatever the methods, economic conditions and policies are very likely to be involved. Certainly the economic policies of a government have a marked impact on the amount of power that it can muster; similarly, the economic policies of one government may have considerable effect on the power that other governments can command. Ideologies and economics are also intertwined; economic deprivations help make people susceptible to the appeals of extremist political movements, whereas economic satisfaction reinforces the going system. Obviously, economic conditions and policies have much to do with both the persuasive and the coercive influence that governments can bring to bear abroad. Obviously too, a government's policies in the economic field are likely to have much to do with the level of well-being achieved at home, and they may also affect well-being abroad; in fact, recent years have witnessed vastly increased international efforts to promote economic and other growth in underdeveloped countries.

In this book on international politics we are not concerned with the whole field of economics or even with all the economic policies of governments. Most aspects of the subject are best left to the economists and to students of domestic politics. We are, however, concerned with economic policies that enter directly into the field of international relations, i.e., with those economic means by which governments seek to promote foreign policy objectives or by which they seek to promote other objectives in cooperation or conflict with foreign states. This means that we are concerned with national policies and international agreements relating to: (1) foreign exchange, that is, the purchase or sale of the money of one state in exchange for the money of another; (2) the international exchange of goods and services; and (3) foreign investments.

These subjects are vast. Again it is best to leave a substantial portion of the relevant material to the economists, especially the discussion of the rather complex theories which are associated with foreign economic policies. We can, however, draw on some conclusions of the economists, and we can see what states in fact do, and what they hope to accomplish, in promoting or regulating international commercial transactions.

Note might be made at the outset of the fact that general international law (i.e., law applicable to all states, as distinct from treaty law, which is applicable only to the parties to the treaty) leaves each government substantially free to regulate international commercial transactions as it sees fit. It may monopolize the field itself, establishing state trading agencies and prohibiting its nationals from engaging in international trade on a private basis. If it permits private trade, it may fix the conditions on the basis of which it occurs. It may prohibit either the import or export of some or all goods, or adopt less severe regulations—for example, regulations permitting goods to be imported only if a tariff duty is paid. A government, within the limits of its jurisdiction, may prohibit or regulate the purchase or sale of its currency. With some qualifications to be noted later, each government is free to prohibit or regulate the commercial activities of foreigners in its territory. Measures taken to regulate international trade may discriminate among foreign states; thus a higher tariff rate may be imposed on wood products from the Soviet Union than on the same products from Canada, and the export of oil may be made legal or illegal, depending on whether the destination of the oil is China or Britain. It goes without saying that economic aid of various kinds may be extended to one state though denied to another. The freedom of states to regulate international commercial activities, and to do so on a discriminatory basis, means that economics can easily be made a weapon in dealings with foreign states.

# FOREIGN EXCHANGE

## Some Bases for Governmental Action

The obvious fact should be stressed that international economic activities involve relationships among different economies. Each sovereign state maintains its own monetary system, pursues its own fiscal and tax policies, and develops its own price and income structure. Nevertheless, the very fact that goods, services, and capital are exchanged means that the various national economies are not entirely independent of each other. The expansion and contraction of foreign commerce are factors that affect both the level of well-being and the level of power that states attain.

Though barter deals among countries occur, international transactions ordinarily involve the use of money. The importer pays money for what he gets—the money of his own country, of the exporter's country, or of a third country, depending on the terms of the bargain. For one party or both, a foreign currency is thus involved. If the importer is to pay in foreign currency, he will presumably have to buy it first. If the exporter is paid in a foreign currency, he may want to sell it and repatriate the proceeds. The buying and selling of foreign currency are foreign exchange transactions. The price of one currency in terms of another is its foreign exchange rate.

Governments may interfere or participate in foreign exchange transactions just as they may interfere or participate in foreign trade. A government may, for example, permit its currency to be bought and sold freely, in which case its currency is said to be freely convertible, or it may impose limitations and restrictions. It may take action to fix or regulate the foreign exchange rate of its currency.

Now obviously the convertibility of a currency and its foreign exchange rate have much to do with the foreign trade of the country involved. A Frenchman who cannot convert his francs into dollars faces an obstacle if he wants to make a purchase in the United States. He may or may not be able to find an American exporter who is willing to receive inconvertible francs. If conversion is possible, the foreign exchange rate becomes all-important. Is the rate a stable one? Stability is generally regarded as the best basis for trade, though speculators may be attracted to the gambling possibilities of a situation in which rates are fluctuating. Is the rate high or low? The more dollars a British subject can buy with his pounds sterling, the more he will be encouraged to make purchases in the United States; conversely, the fewer pounds Americans can buy with dollars, the less will they want to import from Britain. These statements assume some elasticity of demand.

Closely associated with the problem of exchange rates is the problem of

the balance of payments, that is, the relationship between payments and receipts in connection with the international exchange of goods, services, and capital. The so-called balance may or may not be in equilibrium. When all of a country's exports pay for all of its imports, with gold holdings and other reserves neither increased nor reduced, equilibrium exists; otherwise there is disequilibrium. Over any short term, some disequilibrium is virtually inevitable. Over a long period, however, substantial equilibrium must be maintained, for nations must pay their way.[1]

What kinds of actions do governments take concerning the convertibility and the exchange rates of their currencies? What objectives do they seek to serve in so doing? We shall not attempt to explore and explain many of the forces at work in influencing governmental policies, for an understanding of them requires considerable knowledge of economics. Neither shall we describe all the possible lines of governmental action. A few will be sufficient.

## Governmental Policies: The Gold Standard

As a basis for foreign exchange, the gold standard is the archetype. Most governments based their currencies on the gold standard in the decades prior to World War I and again from 1925 to 1931. With some reservations and qualifications it has become common again since World War II, and more particularly since the late 1950's.

A country on the gold standard buys and sells gold at a fixed price on request and permits it to be imported and exported freely. When a number of countries are on the gold standard, their currencies have a common denominator, and foreign exchange rates become obvious and stable. Thus a reliable and predictable basis is provided for all sorts of international commercial transactions. Importers and exporters can use whatever currency happens to be convenient, knowing that each of them is convertible into the others at a stable rate and that profits can always be repatriated in the home currency. Exchange rates fluctuate some, depending on supply and demand, but any considerable deviation from the standard rate simply leads to a shipment of gold. According to traditional gold standard theory, such adjustments as are needed to keep the balance of payments in substantial equilibrium are to occur in the domestic economies of the various states. They are to allow domestic price and income levels to rise and fall, even if it means inflation or deflation. The expectation is that changes in price and income levels will counteract the forces making for disequilibrium, and that international commercial relationships can proceed on the adjusted basis. The underlying assumption

---

[1] Delbert A. Snider, *Introduction to International Economics* (Homewood, Ill., Irwin, 1963), Parts II and III. P. T. Ellsworth, *The International Economy* (New York, Macmillan, 1964), Part IV.

obviously is that countries on the gold standard will accept fluctuations in their domestic economy, even if it means substantial unemployment, in order to keep foreign exchange rates stable.

There is a qualification on the above. Though the gold standard implies a fixed price of gold, the price is not necessarily fixed for all time. A government can devalue its currency. The United States devalued the dollar during the depression, meaning that it declared that each ounce of gold was worth more in dollars than had previously been the case. In principle, it then took more dollars to equal the value of a given amount of gold or a given amount of a foreign currency, which meant in effect that the price of anything bought abroad went up. Conversely, in principle, it took less gold or less of a foreign currency to equal the value of a given number of dollars, which meant in effect that for people abroad American prices went down. Obviously, then, one of the hopes connected with devaluation was that Americans would find it less desirable to buy abroad, and that foreigners would find it more desirable to buy in the United States; as some put it, the idea was to export unemployment. The difficulty was that many other countries also devalued their currencies, and competitive devaluations turned out to be a losing game.

Regardless of the possibility of manipulating the price of gold, the international gold standard broke down for many reasons. The principal one was that, as World War I and the depression disrupted trade patterns, governments became unwilling to allow the violent fluctuations in the domestic economy which adherence to the gold standard entailed. Generally, they were determined to stress domestic stability and full employment, seeking equilibrium in the international balance of payments or "controlled disequilibrium," through actions affecting foreign exchange.[2] As a higher degree of prosperity and stability came to prevail in the years following World War II, more and more governments reverted to a gold standard, often with qualifications. But before treating this development, we should note some of the alternatives to the gold standard.

Various alternatives are available. Governments may adopt a paper currency standard, under which foreign exchange rates find their own level through the operation of the law of supply and demand, and under which considerable fluctuation in exchange rates may occur. Alternatively, governments may adopt regulatory devices or controls of one kind or another. They may seek to "peg" foreign exchange rates, which means that they seek to modify the fluctuations to which a paper currency standard might lead by entering the foreign exchange market themselves,

---

[2] Lloyd A. Metzler, "The Theory of International Trade," in Howard S. Ellis, ed., *A Survey of Contemporary Economics* (New York, McGraw-Hill-Blakiston, 1948), pp. 211-240.

buying and selling (within limits) to compensate for shifts in supply and demand. They may adopt exchange control.

## Governmental Policies: Exchange Control

Under a thorough system of exchange control, the government monopolizes the buying and selling of foreign currency. Those needing foreign currency may get it only from the government, and those who acquire foreign currency must sell it to the government. This puts the government in a position to control and direct all legal international commercial transactions, including foreign travel on the part of its citizens. It may provide foreign exchange for purchases in one country, but refuse to provide it for purchases in another. It may provide foreign exchange for the importation of one type of goods, but refuse to provide it for the importation of another type. If foreigners acquire currency of the country, "blocked accounts" may develop, that is, currency holdings which cannot be converted. Differential foreign exchange rates may be adopted, meaning that the government may make foreign exchange available at a bargain rate for certain purposes, and charge a stiff price in other connections.

Through exchange control, if it is rigorous enough, a government can achieve equilibrium in the international balance of payments, or it may maintain "controlled disequilibrium." It will forgo the advantages of buying in the cheapest market and selling in the dearest, and will thus sacrifice one of the bases of domestic prosperity, but at the same time it can prevent developments in the field of international commerce which might have an adverse effect on the domestic economy. There may be political compensations, too. The very fact of stability in the domestic economy has domestic political advantages; governments which permit deflation and unemployment on a substantial scale jeopardize the support on which their continuance in office may depend. Moreover, exchange controls permit governments to direct international trade so as to serve diplomatic ends. They can refuse to make foreign exchange available for purchases in unfriendly states, and can encourage trade with other states. They can use control over foreign exchange as a bargaining counter in negotiations with other governments, whatever the main issue in the negotiations may be. Germany under Hitler manipulated exchange controls and blocked accounts in such a way as to obtain a strangle hold on the economies of some of the states of southeastern Europe. If such ends could not also be promoted by other means, such as boycotts, embargoes, quotas, and the licensing of imports and exports, which we shall soon discuss, it is probable that exchange control would become even more widespread than it is.

## International Agreement: The International Monetary Fund

Toward the end of World War II the International Monetary Fund was created, now inclusive of most of the states of the free world. The objectives were to eliminate exchange controls and promote stability in exchange rates while still assuring a reasonable degree of national independence with regard to monetary and fiscal policy. To accomplish these rather disparate if not contradictory objectives, members agreed to put a price on their currency in terms of gold. Thus exchange rates were tentatively fixed. Those participants in a position to do so would then allow free convertibility; the United States did this from the first, and by 1958 most of the European countries had followed suit. Participants unable to accept convertibility might "manage" their currency, usually by a combination of partial exchange control and the use of a stabilization fund, that is, a fund with which the member government can enter the foreign exchange market with a view to compensating for shifts in supply and demand. The International Monetary Fund itself is a stabilization fund, to which the members make contributions and from which they can obtain assistance in counteracting short-term pressures against the exchange rate of their currency. If a fundamental disequilibrium appears which these measures do not counteract, a member may devalue its currency; a devaluation by not more than 10 per cent may occur through unilateral action, but a more severe devaluation requires the consent of the Fund. Voting rights in the Fund are weighted on the basis of various criteria, the United States alone casting 30 per cent of the votes. A common interest in the stability of exchange rates has thus been recognized, and qualified assurances have been exchanged against the competitive devaluation of currencies.[3]

# THE INTERNATIONAL EXCHANGE OF
# GOODS AND SERVICES

Governments pursue various kinds of policies in connection with the international exchange of goods and services, depending on the economic system of the state, the objectives pursued, and estimates of the probable effect of given lines of action.

## Free Trade

Where free enterprise prevails, governments may allow free trade. A country is said to follow a policy of free trade when its government interposes no special obstacles to the international exchange of goods and

[3] Snider, *op. cit.*, pp. 482–504.

services. There may be low tariffs on imports for the purpose of raising revenue, but there will be none designed to give domestic enterprise protection against foreign competition, nor will other protective measures be adopted. There will be no bounties or subsidies to encourage exports. Private traders will be allowed to buy and sell abroad as they please, importing or exporting freely for their own profit or pleasure.[4] Of course, even with free trade governments adopt policies which affect foreign exchange rates, and, as we have seen, this means that governments fix an important condition on which trade proceeds.

Though the ideal of the classical economists, free trade has never been generally accepted by governments. Great Britain came closest to doing so during most of the nineteenth and the early part of the twentieth century, and others approached the policy more or less closely.[5] Now none do so. The general rule now is that governments regulate, and participate in, international commercial activities. The reasons for this will appear as we see what kinds of policies they in fact pursue.

## The National Regulation of Imports

*1. Tariffs and the reasons for adopting them.* Outside the Communist world, governments generally adopt protective tariffs on imports. They do so for various purposes. The desire of governing groups to promote their own domestic political advantage is important among them. After all, these groups face pressures for the adoption of tariffs. For all the glorification of competition which capitalism involves, few free enterprisers really want it. If they can eliminate or reduce competition by inducing the government to adopt a high tariff, they are usually glad to do so, and they are ready to give or withhold support to a political party or faction, depending on its willingness to go along. The adoption of a protective tariff generally means that consumers will have to pay higher prices than otherwise for the protected items, but this loss is spread among many who are often hardly aware of the fact that they are being burdened with it. The gain goes to a few, to whom the matter may be really vital. Support from those who want a tariff may in turn be vital to an officeholder, a party, or a government.

Protective tariffs may also be adopted for other reasons. It would be quite difficult to establish some productive activities in a country, even if it were well suited for them, unless protection were afforded against established foreign competition; this is the "infant industry" argument for tariffs, which, though often misused, is theoretically defensible. In the

---

4 *Ibid.*, pp. 23-68. Ellsworth, *op. cit.*, pp. 59-180.

5 A descriptive history of the commercial policies of many states may be found in Asher Isaacs, *International Trade: Tariff and Commercial Policy* (Chicago, Irwin, 1948).

interest of domestic economic stability, tariffs may be adopted to give protection against "dumping," that is, against the sporadic importation of products sold by a foreign merchant at prices lower than those he charges to buyers in his own country. Tariffs are sometimes designed to improve the terms of trade for the country imposing them, that is, through them in some circumstances it may be possible to pay for more imports with fewer exports. The possibility of gaining this advantage through tariffs is reduced, however, when many countries attempt it at the same time.[6] Governments sometimes adopt tariffs simply as a measure of retaliation, perhaps with a view to negotiating reciprocal reductions with other governments. Entirely aside from the question of favoring the producers of certain items at the expense of consumers, governments may adopt tariffs as a means of affecting the distribution of income among various economic groups in the population; for example, the portion of the national income going to labor or to agriculture may be increased or reduced, depending on the tariff policy pursued.[7] Power considerations may also lead to the adoption of tariffs. The governments of sovereign states must think in terms of the possibility of war, defensive if not offensive. They must therefore manage economic affairs so as to be prepared for war, which sometimes means that they must develop and maintain domestic sources of supply even though it is uneconomic to do so. Frequently the tariff is chosen as a means by which this can be done.

Whatever the original objective in adopting tariffs, governments are necessarily cautious about reducing or eliminating them once they have been established. If a protected industry were suddenly deprived of its protection, considerable unemployment and loss of invested capital might well occur; these are developments which governments are understandably loath to bring about.

2. *Other devices.* Governments frequently supplement tariffs with other devices for restricting or regulating imports. A tariff does not fix the quantity of an item which may be imported; those willing to pay the price may import as much as they please. Other devices, such as quotas, licensing systems, and exchange controls, involve quantitative restrictions. When a government fixes import quotas, it specifies the amount of a commodity that can be imported within a given period of time; the quota may be global, or it may be fixed on a country-by-country basis. Under licensing systems, importers bring specified goods into a country only on the basis of licenses which the government may grant or withhold as it sees fit. Exchange controls have already been described.

These supplementary devices for regulating imports may be applied for exactly the same purposes as tariffs. They have generally been

6 Metzler, *op. cit.,* pp. 241-244.
7 *Ibid.,* pp. 244-249.

adopted, however, in response to special situations. The United States has employed quotas mainly in connection with its program of giving price support to certain agricultural products; it is willing to give the American farmer the benefit of artificially high prices at the expense of the taxpayers and consumers, but does not want to extend the benefit to foreign producers.[8] Most countries that have placed quantitative restrictions on imports have done so because of balance-of-payments difficulties. They have not been able to export enough to pay for all the desired imports, and so they have simply curtailed imports rather than accept the economic consequences of imbalance. At the same time, they have exercised their controls so as to avoid frittering away scarce foreign exchange and so as to require that it be devoted only to the purchase of imports regarded as necessary. Especially after World War II, many governments used quotas, licenses, and foreign exchange controls to make sure that only those things would be imported which would contribute most to national rehabilitation and recovery.

As suggested earlier, all these devices for regulating imports may be applied on a discriminatory basis. A government can select the countries from which it is willing to have imports come; it can exclude certain foreign countries from its markets, completely or partially, and it can adopt measures to facilitate the importation of goods from others. Thus it can affect the level of well-being and power that it is possible for other countries to achieve.

*3. Indirect restrictions.* So far, we have been speaking mainly of direct restrictions on the importation of goods. There are also indirect restrictions. The very process of clearing goods through customs sometimes impedes international trade more than the customs duty itself, for it often involves uncertainty about the tariff rate which will be applied and delay in making the decision. Propaganda may be issued to induce popular boycotts of goods made in certain countries. The law may require that imports bear a label indicating their country of origin, and sometimes this requirement has proved to be very onerous. The United States government insists on the "Buy American" principle, meaning that federal agencies (and many state and local agencies as well) commonly procure what they need from domestic producers, even if the same item can be purchased abroad at a substantial saving. Quarantine and sanitary requirements, ostensibly designed to protect domestic plant and animal life from disease, may be administered so as to make them primarily instruments for protecting domestic producers against foreign competition. Thus American beef producers have been protected from Argentine competition by a ruling which excludes fresh beef from any part of Argentina because of the presence of hoof-and-mouth disease in one part.

8 Snider, *op. cit.,* pp. 389-391.

## International Agreements on Import Policies

International trade is regulated not only by national but also by international action. General international law contains a number of rules and principles regulating the treatment of persons engaged in travel, trade, and commerce outside the boundaries of the state of which they are nationals. In addition, most states have found it desirable to conclude treaties with each other on the subject.

*1. General treaties of commerce and navigation.* Such treaties have traditionally dealt with any or all of a wide variety of problems: the rights of the ships of one party in the ports of the other; the rights of nationals of one party engaged in travel, trade, or commerce in the territory of the other; protection by one government of the patent, copyright, and similar rights assured by the other government to its nationals; fishing rights; consular activities; tariffs.

Two principles are especially common in commercial treaties. One calls for "national treatment" and the other for "most-favored-nation treatment."

A pledge of national treatment is a pledge by one party to treat the nationals of the other party as well as it treats its own nationals; the pledge is usually reciprocal. In all matters to which it relates, equal rights and privileges are to be afforded. Thus the nationals of one state may be assured of the right to engage in commercial activities in the territory of the other, free from any discrimination because they are aliens. Reservations or exceptions may, however, be made; the United States, for example, regularly refuses to extend national treatment to foreigners so far as participation in the coastwise carrying trade is concerned. Similarly, exceptions to the principle may be made for the benefit of foreigners, as when they are exempted from military service.

The most-favored-nation clause in a treaty obliges one party to treat nationals of the other party as well as it treats the nationals of any third state; as in the case of national treatment, the pledge is usually reciprocal. The general object is equal and nondiscriminatory treatment. The principle may be adopted in relation to any or all aspects of international commercial relationships; it is most commonly related to tariff rates. Suppose, for example, that France and the United States are bound in tariff matters to extend most-favored-nation treatment to each other. France then makes a special tariff concession to Belgium, which makes Belgium most favored. France will then be obliged to extend the same concession to the United States. There are, however, two forms, or two interpretations, of the most-favored-nation clause. Sometimes the obligation is unconditional, and sometimes it is conditional. When unconditional, it requires that each party automatically extend to the other any tariff concession which it extends to a third state. When conditional, it requires the extension of the concession only for the same or equivalent compensation, if any, which the third state has granted. Thus the conditional form may or may not produce equal and nondiscriminatory treatment.

2. *Special trade agreements.* In addition to general treaties on trade, navigation, and commerce, states also conclude special treaties of various kinds dealing with international economic relations. Bilateral agreements providing for the reciprocal reduction of specific tariff rates have long been common. The promotion of such agreements became a regular feature of American foreign policy in 1934, with the adoption of the Reciprocal Trade Agreements program. Under this program the President concluded agreements with other states reducing American tariffs by as much as 50 percent in return for satisfactory reciprocal tariff concessions; after most of the possible reductions had been made on the basis of the 1934 tariff rates, Congress permitted further reductions of as much as 50 percent of the 1945 rates. Whereas in 1934 the average level of import duties was 53 percent, by 1958 it was 12 percent. The reduction is to be attributed not only to trade agreements, but also to the effects of inflation. Agreements under the program included the most-favored-nation clause in its unconditional form.

The Trade Expansion Act of 1962 is now the principal basis of American foreign trade policy. On the one hand, it renews the authority of the President to make reciprocity agreements providing for a reduction of up to 50 percent in American tariff rates—this time with the 1962 rates as the base—and in limited areas it permits him to eliminate tariffs entirely. Moreover, he can apply the reductions not simply article by article, but category by category. On the other hand, if the Tariff Commission finds that increased imports brought about by tariff concessions are causing serious injury to domestic concerns, the President may raise tariffs up to a level 50 percent higher than they were in 1934. The act provides two alternatives to such increases: the government may grant "adjustment assistance" to firms and workers injured by tariff reductions, or it can seek "orderly marketing agreements" with other countries under which they "voluntarily" limit their exports to the United States.

3. *The GATT.* By 1963 forty-four states, conducting over 80 percent of the world's international trade, had become parties to the General Agreement on Tariffs and Trade (GATT), originally concluded in 1947. Moreover, they had established a secretariat and a permanent Council of Representatives, making the GATT not only a treaty but also an international organization.[9] The principal purpose of the GATT is to increase international trade. To this end the parties agree to negotiate with a view to reducing trade barriers; among other things, they subscribe to the principle that trade is to be conducted in a nondiscriminatory way and that

9 Ellsworth, *op. cit.,* pp. 512-514. Snider, *op. cit.,* pp. 380-383.

quantitative restrictions are, in general, to be condemned. "In the hundreds of individual negotiations that have been carried on under GATT, covering tens of thousands of commodities, tariff concessions have been made applying to products constituting more than two-thirds of the total import trade of the participating countries and considerably more than half of the total import trade of the world." [10] Equally significant is the fact that GATT provides a routine method by which complaints and differences relating to trade policy can be discussed and settled.

4. *The Common Market in Europe.* What later came to be called the "Inner Six" (Belgium, Netherlands, Luxembourg [the Benelux countries], France, West Germany, and Italy) in 1953 established a coal and steel community, eliminating barriers and discriminatory practices affecting the coal and steel trade among themselves. The parties declared that they were:

Resolved to substitute for historical rivalries a fusion of their essential interests; to establish, by creating an economic community, the foundation of a broad and independent community among peoples long divided by bloody conflicts; and to lay the bases of institutions capable of giving direction to their future common destiny.[11]

Three years later, in 1957, the same states concluded the Treaties of Rome providing for a European Economic Community (EEC) and a European Atomic Community (Euratom). The EEC, ordinarily labelled the Common Market, is being created by stages. The end point is a unified economy for all six countries, more or less analogous to that of the United States. The Common Market includes a customs union, that is, the elimination of tariffs between members and the adoption of a common tariff applicable to imports from the outside. Necessarily, it also includes something much more difficult to achieve: the harmonizing of a considerable variety of national policies, e.g., those pertaining to taxes, to social security, to monetary and fiscal matters. There is to be free movement of both capital and labor within the Community. Several special funds are drawn upon to ease the adjustment pains for industries and workers, to help finance large projects of general importance to the Community, and to assist in the development of overseas territories. Various international agencies established by the six supervise the implementation of their agreement: an executive council, on which each state is represented; a commission that assists the council; a legislative assembly; and a court of justice. The purposes are political as well as economic, as indicated by the quotation cited above. The EEC reflects a determination, especially on the part of France and West Germany, to overcome old hatreds and to eliminate the thought of war between them. At the same

[10] Snider, *op. cit.,* p. 382.
[11] *Ibid.,* pp. 418-420. Ellsworth, *op. cit.,* pp. 514-524.

time, implementation of the principles involves severe problems, both in terms of the necessary economic readjustments and in terms of traditional nationalist emotions. Britain is on the outside. It refused to join the coal and steel community back in 1953 and declined to participate in the development of the EEC. In 1959, it led in the European Free Trade Association, consisting of the "Outer Seven"—Britain and six of the smaller states on the continent surrounding the "Inner Six." But Britain then changed its mind, applying for membership in the EEC and engaging in prolonged negotiations to fix the terms of admission. The effort came to nothing, for early in 1963 De Gaulle interposed a French veto.

5. *Economic Cooperation in Latin America.* Almost half of the states of Latin America are parties to a treaty designed to promote their trade.[12] They plan gradually to eliminate trade barriers among themselves and to make "complementarity agreements," assigning industries on a country-by-country basis. How much economic integration will occur remains to be seen. The five Central American republics have gone farther, establishing substantial free trade among themselves, aiming at a customs union, and making agreements concerning the allocation of industry.

## The National Regulation of Exports

In addition to measures that relate primarily to the importation of goods, governments sometimes act directly either to expand or to curtail exports.

The expansion of exports may be brought about in various ways and for various purposes. Governments sometimes provide bounties to encourage exports, perhaps for the purpose of stimulating prosperity at home. They sometimes subsidize service activities, such as merchant shipping, perhaps so that the ships will be available under the national flag in the event of war. They sometimes extend loans to make the export of goods possible. The United States, for example, operates the Export-Import Bank, which extends loans primarily to foreign governments but also to both domestic and foreign corporations engaged in foreign trade. The principal purpose is to facilitate the export of American goods. Obviously, too, measures which a state takes to encourage imports, such as a reduction in its tariffs, are likely to increase exports, for the foreigners who have sold the goods imported will acquire money with which to buy goods which they want in return.

The expansion of exports sometimes occurs in connection with measures taken primarily for other reasons. Thus during World War II the United States, through its "lend-lease" program supplied goods and services to many other countries on a vast scale; but the object was really not the expansion of exports but a contribution to the defeat of the Axis

12 Ellsworth, *op. cit.*, pp. 524-526.

powers. At the close of the war, the United States became a leading contributor to the United Nations Relief and Rehabilitation Administration (UNRRA). Later it undertook a program of aid to Greece and Turkey under the Truman Doctrine, and contributed to the recovery of Western Europe through the Marshall Plan. These programs were supplemented and later supplanted by others designed to contribute to the strength of the "free world" and to promote economic and social development. We will revert to them shortly.

Governments not only take measures that increase exports, but they also impose restrictions or prohibitions. The object may simply be to keep at home goods that are regarded as vital to military preparedness. It may be to deny the goods to other states, so as to avoid assisting them in the development of their welfare or power. For many years, especially under the Battle Act, the United States has imposed an embargo on the shipment of strategic goods to the Soviet Union, mainland China, and other Communist states, and it has insisted that foreign countries receiving American aid impose similar embargoes. More recently, it has imposed a much more extensive embargo on shipments to Cuba. A government may make it illegal for its nationals to sell goods to other states, even though the goods never enter its territory. It may prohibit ships flying its flag from carrying forbidden goods to another state, and can bar from its ports foreign ships engaged in obnoxious trading operations. It can freeze the assets that foreign governments and their nationals have deposited in its territory, thus preventing further purchases. Needless to say, lesser measures may also be taken, such as prohibiting the sale to a country of a greater quantity of a given item than is thought necessary to it for serving normal and proper purposes.[13]

## International Commodity Agreements

International agreements have been made, designed to regulate the marketing of a few commodities (commodities supplied by a relatively small number of countries, and for which no substitute is readily available, e.g., tin, sugar, wheat, and coffee).[14] Several schemes are employed. One calls for the establishment of a buffer stock, the plan being to sell from the stock to prevent prices from going too high and to buy for the stock to prevent them from going too low. Another calls for price maintenance by restricting the total amount offered on the world market, each exporting country being restricted to a given quota. Still another

[13] Yuan-li Wu, *Economic Warfare* (Englewood Cliffs, N.J., Prentice-Hall, 1952), esp. pp. 16-85. For a study of American policies of economic warfare during World War II, see David L. Gordon and Royden Dangerfield, *The Hidden Weapon* (New York, Harper & Row, 1947).

[14] Robert M. Stern, "Policies for Trade and Development," *International Conciliation*, No. 548 (May, 1964), pp. 45-53.

calls for a long-term contract between exporters and importers under which they obligate themselves to sell and buy agreed quantities in given circumstances in the hope of keeping prices within desired limits. Efforts along these lines have so far achieved rather indifferent success.

## State Trading

With qualifications, the discussion of trade arrangements has so far assumed that the system is one in which government stands apart from private enterprise, imposing regulations and restrictions on private operators. However, considerable state trading also occurs. The international trade of Communist states is conducted exclusively by agencies under governmental control, and in many other countries governments are merchants at one time or another, and in respect to one commodity or another. Armaments are generally exported and imported by governments. A number of the governments in Europe have established a tobacco monopoly, and some monopolize the purchase and sale of alcohol as well. After World War II some governments made bulk purchases abroad, e.g., the British purchase of Argentine meat. Merchant shipping is frequently government-owned and -operated. The agricultural support program in the United States has as one of its features the sale of surplus products abroad by the government.[15]

If anything, state trading enhances opportunities to make economics a weapon. The possibility is implicit in every bargain which is made or avoided. Unfriendly states can be boycotted, and friendly states can be patronized. The terms of the bargains which are made can be generous or hard. Goods can be bought abroad simply to prevent them from falling into the hands of another state which also wants them; they can be sold or otherwise disposed of in such a way as to disrupt the economy of another state or to help it out of difficulties. The possible political advantages are obvious. At the same time, there are dangers, for a system which gives political significance to all commercial transactions may well increase international friction.

## FOREIGN INVESTMENTS

So far in this chapter we have been asking how governments can pursue whatever objectives they have by actions directly affecting foreign exchange and international trade in goods and services. The international exchange of capital also occurs, and offers further means by which the achievement of public objectives can be promoted. Foreign investments

---

[15] Charles P. Kindleberger, *Foreign Trade and the National Economy* (New Haven, Conn., Yale University Press, 1962), pp. 134-136.

may be made by private persons, by governments themselves, or by international agencies established by governments.

## Policies of Capital Exporters

*1. Encouraging investments abroad.* Governments have various means at their disposal for encouraging, regulating, or restricting foreign investments by private persons. Both the means and the objectives which governments hope to promote in this way have been exhaustively analyzed and illustrated by Eugene Staley, in his *War and the Private Investor.*[16] Governments themselves may participate along with private investors in financing foreign projects in order to encourage private investments or to serve other interests of state. For example, the Japanese government for several decades owned a controlling interest in the Oriental Development Co., a firm engaged in extensive overseas commercial operations. The British government in 1913 acquired stock in the Anglo-Iranian Oil Co. and held it until the property was nationalized by Iran. The U.S. Export-Import Bank makes loans to promote American foreign trade and, in association with the Foreign Credit Insurance Association, insures loans made for the same purpose by private banks. Also, governments sometimes subsidize private companies engaged in investment and other activities abroad. Sometimes they guarantee a foreign investment or earnings on the investment, or the convertibility of earnings (i.e., the opportunity to repatriate earnings by exchanging a foreign currency for money of the home state). They may either encourage or discourage foreign investing and foreign economic operations of all kinds by the tax policies which they pursue, and by the arrangements which they make with other governments (or fail to make) concerning double taxation. They may offer informal inducements to private lending, government officials taking advantage of personal, social, and business connections, appealing to patriotism, or tacitly holding out the possibility of public distinction and prestige to investors who serve their country well. Promises of firm diplomatic and consular support may be made. Governments of investing countries normally insist vigorously that other governments adhere to the legal principle that private property is not to be nationalized without just compensation.

*2. Discouraging investments abroad.* Governments may also exert negative influences over foreign investments. The objection of a government is in itself usually enough to induce bankers and others to refuse to make a

16 Treatment of the subject here is based largely on Staley's work. See especially his Chapters 4 and 10: "How Investments Serve Diplomacy," and "How Governments Influence Their Investors." See also Jacob Viner, "International Finance and Balance of Power Diplomacy, 1880-1914," *Southwestern Political and Social Science Quarterly,* Vol. 9 (March, 1929), pp. 407-451; *idem,* "Political Aspects of International Finance," *Journal of Business,* Vol. 1 (April, 1928), pp. 141-173.

loan to foreign governments. The law may preclude the listing of foreign securities on the stock exchange unless prior authorization is received from the appropriate governmental agency. In 1934 Congress enacted the Johnson Act, making it a criminal offense to lend money to a foreign government in default on its financial obligations to the United States government. The various American "neutrality" acts of the 1930's prohibited the lending of money to belligerents under certain stipulated conditions.

3. *Objectives served by governmental measures.* Governments may pursue many objectives through their influence or control over the direction and size of foreign investments. Foreign investments, whether private or public, may contribute to the prosperity of the creditor country in various ways, for example, by making available raw material or other resources which otherwise would have gone untapped. They usually enhance the creditor country's prestige and power. Investments in backward and weak areas, especially, may facilitate the extension of the civilization and culture of the more advanced country. Foreign investments have frequently been instruments for penetrating and acquiring political influence in foreign areas. They have provided excuses for intervention and have sometimes been the prelude to conquest. Both Russia and Japan, for example, have at different times acquired great influence and control in Manchuria through the contractual rights which went along with the construction and operation of railways in the region. In the early decades of this century, the United States frequently intervened in various Caribbean republics to protect the rights of investors there. The knowledge of foreign areas gained by citizens who are active in commercial operations abroad is sometimes of considerable value from an intelligence point of view. The threat that loans would be denied or that existing short-term loans would be withdrawn has, on occasion, served as a bargaining weapon. At times, one government has been able to bring about the downfall of another by preventing the extension of loans to it; and frequently embargoes on loans, like embargoes on trade, have presumably impeded the economic or military strengthening of unfriendly states. Investments directed toward friendly and allied states may, of course, enhance both their welfare and their power.

4. *The International Bank for Reconstruction and Development.* At the close of World War II a number of Allied nations joined in establishing the International Bank for Reconstruction and Development (the IBRD, or World Bank), of which most states of the free world are members.[17] The members contribute capital to the bank and have voting power on its Board of Governors roughly in proportion to their contributions. The bank may extend loans to member governments or, if the member government involved guarantees the loan, to private corpora-

[17] Snider, *op. cit.,* pp. 564-579.

tions. Loans must be for specific projects which will contribute to economic growth and development in the borrowing country; in practice, the bank has acted primarily to develop transportation facilities and to increase the output of electric power. Interest rates and provisions for repayment approximate those considered reasonable by commercial standards. In comparison with the vast sums expended by the United States and other countries in various foreign aid programs, the investments of the bank have been small. It is nevertheless a useful agency for the promotion of economic progress. Two affiliated agencies are also in operation. The International Finance Corporation makes loans to private enterprises without any government guarantee. And the International Development Association helps underdeveloped countries that can make effective use of capital but that need especially favorable arrangements as far as interest rates and repayment provisions are concerned.

## Policies of Capital Importers

So far we have spoken of international investments mainly in terms of the policies and purposes of the investor. Borrowers, of course, are also involved, and they may do various things to attract or repel investors. They can attract foreign investments by the stability of their political and economic system, by their reputation for reliability in the payment of debts, and of course, by the opportunities for profit which they provide. They can adopt tax policies which make investment in their territory attractive. Tariffs which they adopt sometimes induce foreign enterprises to make what are called direct investments, that is, the foreign enterprise establishes a branch factory inside the tariff wall. Governments desiring to attract investors may give guarantees that earnings from investments can be converted from their own currency into the currency of the investor and then repatriated. By treaty or contract they can give assurances against nationalization. If none of these conditions or policies prevails, foreign investors are likely to stay away.

Many advanced countries have taken measures against the alienation of control over certain enterprises, and these steps restrict foreign investment. They may regulate or prohibit ownership by aliens of certain kinds of resources, such as land and coal mines. Governments, or private corporations themselves, sometimes require that leading officers of corporations shall not be foreigners. Similarly, less advanced or politically weak countries sometimes seek to protect themselves against economic penetration in various ways. They may use the same devices as the advanced countries. When they need capital or foreign skills, they may give preference to nationals of states deemed least likely to take advantage of the situation for imperialistic purposes. They have also sought acceptance of certain legal principles; they have, in fact, succeeded in establishing the principle that force shall not be used to collect public contract debts, but have not fared so well in efforts to establish the principle, often expressed in a "Calvo clause" in contracts, that the foreign investor shall have no right of diplomatic protection from his home government. Of course, the nationalization or socialization of enterprises or of resources precludes foreign investment in them unless the socializing government itself decides to borrow foreign capital.[18]

## ECONOMIC NATIONALISM AND ECONOMIC INTERNATIONALISM

Foreign economic policies can be classified in several ways. Most frequently they are labeled by the terms *economic nationalism* and *economic internationalism*. Neither term has a fixed and precise meaning.

The term *economic nationalism* is sometimes used to denote policies aimed to produce *Autarkie* or economic self-sufficiency, the object being to reduce or eliminate dependence upon foreign markets and foreign sources of supply. This in turn may be desired to promote the financial gain of influential groups which wish to be shielded against foreign competition, or to insulate the domestic economy from foreign economic instability, or to prepare the country for war, when its foreign commercial ties would be severed in any event.

The term is also sometimes given a broader meaning, to denote "the point of view that it ought to be the object of statesmanship in economic matters to increase the power rather than the economic well-being of a given society." So defined, economic nationalism complements political nationalism, so far as both seek to consolidate and enhance the power of the state.

Whatever the definition, the methods adopted are selected from those which have already been discussed in this chapter. Tariffs, quotas, exchange controls, and the licensing of foreign trade may be chosen. State subsidies may be granted to encourage domestic enterprises, such as the production of synthetic oil. Such foreign trade as continues and such foreign investments as are made may be so directed as to favor potential allies and to avoid strengthening potential enemies. Pronatalist and other population policies may be pursued to increase the manpower available for war.

Economic internationalism is an even vaguer concept. Generally it connotes an emphasis on economic well-being rather than on power, and a belief that well-being can best be promoted by an extensive and a reasonably free international exchange of goods, services, and capital. The economic internationalist accepts the idea that each country should specialize in the production of those things which it is economically best

---

[18] Staley, *War and the Private Investor*, pp. 406-414.

fitted to produce, and should then exchange its products for those which can be produced most advantageously abroad. Barriers to trade and commerce are to be kept at a minimum, and such barriers as exist are to be nondiscriminatory. Immigration and emigration should be free. Mass production is to occur for a world market. Through an international division of labor and reasonably free trade, it is hoped, the world's resources can be exploited and allocated in such a way as to provide the maximum well-being for all. The economic internationalist tends toward the extreme of seeking an integrated world economy, rather than a series of national economies more or less poorly integrated with each other.

The actual policies of states usually fall somewhere between the two extremes. Economic nationalism has generally proved to be more attractive than economic internationalism, especially in relationships among states which regard themselves as potential enemies. Among friends and allies, economic nationalism is likely to be considerably modified. Though the countries of the West since World War II have not exactly pursued a policy of economic internationalism as defined above, they have implemented many cooperative and sometimes very generous policies designed to promote both their well-being and their power.

## THE DEVELOPMENT OF THE UNDERDEVELOPED

The above topics are all discussed on the assumption that direct self-interest is the dominant motive in international economic matters, and that the immediate aim of each state is its own well-being or power. But it is better not to make this assumption in discussing programs of international aid. One of the major questions concerning such programs is why they are or should be undertaken. And the other major question is how they can be made successful—what kinds of aid seem likely to produce what kinds of results.

The motives of international aid have been varied and overlapping, and in most cases two or more of them have operated simultaneously.[19] Some of them are self-regarding. Perhaps the broadest of the motives has been to preserve and to promote a desirable kind of world environment—a world environment that permits the state granting aid to live its own life in its own way, as free as can be from external threats and restraints, or more positively, a world environment that is stimulating and contributes constructively to goal achievement within the state. This broad motive can be subdivided almost indefinitely. It encompasses a concern for power relationships—a concern that has been prominent in connection with foreign aid programs, cited to justify both direct military

[19] Eugene Staley, *The Future of Underdeveloped Countries* (New York, Harper & Row, 1961), pp. 27-64 and 442-466. Robert A. Goldwin, ed., *Why Foreign Aid?* (Chicago, Rand McNally, 1962).

aid (i.e., the giving of military equipment, training, etc. to the armed forces of another state) and every other kind of aid that might affect the foreign policies and power of other states in a desirable way. It also encompasses an overlapping concern for attitudes and ideologies; liberals generally believe that liberalism will flourish at home more surely if it also prevails abroad, and Communists have comparable attitudes. And both may want their respective ideologies to be extended not only for their good at home but also for the good of people abroad. The broad objective also encompasses concern for the fate of specific governments and of specific political leaders, and concern that certain specific policies should be followed or avoided. Thus threats and promises regarding aid are made, and aid is granted or denied or withdrawn in order to sustain or undermine political actors abroad. Further, the broad objective leads some to contemplate the tremendous disparities in the level of development achieved by different peoples over the world and to render the judgment that the disparities are sources of long-run danger, and that reasonable efforts should be made to prevent these disparities from increasing and, even better, to bring about their reduction.

Self-regarding motives of a somewhat different sort operate too. Though aid involves costs and sacrifices, at times it also involves potential advantages, e.g., in gaining access to, or knowledge of, commercial opportunities abroad; it may help alleviate domestic problems, e,g., the problem of disposing of surplus agricultural products in the United States. It may enhance the prestige of the giver around the world and his pride at home; to give aid is in some sense to assume a position of superiority that may be gratifying to the ego. Finally, experience in promoting development abroad may bring knowledge and ideas that help solve problems at home.

Though the above motives are all self-regarding, at least in part, most of them simultaneously reflect concern for the interests of others. Participating in measures designed to create a desirable kind of world may be as advantageous to the receiver as to the giver, if not more. The receiver's security, or his ideology, or political fate, may also be at stake. To say that the philanthropic giver is really seeking to gratify his own ego or to expiate his guilt may in some sense be true; but at the same time to put the philanthropist and the exploiter and the miser all in the same category is to ignore significant moral and practical distinctions. The state that looks for its advantage in a distant and uncertain future by helping others now can be described as pursuing self-interest, but it is self-interest with a difference; the difference is suggested by calling the self-interest enlightened, but it is probably better to say that a considerable degree of altruism is often involved. Sometimes altruism is dominant, the giving of aid occurring at a real sacrifice without any prospect of identifiable reward.

Difficulties in answering questions about the why of foreign aid are more than matched by difficulties in answering questions about how it can be effective, that is, what kinds of aid will produce the desired results. The problems are perhaps simplest in connection with military aid, where the aim is to enhance strength vis-à-vis a common external enemy. But even in this connection it sometimes happens that the enhanced strength of the aided government is significant not so much against a common enemy as against some other country or against the domestic opposition. For example, the United States may enhance Turkey's strength against the Soviet Union, only to find Turkey using its enhanced strength against governments in Cyprus and Greece; and it may enhance Vietnam's strength against Communists only to find that the guns supplied are turned on Buddhists.

The problems associated with foreign aid are vastly greater where the aim is the general development of the underdeveloped. The conditions to be changed are varied and fall roughly in the following categories. (1) Those relating immediately to human resources. A considerable portion of the population may be illiterate, diseased, unskilled, and in the grip of religious or other value systems that militate against what in the West is regarded as progress; further, in recent years throughout much of the world a "population explosion" has been occurring which makes it necessary to run faster just to stay in the same place. (2) Those relating to institutional development. Governmental institutions are commonly inadequate, in varying degrees. Many populations are so loosely organized for governmental purposes, and governmental administration is so meager and distant, that the execution of a plan for development is extremely difficult. Inefficiency and corruption often add to the problems. Educational institutions are also likely to be inadequate at all levels, and commercial and financial institutions may be too few, too small, and too uninspired. (3) Those relating to the attitudes and interests of the elite. In many countries, dominant elites or ruling classes (or important elements within them) fear the results of efforts to develop human resources and governmental and educational institutions, and if they have money to invest they may prefer to send it abroad rather than risk it at home. (4) Those relating immediately to material conditions. Transportation and communication systems are frequently inadequate. Inanimate sources of energy (coal, oil, water power, etc.) and other natural resources are insufficiently exploited. Agricultural methods and tools are primitive. Factories, and machines to put in them, are in short supply.

Given such great and complex problems, it is difficult to know where to start and how to apportion efforts among the various needs. What proportion of the population needs to be educated, and just how much and what kind of education is necessary? What proportion of aid money should go into public health systems and other measures to combat disease? How about birth control? What can be done, if anything, about value systems that make work undignified, that call for a renunciation of material and worldly things, or that lead those who double their hourly wage to work half as long? What can be done, if anything, about political systems that are corrupt or inefficient, or resistant to change, or so lacking in a consensual base that disorder and instability are the rule? This question is particularly acute where there is chronic suspicion of, if not antagonism toward, the efforts of outsiders and "imperialists."

Further, there are other problems. What, after all, is the probable relationship between development, if it can be brought about, and political behavior? Perhaps the least threatening of all people are those without hope. When hope is built up, what may the consequences be? It is quite possible that better health, better education, and somewhat higher standards of living will whet appetites and make people more demanding and more impatient, leading not to peace but to revolution at home and abroad, not to democracy and respect for human rights but to dictatorship.

This raises the question whether revolution and war and dictatorship are always bad. And it also obviously raises the question of how aid can be handled in a manner which not only maximizes the prospect of achieving the intended results but also minimizes the prospect of producing results that are unintended and undesirable.

Though it is doubtful whether anyone has satisfactory answers to the various kinds of questions raised above, a number of governments have adopted aid programs. In 1963 the United States provided aid in the amount of $4.3 billion, of which 63 percent was in grants and the rest in loans at less than 5 percent interest. Corresponding figures for other contributors of aid were as follows: France, $900 million (81 percent in grants); Germany, $700 million (28 percent in grants); United Kingdom, $500 million (52 percent in grants); Japan, $280 million (32 percent in grants). These states are all members of the Development Assistance Committee, as are Belgium, Canada, Denmark, Italy, the Netherlands, Norway, and Portugal. In 1963 their combined assistance to other states totaled over $7.1 billion. French aid went especially to former colonies. The Soviet Union has had an aid program of some magnitude since the latter half of the 1950's, and Communist China has more recently entered the scene. Even Israel plays a role. American aid went to over 70 countries, German aid to about 90.[20] The point is that aid has become a rather widespread feature of foreign policy and international relationships.

Note that we are discussing here development efforts in a chapter on

[20] Organization for Economic Cooperation and Development, *Development Assistance Efforts and Policies of Members of the Development Assistance Committee, 1964 Review* (Report by Willard L. Thorp, September 1964), pp. 41, 46. Staley, *The Future of Underdeveloped Countries*, pp. 408-417. Stern, *op. cit.*, pp. 23-24.

the pursuit of objectives by economic means. This is justifiable, but at the same time might be misleading. Whether the object of aid is better education or better health or better governmental administration or greater agricultural or industrial production, economic means have to be used. At the same time, it is obvious that the problem of development is not solely economic. Virtually every field of learning must be called upon if the problems of developing the underdeveloped countries are to be solved, and many resources must be employed and developed in addition to those ordinarily classified as economic.

## SUGGESTED READINGS

COFFIN, Frank M., *Witness for AID* (Boston, Houghton Mifflin, 1964).

GARDNER, Richard N., *In Pursuit of World Order, U. S. Foreign Policy and International Organizations* (New York, Praeger, 1964).

GOLDWIN, Robert A., ed., *Why Foreign Aid?* (Chicago, Rand McNally, 1962).

HALLOWELL, John H., ed., *Development: For What?* (Durham, N.C., Duke University Press, 1964).

HAMBIDGE, Gove, ed., *Dynamics of Development* (New York, Praeger, 1964).

KORBONSKI, Andrzej, "Comecon," *International Organization*, No. 549 (September, 1964).

LARY, Hal B., *Problems of the United States as World Banker and Trader* (Princeton, N.J., Princeton University Press, 1963).

LISKA, George, *The New Statecraft: Foreign Aid in American Foreign Policy* (Chicago, The University of Chicago Press, 1960).

MEIER, Gerald M., *International Trade and Development* (New York, Harper & Row, 1963).

MONTGOMERY, John D., *The Politics of Foreign Aid, American Experience in Southeast Asia* (New York, Praeger, 1962).

ROSTOW, W. W., *The Stages of Economic Growth* (Cambridge, Cambridge University Press, 1960).

SNIDER, Delbert A., *Introduction to International Economics,* 3rd ed. (Homewood, Ill., Irwin, 1963).

STALEY, Eugene, *The Future of Underdeveloped Countries, Political Implications of Economic Development* (New York, Harper & Row, 1961).

STERN, Robert M., "Policies for Trade and Development," *International Conciliation,* No. 648 (May, 1964).

# 16

# INFORMATIONAL AND
# CULTURAL ACTIVITIES

States have long engaged in informational, propaganda, educational, and cultural activities as means of promoting their foreign policy objectives, and have done so increasingly in recent years. Improved communication facilities make it possible, and the greater significance of mass attitudes in political life make it seem desirable. Moreover, the potentially suicidal character of nuclear war suggests both increased efforts of all sorts to reinforce peace and a search for methods other than war for defending and promoting political goals.

The objectives of informational, propaganda, educational, and cultural activities cover a considerable range. A state engaged in them may aim: (1) simply to enhance knowledge and understanding; (2) to cultivate good will abroad, gain prestige, and perhaps undermine or destroy such good will and prestige as an unfriendly government may enjoy in a third state; (3) to shape mass attitudes in another state so as to influence its government to follow or not to follow a certain course of action; (4) to shape mass attitudes in another state so as to reinforce or undermine its government or its political and social order; if this is the purpose, terrorism and guerrilla warfare may or may not be added as means.

A fifth aim might well be added. Attitudes at home are often a vital factor in a state's international relations. Every government wants a population wholly loyal to it and unresponsive to appeals from foreign governments; and every government wants a population with attitudes that strengthen it in its dealings with other states, whether by allowing for flexibility or by reinforcing adamant stands.

Distinctions between informational, propaganda, educational, and cultural activities are not clear-cut. In fact, a given activity might fall simul-

329

taneously in all four categories. The word *informational* causes little difficulty, suggesting the dissemination of news. *Propaganda* is much more troublesome. The object of propaganda is to influence behavior in a desired way by deliberately shaping attitudes, that is, by affecting judgments on questions of fact or value, or by affecting the manner in which people perceive or interpret conditions or events. The usual connotation is that the mass media of communication are employed and that a mass audience is involved.[1] "Implicit in the word propaganda today is the large-scale promotion of ideas."[2] *Educational* activities and propaganda overlap each other substantially. This is true even in terms of the means of communication employed, for some education is now conducted via mass media. The inculcation of values, which is a feature of every educational system, may be indistinguishable from propaganda. But still, education occurs (or at least the ideal is that it should occur) in an atmosphere of reasoned inquiry, of critical appraisal; and most of what is called education (above all in the sciences and fine arts) commonly goes on without conscious regard for political issues. Moreover, the prime concern of the educator is presumably the truth, whereas the prime concern of the propagandist—even in adhering to the truth—is to shape attitudes on certain issues in a preconceived way. The term *cultural* is also broad and loose. It encompasses educational activities and more. "A nation's culture is the sum total of its achievement; its own expression of its own personality; its way of thinking and acting. Its program of cultural relations abroad is its method of making these things known to foreigners."[3]

Given the overlapping of informational, propaganda, educational, and cultural activities, any organizational plan that we might employ for this chapter has faults. What we will do is to focus first upon what are ordinarily thought of as informational and propaganda activities; they rely mainly on the "quick media" and have short-run uses, and for the most part they are unilateral and involve a one-way flow. Then we will focus on what are ordinarily thought of as educational and cultural activities; they are usually more indirect and longer-run in their effects, and for the most part they are bilateral or multilateral and involve a two-way flow. Further, at the close of the chapter we will take note of the fact that the activities of parties and governments in these realms are supplemented by organized groups abroad—groups which sometimes deserve to be called fifth columns and which sometimes engage in guerrilla war.

[1] Robert T. Holt and Robert W. van de Velde, *Strategic Psychological Operations and American Foreign Policy* (Chicago, The University of Chicago Press, 1960), pp. 26-28.

[2] Terence H. Qualter, *Propaganda and Psychological Warfare* (New York, Random House, 1962), p. 33.

[3] Ruth Emily McMurry and Muna Lee, *The Cultural Approach, Another Way in International Relations* (Chapel Hill, University of North Carolina Press, 1947), p. 2.

# INFORMATIONAL AND PROPAGANDA ACTIVITIES

Governments affect attitudes relevant to international politics both incidentally and deliberately. Incidental effects come simply from the fact that governments act, and it has often been observed that actions speak louder than words; in a great many situations the effects achieved incidentally are so profound that they cannot be altered much by deliberate informational and propaganda activities. Israel, for example, affected the attitudes of surrounding Arab peoples far more by simply establishing its independence than it can possibly do in many decades of information and propaganda activity. And the Soviet Union affected attitudes over the world far more by launching Sputnik into orbit than it possibly could have by any kind of purely verbal efforts. Moreover, various qualities of the domestic life of states, for which governments may or may not have much responsibility, do much to affect attitudes abroad. The cultural and scientific achievements of the United States, the handling of race problems, and the standards of living maintained constitute, in a sense, propaganda of the deed that is far more convincing than propaganda of the word.

Nevertheless, in addition to acting, governments commonly seek to inform people about their actions and to see to it, in so far as they can, that people perceive and interpret developments in a desirable way. They employ various means to this end.

The simplest method is to make public statements. In the natural course of events statements made by the President of the United States get reported around the world. He can command attention in the news media simply by holding a press conference or making a speech. And in one degree or another so can governmental leaders throughout the world. International conferences are sometimes held not so much with a view to solving the problems on the agenda as with a view to obtaining a forum that will assure maximum attention to statements made. Statesmen travel to the United Nations to make pronouncements in order to maximize their propaganda effect. And, for that matter, it is a commonplace that many of the statements of members of the regular delegations at the United Nations are made primarily so that they will be reported over the world, either via news media or in the documents that the United Nations itself distributes. In addition to these kinds of activities, a high proportion of the governments of the world maintain one or more offices—perhaps one or more in each major governmental agency—whose main purpose is to make news available and to offer comments on questions of the day.

News agencies provide one kind of channel through which information and propaganda are gathered and disseminated. There are some 185 of them, varying greatly both in the extent of their operations and in the extent to which they deliberately aim to serve the interests of specific governments.[4] Some, like the AP and UPI, gather and disseminate news throughout most of the world, and others confine their operations to one country only (usually exchanging news with other agencies operating elsewhere). Some are private and others public, though the distinction gets blurred when a "private" agency is subsidized by a government and when a "public" agency is given substantial independence of governmental control. The news agencies most closely controlled for political purposes are no doubt those of the Communist world (e.g., the Soviet agency, Tass); at the same time it should be recognized that those reporting for the AP, for UPI, for Reuters, or for the Agence France-Presse are likely to have attitudes that lead them willingly and naturally to favor one side over another in selecting and interpreting news of international significance.

Radio and more recently TV have come to be used increasingly in international information and propaganda activities. In 1963, for example, the Voice of America was carrying 789 hours of radio broadcasts per week directly to foreign listeners in 36 languages. "In addition, some 14,000 hours a week of programs were prepared in Voice studios and mailed by air to more than 5,000 local overseas stations. These were broadcast on medium wave in more than 60 languages to immense audiences. . . ."[5] The Soviet Union was broadcasting an even greater number of hours directly to foreign listeners in many languages.[6] Program content runs the gamut in the attempt to reflect the culture and policies of the sending country fairly (or to depict it favorably) and, perhaps, in attempting to inculcate unfavorable attitudes toward other governments or social systems. Britain likewise engages extensively in foreign broadcasting, and a great many other countries do so in a more limited way. Where conditions are unsettled and relationships are strained—as they have been at times, for example, in the Arab world—broadcasts may be highly inflammatory, inciting violence and revolution.

Technological factors have so far placed rather severe limits on direct international telecasting, but the shipment of packaged programs for use by foreign TV stations has developed on a rather extensive scale. The United States Information Agency makes programs available both on a regular and a special basis to TV stations abroad, e.g., by supplying them with films of the more spectacular space shots. Various regional groupings of countries have arranged to exchange TV programs, e.g., the 18

[4] See UNESCO, Department of Mass Communications, *World Communications: Press, Radio, Television, Film* (New York, UNESCO Publications Center, 1964).

[5] U. S. Information Agency, *20th Report to Congress, January 1-June 30, 1963*, pp. 9-10.

[6] Frederick C. Barghoorn, *Soviet Foreign Progapanda* (Princeton, N.J., Princeton University Press, 1964), pp. 279-281.

western European countries joined in Eurovision and the Soviet orbit countries joined in Intervision. Experiments with communication satellites suggest that the time is soon coming when the Soviet Premier or the American President can speak directly to everyone in the world who is in reach of a TV set, provided the various networks and stations are willing to carry the program.

Supplementing these methods of disseminating information and propaganda are exhibits, displays, and demonstrations of various sorts. The capsule in which John Glenn orbited the earth was put on display in some 23 countries, and Spacemobiles tour various foreign countries offering demonstrations and talks concerning space and American achievements in space. Governments commonly subsidize the national exhibits at world fairs.

It is not uncommon for the government of one country, or for persons or parties supporting it, to get help within other countries in the dissemination of information and propaganda. It happens in various ways. In the 1930's the Nazi movement in Germany inspired comparable movements in other countries, which conveyed the Nazi line and Nazi attitudes to them. Ever since the Bolshevik Revolution, Communist parties have assisted the Soviet Union in its propaganda efforts abroad, and more recently some of these parties, or splinter groups from them, have assisted Communist China. Various private associations and "front" organizations (e.g., the Society for Friendship with the Soviet Union) have likewise served as transmission belts for Communist propaganda.

Apart from efforts of a subversive sort, there have also been efforts simply to influence policy within the framework of the existing system. A report of the Senate Foreign Relations Committee in 1964 spoke of "persistent efforts by numerous agents of foreign principals to influence the conduct of United States foreign and domestic policies using techniques outside the normal diplomatic channels. This trend has been accompanied by an upsurge in the hiring within this country of public relations men, economic advisers, lawyers, and consultants by foreign interests." The United States has enacted legislation requiring the agents of foreign principals to register, revealing their connection and their identity; and it has applied the requirement to leading Communists, among others. The Senate Foreign Relations Committee has called for a strengthening of the legislation. It wants to prohibit agents of foreign principals from making campaign contributions in primary and general elections and to prohibit "contingent fee contracts between agents and foreign principals based upon success in political activities to be undertaken by the agent." [7]

[7] United States Congress, Senate, *Foreign Agents Registration Act Amendments*, 88th Cong., 2d Sess., 1964, Rpt. 875, pp. 2-4.

## EDUCATIONAL AND CULTURAL ACTIVITIES

A considerable portion of the internationally significant educational and cultural activities are entirely nongovernmental. Government can be permissive or restrictive, or can be permissive in one connection and restrictive in another; and educational and cultural activities and relationships tend to develop accordingly. The ties that bind the English-speaking world developed for the most part without deliberate governmental effort. Similarly, when the people of other countries learn about the culture of the United States through Hollywood movies and American tourists, the role of the government is obviously minimal. But for several centuries before Perry, the role of the Japanese government was quite decisive in isolating Japan from all kinds of contact with the rest of the world, and in more recent times both the Chinese Communist and the Soviet governments have severely restricted the educational and cultural contacts—in fact, all contacts—of their people with the outside world, and particularly with the non-Communist part of the outside world.

Still, many governments play positive roles in promoting international educational and cultural activities. Much of what is done goes under the heading, the exchange of persons. Beyond that, the principal activities relate to libraries, books, and schools.

What is called the exchange of persons is usually not exchange in the sense of a trade but simply the travel of persons from one country to another. Travel provides an obvious opportunity for proselyting. People who come into a given country may well be influenced by what they observe there, and people who go abroad may influence those with whom they come into contact.

Given the fact that the presence of foreigners within a country provides an opportunity to influence their attitudes (and given some other kinds of motives as well), governments and many private agencies commonly encourage them to come. A UNESCO report indicates that in 1963, governments and other agencies in 116 states and territories throughout the world offered some 130,000 awards for international travel and study.[8] If the record of the preceding year is a reliable guide, about a third of these awards went to nationals who were to go abroad, and two-thirds to foreign nationals who were to come to the donor country.[9] The Soviet Union is among the countries that seek to entice foreign students—or at least certain types of foreign students. It was encouraged in this respect from the first, for soon after the revolution in 1917 the Soviet Union succeeded in indoctrinating some of the prisoners of war

---

[8] UNESCO, *Study Abroad, International Handbook, Fellowships, Scholarships, Educational Exchange,* XIV (Paris, UNESCO, 1963), p. 7.

[9] *Ibid.,* p. 666.

over whom it had inherited control and found them to be useful revolutionary agents on their release and repatriation. Subsequently, various schools in the Soviet Union became centers for training foreign students. Though knowledge of Soviet practices in this respect is scant, apparently a considerable portion of the prominent Communists throughout the world have attended these schools. As of 1945, for example, 57 percent of the members of the Central Committee of the Chinese Communist Party were persons who had received some of their education in the Soviet Union.[10] In recent years there has been a sharp increase in the number of students going to the Soviet Union for study. In 1960–1961 almost 1800 students from non-Communist states were studying there (four times as many as in 1956); and, in addition, some 1900 were studying in Communist countries other than the Soviet Union. Ninety-six percent were from the underdeveloped countries.[11] It is not known to what extent their motives in choosing their place of study were ideological. The reverse flow—the flow of Soviet students to the free world—is small.

The United States has a rather extensive exchange program. Legislation associated mainly with the name of Senator Fulbright has enabled some 30,000 Americans to go abroad since 1949 and some 60,000 students to come to the United States for scholarly and educational purposes.[12] In the fiscal year ending June 30, 1963, the Bureau of Educational and Cultural Affairs in the Department of State awarded grants to over 2300 United States citizens to go abroad for the following purposes: 830 for graduate study, 650 for teaching or research at institutions of higher learning, 560 to teach in elementary or secondary schools or to attend foreign-language seminars, and 280 for general lecturing or specialized consultation and advice. In the same year the Bureau issued grants to almost 6000 persons from 130 foreign countries and territories to come to the United States for the following purposes: 2000 for university study, 800 to teach in elementary or secondary schools or for related special training, almost 700 to teach or do research at institutions of higher learning, and 2100 for varied kinds of educational training and experience.[13] The Bureau also sponsors the appearance abroad of individuals and groups in the performing arts. The obvious hope is that the

---

[10] Frederick C. Barghoorn, "The Ideological Weapon in Soviet Strategy," in C. Grove Haines, ed., *The Threat of Soviet Imperialism* (Baltimore, Johns Hopkins Press, 1954), pp. 91-92.

[11] United States Congress, Senate, Committee on Foreign Relations, *Mutual Educational and Cultural Exchange Act*, Hearings . . . on S. 1154, 87th Cong., 1st Sess. March 29 and April 27, 1961, pp. 178-179.

[12] "The Department of State's Educational Exchange Program," Special Report on Federal Programs, American Council on Education, Vol. II, No. 10 (November, 1964), p. 1.

[13] *Open Doors, 1964, Report on International Exchange* (New York, Institute of International Education, 1964), p. 13.

experience of foreigners in the United States and their contact with Americans who go abroad, will create or reinforce attitudes favorable to the country and to the principles for which it stands; further, the obvious hope is that Americans themselves will gain from the experience. The Mutual Educational and Cultural Exchange Act of 1961 (the Fulbright-Hays Act) contains a fuller statement of purpose.

The purpose of this Act is to enable the Government of the United States to increase mutual understanding between the people of the United States and the people of other countries by means of educational and cultural exchange; to strengthen the ties which unite us with other nations by demonstrating the educational and cultural interests, developments, and achievements of the people of the United States and other nations, and the contributions being made toward a peaceful and more fruitful life for people throughout the world; to promote international cooperation for educational and cultural advancement; and thus to assist in the development of friendly, sympathetic, and peaceful relations between the United States and the other countries of the world.

The United States also promotes the exchange of persons outside the framework of the Fulbright legislation. In the fiscal year ending in 1963 the Agency for International Development (AID) brought almost 6000 persons to the United States for the training needed for the implementation of AID programs. Moreover, AID personnel and many other Americans employed by firms and institutions under contract with AID go abroad in considerable number. The Peace Corps has also been sending Americans abroad. Over the years the Department of Defense has operated by far the biggest of the exchange programs by stationing American military personnel overseas and bringing thousands of foreign military personnel to the United States for training. Various other departments and executive agencies have smaller programs.

Many governments, in addition to those of the Soviet Union and the United States, have exchange programs—especially those programs designed to attract foreign students. For example, a report on the activities of Communist China in Latin America in 1964 notes the activities of the New China News Agency, the broadcasts in Spanish and Portuguese from Peking, and the distribution of the Spanish edition of the *Peking Review;* the report then goes on to say:

The most telling line in propaganda is probably the flood of hospitable invitations to Latin Americans to visit China. These are not confined to communists: many left-wing politicians, intellectuals and professional men have been invited to China and found themselves stimulated and impressed by what they saw there. Trade unionists, students and cultural delegations have been enthusiastically welcomed in Peking and returned home with their bags full of Mao Tsetung's writings in Spanish translations. . . .[14]

14 *Economist,* Vol. 213 (October 10, 1964), p. 136.

In addition to exchanging persons, governments pursue international educational and cultural activities principally by supporting libraries and schools abroad. The United States Information Agency operates over 180 libraries abroad, plus some 80 reading rooms and over 150 binational centers. The British Council engages in similar activities and so do the agencies of many other governments. American schools abroad are of varied sorts. The Department of Defense operates many of them primarily for the benefit of the children of military personnel. Some are established by groups of parents, some by an American industry that seeks to attract and hold American employees abroad, and some by religious groups. The government has played only a peripheral role, if any, in connection with these schools (excepting those operated by the Department of Defense), but they nevertheless deserve mention; the student body frequently includes students of other nationalities, and in any event, the example of American educational practices undoubtedly has some influence.

Whether or not in formal schools, both the United States and Britain have extensive programs throughout the world for teaching English to interested people. This is done mainly on a face-to-face basis, but mass media are also employed; for example, the Voice of America beams English lessons to mainland China. Furthermore, the United States, Britain, the Soviet Union, and various other governments have more or less extensive programs for the distribution of books and other literature abroad, by sale and otherwise. The Soviet Union has attracted special attention by its program for distributing abroad the kinds of materials it wants other peoples to read; these materials are usually sold at low prices and are printed in various languages, including English.

Finally, in connection with educational and cultural activities, we should at least note the fact of competition in science. A commentator in 1956 declared that the Soviet leadership was "making a conscious, well-planned attempt to assume the scientific leadership of the world," [15] and the next year Sputnik convinced people all over the world of the success of the endeavor. Soviet scientists have been given much greater freedom to travel abroad than most Soviet citizens, e.g., to attend international scientific conferences. The United States, of course, is active in this realm too. In addition to the extensive domestic program in science, it gives considerable support to scientific research abroad. The Department of Defense, the Department of Agriculture, and the Department of Health, Education, and Welfare all make contracts with (or make grants to) foreign scientists and foreign research agencies for scientific inquiry, and foreign currency surpluses acquired through the sale of American agricultural products (PL-480 Funds) are sometimes used for the same kind of

[15] John Turkevich, quoted by Frederick C. Barghoorn, *The Soviet Cultural Offensive* (Princeton N.J., Princeton University Press, 1960), p. 23.

purposes. Coupled with the tendency to identify scientific achievement with potential military power, these activities have considerable significance.[16]

## SUBVERSION AND GUERRILLA WARFARE

As suggested at the outset, one of the possible purposes of programs of the kinds described above is to undermine and bring about the overthrow of the government or social order of another state. When such a purpose is pursued, the activities may constitute ideological warfare or aggression by subversion; and guerrilla warfare may be added.

Ideological warfare or aggression by subversion is age-old. In modern times it achieved considerable prominence in Europe after the French Revolution. Since then, nationalist movements have frequently brought ideological struggles between governments seeking to bring about the unity and independence of a nation and governments seeking to prevent such a development. Cavour, Prime Minister of Sardinia-Piedmont and chief architect of the unification of Italy a century ago, employed nationalist propaganda against governments standing in the way of unity, inciting domestic insurrection against them. In the decades preceding World War I, the government and private parties in Serbia spread nationalist propaganda in the Austro-Hungarian Empire, trying to induce Slavic people there to transfer their loyalty from the Emperor in Vienna to the idea of a united Serbian (or South Slavic) nation. In the 1930's Hitler and the German Nazis tried to make Nazis out of German-speaking people in other countries—especially in Austria and Czechoslovakia; they used nationalist and other appeals in subversive attacks which threatened the very existence of these countries.

The principal ideological struggle currently in progress is that between the Communist and non-Communist worlds. The Communist program calls for the "liberation" of the masses in all countries from what the Communists regard as capitalist oppression and exploitation, and the liberation of colonial peoples from the "yoke of imperialism." Some influential leaders in the non-Communist world, especially in the United States, feel a comparable urge to liberate those under Communist control from what they regard as a system of tyranny based on deception and hate. Moreover, on each side the missionary spirit is reinforced by other considerations, notably by the belief of each side that it will gain many advantages for itself (e.g., greater security) if those who champion a hostile ideology on the other side are overthrown.

Subversive efforts may have various objectives. They may be designed

[16] Cf., Roger Revelle, "International Cooperation and the Two Faces of Science," in American Assembly, *Cultural Affairs and Foreign Relations* (Englewood Cliffs, N.J., Prentice-Hall, 1963), pp. 133-136.

simply to bring pressure to bear on another government in order to influence its policies. They may be designed to weaken the target state so that it can be defeated more easily in war. Or they may be employed as a substitute for war. If we ask under what conditions, if any, subversive action can serve as a substitute for war, the answer will also shed light on the usefulness of subversion as an instrument for the achievement of lesser objectives.

1. *The need for support from within the target state.* In the first place, if subversion is to substitute for war (or, really, if it is to serve any purpose), the "attacking" state must champion an ideology and a program of action which evoke support within the territory of the victim. In "real" war, a state may win exclusively through the use of its own personnel against the united opposition of the enemy, but in subversion the aggressor must rally people to its cause within the victim state. It is essential in subversion that the people in the target country become disunited, some of them adhering to the enemy.

This requirement poses a question implicitly. What renders people in one country susceptible to subversive appeals emanating from another? An answer can be given in the form of an illustration, drawn from a study of *The Appeals of Communism*, by Gabriel Almond.[17] He classifies the needs and interests which render individuals susceptible to Communist appeals into four major groups: (1) neurotic needs, (2) self-related interests, (3) group-related interests, and (4) ideological interests. The neurotic may, for example, feel rejected by the society in which he lives and may reject it in turn; he may express his rejection in various ways, adherence to an external enemy being among them. Self-related interests include career interests, companionship, and intellectual satisfaction. Group-related interests are illustrated by the example of the trade union official who joins the Communist Party in the belief that he will then be able to promote the objectives of his union more effectively, or by the Negro leader who believes that he can serve his race best by helping to overthrow the system under which it suffers discrimination. Ideological interests which render an individual susceptible to subversive propaganda are exemplified in the person who believes in liberty and equality, but who also believes that these values are not and cannot be adequately realized under the existing social order.

Obviously, the extent of susceptibility to subversive propaganda (i.e., the extent to which the needs and interests of the above types are left unsatisfied) will be different for different persons, different groups or classes, different countries, and different times. Many influencing factors operate. Probably the two most common ones relate to scales of living and to the satisfaction of nationalist aspirations. Susceptibility is likely to be

[17] Gabriel A. Almond, *The Appeals of Communism* (Princeton, N.J., Princeton University Press, 1954), esp. pp. 235-242.

accentuated when people are persistently denied a scale of living that meets their expectations. It is also likely to be accentuated when nationalist aspirations are thwarted—when nations do not enjoy political unity and independence. Communist subversion plays particularly on these vulnerable features of the position of non-Communist states. It also plays on the popular desire for peace, based on the allegation that peace is unobtainable as long as capitalism survives.

2. *The need for organization and coordination.* If aggression by subversion is to substitute for war, it is necessary, in the second place, that the adherents of the "attacking" state in the target country be organized; it is also necessary that they be willing to coordinate their actions with those of the "attacker" or, better, to subordinate themselves to its control. Given these conditions, they are said to constitute a *fifth column,* a term stemming from the remark of a rebel leader in the Spanish Civil War that he controlled four armed columns for an attack on Madrid, plus a fifth column inside the city which would assist him from within. If people abroad are to allow themselves to be used as a fifth column, they must not only believe in the ideology and program of the attacker, but must also obtain, or hope to obtain, assistance from him. Afghanistan would have difficulty winning the support of a fifth column in France, regardless of the merits of the ideology and program it championed, because few Frenchmen would expect Afghanistan to be able to give them aid. The Soviet Union faces much less difficulty. The Soviet Union would probably have some fifth columns abroad even if it did nothing to encourage their development, for people who believe in the need for a Communist revolution in their country would naturally seek to identify themselves with Soviet power and would conduct themselves so as to maximize the prospect of attracting Soviet support.

3. *The need to deter or withstand retaliation.* The third main requirement if aggression by subversion is to substitute for war is that the aggressor must be in a position to deter or withstand retaliatory action by its intended victim, whether the retaliatory action take the form of an ideological counteroffensive, economic pressure, or war. In truth, aggression by subversion is most likely to succeed when the "attacking" state also is able to get what it wants by other methods.

This point is easily illustrated. For some years before 1914 the government of Serbia allowed its territory to serve as a base for subversive propaganda against Austria-Hungary; being militarily more powerful, Austria-Hungary was unwilling to confine the struggle to the ideological level, and finally responded with a declaration of war. Conversely, in the 1930's Hitler's Germany was powerful in every way, whereas Austria was weak; this permitted Hitler to resort to subversion without fear of retaliation and finally led to a bloodless conquest in which, in truth, German military power played a role at least as important as the role of the fifth

column which Hitler had nurtured in Austria. Similarly, after World War II, the Soviet Union was in a virtually unassailable position in relation to the countries of Eastern and Southeastern Europe; it could therefore sponsor fifth-column activities in those countries with impunity. Egypt, Syria, and Saudi Arabia, inciting nationalism throughout North Africa and the Middle East and therefore accentuating antagonisms against Britain and France especially, are in a more vulnerable position, though the events of 1956 proved that both the United Nations and Soviet power give them some degree of safety from retaliatory military action.

*4. The requirement that domestic defenses be ineffective.* Governments threatened by subversion may defend themselves not only by retaliation against the external source of danger but also by purely domestic measures. Thus there is a fourth requirement for successful subversion: that domestic defense measures either not be adopted or not be effective.

Domestic defense measures may be either positive or negative, that is, they may be designed to inculcate loyalty or to prevent subversion. All governments adopt positive defense measures of some sort, however successfully or unsuccessfully. In most countries the major positive defense against subversion is the domestic educational system, together with the various means of mass communication. Through these agencies governments and supporting private agencies exert tremendous influence over political attitudes. Schools commonly inculcate respect for the culture of the country and the political and economic principles on which its social life is based. Similarly, newspapers, periodicals, and radio and TV broadcasts, whether controlled by private persons or public agencies, commonly inculcate and reinforce national loyalties. Even where academic freedom is complete, and where there is complete freedom of speech and press, a strong bias in favor of the prevailing national ideology is the normal thing; usually, though obviously not always, attitudes of loyalty are so thoroughly implanted that subversive appeals emanating from abroad or from a fifth column within the country evoke little response.

Governments which fear that positive domestic measures to inculcate loyalty may not be sufficient are free to adopt negative measures to curtail the flow of subversive ideas from abroad. Different kinds of negative measures can be taken. Contacts with foreigners can be reduced to a minimum by preventing them from coming into the country and by preventing citizens from going abroad. The importation and circulation of printed materials can be regulated. The cultural and informational activities of foreign diplomatic missions can be curtailed. Foreign radio broadcasts can be jammed, or it can be made a criminal offense to listen to such broadcasts. If a foreign government is officially engaged in subversive activities abroad, there is basis for diplomatic protest on the ground that the requirements of international law are being violated.

Governments are rarely completely successful in cutting off the flow of ideas and information from abroad, but they can reduce it very drastically.

Moreover, governments are free to suppress fifth-column activities within their own territory, and strong governments determined to do so have generally succeeded. The dictatorial governments of Europe in the interwar period, for example, outlawed Communist parties and introduced police agents into the underground Communist organizations so successfully that Soviet fifth-column activities became insignificant. Virtually the same results have been achieved in the United States since World War II without the formal outlawry of the Party. Yet, though governments are theoretically free to suppress fifth columns, sometimes they do not act. Perhaps they fail to see the danger. Perhaps they are beset by so many domestic problems and so much domestic opposition that they are simply unable to act effectively. Fear of retaliation may lead a weak country to refrain from suppressing a fifth column sponsored by a powerful neighbor. Difficulties involved in distinguishing a loyal political party from a fifth column may induce a policy of toleration; thus Communists are sometimes regarded as constituting a political party entitled to democratic freedoms, and sometimes they are regarded as members of an international conspiratorial movement aiming at the violent overthrow of non-Communist governments. In short, though each government seems theoretically to have the advantage on its own soil in connection with the problem of fifth columns—as well as in all aspects of struggle in the field of informational, propaganda, educational and cultural activities—circumstances sometimes throw the advantage the other way.

Especially since World War II ideological warfare has come to be supplemented by guerrilla warfare, notably in China (until the Communist victory in 1949), Malaya, Vietnam, Laos, and Algeria. In aggression by subversion the immediate object is to win over the loyalty of the people of the enemy state, or at least to undermine their loyalty to their own government; they are, if possible, to be rendered unwilling to fight in support of their government. Guerrilla warfare has a very similar object. The guerrillas seek to avoid major engagements with government forces, but try to demonstrate to the people that the government can neither govern nor protect them. They thus resort to terroristic threats and attacks against officials and leading citizens who are loyal to the government and engage in hit-and-run raids against vulnerable units of the armed forces deployed against them. At the same time, while trying to paralyze the operations of the regular government and of organizations loyal to it, they attempt to develop a parallel structure through which to take over control. Thus Raoul Girardet describes the techniques employed against the French in Indochina:

They were constant propaganda, systematic terrorism, the deliberate dismemberment of existing social structures, and the establishment of 'parallel hierarchies,' which slowly replaced the hierarchies of legal order and enslaved the population in an increasingly tight web of steel. . . . The French army discovered that its men not only had to be experts in the use of arms, but also, and perhaps above all, had to be political agitators, organizers, and leaders of partisans. In the end, the qualities and methods of the ideological crusader were more effective in obtaining final victory than the qualities and methods of the soldier.[18]

Girardet goes on to say that "the defense of a territory no longer means the defense of frontiers. . . . Defense today must be against the political and ideological forces of internal subversion. Many believe that even a nuclear army is no more than an instrument of intimidation destined to protect the free development and continuance of revolutionary action."[19] This obviously points to the very great importance to every political system or political movement of a doctrine or ideology that commands overwhelming popular support. Societies without a substantial ideological consensus are vulnerable.

We will take up guerrilla warfare briefly again in Chapter 18, "The Utility of War."

## SUGGESTED READINGS

AMERICAN ASSEMBLY, *Cultural Affairs and Foreign Relations* (Englewood Cliffs, N.J., Prentice-Hall, 1963).

BARGHOORN, Frederick C., *The Soviet Cultural Offensive* (Princeton, N.J., Princeton University Press, 1960).

———, *Soviet Foreign Propaganda* (Princeton, N.J., Princeton University Press, 1964).

BARRETT, Edward W., *Truth Is Our Weapon* (New York, Funk & Wagnalls, 1953.

BLACKSTOCK, Paul W., *The Strategy of Subversion: Manipulating the Politics of Other Nations* (Chicago, Quadrangle Books, 1964).

CLEVELAND, Harlan, MANGONE, Gerard J., and ADAMS, John Clarke, *The Overseas Americans* (New York, McGraw-Hill, 1960).

COMMITTEE ON EDUCATIONAL INTERCHANGE POLICY, *Twenty Years of United States Government Programs in Cultural Relations* (New York, Committee on International Interchange Policy, 1959).

DAUGHERTY, William E., ed., *A Psychological Warfare Casebook* (Baltimore, Johns Hopkins Press, for Operations Research Office, 1958).

DIZARD, Wilson P. *The Strategy of Truth, The Story of the U.S. Information Service* (Washington, Public Affairs Press, 1961).

[18] Raoul Girardet, "Civil and Military Power in the Fourth Republic," in Samuel P. Huntington, ed., *Changing Patterns of Military Politics* (New York, Free Press of Glencoe, 1962), p. 130.

[19] *Ibid.*, p. 130.

HOLT, Robert T., and VAN DE VELDE, Robert W., *Strategic Operations and American Foreign Policy* (Chicago, The University of Chicago Press, 1960).

HUNTINGTON, Samuel P., ed., *Changing Patterns of Military Politics* (New York, Free Press of Glencoe, 1962).

INSTITUTE OF INTERNATIONAL EDUCATION, *Open Doors 1965, Report on International Exchange* (New York, Institute of International Education, 1965).

KRUGLAK, Theodore E., *The Two Faces of TASS* (Minneapolis, University of Minnesota Press, 1962).

MCMURRAY, Ruth Emily, and LEE, Muna, *The Cultural Approach, Another Way in International Relations* (Chapel Hill, University of North Carolina Press, 1947).

QUALTER, Terence H., *Propaganda and Psychological Warfare* (New York, Random House, 1962).

THOMSON, Charles A., and LAVES, Walter H. C., *Cultural Relations and U.S. Foreign Policy* (Bloomington, Indiana University Press, 1963).

UNITED STATES CONGRESS, HOUSE, *Twenty-Sixth Semiannual Report on Educational Exchange Activities, Letter from Chairman, Transmitting the 26th Semiannual Report on the Educational Activities. . . .* 87th Cong., 1961, H. Doc. 199.

WHITAKER, Urban, ed., *Propaganda and International Relations* (San Francisco, Chandler, 1960).

WHITTON, John Boardman, *Propaganda and the Cold War* (Washington, Public Affairs Press, 1963).

# 17

# INTELLIGENCE ACTIVITIES
# AND COVERT OPERATIONS

Intelligence is knowledge—knowledge regarding other states —and governments must have it if they are to conduct their foreign relationships successfully. They get it in various ways, both overt and covert. The agencies especially charged with gathering intelligence are also sometimes responsible for covert or illegal activities designed somehow to affect the course of events or the fate of individuals abroad. We will discuss in this chapter how governments obtain intelligence and the kinds of covert operations that they undertake.

## HOW INTELLIGENCE IS OBTAINED

Espionage is obviously one of the methods that states employ to obtain intelligence. It is one of the oldest methods and has about it enough human drama and excitement to create the impression that it is the principal method. This is far from the truth; even the countries that employ spies get far more of their intelligence by other means, and it seems likely that a number do not employ them at all. Still, espionage is important enough in the field of intelligence activities that it deserves attention.

What is espionage? Answers to the question differ. Its essence is a clandestine effort to obtain information. The espionage agent works surreptitiously or on the basis of false pretense or in disguise. He conceals his identity or the true nature and purpose of his activity. He pries into the guarded secrets of one power for the benefit of another power.

Though good enough for most purposes, these statements do not establish a clear borderline between espionage and other kinds of intelligence activity; in any event, states do not always adhere to this definition in their laws. Is the military attaché traveling in uniform on the Trans-Siberian Railway guilty of espionage if he looks out the window and sees something of military significance? If he takes a picture of it? How about Gary Powers, who set out in a high-flying U-2 plane from Pakistan across Soviet territory heading for Norway, taking pictures en route?

The espionage agent may work for or against his own government, at home or abroad. The crucial task of the agent who goes abroad to spy for his government is usually the recruitment of others who actually obtain and deliver the desired information or documents. Potential recruits very often identify themselves in one way or another. Perhaps they want money and so make known the fact that they can provide important information at a price. Perhaps they want a role that gives them a sense of importance. Perhaps their ideological sympathies lead them on. In the countries of the West, Communist parties and front organizations have been pathways into the Soviet intelligence services. In the Communist countries, analogous pathways into Western intelligence services do not exist, but even so, some of the disaffected have found ways of making their availability known. When a recruiter fails to get the voluntary help that he needs, he may recall the existence of sex and try to develop a basis for blackmail, or he may somehow locate a potential informant who is willing to take a bribe. The new recruit may go on with his regular job, or he may seek a new and more strategic one. Sometimes he becomes a "sleeper," lying low for long periods to minimize the risk of discovery and to maximize the prospect of being available for service should an emergency arise.

In relation to the number of persons involved, the human costs of espionage are high. Naturally, no one can know how many spies are entirely successful, but the available evidence suggests that only a small proportion succeed in operating long without getting caught. Moreover, though there have been priceless espionage coups, a considerable portion of the ventures bring no return at all, and it has often happened that even when espionage produced tremendously important information (e.g., that Hitler would attack the Soviet Union, and the date on which he would do it), the government at home has refused to credit its truth. Further, even assuming success, few find the life of the spy attractive.

The upshot is that the number engaged in espionage is relatively limited and so are the purposes for which it is employed. The Soviet government has engaged in industrial espionage, but by and large the concern of governments is with the security of the state. This may lead them to try to plant spies in political parties and other such organizations, particularly in revolutionary parties and organizations whose successes and failures are of great potential significance. It quite commonly leads them to try to penetrate the governmental structure of other states—

above all, of potential enemies—to get fuller information concerning their military power and their intentions. At the same time, there is emphasis on counterespionage work. Among the highest achievements of espionage services is the recruiting or planting of agents in the military or intelligence service of an unfriendly government and the safeguarding of lines of communication with such agents.

Defection is closely related to espionage. One of the jobs of the recruiter is to induce key people to defect spiritually, though staying in place in order to provide information. Defection also takes the form of physical flight, and in East–West relations since World War II many cases of it have occurred, some being of spectacular significance in the realm of intelligence activities. At one time or another the United States, Great Britain, the Soviet Union, Western Germany, and a number of other states have had their own intelligence efforts seriously compromised by the defection of personnel who gave vitally important information to the side to which they fled, e.g., information about the identity and location of espionage agents, or information about developments in the field of nuclear energy and missiles.

"Bugging" is another of the methods of intelligence, that is, the surreptitious planting of microphones and the tapping of telephones. The Soviet Union has made itself notorious in many ways—among others by thoroughly bugging quarters occupied by foreign missions in Moscow, including the United States Embassy. After a trip to Moscow Henry Cabot Lodge once commented that when he and the United States Ambassador to the Soviet Union wanted to be sure of the privacy of their conversation, they went to the middle of the Red Square. The Russians even succeeded in planting a listening device in the wall of a portion of the embassy building that was supposed to be supersecret. Phone tapping is simply assumed. In the perennial struggle going on in Berlin, one of the coups of the United States Central Intelligence Agency —from which it benefited for nearly a year—was the construction of a tunnel permitting it to tap the main telephone line of the Soviet military headquarters in East Berlin.

The fact that a government and its agents abroad must communicate with each other creates the problem of secrecy and at the same time gives enticing opportunities to the intelligence services of other governments. The problems and opportunities are minimal where a diplomatic pouch and a courier can be employed, but various needs lead also to the use of electronic methods of communication, which permit interception. Thus governments develop codes and ciphers, and change them periodically, hoping to safeguard the secrecy of their messages; and at the same time some of them (including the United States government) go to great lengths to break the codes and ciphers that others employ. A code consists of words or other symbols with arbitrarily assigned meanings;

thus *Papa* might mean *H-bomb*. A cipher consists of rules for substituting other symbols (e.g., numbers or other letters) for the letters of the alphabet and perhaps for transposing them or arranging them in some other unusual way. The advantage of a code is that it is extremely difficult to break, but it may not lend itself to flexibility of expression. The advantage of a cipher is that it is suitable for any message, but is liable to be broken. In every language there are regularities in the frequency with which the different letters appear, and the frequency necessarily carries over to enciphered messages. On this basis it is said that every cipher— at least if it is in a known language—can be broken. In the United States the task of developing trustworthy codes and ciphers—and of breaking the codes and ciphers of other governments—is entrusted to the National Security Agency.

Obviously, great advantages come from preserving the secrecy of communications, and great advantages can come from the ability to read the messages exchanged by another government and its agents abroad. At the time of the Washington disarmament conference of 1921-22, the United States was reading the instructions sent by the Japanese government to its representatives and so knew in advance of the conference sessions what terms would and would not be acceptable. Similarly, during part of World War II the United States was reading messages to Japanese forces at different points in the Pacific; knowledge of the Japanese battle plan contributed decisively to the great American naval victory at the Battle of Midway, and knowledge of Admiral Yamamoto's schedule on an inspection trip permitted American forces to intercept his plane and shoot it down.

Picture-taking from above is another method of intelligence. The shooting down of Gary Powers and his U-2 plane in 1960 brought to light the fact that for some four years the United States had been sending U-2's on picture-taking missions over Soviet territory, apparently with great success. Pictures from aircraft confirmed reports of the development of Soviet missile bases in Cuba in the fall of 1962, and flights over Cuba for intelligence purposes have continued ever since. The Chinese Nationalist government has sent U-2 aircraft, and the United States has sent pilotless aircraft (drones), over mainland China on intelligence missions. Since early in the space age, both the United States and the Soviet Union have been developing their capacity to take pictures from orbiting vehicles—again apparently with impressive success—and at least the United States has sought to use such vehicles to obtain earlier warning of the launching of missiles and probably to eavesdrop on the electronic communications of other governments. The legality of the use of orbiting vehicles for such purposes in outer space seems to be tacitly conceded, but peacetime intrusions of the aircraft of one state into the airspace of another have traditionally been regarded as illegal.

Given the importance of all of the above means of gathering intelligence (espionage, promoting defection, bugging, cryptanalysis, and picture-taking from above), it remains true that most intelligence activities and normally the most rewarding intelligence activities are of a more prosaic sort. In a very real sense every diplomat who goes abroad, and every member of his staff, is an intelligence agent, for one of his principal assignments is the acquisition of knowledge that may be useful to the government that sends him. The military attachés connected with diplomatic missions are normally thought of as overt intelligence agents, and it is common knowledge that one or more of the other members of the major diplomatic missions work for their home intelligence services rather than their foreign offices, using their diplomatic status as a cover. But the ambassador himself also gathers intelligence, openly and avowedly.

Moreover, much of the open intelligence activity occurs in home territory. Many of those who work for foreign offices in their home capitals engage in research designed to bring to light the kind of knowledge needed in the management of relationships with other states. In Washington the Central Intelligence Agency can quite properly be thought of as a great research institution, much of the research being based on openly available information, e.g., information from books, periodicals, newspapers, and people. The United States makes it a practice to monitor foreign radio programs, mimeographing voluminous daily releases giving the texts of broadcasts having anything to do with questions of concern to the government. Radar is also employed in open intelligence activities, penetrating quite legally into the airspace of other countries and into outer space. The United States has long maintained radar installations in Turkey, mainly to keep track of missile-testing activities in the Soviet Union; it was these installations that provided crucial evidence of a developing Soviet missile capacity in the early 1950's, leading to a tremendous intensification of comparable American efforts. Similarly, radar and other devices are employed to keep track of missile and space shots today.

It should not be thought, as it sometimes is, that those who gather intelligence go after "all the facts," for the facts are endless; to attempt to gather them all would be like racing for the end of the rainbow. Intelligence activities have to be guided by some conception of the significant, i.e., some notion of actual or potential problems and of the sort of data that may be useful in meeting those problems. The orientation is toward problems, present and future, rather than toward facts. A considerable portion of the problems are so obvious that no one is likely to miss them, and there may be no serious question about the kinds of facts that are relevant, but the identification of others calls for great feats of imagination. Every major change creates problems: the diffusion of nuclear capacities, the development of missiles, the population explosion, the dissolution of empires and the creation of many new states, the "revolution of rising expectations," the Sino–Soviet split, the growing influence of leaders from the rising generation, etc. Every state, at a minimum, wants to do what it can to create or maintain a world environment compatible with its domestic purposes, and this desire shades off into the desire to reshape the world for the good of its peoples.

General problems and general goals take on very concrete forms. How likely is it that Communist China will develop effective means of delivering nuclear bombs to targets abroad? What means? By what time may they be available? What are the intentions of the Communist leaders in Peking, and how may they be affected by changes in the military power at their command? In so far as their power and intentions make them dangerous, now or in the future, how can their power be reduced or countered, and how can their intentions be changed? What must Peking be prevented from doing, even at the cost of war? Should war come, what strategy would be most effective? Given success in war, what persons or groups in China would be acceptable as successors to those who now lead?

It is questions like these, pertaining to China and to all other countries with which significant relationships exist, that intelligence services have to try to answer; and their fact gathering must be guided accordingly. They need data about the values and goals of other peoples, about the constitutional forms and political systems of other countries, about specific political leaders and political groupings, about the functioning of the economy and trends in production, about scientific developments, about the transportation and communication system, about military strength and posture, about individual persons who now or in the future may do good or harm, about specific, immediate policies and goals, and so on. Much of it can be obtained from open sources. Some of it can be obtained, if at all, only by secret means.

## COVERT OPERATIONS

Intelligence activities are sometimes associated, whether in time of peace or in time of war, with covert operations—operations that are deceptive or illegal or otherwise of such a nature that the government engaging in them does not want to admit it officially. Perhaps the very success of the operation depends on concealing the identity of its sponsor. Perhaps the object is simply to avoid the embarrassment or the other difficulties that might follow a public acceptance of responsibility.

Ruses of war are in this sense covert operations. They may begin at the very outset of war. Governments sometimes deliberately create frontier incidents or the appearance of attacks against themselves in the hope of justifying the claim that their own attack is a measure of self-defense. Once war breaks out, members of each side can be expected to tax their imaginations in efforts to deceive the other. Each wants to magnify its own strength, to convince the other that it has a secret weapon or a special method of defense or attack, to give the impression that its weak points are impregnable and perhaps that its strong points are vulnerable, to lead the other to expect attack at the wrong time and place, to create false beliefs on the other side about the amount of damage that its attacks have wrought, etc. The payoff is sometimes handsome.

Whether in war or in peace, some states resort to "black propaganda," that is, to propaganda whose origin is concealed. Radio listeners, for example, may hear a broadcast that purports to come from a station within their own country whereas in fact it comes from abroad. Closely related to this is the practice of secretly supplying money or goods of some kind to influence attitudes and events. Perhaps it is a question of subsidizing newspapers or radio stations, or supplying them with newsprint or equipment. Perhaps it is a question of contributions to a trade union treasury or to the campaign fund of a political party. Recipients do not necessarily sell their souls. The assistance that they get may simply help them to do more effectively what they believe in doing and would want to do in any case. But bribery occurs too: payments designed to induce the recipient to betray his trust in some way or to follow a course of action that he would not otherwise have followed. Special training may be given to foreign nationals, above all, military training. Safe havens may be provided for rebel forces from other countries. And they may be supplied with military equipment of various sorts, either overtly or covertly. Saboteurs may be trained or may receive other kinds of assistance in their destructive pursuits. Kidnappers may be sent to seize persons in other countries who are wanted for some reason but who cannot be brought within the jurisdiction of the state by legal means, and assassins may be employed. Members of the armed forces (even whole divisions) may be sent abroad—or the intimation may be made that they will go abroad—as "volunteers."

The Bay of Pigs fiasco in 1961 is the most notorious of the covert operations in recent years—covert in the sense that the United States government tried (rather badly) to keep its role concealed. Ostensibly, the whole scheme was the work of Cuban refugees, but the United States Central Intelligence Agency was in control. The CIA selected the refugees and provided them with weapons and military training, giving the training principally at "secret" bases in Guatemala. With assistance from the Department of Defense the CIA planned the invasion and provided the ships that carried the invading force. Regular ships of the United States Navy provided escort service. The few air strikes that occurred in connection with the investigation, and the meager air cover, involved planes made available by the United States; some of them were manned by American civilian pilots in the employ of the CIA. Though surreptitious, the role of the United States government was obvious from the first, and

President Kennedy, in effect, admitted it in assuming responsibility for the failure.

Many other covert operations have occurred. Ever since the Bolshevik Revolution the Soviet government or other Soviet agencies have subsidized and given other kinds of assistance secretly to Communist organizations abroad; and they are very probably responsible for the disappearance or murder of a number of persons abroad, e.g., Walter Krivitsky and Trotsky. A Soviet defector reports wholesale bribery of Irani politicians each year to further Soviet interests. It would be surprising if secret American assistance of various sorts did not go to non-Communist and anti-Communist forces in some of the countries of Western Europe after World War II. Apparently the CIA was heavily involved in the overthrow of both the Mossadeq government in Iran and the Arbenz government in Guatemala in the early 1950's. "Since the end of the war, West Berlin and West German authorities have counted 255 cases of successful kidnapping, at least 143 planned or attempted kidnappings and six assassination attempts by East German agents." [1] Persons loyal to Israel abducted Eichmann from Argentina illegally and took him to Israel. Israel then brought him to trial for his part in the extermination of Jews during World War II. "Thanks to the CIA, there is a general of the Indo-Chinese terrorist sect Binh Xuyen now living in comfortable retirement in Paris, after $1 million was reportedly deposited to his account in a Swiss bank. The only condition—that he stay in France to spend it." [2] Many other highly varied kinds of covert operations have occurred —undoubtedly many more than have ever come to light. In specific cases (e.g., the overthrow of the Mossadeq government) it is plausible to think that they have been of fateful significance to national and international politics.

## SUGGESTED READINGS

BLACKSTOCK, Paul W., *The Strategy of Subversion: Manipulating the Politics of Other Nations* (Chicago, Quadrangle Books, 1964).

DALLIN, David J., *Soviet Espionage* (New Haven, Conn., Yale University Press, 1955).

DULLES, Allen W., *The Craft of Intelligence* (New York, Harper & Row, 1963).

FARAGO, Ladislas, *Burn After Reading, The Espionage History of World War II* (New York, Walker, 1961).

———, *War of Wits, The Anatomy of Espionage and Intelligence* (New York, Paperback Library, 1962).

GRAMONT, Sanche de, *The Secret War, The Story of International Espionage Since World War II* (New York, Putnam, 1962).

[1] Sanche de Gramont, *The Secret War, The Story of International Espionage Since World War II* (New York, Putnam 1962), p. 478.

[2] *Ibid.*, p. 197.

HILSMAN, Roger, *Strategic Intelligence and National Decisions* (New York, The Free Press of Glencoe, 1956).

JOHNSON, Haynes, with Manuel Artime *et al., The Bay of Pigs* (New York, Dell, 1964).

KENT, Sherman, *Strategic Intelligence for American World Policy* (Princeton, N.J., Princeton University Press, 1949).

LOMAX, John, *The Diplomatic Smuggler* (London, Arthur Barker, 1965).

McGOVERN, William M., *Strategic Intelligence and the Shape of Tomorrow* (Chicago, Regnery, 1961).

SCOTT, Andrew M., *The Revolution in Statecraft: Informal Penetration* (New York, Random House, 1965).

SETH, Ronald, *Anatomy of Spying* (New York, Dutton, 1963).

STANGER, Roland J., ed., *Essays on Espionage and International Law* (Columbus, Ohio State University Press, 1962).

WEST, Rebecca, *The New Meaning of Treason* (New York, Viking, 1964).

WISE, David, and Ross, Thomas B., *The Invisible Government* (New York, Random House, 1964).

————, *The U-2 Affair* (New York, Random House, 1962).

# THE UTILITY OF WAR

Repeated references have been made throughout this book to the fact that states find war useful. War is the ultimate means by which they seek to make their will prevail—the ultimate expression of power. It is used by those seeking change in the status quo, and by others in defense. It is used by those seeking domination, and by others seeking to establish or preserve a distribution of power which gives them a reasonable chance of preserving independence and other values.

War has occurred persistently throughout history, so persistently that some are inclined to question whether war rather than peace should not be regarded as normal. It has survived new inventions, new scientific discoveries, and new technologies, which have repeatedly brought new and more devastating weapons to the fore. It has survived progress in education, culture, and political organization. War and the threat of war remain a regular preoccupation of the major states of the world, and of many lesser states as well.

War has been so important an instrument of states that the fact deserves to be dwelt upon; we shall do so briefly in this chapter. Then we shall ask what the costs of war have been and whether trends in the costs permit any conclusion as to the probable utility of war in the future. Finally, we shall attempt an appraisal of the probable effects of the development of weapons of mass destruction, especially nuclear weapons, on the usefulness of war.

# THE POLITICAL IMPORTANCE OF WAR

## War and the Birth, Growth, and Extinction of States

The general rule is that states are born in war and that war plays a major role in determining where their boundary lines shall be. In addition, war is a common cause of the extinction of states.

These generalizations are applicable to both ancient and modern times and to all geographical regions of the world—though, as we will note, certain developments since World War II raise questions about them.

The United States itself provides a good illustration. The North American continent was wrested from the Indians by violence. Wars among the colonizing countries largely determined what territory in North America each would hold. The thirteen colonies established their independence from Britain by a revolutionary war, which became an international war when France joined. The first great extension of the territory of the United States was accomplished through purchase, the Louisiana Purchase, but France's fear that she would lose the territory in war was a powerful factor in inducing her to sell. Russia was influenced by somewhat similar considerations when she agreed to sell Alaska. Threats of war were a factor in the settlement of the Oregon boundary controversy. The annexation of Texas led to outright war, as a result of which the entire Southwest was added to the Union. Puerto Rico and the Philippines were acquired by war with Spain. Hawaii was acquired peacefully, but only after American settlers overthrew the native government by force and asked for annexation. World War II led to the establishment of an American trusteeship over the Caroline, Marshall, and Marianas Islands in the Pacific and to American control over Okinawa. In addition, the fact should be recalled that the United States has fought two wars, the War of 1812 and World War I, which produced no change in its boundaries, and it fought a Civil War which determined whether the Union would be preserved.

War has likewise played a powerful role in the history of Russia and the Soviet Union. Muscovy began in the twelfth century as a relatively small principality. By the end of the fifteenth century it had thrown off the yoke of the Mongol hordes and had expanded, largely through violence, to the Arctic, the Ural Mountains, the Caspian Sea, and Lake Ladoga. In subsequent centuries Russia fought many wars, especially with various states of Europe and with the Ottoman Empire, and her boundaries fluctuated back and forth (but in the main were pushed outward) as a result of defeat and victory. World War I brought the collapse of the tsarist regime, made possible the Bolshevik seizure of power, and led to a contraction of the boundaries of the state. World War II not only decided whether the Soviet regime could survive but

brought renewed expansion, accomplished both by the formal annexation of territory and by the establishment of Communist regimes in eastern and southeastern Europe. What began as Muscovy became a great
Soviet state supplemented by satellites or allies stretching from the Elbe
River in the heart of Europe to the Kurile Islands lying north of Japan.

Similarly, war has played a powerful role in the history of the German
people. Frederick the Great succeeded to the throne of the small kingdom
of Prussia in 1740, and forthwith precipitated the War of the Austrian
Succession, in the course of which he seized Silesia. The Seven Years'
War, involving practically all of Europe as well as North America, soon
followed. Later in Frederick's reign he engaged in a brief war with
Austria-Hungary. Prussia was, of course, heavily involved in the wars of
the French Revolution and Napoleon, in the course of which the French
conqueror consolidated many of the small states into which the German
people had been divided. Bismarck brought the remaining German states
into one Reich through a series of wars—with Denmark, with Austria-
Hungary, and with France. World War I brought a reversal of German
fortunes, including the loss of considerable territory to surrounding
states. Hitler took Austria and Czechoslovakia more by the threat than
by the use of violence, and in World War II established a short-lived
empire stretching from the Pyrenees to the gates of Stalingrad. His defeat
led not only to the collapse of his regime and to the loss of great territories but to the end of Germany as a united state.

## War and the Fate of Ideologies, Cultures, and Civilizations

In broader terms, war has also played a powerful role in the struggles
among ideologies, cultures, and civilizations. It figured prominently in
the process through which Christianity was extended over Europe and
over the Western Hemisphere. Islam spread to a large extent through war,
and was prevented from engulfing Europe mainly because of the greater
military power which the Christian states of Europe proved able to command. The civilizations of the Aztecs and Incas collapsed and disappeared as a result of European barbarism and violence. Western ideas
and western technology have accompanied western imperialism in penetrating Africa and Asia. The strongest of the extant ideologies, nationalism, has achieved its triumphs largely in war. Fascism and nazism were
appealing as long as they were powerful, but have been discredited by
defeat. Communism has spread through war, and both the Communists and
the non-Communist worlds view the problem of their survival largely in
military terms.

War, then, has been the instrument by which most of the great facts of political national history have been established and maintained. . . . The map of the
world today has been largely determined upon the battlefield. The maintenance

of civilization itself has been, and still continues to be, underwritten by the insurance of army and navy ready to strike at any time where danger threatens. Thus, even in peace, the war system has to a large degree determined not only international relationships but the character and history of the nations themselves.[1]

Similarly, war has played a powerful role in domestic politics.

There is hardly a national state in this world community, including our own, whose ultimate origins did not lie in acts of violence. The source of every governmental claim to legitimacy will be found to rest in some situation created originally by the arbitrary exertion of armed might. There is hardly a constitution that does not trace its origin to some act which was formally one of insurrection or of usurpation.[2]

The picture should not be overdrawn. After all, historical developments of great significance occur without war. The spread of Buddhism provides an example in one field, and the Industrial Revolution in another. Moreover, the transformation of the political map of so much of Asia and Africa in the last couple of decades raises a question about the role of war. Of course, some of the former colonies, like Indonesia, Indochina, and Algeria, had to fight for their independence, but in most cases it is very difficult to say to what extent the imperial powers granted independence in response to principle and to what extent they did so in response to the fear that otherwise, sooner or later, they would be faced with rebellion. Further, whatever the future holds (and it looks highly uncertain), war has so far not played a major role in bringing about changes in the boundaries that the new states had when they were born. Still, despite the numerous partial or complete exceptions to the generalization stated at the beginning of this section, it remains true that war has been a tremendously powerful force in history—a weapon which peoples and states have persistently used.

## THE INCIDENCE AND COSTS OF WAR

### The Difficulty of Determining Costs

No study is available of the incidence and costs of war throughout the world, even for very recent times. In truth, it is extremely difficult for students of the subject to arrive at reliable findings. Many costs, such as the moral and cultural costs and the costs resulting from wartime dislocations of production and trade, can scarcely be measured in quantitative terms. Estimates of property damage can be no more reliable than the judgment of the many individuals who make the estimates. Govern-

[1] James T. Shotwell, *War as an Instrument of National Policy* (New York, Harcourt, Brace & World, 1929), p. 15.

[2] George F. Kennan, *Realities of American Foreign Policy* (Princeton, N.J., Princeton University Press, 1954), p. 37.

mental expenditures relating to a specific war generally begin long before war breaks out and continue long after it is over, and the selection of the expenditures which should be included in a computation of costs is bound to be somewhat arbitrary. Usually in the case of civilians and often in the case of soldiers it is difficult to determine how many have died as a direct result of a war; if indirect losses are to be included, such as those resulting from wartime epidemics, arbitrary decisions and estimates again become involved. Further, although the absolute costs of war are of interest, relative costs have greater historical significance. For example, it is more significant to know what proportion of the population of a state dies from war than to know precisely how many die, and it more significant to know what proportion of the national income is expended on war than to know precisely how much is spent. This means that additional data must be taken into account, and often the additional data are either unavailable or unreliable. For example, reliable statistics on population, even in Western Europe, do not go very far back in history, and statistics permitting conclusions on the proportion of the national income devoted to war are not available in some countries even in relation to World War II.

## Findings of Wright and Richardson

Both Quincy Wright and Lewis F. Richardson have made studies of the incidence and costs of war.[3] Wright's study is largely confined to the European states and does not take World War II into account; it was published in 1942. Richardson's study focuses on all kinds of deadly quarrels over the world, from murder to war, and covers the period from 1820 to World War II and thereafter.

*1. Who fight?* Virtually all states fight. A search for "organized states that were never belligerent" from 1820 to 1939 led Richardson to conclude that only Sweden and Switzerland could be sensibly named, and even Switzerland had a civil war in 1847. Some states participated in a greater number of wars than others, but without providing sound basis for attributing the problem of war to the persistent aggressiveness of any one of them or any group of them.

*2. Various quantitative trends.* Wright did what he could to discover quantitative trends relating to the size of armies, the proportion of war years to peace years, the intensity and extensity of war, and the costs of war.

"The size of armies has tended to increase during the modern period both absolutely and in proportion to population." In the seventeenth century the European states kept about three persons per thousand under

---

[3] Quincy Wright, *A Study of War* (Chicago, The University of Chicago Press, 1942). Lewis F. Richardson, *Statistics of Deadly Quarrels* (Chicago, Quadrangle Books, 1960).

arms, which is approximately the same ratio as prevailed under the Roman Empire. Before World War I the proportion had risen to about five per thousand, and in 1937 it was about nine per thousand. Individual countries, of course, exceeded the general average; in 1937 "France, with less than half the population of the Roman Empire, maintained almost twice as big an army, some nineteen to one thousand of her European population."

It is clear that during the modern period there has been a trend toward an increase in the absolute and relative size of armies whether one considers the peace army, the number mobilized for war, the number of combatants engaged in battle, or the number of the military and civil populations devoting themselves to war work.

The major European states have been formally at war during a smaller and smaller proportion of the time in the past several centuries. They were at war about 65 percent of the time in the sixteenth and seventeenth centuries; about 38 percent of the time in the eighteenth; about 28 percent in the nineteenth; and about 18 percent from 1900 to 1940. But this tendency to be at peace a greater proportion of the time has been more than counteracted, for the tendency has been to fight harder during war. Battles themselves have lasted longer, and the number of battles per war year has increased. "As a result the total number of battles fought in a century has tended to increase." War has tended to increase not only in intensity but also in extensity, that is, more states tend to become involved. Wright counts 126 wars from 1475 to 1940.

Of these 126 wars, the 42 which began in the late fifteenth and in the sixteenth centuries averaged 2.4 participants each; the 19 which began in the eighteenth century averaged 4.8 participants each; the 32 which began in the nineteenth century averaged 3.1 participants each; and the 11 which began in the twentieth century averaged 5.6 participants each.

Only in the twentieth century have wars occurred which deserved to be called world wars. Although most battles continue to be fought in Europe, an increasingly large proportion occur in other areas.

According to Wright, the net result of various trends pertaining to the wars of European states is that human costs have increased, both absolutely and relative to population. True, a smaller and smaller proportion of those who participate in battle die as a direct result of battle, and military deaths from disease have been strikingly reduced. Moreover, down to World War II civilian deaths resulting directly from battle tended to decline. Yet, as noted above, the proportion of the population mobilized and the number of battles fought have tended to increase. "As a result, the proportion of the population dying as a direct consequence of battle has tended to increase."

Taking all factors into consideration the proportion of deaths attributable to military service and to hostilities has probably increased among European countries from about 2% in the seventeenth to about 3% in the twentieth century.

Wright suggests the probability "that the total of deaths indirectly due to war have been three times as great as direct war deaths in twentieth-century Europe. . . . Probably at least 10% of the deaths in modern civilization can be attributed directly or indirectly to war." Moreover, war has become "progressively more detrimental to the quality of population."

Richardson takes a different approach to the question of trends in the human costs of wars and other deadly quarrels, and comes out with a somewhat different set of conclusions. Focusing on quarrels that led to a large number of deaths in the period 1820 to 1940, he asks about trends in their frequency; and his conclusion is that the evidence "does not indicate any trend towards more, nor towards fewer [of them]. The evidence points instead to a random scatter." For a slightly different period (1820 to 1945) he finds that, of total deaths from all causes all over the world, about 1.6 percent can be attributed to all kinds of quarrels. The heaviest losses of life came from world wars and from murders, small wars contributing relatively less to the total. He points out that opportunities for deadly quarrels increase with increases in population, and makes different kinds of calculations to determine what the relationship in fact has been. As he puts it, his findings constitute "a suggestion, but not a conclusive proof, that mankind has become less warlike since A.D. 1820." One of his most interesting points relates to casualty rates in war. When simpler weapons and smaller numbers of soldiers were involved, as much as half of those engaged in battle might become casualties, but the percentage has gone down sharply as weapons have become more destructive and as greater numbers have fought. Richardson cites Wright's figures indicating that in the sixteenth century "the average casualties in battle were probably about 25 percent of those engaged, [while] in the three succeeding centuries the proportion has been estimated as 20, 15, and 10 percent respectively." The net result is that the percentage of the total population killed or wounded in war has remained small and relatively constant. Richardson goes on to compile statistics concerning 22 belligerents defeated or overrun in wars between 1820 and 1945. In 14 of the 22 cases, the war dead constituted from 0.5 percent to 4 percent of the population; in six cases the percentage was below 0.5, and in two cases higher than 4. The record leads Richardson to suggest the following assumption about hypothetical wars:

If two contiguous groups of people began to fight one another, they would, if not restrained by external authority, go on until one side was defeated; and defeat would usually occur when the less populous side had lost in dead some number between 0.05 and 5 per cent of its population, while the larger population having sustained about equal casualties, would therefore have lost a smaller percentage.[4]

The point of principal interest is the inference on which Richardson bases his assumption. It is that "human endurance to suffering has changed much less than weapons," that is, people are not willing to accept casualties beyond a certain point.[5] In other words, Richardson's suggestion is that the greater destructiveness of weapons does not necessarily mean greater losses of life in war; it may simply mean that the limits of acceptable suffering are reached more quickly. But the rule limiting acceptable suffering to the level indicated has not been absolute. Richardson's table indicates that 22 percent of those living in Serbia when war began in 1914 were dead when it ended in 1918, and (more breathtakingly) that some 83 percent of those living in Paraguay when it got involved in war almost a century ago were dead when it ended. Moreover, as we will note shortly, the development of nuclear weapons introduces new possibilities.

Reliable comprehensive statistics on the direct and indirect economic costs of war are not available. Certainly both world wars consumed vast quantities of labor, skills, and material resources. In battle areas both caused enormous damage to property of all kinds. Whole nations were impoverished. In many countries economic dislocations occurred from which recovery proved to be very difficult and which might have led to even greater political changes than actually came about, had it not been for the fact that the American economy survived both wars as a source of succor and strength.

*3. Qualitative costs.* Trends in the general social and cultural costs of war are, as Wright says, "even less susceptible to objective measurement." His "highly subjective" conclusion is that:

Wars of large magnitude have been followed by anti-intellectual movements in art, literature, and philosophy; by waves of crime, sexual license, suicide, venereal disease, delinquent youth; by class, racial, and religious intolerance, persecution, refugees, social and political revolution; by abandonment of orderly processes for settling disputes and changing law; and by a decline in respect for international law and treaties.

Wright grants that the standards of some people and groups have been stimulated in the opposite direction, but feels that serious deterioration has been the general rule.

4 Richardson, *op. cit.,* p. 299.
5 *Ibid.,* pp. 160-161.

## PROSPECTIVE COSTS OF NUCLEAR WARFARE

### The Destructiveness of Nuclear Weapons

The development of atomic and thermonuclear weapons and the rockets for delivering them to their targets raises a question whether past costs and trends in those costs provide much of a guide for the future. In terms of destructive power and delivery speeds, the differences between the new weapons and those hitherto employed are so great that they involve an entirely new order of magnitude. Recent years have seen leaping development. The atomic bombs dropped on Hiroshima and Nagasaki at the end of World War II (equivalent to 20,000 tons of TNT in their explosive power) made the giant blockbusters hurled at Hitler's Germany seem like firecrackers. Atomic bombs have since been improved, and hard on the heels of their improvement came a second revolution: the development of thermonuclear bombs. The relationship between atomic and thermonuclear bombs is suggested by the practice of describing the explosive power of the one in kilotons and that of the other in megatons—thousands and millions of tons of TNT equivalent. Apparently there is no theoretical upper limit to the megatonnage of thermonuclear bombs. The Russians have exploded a device of 60 megatons, which reportedly "could be weaponized at about 100 megatons."[6] Bombs of several hundred megatons are a possibility, and if detonated at an altitude of 150 miles or so, could reportedly set fire to vast areas—to the whole area within sight of the point of detonation, except for portions protected at the time by cloud cover.[7] As if this were not enough to stagger the statesmen and generals in the calculations they must make, it is also possible to manufacture and explode thermonuclear weapons so as to spread radioactive particles through the atmosphere; these particles will then be carried by the wind, only to drop down to earth with potentially lethal effects over wide areas.

The nuclear revolution has also gone in another direction since Hiroshima—toward the development of weapons with less explosive power than the bombs dropped on Japan and even less than the explosive power of the largest nonatomic bombs. Moreover, the nuclear warheads are deliverable in various ways—not only by aircraft and both short and long-range rockets but also by artillery shells. The nuclear arsenal thus includes quite a variety of weapons. Troops using the least powerful of them, it is said, might fight their way through a city like Des Moines

[6] Secretary McNamara, quoted by William W. Kaufmann, *The McNamara Strategy* (New York, Harper & Row, 1964), p. 153.

[7] Donald G. Brennan, "Arms and Arms Control in Outer Space," in Lincoln P. Bloomfield, ed., *Outer Space. Prospects for Man and Society,* The American Assembly (Englewood Cliffs N.J., Prentice-Hall, 1962), p. 130.

without completely destroying it, whereas less than ten thermonuclear bombs, depending on the megatonnage involved, could paralyze and perhaps destroy the national life of, for example, the United Kingdom.

Even before the thermonuclear age began, President Eisenhower could claim that the American stockpile of atomic weapons "exceeds by many times the explosive equivalent of the total of all bombs and all shells that came from every plane and every gun in every theatre of war in all the years of World War II." [8] Since then the stockpile has vastly increased. Secretary of Defense McNamara speaks of having "in stockpile or planned for stockpile tens of thousands of nuclear explosives for tactical use," and in addition there are atomic and thermonuclear bombs for strategic use. American estimates indicate that the Soviet nuclear arsenal, though perhaps superior in terms of thermonuclear bombs of the greatest megatonnage, is not as great either quantitatively or qualitatively in terms of other nuclear devices. Even so, the Soviet Union, like the United States, controls explosive power absolutely unprecedented in history.

Delivery speeds have also been revolutionized, and altitudes that were far beyond reach not long ago have become militarily significant. The bombers of World War II were all propellor-driven, meaning that they were slow and confined to low altitudes; the B-29 Superfortress flew at about 350 miles per hour at an altitude of 35,000 feet. At the close of the war the Germans introduced jet fighters, opening up new ranges of speed and altitude. Of the jet bombers used by the United States Strategic Air Command in 1965, the B-52 Stratofortress flies more than 650 miles per hour and has a ceiling above 50,000 feet; and the B-58a Hustler flies almost 1400 miles per hour and has a ceiling above 60,000 feet. Prototype bombers and fighters have speeds in excess of 2000 miles per hour and ceilings in excess of 70,000 feet.

The rocket has brought even more revolutionary change. Again it was the Germans who at the close of World War II introduced the V-1 and V-2. The V-1 buzz-bombs went through the atmosphere at about 400 miles per hour, and a reasonably effective defense against them was developed, but the V-2's went through outer space, reaching maximum speeds of up to 3600 miles per hour. There was no defense against them except the capture of the bases from which they were launched. Since then rockets have been as much improved as bombs. When the Russians put Sputnik into orbit in 1957 by boosting it to a speed in excess of 17,000 miles per hour, they proved the claim that they had already made: that their rockets could launch ballistic missiles for intercontinental distances. Missile speeds have become so great—far greater than the speeds of bullets and artillery shells—that escape from the gravitational field of the earth is possible; so both speeds and altitudes now have to be held short of the maximum for military use.

[8] *State Department Bulletin*, Vol. 29 (December 21, 1953), p. 848.

So far, of course, relatively few states have developed the capabilities described above, and even if their number doubles or triples, the overwhelming majority of states will still have only conventional weapons. Wars among them would necessarily be fought in conventional ways. But it is also possible that states lacking the new weapons might get help from states possessing them. Further, states already possessing them, e.g., the Soviet Union and the United States, might fight among themselves.

## The Potentially Suicidal Character
## of Unrestricted Nuclear War

If war were to break out between East and West, with all parties doing the maximum damage to each other (meaning, among other things, that cities would be on the list of targets for thermonuclear bombs), the result would be hideous beyond present imagination and description. President Kennedy once declared that "a full-scale nuclear exchange lasting less than 60 minutes, with weapons now in existence, could wipe out more than 300,000,000 Americans, Europeans, and Russians." [9] Simultaneously, millions of homes and factories would be destroyed. A British analyst, Air Marshal Slessor, speaks of such a war as "general suicide and the end of civilization as we know it." According to Bernard Brodie,

The minimum destruction one can reasonably expect from any unrestricted strategic attack will inevitably be too high to permit further meaningful mobilization of resources, perhaps too high even to permit the effective use of surviving military units. . . . If strategic bombing occurs on the grand scale, other kinds of military operations will prove either unfeasible or superfluous and most likely both.[10]

The problem of the survivors of an all-out nuclear attack will be to continue to live. "They are unlikely to be much concerned with the further pursuit of political-military objectives." The implication is that values which had seemed so precious, including those on behalf of which the war was undertaken, are likely to become relatively insignificant to those surviving after nuclear missiles have transformed the conditions under which remaining life proceeds.

We might note that the principal difference made by nuclear missiles is not so much in the amount of damage that can be done as in the speed with which it can be done. War was violent before rockets and nuclear warheads came along, but deaths were spaced out over a considerable period of time, permitting suffering to be felt and attitudes to change. This no doubt explains Richardson's finding that almost all belligerents have terminated war before more than 5 percent of the population have died.

[9] Kaufmann, The McNamara Strategy, p. 165.
[10] Bernard Brodie, "Strategy Hits a Dead End," Harper's, Vol. 211 (October, 1955), p. 35.

But belligerents firing thermonuclear rockets at each other might kill off far higher percentages before either side could determine how much damage had been done.

## Restricted Nuclear War

Unrestricted nuclear war with cities as targets is by no means the only possible strategy. In fact, the United States has indicated that it would like to avoid such a strategy. According to Secretary of Defense McNamara,

The United States has come to the conclusion that to the extent feasible, basic military strategy in a possible general nuclear war should be approached in much the same way that more conventional military operations have been regarded in the past. That is to say, principal military objectives, in the event of a nuclear war stemming from a major attack on the [North Atlantic] Alliance, should be the destruction of the enemy's military forces, not of his civilian population.[11]

Given reciprocity, the United States would presumably adhere to this strategy, but should the enemy strike at American cities, the implication is that there would be retaliation in kind. And McNamara's claim is that "we would utterly destroy them, and I mean completely destroy them . . . I am talking about completely destroying the Soviet Union as a civilized nation." [12] In indicating that we would prefer to make the destruction of military forces the principal aim, but in the absence of reciprocity would switch to a different strategy, "we are giving a possible opponent the strongest imaginable incentive to refrain from striking our own cities."

This kind of restriction on nuclear strategy obviously involves numerous problems. Mr. McNamara's statement was itself somewhat ambiguous, including the phrase "to the extent feasible" and referring to "the principal" military objectives. He did not necessarily rule out "strategic" as opposed to "tactical" bombardment; that is, he left the possibility open that the United States would bomb such military targets as air bases and missile launching sites. But such targets are not always very far away from cities, and the aiming of missiles and other weapons may not always be reliable. In a crisis leading up to nuclear war, and in the war itself, decision makers on both sides would be under terrible strain and pressure, and might or might not always manage to act rationally. Mistakes due to human error and mechanical faults would surely occur. The destruction of a city by mistake might or might not be greeted with tolerant indulgence, and retaliation might or might not be accepted as such and prevented from shifting the war to a new level of intensity. Moreover, the

11 Quoted by Kaufmann, *The McNamara Strategy*, p. 116.
12 *Ibid.*, p. 96.

"tactical" use of nuclear weapons in what is thought of as a "battle zone" would have uncertain consequences. How would the "battle zone" be delimited? Would it include supply lines leading to the points of belligerent contact? What would be the explosive power of the nuclear weapons used for tactical purposes? How much radioactivity would be thrown into the atmosphere? What would happen to cities in or close to the points of belligerent contact and along the supply lines? "Tactical" nuclear war might be indistinguishable from "strategic" nuclear war in the area in which it is waged. There might be problems, too, in terminating a nuclear war fought on a restricted basis. If one side is doomed to defeat, given the restrictions, it would certainly consider throwing them off and fighting on an unrestricted basis. Of course, it might be deterred from doing so by such warnings as those cited above by Secretary McNamara; and, for that matter, the potential victor might give assurances of terms of peace that would be more acceptable than the risks and costs of intensifying the war.

Certainly the United States has not proposed the restricted strategy lightly. At the same time, Secretary McNamara himself seems to doubt that the Soviet Union will follow the kind of strategy that he suggests. Should it launch a nuclear attack on American military targets, he considers it an "unlikely contingency" that it would delay attacks on American urban centers by as much as an hour.[13]

## Defending Against Nuclear Attack

A point assumed above should be made explicit: that in a nuclear war between East and West defensive efforts will not save either side from terrible losses.

In principle, both active and passive defense might be undertaken. The object in active defense is to ward off the blows of the enemy or to reduce his capacity to inflict them, and the object in passive defense is to reduce the destructive effect of the blows that strike home—to increase your capacity to absorb them.[14]

If nuclear bombs were now to be delivered to their targets by World War II type aircraft, an effective active defense might be possible: anti-aircraft missiles with nuclear warheads might knock all, or nearly all, of them out of the sky before they reached their targets. It is also possible that they might knock out even the aircraft of today and tomorrow, despite their vastly greater speeds and altitudes. But intercepting missiles is

[13] United States Congress, House, Committee on Armed Services, *Hearings on Military Posture and H. R. 4016*, 89th Cong., 1st Sess., February 4, 1965, P. 174. Cf., Thomas W. Wolfe, *Soviet Strategy at the Crossroads* (Cambridge, Harvard University Press, 1964), esp. pp. 163-165.

[14] Bernard Brodie, *Strategy in the Missile Age* (Princeton, N.J., Princeton University Press, 1959), pp. 180-181.

another matter. Both the United States and the Soviet Union are attempting to develop "antimissile missiles," apparently with some success. Each may be able to intercept and destroy some incoming missiles, especially if they come one at a time. But if the attack is so managed that a number of missiles, along with a number of decoys, approach each target simultaneously, the prospect of anything resembling an effective defense seems very remote. In World War II, active defense against bombers was considered successful when 10 percent of them were shot down, but even if 90 percent of the incoming nuclear missiles could be intercepted (and there is no prospect that the proportion could be anything like that high) those that struck home might still inflict unacceptable damage. Nor is it likely that either side could defend itself sufficiently by destroying the launching sites of the other. The United States has been hardening such sites, aiming to keep them usable after everything except a direct hit, and the Soviet Union has presumably been doing the same. Moreover, the United States has developed nuclear submarines capable of firing the Polaris missile while still submerged, and the Soviet Union no doubt has or will soon have a more or less comparable capability. Such vessels are vulnerable, of course, if they can be located, but the probability is that they could do vast damage before being located.

Measures of passive defense are no more promising. The dispersion of urban populations is not feasible either economically or politically. A shelter system might save many lives, especially if the principal danger is from radioactive particles. At the same time the existence of shelters is an invitation to the enemy to increase the destructive power of the bombs that he employs.

## PREVENTIVE AND PREEMPTIVE WAR

The idea of "preventive war" is somewhat vague. One underlying assumption is that at some point the other side is going to attack—that war is inevitable, the only question being when it will come. The other underlying assumption is that time is on his side—that it is crucial to bring the war on before the advantage shifts too much in his direction. Obviously, then, preventive war does not prevent war. At most, it prevents the other side from choosing the time and manner for initiating war.

Preemptive war is similar; in fact, the terms preventive and preemptive are sometimes used interchangeably. When a distinction is made, it turns on the question whether the enemy has started the sequence of steps that directly precede attack. If he has, and if quick action on your part permits you to get in the first blow, your attack is called preemptive.

Suggestions that preventive or preemptive war be undertaken raise factual questions, among others.[15] Actually, no one can be entirely certain

15 *Ibid.*, pp. 229-248.

that a particular war is inevitable—that some time another state is going to attack. Preventive action may thus bring on a war that otherwise would have been avoided. The same may be true of preemptive action, for steps that look as though they are leading to war do not always do so. Once shells and missiles are en route they are not recallable, of course, but aircraft and troops are. Further, there may well be a factual question concerning the advantage to be gained by preventive or preemptive action or by surprise attack. Calculations indicating that time is on the side of the potential enemy are subject to error; at best, such calculations suggest varying degrees of probability. Moreover, so far as nuclear exchanges are concerned, the United States has gone to great lengths to reduce the temptation that another state might be under to try to gain an advantage by striking the first blow. As noted above, American missile bases have been hardened. Secretary McNamara roundly asserts that the United States could absorb any first blow that the Soviet Union could inflict and still have enough retaliatory power to destroy Soviet society. If this is the case, preventive or preemptive action by the Soviet Union would not be rational. And presumably the Soviet Union is taking comparable measures to deter the United States.

The possibility of preventive or preemptive action raises moral questions, too, especially if unrestricted nuclear attack is what is contemplated. Given the factual questions about the underlying assumptions, what responsible person could claim that action of these types—designed to bring death to tens of millions if not to hundreds of millions—is morally justifiable?

## DETERRENCE

What is the prospect that the terrible costs of nuclear war can be avoided by a policy of deterrence? We have already discussed the question to some extent, but it needs a more searching examination.

To deter another party is to induce him to refrain from an action that he otherwise would take. Almost any kind of action might be at issue, but for present purposes the problem is to deter another party from choosing war or from choosing certain weapons or strategies in war. The object is to convince him that he will lose prohibitively if he resorts to war or chooses the weapon or strategy in question, that his suffering will be unacceptably great. Of course, he might have his own reasons for refraining, in which case deterrence is superfluous, perhaps justified as a kind of contingency insurance.

Deterrence is based on predictions.[16] More specifically, it is based

16 Cf., William W. Kaufmann, "The Requirements of Deterrence," in William W. Kaufmann, ed., *Military Policy and National Security* (Princeton, N.J., Princeton University Press, 1956), pp. 12-38. Brodie, *Strategy in the Missile Age*, pp. 264-304.

largely or entirely on threats and on their counterpart, fear. The problem for the state attempting deterrence is to pose threats that are both credible and effective. If the antagonist is to find them credible, he must be convinced of both the determination and the ability of the threatening state to do what it predicts; and if they are to be effective, he must find the predicted damage too great to be risked.

The problem of convincing the antagonist of a determination to execute retaliatory threats varies with the purpose and nature of the anticipated attack. Suppose, on the one hand, that the anticipated attack is of a mortal sort. For example, suppose that the United States anticipates a Soviet nuclear attack, with American cities among the targets. In this situation, the Soviet Union would surely find it credible that the United States was determined to retaliate, if it could, by destroying Soviet society. Suppose, on the other hand, that the anticipated attack, though deplorable, is of much lesser moment to the state that would like to deter it. For example, suppose that the United States anticipates a Soviet attack on Afghanistan; no nuclear weapons are to be used, and the object is very limited—perhaps to take the narrow neck of mountainous land separating the Soviet Union from Pakistan. In this situation, would the Soviet Union find it credible if the United States threatened to retaliate by raining nuclear missiles down on Soviet cities? After all, such an action on the part of the United States would surely bring the destruction of a number of American cities in return, and it is unlikely that anybody in Moscow or elsewhere would believe that the government in Washington would risk so much for so little.

Between these extremes are infinite possibilities. Consider a situation where the Soviet Union seems likely to attempt a conquest of Western Europe (a) with conventional weapons only or (b) using nuclear weapons, while promising not to attack any target within the United States. What kind of deterrent threat on the part of the United States would be credible in Moscow (and elsewhere)? Suppose that the Soviet Union seems likely to attempt a quick seizure of West Berlin, or of the Danish island of Bornholm. Or suppose that Communist China seems likely to try more seriously than ever before to take Quemoy and Matsu, or Taiwan itself, with or without the use of nuclear weapons. How credible would it be in Peking if the United States were to threaten a strategic nuclear attack on military targets throughout China? And how credible would it be in Washington if the Soviet Union were then to declare that any American nuclear attack on targets in China would lead to comparable Soviet attacks on targets within the United States?

Answers to most of these questions are far from easy. It is quite obvious that a state relying largely or solely on nuclear power might suffer a paralysis of will when confronted by acts of aggression not directly affecting its own vital interests. Both moral and expediential considerations might well restrain it. The moral principle that punishment shall fit the crime also requires that retaliatory action be proportionate to the damage done or threatened; governments guided by this moral principle would find it unacceptable to retaliate against a pinprick with a thermonuclear bomb. The expediential consideration is that the use of nuclear weapons in response to nonnuclear challenges and attacks would carry with it the danger of escalation: a minor affray might expand or explode into a catastrophic conflict. Where such considerations are clearly applicable, nuclear deterrent threats lose much of their value.

The above discussion of the credibility of deterrent threats focuses on the purpose and nature of the anticipated attack. There are related considerations, too. A government increases the credibility of its pronouncements if it speaks firmly and with one voice, and if it clearly has solid support for its stand both at home and among its friends and allies. Evidence of indecision and doubt and division automatically raise a question whether a threat will in fact be implemented. Similarly, a government increases the credibility of its pronouncements if it has a reputation for trustworthiness and vigor. Though bluffing is not to be entirely ruled out, still a reputation for it undermines deterrent threats. And failure to respond promptly and vigorously when events test intentions in a symbolic way has the same effect. At best, however, when the costs of implementing a threat are sure to be high, that is, when implementing it brings on the very damage it was supposed to avert, or when it precipitates damage that might have been postponed, it is difficult for a government to make a threat that is sure to be believed. It is this that has led some to cast about for ways of making the commitment absolute and irrevocable— ways of taking the final choice out of the hands of the government attempting deterrence and of convincing the potential enemy that this has been done. It is not terribly difficult to imagine devastating nuclear war occurring because each side expected the other at the last minute to suffer a failure of nerve.

In addition to its determination, a government seeking to make its threats credible must have the necessary capabilities, and it must convince others of the fact. It may want to keep some military secrets, but the emphasis must be on releasing information and on actual demonstrations. Sputnik was, for example, a dramatic and telling proof that the Soviet Union had rockets that could send nuclear warheads across intercontinental distances, and the landing of Cooper's Mercury capsule within about $4\frac{1}{2}$ miles of the main recovery ship gave information concerning the potential accuracy of missiles. Tests of nuclear devices by France and China dramatize their growing capabilities.

Obviously, the idea of deterrence is a close relative of the idea of the balancing of power, discussed in Chapter 12. Many of the same assumptions, methods, and purposes are involved, and meanings are given to both terms that make them virtually synonymous. But sometimes distinctions are made, mainly in terms of the purposes pursued. The prime object in balancing power is more to create and maintain a satisfactory relative power position than to preserve peace; it is compatible with the outbreak of war with a major antagonist and may in fact call for war. In contrast, the prime object in deterrence is to deter the antagonist from taking a specified action, e.g., resort to war or the use of a given weapon or strategy once war has broken out. The outbreak of war with him is thus not compatible with deterrence but instead marks its failure. There is a corollary, too, so far as what is sometimes called the Grand Deterrent is concerned, i.e., the effort to deter unrestricted nuclear war by threatening unrestricted nuclear retaliation: that it must not fail. For failure means mutual suicide. Another distinction is sometimes made, too: that once war breaks out the idea of the balancing of power loses most or all of its relevance, whereas the idea of deterrence remains applicable to the choice of weapons and strategies.

The case for a policy of deterrence rests more on its logical plausibility than on proof. It is rarely if ever possible to demonstrate that a policy of deterrence by one state induced another to refrain from an aggressive act. To illustrate the point more specifically, it is impossible to demonstrate that in the absence of the American nuclear deterrent the Soviet Union would have attempted to occupy the European continent. But whatever judgment one makes on such specific questions, still the rationale for deterrence is plausible.[17]

At the same time, the record demonstrates that the nuclear deterrent is not plausible in connection with all kinds of challenges. Even when the United States had a monopoly of nuclear weapons the Soviet Union blockaded West Berlin; in 1953 it crushed an uprising in East Germany; in 1956 it reimposed Communist control on Hungary; and in 1961 East Germany built a wall around West Berlin. In the Far East the North Koreans attacked in 1950. The Chinese Communists, despite the warnings of John Foster Dulles, aided their cohorts in Indochina who were rebelling against the French, and nuclear weapons later proved equally irrelevant when the United States came closer to a direct confrontation with rebels in Vietnam and Laos. Sukarno challenges Malaysia, and the Congolese continue in their unruly ways, in blitheful disregard of the fact that American nuclear weapons could wipe them out. No one finds it credible that in connection with these kinds of challenges nuclear weapons would be employed.

In sum, given danger of nuclear attack on vital interests, the threat of nuclear retaliation is the favored method of deterrence. And it is a

17 See, however, Karl W. Deutsch, *The Nerves of Government* (New York, Free Press of Glencoe, 1963), pp. 71-72. Arthur I. Waskow, *The Limits of Defense* (Garden City, N.Y., Doubleday, 1962).

logically plausible method. If the potential aggressor is rational, maintains full control of his actions and is convinced of both the determination and the ability of the potential victim to retaliate in devastating fashion, the high probability is that the aggression will be deterred. These "if's" may or may not prevail in practice.

Given lesser kinds of dangers, nuclear deterrence loses much of its credibility. A government relying solely on the nuclear deterrent might find itself helpless in the face of many of the kinds of challenges and attacks that actually occur—unable to react suitably, and unwilling to accept the guilt and the danger of an unsuitable nuclear response.

## LIMITED WAR

All wars are limited in one way or another from the point of view of one or both sides. They are limited in duration, in the area engulfed, in the targets attacked, in the weapons employed, in the goals pursued, in the proportion of potentially available resources actually marshaled or expended, etc. The term is thus a slippery one and is sometimes given such a broad meaning that it becomes confusing.

As the preceding section intimates, we are applying the term to a war in which a major belligerent deliberately limits the damage that he does; he stops short of the maximum that the weapons at his immediate disposal would permit.[18] But how far short of the maximum must he stop if his action is to qualify sensibly as limited? Where is the dividing line between the unlimited and the limited? In fact, there are an infinite number of possible gradations, and people differ in picking out the crucial point on the scale. The question arises mainly in connection with the possible use of nuclear weapons. Some speak of "limited strategic war," and would so classify a nuclear war fought according to the McNamara strategy, described above.[19] Others incline toward treating nuclear war as limited only when the restraint is much more severe, e.g., when "strategic" uses of nuclear weapons are forsworn and when the only uses are "tactical." Still others go farther, treating war as limited only when a belligerent possessing nuclear weapons makes no use of them at all. Moreover, it is also possible to speak of limiting the damage done with conventional weapons and thus to speak of limited war where the use of nuclear weapons is not the issue.

The problem of limitations arises in connection with a number of possible kinds of situations. Our concern here is with the major powers and above all with the nuclear powers. They might fight by proxy, each giving aid to an ally or satellite, as the United States and China are doing

18 Brodie, *Strategy in the Missile Age*, pp. 305-357.
19 Klaus Knorr and Thornton Read, eds., *Limited Strategic War* (New York, Praeger, for the Center of International Studies, Princeton University, 1962).

in Vietnam, and as the Soviet Union did in Korea. They might become directly involved, as the United States and China did in Korea. Involvement might be direct on the one side and remote or indirect on the other; thus Britain and France attacked Egypt in a limited way in 1956, and the United States took part in the Bay of Pigs attack of 1961, with no more than a remote Soviet involvement in either case. In principle, as is suggested by the Berlin blockade and the Cuban missile crisis, great nuclear powers might be locked in some kind of struggle or direct confrontation that they manage to keep localized. They might even become involved in major war without attacking each other's homelands; e.g., the Soviet Union and the United States might fight it out in Europe. And, as Secretary McNamara has shown, it is thinkable that targets in the homelands might be attacked, even with nuclear weapons, but still on a limited, selective basis.

As the above illustrations suggest, the problem of limiting war is sometimes largely or entirely a problem of self-restraint, which may make it manageable. Thus Britain and France had the capacity to do far more damage to Egypt than they in fact did in 1956, the Soviet Union could have done far more damage to Hungary, and the United States could have easily overwhelmed Cuba. Presumably the Soviet Union was guided in Hungary by the old principle of avoiding the infliction of unnecessary suffering; it limited the damage it did to what it considered necessary for the achievement of its objective. Something more than this operated in Egypt and Cuba, for the attacking powers did not even do what was necessary to achieve success. Perhaps they simply made mistakes in their calculations. Perhaps a sense of guilt over the violation of acknowledged moral or legal principles restrained them; or, if not guilt, then a fear of the consequences of undermining the principles to which they in general subscribed. Probably they were restrained to some extent by their own allies, and perhaps by Soviet threats.

But self-restraint is the answer to the problem only in situations of very unequal power. In other situations both sides have significant choices to make, and the question is how a state that wants to keep war limited can maximize the prospect that the enemy will agree to the desired limits and actually observe them. What strategies and conditions give the most promise of success?

One of the requirements is that the desire to limit the war be made clear, and this can be attempted in various ways. Open discussion of the subject in peacetime is likely to be helpful: the kinds of limitations envisaged, the reasons for them, and the signals that can be taken to indicate that they are being observed or ignored. Unofficial public discussion serves the purpose to some extent, but official public pronouncements are even better. Advance understandings may even be possible, whether explicit or tacit. Once war breaks out, it is all the more important that no doubt be left about the desire to keep it limited. Communication between the belligerents should be maintained—perhaps by open pronouncements, perhaps via third parties, or perhaps even by maintaining diplomatic relations and special lines of direct, secret communication. Not only words but also deeds should signal the desire that limits be observed. The problem is to identify acts of omission or commission that are most likely to point clearly to a limit that is mutually acceptable. The most obvious possibility is to pledge to refrain, and actually to refrain, from using nuclear weapons unless the enemy uses them first. If only low-yield nuclear weapons are employed, or if nuclear weapons are employed only for "tactical" purposes or only against "military" targets, it is possible that the limit will be understood and observed, but the chance of misunderstanding and escalation is considerably greater. Geographical limits are among the others that are most likely to be clear and acceptable: that there should be no crossing of a well-known line such as a political boundary or a river or a mountain chain.

The desire to keep war limited is not enough, even if shared by both sides. Each side is likely to want only those limits that it expects to find advantageous, and each will be tempted to abandon any limits that turn out to be disadvantageous. The theoretical solution to this problem is that the state set on keeping war limited should possess a sufficient range of capabilities to be able to fight more effectively than the enemy no matter what the limits are. If the enemy clearly cannot gain by rejecting or abandoning desired limits, then he presumably will accept them. This means that the idea of deterrence continues to be applicable to a time of limited war. The statements of Secretary McNamara, cited above, illustrate the point. They announce the desire of the United States to limit any general nuclear war that occurs; the object in such a war is to be "the destruction of the enemy's military forces, not of his civilian population." And Secretary McNamara threatens the destruction of the Soviet Union as a civilized nation if it ignores this limitation.

Military capabilities are important to the limitation of war in another way, too. The general assumption is that a strategy of denial offers a better basis for limiting war than a strategy of rollback; that is, it is better to be able to prevent the enemy from occupying territory than to rely on an effort to oust him once he has come in. This means that it is important to have military power-in-being at the moment of the outbreak of war and either to have it on the spot or be sufficiently mobile to get it to the spot in short order. Further, if the initial attack is on a third country whose defense is important, that country should have sufficient armed power of its own to hold until help can arrive.

To these requirements for limiting war another should be added: the goals pursued in the war should be reasonably moderate. An enemy confronted with extreme demands, e.g., for unconditional surrender, might choose a desperate gamble instead—expanding or exploding the war, either in the hope of improving his fate or in a spirit of hopeless vindictiveness.

If possible still another element belongs in a strategy for limiting war: one side or preferably both should limit the extent to which pride and honor are staked upon the outcome, for all limits are endangered if the observance of them leads toward humiliation and shame. A number of military encounters suggest ways of minimizing the commitment of pride and honor. One is to fight by proxy, giving assistance to the forces of third parties and trying to maintain the appearance that the war is local, involving only local issues. The Soviet Union managed this in Korea, and the United States (in a very formal sense) is doing so in Vietnam, or at least was until the spring of 1965. Another method is to fight without declaring war and without accepting the fighting as war; the Soviet Union and Japan managed this in the late 1930's, and both found it possible to terminate the fighting without a feeling of national disgrace. A related method is to describe the fighters as volunteers, as Mussolini did in the Spanish Civil War and as the Chinese Communists did in Korea, or to disclaim responsibility and attribute it to others as the United States did in connection with the Bay of Pigs fiasco. Another method is to fight in the name of the United Nations, as the United States and others did in Korea, giving basis for the claim that a decision to accept unpopular limits or an unpalatable final settlement is not, after all, a national decision. Such devices may be fictions, even very thin fictions, but where the emotions of pride and honor are involved fiction sometimes turns out to be of considerable importance.

Obviously, there is no assurance that these strategies for limiting war will be effective. The principal consideration suggesting that they might be is that each side wants to survive; and to assure survival each may have to concede it to the other, limiting the struggle accordingly. At the same time, it should be acknowledged that the meaning of "survival" is open to some question. Even in the case of a man, there is sometimes room for doubt on the question whether he is dead or alive, and what are the marks of the survival of a state?

## GUERRILLA WAR

In the kinds of warfare described above, the assumption is that regular armed forces in one geographical area attack targets in another geographical area. The object is to weaken and destroy the enemy's will to fight, and this is attempted in the main by destroying his capacity to fight. Occupation of territory, or at least control over it, is an important matter; each side seeks to deny the other access to its own territory and, conversely, each side seeks to occupy or control the territory of the enemy.

As we noted briefly at the end of Chapter 16, guerrilla warfare is another possibility, at least in certain situations.[20] The assumption is that one side consists of irregular, guerrilla forces and the other of armed forces of the more conventional type. The guerrillas operate in relatively small groups and aim to hit and run; they seek to avoid general, large-scale battle and make no very serious attempt to deny the enemy access to territory. If the enemy masses his forces and advances, the guerrillas simply retreat or disperse, offering no single target that is worth a major effort. They aim at surprise attack on especially vulnerable units of the enemy, seizing whatever matériel they can use, destroying the rest, and then withdrawing before the enemy can arrive in force for counterattack. The object is the same as in regular war—to undermine the will of the enemy to fight—but it is attempted not so much by the destruction of his fighting capacity as by persistent harassment designed to undermine the morale of the enemy soldiers and to demonstrate to the enemy government the futility of the effort to establish stable, peaceful control.

Guerrilla warfare is feasible only in certain kinds of situations. The guerrillas must be able to elude the enemy. Moreover, though they may be able to capture supplies by their surprise attacks on the enemy, they are likely to need other sources as well. Thus it is important that they have very substantial support from the local population, in terms of a willingness to offer them safe havens and a willingness to provide necessary supplies. They can control the attitudes of the local population to some extent by terrorism and can take supplies, perhaps as "taxes"; and sometimes the toll that they exact is very high. But still they need substantial voluntary support. Further, their chances are much greater if the terrain offers concealment. And they are still better off if they have access to a foreign state whose government is willing to provide a haven along with training and matériel, most particularly if the foreign state in turn is confident of the sympathy and support of various peoples and governments throughout the world.

Those opposing the guerrillas face problems ranging from the easily solvable to the extremely frustrating. The problem is easy if the guerrillas lack most or all of the advantages listed above. But if they in fact have a substantial amount of support from the local population, what are the opposing armed forces to do? Inflict terrible reprisals on whole villages and towns suspected of giving aid to the guerrillas, killing the innocent and guilty alike? Herd them into concentration camps? Of course, one answer is that those opposing the guerrillas should win the support of the population by political means: by providing an effective government championing an attractive ideology and giving assurance of a happy fu-

[20] Andrew C. Janos, "Unconventional Warfare, Framework and Analysis," *World Politics*, Vol. 15 (July, 1963), pp. 636-646.

ture. But this is not always possible, as Algeria and Vietnam attest. If the terrain provides cover for guerrillas, should nuclear bombs be used to lay it bare? If the guerrillas obtain support from a neighboring state, is war to be launched against that state? One of the principles of the neighboring state is that the kind and quantity of the aid that it gives should not be such as to make war an appropriate response. And what if the war might start a chain reaction? Is the world to be engulfed in war because of guerrillas in one little country?

The problem described above is sometimes mainly or entirely a problem of domestic politics. But this is not always true. Sometimes neighboring states have instigated the guerrilla action in the first place, or at least given assurance of support in advance, in which case they are said to be guilty of "indirect aggression" or "aggression by subversion." Sometimes, too, the government and the armed forces opposed to the guerrillas obtain help from the outside, as was the case in Greece and Vietnam. So the problem may, and often does, enter the realm of international politics.

In some circumstances, then, the instigation and support of guerrilla war in another state may be an alternative to international war, whether conventional or nuclear, limited or unlimited. And assistance to a government beleaguered by guerrillas may be equivalent to support for an ally or any other victim of aggression. Given a desire to avoid unrestricted nuclear warfare, and given the danger that any formal international war might escalate, the attractiveness of indirect forms of aggression is increased.

## WARS OF NATIONAL LIBERATION

Communists speak of wars of national liberation, meaning any war that in their eyes aims at liberating people from the "chains of capitalism" or the "yoke of imperialism." Guerrilla wars may be wars of national liberation in this sense. We should note, however, that other kinds of military actions may also qualify, in Communist eyes, as wars of national liberation. Revolutionary armies may be organized in much the same fashion as national armies and may adopt military strategies akin to those adopted in traditional international war. The principal international question raised by such wars concerns the extent to which each side in the civil war receives aid from the governments of other states, and the nature of such aid. From the Communist point of view it is proper for Communist governments to aid the revolutionary forces in "wars of national liberation," but unacceptable for non-Communist governments to aid the other side.

# DOES WAR REMAIN A USEFUL INSTRUMENT?

War and the danger of war continue despite the possibility of holocaust. Both within and among states, political leaders pursue conflicting objectives; some of them find it useful to press their demands by making subtle or brutal threats of war, while others find it imperative to resist demands even at the risk of war. Whether or not anyone ever deliberately wants war, it occurs and the danger of its occurrence persists.

Sir Winston Churchill said in 1953 that he sometimes had

the odd thought that the annihilating character of these agencies [nuclear weapons] may bring an utterly unforeseeable security to mankind. . . . It may be that when the advance of destructive weapons enables everyone to kill everybody else no one will want to kill anyone at all.

Churchill reverted to the same thought again in 1955, taking the development of thermonuclear weapons into account.

After a certain point has been passed, it may be said, the worse things get the better. . . . Then it may be that we shall, by a process of sublime irony, have reached a stage in this story where safety will be the sturdy child of terror, and survival the twin brother of annihilation.

Churchill's anticipations might yet prove sound. It seems highly probable that the United States and the Soviet Union have been more restrained in their dealings with each other than they would have been in the absence of nuclear weapons. But the weight of evidence and the force of reason point not so much to the view that the revolutionary developments of recent decades rule war out as to the view that the methods of waging it must if at all possible be limited. As Bernard Brodie has put it, "In a world still unprepared to relinquish the use of military power, we must learn to effect that use through methods that are something other than self-destroying." The problem is least acute, of course, in relations between states that lack nuclear weapons, though one or more of them might have nuclear allies. Conventional war will presumably remain about as useful and about as dangerous to such states as it has been in the past. Similarly, the dangers of "mutual suicide" are limited when only one side possesses nuclear weapons; it may exercise self-restraint whether out of genuine choice or by force of circumstances, or the other side may concede. The great danger of Armageddon obviously lies in confrontations between the great nuclear powers—the "eyeball to eyeball" showdowns. Such a showdown occurred in the fall of 1962 in connection with the Cuban missile crisis. Whether other such showdowns can be avoided, or whether they can be resolved without major conflict, remains to be seen.

The possibility of "mutual suicide" cannot be excluded. Massive risks attend a policy, even if a purely defensive policy, resting on the threat of the use of force. So far, however, almost all men have judged these risks to be more acceptable—whether or not less serious—than the risks that would attend a policy based on unilateral disarmament and a renunciation of violence.

## SUGGESTED READINGS

BLACK, Cyril E., and THORNTON, Thomas P., eds., *Communism and Revolution, The Strategic Uses of Political Violence* (Princeton, N.J., Princeton University Press, 1964).

BONDURANT, Joan V., *Conquest of Violence. The Gandhian Philosophy of Conflict* (Princeton, N.J., Princeton University Press, 1958).

BRODIE, Bernard, *Strategy in the Missile Age* (Princeton, N.J., Princeton University Press, 1959).

GOLDWIN, Robert A., ed., *America Armed, Essays on United States Military Policy* (Chicago, Rand McNally, 1961).

HALPERIN, Morton H., *Limited War in the Nuclear Age* (New York, Wiley, 1963).

KAHN, Herman, *On Escalation: Metaphors and Scenarios* (New York, Praeger, 1965).

——, *On Thermonuclear War* (Princeton, N.J., Princeton University Press, 1960).

——, *Thinking About the Unthinkable* (New York, Horizon Press, 1962).

KAUFMANN, William W., *The McNamara Strategy* (New York, Harper & Row, 1964).

KAUFMANN, William W., ed., *Military Policy and National Security* (Princeton, N.J., Princeton University Press, 1956).

KISSINGER, Henry A., *The Necessity for Choice, Prospects of American Foreign Policy* (New York, Anchor Books, Doubleday, 1962).

KNORR, Klaus, and READ, Thornton, eds., *Limited Strategic War* (New York, Praeger, 1962).

MAO Tse-tung, *On Guerrilla Warfare* (New York, Praeger, 1961).

MILLIS, Walter, and REAL, James, *The Abolition of War* (New York, Macmillan, 1963).

RICHARDSON, Lewis F., *Statistics of Deadly Quarrels*, ed. by Quincy Wright and C. C. Lienau (Chicago, Quadrangle Books, 1960).

ROSENAU, James N., ed., *International Aspects of Civil Strife* (Princeton, Princeton University Press, 1964).

SCHELLING, Thomas C., *The Strategy of Conflict* (New York, Oxford, 1963).

THAYER, Charles W., *Guerrilla* (New York, Harper & Row, 1963).

WASKOW, Arthur I., *The Limits of Defense* (Garden City, N.Y., Doubleday, 1962).

WRIGHT, Quincy, *A Study of War* (Chicago, The University of Chicago Press, 1942).

Gromyko, Robert A., ed. America Armed. Essays on United States Military Policy (Chicago, Rand McNally, 1961).

# 19

# ARMAMENTS, ARMS CONTROL, AND DISARMAMENT

Governments act in the belief that armed establishments serve useful functions and important purposes, and intelligent consideration of questions relating to armaments, arms control, and disarmament requires acknowledgment of this fact. Governments do not engage lightly in either arming or disarming. Irrationality and perversity play a part in this area of human activity as they do in many others, but they are not the controlling factors. It is a mistake to think that states arm capriciously or to think that disarmament would occur if only those dedicated to the truth and the right had the power of decision. At the same time, it should also be acknowledged that some individuals challenge the belief that armed establishments are needed and justified, and the number who pose the challenge has considerably increased since the catastrophic potentialities of missiles with nuclear warheads have come to be more widely appreciated.

## THE FUNCTIONS AND PURPOSES
## OF ARMED FORCES

The possible functions and purposes of armed forces have already been mentioned, implicitly or explicitly, at various points, but a brief summary is in place here.

In the domestic field, governments regularly seek to command such armed forces as will give them reasonable security against rebellion. They may, if they choose, manipulate expenditures on armed forces as a means of regulating the national economy, expanding armies to avoid or relieve unemployment and reducing the amount spent on armed forces as means of combating inflation. They can confer officers' commissions as a means of assuring prestige and income to influential persons who might otherwise be fractious and even rebellious. They can use the armed services and military training in various ways to promote health, education, and welfare. There have been rulers and other leading personages to whom an army was a source of pride and pleasure, to be drilled and commanded and paraded for the psychological satisfaction involved; even in modern democratic societies many obviously enjoy and take pride in military ceremony and panoply. It is plain that some of these domestic functions of military establishments are important, but means do not exist for measuring their importance with any precision; it naturally varies at different times and in different countries.

The functions and purposes of armed establishments in the international field are generally more important. The over-all purpose is to protect and promote what are regarded as the rights and interests of the state. To accomplish this purpose, the possession and display of armed strength may be enough, but the record shows that states have also frequently found it necessary or desirable to resort to violence, whether in military action short of war or in war itself.

The possession, display, and employment of armed strength are so important in international affairs that they deserve to be dwelt upon. They do much to govern the extent to which a state can work its will. Consider, for example, the position of the belligerents at the end of a war. If the test of war has proved one side to be militarily inferior, and if it has therefore capitulated, it is at the mercy of the victors. They may seize and annex territory, occupy remaining territory, insist on changes in the personnel of the government or in the form of the political and social system, take an indemnity or reparations, disarm the defeated, and impose other measures as they see fit. Among the victors themselves, influence over the terms of the peace is apt to be proportionate to the military power at their command. Brazil and the United States, for example, both declared war against Germany in the two world wars, but the equality of their legal status by no means led to equality of influence over the terms of the peace. The role of military power in determining relative influence over peace settlements is illustrated by Winston Churchill's remark at the Yalta Conference, toward the end of World War II, that the conference was "a very exclusive club, the entrance fee being at least five million soldiers or the equivalent." [1]

The reestablishment of peace does not terminate the significance of armed power. Its influence is still likely to be great. Certainly the dominance of the Red Army in eastern and southeastern Europe after World War II was the major factor in making the victory of Communism possible there, and action by the Red Army was vital to the survival of the

[1] James F. Byrnes, *Speaking Frankly* (New York, Harper & Row, 1947), p. 25.

Communist regimes when rebellions occurred in East Germany (1953) and Hungary (1956). Similarly, Anglo–American power was a major factor in permitting non-Communist groups to gain and maintain control in other parts of Europe, and American armed power has obviously been a vital factor in the fate of Japan, South Korea, and Taiwan. Both sides have spent huge sums to develop and display their nuclear power and missile delivery systems. When Khrushchev sought to emplace Soviet nuclear missiles in Cuba in 1962, and when Kennedy forced him to withdraw, both demonstrated the importance that they attached to armed power. Through spectacular achievements in space, both the Soviet Union and the United States seek (among other things) to impress the world with a prowess that has connotations for military power.

The importance of armaments in times of peace is brought out especially by Salvador de Madariaga.

The fact is that armaments are more useful in time of peace than in time of war. The normal wielders of armaments are not the soldiers, but the diplomats. The gun that does not shoot is more eloquent than the gun that has to shoot and above all than the gun which has shot. There is a Spanish light comedy in which a man is made to agree with a particular course of action by the liberal exhibition of a revolver before his frightened eyes, and as the victim is asked by a third party whether he has at last been convinced: "Yes. He brought me round by means of a 5-bullet argument." Yet no shot had been fired. The diplomacy of the great powers is carried out not exclusively, not always openly, not even always consciously, but always nevertheless on such a principle. The foreign secretary of this or that nation may be the most conciliatory man on earth; yet the minimum which will be granted to him by his adversaries will be considerably higher for the fact of his armaments. At their lowest, therefore, armed forces are one of the most formidable tacit elements in international policy; at their highest . . . the determining factor.[2]

States not only gain their ends simply by possessing armed power; sometimes they actually use it. The steps taken may be short of war. On many occasions strong naval powers have established a so-called pacific blockade as a means of coercing weaker countries; by such a blockade, vessels of the blockaded state are prevented from entering or leaving home ports. The hope is that the disruption of commerce will bring the weaker state to terms. Especially in the decades from 1910 to 1930, the United States repeatedly engaged in military intervention in several of the Caribbean republics, virtually assuming the prerogatives of government in some instances. Time and again, too, states which believe that their legal rights have been violated have used their military forces to inflict reprisals.

Whether to avert a war by balancing power or to create power rela-

2 Salvador de Madariaga, *Disarmament* (New York, Coward-McCann, 1929), pp. 57-58.

tionships in which aggressive war can be launched with the best prospect of success, states also arrange, as we have seen, to combine their physical strength by making alliances, pledging cooperative military operations in certain contingencies.

The ultimate function of armed establishments is, of course, the waging of war. War is the ultimate means by which states defend their rights and interests. It is also the ultimate means by which states prosecute what they consider to be justice, that is, by which they seek to gain new rights against the opposition of others. It is analogous to revolution in the domestic field, and is likely to be regarded as necessary and useful in international politics at least as long as revolutions are thought to be necessary and useful in domestic politics. War may also be thought of as a substitute for legislative, executive, and judicial agencies; it is a means of enforcing law, and a means of determining whose desires shall prevail concerning the content and interpretation of law.

There are likely to be differences of opinion concerning the importance of some of the domestic uses of armed power. It may not seem vital to gratify the ego of certain persons by giving them troops to command, or vital to arouse patriotic spirit through military panoply. There is less room for disagreement, however, on the importance of armed strength for purposes of international relations. States which do not have good arms or good friends, or both, are apt to live in considerable jeopardy, if they survive at all. It is no wonder that such a large proportion of the money spent by national governments goes to military establishments. Neither is it any wonder that international negotiations concerning disarmament have produced little result, even though they have occupied much of the time of statesmen and diplomats of the twentieth century.

## THE MEANING OF ARMS CONTROL AND DISARMAMENT

Disarmament is a popular word. At the same time, it is a misleading one. In a literal sense, governments never disarm and cannot be expected to. They always need some armed power at their disposal, if for no other reason than to guard the frontier against bandit forays. Even when the United States and the Soviet Union agreed in 1961 that "general and complete" disarmament was their objective, they went on to specify that states should be free to have such armed power as is "necessary to maintain internal order and protect the personal security of citizens." Common sense suggests that *disarmament* should be made to mean some reduction of armaments, if not their abolition, but in fact the term is used more loosely. For example, the test ban treaty is sometimes classified as a disarmament measure. It forbids the testing of nuclear weapons in the atmosphere and outer space, and so may impede their improvement, but it does not provide for their reduction or elimination. Thus, according to rather common usage, any regulation or limitation having to do with armed power is treated as a measure of disarmament.

The Soviet–American agreement endorsing "general and complete" disarmament also provided that states should join in creating "an international peace force equipped with agreed types of armaments." Thus, in principle, the quantitative reduction in the armed power of individual states might be accompanied by the simultaneous increase in the armed power of an international organization. "Disarmament" might thus be indistinguishable from the centralization of control over armaments— indistinguishable from the establishment of an armed peace—as is the case within countries.

The Soviet–American agreement further specified that disarmament measures should be implemented under "strict and effective international control," i.e., that there should be verification and inspection. This suggests one of the meanings given to *arms control.* By a slight extension, *arms control* refers to the concerting of armaments policies by potential enemies, with or without formal agreement, for the purpose of promoting stable, orderly relationships; and sometimes it is even made to refer to unilateral policies of self-restraint, followed in the hope that other states will reciprocate. *Arms control* connotes measures of a positive sort, pursued deliberately and persistently with a view to preserving peace, whereas *disarmament* connotes measures of a negative and restrictive sort which will presumably have automatic consequences.[3]

We will discuss armaments, disarmament, and arms control first in terms of the unilateral measures that can be taken and then in terms of international agreement.

## UNILATERAL ACTION AFFECTING ARMED POWER AT HOME AND ABROAD

Unilateral action occurs on the basis of the fact that general international law leaves each government free to choose its weapons and to arm itself with them as heavily or as lightly as it pleases. A government may confine itself to spears, or may concentrate on thermonuclear bombs. It may maintain a bare minimum of armed power, or it may devote so much of its resources to military purposes that a substantial portion of its population starves. Within countries, governments may specify the kind and quantity of weapons that private persons may legally possess. Among countries no agency has developed which exercises comparable functions.

[3] Lincoln P. Bloomfield, "Arms Control Theory," in Walter R. Fisher and Richard Dean Burns, eds., *Armament and Disarmament: The Continuing Dispute* (Belmont, Calif., Wadsworth, 1964), pp. 258-259. Hedley Bull, *The Control of the Arms Race, Disarmament and Arms Control in the Missile Age* (New York, Praeger, 1961), p. ix.

Such international regulations as exist concerning armaments depend on treaties agreed to by the affected states.

Not only can states take unilateral action determining the extent of their own military preparations, but they can also take unilateral actions which affect the military strength of others. Specifically, under general international law each state is free in time of peace to export and import armaments and other war materials as it sees fit. It may buy peashooters and nuclear missiles from anyone who will sell them, and it may sell or give such weapons to anyone who will take them. It may also refuse to buy or sell, and it is free to do so on a discriminatory basis. A government which wishes to strengthen the economy or productive power of an ally may place orders with it or its citizens for matériel, and may withhold such orders from uncooperative or unfriendly states. Likewise, a government may regulate the exportation of its own products so as to make them available to favored states and unavailable to others. Again, such international regulations as exist concerning these matters depend on treaties agreed to by the affected states.

Such rights and powers have been exercised increasingly in recent years. One purpose is to weaken, or at least to avoid strengthening, a potentially hostile state. The United States, for example, refuses to allow the exportation of strategic materials to the Soviet Union and Communist China, and it tries to get recipients of American aid to follow the same policy. The Communist states enforce analogous restrictions. The result is that trade in strategic materials between East and West has substantially ceased. Presumably both sides are somewhat weaker militarily than they would be if such trade restrictions did not exist, yet the effect is necessarily marginal.

Another purpose that both the Soviet Union and the United States have pursued in reciprocal unilateral policies is the control of nuclear dangers. For example, both apparently fear the consequences of the diffusion of nuclear weapons, and both have apparently refrained from contributing to their diffusion. The Soviet Union started out in the 1950's to assist China in developing the capacity to produce nuclear weapons, only to withdraw. The United States has very pointedly refrained from assisting De Gaulle in his similar effort. Moreover, apparently neither the United States nor the Soviet Union has turned completed nuclear weapons over to the control of an ally. Each might pursue such policies even in the absence of reciprocity, but certainly reciprocity makes the position of each country easier than it otherwise would be. Further, despite episodes suggesting the contrary, both sides have tried to give the impression of full self-control and an acute sense of responsibility in their own handling of nuclear weapons.

Still another purpose pursued at times in unilateral policies is the reduction of armaments. Soviet leaders have spoken of achieving this through "mutual example." One leader, in announcing a cut in the defense budget, referred to his understanding that the United States would also make a cut.

A psychologist, Charles E. Osgood, has argued that "tension reduction" in general should be attempted through mutual example.[4] His thought is that if East and West got themselves into an arms race by unilateral actions that accentuated tensions, they ought to be able to reverse the process and bring about disarmament by unilateral actions designed to relieve tensions. Within limits, the possibility does obviously exist. But there are limits. Osgood seems to accept the view that East–West tensions arise not from genuine conflicts of purpose but from "psycho–logic," i.e., from unfounded fear on one side leading to actions that produce unfounded fear on the other; his view seems to be that the tensions and dangers arise from profound misunderstandings and pathological conceptions, not from realistic appraisals of intentions and capabilities. But few American students of Soviet behavior would agree. Moreover, even if Soviet attitudes have mellowed enough to make possible the kind of graduated reciprocal measures of tension reduction that Osgood proposes, there is still Communist China. What states can achieve by mutual example is limited by the extent to which they think they have mutual interests. When genuine conflicts of interest or purpose exist, and when armaments are actually or potentially useful as instruments of struggle, disarmament by mutual example is not to be expected.

## INTERNATIONAL AGREEMENTS ON ARMAMENTS

International agreements are commonly regarded as a more promising basis for disarmament than unilateral action. Such agreements may be concluded in several types of circumstances: (1) those existing at the end of a war in which one side has achieved victory and can largely dictate the terms of peace; (2) those existing in the absence of an expectation of war; and (3) those existing in the presence of an expectation of war.

*1. Imposing disarmament on the defeated.* It is common for victors in war to disarm the defeated. Both the incentive and the power to do so are there. Victors normally wish to reduce to a minimum any prospect that the defeated might rebuild their power and seek revenge, and they therefore include in the treaty of peace provisions which impose more or less strict limits on the possession of armed power. After World War I, for example, the Allies reduced Germany's army to 100,000 men and restricted the German navy to a total of 36 ships. The air force was completely abolished, and Germany was prohibited from possessing certain specified weapons—tanks, for example. The whole Rhineland region, a

[4] Charles E. Osgood, *An Alternative to War or Surrender* (Urbana, University of Illinois Press, 1962), pp. 26-30, 85-89, and *passim*.

rich industrial region lying along Germany's border with France and Belgium, was demilitarized, meaning that Germany could neither build fortifications nor station troops there. In effect, this made the Rhineland a hostage to Germany's good behavior, open to military occupation at the will of France and Belgium. After World War II, the Allies divided Germany and subjected it to military occupation, eliminating German armed power completely. Japanese armed power was likewise destroyed, and the armed establishments of other defeated countries were severely limited.

After neither of the world wars has the disarmament of the defeated countries proved to be enduring. After World War I the Allies failed to adopt effective means of detecting and preventing evasions and violations of the treaty on the part of Germany. Moreover, as time went on they gradually lost their determination to enforce the disarmament which they had imposed. Persistent evasions and violations finally led in 1935 to an open announcement by Hitler that Germany would no longer regard itself as bound by the disarmament provisions of the Treaty of Versailles, and in the following year he similarly repudiated the provisions calling for the demilitarization of the Rhineland. By 1936, therefore, Germany had thrown off the limitations on its armed power with impunity.

The disarmament of the defeated in World War II has likewise been short-lived. With the coming of the East-West struggle, victors on both sides have sought allies wherever they could find them, even among the former enemy states, and they have naturally not wished to enforce the disarmament of an ally. The problem has been not how to enforce disarmament but how and under what conditions to bring about rearmament.

In short, powerful forces work to undermine imposed arrangements for unequal disarmament. Victors tend to lose their determination to enforce such arrangements; they tend also to become divided against each other, and then some or all of them may reverse themselves and actively seek the rearmament of former enemies who are willing to cooperate. Moreover, the defeated states which have been disarmed are likely to chafe under the restrictions imposed upon them and to seek release, whether with the connivance or against the opposition of other states.

If the disarmament of the defeated is unlikely to endure, it is still less likely to lead to general disarmament, even when the victors regard themselves as peace-loving states which have now eliminated the power of the warlike. The victors normally either retain fear of the defeated or develop fear of each other, or both. Despite professions of a love of peace, some of them may also develop aggressive aspirations, which require that they be armed and that others retain arms in self-defense.

2. *Agreements between states not expecting war with each other.* The second of the types of circumstances in which disarmament may be sought

is characterized by an absence of an expectation of war. Unfortunately for the prospects of disarmament, the absence of this expectation is never a general condition. Two states, or even a grouping of a number of states, may enjoy such harmonious relationships that they have no expectation of war with each other. They may therefore leave boundaries which they have in common substantially unguarded and may estimate their military needs without regard to the possibility of war among themselves. Canada and the United States provide the usual example of this kind of situation; under the Rush-Bagot agreement of 1817 the Great Lakes remain demilitarized, and by tacit accord the principle of demilitarization has been extended to the remainder of the common boundary as well. A similar situation, though not based on formal agreement, exists in the relationships of a number of other states, for example, Norway and Sweden. But neither Canada and the United States nor any other combination of states live in the complete absence of an expectation of war. Though Canada and the United States may have no fear of each other, they both have had to recognize the possibility of war with outside powers —with Germany or Japan or the Soviet Union. The disarmament to which their mutual trust has led has therefore been strictly limited. Assured of peace with each other, they can simply devote their resources more fully to military preparedness against an outside power.

3. *Negotiations between potential enemies.* The last of the three types of circumstances in which disarmament may be sought is characterized by the existence of an expectation of war among the parties trying to negotiate the disarmament agreement. Since World War II, for example, the United States and the Soviet Union have negotiated endlessly about disarmament, but all the while both have had the possibility of war between them in the foreground of their thoughts, and it is obvious that their proposals and their reactions to proposals have been conditioned at least as much by concern for relative power positions as by a desire for a regulation and limitation of arms.

What kinds of proposals are made? Some are of a quantitative sort, e.g., fixing the maximum number of men that a country may have in its armed forces or limiting expenditures; between the wars the naval powers kept negotiating about the number of warships of various sorts that their navies might include. Some proposals are of a qualitative sort, for example, to limit or eliminate "aggressive" weapons or weapons of mass destruction. The Soviet Union long sought an agreement to "ban the bomb." Some proposals focus on given geographical areas, calling for a limitation on the armaments or armed forces that can be placed within them or on the kinds of activities that can be conducted. For example, there has been talk of "disengagement" in Central Europe and of the establishment of zones in which nuclear weapons will not be placed; and there have been proposals that all armed forces be kept within the boundaries of their home country, foreign bases being abandoned. Numerous proposals relate to the question of inspection and verification, or more generally, to the access to knowledge of the activities of the various countries involved. Some proposals include specifications concerning successive steps to be taken in implementing the measures agreed upon, so that balance can be maintained throughout, no state gaining special military advantage at any point in the process. Finally, proposals, both for the settlement of disputes by peaceful means and for the establishment of an international peace force, are associated with disarmament efforts, whether or not they should be considered aspects of disarmament.

Though hundreds of able men have devoted thousands of hours to thought, discussion, and negotiation about the problems involved in concluding agreements along these lines, the results have so far been very meager. States acting on the assumption that they may become involved in war with each other find it very difficult to agree on any plan for regulating and limiting their armed power. In the sections below we shall see why this is so.

## WHY STATES PROPOSE DISARMAMENT

States which propose general agreements for disarmament do so for various reasons. Some, but not all, of them are good reasons, compatible with the end sought.

### To Save Money

The desire to save money or, more properly, to permit the diversion of resources to purposes which are socially more desirable is a common reason for disarmament proposals. Anyone familiar with governmental budgets will realize that a very large proportion of national expenditures is devoted to defense. The Department of Defense spends roughly half of the total expenditure of the United States government, and other federal agencies (e.g., the Department of State, including USIA and AID; the Veterans' Administration; and NASA) spend additional billions that can reasonably be charged to past or possible future wars. The extent of the burden is perhaps more realistically indicated by the percentage of the Gross National Product that is devoted to defense. The figures for a number of countries in the calendar year 1963 (or in the nearest fiscal year) are as follows: Belgium, 3.7%; Costa Rica, 0.3%; France, 5.5%; India, 4.7%; Indonesia, 11.7%; Israel, 10.3%; Jordan, 16.3%; Sweden, 5.0%; United Arab Republic (Egypt), 8.6%; United Kingdom, 6.5%; United States, 9.1%.[5]

[5] Statistics and Reports Division, Agency for International Development. Cf., Bull. *op. cit.*, p. 71.

Thus, the burden of maintaining armed strength is clearly a heavy one for most states. And for the most part expenditures for armaments are unproductive. The millions of men recruited for the armed forces of various countries do not produce things which make life better either for themselves or for the remainder of the population. On the contrary, they consume the production of others. Resources devoted to the building of battleships and aircraft carriers cannot be devoted to the construction of schools and hospitals. Men who are manning guns cannot at the same time make refrigerators and air-conditioning units. Talents devoted to the science and art of war cannot, except as an incidental by-product, improve the social and cultural well-being of a people. While millions and millions of people throughout the world are poorly clothed, poorly fed, poorly housed, poorly educated, and poorly safeguarded from disease, millions and millions of others devote themselves to developing means of destroying life and property. The tragic anachronism is so obvious that demands for disarmament naturally follow. Except perhaps where armament programs serve as regulators of the domestic economy, this motive for disarmament is genuine.

At the same time, it would be easy to exaggerate the prospective savings that disarmament might achieve. The savings cannot be greater than the extent of the disarmament permits, and nothing even approaching "complete" disarmament is to be expected. Moreover, any disarmament agreed upon is likely to call for measures of inspection and verification, and they cost money; in fact, some speak of costs so great as to eat up virtually all of the prospective savings.[6] Further, an international peace force, if established, will also cost money. Thus, though the motive is compatible with the end sought, it is not, when examined, as compelling as it might be.

## To Reduce Tensions and the Danger of War

The desire to reduce international tensions and the danger of war is another reason for proposals for disarmament. This desire is no doubt often as genuine as the desire to reduce costs, but it rests on one or more assumptions that do not always hold true and that, even when true, are often not as significant as they are thought to be. One set of related assumptions is that armaments themselves induce or exacerbate tensions, that the possession of power creates a temptation to wield it, and most particularly, that the development of an arms race increases the probability of war. Another set of assumptions relates more specifically to nuclear weapons and delivery systems: that it is important to give states reassurance against surprise attack, and more broadly, important to

[6] Sir Michael Wright, *Disarm and Verify, An Explanation of the Central Difficulties and of National Policies* (New York, Praeger, 1964), esp. pp. 50-51.

create conditions that minimize the possibility of trigger-happy behavior and maximize the assurance of prudent self-control.

*1. Do armaments cause tension and war?* The easy answer to the question is, yes. When a government arms, it gives tangible evidence of thoughts of war; this very fact may increase the fears of another government, forcing it also to think in terms of war and leading it to arm itself more heavily. A vicious circle (or spiral) may thus be created, in which the military preparations of one state accentuate the fears of another, leading it to engage in military preparations, which in turn accentuate the fears of the first. As we have seen, a balance of power may be maintained in which neither state will feel that it dares to resort to war. But those who are militarily minded will have been brought to the fore. A military machine and perhaps a military class or caste may have been created which may feel the need of war; Schumpeter's theory of imperialism should be recalled in this connection. If time seems to be running against one side in the armaments race, even those among its leaders who are peacefully inclined may conclude that the risks of postponing a showdown are too great. Thus, though an armaments program may contribute to a balancing of power, it may also exacerbate tensions and accentuate forces making for war.

Yet, though there is some basis for the assumption that disarmament might relieve tensions and reduce the dangers of war, there are considerations of a more fundamental sort which must be taken into account. We have already seen that states arm themselves for various reasons, and that not all these reasons can be denounced as capricious. A state may arm itself in a desire to bring about changes in the status quo, in which case it will hardly be attracted to disarmament by the thought that disarmament might relieve international tensions. Another state may arm itself to preserve existing rights and interests, in which case it will understandably insist on a reduction or elimination of dangers as a prerequisite to disarmament. In other words, armaments reflect the fact that governments pursue conflicting purposes, wanting either to defend or to promote their interests, and therefore they find military capabilities useful if not vital in this connection. And the conflicting purposes would still be there even if disarmament occurred.

It is said that arms races tend to culminate in war, and undoubtedly they sometimes do. But the question then is whether the war is to be attributed to the arms race or to the conflicting purposes that gave rise to the race. And, if one side in the race has aggressive intentions, the question can also be asked what is likely to happen to the other side if it fails to undertake measures of defense.

Students of the subject differ in their emphasis and conclusions. Some stress the point that armaments produce or accentuate tensions and make war more likely, and so attach the highest priority to disarmament.

Others stress the point that conflicting purposes and the usefulness of armaments in pursuing them are at the root of the problem and so they attach highest priority either to bringing about a change in the purposes that are thought worth pursuing or to the development of reliable peaceful procedures for resolving conflict—or both. In fact efforts reflecting each point of view have gone on simultaneously over many years. Obviously, the efforts aiming directly at disarmament have produced little result. Efforts to change the minds of men and to develop peaceful procedures for resolving conflict may or may not have been more effective; they appear to be more promising, but the problem may well prove to be insoluble.

We ought to note the prospect that just as armaments may help to bring war on so might disarmament. In the first place, if disarmament were so carried out as to change power relationships (and in some degree this would be virtually inevitable), the states making relative gains might be tempted to take advantage of their improved circumstances; disarmament might do no more than reduce the destructiveness of the early stages of a war, and then give victory to the side that managed to rearm the fastest. In the second place, a significant degree of disarmament might encourage some governments to believe that the risks and costs of war have been reduced, making it more acceptable as a means of pursuing their goals. Moreover, if arms races sometimes culminate in war, so does the neglect of arms. World War II, for example, is not in any reasonable sense attributable to an arms race. It stemmed much more from German aggressiveness and from the physical, intellectual, and moral weakness of the United States, Britain, and France.

2. *Would reduced necessity for quick response make war less likely?* The early period of the missile age produced very special anxieties. In the United States the fear was that the Soviet Union might launch a surprise attack with nuclear missiles in the hope of destroying American nuclear retaliatory capacity, and in the Soviet Union there no doubt were comparable fears. If either side had succeeded in such an attack, thus becoming the sole power with significant strategic nuclear capacity, the possibilities open to it would have been breathtaking. As we have noted in discussing deterrence, the United States, and no doubt also the Soviet Union, took domestic measures to reduce the possibility that it might be so victimized. It maintained both an air-borne alert and an under-the-seas alert—keeping bombers in the air and Polaris submarines in the water—all presumably safe from surprise attack; and as quickly as it could, it hardened American missile-launching sites. The object was to make it possible to absorb a surprise attack and still have enough retaliatory capacity left to inflict unacceptable damage on the Soviet Union. And the further object was to make a trigger-happy response to danger signals unnecessary—to make it possible to withhold retaliatory action

until evidence was incontrovertible that an attack was under way. To reduce still further the possibility that an accident or false alarm might precipitate war by mistake, international measures were discussed. One of them was adopted: the establishment of a "hot line" between Washington and Moscow to speed communications between them in an emergency situation. And various sorts of inspection schemes were proposed. Eisenhower suggested that each side give the other a "blueprint" of its armed establishment and accept the idea of "open skies," that is, permit the aircraft of the other to range over its territory so as to keep reassured that no movement for a surprise attack was under way. There were also proposals for the stationing of observers at various critical sites on the surface. Many have commented that what is really needed for maximum reassurance against surprise attack is the general acceptance of the idea of "open societies," that is, free and unrestricted travel and communication for nationals and foreigners alike.

As more countries come to possess nuclear weapons, the danger of war by mistake may well increase. If a nuclear attack might be made by any of twenty-five countries, will it always be clear which one in fact launched the attack? What is the prospect of "catalytic war," a war between major powers precipitated by the action of a third party?

Obviously, international agreements concerning arms control and disarmament might, in principle, reduce fears and dangers of these sorts. At the same time, the United States is doing a great deal through unilateral action. In addition to the measures cited above, it is using picture-taking satellites (and so is the Soviet Union) to achieve part of what Eisenhower suggested in his "open skies" proposal.

## To Symbolize a Desire for Détente

Regardless of the question whether armaments are in fact a significant source of tensions and dangers, they can be given special symbolic significance; inevitably they have some. A state that wants to appear either threatening or reassuring can adjust its arms policies accordingly. A state that has been pressing hard for a gain of some sort, thus accentuating tensions, can intimate an abandonment of the effort and a desire for a détente by making some kind of a gesture in the realm of arms control and disarmament. The nuclear test ban treaty has been interpreted in part in these terms. In accepting the treaty, both the United States and the Soviet Union are thought to have symbolized their desire for less strained relationships and perhaps for some kind of accommodation. Moreover, some of the American commentators who assume that the United States is ahead in nuclear science and technology interpret the Soviet acceptance of the test ban treaty as symbolizing the abandonment of the effort to achieve a nuclear breakthrough and to overcome the

American lead. Thus proposals and agreements in the realm of arms control and disarmament may have a symbolic meaning that is more or less independent of their intrinsic, substantive importance.

## To Reduce Health Hazards

The test ban treaty was also motivated in part by a desire to reduce health hazards. Atmospheric testing increased the amount of radioactivity to which people at home and abroad were exposed. The widespread agitation that developed against nuclear testing was undoubtedly based more on fear of the consequences of using nuclear weapons in war than of the consequences of testing them in peace, but still concern for health also played a role.

## To Reduce the Destructiveness of War

The purpose of some arms control and disarmament proposals is not so much to relieve tensions or to prevent war as to reduce suffering and destruction when war comes. Rules regulating the conduct of warfare accepted by most of the states of the Western world have this general purpose. Some states have ratified agreements banning the use in war of certain kinds of weapons, e.g., chemical and bacteriological weapons; and the destruction and outlawry of nuclear weapons has been proposed.

The record shows that peacetime agreements fixing rules for the conduct of warfare come under extreme strain when war breaks out. It is an accepted principle that "military necessity" supersedes the rules in some circumstances; and even where this principle is not applicable, the belief of a belligerent that he will gain a significant military advantage by violating the rules involves a temptation that is extremely difficult to resist. Moreover, technological change is always occurring, creating possibilities that were not envisaged when the rules were agreed to, thus rendering them more or less obsolete.

It is true that poison gas was not used in World War II, and some cite this to support the argument that the prohibition of certain weapons can be effective. But the question is to what extent decisions to refrain from using poison gas reflected respect for peacetime agreements and to what extent they reflected wartime calculations of advantage. The odds are heavily in favor of the proposition that the wartime calculations were by far the most important, and the same would no doubt hold true if there ever were an agreement to "ban the bomb." Even if the possession of nuclear weapons were prohibited, and even if the prohibition were observed in peacetime, the probability is high that on the outbreak of war those belligerents that could manufacture such weapons would race to do so, and victory might well go to the side that won the race.

## To Achieve a Power Advantage

The desire of states to improve their relative power position, or to avert a decline in relative power, is another factor which prompts disarmament proposals. In the discussion of the balancing of power, we have already seen that statesmen seek a satisfactory, relative power position for their states. One possible way of achieving or preserving it is through international agreements on the reduction and limitation of armaments. It is obviously less costly from several points of view to weaken a potential enemy at a conference, if it can be done there, than to attempt it on the battlefield. But a conference at which each participant is seeking greater relative strength for himself, and greater relative weakness for others, is not a conference which has good prospects of success. Where one state's gain is another state's loss, and where nothing can be done except by unanimous consent, impasse is the most likely result.

This, in fact, has been the usual outcome of disarmament conferences and proposals. The first of the great modern disarmament conferences, held at The Hague in 1899, was called by the Russian Tsar. Among the considerations influencing him and his government was the fact that Germany was equipping its army with rapid-firing artillery and that the state of Russian finances made it very difficult for Russia to keep pace. Moreover, the Russian Foreign Minister felt that the distribution of power at the time was favorable and that "an agreement not to increase forces would leave Russia her great preponderance." [7] Naturally, however, the Tsar found the Germans (and others) uncooperative about limiting their armed power for the advantage of Russia. The results, in terms of agreement on armaments, were negligible. The conference did, however, succeed in concluding a series of conventions (treaties) codifying the laws and customs of war.

The situation was reversed at the time of the Conference on the Reduction and Limitation of Naval Armaments, held in Washington in 1921-1922.[8] The initiator this time was the United States, which had no fear of being outdistanced by others; in fact, it had a naval building program under way which other states could scarcely have matched. They were therefore receptive to American proposals. Moreover, the possibility of war among the participants in the Washington Conference was rather far in the background, and this facilitated agreement. Notwithstanding the favorable circumstances, however, agreement was reached only on the number of capital ships (battleships and heavy carriers) that the parties might have.

[7] William L. Langer, *The Diplomacy of Imperialism. 1890-1902* (New York, Knopf, 1935), Vol. II, p. 583.

[8] See Harold and Margaret Sprout, *Toward a New Order of Sea Power* (Princeton, N.J., Princeton University Press, 1940).

Subsequent conferences, called to extend the arrangement so as to make it cover all kinds of naval vessels, proved futile for various reasons, and Japan terminated the Washington agreement as soon as it was legally free to do so. The record largely justifies the conclusion that "a naval disarmament conference becomes . . . a paper war in which each delegation tries to preserve its own fleet and to sink as much of the other fleets as possible." [9]

The desire of states to improve their relative power position, or to avert a decline in relative power, operated also in connection with the efforts of the League of Nations to bring about general disarmament. It became evident, as the same observer put it, that "states are always perfectly willing to disarm provided their potential enemies disarm more." [10] When many states tacitly insist on such a proviso, it is obviously improbable that agreement can be reached. In fact, the League's efforts resulted in complete failure.

Negotiations since World War II concerning nuclear weapons have been influenced by the same desire. Particularly during the period when the United States enjoyed a monopoly of atomic weapons, the Kremlin's proposals to outlaw their possession and use were obviously calculated to improve the relative power position of the Soviet Union. Even since the termination of the American monopoly, outlawry would still presumably work to the advantage of the Communist states. Given their totalitarian controls, they could probably violate the agreement with less risk of detection. Moreover, if the agreement were observed, an important counterweight to their tremendous manpower would be removed. On the other side, the proposals championed by the United States and by the non-Communist members of the United Nations Atomic Energy Commission would probably have worked to the advantage of the West from a power point of view, for several reasons. In the first place, neither the specific agreement proposed nor any other could have deprived the United States of the advantage which it held for a time in terms of scientific knowledge and technical, manufacturing know-how; had the Soviet Union accepted the American proposals when they were first made, it probably could not have caught up with the United States as fast as it seems to have done by retaining full freedom of action. In the second place, the Western proposals would probably have worked out to the power advantage of the West through decisions concerning the location of atomic plants and laboratories, if not also through decisions concerning the location of nuclear weapons placed in the hands of a United Nations agency. It is a fair guess, at least, that the West would have sought criteria for locating and manning nuclear installations so as to give itself an advantage if seizures

---

[9] Nicholas J. Spykman, *America's Strategy in World Politics* (New York, Harcourt, Brace & World, 1942), p. 168.
[10] *Ibid.*

of such installations ever occurred. In the third place, a power advantage would probably have accrued to the West from the very extensive piercing (if not the elimination) of the Iron Curtain, for which the American proposals called. If it is true that the proposals of each side would have worked to the disadvantage of the other from a power point of view, it is understandable why agreement has not been reached.

## To Achieve a Propaganda Advantage

Another common reason for proposals of disarmament relates to public opinion. As we have seen, public attitudes at home and abroad are an element in the power position of a state. The common assumption is that the public favors disarmament. It is therefore assumed that people at home and abroad will be inclined to give sympathy and support to a government which champions disarmament, and be inclined to withhold sympathy and support from a government which can be made to appear to obstruct disarmament. Disarmament proposals may therefore be made with no expectation whatever that they will be accepted, but only for the purpose of winning friends and influencing people. For example, after the Soviet Union proposed total disarmament in 1927, a world congress of the Communist International explained that there had been no expectation that the proposal would be accepted. Rather, the objectives had been to enlist sympathy for the Soviet Union as the champion of peace, to expose the "imperialists" as enemies of peace, to eradicate alleged pacifist illusions, and to provide a basis for propaganda in support of "the only way toward disarmament and the abolition of war, viz., arming the proletarian dictatorship." [11] The aim at disarmament conferences may thus be more to secure good publicity for one's own side and bad publicity for the potential enemy than to secure agreement. This consideration was surely basic to the 1961 agreement between the United States and the Soviet Union that "general and complete" disarmament was their objective. Given Soviet championship of the principle, the United States chose (wisely or not) to accept it rather than permit the Soviet Union to gain a propaganda triumph. When negotiations that ostensibly aim at arms control and disarmament are actually carried on as aspects of a propaganda struggle, it is not surprising that they seem to fail.

In sum, proposals for arms control and disarmament by international agreement are based on one or more desires: (1) to save money, or to permit the use of resources for more constructive purposes; (2) to reduce tensions and so to diminish the danger of war; (3) to symbolize the desire for a détente; (4) in the case of the nuclear test ban treaty, to reduce

11 *International Press Correspondence*, Vol. 8 (November 28, 1928), pp. 1596-1597.

health hazards; (5) to reduce the destructiveness of war; (6) to improve the relative power position of the state, or to avert a decline in power; and (7) to gain a propaganda advantage. These desires vary considerably in the extent to which they are well-reasoned and compatible with the objective ostensibly sought. Arms control or disarmament might or might not save significant amounts of money, or reduce the destructiveness of war. It probably would not do much to alleviate tensions and the danger of war unless it reflects some kind of change of heart or change of circumstances and so has symbolic significance. The desire to gain a power advantage by means of a disarmament agreement can be effectuated only if the other side is willing or if its calculations of the effect of the agreement on power relationships differ. The search for a propaganda advantage can obviously contribute little or nothing to the actual achievement of agreement.

## OBSTACLES TO AGREEMENT ON DISARMAMENT

Voluntary agreement on disarmament is difficult to achieve only in part because the underlying desires are not all well-reasoned and fully compatible with the objective. There are additional obstacles.

### Armaments Are Needed

A fundamental one relates to a consideration advanced at the beginning of this chapter: that armaments have useful functions and that they serve a number of important purposes. States depend upon them, and are not likely to give them up or accept serious restrictions on them until alternative means of serving the same functions and purposes have been established. During the interwar period, there was a prolonged and important argument over the order in which arbitration, security, and disarmament should be sought. (The term *arbitration* in this context referred to the various means by which the peaceful settlement of international disputes is assured.) As matters turned out, the half-measures adopted to promote arbitration and security proved to be an inadequate basis for disarmament. Most of the states involved believed that they had to remain armed to safeguard their own rights and interests. They believed that they needed armed power both as an inducement to other states to accept the peaceful settlement of disputes and as something to fall back on in the event that efforts to achieve satisfactory peaceful settlement failed. Further, as events proved, a few of the states wanted to retain and build up their armaments for purposes of aggression.

In other words, one of the major obstacles to disarmament is the absence of reliable substitutes for armed power for the achievement of a number of the objectives which states seek. Within countries, people disarm only after a police force has been established to assure them protection, and only after executive, legislative, and judicial methods have been adopted by which rights and interests can be safeguarded and promoted. Analogous substitutes for armed power will probably have to be found internationally before states can be induced to disarm.

## The Problem of Agreement on Ratios of Strength

Another fundamental obstacle to disarmament by voluntary consent derives from the fact that agreement on disarmament presupposes agreement on ratios of strength among armed establishments. What basis is there for determining the ratios that ought to prevail? By what criteria is it to be decided that one state "needs" or ought to be allowed to have fifteen units of armed power, another state twelve units, and another state two?

Attempts to answer the question fall into two general categories. The first category includes answers plainly designed to serve the power interests of a particular state or group of states. Salvador de Madariaga tells of negotiations which once occurred over the limitation of naval armaments. Various states, including Great Britain, had built up their naval power during World War I. Others, including Spain, had been unable to do so. Britain wanted Spain to accept the status quo so far as relative naval strength was concerned, but Spain was reluctant.

> One day the Spanish Admiral accosted the British Admiral at the end of the sitting and declared himself ready to accept the status quo. His British colleague was very much elated. Then the Spaniard added: "But we must discuss one point, the year to be chosen to define the status quo." "Why," said the Englishman, "1921." "Oh, no," said the Spaniard: "I suggest 1588."[12]

A state which finds existing power ratios satisfactory to it and its allies will naturally want to preserve them. It is likely to be favorably disposed toward a standstill arrangement or toward the reduction of armed strength on a percentage basis. It will thus preserve a favorable position. By the same token, states which regard the existing power ratio as unsatisfactory are likely to reject it as a basis for agreement. If they favor disarmament at all, it will be on the basis of a more advantageous ratio which prevailed in earlier years, or on the basis of a new ratio considered desirable for the future. The same kinds of considerations operate when qualitative disarmament is considered; states are likely to favor disarmament in those weapons in which potential enemy states have an advantage.

The second category of answers includes those seriously designed to bring about the reduction and limitation of armaments on an equitable

12 de Madariaga, op. cit., p. 106.

basis. They reflect the subjective judgments of individuals—based on a wide variety of possible considerations—on the question of appropriate and acceptable power ratios. If the judgments are wise, and particularly if, in addition, war seems remote, the proposals might be accepted. However, this combination of circumstances is very rare. What judgments about ratios of power can be wise when most or all of the states involved want to gain or maintain a power advantage at the expense of the others? [13]

## The Problem of Implementing Agreement on Ratios

Even if there were agreement on the ratios of power that ought to prevail among states seeking disarmament, there would still be great obstacles to agreement. The above reference to units of power was figurative. There is no such thing. Weights and distances can be measured; speed can be clocked; the energy available in coal and oil can be transformed arithmetically into kilowatt-hours of electricity equivalent, but there is no standard unit for computing power. If all states had precisely the same weapons and trained equally capable men in precisely the same way, it would be more nearly possible to say what quantities of this and that would produce the agreed ratios of power. But this is not the situation. Some states have thermonuclear bombs and others do not. Some have rockets and others do not. Some stress tanks that are heavy and slow, and others stress tanks that are light and fast. Some naval powers are strong in submarines; others are strong in battleships. Some give relatively brief periods of training to vast numbers of men; others give more intensive training to fewer men. How many submarines equal one battleship in terms of power? How many mortars equal one thermonuclear bomb? How many poorly trained soldiers equal one professional? No precise and reliable answer to such questions is possible. There is no known way of reducing the power of battleships, submarines, nuclear rockets, and rifles to comparable terms. Moreover, as we have seen, armed establishments are not the only elements of national power, and, once armaments are reduced, other elements of power become proportionately more important. How much allowance should be made for the fact that the frontiers of one state are naturally less defensible than the frontiers of another? What weight should be given in the scales of power to such items as commercial aircraft and merchant ships, which can be converted for military purposes when need arises? How much allowance should be made for the prospect that, if a disarmament agreement were violated, one state would be able to rearm more rapidly than another? As Salvador de Madariaga says, the destruction of the eggs of armaments would still leave some

[13] Quincy Wright, *A Study of War* (Chicago, The University of Chicago Press, 1942), Vol. II, p. 803.

states in a favored position in terms of the possession of hens. Given good feeling and an absence of expectation of war, problems of this kind would be easily resolved, and it would not matter much how they were resolved. But an expectation of war necessitates jealous regard for every aspect of the power position of the state; even if we assume that there has been an agreement on what the ratio of power should be, this attitude is likely to lead states into an impasse when it comes to determining precisely how many men each may have under arms in each branch of the armed forces and precisely how many of which weapons each may have.

## The Problem of Distrust

Even if all these obstacles were somehow overcome, there would still be another: that distrust ordinarily goes with fear. This has been particularly true since World War II in relations between the United States and the Soviet Union. For that matter, both of these countries also distrust Communist China, and the distrust is likely to be intensified as Communist China gets relatively stronger. Moreover, the Soviet Union and many of the peoples of Europe fear and distrust the Germans. And when the issues are as portentous as they are in the realms of war and peace, governments want dependable assurances before they are willing to proceed.

The problem has been especially acute in connection with the question of nuclear weapons, for the temptation to violate an agreement concerning them would be particularly strong. In this field, negotiating states have simply assumed that they could not rely upon each other's good faith. They accept the principle that international inspection or verification or control is a necessary corollary of a disarmament agreement. But they have not been able to agree on the interpretation and application of the principle, even in connection with the question of the underground testing of nuclear weapons let alone in connection with other military programs. The United States, supported by its allies, has insisted on more thorough-going inspection than the Soviet Union has been willing to concede. The Soviet Union makes a distinction between "control over disarmament" and "control over armaments." For example, if an agreement called for the destruction of a certain number of bombing planes, the Soviet Union would apparently be willing to have their destruction verified by foreign observers, but it will not permit counting by international inspectors to determine how many bombers remain and whether new ones soon replace those destroyed. "Control over armaments," the Soviet Union holds, "would turn into an international system of legalized espionage, which would naturally be unacceptable . . ." [14]

Where distrust runs so deep that no reliance is placed on the good faith

14 Sir Michael Wright, *op. cit.*, p. 34.

of other states, impasse is the likely result. The search for sure guarantees against violation leads almost necessarily to plans of inspection and control that involve extensive foreign interference and participation in the domestic affairs of states. In the best of situations, the interference and participation is likely to be very unwelcome, and it is likely to be completely unacceptable when hatred and distrust of some of the foreigners who would be engaged in inspection and control activities is intense. In other words, another vicious circle is involved. Severe tension and distrust make extensive international interference in domestic affairs necessary if disarmament is to be achieved, but the same tension and distrust make such interference unacceptable. In truth, it is not at all sure that the United States itself would accept an arrangement for inspection that brought large numbers of Russian or Chinese Communists into the country and permitted them to snoop freely.

## DISARMAMENT AND POLITICAL SETTLEMENT

As we have already suggested implicitly, the problem of disarmament may be tackled either directly or indirectly. We have already explored the difficulties in the way of the direct approach. When states regard armaments as useful and necessary, whether to give latent support to peaceful diplomacy or to provide strength in war, they are naturally reluctant to disarm, and determined that any disarmament which occurs shall not have an adverse effect on their power position. To expect states to disarm before the need for armaments is removed or reduced is like expecting an American frontiersman to abandon his musket in the face of a threat from the Indians and in the absence of police protection.

For the frontiersman, disarmament was brought about largely by indirect means. Threats from Indians and from other sources were reduced or eliminated. Police forces were organized. Legislative, executive, and judicial agencies were established through which rights and interests could be protected or promoted. The frontiersman became a citizen in an organized community, and then he no longer needed to rely on private weapons.

Something similar is probably necessary if disarmament by international agreement is ever to occur on an extensive scale. As Salvador de Madariaga put it, "The problem of disarmament is not the problem of disarmament. It really is the problem of the organization of the World-Community." [15] Quincy Wright comes to a similar conclusion:

Successful disarmament treaties have always been accompanied by political arrangements which were believed by the parties to augment their political security or to settle their outstanding political problems. The two have gone hand in

---

[15] de Madariaga, op. cit., p. 56.

hand, and, considering the conditions of successful negotiation, it is unlikely that agreement will ever be reached on the technical problems of disarmament unless the parties have lessened tensions by political settlements or by general acceptance of international procedures creating confidence that such settlements can be effected peacefully.[16]

Likewise, the Commission for Conventional Armaments, established by the Security Council of the United Nations, concluded in 1948 that

A system of regulation and reduction of armaments and armed forces can only be put into effect in an atmosphere of international confidence and security. Measures for the regulation and reduction of armaments which would follow the establishment of the necessary degree of confidence might in turn be expected to increase confidence and so justify further measures of regulation and reduction.[17]

The possibility of organizing the world community or of establishing the political prerequisites of disarmament is a topic which will be explored in the following chapters.

## THE ARMS DEBATE

The above analysis focuses largely on governments: why they arm, why they propose disarmament, and what obstacles they face. It is worth while to shift the focus briefly to private persons and their attitudes. We will do so largely on the basis of Robert A. Levine's The Arms Debate.[18]

Levine classifies those engaged in the arms debate as "systemists" and "marginalists." Systemists seek relatively drastic change in the attitudes and practices that now call for armaments, while marginalists seek relatively small, incremental changes.

Among the systemists, for example, are those who reject an assumption underlying the policies of all governments: that in certain circumstances it may be justifiable to pursue national purposes through war. That this is a governmental assumption should be emphasized. When a government maintains an armed establishment, the minimal implication is that it might fight. When it stocks thermonuclear bombs in its arsenal, the minimal implication is that it might use them. And a stronger implication is probable in each case: that in certain circumstances, the government actually will fight and actually will use the bomb.

Many private persons find this unacceptable. They hold that war is immoral—that nothing justifies the mass killing and mass destruction that war involves. Some took this view, usually on religious grounds, before nuclear weapons were developed. Surely their number has grown

---

[16] Quincy Wright, op. cit. (copyright 1942 by The University of Chicago), Vol. II, pp. 800-801.

[17] Andrew Martin, Collective Security (Paris, UNESCO, 1952), p. 83.

[18] Robert A. Levine, The Arms Debate (Cambridge, Harvard University Press, 1963).

during the nuclear age, though no count is available; and their number may well grow still more as realization spreads of the potentially awful consequences of the kind of war that nuclear and missile technologies make possible. If war is to be renounced unconditionally, unilateral disarmament is the logical implication, and some specifically urge it.[19] They recognize (or at least should recognize) that unilateral disarmament involves risks. It might mean the loss of national independence and the triumph of the ruthless—presumably the Communists. It might mean the extermination of whole classes of the population, or whole races, and the enslavement of a considerable portion of those allowed to live. The advocates of a renunciation of war and armaments hope to avoid the triumph of the ruthless, or to make their rule no more than transitory, by threatening and employing nonviolent resistance, but they urge acceptance of the risks, arguing that virtually anything is morally more acceptable than policies whose result might be the destruction of half the population of the United States and the Soviet Union and tens if not hundreds of millions of people elsewhere.

In contrast to the systemists who can imagine nothing worse than war, especially thermonuclear war, are the systemists who can imagine nothing worse than the spread of Communism—or perhaps nothing worse than its continued control in countries where it already prevails. These systemists hold that a mortal struggle between Communists and non-Communists is in progress in which one side will triumph and the other disappear. From their point of view, all kinds of weapons, including nuclear weapons and missiles, are to be maintained, brandished, and if need be used in order to see to it that the anti-Communist cause prevails.

Most American observers are marginalists, taking positions between these extremes. They want to avoid war, above all unrestricted thermonuclear war, but they also want to develop and maintain a desirable kind of world in which human welfare can be promoted and progress occur. More concretely, while wanting to avoid war, they also want to create and maintain a world environment suitable for liberalism and democracy at home, and to avoid having to submit to foreign demands and foreign control. They want peace, but they also want freedom, for themselves and for others. And they pursue other values as well. They are, in general, unwilling to select some one goal, such as peace or the freedom of people from Communist control and pursue it regardless of cost. They pursue various goals simultaneously, even if the pursuit of each one means some sacrifice of others and some risk to others. They are said to be optimizers rather than maximizers, aiming at the optimum

19 Mulford Q. Sibley, ed., *The Quiet Battle, Writings on the Theory and Practice of Non-Violent Resistance* (Garden City, N.Y., Doubleday-Anchor, 1963). And Mulford Q. Sibley, "Unilateral Disarmament," in Robert A. Goldwin, ed., *America Armed, Essays on United States Military Policy* (Chicago, Rand McNally, 1963), pp. 112-140.

achievement of a number of competing values rather than the maximum achievement of a few noncompeting values.

Marginalists want both to avoid war and to oppose Communism; they want to preserve both peace and freedom. But they differ in emphasis and in choice of method. The antiwar marginalists—those whose emphasis is on peace—tend to concentrate on the possibility of thermonuclear war, fearing that irrationality or accident or miscalculation will bring it on and that efforts to keep war limited will prove futile. They tend to believe that an accommodation with the Soviet Union is possible or at least that the Soviet Union is opportunistic rather than implacable in its efforts to extend Communism. They point to fissures in the Communist bloc and see opportunities to cooperate with the least truculent Communist countries. They are respectful of military power and consider it necessary, but want to play it down, seeking arms control and disarmament. Above all, they want to reduce nuclear dangers, preferably by eliminating nuclear weapons. They prefer to put the stress on the role of ideas in human affairs rather than on the role of power, and they prefer to emphasize geographical regions other than Europe—regions where the military confrontation between the United States and the Soviet Union is ordinarily not so direct. They fear the domestic effects of emphasis on the military. Politically, they tend toward the Left and are fearful of the Right.

In contrast, the anti-Communist marginalists discount the possibility of an accommodation with the Soviet Union and think in terms of implacable struggle. They put little stress on the signs of discord in the Communist world, assuming its fundamental unity against non-Communists. As they see it, the struggle calls for firmness and determination in the West and possession of a full range of deterrent power, permitting appropriate retaliation for any kind of attack; they specifically include an emphasis on the Grand Deterrent in the form of an invulnerable second-strike capacity. They are dubious of the possibility of arms control, but are willing to use arms policies and disarmament conferences as instruments in the struggle. They are inclined to stress the vital strategic importance of Europe and show little fear of the domestic political consequences of an emphasis on the military. Politically, they tend toward the Right.

Naturally, some marginalists take a middle position, putting approximately equal emphasis on peace and freedom. They want to preserve vital national interests against Communist threats, but hope to do so without war. They interpret the Soviet Union as aggressive but rational and calculating. They stress deterrence, and the desirability and possibility of keeping war limited, if deterrence should fail. Their inclination is to look for interests that East and West share (e.g., the avoidance of mutual suicide), to attempt to handle the problems of the day without looking for definitive solutions, and to accept the view that "control" is preferable to "disarmament"—the view that armed power (preferably stable, and preferably based on some kind of international concerting of arms policies) is more likely than disarmed weakness to safeguard both peace and freedom.

## SUGGESTED READINGS

BEATON, Leonard, and MADDOX, John, *The Spread of Nuclear Weapons* (New York, Praeger, 1962).

BECHHOEFER, Bernhard G., *Postwar Negotiations for Arms Control* (Washington, Brookings Institution, 1961).

BRENNAN, Donald G., ed., *Arms Control, Disarmament, and National Security* (New York, Braziller, 1961).

BULL, Hedley, *The Control of the Arms Race, Disarmament and Arms Control in the Missile Age* (New York, Praeger, for the Institute for Strategic Studies, 1961).

*Daedalus,* Special Issue, Arms Control, Vol. 89 (Fall, 1960), pp. 674-1075.

FALK, Richard A., and BARNET, Richard J., eds., *Security in Disarmament* (Princeton, Princeton University Press, 1965).

FISHER, Walter R., and BURNS, Richard Dean, eds., *Armament and Disarmament: The Continuing Dispute* (Belmont, Calif., Wadsworth, 1964).

GOLDWIN, Robert A., ed., *America Armed, Essays on United States Military Policy* (Chicago, Rand McNally, 1963).

GREEN, Philip, "Method and Substance in the Arms Debate," *World Politics,* Vol. 16 (July, 1964), pp. 642-67.

HENKIN, Louis, ed., *Arms Control, Issues for the Public.* The American Assembly (Englewood Cliffs, N.J., Prentice-Hall, 1961).

LEFEVER, Ernest W., ed., *Arms and Arms Control* (New York, Praeger, for the Washington Center of Foreign Policy Research, 1962).

LEVINE, Robert A., *The Arms Debate* (Cambridge, Harvard University Press, 1963).

MILLIS, Walter, *An End To Arms* (New York, Atheneum, 1965).

OSGOOD, Charles E., *Alternative to War or Surrender* (Urbana, University of Illinois Press, 1962).

ROSECRANCE, R. N., ed., *The Dispersion of Nuclear Weapons, Strategy and Politics* (New York, Columbia University Press, 1964).

SCHELLING, Thomas C., and HALPERIN, Morton H., *Strategy and Arms Control* (New York, Twentieth Century Fund, 1961).

SIBLEY, Mulford Q., ed., *The Quiet Battle, Writings on the Theory and Practice of Non-Violent Resistance* (Garden City, N.Y., Anchor-Doubleday, 1963).

SINGER, David, *Deterrence, Arms Control and Disarmament: Toward a Synthesis in National Security Policy* (Columbus, Ohio State University Press, 1962).

SPANIER, John W., and NOGEE, Joseph L., *The Politics of Disarmament* (New York, Praeger, 1962).

WRIGHT, Michael, *Disarm and Verify* (New York, Praeger, 1964).

WRIGHT, Quincy, EVAN, William M., and DEUTSCH, Morton, eds., *Preventing World War III: Some Proposals* (New York, Simon and Schuster, 1962).

# 20

# INTERNATIONAL
# ORGANIZATION FOR
# SECURITY AND PEACE

At various points we have referred to the United Nations and to some of the hopes and possibilities of promoting peace and security through it. The object here is a fuller and more coherent analysis. The focus will be on: (1) the purposes, structure, and powers of the United Nations; (2) the principles of collective security, and the extent to which the United Nations is or is likely to be an effective agency for promoting collective security; (3) the problems of peaceful settlement and peaceful change; and (4) peacekeeping, policing, and "preventive diplomacy." We will reserve for the next chapter an examination of efforts, through the United Nations and other international organizations, to promote human welfare.

## THE UNITED NATIONS:
## PURPOSES, STRUCTURE, AND POWERS

### Purposes

According to a statement in the Charter of the United Nations, one of its purposes—the one with which we are primarily concerned is:[1]

To maintain international peace and security, and to that end: to take effective collective measures for the prevention and removal of threats to the peace, and for the suppression of acts of aggression or other breaches of the peace, and to bring about by peaceful means, and in conformity with the principles of justice and international law, adjustment or settlement of international disputes or situations which might lead to a breach of the peace.

[1] The full text of the Charter is in the Appendix.

407

Further, members bind themselves to "settle their international disputes by peaceful means in such a manner that international peace and security, and justice, are not endangered." They pledge themselves to "refrain in their international relations from the threat or use of force against the territorial integrity or political independence of any state." The purposes and the obligations are thus obviously very sweeping.

One hundred seventeen political entities subscribe to these purposes and pledges through membership in the United Nations (in 1965). Switzerland has never joined, nor have the divided states (Germany, Korea, and Vietnam). Indonesia has withdrawn. China is a member, but the official United Nations position is that the rights and obligations of membership go to the government in Taipeh, not to the government in Peking.

## The Principal Organs

Like the League of Nations—the predecessor of the United Nations, formed after World War I—the United Nations has a General Assembly, a Security Council, and a Secretariat. In addition, several other agencies are formally declared to be "principal organs": the Economic and Social Council, the Trusteeship Council, and the International Court of Justice. All members of the United Nations are entitled to representation in the General Assembly. According to the original Charter, eleven had seats on the Security Council, but an amendment has now increased that number to fifteen. Five of the fifteen are named in the Charter as permanent members: China, France, the Union of Soviet Socialist Republics, the United Kingdom, and the United States; the other ten are elected for two-year terms by the General Assembly.

## Powers of the Security Council

The Charter requires that the Security Council be "so organized as to be able to function continuously," and assigns it "primary responsibility for the maintenance of international peace and security." It has extensive rights to act in behalf of collective security and the preservation or restoration of peace. Where a dispute exists which might endanger international peace, the Security Council may call upon the parties to seek pacific settlement, may "recommend appropriate procedures or methods of adjustment," or may recommend terms of settlement. The Security Council is also empowered to "determine the existence of any threat to the peace, breach of the peace, or act of aggression." If it finds any such threat, breach, or act, it has wide discretionary powers. It may call upon the parties concerned to comply with provisional measures designed to prevent an aggravation of the situation, or it may apply sanctions, i.e., measures designed to induce the observance of law. The sanctions "may include complete or partial interruption of economic relations and of rail, sea, air, postal, telegraphic, radio, and other means of communication, and the severance of diplomatic relations." If such measures are considered inadequate, the Security Council "may take such action by air, sea, or land forces as may be necessary to maintain or restore international peace and security." Sanctioning measures are to be applied by all United Nations members, or by some of them, as the Security Council determines. The Charter assumed that the Security Council would make special agreements with individual United Nations members by which those members would provide "armed forces, assistance, and facilities" necessary for enforcement action, but no such agreements have actually been concluded.

## Voting Rules in the Security Council

The voting rules of the Security Council are of crucial importance. The Charter gives each member one vote. It sets up two categories into which questions are to be classified: "procedural" and "other"; the "other" questions are commonly referred to as "nonprocedural" or "substantive." The arrangement is that decisions on procedural matters require an affirmative vote of any nine members. Decisions on substantive matters also require nine votes out of the fifteen, but the nine must include the concurring votes of the permanent members; in other words, the five permanent members plus any four of the nonpermanent members may make substantive decisions. The word *veto* does not appear in the Charter, but its use arises from the voting rules. Where a resolution is defeated by the negative vote of a single permanent member, it is said to have been vetoed. The question whether an issue before the Security Council is procedural or substantive is itself considered substantive. Thus a "double veto" is possible: the first negative vote of the permanent member preventing the matter from being classified as procedural, and the second preventing the adoption of the resolution. A custom has developed permitting a permanent member to abstain from voting without blocking action, and action is also not blocked if the delegate of a permanent member deliberately absents himself. When the Security Council is attempting to bring about the pacific settlement of a dispute, parties to the dispute are to abstain from voting. When it is considering enforcement action, however, all members of the Security Council may vote; thus a permanent member is free to veto enforcement action against itself or against any other state.

## The General Assembly: Powers and Voting Rules

The General Assembly of the United Nations meets annually and in special sessions. It may "discuss any questions or any matters within the scope of the present Charter or relating to the powers and functions of any organs" of the United Nations. More particularly, it may "recommend measures for the peaceful adjustment of any situation, regardless of origin, which it deems likely to impair the general welfare or friendly relations among nations." There is a proviso of minor significance in the Charter which, though not curtailing the freedom of the General Assembly to discuss disputes or situations being considered by the Security Council, prohibits it from making recommendations thereon, except by special request of the Security Council.

In the General Assembly, as in the Security Council, each member has one vote. Again the Charter sets up two categories into which questions are to be classified: "important questions" and "other questions." Decisions on "important questions" can be made only by a two-thirds majority of the members present and voting, whereas decisions on "other questions" can be made by a bare majority. The Charter itself lists some questions which are to be considered important, and specifies that additional questions may be placed in this category by a bare majority; in other words, a bare majority may require that a question be so classified that a two-thirds majority is necessary for a decision.

## The Right of Self-defense and Sovereign Equality

It might be noted that the framers of the Charter, fearing that the members of the United Nations might not use it effectively to provide security for each other, included the following statement in Article 51: "Nothing in the present Charter shall impair the inherent right of individual and collective self-defense if an armed attack occurs against a member. . . ."

Further, they included the stipulation that "the Organization is based on the principle of the sovereign equality of all its members," and they specified that "nothing contained in the present Charter shall authorize the United Nations to intervene in matters which are essentially within the domestic jurisdiction of any state. . . ."

## COLLECTIVE SECURITY

### The Meaning of the Term

Especially in the early years after World War II, the United Nations was widely thought of as a system of collective security. Whether it was or not—and, more broadly, whether collective security is feasible and desirable as an international system—depends in part on the meaning assigned to the term.

Speaking very generally, a collective security system is one in which a number of states are bound to engage in collective efforts on behalf of each other's individual security. Such a definition is, however, not very discriminating, covering a considerable range of possibilities. At the one extreme, according to it, an alliance might be said to provide for collective security. And in fact alliances are sometimes so described. Officials in Washington have often been reluctant to say that the United States is a party to balance-of-power arrangements and have preferred to say that such instruments as the North Atlantic Treaty and the Rio Pact provide for collective security. At the other extreme, the definition given above would permit some forms of world government to be described as collective security systems. In truth, the governments that we have within countries could be so described. In the United States, for example, the government is the agency through which citizens engage in collective efforts on behalf of each other's individual security. As noted in Chapter 2, we arm government with a capacity to enforce law; and we accept the principle that, if need be, the people of Maine shall make sacrifices so that law and order can be maintained or restored in, say, Hawaii.

For our purposes it will be best to give the term collective security a narrower meaning and to discuss it first in terms of a possible world-wide (as opposed to a regional) application. We will follow the example of Inis L. Claude, Jr., who describes a hypothetical system that is intermediate between balance of power and world government.[2] The system is universal in membership, or nearly so, and members are bound to spring to each other's defense in case of attack. The basic principle is that an attack on one is an attack on all, and that the inviolability of every frontier throughout the world is as precious to each member as the inviolability of its own frontiers. Any state contemplating aggression would face the sure prospect of struggle not simply with the prospective victim, but with all other members of the system, who would make any necessary sacrifice to save the state attacked. In a hypothetical world of collective security, the assumption is that the members of the system will have such an overwhelming preponderance of power and will be so unreservedly committed to the principles they have endorsed that aggression will become quite irrational; presumably, it will thus not occur, or if it should occur, it will be defeated.

## Collective Security and Balance of Power:
### Similarities and Differences

Systems of balance of power and collective security are alike in some respects, different in others. They are alike in purpose; both are defen-

[2] Inis L. Claude, Jr., *Power and International Relations* (New York, Random House, 1962), Chapters 4 and 5.

sive, aiming to promote the security of states within the system. To some extent they are also alike in method. Both depend on the manipulation or mobilization of power as a means of deterring or, if need be, defeating aggression. Both envisage the possibility of defensive war or of "police actions" that are indistinguishable from war. Both envisage the continued existence of sovereign states that coordinate their actions against aggression. Both assume that states which are not themselves attacked will go to the defense of others in the system that are attacked. Further, the two systems are alike, as we will note shortly, in that their effectiveness is threatened by tremendous concentrations of power in any one state.[3]

Differences between the two kinds of systems are also fairly obvious. The idea of balancing power assumes competitive alignments, that is, assumes a division of states into more or less hostile camps, whereas worldwide collective security calls for universal cooperation. The alliances that go with the balancing of power are likely to be aimed at a specific potential enemy, and the allies know which state they may have to fight, whereas a universal collective security system has to be aimed at any state that turns out to be an aggressor. For either side in a balance of power system, the enemy is outside, whereas in a universal collective security system the enemy is necessarily a member. States joined in a balance of power arrangement agree to defend certain selected frontiers, whereas states joined in a universal collective security system agree to defend all frontiers throughout the world. In the one case the obligation is more limited, and advance planning can occur for the international coordination of defense measures; in the other the obligation is virtually unlimited, and since the potential aggressor is unknown, advance planning of common measures against him is impossible. A balance of power system permits neutrality and the localization of war, whereas a collective security system precludes neutrality and requires that all join in action against the aggressor.

An important difference in underlying assumptions is inherent in the above. The state seeking a balance of power through alliance arrangements assumes that it has vital interests in common with selected states, but not with all states; in fact, it may seek safety at the expense of the territorial integrity or political independence of some states. There is no assumption that an integrated society exists in which each member is obliged to help protect the rights of all. Such an assumption is, however, fundamental to a collective security system.

Finally, a collective security system obviously calls for formal agreement on the part of all or nearly all states, and since so many are involved and face so many possible contingencies, they are likely to find it necessary to make relatively elaborate rules and institutional arrange-

[3] *Ibid.*, pp. 123-133.

ments. In contrast, a state can pursue a balance of power unilaterally; and if it makes alliances, relatively simple rules and institutional arrangements are likely to suffice. In short, in most respects a balance of power system is simpler than a collective security system, and easier to establish and maintain. It is no doubt this that leads Inis L. Claude, Jr., to refer to the balance of power system as a residual system that operates in default of alternatives.[4]

## Why States Reject Collective Security

After World War I many hoped that the states of the world would make the League of Nations a collective security system of the sort described above, and some had the same hope after World War II in connection with the United Nations. They wanted states to abandon narrow conceptions of self-interest as a guide to policy and to regard themselves as units in a world society having an interest in preserving law and order everywhere. They wanted states to accept the view that there was a common vital interest in repressing illegal resort to war, just as, within countries, there is said to be a common vital interest in repressing crime and a common vital interest in supporting the governmental system against revolutionary groups. If one state illegally attacked another, they saw no more basis for neutrality than when one individual murders or robs another. But in fact the members of the League adopted interpretations of the Covenant, explicitly and tacitly, that amounted to a rejection of collective security, and the terms of the Charter scarcely provided for collective security in the first place. The question is, why? Why do states reject collective security?

*1. The absence of a sense of membership in a united world society.* The basic reason is that states do not regard themselves as members of one society having a common vital interest in protecting and preserving each other's rights. Does it really matter very much to Japan if Paraguay and Bolivia destroy each other in war? Is it vital to Chile that Yugoslavia should not attack Albania, or that the attack should be defeated? Within countries analogous questions are answered in the affirmative; all citizens are said to have a vital interest in supporting the system of law enforcement. But the sovereign states that interpreted the League Covenant were not willing to give affirmative answers, nor were the sovereign states that drafted the United Nations Charter, nor are the sovereign states of today. States have demonstrated a willingness to ally themselves with certain other selected states and thus to pledge to defend certain selected frontiers in addition to their own, but the principle of "one for all and all for one" does not commend itself.

*2. The costs and risks of collective security.* Another reason why states

[4] *Ibid.,* pp. 151, 280.

reject collective security is that its risks are great; and the corollary is
that its costs may be very high. The contrasts between the problem within countries and the problem among countries is especially great if the
domestic contenders are assumed to be the government on the one side
against individual law violators on the other. Governments can enforce
law against individuals with little fear. Except in very unusual circumstances, the worst that may happen is that a robber will shoot a policeman. The individual lawbreaker is so nearly helpless in the face of the
might which government commands that he must perforce adopt hit-
and-run tactics, depending on surprise and concealment; he cannot resist
the government in an open, frontal fashion. Moreover, the government,
through the tax structure and in other ways, can see to it not only that citizens share the costs and burdens of law enforcement but that they do it
on what is considered an equitable basis; the costs and burdens do not
become unduly heavy for anyone.

Internationally, however, the situation is quite different. Disparities of
power are much greater. Theoretically, it might be easy for a world society to defeat aggression by a small power like Denmark, but what if one
of the great powers turns aggressor? Repression of the aggression of the
Central Powers after 1914 and of the Axis powers after 1939 might have
been called a police action in each case, but the police actions would
have been world wars nevertheless. If a substantial proportion of the
total military might of the world is concentrated in any one state, and if
that state turns aggressor, the repression of aggression becomes an extremely costly and hazardous undertaking to which other states are understandably loath to commit themselves in advance. It is one thing for
a government to enforce law against a relatively helpless individual, and
another thing for a United Nations to try to enforce the law against a
state which may be almost as strong as the rest of the world combined.
The development of missiles with nuclear warheads makes the problem
all the greater. An aggressor with such weapons could virtually wipe
from the face of the earth a number of the members of a collective security system. Faced with such a possibility, a member whose own most vital
interests were directly threatened might choose proud defiance rather
than surrender. But a member whose own vital interests were not directly
threatened would be very unlikely to be so bold. Nor do states want to
commit themselves in advance to undertake such risks, regardless of the
identity of the aggressor and of his victim.

We might note that governments within countries do not always succeed in keeping law enforcement a problem between them and individual
law violators, though this is the common goal. Sometimes governments
have to confront sizable groups that are defiant if not revolutionary.
They may then bargain, seeking some kind of accommodation; or they
may not. If rebellion occurs, the collective security system goes into oper-

ation, and the struggle takes on the nature of civil war. The possibility of this kind of development is simply a fact of political life. Governments must stand ready to defend themselves against domestic rebellion, but they do not want to take on an analogous sweeping commitment to take action against any aggressor state that challenges the international system.

*3. Probable inequities in sharing costs and risks.* Further, there can be no real assurance that the costs and burdens of collective security will be shared equitably and without undue hardship to individual states. The criteria for determining equity are, of course, vague. Whatever the criteria adopted, there is no real assurance that states, being sovereign, would actually contribute to enforcement measures in conformity with them. In any event, a weak state adjacent to a great power aggressor would be especially exposed to retaliation if it joined in enforcement measures.

*4. Recognition of the need for change.* Another reason why states reject collective security is that they do not want to commit themselves to the indefinite enforcement of existing law. Within countries governments do not attempt this. Rather, they combine executive power for the enforcement of law with legislative power to change the law, and as we saw in Chapter 2, timely adjustments in the law may well contribute as much to the preservation of domestic peace as does provision for enforcement action. But states have not wanted to set up the equivalent of a world legislature. They are too concerned with their own sovereignty and their own territorial and other rights to be willing to give legislative power to an international agency. In sum, states are not willing to provide effective and reliable means for peaceful change, but they know that change is inevitable and often desirable. They deplore aggression, but support justice. The result is a desire to avoid too rigid and strict a commitment to the status quo and, inferentially, an acknowledgment that the pursuit of justice sometimes requires threats and pressures, and even acts of aggression, that the world should not try to repress.

*5. Defense and ancillary ambitions.* Still another difficulty with collective security stems from the fact that states that go to war to defend themselves or others against aggression often either have or develop ancillary ambitions. Given a loose and flexible system, states could take such actual or potential ambitions into account in deciding whether or not joint action against aggression should occur, but collective security as here defined would not permit such a choice.

This consideration can easily be illustrated by reference to the contemporary scene. Suppose, for example, that Pakistan should attack India, and suppose that the Soviet Union were quite willing to send the Red Army through Afghanistan and Iran into Pakistan in the name of collective security. Judging by Communist principles and by the record of the Soviet Union after World War II, it seems likely that Moscow would not confine itself to an effort to defeat an aggressor but would attempt to satisfy an ancillary ambition: the establishment of Communist control over areas that the Red Army enters. The same kind of possibility would exist for the Soviet Union if France should attack Germany, or if Western Germany should attack the Communist regime in Eastern Germany. Had the United Nations authorized the Soviet Union to go to the defense of Egypt in 1956, the imposition of Communist or pro-Soviet control over one or more of the Middle Eastern states would have been a likely consequence. Similarly, if Bulgaria should attack Yugoslavia, the United States might be willing, in the name of collective security, to take action against the aggressor, but there is a question whether resistance to aggression would be kept separate from the ancillary ambition of liberating a Soviet satellite.

In a system of collective security, the United States would presumably be obliged to accept and endorse Soviet action against aggression by Pakistan, and the Soviet Union would presumably be obliged to accept and endorse American action against aggression by Bulgaria. For this reason the United States and the Soviet Union, each fearing the ancillary ambitions of the other, can scarcely favor collective security. Since collective security is ideologically blind, it is hardly acceptable to states locked in an ideological struggle.

Another aspect of the same point was illustrated in the Korean war. Suppose for the moment that the official objective of various powers, including the United States, was to "preserve" South Korea. South Korea wanted to be preserved, of course, but at the same time it wanted to expand—to absorb the territory of the aggressor. How could military action designed to defeat aggression be distinguished from military action designed to extinguish the aggressor government and absorb its territory? In fact, the two objectives were not disentangled until after the intervention of the Chinese Communists rendered the unification of Korea impossible.[5]

Similar problems seem likely to attend every effort to implement collective security. Action taken primarily to resist aggression is also likely to serve other purposes. "It is one of the fallacies of the theory of collective security that war can be waged for the specific and disinterested purpose of 'resisting aggression.' "[6] Where those supporting the principle of collective security are agreed not only on the main objective but also

[5] Leland M. Goodrich, "Korea: Collective Measures Against Aggression," *International Conciliation*, No. 494, (October, 1953).
[6] E. H. Carr, *The Twenty Years' Crisis 1919-1939* (New York, Harper & Row, 1964), p. 113.

on all other objectives, the problem is a minor one, but this is rare. As a general rule, there is disagreement over ancillary ambitions and objectives. This constitutes a serious obstacle to the acceptance of collective security, for it is a relatively inflexible system.

6. *The problem of defining aggression and identifying the aggressor.* Back in the days of the League of Nations the point was made that an officially endorsed definition of aggression might well turn out to be "a trap for the innocent and a signpost for the guilty," and fear of this is no doubt among the reasons why states reject collective security. In many cases, of course, even when each side claims innocence and hurls accusations of guilt at the enemy, third parties have no trouble either in defining aggression or in identifying the aggressor. But difficulties have been encountered in enough actual cases to give reason for hesitation. Further, on top of the definitional problem and the problem of determining the relevant facts, there is a political problem as well. When the aggressor is to be identified by votes, the composition of the body doing the voting may be crucial to the outcome. Communist states accused of aggression cannot be expected to submit themselves to the judgment of non-Communist states, and vice versa; and states of the developing world might or might not be reliable and trustworthy sources of judgment when an "imperialist" state is accused of aggression against one of their own number.

The problem of determining the aggressor becomes especially difficult when the aggression is more or less indirect. North Vietnam in 1965 is clearly giving assistance to rebel forces in South Vietnam. Is it an aggressor? The United States retaliates for the assistance by destroying targets in North Vietnam. Is it an aggressor? The United States is in Vietnam on the basis of an invitation from one of the earlier regimes in Saigon. Suppose that the regime in Saigon should withdraw the invitation and request the United States to leave. Would the United States become an aggressor if it failed to go? Suppose two governments appeared in South Vietnam, one requesting the United States to go and the other requesting it to stay. If the United States stayed on, recognizing the government requesting this, would it be an aggressor?

All of these difficulties suggest that even if a collective security system were established, it could not be relied upon. States would still have to depend for their security on their own power and on alliances; in other words, balance-of-power arrangements would have to exist side by side with collective security arrangements. This would involve still further difficulties, for the requirements of a balance-of-power policy are not always compatible with the requirements of collective security. And there would be danger that the pursuit of incompatible principles would prevent either one from being followed successfully.

# THE UNITED NATIONS AND
# COLLECTIVE SECURITY

## The Security Council

It is perhaps already clear that the Charter does not establish a system of collective security as defined above. To be sure, the Security Council has extensive rights and powers of a relevant sort. In principle, it could enact resolutions obliging all members to apply sanctions against an aggressor. But the Security Council acts only on the basis of a vote; and under the voting rules, as we have seen, any permanent member can block action. As a practical matter then, though the Charter permits the implementation of the principles of collective security, it makes their implementation most unlikely. Obviously, each permanent member would veto enforcement action against itself. In all probability, too, each would veto enforcement action against a friend or ally. More generally, it is probable that the United States and the Soviet Union would each block any action by the Security Council which would call for the use of the armed forces of the other outside their homeland; and Communist China will certainly take the same stand when and if it gets a vote, at least against the United States. It is difficult to think of any situation in which the Communist and non-Communist states would have a common interest in carrying out enforcement action through the United Nations.

In the final analysis, the San Francisco Conference must be described as having repudiated the doctrine of collective security as the foundation for a general, universally applicable system for the management of power in international relations. The doctrine was given ideological lip service, and a scheme was contrived for making it effective in cases of relatively minor importance. But the new organization reflected the conviction that the concept of collective security has no realistic relevance to the problems posed by conflict among the major powers.[7]

True, enforcement action through the United Nations occurred after North Korea attacked South Korea in 1950. But this was possible only because the Soviet delegate at the time was boycotting the meetings of the Security Council. Had he been present, he presumably would have vetoed any action against North Korea. Moreover, the action of the United States and of other United Nations members which supported enforcement action does not necessarily reflect a commitment to resist aggression simply out of belief that the principle of collective security deserved support.

[7] Claude, *op. cit.*, pp. 164-165.

Instead of being a case of nations fighting "any aggressor anywhere" and for no other purpose than to punish aggression and to deter potential aggressors, intervention in Korea was an act of collective military defense against the recognized number-one enemy of the United States and of all the countries which associated themselves with its action.[8]

Had South Korea been the aggressor, it seems unlikely that the non-Communist states in the United Nations would have endorsed enforcement action for the benefit of the Communist regime in North Korea.

Article 43 of the Charter provides that members, in accordance with special agreements to be concluded, are to make available to the Security Council "armed forces, assistance, and facilities, including rights of passage, necessary for the purpose of maintaining international peace and security." But no agreements for the implementation of the article have ever been made.[9] A military staff committee of the Security Council sought to work out the terms of such agreements in the first years after World War II, but the distrust between the United States and the Soviet Union was too great to overcome. The two countries could not agree on the size or the composition of the proposed armed forces—or, for that matter, on various other issues. The Soviet Union wanted relatively weak forces—forces that would not connote any danger for itself—whereas the United States wanted them to be more powerful. The Soviet Union insisted that the contributions of the great powers should be identical, whereas the United States wanted them to be comparable. Underlying this issue was the question of the probable political advantage that each side might gain from the use of the forces: the military predominance of one side in any United Nations action might make it politically predominant as well, and for each side the prospective predominance of the other was intolerable. As it has worked out in practice, the armed forces that the United Nations has employed in the Middle East and in the Congo (to be discussed below) have come entirely from the lesser powers.

In connection with the question of arms control and disarmament, as we have seen, the United States and the Soviet Union agreed on a set of principles in September 1961. One of the principles is that general and complete disarmament is to be accompanied by "the necessary measures to maintain international peace and security, including the obligation of states to place at the disposal of the United Nations agreed power necessary for an international peace force to be equipped with agreed types of armaments." Experience and virtually every relevant consideration suggest that the implementation of this principle is extremely unlikely.

[8] Arnold Wolfers, *Discord and Collaboration* (Baltimore, John Hopkins Press, 1962), p. 176. Cf. Alexander L. George, "American Policy-Making and the North Korean Aggression," *World Politics*, Vol. 7 (January, 1955), pp. 209-232.

[9] Claude, *op. cit.*, pp. 175-190.

## The General Assembly

Anticipating that the Security Council would rarely, if ever, be able to provide for enforcement action, the United States joined with several other states in 1950 in proposing the "Uniting for Peace" resolution to the General Assembly, and it was adopted. This resolution was, in the main, an announcement that, if the Security Council should be unable to act against an aggressor because of the veto, the General Assembly itself would consider the matter with a view to recommending collective measures. The General Assembly could make such recommendations by a two-thirds vote, permitting action despite the opposition of a great power or even against a great power which had committed aggression. The possibility that the United Nations might be used as an agency for authorizing enforcement action was thus markedly increased.

It probably makes little difference that the General Assembly can only recommend enforcement action whereas the Security Council can order it. Though imposing a legal obligation, a Security Council order would, as a practical matter, leave states free to respond or not, as they saw fit. This being so, a recommendation might well be as effective (or as ineffective) as a binding decision. As a matter of fact, the Security Council itself, when it acted in the Korean case, confined itself to the making of recommendations.

But the Uniting for Peace Resolution, though invoked on various occasions, has not in fact proved to be a basis for an effective collective security system. Consensus on it, as Inis L. Claude, Jr., says, was "incomplete, illusory, and ephemeral." The Soviet Union, of course, opposed it; and India abstained. From the point of view of the United States, the resolution was a potential basis not so much for collective security as for resistance to Communism. Many of the smaller countries have had no enthusiasm at all for a principle that might require them to line up with one of the great power blocs against the other. From their point of view—again in the words of Claude—the enactment of the Uniting for Peace Resolution was like putting a penny in the fuse box: the system was not supposed to work against the opposition of a great power. It is probably fair to say that, regardless of the Resolution, the limitation still prevails.

## Regional Collective Security

The above discussion focuses on the problem of collective security on a world-wide basis. We should note, however, that it is possible to have a system that is less than world wide. Any group of states might organize for the purpose of promoting their collective security, within whatever limits they want to fix. In this case, the considerations advanced above with regard to a universal system might or might not all apply. The Organization of the American States (OAS) deserves to be mentioned in this connection. Though an alliance designed to deter or defeat aggression from the outside, it is also a regional collective security system of sorts, offering some promise of collective action against any member who attacks another member. As we have seen in Chapter 14, the OAS has in fact found Cuba guilty of aggression against Venezuela and has called for the application of rather mild sanctions.

## PEACEFUL SETTLEMENT AND PEACEFUL CHANGE

These terms are ambiguous. It is not always clear when settlement or change is "peaceful," for the threat of violence frequently lies in the background, and sometimes "peaceful" action is possible only because of some prior use of violence—as when the United States secured the right to construct the Panama Canal. The terms *settlement* and *change* are sometimes used synonymously. The definition of "peaceful change" offered in Chapter 2 could serve equally as a definition of "peaceful settlement." Yet, though settlement may involve change, it does not always require it. Settlement may involve simply a clarification of existing rights, whereas change necessarily involves the acquisition of a new right by one state, and perhaps, its loss by another. Settlement is likely to be an application of existing law, whereas change is a revision of law or an enactment of new law. Settlement is likely to occur within the status quo whereas change modifies the status quo. Settlement may, and often does, occur through judicial processes; change is normally sought through legislative or executive action. Settlement is reached by more or less voluntary agreement between the disputing states (perhaps aided by third parties); change connotes action likely to be opposed in some manner by the state(s) adversely affected.

The United Nations, of course, has served and presumably will continue to serve, as an agency which promotes the peaceful settlement of international disputes. It does this most simply by providing a meeting place for diplomats and so facilitating communication among them. Agents of parties to an incipient or actual dispute can meet and talk as inconspicuously or as publicly as they please. Third parties have easy opportunities, privately and publicly, to make suggestions and to exert moral pressures; they may recommend terms of settlement or procedures to be followed with a view to agreement on terms. So far, members have not interpreted the Charter in such a way as to permit the imposition of terms of settlement on unwilling parties. Their voluntary agreement is required, and there is no guarantee that it will be forthcoming.

Neither is there any assurance that peaceful change can be accomplished through the United Nations; in fact, it is highly doubtful whether it can be. The precedent set in connection with the Palestine problem in the late 1940's is not encouraging. As we noted in Chapter 14, the General Assembly then recommended the partition of Palestine. But the Arab states rejected the recommendation and went to war to prevent the new state of Israel from implementing it. The Security Council might have ruled, but did not, that resistance to the implementation of the plan was a threat to the peace or breach of the peace, thus calling for enforcement action. For that matter, the General Assembly itself refrained from recommending measures of compulsion. The upshot was that the recommendation for partition served not to bring about peaceful change but to give some shadow of justification to the use of violence by the party desiring the change. In practically all cases where recommendations for change are made, it is to be expected that adversely affected parties will resist, making peaceful change impossible.

In some cases no recommendation is to be expected at all. Repeatedly in history, one state or another has made demands of a completely unacceptable sort—demands that no general international organization could conceivably endorse. Germany under Hitler, for example, demanded that Austria cease to exist as an independent state, accepting incorporation into Germany, and demanded that Czechoslovakia and Poland each give up important portions of their territory. The law was on the side of Austria, Czechoslovakia, and Poland, and so in most eyes were the requirements of justice. Neither the League of Nations nor any other general international organization could possibly have endorsed Hitler's demands. Fear of German military power was such that Hitler took Austria and part of Czechoslovakia "peacefully," but his effort to get what he wanted from Poland brought on World War II.

Correspondingly, disputes that may well arise out of China's territorial claims are probably not solvable on a peaceful basis. For example, China claims considerable Soviet territory. When and if it presses these claims, the United Nations is likely to be helpless. If it were to call upon the Soviet Union to transfer territory to China, which is extremely unlikely, the action would no doubt be a gambit in the East–West conflict rather than a genuine effort at peaceful settlement or peaceful change. The Soviet Union would surely be defiant.

Cuba, too, offers illustrations of the limitations on the United Nations as an agency for peaceful settlement and peaceful change. In 1961 at the Bay of Pigs, the United States assisted Cuban refugees in an invasion aimed at the overthrow of the Castro regime. The change desired was one that the United Nations could not possibly have endorsed. The next year the Soviet Union attempted to establish missile bases in Cuba, and on discovering this, the United States delivered an ultimatum requiring an abandonment of the effort; again the change desired by the Soviet Union and the settlement demanded by the United States were of such a nature that the United Nations could play no more than a very minor role.

In connection with many disputes, the best that can be hoped for is what Inis L. Claude, Jr., calls "pacific nonsettlement" or "peaceful perpetuation." India and Pakistan, for example, have been living with the Kashmir dispute for many years; they called off the fighting long ago, assisted by the United Nations, and did it again when fighting broke out briefly in 1965, but still have been unable to work out a settlement. Similarly, Israel and its neighbors (especially Egypt), assisted by the United Nations, are engaged in what can be called the peaceful perpetuation of their dispute: they are deterred from fighting it out, but are unable to reach a settlement without fighting. The same kind of situation exists in Cyprus, where Greeks and Turks are hostile, with Greece and Turkey supporting their respective compatriots. What the best policy is in connection with such issues is an open question. The United Nations puts the emphasis on peace, even at the cost of the indefinite persistence of the dispute and the indefinite prolongation of crisis. The question is whether in some cases it might not be better to let the disputants fight it out, on the assumption that a settlement providing a basis for enduring stability will be reached more quickly in this way.

## PEACEKEEPING, POLICING, AND "PREVENTIVE DIPLOMACY"

The pacific nonsettlement or perpetuation of disputes may involve no more than the making of speeches and perhaps the enactment of resolutions in the Security Council or the General Assembly. But it may involve formal arrangements for peacekeeping or policing. Moreover, in a few instances the United Nations has confronted situations calling not so much for peaceful settlement or nonsettlement as for action designed to prevent disputes from arising or from becoming more serious.

One of the simplest devices that the United Nations uses is the establishment of a commission or special group to keep watch over a troublesome situation and to make periodic reports. Since 1948, for example, it has maintained a small military observer group in India and Pakistan to watch over Kashmir. In connection with the Lebanese crisis of 1958, the United Nations sent some six hundred observers to patrol the Lebanese–Syrian border. It sponsored a Security Force in West New Guinea in 1962, and had observers in Yemen in 1963. Such observers constitute local reminders of United Nations concern and a source of information for United Nations agencies.[10]

[10] See the address of Secretary-General U Thant, June 13, 1963, reprinted in Lincoln P. Bloomfield *et al.*, *International Military Forces* (Boston, Little, Brown, 1964), pp. 259-267.

The most notable of the United Nations efforts along these lines have been in Palestine and the Congo. Agents of the United Nations helped in the negotiation of a truce between Israel and its Arab neighbors in 1948 and 1949, and the arrangement included provision for a United Nations Truce Supervisory Organization, which has been there ever since. An even more serious crisis arose in 1956 when British, French, and Israeli forces invaded Egypt, and there seemed to be some danger of a major confrontation there with the Soviet Union. Of vital importance in warding off the danger and in inducing a withdrawal of the invading forces was the arrangement under which the United Nations dispatched to Egypt an emergency force, which still watches over the border region in the Gaza strip and the Sinai Desert.

The Congo operation was likewise of great importance.[11] The Congo gained independence from Belgium in 1960, ill-prepared to govern itself. The collapse of public order soon followed, leading to the re-entry of Belgian forces and an appeal from the Congolese government to the United Nations. From the Soviet point of view Belgium was guilty of aggression, and the Soviet delegate on the Security Council voted along with the others to respond to the Congolese appeal. From the point of view of the others, however, the problem was not so much the Belgian action as the disorder that brought it on. The result was that the United Nations force that went into the Congo—totaling some twenty thousand men at the peak of the effort—had an ambiguous kind of assignment. What it in fact did was to forestall a possible East–West confrontation in the Congo, just as the emergency force had already done in the Middle East. And at the same time it helped restore some semblance of order and unity in the face of Katanga's efforts to secede and in the face of widespread tendencies toward lawlessness; and this meant that it strengthened the position of a Congolese government that was oriented toward the West. The United Nations force finally withdrew in 1964.

Though the Soviet Union voted in the Security Council for the United Nations action in the Congo, it was vigorously critical of actions that turned out to be much more beneficial to pro-Western than to neutralist or pro-Soviet forces. It turned bitterly against Secretary-General Hammarskjöld, seeking to transfer the powers of his office to a troika representing the East, the West, and the uncommitted states; and it refused to pay assessments voted by the General Assembly to cover the costs of the Congo operation.

Although at least a qualified success from the Western point of view, the Congo operation plunged the United Nations into a very serious crisis. The financial costs were high—greater each year than the regular United Nations expenses. France and a few other states joined the Soviet

11 Inis L. Claude, Jr., *Swords Into Plowshares, The Problems and Progress of International Organization,* 3rd ed. (New York, Random House, 1964), pp. 287-302.

Union in denying any obligation to help pay the costs, and a number of other members in fact did not pay. These states were unmoved by the ruling of the International Court of Justice that the General Assembly's assessments constituted legally binding obligations. One result was that the UN soon found itself in dire financial straits—in virtual bankruptcy. Equally serious was another dispute that developed. According to the Charter, any member that falls two or more years behind in paying its assessments loses its vote in the General Assembly. By the fall of 1964 the Soviet Union had fallen that far behind, and soon thereafter France had as well. The result was that the General Assembly limped along as best it could without casting votes and adjourned prematurely to avoid a showdown. In the summer of 1965 the United States, though insisting on the legal correctness of the view that members in arrears should lose their votes, announced that it would not insist on the application of the rule.

The crisis involved at least two major issues. One concerns the relative roles of the Security Council and the General Assembly, and therefore the relative roles of the great and small powers. On the one hand, many are unwilling to concede primacy to the Security Council and its permanent members on matters of peace and security. On the other hand, the Soviet Union and France have demonstrated that if they are denied the veto that the Charter grants them they can exercise a kind of financial veto nevertheless. A compromise has been suggested that accepts a more influential role for the General Assembly than was originally envisaged, but that also gives the great powers more influence over its action. Presumably financial support for peacekeeping operations will be purely voluntary. The second issue is suggested by the assertion that "the United Nations in action is largely the free world in action." [12] However welcome this situation may be to those committed to the free world, it is not surprising if others find it unsatisfactory.


## CONCLUSIONS

We have already concluded, virtually as a matter of definition, that the United Nations does not provide for collective security. It does, however, permit action on behalf of security, if the appropriate vote is obtained. If nine members of the Security Council, including the five permanent members, want to take action in the face of a threat to the peace, breach of the peace, or act of aggression, they may do so. Similarly, if two-thirds of the members of the General Assembly want to recommend action, they may do so. But there is no obligation to act, and no assurance that action will occur. Members may vote as they please and are much more likely to be guided by considerations of expediency than by

12 Richard N. Gardner, *In Pursuit of World Order* (New York, Praeger, 1964), p. 43.

the principle that it is vital to resist all acts of aggression everywhere in the world.

This means that members have little assurance of United Nations support should they become victims of aggression. They must rely on their own resources and on such alliances as they find it desirable and possible to make. In no sense has the United Nations security system, if it can be so called, replaced the balance-of-power system. Article 51 of the Charter, confirming "the inherent right of individual and collective self-defense," has turned out to be one of its most important provisions.

At the same time, the United Nations has demonstrated its usefulness in various ways. It has facilitated the settlement of various disputes and has provided a forum in which disputes could be conducted in a public and relatively harmless way. In some cases, it has helped to avert disputes, or helped to keep them from becoming more serious, or helped to dampen them down and confine them. In the process, however, as we have noted, it has not only brought itself to virtual bankruptcy but has also brought on paralysis, at least in the General Assembly, until the issues concerning the distribution of influence and control can somehow be resolved.

## SUGGESTED READINGS

BLOOMFIELD, Lincoln P., et al., International Military Forces, The Question of Peacekeeping in an Armed and Disarming World (Boston, Little, Brown, 1964).

————, The United Nations and U.S. Foreign Policy (Boston, Little, Brown, 1960).

BURNS, Arthur Lee, and HEATHCOTE, Nina, Peace-Keeping by U. N. Forces—From Suez to the Congo (New York, Praeger, 1963).

CLARK, Grenville, and SOHN, Louis B., World Peace Through World Law, 2nd ed., rev. (Cambridge, Harvard University Press, 1960).

CLAUDE, Inis L., Jr., Power and International Relations (New York, Random House, 1962).

————, Swords Into Plowshares, 3rd ed. (New York, Random House, 1964).

DALLIN, Alexander, The Soviet Union at the United Nations (New York, Praeger, 1962).

GARDNER, Richard N., In Pursuit of World Order, U.S. Foreign Policy and International Organizations (New York, Praeger, 1964).

GOODRICH, Leland M., Korea: A Study of U.S. Policy in the United Nations (New York, Council on Foreign Relations, 1956).

————, and SIMONS, Anne P., The United Nations and the Maintenance of International Peace and Security (Washington, The Brookings Institution, 1955).

GORDON, King, The United Nations in the Congo, A Quest for Peace (New York, Carnegie Endowment for International Peace, 1962).

HAAS, Ernst B., "Types of Collective Security: An Examination of Operational Concepts," *American Political Science Review*, Vol. 49 (March, 1955), pp. 40-62.

JOHNSON, Howard C., and NIEMEYER, Gerhart, "Collective Security: The Validity of an Ideal," *International Organization*, Vol. 8 (February, 1954), pp. 19-35.

LEFEVER, Ernest W., *Crisis in the Congo: A United Nations Force in Action* (Washington, The Brookings Institution, 1965).

RAPPARD, William E., *The Quest for Peace* (Cambridge, Harvard University Press, 1940).

ROSNER, Gabriella, *The United Nations Emergency Force* (New York, Columbia University Press, 1963).

SLATER, Jerome, *A Revaluation of Collective Security, The OAS in Action* (Columbus, Ohio State University Press, 1965).

STOESSINGER, John G., "Financing the United Nations," *International Conciliation*, No. 535 (November, 1961).

STONE, Julius, *Legal Controls of International Conflict, A Treatise on the Dynamics of Disputes- and War-Law* (New York, Rinehart, 1954).

STROMBERG, Roland N., *Collective Security and American Foreign Policy, From the League of Nations to NATO* (New York, Praeger, 1963).

WILCOX, Francis O., and HAVILAND, H. Field, Jr., eds., *The United States and the United Nations* (Baltimore, Johns Hopkins Press, 1961).

WOLFERS, Arnold, ed., *Alliance Policy in the Cold War* (Baltimore, Johns Hopkins Press, 1959).

————, *Discord and Collaboration, Essays on International Politics* (Baltimore, Johns Hopkins Press, 1962).

# 21

# INTERNATIONAL ORGANIZATION FOR WELFARE

We have repeatedly noted that states commonly pursue a number of objectives. Some of them, such as security, relate primarily to the state itself. Others, such as prosperity, relate primarily to individuals. There is often an interrelationship between the pusuit of objectives on behalf of the state and their pursuit on behalf of individuals, for the efforts may be mutually reinforcing.

Interrelated concern for the state and for the individual has led governments to cooperate for what can be labeled broadly as the promotion of welfare. Sometimes the immediate concern of each cooperating government is with the welfare of its own citizens. Sometimes some of the governments involved are concerned with people abroad, usually on the basis of mixed motives. One of them is humanitarian; or, to put it somewhat differently, one of them "is undoubtedly a human sympathy which makes the spectacle of pain in others a pain to the spectator." [1] There was a time when pain abroad was ignored because it was unknown, but the communication network now calls much of it to the attention of people in a position to extend help.

Another motive operating in the advanced countries is more directly related to the ideological struggle. The United States, for example, is willing to join in international welfare activities for the benefit of people abroad as a means of influencing their choices about their own future; we want them to choose domestic and foreign policies that contribute to a world environment congenial to our interests. If they do not copy American ways and align themselves with the West, at least they should not go Communist.

[1] P. E. Corbett, *The Individual and World Society* (Princeton, Center for Research on World Political Institutions, 1953), p. 15.

Further, international welfare activities are often called for in the name of peace. Thus the Charter assigns welfare functions to the United Nations "with a view to the creation of conditions of stability and well-being which are necessary for peaceful and friendly relations among nations." Similarly, the constitution of the United Nations Educational, Scientific, and Cultural Organization (UNESCO) provides for what we are broadly calling welfare activities, declaring that they are to be undertaken to promote peace and security. "Since wars begin in the minds of men, it is in the minds of men that the defenses of peace must be constructed."

Those viewing the promotion of welfare as a path to peace may do so for either or both of two reasons. They may contend that better educated, more prosperous, and more healthy people are more likely to be contented and therefore peaceful, even though the world continues to be divided into sovereign states. Or they may contend that as people learn the value of international cooperation for the advancement of welfare they will come to think of themselves more as members of a world society and less as members of distinct national societies. The hope is that "functional integration" will occur, that is, that people all over the world will become united by cooperating in international organizations to perform functions which contribute directly to better living, and, further, that integration at this level may lead to the development of a sense of social unity throughout the world (perhaps even to political integration), thus rendering war less likely.

Numerous motivations and objectives thus combine to produce international cooperation for the promotion of welfare, and the criteria for judging success are therefore complex.

Perhaps it should be noted at the outset of the discussion of international organizations engaged in the promotion of welfare that none of them is empowered to exercise jurisdiction over individuals or to oblige member states to do anything against their will. They are agencies through which voluntary cooperation occurs rather than agencies having an independent existence and a capacity to impose decisions. They can accomplish no more than their members are willing to have them accomplish—and often not as much.

## THE ORGANIZATIONAL ARRANGEMENTS

A considerable number of international (intergovernmental) organizations engage in the promotion of world welfare. The United Nations itself is, of course, the principal one among them. It is charged with promoting:

a. higher standards of living, full employment, and conditions of economic and social progress and development;

b. solutions of international economic, social, health, and related problems; and international cultural and educational cooperation; and

c. universal respect for, and observance of, human rights and fundamental freedoms for all without distinction as to race, sex, language, or religion.

These objectives are pursued primarily by the General Assembly and the Economic and Social Council (ECOSOC). The latter is one of the principal organs of the United Nations and consists of 27 members (formerly 18) elected for three-year terms by the General Assembly. Reelection being permitted, the major powers are regularly represented. Meetings are held semiannually, and decisions are made by a simple majority of those present and voting.

ECOSOC has established various subordinate agencies. Some of them are regional, e.g., the Economic Commission for Europe (ECE), the Economic Commission for Asia and the Far East (ECAFE), the Economic Commission for Latin America (ECLA), and the Economic Commission for Africa (ECA). Others are functional, e.g., the Commission on Human Rights. Moreover, a number of "specialized agencies," established outside the framework of the United Nations, have been brought into relationship with it through agreements with ECOSOC. The International Bank for Reconstruction and Development and the International Monetary Fund, mentioned in an earlier chapter, are among them. Others include the Universal Postal Union (UPU), the International Labor Organization (ILO), the United Nations Educational, Scientific, and Cultural Organization (UNESCO), the World Health Organization (WHO), the Food and Agriculture Organization (FAO), the World Meteorological Organization (WMO), the International Telecommunication Union (ITU), the International Civil Aviation Organization (ICAO), and the International Maritime Consultative Organization (IMCO). The International Atomic Energy Agency is technically not a specialized agency, but is in a similar category.

The division of labor among these various organizations is not clear-cut. The General Assembly, if it chose, could do virtually everything that ECOSOC can do, and either agency may act in some of the same fields with which the specialized agencies are concerned. In fact, the specialized agencies sometimes execute programs selected and financed by the United Nations itself.

Confusion is compounded by the proliferation of programs. For the specific purpose of assisting the developing countries, there is a regular United Nations program, an Expanded Program, a Special Fund, and various programs undertaken by the specialized agencies. Moreover, the notion has been abandoned that development is simply economic, which means that a network of interrelationships has developed among programs and agencies having to do with what superficially appear to be distinct activities: economic, political, social, cultural, and educational. The point is stressed in a statement by Paul G. Hoffman, Managing Director of the United Nations Special Fund.

We soon discovered that economic development is too serious a matter to be left to the economists. . . . Development assistance cannot be effective unless it also takes into account a country's social and political institutions, the way people live and think, the goals they set for themselves, their attitudes toward work, and so forth. Some countries are just emerging from a tradition that frowns on manual labor as beneath the dignity of men and assigns it primarily to women. In some places, education is still looked on more as a social grace for the favored few than as a means to a better material life for a majority. In too many countries, men engaged in industry and commerce are considered as third-class citizens.[2]

Arrangements for financing the various activities of the United Nations and its family of agencies further complicate the picture. Both the United Nations and the specialized agencies have regular budgets to which members contribute on the basis of agreed formulas, and these budgets provide for some of the activities with which we are concerned. But the regular budget of the United Nations does not provide for the Expanded Program or the Special Fund. The Soviet Union and some other members are notably reluctant about developments that seem to make the United Nations a kind of international executive agency, preferring to have it serve primarily as an agency for sponsoring conferences; they thus have insisted on the principle of voluntary contributions to special budgets for the welfare activities.[3] Once raised, much of this money is expended through the specialized agencies. Moreover, in many cases the country in which a project is carried out pays a part of the cost.

The complexity of the organizational arrangements for the promotion of welfare and the interrelationships among the purposes and activities leave us without neat, separate categories to use for descriptive purposes. What we will do is to focus first on the general nature of the programs for promoting development throughout the world and then on some more specific programs and agencies.

## THE UNITED NATIONS DEVELOPMENT DECADE

At the end of 1961 the General Assembly designated the 1960's as the "United Nations Development Decade," declaring that members would intensify their efforts to promote self-sustaining growth. When the resolu-

[2] Paul G. Hoffman, "Forms and Functions of Development Assistance," in Andrew W. Cordier and Wilder Foote, eds., *The Quest for Peace* (New York, Columbia University Press, 1965), p. 232.

[3] Agda Rössel, "Financing the United Nations: Its Economic and Political Implications," in Cordier and Foote, *op. cit.*, p. 140.

tion was enacted, the underdeveloped countries were thought to have a growth rate in their aggregate national incomes of about 3.5 percent per year. The General Assembly suggested that the goal for the end of the decade should be a minimum annual growth rate of 5 percent. According to one estimate, half of the proposed growth could be brought about by international action if the wealthier countries made capital equal to about 1 percent of their combined national incomes available, i.e., if they doubled the amount being made available at the beginning of the decade. Given both the achievement of the growth rate and its continuation, and the continued population increase in the developing countries at the rate prevailing around 1961, "personal living standards can be doubled within twenty-five to thirty years." [4]

We have noted in an earlier chapter that the United States and various other countries have their own national programs for assisting the developing countries. In fact, only a small proportion of the total devoted to such assistance goes through the United Nations and its family of agencies. "Investment" abroad occurs largely through national and private channels, supplemented by the World Bank (IBRD), the International Development Association, and the International Finance Corporation. The United Nations and most of the specialized agencies concentrate, in the main, on "pre-investment" activities and technical assistance.

The preinvestment activities and technical assistance of the Expanded Program have, for the most part, taken the form of the assignment of experts to governments desiring them. From 1950 to 1963, 70 percent of all Expanded Program funds were used for this purpose, allowing an average of some 2500 assignments per year. In addition, in the same period the Expanded Program financed some 24,000 training fellowships.[5]

The purpose of the Special Fund is to assist developing countries with larger-scale pre-investment projects. It finances surveys and studies of natural resources, the use of land and water resources, the possibilities of developing transportation and communication facilities, and the development of fisheries; it assists governments in establishing or strengthening research or advisory services having to do with agricultural or industrial production; it helps in human resource development, i.e., in providing training and education; and it concerns itself with the problem of formulating and implementing national plans for development. The hope is that such activities will set the stage for and encourage the investment of capital by either private or public agencies. As of 1964 the Special Fund was being drawn upon to finance or help finance 374 proj-

[4] United Nations, Department of Economic and Social Affairs, Report of the Secretary-General, *The United Nations Development Decade, Proposals for Action* (New York, United Nations, 1962), p. vi.

[5] United Nations, The Technical Assistance Board, *The Expanded Programme of Technical Assistance for Economic Development of Under-Developed Countries* (New York, United Nations, 1963), pp. vi, 5. *United Nations Yearbook*, 1963, p. 191.

ects in 121 countries and territories. Their total cost was estimated at $837 million, of which $335 million was to come from the Special Fund and the remainder from the recipient governments. The United Nations itself was the executing agency for 64 of these projects, the rest being assigned to one or another of the specialized agencies; UNESCO, for example, was the executing agency for another 64, and FAO for 47. Paul G. Hoffman speaks optimistically of the results of the Special Fund projects.

Our surveys have found huge quantities of water under the desert in Syria, and enormous potentials for irrigation and hydroelectric power in many places in Africa, Asia, and Latin America. Large deposits of minerals have been found in . . . Chile, Uganda, and Pakistan, and unexpected quantities of valuable timber have been discovered. . . . Each day of work strengthens our conviction that we have only just begun to uncover the vast physical resources of the developing nations.[6]

At the beginning of 1964, according to Mr. Hoffman, the United Nations and its family of related agencies employed a total of 23,000 persons. Of these, 20,500 (or 89 percent) were "exclusively engaged in promoting social and economic welfare." [7] The converse of this is that a relatively small proportion of those employed dealt with problems relating directly to security and peace.

In addition to the above activities relating to the problem of development, agencies of the United Nations have interested themselves in patterns of international trade. The most spectacular manifestation of the interest was the United Nations Conference on Trade and Development in 1964—"the biggest international conference ever held, involving 2000 delegates from 119 countries and lasting nearly three months." [8] From the point of view of the developing countries (and they constituted a large majority), the purpose of the conference was to find ways for them to obtain additional foreign exchange—to bridge the gap between their foreign exchange needs and their prospective earnings. Their share of world trade had been declining, and their exports had been paying for less and less of their imports. Rightly or not, many of them concluded that the existing trading system was rigged against them, and they tended to caucus and vote together, seeking concessions from the more developed countries. As Richard N. Gardner points out, the usual East–West confrontation was replaced by a West–South confrontation.[9] The developing countries wanted preferential tariff arrangements, more international commodity agreements designed to raise the prices of the primary products that they exported, automatic compensatory payments when the

6 Hoffman, *loc. cit.*, p. 237.
7 *Ibid.*, p. 234.
8 Richard N. Gardner, *In Pursuit of World Order* (New York, Praeger, 1964), p. 161.
9 *Ibid.*, p. 165.

terms of trade turned against them, and various other adjustments in their favor. They had the votes, but obviously it takes more than the votes of the economically weak to induce the economically powerful to make the concessions demanded. One agreement reached was that a United Nations Conference on Trade and Development should meet every three years, that a Trade and Development Board should meet between conferences, and that a secretariat within the United Nations Secretariat should serve the new institutions. How constructive their work will be remains to be seen.

Finally, in connection with various kinds of economic problems, including those pertaining to development, the regional commissions should be noted. They are, in the main, research organizations, gathering and disseminating data of all sorts about economic problems and developments relating to the region of their concern. The scope of their studies is suggested by the committees created by ECE: on agricultural problems, on coal, on gas, on electric power, on housing, building, and planning, on steel, on timber, on the development of trade, and on inland transport. But the commissions also do more. They engage directly in institution-building, in training, and in promotional activities. Most notably, ECLA promoted and sponsored the negotiations leading to the establishment of the Latin American Free Trade Association (LAFTA) and to the agreement for economic integration in Central America. ECLA, ECAFE, and ECA have all established Institutes for Economic Development and Planning to undertake the training of actual and potential government officials and to engage in research and advisory services. ECA led in the establishment of the African Development Bank. All of the regional commissions are concerned with the problem of uniformity or comparability in statistical data and methods. All are executing agencies for programs of technical assistance.

## THE SPECIALIZED AGENCIES

As suggested above, many of the activities in which the General Assembly and ECOSOC might engage are in fact undertaken by the specialized agencies, either independently or on behalf of the United Nations. For most of them a conference is the supreme governing body, meeting at intervals ranging from one to five years, and in most of the conferences each member has one vote. Decisions are sometimes taken by a simple majority, sometimes by a two-thirds majority. The conference elects a smaller body which directs the affairs of the organization until the next conference occurs. Each organization also has a secretariat or staff. Members contribute to expenses according to various assessment formulas, and most of the organizations also obtain money from the Expanded Program or Special Fund for administering preinvestment or technical assistance projects. Brief sketches of some of the specialized agencies follow.[10] Those that have been dealt with elsewhere (e.g., the World Bank and the International Monetary Fund) are ignored.

## International Transportation and Communication: UPU, ITU, ICAO

As can be easily imagined, problems developed long ago in connection with the international exchange of mail. To assist in their solution, a number of states joined in 1874 in establishing what is now called the Universal Postal Union (UPU), with over 125 members.[11] "The purpose of the Union," according to its constitution, "is to assure the organization and improvement of the various postal services and to promote, in that sphere, the development of international cooperation." The members regard themselves as constituting a single postal territory. Each accepts mail for delivery abroad. Each assures a right of transit across its domain. Agreements have been reached concerning a multitude of details, for example, the permissible size of envelopes. "Regular" international mail is handled on the basis of substantially uniform rules throughout the world, and many countries are party to arrangements under which special services are provided, for example, sending money abroad through international money orders. The UPU itself does not carry mail, but the members have been highly successful through it in their efforts to arrange for smooth and efficient cooperation in postal matters.

The UPU is based upon a constitution and a convention, adopted at the Vienna Congress of 1964. The constitution concerns the structure, powers, and responsibilities of the Union, and the convention sets forth the rules and principles agreed upon for the international postal service. Supplementary agreements provide for special services. Although adherence to the supplementary agreements is optional, all members must perforce accept the two main documents. In this connection a form of international majority rule has developed, for a majority suffices to amend the convention. Theoretically, states that object could withdraw from the UPU, but the benefits of membership make this extremely unlikely. The work of the organization is generally regarded as technical and administrative rather than political; at least, it has so little to do with national prestige and power that members are commonly repre-

---

[10] Summary sketches of the work of the various specialized agencies may be found in the annual editions of the *United Nations Yearbook*. Fuller statements may be found in the annual reports issued by each agency. See also the current edition of the *Yearbook of International Organizations*.

[11] M. A. K. Menon, "Universal Postal Union," *International Conciliation*, No. 552 (March, 1965). George A. Codding Jr., *The Universal Postal Union* (New York, New York University Press, 1964).

sented at the congresses not by personnel from the diplomatic service but rather by postal officials. There is no doubt that the welfare of individuals throughout the world is served. No one has ever been able to determine to what extent these international postal services contribute to the development of a sense of membership in a world society, but it seems plausible that some contribution occurs.

Similarly, problems developed with the coming of the telegraph, the telephone, radio, and TV. On the basis of what kind of arrangements would telegraph and telephone systems in one country handle messages originating in another? What technical specifications should be recommended, for example, concerning the type and quality of equipment used? What radio frequencies should be reserved for different kinds of purposes? What could be done to minimize interference between broadcasting stations? More than 120 political entities throughout the world now attempt to handle problems of these types through the International Telecommunication Union (ITU), which stems from an organization founded in the nineteenth century. They have succeeded pretty well in cooperating in the fields of the telegraph and telephone, for the problems have been mainly technical and administrative in character. Success in connection with radio broadcasting, however, has been more limited. So far, the scientists have not devised means by which each country can do all the broadcasting it wishes to do without interfering with foreign stations, especially in the high-frequency bands, and there is no scientific or technical way of deciding what allocation of frequencies would be equitable; for that matter, even if the rules of equity could be determined, some states might not wish to accept them, for international broadcasting is related to questions of prestige and power. The ITU engages in a continuous attack on problems of the type referred to above; many have been solved, but new problems are always arising and some old ones have proved to be intractable.

The development of aviation also produced problems in the international field. On the basis of what conditions might civil aircraft from one country fly over or land in the territory of another? Should the aircraft of one country be allowed to transport passengers and goods between two other countries? What flight rules should be fixed? What navigational aids should interested countries cooperate in establishing and maintaining? Should they cooperate in collecting and exchanging weather information, and, if so, how? What standards of airworthiness should aircraft meet, and what standards of fitness should pilots and crew members meet? With special regard to financing the purchase and operation of aircraft, what rules should the various countries observe concerning property rights? What rules should be fixed in connection with the problems arising from the loss of life and property because of accidents?

To promote agreement on these and other problems, over one hundred political entities have joined the International Civil Aviation Organization (ICAO), which formally came into existence in 1947. In addition to promoting agreement among states on common problems, it responds to the requests of members for technical assistance in organizing and operating their aeronautical services and in training personnel.

## The International Labor Organization

At the end of World War I, the victors founded not only the League of Nations and a world court but also an International Labor Organization (ILO). It survived World War II and exists today with approximately 110 members. The reason given for the establishment of the ILO was that peace cannot be attained without "social justice," and that to achieve social justice labor conditions must be regulated by international agreement.

The constitution of the ILO lists areas of action for the organization and the general principles to be pursued. The following summary of this portion of the constitution is by P. E. Corbett.

The first and guiding principle is that "labor should not be regarded merely as a commodity or article of commerce." Then follow the right of association; wages "adequate to maintain a reasonable standard of life" as this is understood in the worker's time and country; "an eight hours day or a forty-eight hours week as the standard to be aimed at where it has not already been attained"; a twenty-four hours weekly rest; abolition of child labor and limitation of the labor of young persons to permit continuation of education and ensure proper physical development; equal pay for men and women for work of equal value; equitable economic treatment of all legally resident workers; in every State a system of inspection, with women taking part, to ensure enforcement of laws protecting the employed.[12]

In addition, the constitution lists some "urgently required" improvements.

These specify "the regulation of the labor supply"; "the prevention of unemployment"; "the protection of the worker against sickness, disease, and injury arising out of his employment"; the protection of women; "provision for old age and injury"; "protection of the interests of workers when employed in countries other than their own," and "the organization of vocational and technical education."

Experience demonstrated that the problem of establishing social justice for workers along the above lines was a wide-ranging one, affecting many aspects of the social structure. The ILO therefore became concerned with the question of the kind of society that would have to exist to make its

[12] Corbett, *op. cit.*, p. 18.

objectives in the realm of labor realizable. In a general conference in 1946 the members defined such a society as one in which "all human beings, irrespective of race, creed, or sex, have the right to pursue both their material well-being and their spiritual development in conditions of freedom and dignity, of economic security and equal opportunity. . . ." They declared that the attainment of these conditions was the "central aim" of all national and international policies and measures. "The welfare of the individual in society was thus affirmed as the primary purpose of all social organization on any plane."[13]

The purposes of the ILO thus cover a considerable range. It seeks to promote human rights and fundamental freedoms, e.g., the freedom of workers to organize in trade unions, freedom from forced labor, and freedom from arbitrary discrimination. It is concerned with labor standards throughout the world and with living and working conditions. In 1962, for example, the conference adopted a recommendation on reducing the work week to 40 hours—a recommendation supplementing earlier conventions that had been referred to the members for ratification. ILO personnel make studies pertaining to such subjects as social security, occupational health and safety, and vocational rehabilitation, and assist states facing problems in these realms. Various committees concern themselves with practices and problems identified with specific vocations, e.g., the Committee of Experts on Conditions of Work in the Fishing Industry. More broadly, the ILO is concerned with "human resources development and the promotion of productive employment," which means, among other things, that it studies manpower requirements and manpower policies in different countries and assists in programs for vocational training, management development, and productivity improvement. In the latter fields, the declared objective is:

to promote among management in developing countries a broader conception of its responsibilities in regard to training of personnel and other labor aspects of higher productivity, as well as knowledge of the techniques of modern management, a better understanding of personnel administration needs and methods, and a progressive outlook toward labor–management relations.[14]

The Andean Indian Program is another illustration of the ILO's involvement in human resources development; it is the coordinator of the program, in which the United Nations, FAO, UNESCO, and WHO also participate, designed to bring about the integration of the Andean Indians into the economic and social life of the countries in which they live.[15]

As the above suggests, the ILO employs various methods in pursuing

[13] *Ibid.*, p. 19.
[14] International Labor Organization, *Seventeenth Report of the International Labor Organization to the United Nations* (Geneva, 1963), p. 19.
[15] *Ibid.*, p. 33.

its objectives. It engages in studies of many different kinds relating to labor over the world and publishes its findings. It compiles and disseminates statistical and other relevant information. It makes recommendations (119 of them by 1963) and endorses conventions (again 119 by 1963, with over 2800 ratifications registered). It launches special investigations when one member complains that another is not observing a convention that it has ratified, and in this way has in fact induced states to change their behavior.[16] In 1961 the conference asked South Africa to withdraw from the ILO until it abandoned *apartheid;* and when South Africa failed to comply the governing body voted to exclude South African delegates from all ILO meetings except the conference.

The ILO is distinctive in the composition of its leading organs. To the conference the government of each member state appoints four delegates, two being governmental representatives and the other two being representatives of workers and employers, respectively. The smaller governing body also includes representatives of governments, workers, and employers.

There is no doubt that purely national activities in the field of labor are of more vital significance than the activities conducted internationally through the ILO. Yet it cannot be doubted either that through international cooperation the welfare of labor in many countries has been improved.

## The Food and Agriculture Organization

The Food and Agriculture Organization (FAO), now with more than 105 members, was established at the close of World War II. The preamble of the Constitution of the FAO declares that the members are "determined to promote the common welfare by furthering separate and collective action for the purposes of"

raising levels of nutrition and standards of living of the peoples under their respective jurisdictions,

securing improvements in the efficiency of the production and distribution of all food and agricultural products,

bettering the condition of rural populations,
and thus contributing toward an expanding world economy.

To promote these purposes, FAO is active over much of the world in the fields of agriculture, fisheries, forestry, nutrition, and education and information; it also collects and disseminates statistics relevant to its purposes and undertakes studies concerning the distribution and marketing of agricultural products.

[16] Ernst B. Haas, *Beyond the Nation-State, Functionalism and International Organization* (Stanford, Stanford University Press, 1964), pp. 361-370.

A large proportion of its work, performed in cooperation with ECOSOC, takes the form of technical assistance provided to members on their request. For example, Iraq has received FAO assistance in connection with the problem of soil erosion. India has received assistance in training mechanics in the maintenance of agricultural machinery and irrigation equipment. A number of European countries have secured FAO help in connection with the introduction and development of hybrid seed corn. The entire Middle East, as well as some countries in other regions, have benefited from the locust-control activities of FAO. Egypt and other countries have secured the services of FAO experts regarding problems connected with the production of rice. Widespread cooperation has occurred through FAO in combating various animal and plant diseases. Agricultural extension specialists have been assigned to a number of the fundamental education centers sponsored by UNESCO. Turkey has received assistance in improving the organization and administration of its fishing industry, and Ceylon, India, and Liberia have sought FAO help in improving fishing gear and methods. Missions have been sent to Brazil, Chile, Paraguay, Libya, and Ethiopia to advise on forestry policy. In cooperation with the World Health Organization, FAO has attacked the problem of Kwashiorkor in Africa, a children's disease resulting from malnutrition. These are simply examples of the types of technical assistance that FAO provides. In conjunction with such assistance and in addition to it, FAO conducts extensive educational and informational activities, and sponsors conferences of experts on numerous problems in its field.[17]

In 1960 FAO launched the Freedom From Hunger Campaign, aiming "first, to create a world-wide awareness of the problems of hunger and malnutrition which afflict more than half of the world's population and which, apart from the human suffering and human degradation that they involve, pose a serious threat to peace and orderly progress, and second, to promote a climate of opinion in which solutions to these problems can be organized both on a national and on an international basis."[18] The campaign added an element of agitation to the research and assistance programs in which the FAO normally engaged. In 1963 FAO and the United Nations together launched the World Food Program for the use of food in cooperative programs for social and economic development.

## The World Health Organization

The World Health Organization (WHO), with some 120 members, formally came into existence in 1948. Like FAO, it engages in educational

[17] See Gove Hambidge, *The Story of FAO* (Princeton, N.J., Van Nostrand, 1955).

[18] B. R. Sen, Director-General of FAO, in Freedom From Hunger Campaign Basic Study, No. 12, *Malnutrition and Disease, A Major Problem of the Human Race* (Geneva, World Health Organization, 1963), p. 1.

and informational activity, in research, and in action programs. It co-operates with member countries in combating such diseases as malaria, syphilis, yaws, and tuberculosis. It concerns itself with public health and health education programs, with the clinical and pharmacological evaluation of drugs, with community water supply programs, with air and water pollution, and with various kinds of training programs.

## The United Nations Educational, Scientific, and Cultural Organization

The United Nations Educational, Scientific, and Cultural Organization (UNESCO), now including some 113 members, came into existence at the end of World War II and is active in the fields indicated by its name. Most member states have established national commissions which seek to promote the purposes of UNESCO within their territory.

As with the other specialized agencies, the work of UNESCO can only be briefly illustrated here. It is, of course, concerned with education: with primary and secondary education, technical and vocational education, higher education, and adult education. It engages in research and offers advisory services and assistance to members. It has long sought to eradicate illiteracy, and in 1962 launched a World Campaign for Universal Literacy. In 1963 it established an International Institute for Educational Planning. It engages widely, among other things, in teacher training activities. It conducts various regional programs and operates various regional centers, e.g., the Regional Fundamental Education Centre for Community Development in Latin America.

Other activities relate to the natural and social sciences. UNESCO helps to finance private international organizations in both areas, for example, the International Council of Scientific Unions. It maintains centers and sponsors conferences designed to stimulate and coordinate research in various fields, and it promotes liaison among scholars in different countries, for example, by helping to finance the publication of *International Political Science Abstracts* and by subsidizing the International Political Science Association.

The constitution of UNESCO, which is reprinted in the appendix of this book, enjoins it to seek the "preservation and utilization of the cultural heritage of mankind." In the cultural realm, as in the other realms of its activity, UNESCO operates in part through nongovernmental organizations that it subsidizes, e.g., the International Council for Philosophy and Humanistic Studies. It concerns itself with the cultures of various regions, e.g., with African cultures; in this connection it is conducting the Campaign to Save the Monuments of Nubia. One of its "major projects" aims to cultivate "mutual appreciation of Eastern and Western cultural values."

In the field of mass communication, UNESCO's activities include efforts to promote the free flow of information and ideas, the development of information media (e.g., initiating steps leading to the formation of the Union of African News Agencies), assistance and training in the use of mass media for educational purposes, the issuance of various publications (e.g., the UNESCO *Courier*), and the making and distribution of films, exhibits, and radio and TV programs.

Finally, UNESCO sponsors an International Exchange Service, preparing various publications (e.g., *Teachers for Africa* and the *Handbook on International Exchanges in Education, Science, Culture and Mass Communications*) and administering various fellowship programs.

## The International Atomic Energy Agency

The International Atomic Energy Agency, established in 1956 and now including some 85 members, is concerned with the potential nonmilitary contributions of atomic energy to human welfare. It sponsors research and conferences and serves as the agency through which the leading nuclear powers transfer fissionable materials and related equipment to other countries. On arrangement with the appropriate governments, it administers safeguards and engages in inspections designed to give reassurance against the diversion of nuclear fuels to military purposes. It seeks to minimize nuclear hazards to health and safety. And it provides technical assistance and information to its members, and training and fellowships to their nationals.

# HUMAN RIGHTS

The most notable functional agency of ECOSOC, as distinct from its regional commissions, is the Commission on Human Rights, established in 1946 in conformity with the specific requirements of the Charter. The Commission proceeded with remarkable dispatch to formulate a Universal Declaration of Human Rights, which the General Assembly formally approved at the end of 1948. Two Covenants—one on civil and political rights and the other on economic, social, and cultural rights—remain to be approved. The three documents together are to constitute an International Bill of Rights.

The Declaration of Human Rights is a major additional step along a road that men began to travel centuries ago.[19] Its antecedents within individual nations include the Magna Charta, the United States Constitution and its Bill of Rights, and the French Declaration of the Rights of

19 See Egon Schwelb, *Human Rights and the International Community, The Roots and Growth of the Universal Declaration of Human Rights* (Chicago, Quadrangle Books, 1964), pp. 13-25.

Man and of the Citizen. Its antecedents internationally include numerous acts of "humanitarian intervention" on the part of the major powers, the prohibition of the slave trade, and numerous agreements and treaties relating to the treatment of labor, women and children, and racial, religious, and national minorities. At the end of World War I the Japanese attempted, but failed, to get a provision into the League of Nations Covenant banning discrimination because of race or nationality. By the end of World War II, however, a profound change had occurred, brought about above all by the horrors of Hitler's racialism. There was no question but that the United Nations Charter would somehow espouse human rights, and it in fact does at a number of points. Article 55, for example, enjoins the United Nations to "promote . . . universal respect for, and observance of, human rights and fundamental freedoms for all without distinction as to race, sex, language, or religion," and Article 56 pledges all members to take joint and separate action for the achievement of this purpose. At the same time, we should recall the stipulation that nothing in the Charter authorizes the United Nations to intervene in matters which are essentially within the domestic jurisdiction of states.

The text of the Universal Declaration of Human Rights is in the appendix of this book. Articles 3 through 21 cover the kinds of civil and political rights commonly assured in Western practice. In brief, everyone is said to have the right to life, liberty, personal security, equality before the law, nationality, and property; slavery is prohibited, and there is to be freedom of thought, conscience, religion, expression, and peaceful assembly, and freedom from arbitrary arrest, detention, or exile. Moreover, everyone is said to have the right to take part in the government of his country. "The will of the people shall be the basis of the authority of government; this will shall be expressed in periodic and genuine elections which shall be by universal and equal suffrage and shall be held by secret vote or by equivalent free voting procedures." Articles 22 through 27 cover social, economic, and cultural rights—not so commonly regarded in American and European practice as basic, enforceable human rights.[20] Everyone is said to have the right to social security and to the realization of the rights indispensable for his dignity and the free development of his personality. Everyone is said to have the right to work, to free choice of employment, to just and favorable conditions of work and to protection against unemployment. There is to be equal pay for equal work, and freedom to form and join trade unions. "Everyone has the right to rest and leisure, including reasonable limitation of working hours and periodic holidays with pay." Everyone is said to have the right to an adequate standard of living and the right to edu-

[20] See Maurice Cranston, *What Are Human Rights?* (New York, Basic Books, 1962), esp. pp. 34-39.

cation. "Education shall be directed to the full development of the human personality and to the strengthening of respect for human rights and fundamental freedoms. It shall promote understanding, tolerance and friendship among all nations, racial or religious groups, and shall further the activities of the United Nations for the maintenance of peace."

Preceding the above articles is one enjoining men to act towards one another in a spirit of brotherhood and another stipulating that "everyone is entitled to all the rights and freedoms set forth in this Declaration, without distinction of any kind, such as race, color, sex, language, religion, political or other opinion, national or social origin, property, birth or other status."

We might note that the Ninth International Conference of American States, meeting at Bogota in the spring of 1948, adopted an American Declaration of the Rights and Duties of Man similar in most respects to the Universal Declaration that the General Assembly endorsed some months later.

The General Assembly proclaimed the Universal Declaration "as a common standard of achievement for all peoples and all nations." The document was not a treaty and was generally regarded as a statement of desirable goals rather than a statement of legally binding rules and obligations. The legally binding documents were to be the covenants, which have not been endorsed. There are two of them—one on civil and political rights and another on economic, social, and cultural rights, each including provision for measures of implementation. But the opportunity that this will give to states to accept one without the other does not solve all problems. The United States Senate might well object to both. Moreover, individual provisions raise troublesome questions.[21] As drafted, each covenant guarantees the right of self-determination, to which some object. Some fear that an article prohibiting "any advocacy of national, racial or religious hostility that constitutes an incitement to hatred and violence" might lead to censorship. Conclusion of the covenants would create problems in federal systems, for some of the articles cover matters now under the jurisdiction of the subdivisions rather than the central government. Various problems exist, too, about appropriate measures for implementing or enforcing covenants. Whether the General Assembly will endorse the covenants, and how many states will then ratify them, remains to be seen.

The states of Western Europe have already acted on covenants of their own. In 1950 they concluded a Convention for the Protection of Human Rights and Fundamental Freedoms which not only identified the civil

---

[21] See Leland M. Goodrich, *The United Nations* (New York, Crowell, 1959), pp. 250-253. For a composite text of the draft international covenants, see *American Journal of International Law*, Vol. 58, (July, 1964), pp. 857-872.

and political rights to be guaranteed but also called into being two international institutions, a commission and a court, to watch over the implementation of the guarantees. And in 1961 they concluded the European Social Charter identifying social, economic, and cultural rights.[22]

A reasonably good case can be made for the view that the Universal Declaration itself has been gradually taking on a quasi-obligatory character. Egon Schwelb is among those who champion this view.[23] He points to the extent to which individual provisions have been incorporated into treaties, such as those concluded by the states of Western Europe. And he also cites other supporting considerations. Many new states, most of them in Africa, endorse the Declaration in their constitutions, and so does the Charter of the Organization of African Unity. A number of United Nations Declarations made since 1948 can be construed to reflect the view that the Universal Declaration of Human Rights is declaratory of existing law rather than of an aspiration or standard of achievement. Thus the General Assembly's Declaration on the Elimination of All Forms of Racial Discrimination (1963) asserts:

> Discrimination between human beings on the grounds of race, color or ethnic origin is an offense to human dignity and shall be condemned as a denial of the principles of the Charter of the United Nations, as a violation of the human rights and fundamental freedoms proclaimed in the Universal Declaration of Human Rights, as an obstacle to friendly and peaceful relations among nations and as a fact capable of disturbing peace and security among peoples.

Similarly, the Declaration on the Granting of Independence to Colonial Countries and Peoples (1960) enjoined all states "to observe faithfully and strictly . . . the Universal Declaration of Human Rights. . . ." And the Office of Legal Affairs in the United Nations Secretariat has expressed the view that even if a declaration is not binding in the same sense as a treaty, there is nevertheless a strong expectation that states will observe the principles endorsed.

This is not to say that all states do in fact observe the principles of the Declaration of Human Rights. South Africa has been most egregiously defiant of it in following a policy of *apartheid* and has provoked the condemnation of the General Assembly, the Security Council, and of a number of the specialized agencies. The Security Council declared in 1964 that the policies of *apartheid* are "contrary to the principles and purposes of the Charter of the United Nations and inconsistent with the provisions of the Universal Declaration of Human Rights." It reiterated earlier appeals to the government in Pretoria to liberate those detained because of opposition to *apartheid* and reaffirmed an earlier call upon all

---

[22] Arthur H. Robertson, *Human Rights in Europe* (Dobbs Ferry, N.Y., Oceana Publications, 1963). Cf., Egon Scwelb, "On the Operation of the European Convention on Human Rights," *International Organization,* Vol. 18 (Summer, 1964), pp. 558-585.

[23] Schwelb, *op. cit.,* pp. 73-74.

states to embargo the shipment to South Africa of arms and matériel. The Security Council, showing sufficient willingness to consider the imposition of economic sanctions, appointed a committee of experts to study their potential effectiveness and implications. France did not participate in the work of the committee of experts, asserting that the application of sanctions would constitute intervention in matters essentially within the domestic jurisdiction of South Africa. Delegates from the new states of Africa have been especially insistent on action against South Africa.

If the Declaration really has taken on a kind of quasi-obligatory character, the fact would be suggestive of international legislation—legislation in the enactment of which new states exert influence disproportionate to their power. They are appealing to principles that are at least intimated if not explicity endorsed in traditional liberalism and in the law or practice of the great powers of the West. The difference is that the intimations are now more fully revealed and emphasized, and all states, including the great powers, are asked to give fuller and more general application to principles that until recent times, even within the advanced countries, operated only in restricted and congenial ways. The great powers of the West cannot be entirely true to their own traditions and tendencies if they resist, and further, resistance might well be costly in terms of competition with Moscow and Peking for the world's respect and favor. There is some basis for the speculation that the Declaration "may yet come to be regarded as the Magna Carta of mankind." [24]

## THE VALUE OF INTERNATIONAL WELFARE ACTIVITIES

### Welfare for the Sake of Welfare

At the beginning of this chapter mention was made of the fact that international cooperation for the promotion of welfare occurs for a number of reasons. There is no doubt that the achievement of some of the objectives is being promoted. Certainly it is a convenience and an economic asset to have postal systems integrated and to have arrangements under which international transportation and communication are facilitated. Certainly a humanitarian interest is served when labor standards are improved, when agricultural and industrial production is increased in underdeveloped areas, and when health is promoted. It is generally assumed that the extension of education, science, and culture is good in itself. Very probably the long-run economic advantage both of the advanced and of the less developed countries is served by measures which

[24] C. W. Jenks, *Human Rights and International Labor Standards* (London, Stevens, 1960), pp. 13-14.

enhance the possibilities of future trade among them. The United Nations and the specialized agencies are promoting all these objectives. Some of the services performed are indispensable if a mode of living involving international exchange and interdependence is to be maintained.

## International Welfare Activities
### and National Political Objectives

The extent to which cooperative international welfare activities promote the achievement of objectives that are more definitely political is less certain. These objectives may be classified as "national" and "world-social."

The United States, for example, pursues certain national political objectives in supporting international welfare activities. It wants to do what it reasonably can to create and maintain a world environment compatible with its own interests. But it can and does seek to promote this objective through a national aid program. What considerations guide it in giving emphasis to one line of action or the other? Through which line of action is the greatest political advantage likely to be derived? On the one hand, a national program permits the allocation of aid among foreign countries in accordance with their political and strategic importance to the United States, and it permits the United States to gain the benefit of whatever good will is created. On the other hand, it would scarcely be compatible with support for the United Nations as an organization for the promotion of peace and security if support were denied to its activities in the economic and social realm. Moreover, the fact is that some countries are reluctant to receive aid directly from the United States for fear that it will lead to interference in their affairs or for fear that it will unduly identify them with the United States in the East–West struggle. If aid is to reach them, with the presumed result of reducing the appeals of Communism, use of an international agency as an intermediary is indicated.

These considerations do not lead to a clear-cut answer to the questions asked. There are political advantages and disadvantages in both national and world-social technical assistance programs, which perhaps suggests that both are to be supported for the advantages which they respectively offer.

## International Welfare Activities
### and the Development of a World Society

The world-social objectives which some expect international welfare activities to promote relate to the idea of functional integration and to the hope that enhanced well-being throughout the world will contribute to peace.

It is obvious, in the first place, that the development of a sense of membership in a unified world society is bound to be slow. There has been and there will be no sudden transformation of attitudes because it is possible to mail a letter to Yemen or to telephone a friend in Vienna. Nationalism, Communism, and other divisive forces constitute powerful obstructions to world unity, and, if they are overcome at all by the methods discussed in this chapter, it can only be by a very gradual process of erosion.

In the second place, cooperative international welfare activities are least extensive and effective where, from a world-social point of view, they are most needed. Communist China, whose population constitutes about a fifth of the human race, is not represented at all in the meetings of the United Nations and its specialized agencies. The Soviet Union is represented, of course, and relations between the West and Moscow have been improving, but still the improvement gives little basis for optimism concerning the peaceful emergence of a sense of membership in a united world society. Further, a different kind of cleavage has developed between the Republic of South Africa and other countries, especially the countries of Africa, over the issue of *apartheid.* If the developing countries constitute a "third world," as is sometimes said, then it could also be said that South Africa constitutes a fourth—a little world all to itself—in which it engages in racial policies that are profoundly objectionable to others. Whether the ostracism and other pressures now directed at South Africa will lead to changes giving it better standing in the world community remains to be seen.

In the third place, the problem of war is much more than a problem of educating people and making them healthy and prosperous. Educated, healthy, and prosperous people have often been engaged in war. To bring the peoples of the world up to the social, economic, and cultural standards that have long prevailed in Europe might simply equip them to fight more effectively and destructively, unless somehow the process is accompanied by the development of common attitudes and value patterns which involve stress on tolerance, unity, cooperation, and peace.

Considerations such as the above do not encourage optimism about the possibility that cooperative international welfare activities might create a peaceful world. However, it should be remembered that no other line of action seems promising enough to encourage optimism either. Certainly the direct attacks which have been made on the problem of assuring peace and security—whether in the name of the balance of power or in the name of collective security—have produced very meager results; where they have produced results, they have contributed more to the relative advantage of a few states than to the development of a unified world society. The problem of producing such a society is overwhelmingly difficult. This situation prevailing, even very slight contributions toward its solution are precious. Thus there is reason to emphasize cooperative international welfare activities, for they can be justified in the name of welfare alone, and they may, after all, have supplementary value.

In a period when the mechanisms hopefully devised for universal security are stalled by resurgent conflict, increased emphasis may with profit be placed upon social and humanitarian work. The welfare of the individual in society should be recognized as an end in itself and the purpose of all organization, national or international. But the direct effort to promote it may also prove the speediest road to general and enduring peace.[25]

## SUGGESTED READINGS

ASHER, Robert E., et al., The United Nations and the Promotion of the General Welfare (Washington, The Brookings Institution, 1957).

BALL, M. Margaret, "Issue for the Americas: Non-intervention v. Human Rights and the Preservation of Democratic Institutions," International Organization, Vol. 15 (Winter, 1961), pp. 21-37.

CODDING, George A., Jr., The Universal Postal Union (New York, New York University Press, 1964).

CORBETT, P. E., The Individual and World Society (Princeton, Center for Research on World Political Institutions, 1953).

CORDIER, Andrew W., and FOOTE, Wilder, eds., The Quest for Peace, The Dag Hammarskjöld Memorial Lectures (New York, Columbia University Press, 1965).

CRANSTON, Maurice, What Are Human Rights? (New York, Basic Books, 1962).

GARDNER, Richard N., In Pursuit of World Order, U.S. Foreign Policy and International Organizations (New York, Praeger, 1964).

GOODRICH, Leland M., The United Nations (New York, Crowell, 1959).

HAAS, Ernst B., Beyond the Nation-State, Functionalism and International Organization (Stanford, Stanford University Press, 1964).

HALLOWELL, John H., ed., Development: For What? (Durham, N.C., Duke University Press, 1964).

HAMBIDGE, Gove, ed., Dynamics of Development (New York, Praeger, 1964).

HOFFMAN, Paul G., World Without Want (New York, Harper & Row, 1962).

JACOBSON, Harold K., The USSR and the UN's Economic and Social Activities (Notre Dame, Ind., University of Notre Dame Press, 1963).

JENKS, C. W., Human Rights and International Labour Standards (London, Stevens, 1960).

LANGROD, Georges, The International Civil Service: Its Origins, Its Nature, Its Evolution (New York, Oceana, 1963).

McDOUGAL, Myres S., and BEBR, Gerhard, "Human Rights in the United Nations," American Journal of International Law, Vol. 58 (July, 1964), pp. 603-641.

MENON, M. A. K., "Universal Postal Union," International Conciliation, No. 552 (March, 1965).

25 Corbett, op. cit., p. 59.

ROBERTSON, A. H., *Human Rights in Europe* (Dobbs Ferry, N.Y., Oceana Publications, 1963).

RUBINSTEIN, Alvin Z., *The Soviets in International Organizations, Changing Policy Toward Developing Countries, 1953-1963* (Princeton, Princeton University Press, 1964).

SCHWELB, Egon, *Human Rights and the International Community* (Chicago, Quadrangle Books, 1964).

————, "On the Operation of the European Convention on Human Rights," *International Organization*, Vol. 18 (Summer, 1964), pp. 558-585.

SEGAL, Ronald, ed., *Sanctions Against South Africa* (Baltimore, Penguin Books, 1964).

SHUSTER, George N., *UNESCO: Assessment and Promise* (New York, Harper & Row, 1963).

UNITED NATIONS, Department of Economic and Social Affairs, Report of the Secretary-General, *The United Nations Development Decade, Proposals for Action* (New York, 1962).

UNITED NATIONS, Secretariat, Department of Social Affairs, *Yearbook on Human Rights,* 1946-.

UNITED NATIONS, The Technical Assistance Board, *The Expanded Programme of Technical Assistance for Economic Development of Under-Developed Countries* (New York, 1963).

*United Nations Yearbook,* 1946-47-.

*Yearbook of International Organizations,* 1948-.

# PROSPECTS FOR PEACE

*Part* IV

# 22

# THE PROSPECTS OF PEACE:
# A BALANCE SHEET

The analysis "Domestic Politics, Peace, and Civil War," in Chapter 2, indicated that government and attitudes are crucial in determining whether peace will prevail within countries or whether civil war will occur.

Governments, it was said, contribute to domestic peace in several ways. In the first place, they seek to establish and maintain power relationships within countries which are conducive to peace; specifically, they seek to establish and maintain police and military power that is overwhelming in relation to the physical power that could be mustered by any rebellious group. In the second place, they offer peaceful procedures—executive, legislative, and judicial—by which change can be brought about and by which what is regarded as justice can be achieved. In the third place, they maintain a system of law which tends to reinforce peace by providing a reasonably clear definition of rights and duties and by providing a basis for the development of a network of social relationships.

Certain types of attitudes were likewise found to contribute to peace within countries, the general proposition being that peace is more secure the more widely a set of fundamental attitudes is shared. In the first place, belief in the desirability of law and order, belief in peace, is important. There must be a desire for peace that is stronger than a desire for change which could be brought about only by violence. In the second place, a constitutional consensus is important, reflecting generally accepted fundamental rules and principles in accordance with which social and political life should proceed. In the third place, it is helpful if there is a feeling of membership in a society whose good transcends the good of individuals and groups within it—a belief that in some circumstances it is proper to require individuals and groups within the society to undertake risks and make sacrifices for the good of the whole. Finally, loyalty to the state, a loyalty superseding other loyalties in the event of conflict, contributes to domestic peace.

It is difficult to say whether government or attitudes are more important as bases of peace. Theoretically, either one might suffice at least for a time. Governments might be able to maintain peace within countries even though supporting attitudes were weak or held only by a small portion of the population. Similarly, a common set of shared attitudes might provide a basis of peace among members of large groups, even in the absence of government. Peace, however, is most secure when government and attitudes reinforce each other.

Likewise it is difficult to say which comes first in the development of a peaceful society. There is an interaction, governments seeking to foster the general acceptance of certain common attitudes, and the existence of common attitudes helping to make it possible for governments to exist.

The argument in both Chapters 1 and 2 was that within countries the strong rule. Politics is not a process which is always carried on in a spirit of harmony and cooperation; conflict is an inevitable element in it. Various methods are used in the political struggle within countries, and various tests serve to measure strength and allocate the right to rule. The ultimate test is violence—civil war. Those who win in civil war secure control of government and therefore the right to say what the law shall be. The generalization was made that law within countries commonly reflects the desires of the strong.

Presumably the conditions of peace among countries are similar to the conditions of peace among individuals and groups within countries. In Parts II and III we have, in effect, been asking to what extent those conditions exist in the international field. Now the purpose is to engage in a summary and stock-taking, and to inquire into the prospects of bringing about organizational and attitudinal changes in the world which might render peace more secure than it in fact is.

## THE PROBLEM OF GOVERNMENT
## FOR THE WORLD

A book on international politics was scarcely required to demonstrate the fact that the world is controlled by many governments, not by one. Rather than being concentrated overwhelmingly in central hands, power is dispersed over the world among sovereign states, all of which are potential rebels, potential aggressors. Throughout history international politics, like domestic politics, has involved a power struggle, but the international power struggle has not been mitigated, regulated, and rendered peaceful in anything near the same degree as the power struggle within most states. Naked violence has been much more prominent.

The substitutes which have been developed for world government are pallid and weak. During most of modern history, there has been nothing remotely resembling an international executive—no central agency for administering and enforcing law. States and alliances of states have relied upon their own power to enforce portions of the law of interest to them. The system has been one of self-help. Since World War I, some change has occurred, but it is mild and halting. The victors of World War I attempted to modify the system by creating the League of Nations, only to allow it to fail. The victors of World War II then established the United Nations. In it, the Security Council, which might be a kind of international executive, is bound by voting rules that make it quite unreliable. The General Assembly can recommend all sorts of measures, including measures of an executive sort, but has no formal executive authority; still, it can give a blessing to states that wish to act on behalf of law and order—whether in their own interest or in the general interest. Within the Western Hemisphere, the Organization of the American States can play a comparable role in lending its name to executive-type actions by one or more of its members. International executive authority thus shows some signs of appearing, but it is still very limited and is likely to remain so for the visible future.

During most of modern history the international legislative process has operated without a legislature. Law could be developed and changed only with the explicit or tacit consent of the states to which it applied, given voluntarily or under all sorts of coercive pressures, including war. The United Nations has modified the methods of making and changing law even less than it has the methods of enforcing it. It incorporates the old devices of mediation and conciliation, and the General Assembly may make such recommendations as it pleases. Peaceful change in the law may follow, but only if the affected states consent, and the consent of the adversely affected is rarely given.

During the same period, also, the international judicial process has operated without a judiciary. States involved in legal disputes might somehow reach agreement by negotiation, or by resort to *ad hoc* arbitral tribunals. Since World War I an international court has existed (now named the International Court of Justice); as we have seen, advance consent gives it some compulsory jurisdiction, but in the main the Court can decide a dispute only if the parties at the time consent.

Since World War I states have agreed in various documents, most notably in the United Nations Charter, to restrict themselves to peaceful methods of pursuing their needs and wants. But the agreements have been unreliable, and it was predictable that they would be. Peace is not maintained within countries simply through an exchange of promises not to go to war, and there is no hope of maintaining it throughout the world by this means.

In the world as a whole, as within countries, the strong are to be expected to demand that the law reflect their desires. The development of
conditions and procedures by which they can achieve this peacefully has
been a slow process within countries, and it is probably a never-ending
one. Some countries have been far from successful, as the occurrence and
the threats of civil war attest. Internationally the process has barely begun. Though there has been some erosion of the unanimity rule, there
is nothing comparable to the elections staged in democratic countries as
measurements of strength and therefore as methods of allocating law-
making and law-enforcing authority. For that matter, there is no agreement on a set of constitutional powers and limitations within which the
strong could exercise such authority even if they could be peacefully identified. The established test of strength and therefore of the "right" to
shape law is military power and war.

## THE PROBLEM OF ATTITUDES

Just as the world is poorly organized for peace, so are prevailing attitudes poorly shaped. Over the world there has not existed in the past,
and there does not exist today, a desire for peace which is stronger than
a desire for change. Periodically, one state or another has wanted change
with sufficient urgency to feel justified in resorting to violence to get it,
and it is to be expected that adamant demands for change will continue
to be made, now by this state and now by that. Such demands are more
likely to be deterred by a belief that the risks and costs of pressing them
are too great (i.e., by a belief that power relationships are unfavorable)
than by dedication to peace. The threat of nuclear warfare may be especially effective as a deterrent. Yet, even within countries, where governments exist which attempt to preserve a preponderance of violence, it
has often proved impossible to maintain such a deterrent, and the difficulties of doing it are much greater in a world of sovereign states. It
takes only one aggressive government to plunge others—perhaps all the
rest of the world—into war.

A constitutional consensus exists among some states, just as a strong
desire for peace exists within some. Among those states which share a
constitutional consensus, peace has a good chance of prevailing. The
United States and Canada share such a consensus, as do Norway and
Sweden; there are other such combinations of states as well. It is difficult
to say just what elements must be included in a constitutional consensus
to provide a basis for peace. Presumably there must be substantial agreement among the states involved in defining their respective rights and
interests; some interests must be shared, and those which are not shared
(particularly if they are regarded as vital) must at least be compatible.
Given agreement in defining rights and interests, there must be mutual

respect for them. Agreement on interests would presumably include agreement concerning objectives to be pursued and the methods to be adopted in pursuing them. There must be tolerance of some degree of diversity, and there must be no thought of settling such disputes as arise by anything other than peaceful means.

Although such elements of consensus exist among restricted groups of states, there is no one consensus for the world as a whole, as the record of international tension and war demonstrates. Attitudes frequently differ on questions pertaining to legal rights and obligations, and on the importance of paying attention to law. They differ on the location of boundary lines, on the question of reuniting divided states, on the question of what constitutes intervention, on the question of the tests of self-determination, and on a myriad of other questions. Conflicting aspirations are pursued, and even where objectives are agreed to, there may be differences over the choice of method in striving to achieve them. Prestige and power, so widely sought, are values which can be obtained only at the relative expense of others. Communists want a world of Communists, and liberals want a world of liberals. So many conflicts of important and vital interests exist that threats of war are regularly present in one area or another, and somewhere in the world war is usually being fought. The expectation of war leads to additional tensions and conflicts, as states try to maintain or improve their relative power positions. The absence of a world constitutional consensus means that the world lacks an important basis of peace.

Within countries, we have seen, people are expected to regard themselves as members of a society whose good transcends the good of individual parts. They are expected to make sacrifices, voluntarily or on demand, for the good of the society, including the risk of life itself. For the world as a whole, such expectations are weak, if they exist at all. Individuals may have a vague feeling that they belong to something called the human race, and they may feel some affinity to mankind. Both privately and through governments they sometimes respond to charitable impulses to help those in distress and to uplift the benighted. Statesmen, as we have seen, frequently justify policies they pursue in the name of universal values, and they speak of duties to mankind. Still, when help is given to those beyond the borders of the state, it is given to people who are regarded as foreign, rather than to people who are regarded as comembers of one society; when help is received across political boundaries, it is received from foreigners. The sense of disunity, reflecting differences in culture, in value patterns, and in social and political organization, seems to be much stronger than any sense of unity. It is even doubtful whether a world society can be said to exist.

There is even less sign of anything that could be called world loyalty than there is of a sense of membership in a world society. Literally none of the forces and conditions which give rise to loyalty to states and lesser groups operate significantly to produce world loyalty. The closest approximation occurs in connection with the United Nations, to which some small degree of loyalty may have developed because of the hope that it would serve effectively as a means of preserving peace. Such loyalty as the United Nations has aroused may or may not be maintained, depending on attitudes toward its utility.

Thus the principal generalization which can be made is that the attitudinal basis for peace over the world as a whole is very weak.

Persistence of this situation is not necessarily inevitable. Theoretically it is possible to develop in all men attitudes that would provide a basis for peace. This is so because attitudes are not congenital but socially and culturally determined. They develop through the learning process. They result from communications of some kind reaching individuals after their birth. This is true of loyalty as well as of other attitudes. If the right things were communicated—if the learning process were properly controlled—all mankind could be led to adopt attitudes conducive to peace. Hope of this is implicit in the constitution of UNESCO which, as we have seen, assumes that wars begin in the minds of men and that it is in those minds that the defenses of peace must be constructed.

However, results which are theoretically possible are often difficult to achieve in practice, and this is true above all with the problem of changing attitudes. Who would decide which attitudes to sponsor? Could the Soviet Union and the United States agree in selecting them? Would other states agree? It seems virtually out of the question. Nationalists would have to cease being nationalists, and Communists would have to cease being Communists (or at least the adherents of these and other ideologies would have to accept severe modifications of them) if agreement on the attitudes essential to peace were to be reached. Governments would have to risk and perhaps accept subversion. Notions of the sources of prestige and glory, or of the importance of these values, would have to be changed. The obstacles to agreement are formidable. Again, even if agreement could be reached on the nature of the attitudes to be sponsored, who would sponsor them, and how? What chance is there that all people throughout the world whose attitudes are important to peace could be reached and induced to accept attitudes somehow agreed upon? Even if totalitarian controls governed an indoctrination process, it is doubtful whether success could be achieved, and such controls would be unacceptable to significant portions of mankind in any event. The development of appropriate attitudes in free and thinking minds, which would probably be essential to a stable peace, would require a very long time, tremendous effort, and unwonted cooperation among many governments and vast numbers of people.

## SECURITY-COMMUNITY

The concept of the security-community has been suggested in connection with the problem of war and peace.

A security-community is considered to be a group which has become integrated, where integration is defined as the attainment of a sense of community, accompanied by formal or informal institutions or practices, sufficiently strong and widespread to assure peaceful change among members of a group with "reasonable" certainty over a "long" period of time.[1]

Security-communities are described as amalgamated or pluralistic. The United States is an amalgamated security-community, having come into existence as a single entity under one government through the merger of formerly independent entities. The United States and Canada together comprise a pluralistic security-community, pluralistic because they are under separate governments.

The fact that security-communities have somehow come into existence in the past suggests that the process is one which might be repeated and extended. States which are not now security-communities might be integrated so as to constitute one, or existing security-communities might be expanded through the addition of other states. The thought is that the development of security-communities would at least solve the problem of war among the members, and that if one security-community could come to encompass most or all of the world the problem of war would be solved for mankind.

The process and the possibility have already been discussed, though the term *security-community* has not appeared. The problems involved have been shown to be tremendous. A further point might be added. It is that the problem of developing a series of security-communities is no doubt much less difficult than the problem of expanding one such community over most or all of the world. This is demonstrated by the very fact that some security-communities, each including a few states, have come into existence, whereas obviously none has spread over the world. Various factors which we have already discussed, to be described collectively as common interests, have repeatedly brought a few states into stable and peaceful relationships with each other. Many alliances are among states which constitute a security-community. Yet, just as alliances tend to produce counteralliances, so is it likely that security-communities would tend to produce rivals. Even if the whole world were organized in a series of security-communities, the likelihood is that at least one of them would

[1] Richard W. Van Wagenen, *Research in the International Organization Field, Some Notes on a Possible Focus* (Princeton, Center for Research on World Political Institutions, 1952), pp. 10-11.

define its interests in such a way as to create friction and a danger of war with others. Consensus among such diverse alignments of states as those in the North Atlantic Treaty Organization and those in the Communist world seems remote.

## WORLD FEDERALISM

Plans for joining sovereign states in some kind of international organization which would to some degree substitute for world government have been proposed throughout the centuries. The League of Nations was, and the United Nations is, such an organization. A number of proposals have been made to go beyond them in the establishment of international or world government. Such plans usually contemplate a federal structure. Some are "partialist," in that they call for a plan including only a part of the states of the world in the structure; others are "universalist." Some are "minimalist," in that they would assign few powers to the federal government; others are "maximalist." Since World War II the United World Federalists have been the most prominent advocates of world government in the United States. Their plan is universalist, and once their world federation is organized they would deny a right of secession. At least in the early phases of its operation, their plan is also minimalist. They start with the UN Charter, seeking action under it and amendments to it, emphasizing universal and complete disarmament, judicial settlement, and "an adequate armed peace force." They would eliminate the veto in the Security Council, and make it "responsible" to the General Assembly. In the latter body they would abandon the one-member-one-vote formula and adopt a formula that is "more just and realistic." Understandably, the many elements of the program are left vague. Overlapping the movement for world federation is a movement for "peace through law."

For the foreseeable future, plans for world federation or world government have no chance of adoption. Reasons for this conclusion have been presented, implicitly or explicitly, throughout this book. Several of the most important deserve emphasis.

In the first place, the minimum essential attitudinal basis does not exist and seems unlikely to be created for a long time to come.

In the second place, no acceptable and feasible solution has been found to the problem of allocating votes (or, more generally, shares of control over decisions). The authority of a world government would have to be exercised in conformity with the desires of the strong, just as within countries. One of the assumptions on which democracy rests, that men are equally strong and therefore entitled to equal voting power, is not acceptable on a world scale. People in the more advanced and powerful countries, extending through the geographic region from the Soviet

Union to the United States, would not accept a distribution of votes in proportion to population; they would not believe that India should have more than double the voting strength of the United States, or Indonesia double the voting strength of Britain or France. To give each state one vote would be even more absurd, since states vary so greatly in strength. If either of these "solutions" could somehow be adopted, it would almost inevitably break down, for those with a majority of the votes would not control a preponderance of power. An apportionment of votes according to the distribution of military strength has much to commend it, but it involves many difficulties; among them is the probability that the principle would not be acceptable to weaker peoples and the fact that it provides no basis for reapportionment in the period following the hoped-for disarmament of the units in the system.

In the third place, it is very difficult to internationalize power or to transfer it to a world federal structure. Many elements of power (plants for producing nuclear fuel, for example) are geographically fixed, and the units and weapons of any armed establishment must be geographically located. States within a world federal structure would necessarily retain some power, actual and potential, power of their own and power ostensibly under the command of the federal government but subject to seizure. Closely related is the fact that potential rebels against the world federation would not be geographically interspersed with supporters of the federation. Within countries, potential rebels are usually interspersed with other elements of the population and lack a geographical base for preparing their rebellion. Within a world federation, each unit would not only command some power inevitably but would also have a definite geographic base as a staging area for revolutionary operations.

The final obstacle to world federation which we shall name is

. . . the unwillingness of governments and peoples to abandon their means of self-defense until they are certain that a world federation can protect them, and the certainty that a world federation cannot protect them until the most powerful have abandoned these means.[2]

The same dilemma has been described in other words.

The status of the international community calls to mind the two trains which met at a crossing where neither would proceed until the other had passed. No state can give up its power of self-defense, or the right to decide when it shall be used, until almost every other state has done the same.[3]

The first three of the obstacles named above combine with other considerations to suggest an additional point: that even world federation or world government, if it could be achieved, would not necessarily keep

[2] Quincy Wright, *Problems of Stability and Progress in International Relations* (Berkeley, University of California Press, 1954), p. 235.
[3] Van Wagenen, *op. cit.*, p. 17.

the peace. After all, civil wars occur within countries despite the existence of government. Nor is peace necessarily to be obtained through law,
any more than it is within countries. Just as individuals and groups defy
government and law in domestic political systems, so might they in a
world political system. The problem of peace is complex; its solution
contains many elements. We described them in a succinct way in Chapter 2 and have been talking about them throughout the book. A constitutional consensus is what is needed, and the consensus has to provide
for much more than simply disarmament or law or even governmental
structure, and more than all three of these combined. In fact, other elements of consensus—if they can be developed in full enough measure—
may go very far toward assuring peace even in the absence of these three.
Among some countries, they have done so already. But among others
they obviously have not.

## CRISIS

Clearly the peoples and governments of the world today face a crisis.
Comfort may be derived from the fact that they have pretty regularly
faced crises throughout history, yet somehow have survived, but today's
crisis seems to be of a different order of magnitude from any which have
been faced before.

In varying degrees sovereign states perform useful functions. They
provide a stable order for large groups of people over the world, and
within the framework of the stable order they provide for peaceful
change. They afford protection for life and property. They permit and
stimulate educational, scientific, and cultural pursuits, and the development of systems of production and distribution. If by some evil incanta-
tion the sovereign state and its agent, government, could somehow be
destroyed and if no substitute were provided (i.e., if complete anarchy
could be brought into existence), unimaginable damage would be done.

In rough measure the division of the world into sovereign states reflects actual diversities among men. Men differ in the languages they
speak, the religions they profess, the aspirations which they pursue, the
skills which they have acquired, the social customs which they follow,
the ideologies to which they adhere, the loyalties which they develop,
and in a multitude of other ways. They have differing and often conflicting values. On many fundamental questions they hold attitudes which
sharply clash. Even within many states differences and conflicts are so
great and fundamental that stability and order are difficult to maintain;
civil wars occur. Among many states, though not between all of them, the
differences and conflicts are still greater. The system of sovereign states
is to a considerable degree adapted to the diversities among men, per-

mitting different societies to be governed more or less in accordance with the characteristics which are peculiar to them.

At the same time, although sovereign states perform useful and important functions within their own territory, it is obvious that for the world as a whole the system of sovereign states fails to provide adequately for stability, order, and individual welfare. In a multitude of ways the things done by men in one state affect men in other states. Many aspirations can be pursued only through cooperation or conflict with people abroad. And the system of sovereign states does not lend itself to the development of the kinds of attitudes and organizational arrangements that maximize the prospects of peace.

The statement was just made that comfort might be taken from the fact that men have survived crises in the past. The statement should be qualified by recognizing that some states, and even some civilizations, have not survived. A number have perished, and prominent among the reasons has been the inadequacy of interstate arrangements for stability, order, and peaceful change. "The failure to solve the problem of war has been the death of most civilizations that have died since civilizations first came into existence." [4]

The great powers of today, and the civilizations which they help maintain, face greater danger of cataclysmic destruction than have any of the states or civilizations which have perished in the past. For the first time in history, the possibility exists that war may bring death to people by the hundreds of millions, if not to all mankind. Although science and technology have produced a revolutionary increase in the dangers men face, the methods which men have been willing to adopt to ward off the dangers have improved relatively little for decades and centuries. Better methods are known, but prevailing attitudes make them unacceptable and would probably doom them to failure even if an attempt could somehow be made to use them.

Though a crisis exists for which no acceptable solution is in sight, the prospects are not necessarily hopeless. There have been prolonged periods of substantial peace in the past (witness the century from 1815 to 1914), which suggests that they are possible in the future even if no major change in the political structure of the world occurs. When war comes, as it undoubtedly sometime will, it is not to be assumed that it will necessarily involve the unrestricted use of nuclear weapons or other weapons of mass destruction. The longer utter catastrophe can be postponed, the greater is the possibility that attitudes can be shaped over the world in such a way as to make the postponement indefinite. Moreover, though the prospect now seems remote, changing attitudes plus creative imagina-

[4] Arnold J. Toynbee, as quoted by Kenneth W. Thompson, "Mr. Toynbee and World Politics: War and National Security," *World Politics*, Vol. 8 (April, 1956), p. 383.

tion may yet lead to the development of some kind of a world political system which will provide for both stability and change.

More somber possibilities also exist. Surely very drastic changes will occur if major powers engage in unrestricted nuclear warfare. If one side should succeed in laying waste the other while remaining relatively unscathed itself, it might conceivably unite the world politically through the threat of its power; men who are unwilling to agree to something akin to world government might find themselves included in a world empire dominated by the victor. If the belligerents succeed in laying each other waste without destroying all human life, leadership in what is left of the world may well be transferred to peoples now on the periphery of the power struggle, to peoples who are now too weak or backward or uncivilized to take part in suicidal war.

## SUGGESTED READINGS

CLAUDE, Inis L., Jr., *Power and International Relations* (New York, Random House, 1962).

DEUTSCH, Karl W., *et al.*, *The Integration of Political Communities* (Philadelphia, Lippincott, 1964).

————, *Political Community at the International Level, Problems of Definition and Measurement* (Garden City, N.Y., Doubleday, 1954).

GUETZKOW, Harold, *Multiple Loyalties: Theoretical Approach to a Problem in International Organization* (Princeton, Center for Research on World Political Institutions, 1955).

KAPLAN, Morton A., ed., *The Revolution in World Politics* (New York, Wiley, 1962).

MANNING, Charles A. W., *The Nature of International Society* (New York, Wiley, 1962).

PLISCHKE, Elmer, ed., *Systems of Integrating the International Community* (Princeton, Van Nostrand, 1964).

VAN WAGENEN, Richard W., *Research in the International Organization Field, Some Notes on a Possible Focus* (Princeton, Center for Research on World Political Institutions, 1952).

WALTZ, Kenneth N., *Man, the State, and War: A Theoretical Analysis* (New York, Columbia University Press, 1959).

# INTERNATIONAL
# DOCUMENTS

APPENDIX

# CHARTER OF
# THE UNITED NATIONS

*WE THE PEOPLES*
*OF THE UNITED NATIONS*
*DETERMINED*

to save succeeding generations from the scourge of war, which twice in our lifetime has brought untold sorrow to mankind, and

to reaffirm faith in fundamental human rights, in the dignity and worth of the human person, in the equal rights of men and women and of nations large and small, and

to establish conditions under which justice and respect for the obligations arising from treaties and other sources of international law can be maintained, and

to promote social progress and better standards of life in larger freedom,

*AND FOR THESE ENDS*

to practice tolerance and live together in peace with one another as good neighbors, and

to unite our strength to maintain international peace and security, and

to ensure, by the acceptance of principles and the institution of methods, that armed force shall not be used, save in the common interest, and

to employ international machinery for the promotion of the economic and social advancement of all peoples,

*HAVE RESOLVED TO*
*COMBINE OUR EFFORTS TO*
*ACCOMPLISH THESE AIMS.*

Accordingly, our respective Governments, through representatives assembled in the city of San Francisco, who have exhibited their full powers found to be in good and due form, have agreed to the present Charter of the United Nations and do hereby establish an international organization to be known as the United Nations.

467

CHAPTER I

## PURPOSES AND PRINCIPLES

*Article 1*

The Purposes of the United Nations are:

1.  To maintain international peace and security, and to that end: to take effective collective measures for the prevention and removal of threats to the peace, and for the suppression of acts of aggression or other breaches of the peace, and to bring about by peaceful means, and in conformity with the principles of justice and international law, adjustments or settlement of international disputes or situations which might lead to a breach of the peace;

2.  To develop friendly relations among nations based on respect for the principle of equal rights and self-determination of peoples, and to take other appropriate measures to strengthen universal peace;

3.  To achieve international cooperation in solving international problems of an economic, social, cultural, or humanitarian character, and in promoting and encouraging respect for human rights and for fundamental freedoms for all without distinction as to race, sex, language, or religion; and

4.  To be a center for harmonizing the actions of nations in the attainment of these common ends.

*Article 2*

The Organization and its Members, in pursuit of these Purposes stated in Article 1, shall act in accordance with the following Principles.

1.  The Organization is based on the principle of the sovereign equality of all its Members.

2.  All Members, in order to ensure to all of them the rights and benefits resulting from membership, shall fulfil in good faith the obligations assumed by them in accordance with the present Charter.

3.  All Members shall settle their international disputes by peaceful means in such a manner that international peace and security, and justice, are not endangered.

4.  All Members shall refrain in their international relations from the threat or use of force against the territorial integrity or political independence of any state, or in any other manner inconsistent with the Purposes of the United Nations.

5.  All Members shall give the United Nations every assistance in any action it takes in accordance with the present Charter, and shall refrain from giving assistance to any state against which the United Nations is taking preventive or enforcement action.

6.  The Organization shall ensure that states which are not Members of the United Nations act in accordance with these Principles so far as may be necessary for the maintenance of international peace and security.

7.  Nothing contained in the present Charter shall authorize the United

Nations to intervene in matters which are essentially within the domestic jurisdiction of any state or shall require the Members to submit such matters to
settlement under the present Charter; but this principle shall not prejudice the
application of enforcement measures under Chapter VII.

## CHAPTER II

## MEMBERSHIP

### Article 3

The original Members of the United Nations shall be the states which, having
participated in the United Nations Conference on International Organization
at San Francisco, or having previously signed the Declaration by United Nations
of January 1, 1942, sign the present Charter and ratify it in accordance with
Article 110.

### Article 4

1. Membership in the United Nations is open to all other peace-loving states
which accept the obligations contained in the present Charter and, in the judgment of the Organization, are able and willing to carry out these obligations.

2. The admission of any such state to membership in the United Nations
will be effected by a decision of the General Assembly upon the recommendation of the Security Council.

### Article 5

A member of the United Nations against which preventive or enforcement
action has been taken by the Security Council may be suspended from the
exercise of the rights and privileges of membership by the General Assembly
upon the recommendation of the Security Council. The exercise of these rights
and privileges may be restored by the Security Council.

### Article 6

A Member of the United Nations which has persistently violated the Principles contained in the present Charter may be expelled from the Organization
by the General Assembly upon the recommendation of the Security Council.

## CHAPTER III

## ORGANS

### Article 7

1. There are established as the principal organs of the United Nations; a
General Assembly, a Security Council, an Economic and Social Council, a Trusteeship Council, an International Court of Justice, and a Secretariat.

2. Such subsidiary organs as may be found necessary may be established in
accordance with the present Charter.

### Article 8

The United Nations shall place no restrictions on the eligibility of men and
women to participate in any capacity and under conditions of equality in its
principal and subsidiary organs.

## CHAPTER IV

## THE GENERAL ASSEMBLY

*Composition*

### Article 9

1. The General Assembly shall consist of all the Members of the United Nations.

2. Each Member shall have not more than five representatives in the General Assembly.

*Functions and Powers*

### Article 10

The General Assembly may discuss any questions or any matters within the scope of the present Charter or relating to the powers and functions of any organs provided for in the present Charter, and, except as provided in Article 12, may make recommendations to the Members of the United Nations or to the Security Council or to both on any such questions or matters.

### Article 11

1. The General Assembly may consider the general principles of cooperation in the maintenance of international peace and security, including the principles governing disarmament and the regulation of armaments, and may make recommendations with regard to such principles to the Members or to the Security Council or to both.

2. The General Assembly may discuss any questions relating to the maintenance of international peace and security brought before it by any Member of the United Nations, or by the Security Council, or by a state which is not a Member of the United Nations in accordance with Article 35, paragraph 2, and, except as provided in Article 12, may make recommendations with regard to any such question to the state or states concerned or to the Security Council or to both. Any such question on which action is necessary shall be referred to the Security Council by the General Assembly either before or after discussion.

3. The General Assembly may call the attention of the Security Council to situations which are likely to endanger international peace and security.

4. The powers of the General Assembly set forth in this Article shall not limit the general scope of Article 10.

### Article 12

1. While the Security Council is exercising in respect to any dispute or situation the functions assigned to it in the present Charter, the General Assembly shall not make any recommendations with regard to that dispute or situation unless the Security Council so requests.

2. The Secretary-General, with the consent of the Security Council, shall notify the General Assembly at each session of any matters relative to the maintenance of international peace and security which are being dealt with by the Security Council and shall similarly notify the General Assembly, or the Members of the United Nations if the General Assembly is not in session, immediately the Security Council ceases to deal with such matters.

## *Article 13*

1. The General Assembly shall initiate studies and make recommendations for the purpose of:

    a. promoting international cooperation in the political field and encouraging the progressive development of international law and its codification;

    b. promoting international cooperation in the economic, social, cultural, educational, and health fields, and assisting in the realization of human rights and fundamental freedoms for all without distinction as to race, sex, language, or religion.

2. The further responsibilities, functions and powers of the General Assembly with respect to matters mentioned in paragraph 1(b) above are set forth in Chapters IX and X.

## *Article 14*

Subject to the provisions of Article 12, the General Assembly may recommend measures for the peaceful adjustment of any situation, regardless of origin, which it deems likely to impair the general welfare or friendly relations among nations, including situations resulting from a violation of the provisions of the present Charter setting forth the Purposes and Principles of the United Nations.

## *Article 15*

1. The General Assembly shall receive and consider annual and special reports from the Security Council; these reports shall include an account of the measures that the Security Council has decided upon or taken to maintain international peace and security.

2. The General Assembly shall receive and consider reports from the other organs of the United Nations.

## *Article 16*

The General Assembly shall perform such functions with respect to the international trusteeship system as are assigned to it under Chapters XII and XIII, including the approval of the trusteeship agreements for areas not designated as strategic.

## *Article 17*

1. The General Assembly shall consider and approve the budget of the Organization.

2. The expenses of the Organization shall be borne by the Members as apportioned by the General Assembly.

3. The General Assembly shall consider and approve any financial and budgetary arrangements with specialized agencies referred to in Article 57 and shall examine the administrative budgets of such specialized agencies with a view to making recommendations to the agencies concerned.

*Voting*

## *Article 18*

1. Each member of the General Assembly shall have one vote.

2. Decisions of the General Assembly on important questions shall be made by a two-thirds majority of the members present and voting. These questions

shall include: recommendations with respect to the maintenance of international peace and security, the election of the non-permanent members of the Security Council, the election of the members of the Economic and Social Council, the election of members of the Trusteeship Council in accordance with paragraph 1(c) of Article 86, the admission of new Members to the United Nations, the suspension of the rights and privileges of membership, the expulsion of Members, questions relating to the operation of the trusteeship system, and budgetary questions.

3.  Decisions on other questions, including the determination of additional categories of questions to be decided by a two-thirds majority, shall be made by a majority of the members present and voting.

### Article 19

A Member of the United Nations which is in arrears in the payment of its financial contributions to the Organization shall have no vote in the General Assembly if the amount of its arrears equals or exceeds the amount of the contributions due from it for the preceding two full years. The General Assembly may, nevertheless, permit such a Member to vote if it is satisfied that the failure to pay is due to conditions beyond the control of the Member.

*Procedure*

### Article 20

The General Assembly shall meet in regular annual sessions and in such special sessions as occasion may require. Special sessions shall be convoked by the Secretary-General at the request of the Security Council or of a majority of the Members of the United Nations.

### Article 21

The General Assembly shall adopt its own rules of procedure. It shall elect its President for each session.

### Article 22

The General Assembly may establish such subsidiary organs as it deems necessary for the performance of its functions.

### Chapter V

## THE SECURITY COUNCIL

*Composition*

### Article 23 (As amended)

1.  The Security Council shall consist of fifteen [originally eleven] Members of the United Nations. The Republic of China, France, the Union of Soviet Socialist Republics, the United Kingdom of Great Britain and Northern Ireland, and the United States of America shall be permanent members of the Security Council. The General Assembly shall elect ten [originally six] other Members of the United Nations to be non-permanent members of the Security Council, due regard being specially paid, in the first instance to the contribution of Members of the United Nations to the maintenance of international peace and security and to the other purposes of the Organization, and also to equitable geographical distribution.

2.  The non-permanent members of the Security Council shall be elected

for a term of two years. In the first election of the non-permanent members after the increase of the membership of the Security Council from eleven to fifteen, two of the four additional members shall be chosen for a term of one year. A retiring member shall not be eligible for immediate re-election.

3. Each member of the Security Council shall have one representative.

*Functions and Powers*

### Article 24

1. In order to ensure prompt and effective action by the United Nations, its Members confer on the Security Council primary responsibility for the maintenance of international peace and security, and agree that in carrying out its duties under this responsibility the Security Council acts on their behalf.

2. In discharging these duties the Security Council shall act in accordance with the Purposes and Principles of the United Nations. The specific powers granted to the Security Council for the discharge of these duties are laid down in Chapters VI, VII, VIII, and XII.

3. The Security Council shall submit annual and, when necessary, special reports to the General Assembly for its consideration.

### Article 25

The Members of the United Nations agree to accept and carry out the decisions of the Security Council in accordance with the present Charter.

### Article 26

In order to promote the establishment and maintenance of international peace and security with the least diversion for armaments of the world's human and economic resources, the Security Council shall be responsible for formulating, with the assistance of the Military Staff Committee referred to in Article 47, plans to be submitted to the Members of the United Nations for the establishment of a system for the regulation of armaments.

*Voting*

### Article 27 (As amended)

1. Each member of the Security Council shall have one vote.

2. Decisions of the Security Council on procedural matters shall be made by an affirmative vote of nine [originally seven] members.

3. Decisions of the Security Council on all other matters shall be made by an affirmative vote of nine [originally seven] members including the concurring votes of the permanent members; provided that, in decisions under Chapter VI, and under paragraph 3 of Article 52, a party to a dispute shall abstain from voting.

*Procedure*

### Article 28

1. The Security Council shall be so organized as to be able to function continuously. Each member of the Security Council shall for this purpose be represented at all times at the seat of the Organization.

2. The Security Council shall hold periodic meetings at which each of its members may, if it so desires, be represented by a member of the government or by some other specially designated representative.

3. The Security Council may hold meetings at such places other than the seat of the Organization as in its judgment will best facilitate its work.

### Article 29

The Security Council may establish such subsidiary organs as it deems necessary for the performance of its functions.

### Article 30

The Security Council shall adopt its own rules of procedure, including the method of selecting its President.

### Article 31

Any Member of the United Nations which is not a member of the Security Council may participate, without vote, in the discussion of any question brought before the Security Council whenever the latter considers that the interests of that Member are specially affected.

### Article 32

Any Member of the United Nations which is not a member of the Security Council or any state which is not a Member of the United Nations, if it is a party to a dispute under consideration by the Security Council, shall be invited to participate, without vote, in the discussion relating to the dispute. The Security Council shall lay down such conditions as it deems just for the participation of a state which is not a Member of the United Nations.

## CHAPTER VI
## PACIFIC SETTLEMENT OF DISPUTES
### Article 33

1. The parties to any dispute, the continuance of which is likely to endanger the maintenance of international peace and security, shall, first of all, seek a solution by negotiation, enquiry, mediation, conciliation, arbitration, judicial settlement, resort to regional agencies or arrangements, or other peaceful means of their own choice.

2. The Security Council shall, when it deems necessary, call upon the parties to settle their dispute by such means.

### Article 34

The Security Council may investigate any dispute, or any situation which might lead to international friction or give rise to a dispute, in order to determine whether the continuance of the dispute or situation is likely to endanger the maintenance of international peace and security.

### Article 35

1. Any Member of the United Nations may bring any dispute, or any situation of the nature referred to in Article 34, to the attention of the Security Council or of the General Assembly.

2. A state which is not a Member of the United Nations may bring to the attention of the Security Council or of the General Assembly any dispute to which it is a party if it accepts in advance, for the purposes of the dispute, the obligations of pacific settlement provided in the present Charter.

3. The proceedings of the General Assembly in respect of matters brought to its attention under this Article will be subject to the provisions of Articles 11 and 12.

### Article 36

1. The Security Council may, at any stage of a dispute of the nature referred to in Article 33 or of a situation of like nature, recommend appropriate procedures or methods of adjustment.

2. The Security Council should take into consideration any procedures for the settlement of the dispute which have already been adopted by the parties.

3. In making recommendations under this Article the Security Council should also take into consideration that legal disputes should as a general rule be referred by the parties to the International Court of Justice in accordance with the provisions of the Statute of the Court.

### Article 37

1. Should the parties to a dispute of the nature referred to in Article 33 fail to settle it by the means indicated in that Article, they shall refer it to the Security Council.

2. If the Security Council deems that the continuance of the dispute is in fact likely to endanger the maintenance of international peace and security, it shall decide whether to take action under Article 36 or to recommend such terms of settlement as it may consider appropriate.

### Article 38

Without prejudice to the provisions of Articles 33 to 37, the Security Council may, if all the parties to any dispute so request, make recommendations to the parties with a view to a pacific settlement of the dispute.

## CHAPTER VII

### ACTION WITH RESPECT TO THREATS TO THE PEACE, BREACHES OF THE PEACE, AND ACTS OF AGGRESSION

### Article 39

The Security Council shall determine the existence of any threat to the peace, breach of peace, or act of aggression and shall make recommendations, or decide what measures shall be taken in accordance with Articles 41 and 42, to maintain or restore international peace and security.

### Article 40

In order to prevent an aggravation of the situation, the Security Council may, before making the recommendations or deciding upon the measures provided for in Article 39, call upon the parties concerned to comply with such provisional measures as it deems necessary or desirable. Such provisional measures shall be without prejudice to the rights, claims, or position of the parties concerned. The Security Council shall duly take account of failure to comply with such provisional measures.

### Article 41

The Security Council may decide what measures not involving the use of armed force are to be employed to give effect to its decisions, and it may call upon the Members of the United Nations to apply such measures. These may include complete or partial interruption of economic relations and of rail, sea, air, postal, telegraphic, radio, and other means of communication, and the severance of diplomatic relations.

### Article 42

Should the Security Council consider that measures provided for in Article 41 would be inadequate or have proved to be inadequate, it may take such action by air, sea, or land forces as may be necessary to maintain or restore international peace and security. Such action may include demonstrations, blockade, and other operations by air, sea, or land forces of Members of the United Nations.

### Article 43

1. All Members of the United Nations, in order to contribute to the maintenance of international peace and security, undertake to make available to the Security Council, on its call and in accordance with a special agreement or agreements, armed forces, assistance, and facilities, including rights of passage, necessary for the purpose of maintaining international peace and security.

2. Such agreement or agreements shall govern the numbers and types of forces, their degree of readiness and general location, and the nature of the facilities and assistance to be provided.

3. The agreement or agreements shall be negotiated as soon as possible on the initiative of the Security Council. They shall be concluded between the Security Council and Members or between the Security Council and groups of Members and shall be subject to ratification by the signatory states in accordance with their respective constitutional processes.

### Article 44

When the Security Council has decided to use force it shall, before calling upon a Member not represented on it to provide armed forces in fulfillment of the obligations assumed under Article 43, invite that Member, if the Member so desires, to participate in the decisions of the Security Council concerning the employment of contingents of that Member's armed forces.

### Article 45

In order to enable the United Nations to take urgent military measures, Members shall hold immediately available national air-force contingents for combined international enforcement action. The strength and degree of readiness of these contingents and plans for their combined action shall be determined, within the limits laid down in the special agreement or agreements referred to in Article 43, by the Security Council with the assistance of the Military Staff Committee.

### Article 46

Plans for the application of armed force shall be made by the Security Council with the assistance of the Military Staff Committee.

### Article 47

1. There shall be established a Military Staff Committee to advise and assist the Security Council on all questions relating to the Security Council's military requirements for the maintenance of international peace and security, the em-

ployment and command of forces placed at its disposal, the regulation of armaments, and possible disarmament.

2. The Military Staff Committee shall consist of the Chiefs of Staff of the permanent members of the Security Council or their representatives. Any Member of the United Nations not permanently represented on the Committee shall be invited by the Committee to be associated with it when the efficient discharge of the Committee's responsibilities requires the participation of that Member in its work.

3. The Military Staff Committee shall be responsible under the Security Council for the strategic direction of any armed forces placed at the disposal of the Security Council. Questions relating to the command of such forces shall be worked out subsequently.

4. The Military Staff Committee, with the authorization of the Security Council and after consultation with appropriate regional agencies, may establish regional subcommittees.

## Article 48

1. The action required to carry out the decisions of the Security Council for the maintenance of international peace and security shall be taken by all the Members of the United Nations or by some of them, as the Security Council may determine.

2. Such decisions shall be carried out by the Members of the United Nations directly and through their action in the appropriate international agencies of which they are members.

## Article 49

The Members of the United Nations shall join in affording mutual assistance in carrying out the measures decided upon by the Security Council.

## Article 50

If preventive or enforcement measures against any state are taken by the Security Council, any other state, whether a Member of the United Nations or not, which finds itself confronted with special economic problems arising from the carrying out of those measures shall have the right to consult the Security Council with regard to a solution of those problems.

## Article 51

Nothing in the present Charter shall impair the inherent right of individual or collective self-defense if an armed attack occurs against a Member of the United Nations, until the Security Council has taken measures necessary to maintain international peace and security. Measures taken by Members in the exercise of this right of self-defense shall be immediately reported to the Security Council and shall not in any way affect the authority and responsibility of the Security Council under the present Charter to take at any time such action as it deems necessary in order to maintain or restore international peace and security.

## CHAPTER VIII

## REGIONAL ARRANGEMENTS

## Article 52

1. Nothing in the present Charter precludes the existence of regional arrangements or agencies for dealing with such matters relating to the maintenance

of international peace and security as are appropriate for regional action, provided that such arrangements or agencies and their activities are consistent with the Purposes and Principles of the United Nations.

2. The Members of the United Nations entering into such arrangements or constituting such agencies shall make every effort to achieve pacific settlement of local disputes through such regional arrangements or by such regional agencies before referring them to the Security Council.

3. The Security Council shall encourage the development of pacific settlement of local disputes through such regional arrangements or by such regional agencies either on the initiative of the states concerned or by reference from the Security Council.

4. This Article in no way impairs the application of Articles 34 and 35.

### Article 53

1. The Security Council shall, where appropriate, utilize such regional arrangements or agencies for enforcement action under its authority. But no enforcement action shall be taken under regional arrangements or by regional agencies without the authorization of the Security Council, with the exception of measures against any enemy state, as defined in paragraph 2 of this Article, provided for pursuant to Article 107 or in regional arrangements directed against renewal of aggressive policy on the part of any such state, until such time as the Organization may, on request of the Governments concerned, be charged with the responsibility for preventing further aggression by such a state.

2. The term enemy state as used in paragraph 1 of this Article applies to any state which during the Second World War has been an enemy of any signatory of the present Charter.

### Article 54

The Security Council shall at all times be kept fully informed of activities undertaken or in contemplation under regional arrangements or by regional agencies for the maintenance of international peace and security.

### CHAPTER IX

### INTERNATIONAL ECONOMIC AND SOCIAL COOPERATION

### Article 55

With a view to the creation of conditions of stability and well-being which are necessary for peaceful and friendly relations among nations based on respect for the principle of equal rights and self-determination of peoples, the United Nations shall promote:

    a. higher standards of living, full employment, and conditions of economic and social progress and development;

    b. solutions of international economic, social, health, and related problems and international cultural and educational cooperation; and

    c. universal respect for, and observance of, human rights and fundamental freedoms for all without distinction as to race, sex, language, or religion.

## Article 56

All Members pledge themselves to take joint and separate action in cooperation with the Organization for the achievement of the purposes set forth in Article 55.

## Article 57

1. The various specialized agencies, established by intergovernmental agreement and having wide international responsibilities, as defined in their basic instruments, in economic, social, cultural, educational, health, and related fields, shall be brought into relationship with the United Nations in accordance with the provisions of Article 63.

2. Such agencies thus brought into relationship with the United Nations are hereinafter referred to as specialized agencies.

## Article 58

The Organization shall make recommendations for the coordination of the policies and activities of the specialized agencies.

## Article 59

The Organization shall, where appropriate, initiate negotiations among the states concerned for the creation of any new specialized agencies required for the accomplishment of the purposes set forth in Article 55.

## Article 60

Responsibility for the discharge of the functions of the Organization set forth in this Chapter shall be vested in the General Assembly and, under the authority of the General Assembly, in the Economic and Social Council, which shall have for this purpose the powers set forth in Chapter X.

## CHAPTER X

### THE ECONOMIC AND SOCIAL COUNCIL

*Composition*

### Article 61 (As amended)

1. The Economic and Social Council shall consist of twenty-seven Members of the United Nations elected by the General Assembly.

2. Subject to the provisions of paragraph 3, nine members of the Economic and Social Council shall be elected each year for a term of three years. A retiring member shall be eligible for immediate re-election.

3. At the first election after the increase in the membership of the Economic and Social Council from eighteen to twenty-seven members, in addition to the members elected in place of the six members whose term of office expires at the end of that year, nine additional members shall be elected. Of these nine additional members, the term of office of three members so elected shall expire at the end of one year, and of three other members at the end of two years, in accordance with arrangements made by the General Assembly.

4. Each member of the Economic and Social Council shall have one representative.

*Functions and Powers*

### Article 62

1. The Economic and Social Council may make or initiate studies and reports with respect to international economic, social, cultural, educational, health, and related matters and may make recommendations with respect to any such matters to the General Assembly, to the Members of the United Nations, and to the specialized agencies concerned.

2. It may make recommendations for the purpose of promoting respect for, and observance of, human rights and fundamental freedoms for all.

3. It may prepare draft conventions for submission to the General Assembly, with respect to matters falling within its competence.

4. It may call, in accordance with the rules prescribed by the United Nations, international conferences on matters falling within its competence.

### Article 63

1. The Economic and Social Council may enter into agreements with any of the agencies referred to in Article 57, defining the terms on which the agency concerned shall be brought into relationship with the United Nations. Such agreements shall be subject to approval by the General Assembly.

2. It may coordinate the activities of the specialized agencies through consultation with and recommendations to such agencies and through recommendations to the General Assembly and to the Members of the United Nations.

### Article 64

1. The Economic and Social Council may take appropriate steps to obtain regular reports from the specialized agencies. It may make arrangements with the Members of the United Nations and with the specialized agencies to obtain reports on the steps taken to give effect to its own recommendations and to recommendations on matters falling within its competence made by the General Assembly.

2. It may communicate its observations on these reports to the General Assembly.

### Article 65

The Economic and Social Council may furnish information to the Security Council and shall assist the Security Council upon its request.

### Article 66

1. The Economic and Social Council shall perform such functions as fall within its competence in connection with the carrying out of the recommendations of the General Assembly.

2. It may, with the approval of the General Assembly, perform services at the request of Members of the United Nations and at the request of specialized agencies.

3. It shall perform such other functions as are specified elsewhere in the present Charter or as may be assigned to it by the General Assembly.

*Voting*

### Article 67

1. Each member of the Economic and Social Council shall have one vote.

2. Decisions of the Economic and Social Council shall be made by a majority of the members present and voting.

*Procedure*

## Article 68

The Economic and Social Council shall set up commissions in economic and social fields and for the promotion of human rights, and such other commissions as may be required for the performance of its functions.

## Article 69

The Economic and Social Council shall invite any Member of the United Nations to participate, without vote, in its deliberations on any matter of particular concern to that Member.

## Article 70

The Economic and Social Council may make arrangements for representatives of the specialized agencies to participate, without vote, in its deliberations and in those of the commissions established by it, and for its representatives to participate in the deliberations of the specialized agencies.

## Article 71

The Economic and Social Council may make suitable arrangements for consultation with non-governmental organizations which are concerned with matters within its competence. Such arrangements may be made with international organizations and, where appropriate, with national organizations after consultation with the Member of the United Nations concerned.

## Article 72

1. The Economic and Social Council shall adopt its own rules of procedure, including the method of selecting its President.

2. The Economic and Social Council shall meet as required in accordance with its rules, which shall include provision for the convening of meetings on the request of a majority of its members.

## Chapter XI

## DECLARATION REGARDING NON-SELF-GOVERNING TERRITORIES

### Article 73

Members of the United Nations which have or assume responsibilities for the administration of territories whose peoples have not yet attained a full measure of self-government recognize the principle that the interests of the inhabitants of these territories are paramount, and accept as a sacred trust the obligation to promote to the utmost, within the system of international peace and security established by the present Charter, the well-being of the inhabitants of these territories, and, to this end:

a. to ensure, with due respect for the culture of the peoples concerned, their political, economic, social, and educational advancement, their just treatment, and their protection against abuses;

b. to develop self-government, to take due account of the political aspirations of the peoples, and to assist them in the progressive development of their free political institutions, according to the particular circumstances of each territory and its peoples and their varying stages of advancement;

c.  to further international peace and security;

d.  to promote constructive measures of development, to encourage research, and to cooperate with one another and, when and where appropriate, with specialized international bodies with a view to the practical achievement of the social, economic, and scientific purposes set forth in this Article; and

e.  to transmit regularly to the Secretary-General for information purposes, subject to such limitation as security and constitutional considerations may require, statistical and other information of a technical nature relating to economic, social, and educational conditions in the territories for which they are respectively responsible other than those territories to which Chapters XII and XIII apply.

## Article 74

Members of the United Nations also agree that their policy in respect of the territories to which this Chapter applies, no less than in respect of their metropolitan areas, must be based on the general principle of good-neighborliness, due account being taken of the interests and well-being of the rest of the world, in social, economic, and commercial matters.

## CHAPTER XII

### INTERNATIONAL TRUSTEESHIP SYSTEM

#### Article 75

The United Nations shall establish under its authority an international trusteeship system for the administration and supervision of such territories as may be placed thereunder by subsequent individual agreements. These territories are hereinafter referred to as trust territories.

#### Article 76

The basic objectives of the trusteeship system, in accordance with the Purposes of the United Nations laid down in Article 1 of the present Charter, shall be:

a.  to further international peace and security;

b.  to promote the political, economic, social, and educational advancement of the inhabitants of the trust territories, and their progressive development towards self-government or independence as may be appropriate to the particular circumstances of each territory and its peoples and the freely expressed wishes of the peoples concerned, and as may be provided by the terms of each trusteeship agreement;

c.  to encourage respect for human rights and for fundamental freedoms for all without distinction as to race, sex, language, or religion, and to encourage recognition of the interdependence of the peoples of the world; and

d.  to ensure equal treatment in social, economic, and commercial matters for all Members of the United Nations and their nationals, and also equal treatment for the latter in the administration of justice, without prejudice to the attainment of the foregoing objectives and subject to the provisions of Article 80.

## Article 77

1. The trusteeship system shall apply to such territories in the following categories as may be placed thereunder by means of trusteeship agreements:

    a. territories now held under mandate;

    b. territories which may be detached from enemy states as a result of the Second World War; and

    c. territories voluntarily placed under the system by states responsible for their administration.

2. It will be a matter for subsequent agreement as to which territories in the foregoing categories will be brought under the trusteeship system and upon what terms.

## Article 78

The trusteeship system shall not apply to territories which have become Members of the United Nations, relationship among which shall be based on respect for the principle of sovereign equality.

## Article 79

The terms of trusteeship for each territory to be placed under the trusteeship system, including any alteration or amendment, shall be agreed upon by the states directly concerned, including the mandatory power in the case of territories held under mandate by a Member of the United Nations, and shall be approved as provided for in Articles 83 and 85.

## Article 80

1. Except as may be agreed upon in individual trusteeship agreements, made under Articles 77, 79, and 81, placing each territory under the trusteeship system, and until such agreements have been concluded, nothing in this Chapter shall be construed in or of itself to alter in any manner the rights whatsoever of any states or any peoples or the terms of existing international instruments to which Members of the United Nations may respectively be parties.

2. Paragraph 1 of this Article shall not be interpreted as giving grounds for delay or postponement of the negotiation and conclusion of agreements for placing mandated and other territories under the trusteeship system as provided for in Article 77.

## Article 81

The trusteeship agreement shall in each case include the terms under which the trust territory will be administered and designate the authority which will exercise the administration of the trust territory. Such authority, hereinafter called the administering authority, may be one or more states or the Organization itself.

## Article 82

There may be designated, in any trusteeship agreement, a strategic area or areas which may include part or all of the trust territory to which the agreement applies, without prejudice to any special agreement or agreements made under Article 43.

*Article 83*

1. All functions of the United Nations relating to strategic areas, including the approval of the terms of the trusteeship agreements and of their alteration or amendment, shall be exercised by the Security Council.

2. The basic objectives set forth in Article 76 shall be applicable to the people of each strategic area.

3. The Security Council shall, subject to the provisions of the trusteeship agreements and without prejudice to security considerations, avail itself of the assistance of the Trusteeship Council to perform those functions of the United Nations under the trusteeship system relating to political, economic, social, and educational matters in the strategic areas.

*Article 84*

It shall be the duty of the administering authority to ensure that the trust territory shall play its part in the maintenance of international peace and security. To this end the administering authority may make use of volunteer forces, facilities, and assistance from the trust territory in carrying out the obligations towards the Security Council undertaken in this regard by the administering authority, as well as for local defense and the maintenance of law and order within the trust territory.

*Article 85*

1. The functions of the United Nations with regard to trusteeship agreements for all areas not designated as strategic, including the approval of the terms of the trusteeship agreements and of their alteration or amendment, shall be exercised by the General Assembly.

2. The Trusteeship Council, operating under the authority of the General Assembly, shall assist the General Assembly in carrying out these functions.

CHAPTER XIII

THE TRUSTEESHIP COUNCIL

*Composition*

*Article 86*

1. The Trusteeship Council shall consist of the following Members of the United Nations:

    a. those Members administering trust territories;

    b. such of those Members mentioned by name in Article 23 as are not administering trust territories; and

    c. as many other Members elected for three-year terms by the General Assembly as may be necessary to ensure that the total number of members of the Trusteeship Council is equally divided between those Members of the United Nations which administer trust territories and those which do not.

2. Each member of the Trusteeship Council shall designate one specially qualified person to represent it therein.

*Functions and Powers*

*Article 87*

The General Assembly and, under its authority, the Trusteeship Council, in carrying out their functions, may:

a.   consider reports submitted by the administering authority;

b.   accept petitions and examine them in consultation with the administering authority;

c.   provide for periodic visits to the respective trust territories at times agreed upon with the administering authority; and

d.   take these and other actions in conformity with the terms of the trusteeship agreements.

### Article 88

The Trusteeship Council shall formulate a questionnaire on the political, economic, social, and educational advancement of the inhabitants of each trust territory, and the administering authority for each trust territory within the competence of the General Assembly shall make an annual report to the General Assembly upon the basis of such questionnaire.

*Voting*

### Article 89

1.   Each member of the Trusteeship Council shall have one vote.

2.   Decisions of the Trusteeship Council shall be made by a majority of the members present and voting.

*Procedure*

### Article 90

1.   The Trusteeship Council shall adopt its own rules of procedure, including the method of selecting its President.

2.   The Trusteeship Council shall meet as required in accordance with its rules, which shall include provision for the convening of meetings on the request of a majority of its members.

### Article 91

The Trusteeship Council shall, when appropriate, avail itself of the assistance of the Economic and Social Council and of the specialized agencies in regard to matters with which they are respectively concerned.

### Chapter XIV

### THE INTERNATIONAL COURT OF JUSTICE

### Article 92

The International Court of Justice shall be the principal judicial organ of the United Nations. It shall function in accordance with the annexed Statute, which is based upon the Statute of the Permanent Court of International Justice and forms an integral part of the present Charter.

### Article 93

1.   All Members of the United Nations are *ipso facto* parties to the Statute of the International Court of Justice.

2.   A state which is not a Member of the United Nations may become a party to the Statute of the International Court of Justice on condition to be determined in each case by the General Assembly upon the recommendation of the Security Council.

### Article 94

1. Each Member of the United Nations undertakes to comply with the decision of the International Court of Justice in any case to which it is a party.

2. If any party to a case fails to perform the obligations incumbent upon it under a judgment rendered by the Court, the other party may have recourse to the Security Council, which may, if it deems necessary, make recommendations or decide upon measures to be taken to give effect to the judgment.

### Article 95

Nothing in the present Charter shall prevent Members of the United Nations from entrusting the solution of their differences to other tribunals by virtue of agreements already in existence or which may be concluded in the future.

### Article 96

1. The General Assembly or the Security Council may request the International Court of Justice to give an advisory opinion on any legal question.

2. Other organs of the United Nations and specialized agencies, which may at any time be so authorized by the General Assembly, may also request advisory opinions of the Court on legal questions arising within the scope of their activities.

## CHAPTER XV

## THE SECRETARIAT

### Article 97

The Secretariat shall comprise a Secretary-General and such staff as the Organization may require. The Secretary-General shall be appointed by the General Assembly upon the recommendation of the Security Council. He shall be the chief administrative officer of the Organization.

### Article 98

The Secretary-General shall act in that capacity in all meetings of the General Assembly, of the Security Council, of the Economic and Social Council, and of the Trusteeship Council, and shall perform such other functions as are entrusted to him by these organs. The Secretary-General shall make an annual report to the General Assembly on the work of the Organization.

### Article 99

The Secretary-General may bring to the attention of the Security Council any matter which in his opinion may threaten the maintenance of international peace and security.

### Article 100

1. In the performance of their duties the Secretary-General and the staff shall not seek or receive instructions from any government or from any other authority external to the Organization. They shall refrain from any action which might reflect on their position as international officials responsible only to the Organization.

2. Each Member of the United Nations undertakes to respect the exclusively international character of the responsibilities of the Secretary-General and the staff and not to seek to influence them in the discharge of their responsibilities.

## Article 101

1. The staff shall be appointed by the Secretary-General under regulations established by the General Assembly.

2. Appropriate staffs shall be permanently assigned to the Economic and Social Council, the Trusteeship Council, and, as required, to other organs of the United Nations. These staffs shall form a part of the Secretariat.

3. The paramount consideration in the employment of the staff and in the determination of the conditions of service shall be the necessity of securing the highest standards of efficiency, competence, and integrity. Due regard shall be paid to the importance of recruiting the staff on as wide a geographical basis as possible.

### CHAPTER XVI

### MISCELLANEOUS PROVISIONS

## Article 102

1. Every treaty and every international agreement entered into by any Member of the United Nations after the present Charter comes into force shall as soon as possible be registered with the Secretariat and published by it.

2. No party to any such treaty or international agreement which has not been registered in accordance with the provisions of paragraph 1 of this Article may invoke that treaty or agreement before any organ of the United Nations.

## Article 103

In the event of a conflict between the obligations of the Members of the United Nations under the present Charter and their obligations under any other international agreement, their obligations under the present Charter shall prevail.

## Article 104

The Organization shall enjoy in the territory of each of its Members such legal capacity as may be necessary for the exercise of its functions and the fulfillment of its purposes.

## Article 105

1. The Organization shall enjoy in the territory of each of its Members such privileges and immunities as are necessary for the fulfillment of its purposes.

2. Representatives of the Members of the United Nations and officials of the Organization shall similarly enjoy such privileges and immunities as are necessary for the independent exercise of their functions in connection with the Organization.

3. The General Assembly may make recommendations with a view to determining the details of the application of paragraphs 1 and 2 of this Article or may propose conventions to the Members of the United Nations for this purpose.

## Chapter XVII

## TRANSITIONAL SECURITY ARRANGEMENTS

### Article 106

Pending the coming into force of such special agreements referred to in Article 43 as in the opinion of the Security Council enable it to begin the exercise of its responsibilities under Article 42, the parties of the Four-Nation Declaration, signed at Moscow, October 30, 1943, and France, shall, in accordance with the provisions of paragraph 5 of that Declaration, consult with one another and as occasion requires with other Members of the United Nations with a view to such joint action on behalf of the Organization as may be necessary for the purpose of maintaining international peace and security.

### Article 107

Nothing in the present Charter shall invalidate or preclude action, in relation to any state which during the Second World War has been an enemy of any signatory to the present Charter, taken or authorized as a result of that war by the Governments having responsibility for such action.

## Chapter XVIII

## AMENDMENTS

### Article 108

Amendments to the present Charter shall come into force for all Members of the United Nations when they have been adopted by a vote of two-thirds of the members of the General Assembly and ratified in accordance with their respective constitutional processes by two-thirds of the Members of the United Nations, including all the permanent members of the Security Council.

### Article 109

1. A General Conference of the Members of the United Nations for the purpose of reviewing the present Charter may be held at a date and place to be fixed by a two-thirds vote of the members of the General Assembly and by a vote of any seven members of the Security Council. Each Member of the United Nations shall have one vote in the conference.

2. Any alteration of the present Charter recommended by a two-thirds vote of the conference shall take effect when ratified in accordance with their respective constitutional processes by two-thirds of the Members of the United Nations including all the permanent members of the Security Council.

3. If such a conference has not been held before the tenth annual session of the General Assembly following the coming into force of the present Charter, the proposal to call such a conference shall be placed on the agenda of that session of the General Assembly, and the conference shall be held if so decided by a majority vote of the members of the General Assembly and by a vote of any seven members of the Security Council.

## Chapter XIX

## RATIFICATION AND SIGNATURE

### Article 110

1. The present Charter shall be ratified by the signatory states in accordance with their respective constitutional processes.

2. The ratifications shall be deposited with the Government of the United States of America, which shall notify all the signatory states of each deposit as well as the Secretary-General of the Organization when he has been appointed.

3. The present Charter shall come into force upon the deposit of ratifications by the Republic of China, France, the Union of Soviet Socialist Republics, the United Kingdom of Great Britain and Northern Ireland, and the United States of America, and by a majority of the other signatory states. A protocol of the ratifications deposited shall thereupon be drawn by the Government of the United States of America which shall communicate copies thereof to all the signatory states.

4. The states signatory to the present Charter which ratify it after it has come into force will become original Members of the United Nations on the date of the deposit of their respective ratifications.

### Article 111

The present Charter, of which the Chinese, French, Russian, English, and Spanish texts are equally authentic, shall remain deposited in the archives of the Government of the United States of America. Duly certified copies thereof shall be transmitted by that Government to the Governments of the other signatory states.

IN FAITH WHEREOF the representatives of the Governments of the United Nations have signed the present Charter.

DONE at the city of San Francisco the twenty-sixth day of June, one thousand nine hundred and forty-five.

# STATUTE OF THE INTERNATIONAL COURT OF JUSTICE

## Article 1

The International Court of Justice established by the Charter of the United Nations as the principal judicial organ of the United Nations shall be constituted and shall function in accordance with the provisions of the present Statute.

## Chapter I

## ORGANIZATION OF THE COURT

### Article 2

The Court shall be composed of a body of independent judges, elected regardless of their nationality from among persons of high moral character, who possess the qualifications required in their respective countries for appointment to the highest judicial offices, or are juris-consults of recognized competence in international law.

### Article 3

1. The Court shall consist of fifteen members, no two of whom may be nationals of the same state.

2. A person who for the purposes of membership in the Court could be regarded as a national of more than one state shall be deemed to be a national of the one in which he ordinarily exercises civil and political rights.

### Article 4

1. The members of the Court shall be elected by the General Assembly and by the Security Council from a list of persons nominated by the national groups in the Permanent Court of Arbitration, in accordance with the following provisions.

2. In the case of Members of the United Nations not represented in the Permanent Court of Arbitration, candidates shall be nominated by national groups appointed for this purpose by their governments under the same conditions as those prescribed for members of the Permanent Court of Arbitration by Article 44 of the Convention of The Hague of 1907 for the pacific settlement of international disputes.

3. The conditions under which a state which is a party to the present Statute but is not a Member of the United Nations may participate in electing the members of the Court shall, in the absence of a special agreement, be laid down by the General Assembly upon recommendation of the Security Council.

### Article 5

1. At least three months before the date of the election, the Secretary-General of the United Nations shall address a written request to the members of the Permanent Court of Arbitration belonging to the states which are parties to the present Statute, and to the members of the national groups appointed under Article 4, paragraph 2, inviting them to undertake, within a given time, by national groups, the nomination of persons in a position to accept the duties of a member of the Court.

2. No group may nominate more than four persons, not more than two of whom shall be of their own nationality. In no case may the number of candidates nominated by a group be more than double the number of seats to be filled.

### Article 6

Before making these nominations, each national group is recommended to consult its highest court of justice, its legal faculties and schools of law, and its national academies and national sections of international academies devoted to the study of law.

### Article 7

1. The Secretary-General shall prepare a list in alphabetical order of all the persons thus nominated. Save as provided in Article 12, paragraph 2, these shall be the only persons eligible.

2. The Secretary-General shall submit this list to the General Assembly and to the Security Council.

### Article 8

The General Assembly and the Security Council shall proceed independently of one another to elect the members of the Court.

### Article 9

At every election, the electors shall bear in mind not only that the persons to be elected should individually possess the qualifications required, but also that in the body as a whole the representation of the main forms of civilization and of the principal legal systems of the world should be assured.

### Article 10

1. Those candidates who obtain an absolute majority of votes in the General Assembly and in the Security Council shall be considered as elected.

2. Any vote of the Security Council, whether for the election of judges or for the appointment of members of the conference envisaged in Article 12, shall be taken without any distinction between permanent and non-permanent members of the Security Council.

3. In the event of more than one national of the same state obtaining an absolute majority of the votes both of the General Assembly and of the Security Council, the eldest of these only shall be considered as elected.

## Article 11

If, after the first meeting held for the purpose of the election, one or more seats remain to be filled, a second and, if necessary, a third meeting shall take place.

## Article 12

1. If, after the third meeting, one or more seats still remain unfilled, a joint conference consisting of six members, three appointed by the General Assembly and three by the Security Council, may be formed at any time at the request of either the General Assembly or the Security Council, for the purpose of choosing by the vote of an absolute majority one name for each seat still vacant, to submit to the General Assembly and the Security Council for their respective acceptance.

2. If the joint conference is unanimously agreed upon any person who fulfils the required conditions, he may be included in its list, even though he was not included in the list of nominations referred to in Article 7.

3. If the joint conference is satisfied that it will not be successful in procuring an election, those members of the Court who have already been elected shall, within a period to be fixed by the Security Council, proceed to fill the vacant seats by selection from among those candidates who have obtained votes either in the General Assembly or in the Security Council.

4. In the event of an equality of votes among the judges, the eldest judge shall have a casting vote.

## Article 13

1. The members of the Court shall be elected for nine years and may be re-elected, provided, however, that of the judges elected at the first election, the terms of five judges shall expire at the end of three years and the terms of five more judges shall expire at the end of six years.

2. The judges whose terms are to expire at the end of the above-mentioned initial periods of three and six years shall be chosen by lot to be drawn by the Secretary-General immediately after the first election has been completed.

3. The members of the Court shall continue to discharge their duties until their places have been filled. Though replaced, they shall finish any cases which they may have begun.

4. In the case of the resignation of a member of the Court, the resignation shall be addressed to the President of the Court for transmission to the Secretary-General. This last notification makes the place vacant.

## Article 14

Vacancies shall be filled by the same method as that laid down for the first election, subject to the following provision: the Secretary-General shall, within one month of the occurrence of the vacancy, proceed to issue the invitations provided for in Article 5, and the date of the election shall be fixed by the Security Council.

## Article 15

A member of the Court elected to replace a member whose term of office has not expired shall hold office for the remainder of his predecessor's term.

## Article 16

1. No member of the Court may exercise any political or administrative function, or engage in any other occupation of a professional nature.

2. Any doubt on this point shall be settled by the decision of the Court.

## Article 17

1. No member of the Court may act as agent, counsel, or advocate in any case.

2. No member may participate in the decision of any case in which he has previously taken part as agent, counsel, or advocate for one of the parties, or as a member of a national or international court, or of a commission of enquiry, or in any other capacity.

3. Any doubt on this point shall be settled by the decision of the Court.

## Article 18

1. No member of the Court can be dismissed unless, in the unanimous opinion of the other members, he has ceased to fulfil the required conditions.

2. Formal notification thereof shall be made to the Secretary-General by the Registrar.

3. This notification makes the place vacant.

## Article 19

The members of the Court, when engaged on the business of the Court, shall enjoy diplomatic privileges and immunities.

## Article 20

Every member of the Court shall, before taking up his duties, make a solemn declaration in open court that he will exercise his powers impartially and conscientiously.

## Article 21

1. The Court shall elect its President and Vice-President for three years; they may be re-elected.

2. The Court shall appoint its Registrar and may provide for the appointment of such other officers as may be necessary.

## Article 22

1. The seat of the Court shall be established at The Hague. This, however, shall not prevent the Court from sitting and exercising its functions elsewhere whenever the Court considers it desirable.

2. The President and the Registrar shall reside at the seat of the Court.

## Article 23

1. The Court shall remain permanently in session, except during the judicial vacations, the dates and duration of which shall be fixed by the Court.

2. Members of the Court are entitled to periodic leave, the dates and duration of which shall be fixed by the Court, having in mind the distance between The Hague and the home of each judge.

3. Members of the Court shall be bound, unless they are on leave or prevented from attending by illness or other serious reasons duly explained to the President, to hold themselves permanently at the disposal of the Court.

### Article 24

1. If, for some special reason, a member of the Court considers that he should not take part in the decision of a particular case, he shall so inform the President.

2. If the President considers that for some special reason one of the members of the Court should not sit in a particular case he shall give him notice accordingly.

3. If in any such case the member of the Court and the President disagree, the matter shall be settled by the decision of the Court.

### Article 25

1. The full Court shall sit except when it is expressly provided otherwise in the present Statute.

2. Subject to the condition that the number of judges available to constitute the Court is not thereby reduced below eleven, the Rules of the Court may provide for allowing one or more judges, according to circumstances and in rotation, to be dispensed from sitting.

3. A quorum of nine judges shall suffice to constitute the Court.

### Article 26

1. The Court may from time to time form one or more chambers, composed of three or more judges as the Court may determine, for dealing with particular categories of cases; for example, labor cases and cases relating to transit and communications.

2. The Court may at any time form a chamber for dealing with a particular case. The number of judges to constitute such a chamber shall be determined by the Court with the approval of the parties.

3. Cases shall be heard and determined by the chambers provided for in this Article if the parties so request.

### Article 27

A judgment given by any of the chambers provided for in Articles 26 and 29 shall be considered as rendered by the Court.

### Article 28

The chambers provided for in Articles 26 and 29 may, with the consent of the parties, sit and exercise their functions elsewhere than at The Hague.

### Article 29

With a view to the speedy despatch of business, the Court shall form annually a chamber composed of five judges which, at the request of the parties, may hear and determine cases by summary procedure. In addition, two judges shall be selected for the purpose of replacing judges who find it impossible to sit.

### Article 30

1. The Court shall frame rules for carrying out its functions. In particular, it shall lay down rules of procedure.

2.  The Rules of the Court may provide for assessors to sit with the Court or with any of its chambers, without the right to vote.

## Article 31

1.  Judges of the nationality of each of the parties shall retain their right to sit in the case before the Court.

2.  If the Court includes upon the Bench a judge of the nationality of one of the parties, any other party may choose a person to sit as judge. Such person shall be chosen preferably from among those persons who have been nominated as candidates as provided in Articles 4 and 5.

3.  If the Court includes upon the Bench no judge of the nationality of the parties, each of these parties may proceed to choose a judge as provided in paragraph 2 of this Article.

4.  The provisions of this Article shall apply to the case of Articles 26 and 29. In such cases, the President shall request one or, if necessary, two of the members of the Court forming the chamber to give place to the members of the Court of the nationality of the parties concerned, and, failing such, or if they are unable to be present, to the judges specially chosen by the parties.

5.  Should there be several parties in the same interest, they shall, for the purpose of the preceding provisions, be reckoned as one party only. Any doubt upon this point shall be settled by the decision of the Court.

6.  Judges chosen as laid down in paragraphs 2, 3, and 4 of this Article shall fulfil the conditions required by Articles 2, 17 (paragraph 2), 20, and 24 of the present Statute. They shall take part in the decision on terms of complete equality with their colleagues.

## Article 32

1.  Each member of the Court shall receive an annual salary.

2.  The President shall receive a special annual allowance.

3.  The Vice-President shall receive a special allowance for every day on which he acts as President.

4.  The judges chosen under Article 31, other than members of the Court, shall receive compensation for each day on which they exercise their functions.

5.  These salaries, allowances, and compensation shall be fixed by the General Assembly. They may not be decreased during the term of office.

6.  The salary of the Registrar shall be fixed by the General Assembly on the proposal of the Court.

7.  Regulations made by the General Assembly shall fix the conditions under which retirement pensions may be given to members of the Court and to the Registrar, and the conditions under which members of the Court and the Registrar shall have their traveling expenses refunded.

8.  The above salaries, allowances, and compensation shall be free of all taxation.

## Article 33

The expenses of the Court shall be borne by the United Nations in such a manner as shall be decided by the General Assembly.

CHAPTER II

## COMPETENCE OF THE COURT

*Article 34*

1.   Only states may be parties in cases before the Court.

2.   The Court, subject to and in conformity with its Rules, may request of public international organizations information relevant to cases before it, and shall receive such information presented by such organizations on their own initiative.

3.   Whenever the construction of the constituent instrument of a public international organization or of an international convention adopted thereunder is in question in a case before the Court, the Registrar shall so notify the public international organization concerned and shall communicate to it copies of all the written proceedings.

*Article 35*

1.   The Court shall be open to the states parties to the present Statute.

2.   The conditions under which the Court shall be open to other states shall, subject to the special provisions contained in treaties in force, be laid down by the Security Council, but in no case shall such conditions place the parties in a position of inequality before the Court.

3.   When a state which is not a Member of the United Nations is a party to a case, the Court shall fix the amount which that party is to contribute towards the expenses of the Court. This provision shall not apply if such state is bearing a share of the expenses of the Court.

*Article 36*

1.   The jurisdiction of the Court comprises all cases which the parties refer to it and all matters specially provided for in the Charter of the United Nations or in treaties and conventions in force.

2.   The states parties to the present Statute may at any time declare that they recognize as compulsory *ipso facto* and without special agreement, in relation to any other state accepting the same obligation, the jurisdiction of the Court in all legal disputes concerning:

   a.   the interpretation of a treaty;

   b.   any question of international law;

   c.   the existence of any fact which, if established, would constitute a breach of an international obligation;

   d.   the nature or extent of the reparation to be made for the breach of an international obligation.

3.   The declarations referred to above may be made unconditionally or on condition of reciprocity on the part of several or certain states, or for a certain time.

4.   Such declarations shall be deposited with the Secretary-General of the United Nations, who shall transmit copies thereof to the parties to the Statute and to the Registrar of the Court.

5. Declarations made under Article 36 of the Statute of the Permanent Court of International Justice and which are still in force shall be deemed, as between the parties to the present Statute, to be acceptances of the compulsory jurisdiction of the International Court of Justice for the period which they still have to run and in accordance with their terms.

6. In the event of a dispute as to whether the Court has jurisdiction, the matter shall be settled by the decision of the Court.

## Article 37

Whenever a treaty or convention in force provides for reference of a matter to a tribunal to have been instituted by the League of Nations, or to the Permanent Court of International Justice, the matter shall, as between the parties to the present Statute, be referred to the International Court of Justice.

## Article 38

1. The Court, whose function is to decide in accordance with international law such disputes as are submitted to it, shall apply:

    a. international conventions, whether general or particular, establishing rules expressly recognized by the contesting states;

    b. international custom, as evidence of a general practice accepted as law;

    c. the general principles of law recognized by civilized nations;

    d. subject to the provisions of Article 59, judicial decisions and the teachings of the most highly qualified publicists of the various nations, as subsidiary means for the determination of rules of law.

2. This provision shall not prejudice the power of the Court to decide a case *ex aequo et bono,* if the parties agree thereto.

## CHAPTER III

## PROCEDURE

### Article 39

1. The official languages of the Court shall be French and English. If the parties agree that the case shall be conducted in French, the judgment shall be delivered in French. If the parties agree that the case shall be conducted in English, the judgment shall be delivered in English.

2. In the absence of an agreement as to which language shall be employed, each party may, in the pleadings, use the language which it prefers; the decision of the Court shall be given in French and English. In this case the Court shall at the same time determine which of the two texts shall be considered as authoritative.

3. The Court shall, at the request of any party, authorize a language other than French or English to be used by that party.

### Article 40

1. Cases are brought before the Court, as the case may be, either by the notification of the special agreement or by a written application addressed to the Registrar. In either case the subject of the dispute and the parties shall be indicated.

2. The Registrar shall forthwith communicate the application to all concerned.

3. He shall also notify the Members of the United Nations through the Secretary-General, and also any other states entitled to appear before the Court.

### Article 41

1. The Court shall have the power to indicate, if it considers that circumstances so require, any provisional measures which ought to be taken to preserve the respective rights of either party.

2. Pending the final decision, notice of the measures suggested shall forthwith be given to the parties and to the Security Council.

### Article 42

1. The parties shall be represented by agents.

2. They may have the assistance of counsel or advocates before the Court.

3. The agents, counsel, and advocates of parties before the Court shall enjoy the privileges and immunities necessary to the independent exercise of their duties.

### Article 43

1. The procedure shall consist of two parts: written and oral.

2. The written proceedings shall consist of the communication to the Court and to the parties of memorials, counter-memorials and, if necessary, replies; also all papers and documents in support.

3. These communications shall be made through the Registrar, in the order and within the time fixed by the Court.

4. A certified copy of every document produced by one party shall be communicated to the other party.

5. The oral proceedings shall consist of the hearing by the Court of witnesses, experts, agents, counsel, and advocates.

### Article 44

1. For the service of all notices upon persons other than the agents, counsel, and advocates, the Court shall apply direct to the government of the state upon whose territory the notice has to be served.

2. The same provision shall apply whenever steps are to be taken to procure evidence on the spot.

### Article 45

The hearing shall be under the control of the President or, if he is unable to preside, of the Vice-President; if neither is able to preside, the senior judge present shall preside.

### Article 46

The hearing in Court shall be public, unless the Court shall decide otherwise, or unless the parties demand that the public be not admitted.

### Article 47

1. Minutes shall be made at each hearing and signed by the Registrar and the President.

2. These minutes alone shall be authentic.

### Article 48

The Court shall make orders for the conduct of the case, shall decide the form and time in which each party must conclude its arguments, and make all arrangements connected with the taking of evidence.

### Article 49

The Court may, even before the hearing begins, call upon the agents to produce any document or to supply any explanations. Formal note shall be taken of any refusal.

### Article 50

The Court may, at any time, entrust any individual, body, bureau, commission, or other organization that it may select, with the task of carrying out an enquiry or giving an expert opinion.

### Article 51

During the hearing any relevant questions are to be put to the witnesses and experts under the conditions laid down by the Court in the rules of procedure referred to in Article 30.

### Article 52

After the Court has received the proofs and evidence within the time specified for the purpose, it may refuse to accept any further oral or written evidence that one party may desire to present unless the other side consents.

### Article 53

1. Whenever one of the parties does not appear before the Court, or fails to defend its case, the other party may call upon the Court to decide in favor of its claim.

2. The Court must, before doing so, satisfy itself, not only that it has jurisdiction in accordance with Articles 36 and 37, but also that the claim is well founded in fact and law.

### Article 54

1. When, subject to the control of the Court, the agents, counsel, and advocates have completed their presentation of the case, the President shall declare the hearing closed.

2. The Court shall withdraw to consider the judgment.

3. The deliberations of the Court shall take place in private and remain secret.

### Article 55

1. All questions shall be decided by a majority of the judges present.

2. In the event of an equality of vote, the President or the judge who acts in his place shall have a casting vote.

### Article 56

1. The judgment shall state the reasons on which it is based.

2. It shall contain the names of the judges who have taken part in the decision.

### Article 57

If the judgment does not represent in whole or in part the unanimous opinion of the judges, any judge shall be entitled to deliver a separate opinion.

### Article 58

The judgment shall be signed by the President and by the Registrar. It shall be read in open court, due notice having been given to the agents.

### Article 59

The decision of the Court has no binding force except between the parties and in respect of that particular case.

### Article 60

The judgment is final and without appeal. In the event of dispute as to the meaning or scope of the judgment, the Court shall construe it upon the request of any party.

### Article 61

1. An application for revision of a judgment may be made only when it is based upon the discovery of some fact of such a nature as to be a decisive factor, which fact was, when the judgment was given, unknown to the Court and also to the party claiming revision, always provided that such ignorance was not due to negligence.

2. The proceedings for revision shall be opened by a judgment of the Court expressly recording the existence of the new fact, recognizing that it has such a character as to lay the case open to revision, and declaring the application admissible on this ground.

3. The Court may require previous compliance with the terms of the judgment before it admits proceedings in revision.

4. The application for revision must be made at latest within six months of the discovery of the new fact.

5. No application for revision may be made after the lapse of ten years from the date of the judgment.

### Article 62

1. Should a state consider that it has an interest of a legal nature which may be affected by the decision in the case, it may submit a request to the Court to be permitted to intervene.

2. It shall be for the Court to decide upon this request.

### Article 63

1. Whenever the construction of a convention to which states other than those concerned in the case are parties is in question, the Registrar shall notify all such states forthwith.

2. Every state so notified has the right to intervene in the proceedings; but if it uses this right, the construction given by the judgment will be equally binding upon it.

### Article 64

Unless otherwise decided by the Court, each party shall bear its own costs.

## Chapter IV

## ADVISORY OPINIONS

### Article 65

1. The Court may give an advisory opinion on any legal question at the request of whatever body may be authorized by or in accordance with the Charter of the United Nations to make such a request.

2. Questions upon which the advisory opinion of the Court is asked shall be laid before the Court by means of a written request containing an exact statement of the question upon which an opinion is required, and accompanied by all documents likely to throw light upon the question.

### Article 66

1. The Registrar shall forthwith give notice of the request for an advisory opinion to all states entitled to appear before the Court.

2. The Registrar shall also, by means of a special and direct communication, notify any state entitled to appear before the Court or international organization considered by the Court, or, should it not be sitting, by the President, as likely to be able to furnish information on the question, that the Court will be prepared to receive, within a time limit to be fixed by the President, written statements, or to hear, at a public sitting to be held for the purpose, oral statements relating to the question.

3. Should any such state entitled to appear before the Court have failed to receive the special communication referred to in paragraph 2 of this Article, such state may express a desire to submit a written statement or to be heard; and the Court will decide.

4. States and organizations having presented written or oral statements or both shall be permitted to comment on the statements made by other states or organizations in the form, to the extent, and within the time limits which the Court, or, should it not be sitting, the President, shall decide in each particular case. Accordingly, the Registrar shall in due time communicate any such written statements to states and organizations having submitted similar statements.

### Article 67

The Court shall deliver its advisory opinions in open court, notice having been given to the Secretary-General and to the representatives of Members of the United Nations, of other states and of international organizations immediately concerned.

### Article 68

In the exercise of its advisory functions the Court shall further be guided by the provisions of the present Statute which apply in contentious cases to the extent to which it recognizes them to be applicable.

CHAPTER V

AMENDMENT

*Article 69*

Amendments to the present Statute shall be effected by the same procedure as is provided by the Charter of the United Nations for amendments to that Charter, subject however to any provisions which the General Assembly upon recommendation of the Security Council may adopt concerning the participation of states which are parties to the present Statute but are not Members of the United Nations.

*Article 70*

The Court shall have power to propose such amendments to the present Statute as it may deem necessary, through written communications to the Secretary-General, for consideration in conformity with the provisions of Article 69.

# CONSTITUTION OF THE UNITED NATIONS EDUCATIONAL, SCIENTIFIC AND CULTURAL ORGANISATION

THE GOVERNMENTS of the States parties of this Constitution on behalf of their peoples declare

that since wars begin in the minds of men, it is in the minds of men that the defences of peace must be constructed;

that ignorance of each other's ways and lives has been a common cause, throughout the history of mankind, of that suspicion and mistrust between the peoples of the world through which their differences have all too often broken into war;

that the great and terrible war which has now ended was a war made possible by the denial of the democratic principles of the dignity, equality and mutual respect of men, and by the propagation, in their place, through ignorance and prejudice, of the doctrine of the inequality of men and races;

that the wide diffusion of culture, and the education of humanity for justice and liberty and peace are indispensable to the dignity of man and constitute a sacred duty which all the nations must fulfil in a spirit of mutual assistance and concern;

that a peace based exclusively upon the political and economic arrangements of governments would not be a peace which could secure the unanimous, lasting and sincere support of the peoples of the world, and that the peace must therefore be founded, if it is not to fail, upon the intellectual and moral solidarity of mankind.

For these reasons, the States parties to this Constitution, believing in full and equal opportunities for education for all, in the unrestricted pursuit of objective truth, and in the free exchange of ideas and knowledge, are agreed and determined to develop and to increase the means of communication between their peoples and to employ these means for the purposes of mutual understanding and a truer and more perfect knowledge of each other's lives;

In consequence whereof they do hereby create the United Nations Educational, Scientific and Cultural Organisation for the purpose of advancing.

503

through the educational and scientific and cultural relations of the peoples of the world, the objectives of international peace and of the common welfare of mankind for which the United Nations Organisation was established and which its Charter proclaims.

## ARTICLE I

## PURPOSES AND FUNCTIONS

1. The purpose of the Organisation is to contribute to peace and security by promoting collaboration among the nations through education, science and culture in order to further universal respect for justice, for the rule of law and for the human rights and fundamental freedoms which are affirmed for the peoples of the world, without distinction of race, sex, language or religion, by the Charter of the United Nations.

2. To realise this purpose the Organisation will:

a. collaborate in the work of advancing the mutual knowledge and understanding of peoples, through all means of mass communication and to that end recommend such international agreements as may be necessary to promote the free flow of ideas by word and image;

b. give fresh impulse to popular education and to the spread of culture;

by collaborating with Members, at their request, in the development of educational activities;

by instituting collaboration among the nations to advance the ideal of equality of educational opportunity without regard to race, sex or any distinctions, economic or social;

by suggesting educational methods best suited to prepare the children of the world for the responsibilities of freedom:

c. maintain, increase and diffuse knowledge;

by assuring the conservation and protection of the world's inheritance of books, works of art and monuments of history and science, and recommending to the nations concerned the necessary international conventions;

by encouraging cooperation among the nations in all branches of intellectual activity, including the international exchange of persons active in the fields of education, science and culture and the exchange of publications, objects of artistic and scientific interest and other materials of information;

by initiating methods of international cooperation calculated to give the people of all countries access to the printed and published materials produced by any of them.

3. With a view to preserving the independence, integrity and fruitful diversity of the cultures and educational systems of the States Members of this Organisation, the Organisation is prohibited from intervening in matters which are essentially within their domestic jurisdiction.

## ARTICLE II

## MEMBERSHIP

1. Membership of the United Nations Organisation shall carry with it the right to membership of the United Nations Educational, Scientific and Cultural Organisation.

2.   Subject to the conditions of the agreement between this Organisation and the United Nations Organisation, approved pursuant to Article X of this Constitution, States not members of the United Nations Organisation may be admitted to membership of the Organisation, upon recommendation of the Executive Board, by a two-thirds majority vote of the General Conference.

3.   Members of the Organisation which are suspended from the exercise of the rights and privileges of membership of the United Nations Organisation shall, upon the request of the latter, be suspended from the rights and privileges of this Organisation.

4.   Members of the Organisation which are expelled from the United Nations Organisation shall automatically cease to be members of this Organisation.

## ARTICLE III

## ORGANS

The Organisation shall include a General Conference, an Executive Board and a Secretariat.

## ARTICLE IV

## THE GENERAL CONFERENCE

*A.   Composition*

1.   The General Conference shall consist of the representatives of the States Members of the Organisation. The Government of each Member State shall appoint not more than five delegates, who shall be selected after consultation with the National Commission, if established, or with educational, scientific and cultural bodies.

*B.   Functions*

2.   The General Conference shall determine the policies and the main lines of work of the Organisation. It shall take decisions on programmes drawn up by the Executive Board.

3.   The General Conference shall, when it deems it desirable, summon international conferences on education, the sciences and humanities and the dissemination of knowledge.

4.   The General Conference shall, in adopting proposals for submission to the Member States, distinguish between recommendations and international conventions submitted for their approval. In the former case a majority vote shall suffice; in the latter case a two-thirds majority shall be required. Each of the Member States shall submit recommendations or conventions to its competent authorities within a period of one year from the close of the session of the General Conference at which they were adopted.

5.   The General Conference shall advise the United Nations Organisation on the educational, scientific and cultural aspects of matters of concern to the latter, in accordance with the terms and procedure agreed upon between the appropriate authorities of the two Organisations.

6.   The General Conference shall receive and consider the reports submitted periodically by Member States as provided by Article VIII.

7.   The General Conference shall elect the members of the Executive Board, and, on the recommendation of the Board, shall appoint the Director-General.

*C. Voting*

8.  Each Member State shall have one vote in the General Conference. Decisions shall be made by a simple majority except in cases in which a two-thirds majority is required by the provisions of this Constitution. A majority shall be a majority of the Members present and voting.

*D. Procedure*

9.  The General Conference shall meet annually in ordinary session; it may meet in extraordinary session on the call of the Executive Board. At each session the location of its next session shall be designated by the General Conference and shall vary from year to year.

10.  The General Conference shall, at each session, elect a President and other officers and adopt rules of procedure.

11.  The General Conference shall set up special and technical committees and such other subordinate bodies as may be necessary for its purposes.

12.  The General Conference shall cause arrangements to be made for public access to meetings, subject to such regulations as it shall prescribe.

*E. Observers*

13.  The General Conference, on the recommendation of the Executive Board and by a two-thirds majority may, subject to its rules of procedure, invite as observers at specified sessions of the Conference or of its commissions representatives of international organisations, such as those referred to in Article XI, paragraph 4.

## ARTICLE V

## EXECUTIVE BOARD

*A. Composition*

1.  The Executive Board shall consist of eighteen members elected by the General Conference from among the delegates appointed by the Member States, together with the President of the Conference who shall sit *ex officio* in an advisory capacity.

2.  In electing the members of the Executive Board the General Conference shall endeavour to include persons competent in the arts, the humanities, the sciences, education and the diffusion of ideas, and qualified by their experience and capacity to fulfil the administrative and executive duties of the Board. It shall also have regard to the diversity of cultures and a balanced geographical distribution. Not more than one national of any Member State shall serve on the Board at any one time, the President of the Conference excepted.

3.  The elected members of the Executive Board shall serve for a term of three years, and shall be immediately eligible for a second term, but shall not serve consecutively for more than two terms. At the first election eighteen members shall be elected of whom one-third shall retire at the end of the first year and one-third at the end of the second year, the order of retirement being determined immediately after the election by the drawing of lots. Thereafter six members shall be elected each year.

4.  In the event of the death or resignation of one of its members, the Executive Board shall appoint, from among the delegates of the Member State con-

cerned, a substitute, who shall serve until the next session of the General Conference which shall elect a member for the remainder of the term.

*B. Functions*

5. The Executive Board, acting under the authority of the General Conference, shall be responsible for the execution of the programme adopted by the Conference and shall prepare its agenda and programme of work.

6. The Executive Board shall recommend to the General Conference the admission of new Members to the Organisation.

7. Subject to decisions of the General Conference, the Executive Board shall adopt its own rules of procedure. It shall elect its officers from among its members.

8. The Executive Board shall meet in regular session at least twice a year and may meet in special session if convoked by the Chairman on his own initiative or upon the request of six members of the Board.

9. The Chairman of the Executive Board shall present to the General Conference, with or without comment, the annual report of the Director-General on the activities of the Organisation, which shall have been previously submitted to the Board.

10. The Executive Board shall make all necessary arrangements to consult the representatives of international organisations or qualified persons concerned with questions within its competence.

11. The members of the Executive Board shall exercise the powers delegated to them by the General Conference on behalf of the Conference as a whole and not as representatives of their respective Governments.

## Article VI
### SECRETARIAT

1. The Secretariat shall consist of a Director-General and such staff as may be required.

2. The Director-General shall be nominated by the Executive Board and appointed by the General Conference for a period of six years, under such conditions as the Conference may approve, and shall be eligible for re-appointment. He shall be the chief administrative officer of the Organisation.

3. The Director-General, or a deputy designated by him, shall participate, without the right to vote, in all meetings of the General Conference, of the Executive Board, and of the committees of the Organisation. He shall formulate proposals for appropriate action by the Conference and the Board.

4. The Director-General shall appoint the staff of the Secretariat in accordance with staff regulations to be approved by the General Conference. Subject to the paramount consideration of securing the highest standards of integrity, efficiency and technical competence appointment to the staff shall be on as wide a geographical basis as possible.

5. The responsibilities of the Director-General and of the staff shall be exclusively international in character. In the discharge of their duties they shall not seek or receive instructions from any government or from any authority external to the Organisation. They shall refrain from any action which might

prejudice their position as international officials. Each State Member of the Organisation undertakes to respect the international character of the responsibilities of the Director-General and the staff, and not to seek to influence them in the discharge of their duties.

6. Nothing in this Article shall preclude the Organisation from entering into special arrangements within the United Nations Organisation for common services and staff and for the interchange of personnel.

## ARTICLE VII
## NATIONAL COOPERATING BODIES

1. Each Member State shall make such arrangements as suit its particular conditions for the purpose of associating its principal bodies interested in educational, scientific and cultural matters with the work of the Organisation, preferably by the formation of a National Commission broadly representative of the Government and such bodies.

2. National Commissions or national cooperating bodies, where they exist, shall act in an advisory capacity to their respective delegations to the General Conference and to their Governments in matters relating to the Organisation and shall function as agencies of liaison in all matters of interest to it.

3. The Organisation may, on the request of a Member State, delegate, either temporarily or permanently, a member of its Secretariat to serve on the National Commission of that State, in order to assist in the development of its work.

## ARTICLE VIII
## REPORTS BY MEMBER STATES

Each Member State shall report periodically to the Organisation, in a manner to be determined by the General Conference, on its laws, regulations, and statistics relating to educational, scientific and cultural life and institutions, and on the action taken upon the recommendations and conventions referred to in Article IV, paragraph 4.

## ARTICLE IX
## BUDGET

1. The budget shall be administered by the Organisation.

2. The General Conference shall approve and give final effect to the budget and to the apportionment of financial responsibility among the States Members of the Organisation subject to such arrangement with the United Nations as may be provided in the agreement to be entered into pursuant to Article X.

3. The Director-General, with the approval of the Executive Board, may receive gifts, bequests, and subventions directly from governments, public and private institutions, associations and private persons.

## ARTICLE X
## RELATIONS WITH THE UNITED NATIONS ORGANISATION

This Organisation shall be brought into relation with the United Nations Organisation, as soon as practicable, as one of the specialised agencies referred to in Articles 57 of the Charter of the United Nations. This relationship shall be effected through an agreement with the United Nations Organisation under Article 63 of the Charter, which agreement shall be subject to the approval of the General Conference of this Organisation. The agreement shall provide for effective cooperation between the two Organisations in the pursuit of their common purposes, and at the same time shall recognise the autonomy of this Organisation, within the fields of its competence as defined in this Constitution. Such agreement may, among other matters, provide for the approval and financing of the budget of the Organisation by the General Assembly of the United Nations.

## ARTICLE XI

### RELATIONS WITH OTHER SPECIALISED ORGANISATIONS AND AGENCIES

1. This Organisation may cooperate with other specialised inter-governmental organisations and agencies whose interests and activities are related to its purposes. To this end the Director-General, acting under the general authority of the Executive Board, may establish effective working relationships with such organisations and agencies and establish such joint committees as may be necessary to assure effective cooperation. Any formal arrangements entered into with such organisations or agencies shall be subject to the approval of the Executive Board.

2. Whenever the General Conference of this Organisation and the competent authorities of any other specialised inter-governmental organisations or agencies, whose purposes and functions lie within the competence of this Organisation, deem it desirable to effect a transfer of their resources and activities to this Organisation, the Director-General, subject to the approval of the Conference, may enter into mutually acceptable arrangements for this purpose.

3. This Organisation may make appropriate arrangements with other inter-governmental organisations for reciprocal representation at meetings.

4. The United Nations Educational, Scientific and Cultural Organisation may make suitable arrangements for consultation and cooperation with non-governmental international organisations concerned with matters within its competence, and may invite them to undertake specific tasks. Such cooperation may also include appropriate participation by representatives of such organisations on advisory committees set up by the General Conference.

## ARTICLE XII

### LEGAL STATUS OF THE ORGANISATION

The provisions of Articles 104 and 105 of the Charter of the United Nations Organisation concerning the legal status of that Organisation, its privileges and immunities shall apply in the same way to this Organisation.

## ARTICLE XIII

### AMENDMENTS

1. Proposals for amendments to this Constitution shall become effective upon receiving the approval of the General Conference by a two-thirds majority; provided, however, that those amendments which involve fundamental alterations in the aims of the Organisation or new obligations for the Member States shall

require subsequent acceptance on the part of two-thirds of the Member States before they come into force. The draft texts of proposed amendments shall be communicated by the Director-General to the Member States at least six months in advance of their consideration by the General Conference.

2.    The General Conference shall have power to adopt by a two-thirds majority rules of procedure for carrying out the provisions of this Article.

## Article XIV

## INTERPRETATION

1.    The English and French texts of this Constitution shall be regarded as equally authoritative.

2.    Any question or dispute concerning the interpretation of this Constitution shall be referred for determination to the International Court of Justice or to an arbitral tribunal, as the General Conference may determine under its rules of procedure.

## Article XV

## ENTRY INTO FORCE

1.    This Constitution shall be subject to acceptance. The instruments of acceptance shall be deposited with the Government of the United Kingdom.

2.    This Constitution shall remain open for signature in the archives of the Government of the United Kingdom. Signature may take place either before or after the deposit of the instrument of acceptance. No acceptance shall be valid unless preceded or followed by signature.

3.    This Constitution shall come into force when it has been accepted by twenty of its signatories. Subsequent acceptances shall take effect immediately.

4.    The Government of the United Kingdom will inform all members of the United Nations of the receipt of all instruments of acceptance and of the date on which the Constitution comes into force in accordance with the preceding paragraph.

In faith whereof, the undersigned, duly authorised to that effect, have signed this Constitution in the English and French languages, both texts being equally authentic.

Done in London the sixteenth day of November 1945 in a single copy, in the English and French languages, of which certified copies will be communicated by the Government of the United Kingdom to the Governments of all the Members of the United Nations.

# UNIVERSAL DECLARATION
# OF HUMAN RIGHTS

## PREAMBLE

WHEREAS recognition of the inherent dignity and of the equal and inalienable rights of all members of the human family is the foundation of freedom, justice and peace in the world,

WHEREAS disregard and contempt for human rights have resulted in barbarous acts which have outraged the conscience of mankind, and the advent of a world in which human beings shall enjoy freedom of speech and belief and freedom from fear and want has been proclaimed as the highest aspiration of the common people,

WHEREAS it is essential, if man is not to be compelled to have recourse, as a last resort, to rebellion against tyranny and oppression, that human rights should be protected by the rule of law,

WHEREAS it is essential to promote the development of friendly relations between nations,

WHEREAS the peoples of the United Nations have in the Charter reaffirmed their faith in fundamental human rights, in the dignity and worth of the human person and in the equal rights of men and women and have determined to promote social progress and better standards of life in larger freedom,

WHEREAS Member States have pledged themselves to achieve, in cooperation with the United Nations, the promotion of universal respect for and observance of human rights and fundamental freedoms,

WHEREAS a common understanding of these rights and freedoms is of the greatest importance for the full realization of this pledge,

NOW, THERFORE,

## THE GENERAL ASSEMBLY

### proclaims

This Universal Declaration of Human Rights as a common standard of achievement for all peoples and all nations, to the end that every individual and every organ of society, keeping this Declaration constantly in mind, shall strive by teaching and education to promote respect for these rights and freedoms and by progressive measures, national and international, to secure their universal

511

and effective recognition and observance, both among the peoples of Member States themselves and among the peoples of territories under their jurisdiction.

## Article 1

All human beings are born free and equal in dignity and rights. They are endowed with reason and conscience and should act towards one another in a spirit of brotherhood.

## Article 2

Everyone is entitled to all the rights and freedoms set forth in this Declaration, without distinction of any kind, such as race, colour, sex, language, religion, political or other opinion, national or social origin, property, birth or other status.

Furthermore, no distinction shall be made on the basis of the political, jurisdictional or international status of the country or territory to which a person belongs, whether it be independent, trust, non-self-governing or under any other limitation of sovereignty.

## Article 3

Everyone has the right to life, liberty and security of person.

## Article 4

No one shall be held in slavery or servitude; slavery and the slave trade shall be prohibited in all their forms.

## Article 5

No one shall be subjected to torture or to cruel, inhuman or degrading treatment or punishment.

## Article 6

Everyone has the right to recognition everywhere as a person before the law.

## Article 7

All are equal before the law and are entitled without any discrimination to equal protection of the law. All are entitled to equal protection against any discrimination in violation of this Declaration and against any incitement to such discrimination.

## Article 8

Everyone has the right to an effective remedy by the competent national tribunals for acts violating the fundamental rights granted him by the constitution or by law.

## Article 9

No one shall be subjected to arbitrary arrest, detention or exile.

## Article 10

Everyone is entitled in full equality to a fair and public hearing by an independent and impartial tribunal, in the determination of his rights and obligations and of any criminal charge against him.

## Article 11

1. Everyone charged with a penal offence has the right to be presumed innocent until proved guilty according to law in a public trial at which he has had all the guarantees necessary for his defence.

2. No one shall be held guilty of any penal offence on account of any act or omission which did not constitute a penal offence, under national or international law, at the time when it was committed. Nor shall a heavier penalty be imposed than the one that was applicable at the time the penal offence was committed.

## Article 12

No one shall be subjected to arbitrary interference with his privacy, family, home or correspondence, nor to attacks upon his honour and reputation. Everyone has the right to the protection of the law against such interference or attacks.

## Article 13

1. Everyone has the right to freedom of movement and residence within the borders of each state.

2. Everyone has the right to leave any country, including his own, and to return to his country.

## Article 14

1. Everyone has the right to seek and to enjoy in other countries asylum from persecution.

2. This right may not be invoked in the case of prosecutions genuinely arising from non-political crimes or from acts contrary to the purposes and principles of the United Nations.

## Article 15

1. Everyone has the right to a nationality.

2. No one shall be arbitrarily deprived of his nationality nor denied the right to change his nationality.

## Article 16

1. Men and women of full age, without any limitation due to race, nationality or religion, have the right to marry and to found a family. They are entitled to equal rights as to marriage, during marriage and at its dissolution.

2. Marriage shall be entered into only with the free and full consent of the intending spouses.

3. The family is the natural and fundamental group unit of society and is entitled to protection by society and the State.

## Article 17

1. Everyone has the right to own property alone as well as in association with others.

2. No one shall be arbitrarily deprived of his property.

*Article 18*

Everyone has the right to freedom of thought, conscience and religion; this right includes freedom to change his religion or belief, and freedom, either alone or in community with others and in public or private, to manifest his religion or belief in teaching, practice, worship and observance.

*Article 19*

Everyone has the right to freedom of opinion and expression; this right includes freedom to hold opinions without interference and to seek, receive and impart information and ideas through any media and regardless of frontiers.

*Article 20*

1.  Everyone has the right to freedom of peaceful assembly and association.

2.  No one may be compelled to belong to an association.

*Article 21*

1.  Everyone has the right to take part in the government of his country, directly or through freely chosen representatives.

2.  Everyone has the right of equal access to public service in his country.

3.  The will of the people shall be the basis of the authority of government; this will shall be expressed in periodic and genuine elections which shall be by universal and equal suffrage and shall be held by secret vote or by equivalent free voting procedures.

*Article 22*

Everyone, as a member of society, has the right to social security and is entitled to realization, through national effort and international cooperation and in accordance with the organization and resources of each State, of the economic, social and cultural rights indispensable for his dignity and the free development of his personality.

*Article 23*

1.  Everyone has the right to work, to free choice of employment, to just and favourable conditions of work and to protection against unemployment.

2.  Everyone, without any discrimination, has the right to equal pay for equal work.

3.  Everyone who works has the right to just and favourable remuneration ensuring for himself and his family an existence worthy of human dignity, and supplemented, if necessary, by other means of social protection.

4.  Everyone has the right to form and to join trade unions for the protection of his interests.

*Article 24*

Everyone has the right to rest and leisure, including reasonable limitation of working hours and periodic holidays with pay.

*Article 25*

1.  Everyone has the right to a standard of living adequate for the health and well-being of himself and of his family, including food, clothing, housing and medical care and necessary social services, and the right to security in the event

of unemployment, sickness, disability, widowhood, old age or other lack of livelihood in circumstances beyond his control.

2. Motherhood and childhood are entitled to special care and assistance. All children, whether born in or out of wedlock, shall enjoy the same social protection.

## Article 26

1. Everyone has the right to education. Education shall be free, at least in the elementary and fundamental stages. Elementary education shall be compulsory. Technical and professional education shall be made generally available and higher education shall be equally accessible to all on the basis of merit.

2. Education shall be directed to the full development of the human personality and to the strengthening of respect for human rights and fundamental freedoms. It shall promote understanding, tolerance and friendship among all nations, racial or religious groups, and shall further the activities of the United Nations for the maintenance of peace.

3. Parents have a prior right to choose the kind of education that shall be given to their children.

## Article 27

1. Everyone has the right freely to participate in the cultural life of the community, to enjoy the arts and to share in scientific advancement and its benefits.

2. Everyone has the right to the protection of the moral and material interests resulting from any scientific, literary or artistic production of which he is the author.

## Article 28

Everyone is entitled to a social and international order in which the rights and freedoms set forth in this Declaration can be fully realized.

## Article 29

1. Everyone has duties to the community in which alone the free and full development of his personality is possible.

2. In the exercise of his rights and freedoms, everyone shall be subject only to such limitations as are determined by law solely for the purpose of securing due recognition and respect for the rights and freedoms of others and of meeting the just requirements of morality, public order and the general welfare in a democratic society.

3. These rights and freedoms may in no case be exercised contrary to the purposes and principles of the United Nations.

## Article 30

Nothing in this Declaration may be interpreted as implying for any State, group or person any right to engage in any activity or to perform any act aimed at the destruction of any of the rights and freedoms set forth herein.

# NORTH ATLANTIC TREATY

The Parties to this Treaty reaffirm their faith in the purposes and principles of the Charter of the United Nations and their desire to live in peace with all peoples and all governments.

They are determined to safeguard the freedom, common heritage and civilization of their peoples, founded on the principles of democracy, individual liberty and the rule of law.

They seek to promote stability and well-being in the North Atlantic area.

They are resolved to unite their efforts for collective defense and for the preservation of peace and security.

They therefore agree to this North Atlantic Treaty:

## Article 1

The Parties undertake, as set forth in the Charter of the United Nations, to settle any international disputes in which they may be involved by peaceful means in such a manner that international peace and security, and justice, are not endangered, and to refrain in their international relations from the threat or use of force in any manner inconsistent with the purposes of the United Nations.

## Article 2

The Parties will contribute toward the further development of peaceful and friendly international relations by strengthening their free institutions, by bringing about a better understanding of the principles upon which these institutions are founded, and by promoting conditions of stability and well-being. They will seek to eliminate conflict in their international economic policies and will encourage economic collaboration between any or all of them.

## Article 3

In order more effectively to achieve the objectives of this Treaty, the Parties, separately and jointly, by means of continuous and effective self-help and mutual aid, will maintain and develop their individual and collective capacity to resist armed attack.

## Article 4

The Parties will consult together whenever, in the opinion of any of them, the territorial integrity, political independence or security of any of the Parties is threatened.

## Article 5

The Parties agree that an armed attack against one or more of them in Europe or North America shall be considered an attack against them all; and consequently they agree that, if such an armed attack occurs, each of them, in exercise of the right of individual or collective self-defense recognized by Article 51 of the Charter of the United Nations, will assist the Party or Parties so attacked by taking forthwith, individually and in concert with the other Parties, such action as it deems necessary, including the use of armed force, to restore and maintain the security of the North Atlantic area.

Any such armed attack and all measures taken as a result thereof shall immediately be reported to the Security Council. Such measures shall be terminated when the Security Council has taken the measures necessary to restore and maintain international peace and security.

### Article 6

For the purpose of Article 5 an armed attack on one or more of the Parties is deemed to include an armed attack on the territory of any of the Parties in Europe or North America, on the Algerian departments of France, on the occupation forces of any Party in Europe, on the islands under the jurisdiction of any Party in the North Atlantic area north of the Tropic of Cancer or on the vessels or aircraft in this area of any of the Parties.

### Article 7

This Treaty does not affect, and shall not be interpreted as affecting, in any way the rights and obligations under the Charter of the Parties which are members of the United Nations, or the primary responsibility of the Security Council for the maintenance of international peace and security.

### Article 8

Each Party declares that none of the international engagements now in force between it and any other of the Parties or any third state is in conflict with the provisions of this Treaty, and undertakes not to enter into any international engagement in conflict with this Treaty.

### Article 9

The Parties hereby establish a council, on which each of them shall be represented, to consider matters concerning the implementation of this Treaty. The council shall be so organized as to be able to meet promptly at any time. The council shall set up such subsidiary bodies as may be necessary; in particular it shall establish immediately a defense committee which shall recommend measures for the implementation of Articles 3 and 5.

### Article 10

The Parties may, by unanimous agreement, invite any other European state in a position to further the principles of this Treaty and to contribute to the security of the North Atlantic area to accede to this Treaty. Any state so invited may become a party to the Treaty by depositing its instrument of accession with the Government of the United States of America. The Government of the United States of America will inform each of the Parties of the deposit of each such instrument of accession.

### Article 11

This Treaty shall be ratified and its provisions carried out by the Parties in accordance with their respective constitutional processes. The instruments of ratification shall be deposited as soon as possible with the Government of the United States of America, which will notify all the other signatories of each deposit. The Treaty shall enter into force between the states which have ratified it as soon as the ratifications of the majority of the signatories, including the ratifications of Belgium, Canada, France, Luxembourg, the Netherlands, the United Kingdom and the United States, have been deposited and shall come into effect with respect to other states on the date of the deposit of their ratifications.

## Article 12

After the Treaty has been in force for ten years, or at any time thereafter, the Parties shall, if any of them so requests, consult together for the purpose of reviewing the Treaty, having regard for the factors then affecting peace and security in the North Atlantic area, including the development of universal as well as regional arrangements under the Charter of the United Nations for the maintenance of international peace and security.

## Article 13

After the Treaty has been in force for twenty years, any Party may cease to be a party one year after its notice of denunciation has been given to the Government of the United States of America, which will inform the Governments of the other Parties of the deposit of each notice of denunciation.

## Article 14

This Treaty, of which the English and French texts are equally authentic, shall be deposited in the archives of the Government of the United States of America. Duly certified copies thereof will be transmitted by that Government to the Governments of the other signatories.

IN WITNESS WHEREOF, the undersigned plenipotentiaries have signed this Treaty. DONE at Washington, the fourth day of April, 1949.

# JOINT STATEMENT BY THE UNITED STATES AND THE U.S.S.R. OF AGREED PRINCIPLES FOR DISARMAMENT NEGOTIATIONS 20TH SEPTEMBER 1961

Having conducted an extensive exchange of views on disarmament pursuant to their agreement announced in the General Assembly on 30th March 1961.

Noting with concern that the continuing arms race is a heavy burden for humanity and is fraught with dangers for the cause of world peace.

Reaffirming their adherence to all the provisions of the General Assembly resolution 1378 (XIV) of 20th November 1959.

Affirming that to facilitate the attainment of general and complete disarmament in a peaceful world it is important that all States abide by existing international agreements, refrain from any actions which might aggravate international tensions, and that they seek settlement of all disputes by peaceful means.

The United States and the U.S.S.R. have agreed to recommend the following principles as the basis for future multilateral negotiations on disarmament and to call upon other states to co-operate in reaching early agreement on general and complete disarmament in a peaceful world in accordance with these principles.

1. The goal of negotiations is to achieve agreement on a programme which will ensure that (a) disarmament is general and complete and war is no longer an instrument for settling international problems, and (b) such disarmament is accompanied by the establishment of reliable procedures for the peaceful settlement of disputes and effective arrangements for the maintenance of peace in accordance with the principles of the United Nations Charter.

2. The programme for general and complete disarmament shall ensure that states will have at their disposal only those non-nuclear armaments, forces, facilities, and establishments as are agreed to be necessary to maintain internal order and protect the personal security of citizens; and that states shall support and provide agreed manpower for a United Nations peace force.

3. To this end, the programme for general and complete disarmament shall contain the necessary provisions, with respect to the military establishment for every nation, for:

(a) Disbanding of armed forces, dismantling of military establishments, including bases, cessation of the production of armaments as well as their liquidation or conversion to peaceful uses;
(b) Elimination of all stockpiles of nuclear, chemical, bacteriological, and other weapons of mass destruction and cessation of the production of such weapons;
(c) Elimination of all means of delivery weapons of mass destruction;
(d) Abolishment of the organization and institutions designed to organize the military effort of states, cessation of military training, and closing of all military training institutions;
(e) Discontinuance of military expenditures.

4.   The disarmament programme should be implemented in an agreed sequence, by stages until it is completed, with each measure and stage carried out within specified time-limits. Transition to a subsequent stage in the process of disarmament should take place upon a review of the implementation of measures included in the preceding stage and upon a decision that all such measures have been implemented and verified and that any additional verification arrangements required for measures in the next stage are, when appropriate, ready to operate.

5.   All measures of general and complete disarmament should be balanced so that at no stage of the implementation of the treaty could any state or group of states gain military advantage and that security is ensured equally for all.

6.   All disarmament measures should be implemented from beginning to end under such strict and effective international control as would provide firm assurance that all parties are honouring their obligations. During and after the implementation of general and complete disarmament, the most thorough control should be exercised, the nature and extent of such control depending on the requirements for verification of the disarmament measures being carried out in each stage. To implement control over and inspection of disarmament, an International Disarmament Organization including all parties to the agreement should be created within the framework of the United Nations. This International Disarmament Organization and its inspectors should be assured unrestricted access without veto to all places as necessary for the purpose of effective verification.

7.   Progress in disarmament should be accompanied by measures to strengthen institutions for maintaining peace and the settlement of international disputes by peaceful means. During and after the implementation of the programme of general and complete disarmament, there should be taken, in accordance with the principles of the United Nations Charter, the necessary measures to maintain international peace and security, including the obligation of states to place at the disposal of the United Nations agreed manpower necessary for an international peace force to be equipped with agreed types of armaments. Arrangements for the use of this force should ensure that the United Nations can effectively deter or suppress any threat or use of arms in violation of the purposes and principles of the United Nations.

8.   States participating in the negotiations should seek to achieve and implement the widest possible agreement at the earliest possible date. Efforts should continue without interruption until agreement upon the total programme has been achieved, and efforts to ensure early agreement on and implementation of measures of disarmament should be undertaken without prejudicing progress on agreement on the total programme and in such a way that these measures would facilitate and form part of that programme.

# INDEX

Acheson, Dean, 267-268
Adjudication, 260
Adler, Alfred, 141
African Development Bank, 434
Agency for International Development
    (AID), 336, 447
Aggrandizement, 183-185, 189
    see also Aggression, Imperialism, Na-
    tionalism
Aggression, difficulties of definition, 417
    the moral issue, 301
    through subversion, 84, 338-343, 377
    psychological explanations, 144-150
*Agréation,* 251
Aid, economic, motives and purposes, 324
    problems, 326-327
    see also Agency for International Devel-
    opment, Development, Welfare
Alliances, and the balancing of power, 233-
    235
Almond, Gabriel, 339
Animism, and aggression and war, 148-149
*Apartheid,* 439, 445, 448
Appeasement, defined, 258
    of Hitler by Chamberlain, 178, 226
Arbitration, 259-260, 398
Armaments, and the balancing of power,
    235, 391
    and domestic prosperity, 103-104
    and war, 122-123, 391
    as a domestic matter, 384-386
    costs, 389
    functions and purposes, 380-383
    *See also* Arms control, Disarmament
Arms control, and inspection, 401-402
    and surprise attack, 392-393
    meaning, 383-384
    policies followed, 384-386
Attitudes, and domestic peace, 19-22
    and world peace, 456-458

Balance of payments, 307, 309, 313
Balancing of power, and arms races, 391
    and collective security, 411-413
    and deterrence, 371

and disarmament proposals, 395-397
and expectation of war, 123-126
and nuclear weapons, 241-243
appraisal, 239-244
meanings of balance, 219-221
methods, 232-238, 382-383
purposes, 221-222
underlying assumptions, 222-232
Banfield, Edward C., 5
Banse, E., 133
Bargaining, strategy of, 256-258
Bay of Pigs, 240, 351-352, 422
Beveridge, Albert J., 55-56, 97
Bismarck, 192, 356
Briand, Aristide, 292
Brierly, J. L., 286
Brodie, Bernard, 378
Buffer states, 236, 237
Bugging, 347

Carr, E. H., 87-89, 284, 294-295
Cavour, 338
Central Intelligence Agency, and Bay of
    Pigs, 351-352
    and bugging, 347
    and research, 349
    in Iran, 237
    other covert operations, 348, 352
Chamberlain, Neville, 226, 292
Change, peaceful, *see* Peaceful change
Churchill, Sir Winston, 239, 242, 378, 381
Claude, Inis L., Jr., 220, 243, 411, 413, 420,
    423
Cobden, Richard, 166
Coexistence, Sino-Soviet views on, 80-81, 85
    meanings of, 179
Coleman, James S., 170
Collective security, and the United Na-
    tions, 418-421
    compared to balance of power, 411-413
    defined, 410-411
    peace as a goal of, 222
    regional, 420-421
    why rejected, 413-417
    *See also* Security

521